Following Christ

Teacher's Manual

Following Christ

Teacher's Manual

Faith and Life Series

Third Edition

BOOK SIX

Ignatius Press, San Francisco

Catholics United for the Faith, Steubenville, Ohio

Nihil Obstat: Reverend James M. Dunfee
Censor Librorum

Imprimatur: Reverend Monsignor Kurt H. Kemo
Diocesan Administrator of Steubenville

Director of First Edition: The late Rev. Msgr. Eugene Kevane, Ph.D.
Assistant Director and General Editor of First Edition: Patricia Puccetti Donahoe, M.A.
First Edition Writer: Sister Mary Ann Kirkland, I.H.M.

Revision Writers: Colette Ellis, M.A. and Matthew Ramsay
Director and General Editor of Revision: Caroline Avakoff, M.A.
Editor of Revision: Christopher Bess

2013 reprint
See www.faithandlifeseries.com for additional tools and resources
© 1987, 2004, 2009, 2011 Catholics United for the Faith, Inc.
All rights reserved
ISBN 978-1-58617-584-9
Printed in Canada

Contents

Foreword

After a long process of updating, reformatting, editing, proofreading, and seeking ecclesiastical guidance and approval, the editorial staff of Ignatius Press gladly presents to you this Third Edition of the *Faith and Life* series. Our staff works from locations all across the country: from Florida and Michigan in the East, to Texas in the South, to California in the West. Wherever our location, we brought to the service of this project of creating a Third Edition our various talents and backgrounds, and hope to offer to you here a catechetical series that will earn the same kind of accolades we received for the Revised Edition:

"For the past two decades, *Faith and Life* has proven to be an excellent series for religious instruction in schools and family catechesis in the home. I know families who use this faith series and bear witness to the excellent fruit it has brought forth. To all who wish to transmit the faith to children in schools or in the home, I recommend the *Faith and Life* series as a textbook of refreshing and high quality" (Cardinal Christoph Schönborn).

"The *Faith and Life* series from Catholics United for the Faith provides a clear and informative presentation of what we as Catholics believe, live, and teach. With a firm grounding in the *Catechism of the Catholic Church*, *Faith and Life* reaffirms that the faith is indeed alive, a gift to be cherished, and as relevant today as when Our Lord Jesus Christ called Peter and Andrew to 'Come after me'" (Most Rev. John J. Myers, Archbishop of Newark).

"At a time when our young people so desperately need sound teaching, the *Faith and Life* catechism series is the answer to prayers. I will strongly recommend this series for use in our schools and parish-based religious education programs" (Most Reverend Michael J. Sheridan, Bishop of Colorado Springs).

"I believe that the *Faith and Life* series is a very good catechetical tool. Students who finish this series will have an excellent grasp of the deposit of faith. The material is sound and is faithful to the Magisterium of our holy Church" (Most Reverend Thomas J. Olmsted, Bishop of Phoenix, AZ).

"When CUF came out with its *Faith and Life* series, printed by Ignatius Press, and I began using it in my parish, within one year I could tell the difference for the better in the knowledge of true faith among the children of my parish" (Fr. Robert J. Fox, Fatima Family Apostolate).

"It's hard to think of anything more important than forming children in the faith. *Faith and Life* does it, and does it well" (Russell Shaw, Editor, *Encyclopedia of Catholic Doctrine*).

"Marvelous—this series will help you follow the Holy Father's desire that you teach your children" (Mother Angelica, Founder of EWTN).

"I give the *Faith and Life* series my highest recommendation. We teach our children with these texts and encourage others to do the same... [It] presents the faith with clarity, depth, and great beauty" (Scott Hahn, Steubenville, OH).

We joyfully offer this series in the spirit of our patron, Saint Ignatius of Loyola, for the greater honor and glory of God. We offer it to Catholic families, schools, and parishes in the hope of faithfully fulfilling the command of our Lord to "let the children come to me, and do not hinder them" (Mt 19:14).

The *Faith and Life* Series Editorial Staff
Ignatius Press

Introduction to the *Faith and Life* Third Edition

The *Faith and Life* series, which now includes a student text, teacher's manual, and activity book for grades one through eight, has been used in schools, parishes, and homes across the country since its original publication in 1984. This edition of the original series continues our commitment to the faithful transmission of the teachings of the Roman Catholic Church, placing special emphasis on the importance of Scripture and the *Catechism of the Catholic Church*. This edition of the series has been updated to incorporate the new translations of the Roman Missal introduced into the Mass in Advent 2011. It is our hope that additional recent changes, such as updating photographs and reformatting the teacher's manuals, will continue to make *Faith and Life* a valuable tool in catechesis.

Text and Grade Level

The sixth grade text, *Following Christ*, is devoted to the Ten Commandments and the Mass. Sixth graders are making the transition from childhood to adulthood. This period of tension is also a time when they are able to understand the Faith more clearly and make it truly their own. The students are able to think independently and to participate in reasoned discussion. At this turning point in their lives, the students need to be guided to follow Christ with their whole mind and will. Thus, instructing the students in the formation of conscience and in the liturgical life of the Church is vitally important.

The Student Textbook

The *Faith and Life* student texts are intentionally written at an advanced reading level. Doctrine is presented in a way that both challenges the student's intellect and avoids the boredom that is often fatal in catechetical efforts. The text of these books is elucidated by the material in the *Teacher's Manual*.

Each chapter opens with a passage from Sacred Scripture. Additional quotations are interspersed throughout the books to help demonstrate the Biblical backing for the Faith. The chapters close with memorization questions dealing with Church doctrines as they are presented in the *Catechism of the Catholic Church*. As students regularly review these questions they will come to recognize the significance of the *Catechism of the Catholic Church*, a fruit of the Second Vatican Council.

Each book also offers vocabulary words indicated in bold type and defined in a glossary, and a section of common Catholic prayers.

One of the first things you will notice about the *Faith and Life* student texts is the beautiful and inspiring religious artwork. Faith has inspired art for centuries, and religious art has, in turn, inspired our faith. Art is a valuable educational tool, especially in the teaching of religious truths to children, for, in addition to the oral and written word, it offers a visual image of the subject manner. Art can also be a source of meditation for students and teachers alike as they investigate the paintings, discuss the religious imagery, and come to understand the beautiful symbols and the artistic expressions of the realities they communicate.

The Activity Book

The *Faith and Life* activity books contain supplemental activities for each chapter in each grade. They offer the teacher a variety of reinforcement tools, in a text separate from the student textbook. Their purpose is to reinforce and interest the students in a new way in the material found in the student textbook.

In the primary grades, the activities focus upon drawing, coloring, and simple puzzles and exercises. In the middle grades, the activities focus on reading comprehension and integration; memorization is also emphasized. In the final grades the activities focus on comprehension and synthesis of the ideas expressed, as students are encouraged to make their own, both intellectually and actively, what they have been taught.

The Teacher's Manual

This book will be imperative for you as you guide your students through the *Faith and Life* series.

Each chapter of the teacher's manuals begins with a list of important references to the *Catechism of the Catholic Church* and Sacred Scripture that support the chapter's lessons. These are available for your own preparation, research, and reflection. You are encouraged to incorporate them into the lessons as you see fit.

This is followed by a clear and succinct summary of the doctrine discussed in the chapter's four lessons. Each chapter provides a full week of detailed color-coded lesson plans, with four days for presenting new material and one day for review and assessment.

The lesson plans are designed to be guides in teaching even the most complex truths of the Faith with age-appropriate examples. The lessons begin in the Aims section with a clear statement of the main doctrines to be discussed that day. This is accompanied by a Materials section, which allows you to know beforehand how to prepare for the various exercises and activities in the day's lesson. The Begin section provides introductory material that will help you to broach the day's topic with your students. The Develop section begins by listing the paragraphs that your students should read together in class. The student textbook pages that are used that day appear on the facing page of the *Teacher's Manual*. The specific paragraphs to be read are highlighted in accord with the color code for your easy reference.

The content of the lesson is explained in the Develop section, which also provides useful review and questions for discussion. This is supplemented with "Catholic Culture and Tradition" boxes, which include materials for the teacher, lives of the saints, explanation of terms, descriptions of Church traditions and rituals, relevant citations, suggestions for activities, additional resources, and prayers.

The Reinforce and Conclude sections help you to draw together the material covered, apply it to life, and end the classroom discussion in prayer.

Comprehensive chapter quizzes and optional unit tests are also part of each lesson and chapter. Black line masters, from which you may make copies for your students, are found in Appendix A. In addition to the review and assessment provided in the *Teacher's Manual*, each chapter's content may be reviewed and reinforced by using the *Activity Book*. The answer keys for the activities are found at the end of each chapter in this manual.

Appendix B contains additional activities such as stories, games, crafts, and skits that are often suggested in the various sections of the lesson plans.

The "Words to Know" glossary and Prayer sections from the student textbook are also available for you to view at the end of the *Teacher's Manual*, just prior to Appendix A.

Using the *Teacher's Manual* in the parish setting:
To assist Parish and CCD Programs, "once-a-week lesson plans" have been formulated and are available online at www.faithandlifeseries.com. These lesson plans cover the essential material and doctrines of each chapter in a one hour format.

In addition to following the online lesson plans, you may wish to spend time reinforcing the material learned by having students memorize questions, vocabulary words, and prayers. The quizzes can then be sent home for family reinforcement and review. The unit quizzes can still be administered in class once a month to assist the teacher in assessing the students' understanding.

Additional resources to be used with the *Faith and Life* series can be found online at www.faithandlifeseries.com.

The *Faith and Life* series Third Edition aspires to aid teachers and parents (the primary educators) in transmitting the truths, doctrines, wealth of traditions, and richness of culture found in the Roman Catholic Church.

A Note for Teachers and Catechists

Catechesis: Nature and Purpose

In recent decades the Catholic Church has given its members numerous documents and resources defining and explaining the role of catechesis in the life of Catholics. Among these are the documents of the Second Vatican Council, the *General Directory for Catechesis*, the *National Directory for Catechesis*, and *Catechesi Trandendae*. The authors and editors of the *Faith and Life* series have taken these teachings to heart in preparing a catechism for students in the first through eighth grades.

Catechesis is the systematic instruction of children, young people, and adults in the Catholic Faith and the teachings of the Church with the goal of making them into Christ's disciples (cf. CCC 5). It is the handing-on of Christ's message to his people. The *General Catechetical Directory* describes catechesis as a form of ministry of God's Word, "which is intended to make men's faith living, conscious, and active, through the light of instruction" (GCD 17; 1971).

The Role of Parents: The First Catechists

The family provides the first and most important introduction to Christian faith and practice for any child, since parents are the primary educators of their children. Instruction in the Faith, which begins at an early age, should include not only the parents' good Christian example, but also a formation in prayer and an explanation and review of what students have learned from religious instruction and from attending liturgical events, such as Mass.

Parental cooperation is very important to a teacher's success as a catechist. You should try to involve parents in their children's instruction. Discuss with them the program and methods you are using, consult them about better ways to teach their children, and ask for assistance if problems arise. Let parents know that you are there to help them fulfill their duties in forming and educating their children in Christ (cf. GCD 78, 79).

The Role of the Catechist

Put simply, "catechesis is an education in the faith" (CCC 5). To be a catechist is to be God's instrument. Every catechist has a responsibility to teach the fullness of the truth faithfully, while witnessing to those entrusted to his care. A fervent sacramental life and regular prayer life are the catechist's best personal preparation. Any instructor can use textbooks and teaching tools, learn various methods for effective classroom participation, and develop lesson plans to facilitate an academic environment. But nothing is as important as witnessing through your words and deeds and petitioning God for the on-going formation and spiritual growth of the students. No matter how much knowledge you impart to your students, you should recognize that you merely plant the seeds of faith that God himself must cultivate in their souls.

Catechesis in today's ministry is often coupled with evangelization—a first hearing of the Good News of Salvation. Through catechesis, you should guide your students to seek, accept, and profoundly investigate the Gospel so that they in turn may become witnesses to Christ. The *Catechism of the Catholic Church*, together with Sacred Scripture, provide catechists with the tools necessary to achieve this.

John Paul II states in *Catechesi Tradendae*: "at the heart of catechesis we find . . . the Person of Jesus of Nazareth . . . in catechesis it is Christ . . . who is taught . . . and it is Christ alone who teaches . . ." (CT 5, 6). Religious education must always be centered on the Triune God and on Christ himself. God chose to reveal himself throughout salvation history, through his creation, the prophets, the Scriptures, and most perfectly in the Person of Jesus Christ. This revelation, preserved faithfully through Sacred Scripture and Tradition, has been entrusted to the Church that every catechist is called to serve.

As you teach, you will find that your students, like all men, have a deep desire for God and are searching for the truth. As you bring them into an environment of docility to the Holy Spirit, you will be echoing the fullness of God's revelation in Christ and helping to immerse your students into the mystery of Christ and the salvation he offers. This mirrors the divine pedagogy which ends in our salvation. Likewise, you will be creating an environment of study and prayer in which your students will be able to respond with a deepening conversion and a cultivation of the life of virtue.

Pedagogical Tools

The *General Catechetical Directory* provides an overview of various successful methodologies you may find useful. Knowledge can be transmitted through prayer and liturgy, through words and deeds, or through texts and activities, but the students learn it primarily from you, the catechist.

Induction and Deduction: Inductive methods serve well in the presentation of facts and in considering and examining those facts in order to recognize their Christian meaning. Induction is the process of reasoning from a part to a whole, from particular to general principles. It is not independent of deductive methods, which reason from the general to the particular and include interpretation and determining cause and effect. These two methods, taken together, aid in the students' understanding of the unity of the Faith, the inter-relation of topics, and, most importantly, their practical applications.

Formulas: Expressing thoughts or ideas succinctly and accurately in a memorable form allows for ease of memorization and better understanding of a topic. In the early stages of education, memorization should be utilized more frequently since children first need language to communicate meaning. In theology, semantics are very important, for Christians have died for their faith and schisms have occurred because of word use (e.g., the *Filioque* in the Nicene Creed still distinguishes Roman Catholics from the Eastern Orthodox). Such formulas also provide a uniform method of speaking among the faithful.

Experience: Personal experience is reflective and practical, and it transforms abstract theories into applicable and memorable concepts. Catechists should use concrete examples in class and encourage their students to judge personal experience with Christian values.

Creativity: Creative activities enable students to meditate upon and express, in their own words, the messages they have learned.

Groups: In catechesis the importance of group instruction is becoming more apparent. Groups aid the social and ecclesial formation of students, and they foster a sense of Christian co-responsibility and solidarity.

The *Catechism of the Catholic Church*: An Important Tool

Today's classrooms are filled with children who have various needs and backgrounds. Complicated by an atmosphere of religious indifference, religious hostility, and an apparent absence of Catholic culture, knowledge, and meaningful practice, your catechetical work becomes especially valuable. One important tool that belongs to all the faithful is the *Catechism of the Catholic Church*, which is divided into four sections: the Profession of Faith (the Creed), The Celebration of the Christian Mystery (the Sacraments), Life in Christ (the moral life), and Christian Prayer.

The Creed: The Creed is a summary of the Faith and the Church's baptismal promises. As a public profession of faith, Catholics find in it their identity as members of Christ's Mystical Body. This is the Faith handed down from Christ to the Apostles and to the entire Church.

Sacraments: The seven Sacraments are outward signs instituted by Christ to confer grace. Active participation in the sacramental life of the Church, such as attending Mass prayerfully and faithfully, should be encouraged from a young age.

The Moral Life: The moral life does not limit; instead it provides the boundaries that define the Catholic identity and allow for proper love of God and neighbor. A right moral life is man's gift to God, a response to His unconditional love, and a pathway to true freedom. Every Catholic should be an example to others.

Prayer: Prayer unites a person with God (through words, actions, silence, and presence), and should be encouraged and put into practice from early childhood. There are many forms of prayer, but each brings the soul closer to God.

The *Faith and Life Teacher's Manual* provides much of what you will need to be an effective catechist, but it will only be fruitful depending on how you utilize it and how you teach and minister the Word of God to your students. Take your responsibilities as a catechist very seriously. Call upon Christ frequently, as his witness and disciple, to help you hand on his message. Persevere and draw near to God, bringing your students with you.

Contents

A Note to Parents

Dear Parents,

The *Faith and Life* series was originally published in 1984. The book you hold in your hands is one of over 4.6 million books sold since then. From the beginning, the series was intended to provide schools, parishes, and families with the catechetical tools and essential elements of Catholic doctrine pivotal in the formation of young Catholics.

While the doctrine and Tradition of the Church remain essentially unchanged, as time has passed the editors have provided additional teaching tools that enrich the series and make it even more accessible to all types of students. Since its introduction, the series has seen the addition of activity books, teacher's manuals, numerous online resources, scriptural quotations, and correlations with the *Catechism of the Catholic Church*. Additionally, this edition has been updated to incorporate the new translations of the Roman Missal introduced into the Mass during Advent 2011. These additions were all undertaken with an eye toward the *General Directory for Catechesis'* statement: "It is necessary that religious instruction in schools appear as a scholastic discipline with the same systematic demands and the same rigor as other disciplines. It must present the Christian message and the Christian event with the same seriousness and the same depth with which other disciplines present their knowledge" (GDC, 73; Congregation for the Clergy, 1998).

In this sixth grade student text, *Following Christ*, you will find that emphasis has been given to the scriptural basis of our Faith in accord with Sacred Tradition. Every chapter opens with a Scripture passage, and important verses supplement the text where relevant. Each chapter closes with questions and answers based on Church teaching as found in the *Catechism of the Catholic Church*. Vocabulary words are indicated in bold type and in the Words to Know sections. Their definitions are found in the glossary. Common Catholic prayers are also taught in the lessons, and presented at the end of the book.

It is important to realize that, as parents, you are the primary educators of your child. Your active participation in your child's religious education is highly encouraged by the Church. As a family, you are the first witnesses of God's love to your child. If you provide a model of Catholic living at home, if as a family you participate in the sacramental life of the Church, and if you pray and attend Mass together, your child is more likely to take to heart the lessons he will learn in religion class. Family discussions of current events with a healthy religious perspective will allow your child to grow up with a better understanding of the world around him, and more importantly, help him to be a true Catholic and follower of Christ in the midst of it. As stated in the *General Directory for Catechesis*, "family catechesis precedes . . . accompanies and enriches all forms of catechesis" (GDC, 226). Providing your child with a strong Catholic identity at an early age, while not ensuring a lifetime of devotion, will certainly prepare him for the challenge of becoming a faithful Catholic adult.

We encourage you to use the *Following Christ* student text, along with its resources, to assist you in the task of sharing the Good News with which you have been entrusted. More information and resources can be found at www.faithandlifeseries.com.

We sincerely hope that this series will provide parents, catechists, and teachers with the assistance they need in the task of evangelizing young people and of putting them in "communion and intimacy with Jesus Christ" (GDC, 80).

7

INTRODUCTION

You may spend the first days of class introducing the year's focus to the students. The students will consider love, abundant life, law, and their call to union with God. Have the students read the text together in class, and then discuss any questions they may have.

After reading through the introduction, students will be able to put their study for this class into the context of their union with Jesus.

TEACHER'S NOTES

INTRODUCTION

Jesus has promised that he will be with us to the end of the world. He is with each of us, personally, in every step of our life. What is the special ingredient that Jesus adds to life that changes it from a dull chore to a rich adventure? The special ingredient is love. Jesus tells us that he came so that we "may have life, and have it abundantly" (Jn 10:10).

How do we receive this abundant life that Jesus wants to give us? We receive it by following the plan that God has for us. Before you build a house you need a blueprint. Even God, before he made the first man, had a plan for his body and soul—he planned every bone and every muscle, every nerve, every organ, every blood cell. We have a plan to lay the foundation of our lives: God's law.

Law is necessary if we are to have order in life, and without order there can be no happiness. All life is based on law. God planned the entire universe with very precise laws to guide every part of it, both very little things and very great. But everything we see around us—except human beings—obeys without choice. Men are not machines. We have free will. We have the gift of choice. We are invited to obey God's laws. And it is especially now, at this point in your lives, that the choice is offered to you in a new way. Life in Jesus is not for those who are lazy, indifferent, and selfish. But what would this invitation be without Jesus? Men have never lived together without laws. But no one has ever offered a better reason to live by law than Jesus—and that reason is love. There can be no real love without law; without law, love becomes mere sentimentality. But without love, law can become a fearful burden.

When he was asked which was the greatest commandment of God's law, Jesus said that love of God and neighbor sum up all the laws. We live by God's law, therefore, because we love God and each other. That makes all the difference.

You are being invited here to become closely united with Jesus. The rewards are great. Jesus is always challenging us, always expecting more from us—and always giving us the graces we need to meet his demands.

PART ONE

The Ten Commandments

TEACHER'S NOTES

CHAPTER ONE
GOD GIVES US THE LAW

Catechism of the Catholic Church References

Charity: 1822–29, 1844
Choices Presented to Conscience: 1786–89, 1799–1800
Conscience: 1776–82, 1795–97
Consequences of Original Sin: 55–58, 399–400, 402–9, 416–19
Decalogue: 423, 2052–55, 2057–82
Fall of Man: 385–90, 413
God Creates an Ordered and Good World: 299
God Creates out of Wisdom and Love: 295, 315
God's Promise to Abraham: 705–6, 762
Grace: 1996–2005, 2021–24
Jesus and the Law: 574–82, 592, 2052–55, 2075

Man's Freedom: 1730–42, 1743–48
Moses and the Prayer of the Mediator: 2574–77, 2593
New Law or Law of the Gospel: 1965–74, 1977, 1983–86
Obligation of the Ten Commandments: 2072–74, 2081–82
Old Law: 1961–64, 1975, 1980–82
Original Sin: 388–90, 396–401, 415
Promise of a Redeemer: 410–12, 420–21
Ten Commandments and the Natural Law: 2070–71, 2080
Ten Commandments as Light and Foundation of Conscience: 1962
Ways of Knowing God: 31–38, 46–48, 286

Scripture References

Creation and Fall: Gen 1:1—3:24
Ten Commandments: Ex 19—20:22, 24; 25:10–12; 31:19—32:35

Sermon on the Mount: Mt 5

Summary of Lesson Content

Lesson 1

God created the world to be good and orderly.

God can be recognized in his creation.

God established universal divine laws for his creation.

Man is a unique creature with free will.

Man is called to do good and avoid evil.

Lesson 2

God established divine and natural laws to govern his creation. Following these laws will make us truly happy.

As a result of Original Sin, man has difficulty in recognizing and choosing the true good.

God does not abandon man, but gives us the means of salvation, offered first to the Israelites and then to all people through his covenant.

Lesson 3

Jesus established the New Law and did not set aside the Old Law of the Ten Commandments.

The greatest commandment is to love God and our neighbors as ourselves.

Disobeying God's commandments is a failure to love God and neighbor.

Lesson 4

Conscience is the faculty of judgment applied to a given action to determine whether it is good or evil.

All men have a conscience and are obliged to form it properly.

God has provided the means to know him and his ways and to form our consciences through the teachings of the Church.

3

CHAPTER ONE: GOD GIVES US THE LAW
LESSON ONE: CREATION

Aims

The students will learn that God created the world to be good and orderly, and that God can be recognized in his creation. God established universal divine laws for his creation.

They will learn that man is a unique creature with free will and that man is called to do good and avoid evil.

Materials

• *Activity Book*, p. 1

• Bible

• Art supplies to depict creation (mural paper and paint, colored chalk, etc.)

Optional:
• "Father, we thank thee who has planted," *Adoremus Hymnal*, #515

Begin

Man can know that there is a God by observing the natural world around him. Take the students outside, and have them discover ways to realize that there is a God. Saint Thomas Aquinas gives us 5 ways, or proofs, of knowing of God's existence:
  • Everything comes from something (i.e. generation) and there must have been a first

• Everything is in motion, something must have moved it
• Something holds everything in existence
• Order
• Degrees of perfection

Develop

1. Read paragraphs 1–4 with the students.

2. Review that we can know that God exists from the world around us. All of creation testifies to the glory of God. You may lead the students in prayer, praising God and thanking him for his wondrous gifts.

3. There is a hierarchy within creation. The inanimate objects are the lowest level. Have the students give examples: rocks, metals, etc. Then there are the vegetative creatures, which have life, grow, and turn toward the sun, e.g., trees and flowers. Then are the animals. They grow, live, have mobility and instincts. Animals are not rational. Some may seem smart or expressive, but they are driven by instincts or training. They do not solve math problems, create cities, or laugh at jokes. Humans are above animals in the hierarchy of creation. All of the lower levels of creation were given to man by God for the service of man (e.g., food, shelter). Man is rational. He has free will. He is a body and soul unity. Angels are rational pure spirits that serve God (and part of that service may be to help man, e.g., guardian angels).

4. Have the students do a project (e.g., story board, mural, dramatization, eye-witness report) to demonstrate how God created all things seen and unseen.

5. Review that God made man for a purpose: heaven. To get to heaven, we must do good and avoid evil. We are designed for this and it is written in our hearts. Because of the effects of the Fall we are prone to sin. This is called concupiscence. However, we have free will. We can choose good or evil. To be truly free, we must choose to do good.

Reinforce

1. Have the students work on *Activity Book* p. 1 (see *Teacher's Manual*, p. 13).

2. Explain how law is binding and has consequences, and yet allows freedom. This is different from free will. Free will allows us to choose what to do (good or bad). We often think of freedom from slavery, fear, sin, etc., but we should also think of freedom for liberty, hope, union with God, etc.

3. Give the students various scenarios and have them see how choosing the good (with free will) gives true freedom. E.g., choosing not to steal gives one freedom from guilt and maintains friendship with God.

4. Have the students work on their Memorization Questions and Words to Know (see *Teacher's Manual*, p. 11).

Conclude

1. Teach the students to sing "Father, we thank thee who has planted," *Adoremus Hymnal*, #515.

2. End class by leading the students in the Our Father (see *Teacher's Manual*, p. 396).

CHAPTER 1

God Gives Us the Law

"And if you obey the voice of the Lord your God, being careful to do all his commandments which I command you this day, the Lord your God will set you high above all the nations of the earth."

Deuteronomy 28:1

If we observe the world around us, we will see that there is a certain order in the way things happen. Throw a stone in the air and it falls back to the ground. We say it does that because of the law of gravity. Wild geese will fly for miles and miles to return every year to the same place to nest and hatch their goslings. They do that by instinct. And if we look at men now and through the ages, in different countries and cultures, we find that they always have a rule about right and wrong: "Do good and avoid evil." Human beings all over the earth have the idea that they ought to behave in a certain way.

The difference between this rule of human behavior and the law of gravity or instinct is that the law of gravity or instinct tells us what things *do*, and the rule of human behavior tells us what we *ought* to do. In other words, the stone or goose has no choice in the matter. The stone doesn't decide to fall back to earth—it must. But while the rule of human behavior may tell us what is right and wrong to do, we are still free to decide just what we will do.

This presents two problems. The first problem is that though all men might agree that we should "do good and avoid evil," they don't always agree about what is good and what is evil. In fact, people are often mistaken about what behavior is right and wrong. So how can we know for sure?

The second problem concerns our reasons for following this law of human behavior. Since men aren't forced to act in accord with law but may freely choose, why do they?

The Master Plan

Where can we find the solution to these problems? The best way is to look to the Master Planner and see what he had in mind.

As we all know, God is the Creator and Lord of heaven and earth. In his great wisdom he made the universe and governs it all. Now, just as he made the law of gravity and instinct, he made all men with this idea of doing good and avoiding evil. But he also made men with free will, allowing them to choose to do good and avoid evil.

When Adam and Eve chose to disobey God, their sin affected all men that were to come. One result of Original Sin is that it is harder for us to know what is right and wrong and to behave accordingly. If we read the beginning of the Old Testament we can easily see that men soon made a mess of things.

13

But God promised Adam that he would not abandon us and would give us a means of salvation. So God called upon Abraham and made him the father of his chosen people. God established his covenant with the Israelites, to show that he would be their God and they would be his people. He gave them the **Decalogue**—the **Ten Commandments**. God wanted his people to know what was right and wrong and what was truly good and truly bad for them. He was preparing them for a special role in salvation history.

Some people think that God simply wanted obedience to a set of rules. What he really wanted is a faithful people. He gave his people a law to teach and guide them in every part of their lives. Further, he gave his people a law to prepare them for the coming of the Savior.

Fulfillment of the Law

When Jesus came to establish the New **Covenant**, he did not set aside the Ten Commandments, but completed them. He said: "Do not think that I have come to abolish the law and the prophets; I have come not to abolish them but to fulfill them" (Mt 5:17). Jesus teaches that the foundation of all law is love: to love God above all things, with one's whole mind and heart and soul, and to love one's neighbor as oneself. Jesus wants all men to turn their minds and hearts to God with love. Disobeying any of the Ten Commandments is a failure to love either God or our neighbor. This is because the Ten Commandments sum up our duties to God and our neighbor.

14

Conscience

How do we know that one action is right and another wrong? Along with free will God has given each man the ability to judge if something is right or wrong. This ability is called **conscience**. Our conscience is a very practical tool. It tells us what would be right or wrong behavior in a given situation. We are to obey our conscience, for God gave it to us so that we could live according to his law.

Every person is born with a conscience. Even a member of some primitive tribe that has never come into contact with civilization has the same law in his heart to do good and avoid evil. His tribe will probably have a code of what they think is right and wrong. He will be responsible before God for doing what he thinks is right and not doing what he thinks is wrong. In this way he can please God. But his code of behavior might differ somewhat from the Ten Commandments. Since he has had no contact with the commandments, he will not be held responsible for obeying them. Nonetheless, his conscience is faulty.

A conscience has to be taught—and taught correctly. We call this "forming" a conscience. The conscience of the primitive man, since it was not formed correctly, is called an incorrect conscience. Since he could do nothing about

that, he will not be held responsible for his incorrect conscience. On the other hand, all men who have access to the Word of God have a responsibility to form a correct conscience.

God has given us the means to form our consciences correctly. He has revealed truths about himself and given us the Ten Commandments. To live according to the will of God we must follow and obey the commandments. If we disregard or break God's law we sin. If we deliberately break a commandment in a serious matter, we commit a mortal sin and destroy charity, or the love of God, in our hearts. When we commit a mortal sin, we reject God by choosing to do something seriously contrary to God's will. If we do not repent of mortal sin, we cannot go to heaven and be happy with God forever. Of course, whether or not what we do is a mortal sin depends on whether we know that what we are doing is seriously wrong and we freely chose to do it anyway. And if we do commit a mortal sin, God will forgive us if we truly repent of our sin. He has given us the Sacrament of Penance to forgive our sins and to help us to grow closer to him.

But besides giving us the Law, he has given us reasons why we should want to follow it. First, God is the giver and author of that law, and since he is our Creator he knows what is best for us. Obeying God's law is necessary

The Ten Commandments

1. I am the Lord your God; you shall not have other gods before me.
2. You shall not take the name of the Lord your God in vain.
3. Remember to keep holy the Lord's Day.
4. Honor your father and mother.
5. You shall not kill.
6. You shall not commit adultery.
7. You shall not steal.
8. You shall not bear false witness against your neighbor.
9. You shall not covet your neighbor's wife.
10. You shall not covet your neighbor's goods.

15

KNOWING GOD

1. We can know that God exists through the natural world that surrounds us.

2. We can know about God through his *revelation*:
   - Sacred Scripture is the Word of God written down by men under the inspiration of the Holy Spirit.
   - Sacred Tradition is the entirety of the Word of God.
   - The Magisterium is the teaching Church that safeguards revelation.

Preview

In the next lesson, the students will learn about God's laws.

CHAPTER ONE: GOD GIVES US THE LAW
LESSON TWO: GOD'S LAWS

Aims

The students will learn that God established divine and natural laws to govern his creation and that following these laws will make us truly happy.

They will learn that, as a result of Original Sin, man has difficulty in recognizing and choosing the true good. Nonetheless, God does not abandon man, but gives him the means of salvation, offered first to the Israelites and then to all people through his covenant.

Materials

- *Activity Book*, p. 2

- Bible

- Art supplies for Ark

Optional:
- "Father, we thank thee who has planted," *Adoremus Hymnal*, #515

Begin

From the story of Creation (Gen 1:1—3:24) we know that God created man in the state of original justice. After the Fall, many things changed for man. (See the box, "God's Master Plan," on p. 7, at right.)

Each person is made in God's image and is precious in God's eyes. Each person is a unique gift from God, and has a specific purpose. (God has a plan for each of us.) Have the students share some of their special talents. Our talents help us to see God's plan at work in our lives.

Develop

1. Read the story of Creation (Gen 1:1—3:24) and paragraphs 5–9 of the student text with the students.

2. Review that God promised Adam and Eve a savior (Gen 3:15). Explain to the students that because of Original Sin, there was a separation between God and man. There was nothing that man could do to make up for this great sin. This Original Sin was passed down to all people. A savior would be needed to make up for this sin (redemption) and to reunite man and God (atonement). Remember that God wants us all to be united with him forever. He loves us completely. Throughout history God has provided ways for man to be united with him (through covenants, sacrifices, and worship).

3. In order to live in relationship, we must fulfill certain responsibilities. Can you be best friends with someone if he is always lying to you, or if he steals from you? God gave us the Ten Commandments or Decalogue ("ten words") so that we can live in relationship with God and one another. He did not need to do this, as his law was already written upon our hearts. We had a hard time recognizing the true good due to Original Sin, so, in his love and mercy, God revealed his laws to us.

4. Together, read Exodus 19:5—20:17. These are the Ten Commandments. Discuss the commandments with the students. Explain that we are not simply to be obedient to God's laws; rather, we should want to keep them to show our love for God; we should want to hear and obey his words. You may also discuss that in keeping these commandments, we are made free: free from sin, free to follow God, and free to recognize and follow our Savior.

Reinforce

1. Have the students work on *Activity Book* p. 2 (see *Teacher's Manual*, p. 13).

2. Make a model of the Ark of the Covenant, using a large cardboard box. Decorate the "Ark." Have the students create posters of the Ten Commandments and put them in the Ark.

3. The students should work on the Memorization Questions (see *Teacher's Manual*, p. 11) and the Ten Commandments. Review them with a game, such as matching the number and the commandment. Reward the students who memorize all ten.

Conclude

1. Lead the students in singing "Father, we thank thee who has planted," *Adoremus Hymnal*, #515.

2. End class by leading the students in the Our Father (see *Teacher's Manual*, p. 396).

CHAPTER 1

God Gives Us the Law

"And if you obey the voice of the LORD your God, being careful to do all his commandments which I command you this day, the LORD your God will set you high above all the nations of the earth."

Deuteronomy 28:1

If we observe the world around us, we will see that there is a certain order in the way things happen. Throw a stone in the air and it falls back to the ground. We say it does that because of the law of gravity. Wild geese will fly for miles and miles to return every year to the same place to nest and hatch their goslings. They do that by instinct. And if we look at men now and through the ages, in different countries and cultures, we find that they always have a rule about right and wrong: "Do good and avoid evil." Human beings all over the world have the idea that they ought to behave in a certain way.

The difference between this rule of human behavior and the law of gravity or instinct is that the law of gravity or instinct tells us what things *do*, and the rule of human behavior tells us what we *ought* to do. In other words, the stone or goose has no choice in the matter. The stone doesn't decide to fall back to earth—it must. But while the rule of human behavior may tell us what is right and wrong to do, we are still free to decide just what we will do.

This presents two problems. The first problem is that though all men might agree that we should "do good and avoid evil," they don't always agree about what is good and what is evil. In fact, people are often mistaken about what behavior is right and wrong. So how can we know for sure?

The second problem concerns our reasons for following this law of human behavior. Since men aren't forced to act in accord with law but may freely choose, why do they?

The Master Plan

Where can we find the solution to these problems? The best way is to look to the Master Planner and see what he had in mind.

As we all know, God is the Creator and Lord of heaven and earth. In his great wisdom he made the universe and governs it all. Now, just as he made the law of gravity and instinct, he made all men with this idea of doing good and avoiding evil. But he also made men with free will, allowing them to choose to do good and avoid evil.

When Adam and Eve chose to disobey God, their sin affected all men that were to come. One result of Original Sin is that it is harder for us to know what is right and wrong and to behave accordingly. If we read the beginning of the Old Testament we can easily see that men soon made a mess of things.

13

But God promised Adam that he would not abandon us and would give us a means of salvation. So God called upon Abraham and made him the father of his chosen people. God established his covenant with the Israelites, to show that he would be their God and they would be his people. He gave them the **Decalogue—the Ten Commandments**. God wanted his people to know what was right and wrong and what was truly good and truly bad for them. He was preparing them for a special role in salvation history.

Some people think that God simply wanted obedience to a set of rules. What he really wanted was a faithful people. He gave his people a law to teach and guide them in every part of their lives. Further, he gave his people a law to prepare them for the coming of the Savior.

Fulfillment of the Law

When Jesus came to establish the New **Covenant**, he did not set aside the Ten Commandments, but completed them. He said: "Do not think that I have come to abolish the law and the prophets; I have come not to abolish them but to fulfill them" (Mt 5:17). Jesus teaches that the foundation of all law is love: to love God above all things, with one's whole mind and heart and soul, and to love one's neighbor as oneself. Jesus wants all men to turn their minds and hearts to God with love. Disobeying any of the Ten Commandments is a failure to love either God or our neighbor. This is because the Ten Commandments sum up our duties to God and our neighbor.

14

Conscience

How do we know that one action is right and another wrong? Along with free will God has given each man the ability to judge if something is right or wrong. This ability is called **conscience**. Our conscience is a very practical tool. It tells us what would be right or wrong behavior in a given situation. We are to obey our conscience, for God gave it to us so that we could live according to his law.

Every person is born with a conscience. Even a member of some primitive tribe that has never come into contact with civilization has the same law in his heart to do good and avoid evil. His tribe will probably have a code of what they think is right and wrong. He will be responsible before God for doing what he thinks is right and not doing what he thinks is wrong. In this way he can please God. But his code of behavior might differ somewhat from the Ten Commandments. Since he has had no contact with the commandments, he will not be held responsible for obeying them. Nonetheless, his conscience is faulty.

A conscience has to be taught—and taught correctly. We call this "forming" a conscience. The conscience of the primitive man, since it was not formed correctly, is called an incorrect conscience. Since he could do nothing about

that, he will not be held responsible for his incorrect conscience. On the other hand, all men who have access to the Word of God have a responsibility to form a correct conscience.

God has given us the means to form our consciences correctly. He has revealed truths about himself and given us the Ten Commandments. To live according to the will of God we must follow and obey the commandments. If we disregard or break God's law we sin. If we deliberately break a commandment in a serious matter, we commit a mortal sin and destroy charity, or the love of God, in our hearts. When we commit a mortal sin, we reject God by choosing to do something seriously contrary to God's will. If we do not repent of mortal sin, we cannot go to heaven and be happy with God forever. Of course, whether or not what we do is a mortal sin depends on whether we know that what we are doing is seriously wrong and we freely chose to do it anyway. And if we do commit a mortal sin, God will forgive us if we truly repent of our sin. He has given us the Sacrament of Penance to forgive our sins and to help us to grow closer to him.

But besides giving us the Law, he has given us reasons why we should want to follow it. First, God is the giver and author of that law, and since he is our Creator he knows what is best for us. Obeying God's law is necessary

The Ten Commandments

1. I am the Lord your God; you shall not have other gods before me.
2. You shall not take the name of the Lord your God in vain.
3. Remember to keep holy the Lord's Day.
4. Honor your father and mother.
5. You shall not kill.
6. You shall not commit adultery.
7. You shall not steal.
8. You shall not bear false witness against your neighbor.
9. You shall not covet your neighbor's wife.
10. You shall not covet your neighbor's goods.

15

GOD'S MASTER PLAN

In the beginning:
- In God's image
- Free will
- Rational
- Free from sin
- Preternatural gifts:
  - Infused knowledge
  - Not die
  - Never sick or suffer
  - Knew good from evil
  - Acted with will
  - Lived in harmony
- Supernatural gift:
  - Grace (God's life)

After the Fall:
- Distorted God's image
- Free will
- Rational
- Born with Original Sin
- Preternatural gifts lost:
  - Learning requires labor
  - Would die, return to dust
  - Suffering and illness
  - Intellect is weakened
  - Will is weakened to sin
  - Disharmony with others
- Supernatural gift:
  - Grace is lost

Preview

In the next lesson, the students will learn about Jesus and the Law.

CHAPTER ONE: GOD GIVES US THE LAW
LESSON THREE: JESUS' LAW

Aims

The students will learn that Jesus established the New Law and did not set aside the Old Law of the Ten Commandments.

They will learn that the greatest commandment is to love God and our neighbors as ourselves.

They will learn that disobeying God's commandments is a failure to love God and neighbor.

Materials

- *Activity Book*, p. 3

- Bible

Optional:
- "Father, we thank thee who has planted," *Adoremus Hymnal*, #515

Begin

Review the definition of the term *covenant* (see glossary in student text on *Teacher's Manual* p. 395). A covenant is a binding oath that unites two parties in a relationship. Throughout history, God has called man into relationship with him (see timeline on p. 9, at right). The Ten Commandments were the condition of this covenant. By breaking them, we break our covenant (it is a breach of contract).

Develop

1. Read paragraph 10 from the student text.

2. You may read the major covenants of the Old Testament from your Bible, using the timeline at right as your guide. The students may break into groups, and dramatize these covenants for their fellow students.

3. Discuss a covenant that the students may be familiar with, such as marriage. Marriage is a covenant that a man and woman enter into because of love for one another. Marriage is entered into by the profession of vows before man and God. It is binding. It is possible to break the marriage covenant by breaking the vows to love, honor, and cherish, but breaking vows hurts the marriage relationship.

4. Review the Ten Commandments. The first three commandments teach us how to love God. The last seven teach us how to love our neighbor. Jesus, who is God the Son become man,

established a New Covenant, expanding upon these laws. Read the laws of Jesus in the Beatitudes: Mt 5:1–12, 17; the story of the rich young man: Mt 19:16–21; and the Great Commandment: Lk 10:27. Jesus teaches that beyond the duty of the law is the spirit of the law: love.

5. Have the students discuss and memorize the Beatitudes.

6. Explain to the students that Jesus established the New and Everlasting Covenant. He is the Savior promised by God to Adam and Eve. He redeemed man by dying on the Cross. By his death and Resurrection he offered atonement and reunited man and God through grace. He established his covenant at the Last Supper by giving the disciples his Body and Blood in the Eucharist and fulfilling this self-gift by his sacrifice on the Cross. We enter this covenant through Baptism and commemorate Jesus' sacred meal and sacrifice at Mass.

Reinforce

1. Have the students work on *Activity Book* p. 3 (see *Teacher's Manual*, p. 13).

2. Have the students work on the Memorization Questions, Words to Know (see *Teacher's Manual*, p. 11), and memorization of the Beatitudes. They may do a service project in honor of the blessed in the Beatitudes; e.g., a food collection for the poor, writing get well cards for the sick, sympathy cards for family members of a deceased parishioner.

3. Write prayers, asking God to bless those named in the Beatitudes.

Conclude

1. Lead the students in singing "Father, we thank thee who has planted," *Adoremus Hymnal*, #515.

2. End class by leading the students in praying the Our Father (see *Teacher's Manual*, p. 396).

But God promised Adam that he would not abandon us and would give us a means of salvation. So God called upon Abraham and made him the father of his chosen people. God established his covenant with the Israelites, to show that he would be their God and they would be his people. He gave them the **Decalogue**—the **Ten Commandments**. God wanted his people to know what was right and wrong and what was truly good and truly bad for them. He was preparing them for a special role in salvation history.

Some people think that God simply wanted obedience to a set of rules. What he really wanted is a faithful people. He gave his people a law to teach and guide them in every part of their lives. Further, he gave his people a law to prepare them for the coming of the Savior.

14

Fulfillment of the Law

When Jesus came to establish the New **Covenant**, he did not set aside the Ten Commandments, but completed them. He said: "Do not think that I have come to abolish the law and the prophets; I have come not to abolish them but to fulfill them" (Mt 5:17). Jesus teaches that the foundation of all law is love: to love God above all things, with one's whole mind and heart and soul, and to love one's neighbor as oneself. Jesus wants all men to turn their minds and hearts to God with love. Disobeying any of the Ten Commandments is a failure to love either God or our neighbor. This is because the Ten Commandments sum up our duties to God and our neighbor.

Conscience

How do we know that one action is right and another wrong? Along with free will God has given each man the ability to judge if something is right or wrong. This ability is called **conscience**. Our conscience is a very practical tool. It tells us what would be right or wrong behavior in a given situation. We are to obey our conscience, for God gave it to us so that we could live according to his law.

Every person is born with a conscience. Even a member of some primitive tribe that has never come into contact with civilization has the same law in his heart to do good and avoid evil. His tribe will probably have a code of what they think is right and wrong. He will be responsible before God for doing what he thinks is right and not doing what he thinks is wrong. In this way he can please God. But his code of behavior might differ somewhat from the Ten Commandments. Since he has had no contact with the commandments, he will not be held responsible for obeying them. Nonetheless, his conscience is faulty.

A conscience has to be taught—and taught correctly. We call this "forming" a conscience. The conscience of the primitive man, since it was not formed correctly, is called an incorrect conscience. Since he could do nothing about that, he will not be held responsible for his incorrect conscience. On the other hand, all men who have access to the Word of God have a responsibility to form a correct conscience.

God has given us the means to form our consciences correctly. He has revealed truths about himself and given us the Ten Commandments. To live according to the will of God we must follow and obey the commandments. If we disregard or break God's law we sin. If we deliberately break a commandment in a serious matter, we commit a mortal sin and destroy charity, or the love of God, in our hearts. When we commit a mortal sin, we reject God by choosing to do something seriously contrary to God's will. If we do not repent of mortal sin, we cannot go to heaven and be happy with God forever. Of course, whether or not what we do is a mortal sin depends on whether we know that what we are doing is seriously wrong and we freely chose to do it anyway. And if we do commit a mortal sin, God will forgive us if we truly repent of our sin. He has given us the Sacrament of Penance to forgive our sins and to help us to grow closer to him.

But besides giving us the Law, he has given us reasons why we should want to follow it. First, God is the giver and author of that law, and since he is our Creator he knows what is best for us. Obeying God's law is necessary

> ### The Ten Commandments
> 1. I am the Lord your God; you shall not have other gods before me.
> 2. You shall not take the name of the Lord your God in vain.
> 3. Remember to keep holy the Lord's Day.
> 4. Honor your father and mother.
> 5. You shall not kill.
> 6. You shall not commit adultery.
> 7. You shall not steal.
> 8. You shall not bear false witness against your neighbor.
> 9. You shall not covet your neighbor's wife.
> 10. You shall not covet your neighbor's goods.

15

SALVATION HISTORY TIMELINE

Adam and Eve: Gen 3:15

Noah: Gen 8:20–22

Abraham: Gen 22:15–18

Israel moves to Egypt: Gen 46:1–4

Moses and the Exodus: Ex 19:5

Reign of David: 2 Sam 7:13–17

Kingdom Divides: 1 Kings 12:1–17

Fall of Northern Kingdom; population sent into exile: 2 Kings 17:1–8

Fall and exile of Southern Kingdom: 2 Kings 25:1–7

Return from Exile: Ezra 1:1–4

Jesus: Mk 14:22–25

| CREATION | 2000 BC | 1500 | 1000 | 750 | 500 | 33 AD |

BEATITUDE

The word *beatitude* comes from the Latin word *beatitudo*, which means "the state of being happy" or "felicity."

Preview

In the next lesson, the students will learn about the conscience.

CHAPTER ONE: GOD GIVES US THE LAW
LESSON FOUR: CONSCIENCE

Aims

The students will learn that conscience is the faculty of judgment applied to a given action to determine whether it is good or evil.

They will learn that all men have a conscience and are obliged to form it properly. God has provided the means to know him and his ways and to form our consciences through the teachings of the Church.

Materials

- *Activity Book*, p. 4

- Bible

Optional:
- "Father, we thank thee who has planted," *Adoremus Hymnal*, #515

~~Father~~ Mike Schmitz
What is sin?
Mortal vs. Venial

Begin

Have the students look up the word "conscience" in the glossary of their text (see box on facing page). Explain that every person has a conscience. It is man's moral guide. It is his inner sanctuary, in which God speaks to him. It is the power to judge what course of action to take in any situation. Each of us is obliged to follow his conscience, so everyone has a great duty to properly form his conscience. Because we must never act on a doubtful conscience, we must look to the Church for the proper help to form our consciences well.

Develop

1. Read paragraphs 11–17 from the student text.

2. God has given us his law in the Ten Commandments, revealed to Moses at Mount Sinai. Every person knows God's natural law (do good and avoid evil) through his conscience. Read the following passages from the Bible to see how conscience has been followed: Gen 22:1–19; 2 Mac 6:18–31; 7:1–42; Gen 3; 4:1–16; and 2 Sam 11:1—12:25. (Also 1 Cor 8:12.)

3. If we break the moral law, we sin. We sin when we choose to disobey the moral law. Sinful actions that we choose to do are called "actual sins." (Actual sin differs from Original Sin, which is an inherited stain.) We can sin by thought, word, deed, and omission. To determine if something is sinful we must look at the object (what it is). An object can be moral (good) like praying, immoral (bad) like stealing, or amoral (neither) like walking. An immoral object can never become good. A moral or amoral object can become bad by its intention and or circumstance. For example, eating might seem harmless, but if we are eating the last food to keep it away from someone else to be cruel, eating is bad. On the other hand, if we are eating so little that we starve ourselves, then choosing not to eat is bad. Once we determine that a thought, word, deed or omission is sinful, we must determine if the sin is mortal or venial. (See the box, "Mortal and Venial Sin," at right for abbreviated definitions.)

4. Give the students various scenarios, and have them first determine if an action is sinful. If they determine an action (or omission) to be a sin, they must decide if it is mortal or venial sin. Have the students use the Ten Commandments and the moral teachings of Jesus to make an examination of conscience. (Students may desire to receive the Sacrament of Penance after completing their examinations of conscience.)

Reinforce

1. Have the students complete *Activity Book* p. 4 (see *Teacher's Manual*, p. 13).

2. If possible, arrange for the students to receive the Sacrament of Penance. (Start the year off right!)

3. Discuss how we find God's laws in the Bible (revelation), the Church (Tradition), and in our hearts (conscience).

4. Have the students work on the Memorization Questions and prepare for the quiz.

Conclude

1. Lead the students in singing "Father, we thank thee who has planted," *Adoremus Hymnal*, #515.

2. End class by leading the students in praying the Our Father (see *Teacher's Manual*, p. 396).

Conscience

How do we know that one action is right and another wrong? Along with free will God has given each man the ability to judge if something is right or wrong. This ability is called **conscience**. Our conscience is a very practical tool. It tells us what would be right or wrong behavior in a given situation. We are to obey our conscience, for God gave it to us so that we could live according to his law.

Every person is born with a conscience. Even a member of some primitive tribe that has never come into contact with civilization has the same law in his heart to do good and avoid evil. His tribe will probably have a code of what they think is right and wrong. He will be responsible before God for doing what he thinks is right and not doing what he thinks is wrong. In this way he can please God. But his code of behavior might differ somewhat from the Ten Commandments. Since he has had no contact with the commandments, he will not be held responsible for obeying them. Nonetheless, his conscience is faulty.

A conscience has to be taught—and taught correctly. We call this "forming" a conscience. The conscience of the primitive man, since it was not formed correctly, is called an incorrect conscience. Since he could do nothing about that, he will not be held responsible for his incorrect conscience. On the other hand, all men who have access to the Word of God have a responsibility to form a correct conscience.

God has given us the means to form our consciences correctly. He has revealed truths about himself and given us the Ten Commandments. To live according to the will of God we must follow and obey the commandments. If we disregard or break God's law we sin. If we deliberately break a commandment in a serious matter, we commit a mortal sin and destroy charity, or the love of God, in our hearts. When we commit a mortal sin, we reject God by choosing to do something seriously contrary to God's will. If we do not repent of mortal sin, we cannot go to heaven and be happy with God forever. Of course, whether or not what we do is a mortal sin depends on whether we know that what we are doing is seriously wrong and we freely chose to do it anyway. And if we do commit a mortal sin, God will forgive us if we truly repent of our sin. He has given us the Sacrament of Penance to forgive our sins and to help us to grow closer to him.

But besides giving us the Law, he has given us reasons why we should want to follow it. First, God is the giver and author of that law, and since he is our Creator he knows what is best for us. Obeying God's law is necessary for our eternal salvation. How could we live with God forever if we choose to reject his life and his friendship by serious sin?

But an even greater reason to obey God is that we know his great love for us. Jesus tells us: "If you love me, you will keep my commandments." (Jn 14:15) What better way do we have of showing our love for God than by doing what he asks of us?

God gave us his commandments and our conscience to help us know right from wrong. He gave us the example of his Son Jesus Christ, who perfectly loved and obeyed the Father. At the same time, God gave us the power to keep his commandments. That power is the life of grace that comes from the Holy Spirit who lives within us.

Words to Know:
Decalogue   Ten Commandments
covenant   conscience

The Ten Commandments

1. I am the Lord your God; you shall not have other gods before me.
2. You shall not take the name of the Lord your God in vain.
3. Remember to keep holy the Lord's Day.
4. Honor your father and mother.
5. You shall not kill.
6. You shall not commit adultery.
7. You shall not steal.
8. You shall not bear false witness against your neighbor.
9. You shall not covet your neighbor's wife.
10. You shall not covet your neighbor's goods.

15

Q. 1 *What must we do to live according to the will of God?*
To live according to the will of God, we must believe the truths that he has revealed and with the help of his grace obey his commandments (CCC 1692).

Q. 2 *What are the commandments of God?*
The commandments of God are the Ten Commandments, the moral laws that God gave to Moses on Mount Sinai in the Old Testament, and which Jesus Christ perfected in the New Testament.

Q. 3 *What is the foundation of all our duties toward God and neighbor?*
The foundation of all our duties toward God and neighbor is charity, as Jesus Christ explained: the greatest and first commandment is the love of God, and the second is love of neighbor; upon these two commandments depends the whole law and the prophets. (CCC 2055).

Q. 4 *Why are we obliged to keep the commandments of God?*
We are obliged to keep the commandments of God because they sum up our basic duties toward God and our neighbor (CCC 2072).

Q. 5 *Does one who deliberately breaks a commandment of God in a serious matter sin gravely?*
One who deliberately breaks even one commandment of God in a serious matter sins gravely against God, and thus risks hell (CCC 1855, 2072).

16

SCRIPTURE AND CATECHISM ON MORTAL AND VENIAL SIN

CCC 1855: *Mortal sin* destroys charity in the heart of man by a grave violation of God's law; it turns man away from God, who is his ultimate end and his beatitude, by preferring an inferior good to him.

Venial sin allows charity to subsist, even though it offends and wounds it.

"If anyone sees his brother committing what is not a deadly sin, he will ask, and God will give him life for those whose sin is not deadly. . . . All wrongdoing is sin, but there is sin which is not deadly."
—1 John 5:16–17

MORTAL AND VENIAL SIN

For a sin to be mortal:
- It must be serious matter.
- We must know it is wrong.
- We must freely choose to do it.

For a sin to be venial:
- It must be less serious matter, though we may have knowledge and free will.
- It may be serious, but we are without full knowledge of its seriousness and/or we do not fully consent to the action.

—See CCC 1854–1864.

CONSCIENCE

From the student glossary, the definition of *conscience* is: our ability to know and judge what is right and wrong.

The word *conscience* comes from the Latin words *con*, which means "with" and *scientia*, which means "knowledge."

Preview

In the next lesson, the students' understanding of the material covered in this chapter will be reviewed and assessed.

CHAPTER ONE: GOD GIVES US THE LAW
REVIEW AND ASSESSMENT

Aims

The students' understanding of the material covered in this chapter will be reviewed and assessed.

Materials

- Quiz 1, Appendix, p. A-1

Optional:
- "Father, we thank thee who has planted," *Adoremus Hymnal*, #515.

Review and Enrichment

1. Man can know that God exists from the world around him. We know about God by revelation in Sacred Scripture and Sacred Tradition. This revelation is safeguarded by the Magisterium (the teaching Church).

2. Man is made in the image of God. Man has free will. The students should know the hierarchy of creation.

3. God made man to be united with God forever in heaven. He gave us his law so that we can be free to follow his plan.

4. The students should be familiar with Creation and the Fall of man. The students should understand the need for a savior.

5. God's law includes (but is not limited to) the Ten Commandments, the Beatitudes, the law of love, and conscience.

6. Jesus Christ, God the Son made man, is the Savior, who established the new and everlasting covenant at the Last Supper and the Crucifixion. We enter into this covenant at Baptism and commemorate this covenant at Mass.

7. Conscience is the faculty to judge a given situation as good or evil. Students must be able to define actual sin, mortal sin, and venial sin.

Name: _____

God Gives Us the Law   Quiz 1

Part I: Fill in the blanks.

1. Every man has the law in his heart to do <u>good</u> and avoid <u>evil</u>.

2. Our <u>conscience</u> is the ability to judge if an action is right or wrong.

3. God established a <u>covenant</u> with the Israelites and gave them his laws.

4. God's laws known as the Ten Commandments are also called the <u>Decalogue</u>.

5. Man has <u>free</u> <u>will</u> so that he can love and obey God.

6. Jesus taught us that <u>love</u> is the foundation of all law.

7. Jesus said that all of the commandments can be summed up in this: Love <u>God</u> above all things with our whole mind, heart and soul and love our <u>neighbor</u>.

8. We <u>sin</u> when we choose to break God's law.

Part II: Write the Ten Commandments in order.

1. <u>I am the Lord your God; you shall not have other gods before me.</u>
2. <u>You shall not take the name of the Lord your God in vain.</u>
3. <u>Remember to keep holy the Lord's Day.</u>
4. <u>Honor your father and mother.</u>
5. <u>You shall not kill.</u>
6. <u>You shall not commit adultery.</u>
7. <u>You shall not steal.</u>
8. <u>You shall not bear false witness against your neighbor.</u>
9. <u>You shall not covet your neighbor's wife.</u>
10. <u>You shall not covet your neighbor's goods.</u>

Faith and Life Series • Grade 6 • Appendix A   *A-1*

Assess

1. Distribute the quizzes and read through them with the students to be sure they understand the questions.

2. Administer the quiz. As they hand in their work, you may orally quiz the students on the Memorization Questions from this chapter.

3. After all the quizzes have been handed in, you may wish to review the correct answers with the class.

Conclude

1. Lead the students in singing "Father, we thank thee who has planted," *Adoremus Hymnal*, #515.

2. End class by leading the students in praying the Our Father (see *Teacher's Manual*, p. 396).

Name:_____

God Gives Us the Law

Answer the following questions in complete sentences.

1. What is the first rule of moral law?
   The first rule of moral law is "Do good and avoid evil."

2. What do the rules of moral behavior tell us?
   The rules of moral behavior tell us what we ought to do.

3. Why must we follow the rules of moral behavior?
   Answers will vary.

4. Are we free to choose to do good and avoid evil?
   Yes, we are free to choose to do good and avoid evil.

5. How can we know what the good is?
   To know what the good is, we should look to God for guidance.

6. How does God help us know the moral good?
   Answers wills vary.

Faith and Life Series • Grade 6 • Chapter 1 • Lesson 1   1

Name:_____

God's Laws

Answer the following questions in complete sentences.

1. Why did God give us his law?
   God gave us his law to show us what is right and wrong—to guide us in every part of our lives.

2. What is a covenant?
   A covenant is a solemn agreement.

3. Write out the Ten Commandments in order.
   1. You shall not have other gods before me.
   2. You shall not take the name of the Lord your God in vain.
   3. Remember to keep holy the Lord's Day.
   4. Honor your father and mother.
   5. You shall not kill.
   6. You shall not commit adultery.
   7. You shall not steal.
   8. You shall not bear false witness against your neighbor.
   9. You shall not covet your neighbor's wife.
   10. You shall not covet your neighbor's goods.

2   *Faith and Life Series • Grade 6 • Chapter 1 • Lesson 2*

Name:_____

Fulfillment of the Law

Answer the following questions in complete sentences.

1. When Jesus established the New Covenant, did he set aside the Old Law?
   No, Jesus did not set aside the Old Law, he fulfilled it.

2. What is the foundation of the Old Law?
   The foundation of the Old Law is love.

3. What did Jesus say were the two greatest commandments?
   Jesus said that the two greatest commandments are to love God above all things, and to love one's neighbor as oneself.

4. Which commandment summarizes the first three of the Ten Commandments?
   The commandment to love God above all things summarizes the first three of the Ten Commandments.

5. Which commandment summarizes the last seven of the Ten Commandments?
   The commandment to love one's neighbor as one's self summarizes the last seven of the Ten Commandments.

6. Why is free will necessary if we are to follow Jesus?
   Answers will vary, but should be similar to: Free will allows us to choose freely to follow Jesus.

*The last three questions are not covered in the student text, but students should be able to answer them.

Faith and Life Series • Grade 6 • Chapter 1 • Lesson 3   3

Name:_____

Your Conscience

Answer the following questions in complete sentences.

1. What is your conscience?
   Conscience is the ability to judge whether something is right or wrong.

2. Why did God give you a conscience?
   God gave us a conscience so that we could live according to his law.

3. Does everybody know the Ten Commandments?
   No, not everyone knows the Ten Commandments.

4. Does everybody know God's laws? How?
   Everyone has God's law to "do good and avoid evil" in his heart.

5. How can we form our consciences correctly?
   We can form our consciences by living according to the will of God and following his commandments.

6. What are the three conditions for a mortal sin?
   For a sin to be mortal, it must be a serious matter, we must know it is serious, and we must freely choose to do it.

7. What must we do with our consciences as Catholics?
   We must form our consciences correctly and then follow them.

4   *Faith and Life Series • Grade 6 • Chapter 1 • Lesson 4*

TEACHER'S NOTES

CHAPTER TWO
THE FIRST COMMANDMENT IN OUR OWN DAY

Catechism of the Catholic Church References

Eucharist as Sacrifice: 1356–81, 1414
Eucharist as Thanksgiving and Praise to the Father: 1359–61
Eucharist as Sacrificial Memorial of Christ and of His Body,
the Church: 1362–72, 1408, 1414
Presence of Christ in the Eucharist: 1373–81, 1410, 1418
First Commandment: 2084–2132, 2133–41
"You Shall Worship the Lord Your God": 2084–2141
    Faith: 2087–89
    Hope: 2090–92
    Charity: 2093–94
"Him Only Shall You Serve": 2095–2136
    Worship: 2096–97
    Prayer: 2098
    Sacrifice: 2099–2100

Promises and Vows: 2101–3
Society and Religious Freedom: 2104–9, 2137
"You Shall Have No Other Gods Before Me": 2100
    Superstition: 2111, 2138
    Idolatry: 2112–14, 2138
    Divination and Magic: 2115–17, 2138
    Irreligion: 2118–22, 2139
    Atheism: 2123–26, 2140
    Agnosticism: 2127–28
"You Shall Not Make for Yourself a Graven Image":
2129–32
    Poverty of heart: 2544–47, 2556
    Ways of knowing God: 31–38, 46–48, 286
Original Sin, Consequences: 55–58, 399–400, 402–9, 416–19

Scripture References

Golden Calf: Ex 32:1–28
Cannot Serve Two Masters: Mt 6:24–30

The Rich Young Man: Mk 10:17–22
God Knows Us: Ps 139

Summary of Lesson Content

Lesson 1

The First Commandment teaches that there is one true God, who alone should be worshipped.

God has revealed himself to man and man in return must believe all that God has revealed to him.

The First Commandment forbids superstition, impiety, heresy, and anything contrary to the reverence we owe God.

Lesson 2

Worship of false gods is called idolatry.

Man must not put anything before God. Man must love God above all else.

Lesson 3

The story about the rich young man teaches that we must love God above all creatures. This love requires detachment from worldly possessions.

Lesson 4

The Israelites offered sacrifices to God to acknowledge him as Creator of all and to atone for their sins.

They will learn that because the victim, priest, and intention could not be perfect and in total union with God, no sin offering made by men could fully atone for our sins.

Jesus, the perfect priest, offered the perfect sacrifice of himself, the perfect victim, with the perfect intention, to atone for our sins. This is the Sacrifice of the Mass.

CHAPTER TWO: THE FIRST COMMANDMENT IN OUR OWN DAY
LESSON ONE: FIRST COMMANDMENT

Aims

The students will learn that the First Commandment teaches that there is one true God, who alone should be worshipped.

They will learn that God has revealed himself to man and man in return must believe all that God has revealed to him. The First Commandment forbids superstition, impiety, heresy, and anything contrary to the reverence we owe God.

Materials

- *Activity Book*, p. 5

- Appendix, pp. B-1 and B-2

- Bible

Optional:
- "God Father, praise and glory," *Adoremus Hymnal*, #464

Begin

Review our dependence upon God. You may read Psalm 139 with the students. Discuss God's great love for us and that he cares so greatly for us. How should we respond to this love? What are ways that we can show our love and thanks to God?

Develop

1. Read paragraphs 1–3 with the students.

2. Have the students look up the bold text in the glossary and write down the definitions.

3. Using Appendix, pp. B-1 and B-2, review the gestures used at Mass. Explain clearly that our actions are an outward expression of what is in our hearts. We are called to be reverent at Mass and in church. Reverence means to be respectful toward God and his holy people, places, and things, and to be loving in our thoughts, words, and deeds. Help the students to practice and to better understand the gestures used in church and at Mass, so that they may show God that they worship and adore him.

4. Reread paragraph 2. We must learn about God through his revelation. We have a duty to learn God's laws, and to obey them. We must learn about God to believe in him, to have hope in his teachings, and to live these teachings in love. What are ways we can learn about God? (Go to religion class; listen to homilies; read the Bible, catechism, lives of the saints; etc.)

5. Review what superstition is. Superstition is placing our trust in something other than God. In today's society, we seldom see people worship golden statues, as in the times of Moses. But there are many ways that people show they do not trust in God: through faith in horoscopes, psychics, numerology, tarot cards, ouija boards, etc. Some people willfully worship the devil, through witchcraft and satanism. These are dangerous abominations before God.

6. You may teach the students that heresy is to deny a truth of the Faith; apostasy is to deny or reject the true religion of Catholicism; and schism is to deny the authority of the Church, as it was entrusted by Jesus Christ.

Reinforce

1. Have the students work on *Activity Book* p. 5 (see *Teacher's Manual*, p. 25).

2. Take the students outdoors to draw pictures of things that glorify God in the world. They may record in a journal or on notepaper how they intend to know, love, and serve God.

3. The students should begin to work on the Memorization Questions and Words to Know from the text (see *Teacher's Manual*, p. 23).

Conclude

1. Teach the students to sing "God Father, praise and glory," *Adoremus Hymnal*, #464.

2. End class by leading the students in the Apostles' Creed (see *Teacher's Manual*, p. 396).

CHAPTER 2

The First Commandment In Our Own Day

"I am the LORD your God, who brought you out of the land of Egypt, out of the house of bondage. You shall have no other gods before me."

Exodus 20:2–3

The First Commandment requires all men to recognize or acknowledge God as the one true God, Creator and Lord of all things, and to **worship** and **adore** him as our God. As creatures, we owe everything to God; we are completely dependent on him. By our reverence and worship we acknowledge our debt and gratitude to our Creator.

To give God loving worship we must believe in him and believe all that he has revealed to us. This means that we must learn more about God. If he has given us the means to do this, we have no excuse for being ignorant about God and his truths.

This commandment requires certain behavior from us, it also forbids us to act in any way contrary to what we owe God. It is wrong if we practice **superstition** or impiety. **Impiety** means being irreverent and disrespectful of God or sacred things. It is also wrong if we willfully doubt some truth about God or refuse to know what we should about God and our religion. There are times when some people are so willful that they publicly acknowledge their disbelief in or disagreement with the

truths of the Faith. This is called **heresy**—the denying or disagreeing with one particular truth, or **apostasy**—deserting or leaving the true religion.

Strange Gods

We have read about people in ancient times who used to worship idols—false gods, things like golden calves. Remember when the Israelites worshipped the golden calf in the desert before God gave them the Ten Commandments? This is called **idolatry**. We don't run into too many people who worship golden calves, but many still place "strange gods" before God in their lives.

Not to have "strange gods" means that we are not to love anyone or anything as much as we love God. We are to worship and adore him—that is, give him the special love that is owed to him alone. This is a love that acknowledges his supreme position above all creation.

We must put nothing God has made before our love for him. No creature is to be adored—that is, worshipped with that special love

17

which we owe to God alone. Our love for or attachment to things God has made is not wrong in itself. It is not wrong for a computer or a dog to have a place in our life. But these things must never compete with our love for God or with his plans for us. For example, if we love a computer so much that we steal one, then we have put it before God.

There is a story from the Bible which makes all this clear.

The Rich Young Man

A rich young man received an invitation from our Lord himself to give up his riches and become a follower of Jesus. Saint Mark tells us that Jesus looked at the young man and loved him, for the youth had always kept all of God's commandments and wanted to do even better. Jesus said to him: "You lack one thing; go, sell what you have, and give to the poor, and you will have treasure in heaven; and come, follow me" (Mk 10:21).

But the young man turned away sadly and left Jesus because, as the Bible says, he "had many possessions." He could not follow Jesus

because he loved creatures, or created goods, too much. They may not have been the same creatures we have—not radios or televisions or cars—but whatever they were, he would not give them up. He missed the chance to follow Jesus because creatures were competing in his heart with love for God.

There is danger in having many possessions because they may turn our hearts from God. Our love for such things must be a "detached" love, a love that is ready to let go of things when God asks it of us.

Due Worship

In ages before Christ, the Hebrew people offered public **sacrifice** by slaughtering a valuable animal, like a lamb, upon an altar to honor God, to acknowledge him as Creator of all, and especially to make up for their sins.

The sacrifice of the Hebrew people pleased God but it could never fully make up for sin. As we know, the sin of Adam had closed the gates of heaven. None of the many sacrifices offered by the Hebrews could change this. For sin offends God who is so great, and no

18

offering of man alone, no matter how valuable, can make up for it.

Man's helplessness was no obstacle to God who wanted to save man. God himself became man and offered himself on the Cross as a fitting sacrifice, which was far more than enough to make up for all sins of all men. This sacrifice is renewed daily in every Mass around the world. The sacrifice of Jesus on the Cross is the greatest gift we can offer to God.

The sacrifice we offer in the Mass is the highest possible act of worship. It contains all that is necessary for giving due worship to God. In the Mass we acknowledge God as

Creator, our Lord and Master. We thank him in gratitude for all he has given us. And, in recognition that we are dependent on him, we ask for all we need and for what will help others. Finally, we offer in the Mass the only thing that can make up for our sins and offenses. We offer the sacrifice of Jesus Christ on the Cross.

We can give God the love and worship we owe him when we participate in Holy Mass. Let's do so often!

Words to Know:
worship adore superstition impiety
heresy idolatry sacrifice apostasy

"Bless the Lord, all works of the Lord, sing praise to him and highly exalt him for ever."

Daniel 3:35

19

CHALK TALK: THE FIRST COMMANDMENT

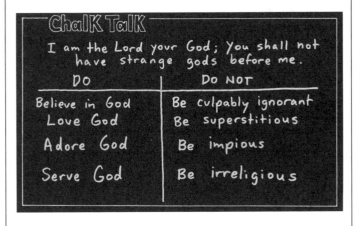

Chalk Talk

I am the Lord your God; You shall not have strange gods before me.

DO	DO NOT
Believe in God	Be culpably ignorant
Love God	Be superstitious
Adore God	Be impious
Serve God	Be irreligious

Preview

In the next lesson, the students will learn more about idolatry.

CHAPTER TWO: THE FIRST COMMANDMENT IN OUR OWN DAY
LESSON TWO: IDOLATRY

Aims

The students will learn that worship of false gods is called idolatry.

They will learn that man must not put anything before God. Man must love God above all else.

Materials

- *Activity Book*, p. 6
- Magazines or catalogues
- Bible

Optional:
- "God Father, praise and glory," *Adoremus Hymnal*, #464

Begin

Read from the Bible (Ex 32:1–28) the story of the Israelites worshipping the golden calf.

Discuss this passage:
- Why did they make a calf?

- Did they not trust God?
- How did God respond?
- What was their punishment?
- What should we learn from this story?
- What are some of our "golden calves" today?

Develop

1. Read paragraphs 4–7 from the student text.

2. Explain to the students that though God created many good things (food, animals, friends, love) we must never place these things before God. The good use of created things is called stewardship. Through stewardship we give glory to God. Show: that every created good is a gift from God; how we might value it more than God; how we should use it to glorify God in good stewardship. Food is a good example:
- Food is a great gift from God. It keeps us alive, it tastes wonderful (what is your favorite food?), etc.
- We can place food before God by choosing to break appointed days and times of fast and abstinence (e.g., breaking the Eucharistic fast, eating meat on Good Friday).
- We can glorify God through food, by thanking him for it, sharing it with those who do not have it, using it well, etc.
Have the students give further examples of things from God's creation that can be wrongly placed above God.

3. Another form of idolatry, the worship of things other than the one true God, has become more common today. Recently, the practice of the occult, particularly in witchcraft and satanism, has increased dramatically. The practice of these superstitious beliefs is not only sinful, but very dangerous. Those who participate in the occult are consenting to cooperate and sometimes even belong to Satan and his demons. Television and movies sometimes glorify the occult, making it appear harmless or even beneficial. This is a lie and an offense against God and his truth.

4. Using magazines and catalogues, have the students find images of things that we often put before God. Discuss why. (Are they expensive? Do they take up a lot of time?)

5. Discuss irreligion: an absence of love for God and not giving to him what we owe as his creatures.

Reinforce

1. Have the students work on *Activity Book* p. 6 (see *Teacher's Manual*, p. 25).

2. Have the students pray an Act of Consecration to Jesus (see facing page).

3. Have the students write letters to God, telling God how they love him above all things and describing ways in which they will overcome their worldly attachments.

4. Have the students work on the Memorization Questions and Words to Know (see *Teacher's Manual*, p. 23).

Conclude

1. Lead the students in singing "God Father, praise and glory," *Adoremus Hymnal*, #464.

2. End class by leading the students in the Apostles' Creed (see *Teacher's Manual*, p. 396).

CHAPTER 2

The First Commandment In Our Own Day

"I am the LORD your God, who brought you out of the land of Egypt, out of the house of bondage. You shall have no other gods before me."

Exodus 20:2–3

The First Commandment requires all men to recognize or acknowledge God as the one true God, Creator and Lord of all things, and to **worship** and **adore** him as our God. As creatures, we owe everything to God; we are completely dependent on him. By our reverence and worship we acknowledge our debt and gratitude to our Creator.

To give God loving worship we must believe in him and believe all that he has revealed to us. This means that we must learn more about God. If he has given us the means to do this, we have no excuse for being ignorant about God and his truths.

This commandment requires certain behavior from us, it also forbids us to act in any way contrary to what we owe God. It is wrong if we practice **superstition** or impiety. **Impiety** means being irreverent and disrespectful of God or sacred things. It is also wrong if we willfully doubt some truth about God or refuse to know what we should about God and our religion. There are times when some people are so willful that they publicly acknowledge their disbelief in or disagreement with the truths of the Faith. This is called **heresy**—the denying or disagreeing with one particular truth, or **apostasy**—deserting or leaving the true religion.

Strange Gods

We have read about people in ancient times who used to worship idols—false gods, things like golden calves. Remember when the Israelites worshipped the golden calf in the desert before God gave them the Ten Commandments? This is called **idolatry**. We don't run into too many people who worship golden calves, but many still place "strange gods" before God in their lives.

Not to have "strange gods" means that we are not to love anyone or anything as much as we love God. We are to worship and adore him —that is, give him the special love that is owed to him alone. This is a love that acknowledges his supreme position above all creation.

We must put nothing God has made before our love for him. No creature is to be adored— that is, worshipped with that special love

17

which we owe to God alone. Our love for or attachment to things God has made is not wrong in itself. It is not wrong for a computer or a dog to have a place in our life. But these things must never compete with our love for God or with his plans for us. For example, if we love a computer so much that we steal one, then we have put it before God.

There is a story from the Bible which makes all this clear.

The Rich Young Man

A rich young man received an invitation from our Lord himself to give up his riches and become a follower of Jesus. Saint Mark tells us that Jesus looked at the young man and loved him, for the youth had always kept all of God's commandments and wanted to do even better. Jesus said to him: "You lack one thing; go, sell what you have, and give to the poor, and you will have treasure in heaven; and come, follow me" (Mk 10:21).

But the young man turned away sadly and left Jesus because, as the Bible says, he "had many possessions." He could not follow Jesus

18

because he loved creatures, or created goods, too much. They may not have been the same creatures we have—not radios or televisions or cars—but whatever they were, he would not give them up. He missed the chance to follow Jesus because creatures were competing in his heart with love for God.

There is danger in having many possessions because they may turn our hearts from God. Our love for such things must be a "detached" love, a love that is ready to let go of things when God asks it of us.

Due Worship

In ages before Christ, the Hebrew people offered public **sacrifice** by slaughtering a valuable animal, like a lamb, upon an altar to honor God, to acknowledge him as Creator of all, and especially to make up for their sins.

The sacrifice of the Hebrew people pleased God but it could never fully make up for sin. As we know, the sin of Adam had closed the gates of heaven. None of the many sacrifices offered by the Hebrews could change this. For sin offends God who is so great, and no

ACT OF CONSECRATION TO JESUS

Lord Jesus Christ, I consecrate myself today anew and without reserve to your divine heart. I consecrate to you my body with all its senses, my soul with all its faculties, my entire being. I consecrate to you all my thoughts, words, and deeds, all my sufferings and labors, all my hopes, consolations, and joys. In particular I consecrate to you this poor heart of mine so that it may love only you and may be consumed as a victim in the fire of your love. I place my trust in you without reserve and I hope for the remission of my sins through your infinite mercy. I place within your hands all my cares and anxieties. I promise to love you and to honor you till the last moment of my life and to spread, as much as I can, devotion to your most Sacred Heart. Do with me what you will, my Jesus. I deserve no other reward except your greater glory and your holy love. Take this offering of myself and give me a place within your divine heart forever. *Amen.*

Many early Christians were martyred for refusing to worship false gods.

"I am a pious man, and I may not worship idols made with hands. Therefore, I do not bow before gold and silver, bronze or iron, or before false gods made of stone or wood."

—from the *Martyrdom of Apollonius*

Preview

In the next lesson, the students will learn from the example of the rich young man.

CHAPTER TWO: THE FIRST COMMANDMENT IN OUR OWN DAY
LESSON THREE: RICH YOUNG MAN

Aims

The students will learn that the story about the rich young man teaches us that we must love God above all creatures. This love requires detachment from worldly possessions.

Materials

- *Activity Book*, p. 7
- Bible

Optional:
- "God Father, praise and glory," *Adoremus Hymnal*, #464

Begin

Begin this class with the story of the rich young man from the Bible (Mk 10:17–22).

The students may dramatize this story as written, or place it into a modern-day setting. They may interview various people from this story (an on-looker, the rich young man, Jesus, an Apostle, etc.)

Develop

1. Read paragraphs 8–10 from the student text.

2. Discuss the lesson from the story of the rich young man:
   - Did the rich young man keep the commandments?
   - Did he know about God?
   - Did he use his things well? (Love them more than God?)
   - Why was the rich young man sad?
   - Do we work hard for the things we have? Do we deserve them?
   - Are our possessions a gift from God?
   - Is it hard to give up our possessions? Why? (What if you had to give up television, video games, the internet, or MP3 players?)
   - Did the rich young man love God? How much?
   - What is a detached love? How can we have a detached love for our possessions?

3. To help explain the need for detachment from worldly goods, use the example taught by Saint John of the Cross.

Saint John of the Cross said that a bird, whether it is tied by a heavy gold chain or the lightest, tiniest thread, will not be able to fly free. So it is with the soul and riches. If we are unduly attached to worldly treasure, we won't be able to love God as we should.

4. Have the students again dramatize the story of the rich young man; only this time, have the rich young man do as Jesus asks. In following Jesus he finds true happiness.

5. Read Matthew 6:24–30 from the Bible. Discuss this passage:
   - What does it mean not to serve two masters?
   - Should we worry about our material things?
   - How should we trust in God?

6. Discuss tithing: we return our riches to God in service for the poor and the Church. Tithing is an act of love for God.

Reinforce

1. Have the students work on *Activity Book* p. 7 (see *Teacher's Manual*, p. 25).

2. Tell the students to imagine that they are the rich young man. Have them write stories of their encounters with Jesus. What would they do? What would they sell? To whom would they give the money? How would they find happiness with Jesus? Would they decide to go away sad?

3. Have the students work on the Memorization Questions and Words to Know (see *Teacher's Manual*, p. 23).

Conclude

1. Lead the students in singing "God Father, praise and glory," *Adoremus Hymnal*, #464.

2. End class by leading the students in the Apostles' Creed (see *Teacher's Manual*, p. 396).

which we owe to God alone. Our love for or attachment to things God has made is not wrong in itself. It is not wrong for a computer or a dog to have a place in our life. But these things must never compete with our love for God or with his plans for us. For example, if we love a computer so much that we steal one, then we have put it before God.

There is a story from the Bible which makes all this clear.

The Rich Young Man

A rich young man received an invitation from our Lord himself to give up his riches and become a follower of Jesus. Saint Mark tells us that Jesus looked at the young man and loved him, for the youth had always kept all of God's commandments and wanted to do even better. Jesus said to him: "You lack one thing; go, sell what you have, and give to the poor, and you will have treasure in heaven; and come, follow me" (Mk 10:21).

But the young man turned away sadly and left Jesus because, as the Bible says, he "had many possessions." He could not follow Jesus

because he loved creatures, or created goods, too much. They may not have been the same creatures we have—not radios or televisions or cars—but whatever they were, he would not give them up. He missed the chance to follow Jesus because creatures were competing in his heart with love for God.

There is danger in having many possessions because they may turn our hearts from God. Our love for such things must be a "detached" love, a love that is ready to let go of things when God asks it of us.

Due Worship

In ages before Christ, the Hebrew people offered public **sacrifice** by slaughtering a valuable animal, like a lamb, upon an altar to honor God, to acknowledge him as Creator of all, and especially to make up for their sins.

The sacrifice of the Hebrew people pleased God but it could never fully make up for sin. As we know, the sin of Adam had closed the gates of heaven. None of the many sacrifices offered by the Hebrews could change this. For sin offends God who is so great, and no

offering of man alone, no matter how valuable, can make up for it.

Man's helplessness was no obstacle to God who wanted to save man. God himself became man and offered himself on the Cross as a fitting sacrifice, which was far more than enough to make up for all sins of all men. This sacrifice is renewed daily in every Mass around the world. The sacrifice of Jesus on the Cross is the greatest gift we can offer to God.

The sacrifice we offer in the Mass is the highest possible act of worship. It contains all that is necessary for giving due worship to God. In the Mass we acknowledge God as Creator, our Lord and Master. We thank him in gratitude for all he has given us. And, in recognition that we are dependent on him, we ask for all we need and for what will help others. Finally, we offer in the Mass the only thing that can make up for our sins and offenses. We offer the sacrifice of Jesus Christ on the Cross.

We can give God the love and worship we owe him when we participate in Holy Mass. Let's do so often!

Words to Know:
worship   adore   superstition   impiety
heresy   idolatry   sacrifice   apostasy

"Bless the Lord, all works of the Lord, sing praise to him and highly exalt him for ever."

Daniel 3:35

SAINTS FRANCIS AND CLARE AND THE PRIVILEGE OF POVERTY

Saint Francis was a popular youth of Assisi, born to wealth and worldly privilege. After being captured in battle, Francis re-thought his life and began giving away his wealth. Finally, he broke completely from his old life and founded the Order of Friars Minor, dedicated to following Christ by living in poverty and preaching about the love of God. Saint Clare was a noble lady, younger than Francis, who greatly admired Francis' teaching and joy in God. She left her home and consecrated her life to God. Francis established a convent for her, and soon the Poor Clare sisters attracted women from many places and backgrounds. In those days, it was common for monasteries to own land and some were very wealthy. Following the spirituality of Saint Francis, Saint Clare and her sisters did not want to live like that. Clare petitioned Pope Innocent III directly and, in 1216, was granted the "Privilege of Poverty" which meant that she and her sisters would own no property.

"Look at the birds of the air: they neither sow nor reap nor gather into barns, and yet your heavenly Father feeds them. Are you not of more value than they?"

—Matthew 6:26

Blessed Pier Giorgio Frassati was born into a well-to-do Italian family in 1901. While never having much spending money of his own, Blessed Pier gave even that away out of love for Christ, present in the poor. Unlike the Gospel's rich young man who refused to give away his earthly goods and went away sad, Blessed Pier Giorgio was known and remembered for his purity, happiness, and enthusiasm about life and everything that is good and beautiful.

Preview

In the next lesson, the students will learn about due worship.

CHAPTER TWO: THE FIRST COMMANDMENT IN OUR OWN DAY
LESSON FOUR: DUE WORSHIP

Aims

The students will learn that the Israelites offered sacrifices to God to acknowledge him as Creator of all and to atone for their sins.

They will learn that because the victim, priest, and intention could not be perfect and in total union with God, no sin offering made by men could fully atone for our sins.

They will learn that Jesus, the perfect priest, offered the perfect sacrifice of himself, the perfect victim, with the perfect intention, to atone for our sins. This is the Sacrifice of the Mass.

Materials

- *Activity Book*, p. 8

- Bibles

- Missals

Optional:
- "God Father, praise and glory," *Adoremus Hymnal*, #464

Begin

Begin the class by assigning the students various passages to look up in the Bible about sacrifice. Have the students read them and summarize them for each other. Example passages include:
  - Cain and Abel: Gen 4:1–5
  - Melchizedek: Gen 14:18–20

- Abraham: Gen 22:9–14
- Passover: Ex 12:24–27
- David: 2 Sam 6:17–19
- Ps 40:6–8, 50:5
- Jesus: Heb 9:24–28

Develop

1. Finish reading the chapter, paragraphs 11–15.

2. Review the effects of Original Sin. Because of this sin, man could not make up for his sin and be reconciled with God. The sin of Adam had closed the gates of heaven. The Hebrews offered worship and sacrifices to show their sorrow for sin—but the offense against God was so great that no offering of man could make up for it.

3. You may review what a sacrifice is—the act of completely giving something back to God. You may review the Old Testament sacrifices.

4. God, in his great love for us, became man in the Divine Person of Jesus Christ, so that he could be the perfect sacrifice by dying on the Cross. This perfect sacrifice would restore man's friendship with God and open the gates of heaven. Jesus died once for all of our sins.

5. The sacrifice of Jesus is made present through the Mass. Just as on the Cross, Jesus is the priest and the victim, so too at Mass, Jesus is the priest through the ministerial priesthood (the priest at Mass acts in the Person of Christ) and Jesus is the victim (the bread and wine become Jesus truly present—Body, Blood, Soul, and Divinity). This perfect offering to the Father is a wonderful gift. We can unite ourselves to this Sacrifice by offering to God our works, joys, sorrows, and suffering, and (most perfectly) by uniting ourselves with Jesus in a worthy Holy Communion.

6. Review the things necessary to give due worship to God: acknowledge that he is God, thank him, ask him to provide for our needs and the needs of others, ask forgiveness (adoration, contrition, thanksgiving, supplication).

Reinforce

1. Have the students work on *Activity Book* p. 8 (see *Teacher's Manual*, p. 25).

2. Go through a missal and find in the parts of the Mass the parts of worship: adoration, contrition, thanksgiving, and supplication.

3. Review the duty to participate in Mass on Sundays and Holy Days of Obligation.

4. The students should review the Memorization Questions and Words to Know in preparation for the quiz.

Conclude

1. Lead the students in singing "God Father, praise and glory," *Adoremus Hymnal*, #464.

2. Play a review game in preparation for the chapter quiz.

3. End class by leading the students in the Apostles' Creed (see *Teacher's Manual*, p. 396).

which we owe to God alone. Our love for or attachment to things God has made is not wrong in itself. It is not wrong for a computer or a dog to have a place in our life. But these things must never compete with our love for God or with his plans for us. For example, if we love a computer so much that we steal one, then we have put it before God.

There is a story from the Bible which makes all this clear.

The Rich Young Man

A rich young man received an invitation from our Lord himself to give up his riches and become a follower of Jesus. Saint Mark tells us that Jesus looked at the young man and loved him, for the youth had always kept all of God's commandments and wanted to do even better. Jesus said to him: "You lack one thing; go, sell what you have, and give to the poor, and you will have treasure in heaven; and come, follow me" (Mk 10:21).

But the young man turned away sadly and left Jesus because, as the Bible says, he "had many possessions." He could not follow Jesus because he loved creatures, or created goods, too much. They may not have been the same creatures we have—not radios or televisions or cars—but whatever they were, he would not give them up. He missed the chance to follow Jesus because creatures were competing in his heart with love for God.

There is danger in having many possessions because they may turn our hearts from God. Our love for such things must be a "detached" love, a love that is ready to let go of things when God asks it of us.

Due Worship

In ages before Christ, the Hebrew people offered public **sacrifice** by slaughtering a valuable animal, like a lamb, upon an altar to honor God, to acknowledge him as Creator of all, and especially to make up for their sins.

The sacrifice of the Hebrew people pleased God but it could never fully make up for sin. As we know, the sin of Adam had closed the gates of heaven. None of the many sacrifices offered by the Hebrews could change this. For sin offends God who is so great, and no

---

offering of man alone, no matter how valuable, can make up for it.

Man's helplessness was no obstacle to God who wanted to save man. God himself became man and offered himself on the Cross as a fitting sacrifice, which was far more than enough to make up for all sins of all men. This sacrifice is renewed daily in every Mass around the world. The sacrifice of Jesus on the Cross is the greatest gift we can offer to God.

The sacrifice we offer in the Mass is the highest possible act of worship. It contains all that is necessary for giving due worship to God. In the Mass we acknowledge God as Creator, our Lord and Master. We thank him in gratitude for all he has given us. And, in recognition that we are dependent on him, we ask for all we need and for what will help others. Finally, we offer in the Mass the only thing that can make up for our sins and offenses. We offer the sacrifice of Jesus Christ on the Cross.

We can give God the love and worship we owe him when we participate in Holy Mass. Let's do so often!

Words to Know:

worship   adore   superstition   impiety
heresy   idolatry   sacrifice   apostasy

"Bless the Lord, all works of the Lord, sing praise to him and highly exalt him for ever."

Daniel 3:35

Q. 6   *What are we required to do by the First Commandment?*
The First Commandment commands us to believe in God, to hope in him, and to love him above all else (CCC 2134).

Q. 7   *What does the First Commandment forbid?*
The First Commandment forbids heresy, apostasy, voluntary doubt, deliberate ignorance of God's truth, despair, presumption, idolatry, indifference to God, hatred of God, superstition, and irreligious behavior (CCC 2110).

Q. 8   *How does the story of the rich young man teach us to avoid putting possessions above God?*
The story of the rich young man showed that he was overly attached to his many possessions and therefore did not follow Jesus. This is an example of how many people, even today, commit idolatry (CCC 2113).

Q. 9   *How did the Hebrews offer worship to God?*
The Hebrews offered worship to God through animal sacrifice (CCC 1539).

Q. 10   *What was the perfect sacrifice made to God?*
The perfect sacrifice made to God was the offering of Jesus Christ upon the Cross, which was the perfect act of worship (CCC 2100).

Q. 11   *How can we participate in Jesus' perfect act of worship due to God?*
We can participate in Jesus' perfect act of worship due to God by participating in the Mass, since the Sacrifice of the Mass and the Sacrifice of the Cross are one and the same sacrifice (CCC 1369, 2100).

"ACTS" OF WORSHIP

A – Adoration: Adoration is the first attitude of man acknowledging that he is a creature before his Creator (CCC 2628).

C – Contrition: Contrition is "sorrow of the soul and detestation for the sin committed, together with the resolution not to sin again" (CCC 1451; citing the Council of Trent).

T – Thanksgiving: The Eucharist is a sacrifice of thanksgiving to the Father, a blessing by which the Church expresses her gratitude to God for all his benefits, for all that he has accomplished through creation, redemption, and sanctification (CCC 1361).

S – Supplication: The vocabulary of supplication in the New Testament is rich in shades of meaning: ask, beseech, plead, invoke, entreat, cry out. . . . Its most usual form, because the most spontaneous, is petition: by prayer of petition we express awareness of our relationship with God. We are creatures who are not our own beginning, not the masters of adversity, not our own last end (CCC 2629).

Preview

In the next lesson, the students' understanding of the material covered in this chapter will be reviewed and assessed.

Aims

The students' understanding of the material covered in this chapter will be reviewed and assessed.

Materials

- Quiz 2, Appendix, p. A-2

Optional:
- "God Father, praise and glory," *Adoremus Hymnal*, #464

Review and Enrichment

1. The students should know the Words to Know for this chapter.

2. Review what the First Commandment demands of us, and what it forbids.

3. The students should be familiar with the strange gods and false idols in today's society.

4. The students should understand that all good things are a gift from God and can be misused. God wills that we use created things according to his plan and will. The good use of created things is called stewardship. Through stewardship we give glory to God.

5. Review the story of the rich young man. The students should have an understanding of detachment in love of created things.

6. The students should understand due worship. They should know their Mass obligation. They should understand sacrifice. Jesus offered the perfect sacrifice of himself to the Father on the Cross. This very same sacrifice is made present at Mass on the altar. We are called to share in this sacrifice by offering ourselves to God and by worthily uniting ourselves with Jesus in Holy Communion.

7. The students should know what is necessary for true worship: adoration, contrition, thanksgiving, and supplication.

Name: _____

The First Commandment in Our Own Day   Quiz 2

Part I: Fill in the word that matches the definition.

apostasy	detachment	idolatry
impiety	superstition	heresy

1. <u>superstition</u> the belief that creatures have supernatural powers
2. <u>impiety</u> the lack of reverence or proper respect for God
3. <u>heresy</u> the willful denial of a truth of Faith
4. <u>apostasy</u> the rejection of the Christian Faith by a baptized person
5. <u>idolatry</u> the sin of worshipping something other than God
6. <u>detachment</u> the ability to let go of things when God asks it of us

Part II: Answer in complete sentences.

1. What can we learn from the story of the rich young man?
<u>From the story of the rich young man, we learn that we must love God more than all our possessions.</u>

2. What are five things in today's world that can easily end up competing with our love for God and become idolatrous?
<u>Answers will vary.</u>

Part III: Yes or No.

1. <u>Yes</u> In the age before Christ did the sacrifice of the Hebrews please God?

2. <u>No</u> In the age before Christ could the sacrifice of the Hebrew people make up for sin?

3. <u>No</u> Can man alone make up for sin?

4. <u>Yes</u> Did God have to become man in order to make up for sin?

A-2   *Faith and Life Series • Grade 6 • Appendix A*

Assess

1. Distribute the quizzes and read through them with the students to be sure they understand the questions.

2. Administer the quiz. As they hand in their work, you may orally quiz the students on the Memorization Questions from this chapter.

3. After all the quizzes have been handed in, you may wish to review the correct answers with the class.

Conclude

1. Lead the students in singing "God Father, praise and glory," *Adoremus Hymnal*, #464.

2. End class by leading the students in the Apostles' Creed (see *Teacher's Manual*, p. 396).

CHAPTER TWO: THE FIRST COMMANDMENT IN OUR OWN DAY
ACTIVITY BOOK ANSWER KEYS

Name:_____

The First Commandment

Answer the following questions in complete sentences.

1. What is the First Commandment?

   <u>The First Commandment is: I am the Lord your God; you shall not have other gods before me.</u>

2. What does this commandment require and why?

   <u>This commandment requires all men to recognize or acknowledge God as the one true God and to worship and adore him. This is because he is God and we are his creatures. We are entirely dependent on him.</u>

3. In what must we believe?

   <u>We must believe in God and in all that he has revealed to us.</u>

4. Do we have any excuse for not knowing about God and his revelation?

   <u>No.</u>

5. What does this commandment forbid?

   <u>The commandment forbids heresy, apostasy, voluntary doubt, deliberate ignorance of God's truth, despair, presumption, idolatry, indifference to God, hatred of God, superstition, and irreligious behavior.</u>

6. Define heresy, apostasy, superstition, and culpable ignorance.

   <u>Heresy is the willful denial of a truth of Faith; apostasy is the rejection by a baptized person of the Christian Faith; superstition is the belief that creatures have supernatural powers, and culpable ignorance is not knowing something that one ought to know.</u>

Faith and Life Series • Grade 6 • Chapter 2 • Lesson 1　　5

Name:_____

Strange Gods

Answer the following questions in complete sentences.

1. What is idolatry?

   <u>Idolatry is the sin of worshipping something other than God.</u>

2. How did the Israelites commit idolatry?

   <u>The Israelites committed idolatry by worshipping the golden calf in the desert.</u>

3. Do we often see idolatry like this in present times?

   <u>No.</u>

4. What does "you shall not have strange gods" mean?

   <u>This means that we are not to love anyone or anything as much as we love God. We are to give him a special love that is owed to him alone.</u>

5. What kind of things do people put before God in present times?

   <u>Answers will vary.</u>

6　　*Faith and Life Series • Grade 6 • Chapter 2 • Lesson 2*

Name:_____

The Rich Young Man

Read the story of the rich young man in Mark 10:17–27 as a class and answer the following questions in complete sentences.

1. What did the rich young man ask Jesus?

   <u>The rich young man asked Jesus, "What must I do to inherit eternal life?"</u>

2. What did Jesus invite the rich young man to do?

   <u>Jesus invited the man to sell what he owned, give to the poor, and follow Jesus.</u>

3. Had the rich young man kept all the commandments?

   <u>Yes.</u>

4. Why did he go away sad?

   <u>He went away sad because he had many possessions and did not want to part with them.</u>

5. What did the rich young man love more than God?

   <u>He loved his possessions more than God.</u>

6. What does Jesus say in Mark 10:25 and what does it mean?

   <u>Jesus said, "It is easier for a camel to go through the eye of a needle than for a rich man to enter the Kingdom of God." Answers will vary as to what it means.</u>

Faith and Life Series • Grade 6 • Chapter 2 • Lesson 3　　7

Name:_____

Due Worship

Answer the following questions in complete sentences.

1. How did the Hebrew people offer worship to God?

   <u>The Hebrew people offered worship to God through animal sacrifice.</u>

2. Did their sacrifices fully atone for sin?

   <u>No.</u>

3. How did God save man from sin?

   <u>God saved man from sin by offering himself on the Cross as a fitting sacrifice.</u>

4. How can we share in this sacrifice?

   <u>We can share in this sacrifice by participating in the Mass.</u>

5. What do we do during the Mass? (Hint: there are four things.)

   <u>During the Mass we acknowledge God as Creator, Lord, and Master; thank him for what he has given us; ask for what we need; and offer to him the sacrifice of Jesus on the Cross.</u>

6. How can we show God that we love and worship him?

   <u>Answers will vary. One important way is to participate in Holy Mass.</u>

7. How often must we go to Mass?

   <u>Answer is not in text, but students should know that is it every Sunday and Holy Day.</u>

8　　*Faith and Life Series • Grade 6 • Chapter 2 • Lesson 4*

25

TEACHER'S NOTES

CHAPTER THREE
PRAYER—HIDDEN TREASURE

Catechism of the Catholic Church References

Childlike Trust in Prayer: 2734–41, 2756
Jesus as True God and True Man: 464–70, 480–83
Jesus Hears and Answers Prayer: 2616, 2621
Jesus Teaches Us to Pray: 2607–15, 2621
Liturgy of the Hours: 1174–78, 1196
Meditation on the Rosary: 2705–8, 2723
Prayer in Union with Mary: 2673–79, 2680–82
Prayers of Blessing and Adoration: 2626–28, 2645

Prayers of Intercession: 2634–36, 2647
Prayers of Petition: 2629–33, 2646
Prayers of Praise: 2639–43, 2649
Prayers of Thanksgiving: 2637–38, 2648
Saints as Companions in Prayer: 2683–84, 2692–93
What Is Prayer? : 2559–65, 2590, 2644
Worship and Prayer: 2096–98, 2135

Scripture References

God Answers Prayer: Mt 6:8; 7:7–11; Ps 139:4; Lk 18:1–8

Summary of Lesson Content

Lesson 1

Prayer is required by the First Commandment. God listens to our prayers.

Prayer is the lifting of the heart and mind to God. It is our conversation with God.

The types of prayer include: blessing and praise, adoration, thanksgiving, petition, and intercession.

The two forms of prayer include vocal and mental prayer.

Lesson 2

We should pray even when it is difficult. We will face distractions, but should not be discouraged in prayer.

God answers all our prayers according to his will.

Lesson 3

The prayer of the Church is the Liturgy of the Hours, or Divine Office. It is comprised of Psalms, Scripture readings, and writings of the saints.

The Rosary is a beautiful prayer, through which we meditate upon mysteries in the lives of Jesus and Mary. While meditating upon these mysteries, vocal prayers are recited.

Lesson 4

The spiritual life, or the devout life, includes a prayer life, reception of the Sacraments, and the performance of good works.

CHAPTER THREE: PRAYER—HIDDEN TREASURE
LESSON ONE: LET US PRAY

Aims

The students will learn that prayer is required by the First Commandment. God listens to our prayers.

They will learn that prayer is the lifting of the heart and mind to God. It is our conversation with God.

They will learn that the types of prayer include: blessing and praise, adoration, thanksgiving, petition, and intercession. The two forms of prayer include vocal and mental prayer.

Materials

• *Activity Book*, p. 9

• Bibles

Optional:
• "Now thank we all our God," *Adoremus Hymnal*, #607

Father Mikes Tips for Prayer

Begin

Lead the students in a discussion on prayer.
• What is prayer?
• When do you pray?
• Do you pray with anyone?
• What is your favorite prayer?
• What do you like to talk to God about?

• How do you like to pray?
• Do you offer your works as prayers?
• Do you ask saints to pray with and for you?
• Do you have a special place to pray?
• How do you feel when you pray?
• How do you feel after you pray?

Develop

1. Read paragraphs 1–3 with the students.

2. Why is prayer included in the First Commandment? Prayer is our conversation with God. Imagine if we said we loved and obeyed our parents, but never took time to listen to them, talk with them, or even tell them we love them! Prayer is important and necessary for us to grow in love with God.

3. Prayer is the lifting up of our hearts and minds to God. It is not just talking at God, but talking with God. We share what is in our hearts and on our minds—all things big and little. We also listen to God in the silence of our hearts. He guides us to do his will by prompting our hearts and minds with peace, joy, and rightness.

4. The three forms of prayer are vocal prayer, meditation, and contemplation. In vocal prayer, we use our voice and say set words that we read or have memorized, such as the Our

Father or Hail Mary. Or we may say personal prayers aloud. In meditation, we use our mind, heart, and imagination to consider God and to seek His will for us. We may also pray about what is happening in our lives. Books, such as the Bible, are often used in meditation. In contemplation, we are simply and lovingly united to God. Since prayer is a way to worship God, it includes things necessary for due worship: adoration (to be in awe of God and to praise and bless him for who he is), contrition (to have sorrow for sin and ask for God's mercy and forgiveness), thanksgiving (to thank God for his many gifts), and supplication (to ask for what we need, and for the needs of others).

5. Read Matthew 6:8; 7:7–11; Psalm 139:4; Luke 18:1–8. Discuss if and how God answers prayers. We can say that God gives three answers for prayer: yes, no, and slow (yes, but in his time). He answers according to his love for us and his will.

Reinforce

1. Have the students work on *Activity Book* p. 9 (see *Teacher's Manual*, p. 37).

2. Have the students begin working on the Memorization Questions and Words to Know (see *Teacher's Manual*, p. 35).

3. Have the students work on memorizing the Acts of Faith, Hope, and Love on *Student Text* pp. 147–148 (see *Teacher's Manual*, p. 396).

4. With the class' assistance, make a prayer station—a sacred place where your class can pray. If possible, have a crucifix, a statue of Mary (or another favorite saint), a box for intentions, a candle, and a Bible. Encourage the students to write their intentions and place them in the box.

Conclude

1. Teach the students to sing "Now thank we all our God," *Adoremus Hymnal*, #607.

2. End class by leading the students in praying the Acts of Faith, Hope, and Love (see facing page or *Teacher's Manual*, p. 396).

CHAPTER 3

Prayer–Hidden Treasure

"Lord, teach us to pray, as John taught his disciples."

Luke 11:1

> The chief exercise of prayer is to speak to God and to hear God speak in the depths of your heart.
>
> —Saint Francis de Sales

Prayer is something required of us by the First Commandment. It is necessary for us to pray, and we must do so every day. God commanded us to pray, and he listens to our prayers.

Prayer is defined as the raising of the mind and heart to God. Our prayer is our conversation with God. It may be done briefly or at length. We must have God in mind when we pray. We must think of something about him which moves us to love him. Then we can talk with him, adore him, tell him we are sorry for our sin, ask him for things we need, and listen to him, too. One of the best ways to do this is to consider something Jesus said or did. Jesus, being man as well as God, can be pictured in the imagination. This helps to stir our heart, and then we can, for instance, make an act of faith, an act of hope, or an act of love.

Three forms of prayer are vocal prayer, meditation, and contemplation. In vocal prayer, we use our voice to express a set prayer (such as the Our Father) or a personal prayer. In meditation we use our mind, heart, and imagi-

nation to consider and seek the Lord and his will for us. Often meditation uses books, such as the Bible, to seek the Lord. In contemplative prayer, we are simply and lovingly united to God.

Our Need to Pray

Jesus strongly encourages us to pray. Saint Luke records, "And he [Jesus] told them a parable, to the effect that they ought always to pray and not lose heart" (Lk 18:1).

This means that we must pray even when we do not feel like it, as well as when we do. We must pray when unwanted thoughts interrupt our concentration or when worries tug us away from our thoughts about God, about Jesus, and about the saints. These interruptions are called "distractions." When they happen, we must return to prayer calmly and patiently. Distractions like these are not our fault. But if we begin to daydream and, after we realize it, continue to daydream instead of pray, we are at fault. If my mind wanders a hundred times, and I direct it back to prayer each time, there is no fault. In fact, there is great merit because this is hard work and shows God that I love him and want to please him. By praying to God—asking for what we need, thanking him for what he has given us—we acknowledge that we are his creatures and that we are totally dependent on him.

21

"Let my prayer be counted as incense before you, and the lifting up of my hands as an evening sacrifice."

Psalm 141:2

Jesus assures us that our prayers will be answered. He says: "Ask, and it will be given you; seek, and you will find; knock, and it will be opened to you" (Mt 7:7).

We will not, of course, get what is bad for us or what is really unnecessary. But God will always give us what is best for us.

Particular Prayers

There is a special prayer of the Church called the Liturgy of the Hours or the **Divine Office**. The Divine Office is a prayer of praise and petition using the Psalms and readings from Scripture and the writings of the saints. Certain members of the Church, such as priests, are required to pray the Divine Office every day, but all of us in the Church are invited to join in the Church's praise of God in this rich and beautiful form of prayer.

Another prayer especially recommended by the Church is the Rosary. For about eight hundred years, countless numbers of the faithful have made it part of their daily prayer. The Rosary is divided into mysteries, episodes in the lives of Jesus and Mary. We are to think

22

ACTS OF FAITH, HOPE, AND LOVE

O my God, I firmly believe that thou art one God in three Divine Persons: Father, Son, and Holy Spirit. I believe that thy Divine Son became man and died for our sins, and that he will come to judge the living and the dead. I believe these and all the truths that the Holy Catholic Church teaches, because thou hast revealed them, who can neither deceive nor be deceived. *Amen.*

O my God, relying on thy infinite goodness and promises, I hope to obtain the pardon of my sins, the help of thy grace, and life everlasting, through the merits of Jesus Christ, my Lord and Redeemer. *Amen.*

O my God, I love thee above all things, with my whole heart and soul, because thou art all good and worthy of all love. I love my neighbor as myself for the love of thee. I forgive all who have injured me and ask pardon of all whom I have injured. *Amen.*

> However softly we speak, He is near enough to hear us. . . . All one need do is go into solitude and look at Him within oneself, and not turn away from so good a Guest but with great humility speak to Him as to a father.
>
> —Saint Teresa of Avila

Preview

In the next lesson, the students will learn that they must always pray.

CHAPTER THREE: PRAYER—HIDDEN TREASURE
LESSON TWO: PRAY ALWAYS

Aims

The students will learn that man should pray even when it is difficult. We often face distractions, but should not be discouraged in prayer.

They will learn that God answers all our prayers according to his will.

Materials

- *Activity Book*, p. 10
- Various prayer aids and sacramentals: prayer books, missals, holy cards and medals, holy images/ statues, music, Bible, etc.

Optional:
- "Now thank we all our God," *Adoremus Hymnal*, #607

Begin   Father Mike S. The Power of Prayer

One of the many beautiful things about our Catholic Faith is that it uses our senses. The Sacraments all have a matter (physical thing used). We have stained glass images in our churches, Stations of the Cross, a crucifix, statues. We have many aids to help us focus on God and his saints. These aids help draw us to prayer and to focus when we are praying. Show your class some sacramentals and discuss how they can help us pray. Is there a printed prayer on a card, an image that reminds us of God's love? Does the church building make us feel close to God?

Develop

1. Read paragraphs 4–7 with the students.

2. How can we pray always? Is this realistic? How can we remain in God's presence throughout the day? Everything should remind us of him and his love for us. We can thank him. Our encounters with other people should lead us closer to him. Our hearts and thoughts should never be apart from God. Even when we are working, or studying, or playing, we can be in union with God.

3. Often when we try to pray, we become distracted. We must try not to give in to these distractions. Some things we can do are:
   - Use a prayerful posture (kneel to pray, fold our hands, sit if we are praying for a long time, etc.).
   - Be in a prayerful place, such as at church, have a prayer station or altar in a room, close your eyes and use your imagination to help you to be with God.

- Use vocal and mental prayer. When we cannot think of what to pray, return to vocal prayer. Prayers like the Rosary or Stations of the Cross guide our meditation. These are very helpful to stay focused.
- Have a prayer book/Bible/some form of spiritual reading to help stay focused or direct our thoughts.
- Look at a holy image.
- Use your senses—bless yourself with holy water (a reminder of our baptismal promises), hold a crucifix and trace your finger over the wounds of Christ, smell incense, light a candle, listen to music—there are many ways to be focused in prayer.

4. God always hears our prayers. We can pray anywhere. However, as Catholics, we have a special gift to be able to pray before Jesus truly present in the Blessed Sacrament reserved in our churches, and sometimes at Adoration. Take your class to visit Jesus in the tabernacle at your church.

Reinforce

1. Have the students work on *Activity Book* p. 10 (see *Teacher's Manual*, p. 37).

2. Have the students list ways they can refocus when they become distracted in prayer. They can create "emergency prayer kits," collecting in a paper bag things to help them focus. Have them include things that draw them back to prayer; e.g., holy cards, a crucifix, holy medal. The students may decorate their emergency prayer kit bags with appropriate symbols of prayer, such as pictures of candles, people in prayer, the Cross.

3. Have the students work on the Memorization Questions and Words to Know (see *Teacher's Manual*, p. 35).

Conclude

1. Lead the students in singing "Now thank we all our God," *Adoremus Hymnal*, #607.

2. End class by leading the students in praying the Acts of Faith, Hope, and Love (see *Teacher's Manual*, p. 29 or p. 396).

CHAPTER 3

Prayer–Hidden Treasure

"Lord, teach us to pray, as John taught his disciples."

Luke 11:1

> The chief exercise of prayer is to speak to God and to hear God speak in the depths of your heart.
> —Saint Francis de Sales

Prayer is something required of us by the First Commandment. It is necessary for us to pray, and we must do so every day. God commanded us to pray, and he listens to our prayers.

Prayer is defined as the raising of the mind and heart to God. Our prayer is our conversation with God. It may be done briefly or at length. We must have God in mind when we pray. We must think of something about him which moves us to love him. Then we can talk with him, adore him, tell him we are sorry for our sin, ask him for things we need, and listen to him, too. One of the best ways to do this is to consider something Jesus said or did. Jesus, being man as well as God, can be pictured in the imagination. This helps to stir our heart, and then we can, for instance, make an act of faith, an act of hope, or an act of love.

Three forms of prayer are vocal prayer, meditation, and contemplation. In vocal prayer, we use our voice to express a set prayer (such as the Our Father) or a personal prayer. In meditation we use our mind, heart, and imagi-

nation to consider and seek the Lord and his will for us. Often meditation uses books, such as the Bible, to seek the Lord. In contemplative prayer, we are simply and lovingly united to God.

Our Need to Pray

Jesus strongly encourages us to pray. Saint Luke records, "And he [Jesus] told them a parable, to the effect that they ought always to pray and not lose heart" (Lk 18:1).

This means that we must pray even when we do not feel like it, as well as when we do. We must pray when unwanted thoughts interrupt our concentration or when worries tug us away from our thoughts about God, about Jesus, and about the saints. These interruptions are called "distractions." When they happen, we must return to prayer calmly and patiently. Distractions like these are not our fault. But if we begin to daydream and, after we realize it, continue to daydream instead of pray, we are at fault. If my mind wanders a hundred times, and I direct it back to prayer each time, there is no fault. In fact, there is great merit because this is hard work and shows God that I love him and want to please him. By praying to God—asking for what we need, thanking him for what he has given us—we acknowledge that we are his creatures and that we are totally dependent on him.

21

Jesus assures us that our prayers will be answered. He says: "Ask, and it will be given you; seek, and you will find; knock, and it will be opened to you" (Mt 7:7).

We will not, of course, get what is bad for us or what is really unnecessary. But God will always give us what is best for us.

Particular Prayers

There is a special prayer of the Church called the Liturgy of the Hours or the **Divine Office**. The Divine Office is a prayer of praise and petition using the Psalms and readings from Scripture and the writings of the saints. Certain members of the Church, such as priests, are required to pray the Divine Office every day, but all of us in the Church are invited to join in the Church's praise of God in this rich and beautiful form of prayer.

Another prayer especially recommended by the Church is the Rosary. For about eight hundred years, countless numbers of the faithful have made it part of their daily prayer. The Rosary is divided into mysteries, episodes in the lives of Jesus and Mary. We are to think

22

ACT OF SPIRITUAL COMMUNION

When we want to receive Jesus sacramentally in Holy Communion but cannot, we can still receive him spiritually. If we desire to be with him and ask him in love to come to us, he will come. The following is a sample prayer of spiritual communion:

My Jesus, I believe that you are in the Blessed Sacrament. I love you above all things and I long for you in my soul. Since I cannot now receive you sacramentally, come at least spiritually into my heart. As though you have already come, I embrace you and unite myself entirely to you; never permit me to be separated from you. *Amen.*

THE LUMINOUS MYSTERIES

On October 16, 2002, the beginning of the 25th year of his pontificate, Pope John Paul II wrote an apostolic letter on the Rosary entitled *Rosarium Virginis Mariae*. His purpose in writing it was to remind Catholics of the beau-tiful prayer of the Rosary and encourage a revival of this age-old prayer. "A prayer so easy and yet so rich truly deserves to be rediscovered by the Christian community." Focusing on the Rosary as a fundamentally Christocentric (Christ-centered) prayer, the Holy Father suggested a new set of mysteries: the Mysteries of Light. These mysteries are an optional addition to the Rosary which allow us to meditate on the ministry of Christ from his baptism to the eve of his Passion.

Lift up your heart to Him, sometimes even at your meals, and when you are in company; the least little remembrance will always be acceptable to Him. You need not cry very loud; he is nearer to us than we are aware of.
—Saint Francis de Sales

Preview

In the next lesson, the students will learn about specific prayers.

CHAPTER THREE: PRAYER—HIDDEN TREASURE
LESSON THREE: PRAYERS

Aims

The students will learn that the prayer of the Church is the Liturgy of the Hours, or Divine Office. It is comprised of Psalms, Scripture readings and writings of the saints.

They will learn that the Rosary is a beautiful prayer, through which we meditate upon mysteries in the lives of Jesus and Mary. While meditating upon these mysteries, vocal prayers are recited.

Materials

- *Activity Book*, p. 11

- Small journals that will be made into prayer books

- Copies of prayers for every student

- Liturgy of the Hours

Optional:
- "Now thank we all our God," *Adoremus Hymnal*, #607

Battle of Prayer

Begin

Begin the class by showing the students a copy of the Liturgy of the Hours. This is the official prayer of the Church, said by religious and those who have been consecrated in Holy Orders. It is said throughout the day, so that those who pray it are uniting themselves and centering their lives upon Christ throughout the day. It is made up of Scripture readings, Psalms, writings of the saints, and hymns. As they pray this, they are united with the prayer of the Church, for all priests and religious around the world (and many lay people, too) are praying the same prayer.

Develop

1. Read paragraphs 8–9 with the students.

2. Today, let the students work on a project. Give each student a small journal and copies of prayers that will fit on these pages. Allow them to use the computer to find holy images, and prayers they like that they can print and paste into their journal. They can also write their own prayers or list their prayer intentions in this book. This may take the entire class. Remind them not to rush and really to make this special. The students may leave their prayer books at the prayer station in your classroom, or take them with them, so that they always have them.

Ideas to help make this fun: use stickers, prayer cards, stamps, markers, ribbons and buttons, put a nice clasp or even a lock on it. Decorate the cover with a foam frame and put the students' pictures in them. You may want the students to put an index in this book, as well.

3. If you have a set of images of the Mysteries of the Rosary, bring them out or have the students draw a set. Teach them the Mysteries of the Rosary. Teach them their proper names, what they mean, and their proper order.

4. The students can make rosaries for themselves, then have a priest visit the class to bless them.

5. Pray a decade of the Rosary. As you pray the mystery appropriate to the day, help the students truly to meditate on the mystery. Have each student imagine he is someone present at the mystery: Mary, someone in the crowd watching, or maybe even Jesus. What does each hear? What does he see? How does he feel? Who is with him? Why is this event so important? Remind the students to pray slowly and concentrate.

Reinforce

1. Have the students work on *Activity Book* p. 11 (see *Teacher's Manual*, p. 37).

2. The students may work on their prayer books or on the construction of rosaries.

3. Have the students work on the Memorization Questions and Words to Know (see facing page and *Teacher's Manual*, p. 35).

Conclude

1. Lead the students in singing "Now thank we all our God," *Adoremus Hymnal*, #607.

2. End class by leading the students in praying the Acts of Faith, Hope, and Love (see *Teacher's Manual*, p. 29 or p. 396).

> *"Let my prayer be counted as incense before you, and the lifting up of my hands as an evening sacrifice."*
>
> *Psalm 141:2*

Jesus assures us that our prayers will be answered. He says: "Ask, and it will be given you; seek, and you will find; knock, and it will be opened to you" (Mt 7:7).

We will not, of course, get what is bad for us or what is really unnecessary. But God will always give us what is best for us.

Particular Prayers

There is a special prayer of the Church called the Liturgy of the Hours or the **Divine Office**. The Divine Office is a prayer of praise and petition using the Psalms and readings from Scripture and the writings of the saints. Certain members of the Church, such as priests, are required to pray the Divine Office every day, but all of us in the Church are invited to join in the Church's praise of God in this rich and beautiful form of prayer.

Another prayer especially recommended by the Church is the Rosary. For about eight hundred years, countless numbers of the faithful have made it part of their daily prayer. The Rosary is divided into mysteries, episodes in the lives of Jesus and Mary. We are to think

22

---

about these mysteries as we say the vocal prayers—mainly the Hail Marys. The prayers should be said slowly as our hearts are moved by what is in our minds. And what could be better suited to help us pray than scenes from the lives of Jesus and Mary?

* * *

A life of prayer is sometimes called the spiritual life or the devout life. Our spiritual life is the sum of all we do to reach heaven, which includes receiving the Sacraments and doing good works. The spiritual life is a way of growing; and the more we grow in prayer, the more joy, peace, and confidence we will have. A life of prayer makes us fully alive!

Jesus said: "These things I have spoken to you, that my joy may be in you, and that your joy may be full" (Jn 15:11).

Words to Know:
prayer   Divine Office (Liturgy of the Hours)

Form the habit of speaking to God as if you were alone with him, familiarly and with confidence and love, as to the dearest and most loving of friends. Speak to him often of your business, your plans, your troubles, your fears—of everything that concerns you. Talk with him confidently and frankly; for God does not often speak to a soul that does not speak to him.

—Saint Alphonsus Liguori

Q. 12   *What is prayer?*
Prayer is the lifting of the mind and heart to God, in order to know him better, to adore him, to thank him, and to ask him for what we need (CCC 2590).

Q. 13   *What kinds of prayer are there?*
There are five kinds of prayer: blessing and adoration, prayer of petition, prayer of intercession, prayer of thanksgiving, and prayer of praise (CCC 2626–49).

Q. 14   *What is mental prayer?*
Mental prayer is that which is said with the mind and heart alone (CCC 2708).

23

THE MYSTERIES OF THE ROSARY

The Joyful Mysteries Monday & Saturday
- The Annunciation
- The Visitation
- The Nativity
- The Presentation
- The Finding in the Temple

The Sorrowful Mysteries Tuesday & Friday
- The Agony in the Garden
- The Scourging at the Pillar
- The Crowning with Thorns
- The Carrying of the Cross
- The Crucifixion

The Glorious Mysteries Wednesday & Sunday
- The Resurrection
- The Ascension
- The Descent of the Holy Spirit
- The Assumption
- The Coronation

The Luminous Mysteries (see p. 31) Thursday
- The Baptism of Christ in the Jordan
- The Wedding Feast at Cana
- The Proclamation of the Kingdom of God
- The Transfiguration of Our Lord
- The Institution of the Holy Eucharist

I look to all of you, brothers and sisters of every state of life, to you, Christian families, to you, the sick and elderly, and to you, young people: *confidently take up the Rosary once again.* Rediscover the Rosary in the light of Scripture, in harmony with the Liturgy, and in the context of your daily lives.

—Pope John Paul II,
Rosarium Virginis Mariae

Preview

In the next lesson, the students will learn about the spiritual life.

CHAPTER THREE: PRAYER—HIDDEN TREASURE
LESSON FOUR: SPIRITUAL LIFE

Aims

The students will learn that the spiritual life, or the devout life, includes a prayer life, reception of the Sacraments, and the performance of good works.

Materials

- *Activity Book*, p. 12

Optional:
- "Now thank we all our God," *Adoremus Hymnal*, #607

Begin

Often when we think of the devout life or the spiritual life, we think of saints and not of ourselves. The spiritual life is a daily process of dying to ourselves and recommitting ourselves to God. It is living our journey to God, in union with him. It is not just prayer, but a lifetime learning about God, receiving the Sacraments, and living the moral life, as well as praying. The students may complete *Activity Book* p. 12 at this point (see *Teacher's Manual*, p. 37).

You may also wish to assign each student to research the spiritual life of a saint and then write a paragraph on how he can follow the saint's example. These saint projects can later be presented to the class.

Develop

1. Finish reading the chapter with the students (paragraphs 10–11).

2. There are three levels to the spiritual life:
- *Purgative way*: This is the primary stage in mental prayer, according to the teaching of Sts. Theresa of Avila and John of the Cross. The soul's chief concern in this stage of perfection is an awareness of its sins, sorrow for the past, and a desire to expiate the offenses against God.

- *Illuminative way*: This is the intermediary stage between purification and union on the path to Christian perfection. The main feature of the Illuminative Way, also called the "Way of the Proficients," is an enlightenment of the mind in the ways of God and a clear understanding of his will in one's state in life.

- *Unitive Way*: The third and final stage of Christian perfection, beyond the purgative and illuminative, is the unitive.

Its principle feature is a more or less constant awareness of God's presence, and a habitual disposition of conformity to the will of God. Although commonly regarded as the last stage in the spiritual life, it is recognized that the three traditional levels of progress in holiness are not chronological. They may be present, in greater or less degree, at any point in a person's growth in sanctity.

From the *Pocket Catholic Dictionary* by John A. Hardon, S.J.

3. The more we strive to be holy, the more God will help us to become holy. In the Catholic Church, we have the fullness of the means of salvation—many gifts and ways to help us to become truly holy: creed and correct teaching through the Church, God's revelation, Sacraments, moral life, and prayer.

4. Have the students share stories of the saints and discuss how they became holy, and how to follow their examples.

Reinforce

1. Have the students work on *Activity Book* p. 12 (see *Teacher's Manual*, p. 37).

2. The students may work on the Memorization Questions and Words to Know to review for the quiz.

3. Have the students finish working on their prayer books.

4. Share stories of the lives of the saints and discuss how we can follow their examples of holiness.

Conclude

1. Lead the students in singing "Now thank we all our God," *Adoremus Hymnal*, #607.

2. Play a review game in preparation for the quiz.

3. End class by leading the students in praying the Acts of Faith, Hope, and Love (see *Teacher's Manual*, p. 29).

about these mysteries as we say the vocal prayers—mainly the Hail Marys. The prayers should be said slowly as our hearts are moved by what is in our minds. And what could be better suited to help us pray than scenes from the lives of Jesus and Mary?

* * *

A life of prayer is sometimes called the spiritual life or the devout life. Our spiritual life is the sum of all we do to reach heaven, which includes receiving the Sacraments and doing good works. The spiritual life is a way of growing; and the more we grow in prayer, the more joy, peace, and confidence we will have. A life of prayer makes us fully alive!

Jesus said: "These things I have spoken to you, that my joy may be in you, and that your joy may be full" (Jn 15:11).

Words to Know:

prayer   Divine Office (Liturgy of the Hours)

Form the habit of speaking to God as if you were alone with him, familiarly and with confidence and love, as to the dearest and most loving of friends. Speak to him often of your business, your plans, your troubles, your fears—of everything that concerns you. Talk with him confidently and frankly; for God does not often speak to a soul that does not speak to him.

—Saint Alphonsus Liguori

Q. 12   What is prayer?
Prayer is the lifting of the mind and heart to God, in order to know him better, to adore him, to thank him, and to ask him for what we need (CCC 2590).

Q. 13   What kinds of prayer are there?
There are five kinds of prayer: blessing and adoration, prayer of petition, prayer of intercession, prayer of thanksgiving, and prayer of praise (CCC 2626–49).

Q. 14   What is mental prayer?
Mental prayer is that which is said with the mind and heart alone (CCC 2708).

23

Q. 15   What is vocal prayer?
Vocal prayer is that which is expressed by spoken words with the participation of the mind and heart (CCC 2700).

Q. 16   How should we pray?
We should pray humbly, attentively, and devoutly (CCC 2559).

Q. 17   Why is it necessary to pray?
It is necessary to pray in order to grow in our faith in God, in our hope in him, and in our love for him, and in this way to receive the grace necessary to be united with him in heaven (CCC 2558).

Q. 18   How should we pray, and what for?
We should give glory, thanksgiving, and praise to God in our daily prayer. We should hallow (make holy) his name. We should ask for whatever is necessary to obtain eternal life, including things necessary for life in this world. We should ask forgiveness for our sins. Jesus Christ taught us to do this in the Our Father (CCC 2857).

Q. 19   What is the most perfect prayer?
The Mass is the most perfect prayer because in it Jesus offers himself to the Father for us. We offer ourselves along with Jesus to the Father by the power of the Holy Spirit (CCC 1358–59, 1369, 1407).

24

SAINT IGNATIUS OF LOYOLA AND THE *SPIRITUAL EXERCISES*

Though Ignatius of Loyola was of noble birth and was more interested in a career in knightly gallantry and soldiering than in Jesus Christ, he would become the founder of the Society of Jesus (the Jesuits) and the author of the *Spiritual Exercises* that have, for centuries, helped many to know Jesus. When Ignatius' leg was injured in battle by a cannonball, his career as a soldier was over. While recovering, he had nothing to read but the lives of Christ and the saints. He saw the error of his prior sins, confessed at Montserrat, and went into a cave to fast and pray. It was during these difficult months of deprivation that Saint Ignatius wrote his *Spiritual Exercises*.

The *Spiritual Exercises* is a short book designed to guide souls in the spiritual life. It is divided into four "weeks" with a different meditation for each day. Through a series of teachings and meditations, this book has led countless people into a deeper relationship with God. Even today, five hundred years after they were written, they are used by many people. One practice related to them today is for people to go on silent retreats for as long as thirty days to undertake the *Spiritual Exercises* of Saint Ignatius of Loyola.

All true and living devotion presupposes the love of God. . . . The difference between love and devotion is just that which exists between fire and flame;—love being a spiritual fire which becomes devotion when it is fanned into a flame;—and what devotion adds to the fire of love is that flame which makes it eager, energetic and diligent, not merely in obeying God's Commandments, but in fulfilling His Divine Counsels and inspirations.

—Saint Francis de Sales

Preview

In the next lesson, the students' understanding of the material covered in this chapter will be reviewed and assessed.

CHAPTER THREE: PRAYER—HIDDEN TREASURE
REVIEW AND ASSESSMENT

Aims

The students' understanding of the material covered in this chapter will be reviewed and assessed.

Materials

• Quiz 3, Appendix, p. A-3

Optional:
• "Now thank we all our God," *Adoremus Hymnal*, #607

Review and Enrichment

1. The students should understand what prayer is and how prayer is related to the First Commandment.

2. The two kinds of prayer are vocal and mental. The students should be able to define these and give examples.

3. The students should be able to give multiple examples of how to stay focused during prayer.

4. The students should be able to name numerous Catholic prayers, especially the Stations of the Cross, the Rosary, and the Liturgy of the Hours. The students should be able to name the Mysteries of the Rosary and know how to pray this important prayer.

5. The students should know who is obliged to pray the Liturgy of the Hours.

6. The students should understand that the devout life/spiritual life and daily conversion require us to know God, to receive the Sacraments, to live the moral life, and to pray. They should be able to explain the life of a saint as an example.

7. The levels of the spiritual life include: the purgative, illuminative, and unitive. They may also know the development of prayer from vocal to meditative, and then to contemplative.

30

Name: _____

Prayer—Hidden Treasure   **Quiz 3**

Part I: Answer in complete sentences.

1. What is prayer?
   Prayer is the raising of the mind and heart to God.

2. What are the three forms of prayer?
   The three forms of prayer are vocal prayer, meditation, and contemplation.

3. What are three prayers that we pray as Catholics?
   Answers will vary. Divine Office (Liturgy of the Hours), Rosary, Our Father, Hail Mary, etc.

Part II: Write the Mysteries of the Rosary in the correct order.

Joyful Mysteries
1. The Annunciation
2. The Visitation
3. The Nativity
4. The Presentation
5. The Finding of Jesus in the Temple

Sorrowful Mysteries
1. The Agony in the Garden
2. The Scourging at the Pillar
3. The Crowning with Thorns
4. The Carrying of the Cross
5. The Crucifixion

Glorious Mysteries
1. The Resurrection
2. The Ascension
3. The Descent of the Holy Spirit
4. The Assumption
5. The Coronation

Luminous Mysteries
1. The Baptism of Christ
2. The Wedding Feast of Cana
3. The Proclamation of the Kingdom
4. The Transfiguration
5. The Institution of the Eucharist

Part III: Write a paragraph on one of the following topics.

1. How can we stay focused when we pray?
2. What is the Divine Office or Liturgy of the Hours and who must pray it?
3. What is the spiritual life?

_____
_____
_____
_____
_____
_____

Faith and Life Series • Grade 6 • Appendix A   *A-3*

Assess

1. Distribute the quizzes and read through them with the students to be sure they understand the questions.

2. Administer the quiz. As they hand in their work, you may orally quiz the students on the Memorization Questions from this chapter.

3. After all the quizzes have been handed in, you may wish to review the correct answers with the class.

Conclude

1. Lead the students in singing "Now thank we all our God," *Adoremus Hymnal*, #607.

2. End class by leading the students in the Acts of Faith, Hope, and Love (see *Teacher's Manual*, p. 29 or p. 396).

Name:_____

Prayer

Answer the following questions in complete sentences.

1. What is prayer?
   <u>Prayer is the raising of the mind and heart to God.</u>

2. What are three forms of prayer?
   <u>Three forms of prayer are vocal prayer, meditation, and contemplation.</u>

3. Why should we pray?
   <u>Answers will vary.</u>

4. Should we pray even if we do not feel like praying?
   <u>Yes.</u>

5. What should we do if we are distracted in prayer?
   <u>We should return to prayer calmly and patiently.</u>

6. Does God hear and answer our prayers?
   <u>Yes, Jesus promised that our prayers will be answered.</u>

7. Does God always give us what we want? Why or why not?
   <u>No, if we want something that is bad for us God will not grant it, but God will always give what is best for us.</u>

Faith and Life Series • Grade 6 • Chapter 3 • Lesson 1 9

Name:_____

Catholic Prayers

Answer the following questions in complete sentences.

1. What is the Divine Office or the Liturgy of the Hours?
   <u>The Divine Office is a prayer of praise and petition using the Psalms and readings from Scripture and the writings of the saints.</u>

2. Who is obliged to say the Liturgy of the Hours?
   <u>Certain members of the Church, such as priests, are required to pray it.</u>

3. What is the Rosary?
   <u>The Rosary is a prayer in which we meditate on episodes in the lives of Jesus and Mary as we pray vocal prayers.</u>

4. How should we say the Rosary?
   <u>We should pray the vocal prayers slowly as our hearts are moved by what is in our minds.</u>

5. What other special prayers do you know?
   <u>Answers will vary.</u>

6. What does Saint Alphonsus Ligouri teach us about prayer?
   <u>Answers will vary but should be based on the quote on p. 23 of the student text.</u>

10 *Faith and Life Series • Grade 6 • Chapter 3 • Lesson 2*

Name:_____

The Rosary

From the list below, write the Mysteries of the Rosary in order.

The Agony in the Garden

The Annunciation

The Proclamation of the Kingdom

The Assumption

The Ascension

The Coronation

The Wedding Feast at Cana

The Visitation

The Crucifixion

The Baptism of Christ in the Jordan

The Nativity

The Institution of the Holy Eucharist

The Descent of the Holy Spirit

The Scourging at the Pillar

The Transfiguration of Our Lord

The Carrying of the Cross

The Finding in the Temple

The Resurrection

The Presentation

The Crowning with Thorns

THE JOYFUL MYSTERIES	THE GLORIOUS MYSTERIES
The Annunciation	The Resurrection
The Visitation	The Ascension
The Nativity	Descent of the Holy Spirit
The Presentation	The Assumption
The Finding in the Temple	The Coronation

THE SORROWFUL MYSTERIES	THE LUMINOUS MYSTERIES
The Agony in the Garden	The Baptism of Christ
The Scourging at the Pillar	The Wedding Feast at Cana
The Crowning with Thorns	Proclamation of the Kingdom
The Carrying of the Cross	The Transfiguration
The Crucifixion	Institution of the Eucharist

Faith and Life Series • Grade 6 • Chapter 3 • Lesson 3 11

Name:_____

The Spiritual Life

Answer the following questions in complete sentences.

1. What does the spiritual life include?
   1. <u>Prayer</u>
   2. <u>Sacraments</u>
   3. <u>Good works</u>

2. How does prayer help us to do good works?
   <u>Answers will vary.</u>

3. How does prayer relate to the sacramental life?
   <u>Answers will vary.</u>

4. How does receiving the Sacraments help us to pray?
   <u>Answers will vary.</u>

5. To whom does prayer unite us?
   <u>Prayer unites us to God.</u>

6. How does prayer make us fully alive?
   <u>A life of prayer fills us with joy, peace, and confidence.</u>

12 *Faith and Life Series • Grade 6 • Chapter 3 • Lesson 4*

TEACHER'S NOTES

CHAPTER FOUR
SAINTS—THEY MADE THE MOST OF IT

Catechism of the Catholic Church References

Angels: 328–36, 350–52
Heaven: 1023–29, 1053
Holiness: 683, 686, 688, 828, 946–59, 1717, 2012–14, 2028–2030, 2156,
Man's Vocation to Beatitude: 1718–24, 1726–29
Mary as Our Mother: 963–70, 973–75

Prayer in Union with Mary: 2673–79, 2682
Prayers of Intercession: 2634–36, 2647
Saints as Guides and Companions in Prayer: 2683–84, 2692–93
Saints as Patrons: 2156

Scripture References

The Kingdom of God: Mt 13:44–46

Stewardship: Mt 25:14–30

Summary of Lesson Content

Lesson 1

Saints are the souls united with God forever in heaven. On earth, the saints lived lives of holiness and special closeness to God. We are all called to become saints.

Conversion is the turning away from sin toward God.

We can only be truly happy if we are in union with God and his will. This is called sanctity (holiness), and is deeply related to our membership in the Kingdom of God.

Lesson 2

The saints in heaven are called the Church Triumphant because their eternal reward is union with God.

As Catholics, we believe in eternal life: not that we will live forever on earth, but that we will share in God's eternal life through grace.

Lesson 3

Intercession is prayer on behalf of another.

We can ask others on earth, those in purgatory, and those in heaven to pray for us. We often ask the saints to intercede for us. Their prayers are powerful before the throne of God.

Lesson 4

The Church has canonized many saints and assures us that they are in heaven. There are also many saints in heaven who are unknown to us.

CHAPTER FOUR: SAINTS—THEY MADE THE MOST OF IT
LESSON ONE: CONVERSION

Aims

The students will learn that saints are the souls united with God forever in heaven. On earth, the saints lived lives of holiness and special closeness to God. We are all called to become saints.

They will learn that conversion is the turning away from sin toward God.

They will learn that we can only be truly happy if we are in union with God and his will.

Materials

- *Activity Book*, p. 13
- Lives of the saints books

Optional:
- "For all the saints," *Adoremus Hymnal*, #590

Begin

Discuss conversion with the students. It is a turning away from sin and turning toward God. We often think of conversion meaning those who were not Catholic, who then become Catholic. We are all called to conversion, to a life of holiness.

We are called to die to sin and to unite ourselves closely with God. We have many aids in this process: Sacraments, prayer/grace, angels and saints, examples of saints, intercessors, the guidance of the Church, etc.

Develop

1. Read paragraphs 1–7 from the text with the students.

2. What does Saint Augustine mean when he says that our hearts are restless until they rest in God? God who created us did so with the plan that we were created to be in union with him. If we are not striving for this union, it is like trying to put a square peg in a round hole. It is like using a car for a paperweight—yes, it would hold down the paper, but it is not what the car was designed for. So, too, we are designed to be in union with God and there is a natural longing in our hearts for this.

3. Have the students research their patron saints. (They will make presentations on their patron saints in another lesson.) How did each saint become united with God? How can we follow his example? Each student should know his saint's biography and reasons why he is a model for holiness.

4. Review that the Sacraments are a very important part of

our conversion. The Sacrament of Penance gives us a new beginning so that we can live in union with God. We are most perfectly united with God through a worthy reception of Holy Communion. You may review the steps to a good confession and worthy Communion with the students.

5. Have the students write a journal entry about a conversion experience in their lives.

6. Using the students' names/patrons, make a litany of the saints to be prayed throughout this chapter. Write this out, and make copies for all the students. You may use the usual formula for the litany.

7. What are the fruits of conversion? How will we know if we are living in friendship with God? We keep his commandments, we pray, we do good works, we receive the Sacraments, we are joyful, etc.

Reinforce

1. Have the students work on *Activity Book* p. 13 (see *Teacher's Manual*, p. 49).

2. Have the students continue to research their patron saints.

3. Have the students begin memorizing the Words to Know and the Memorization Questions for this chapter (see *Teacher's Manual*, p. 43).

4. Have the students make prayer cards for their patron saints, including writing a prayer on the back.

Conclude

1. Teach the students to sing "For all the saints," *Adoremus Hymnal*, #590.

2. End class by leading the students in a litany of saints, using the patron saints of students.

CHAPTER 4

Saints—They Made The Most of It

"After this I looked, and behold, a great multitude which no man could number, from every nation, from all tribes and peoples and tongues, standing before the throne and before the Lamb, clothed in white robes, with palm branches in their hands."

Revelation 7:9

In this life we are all looking for the same thing: *happiness*. **Saints** are those who have found it. They are perfectly happy with God in heaven. On earth they enjoyed a special closeness to God that brought them great happiness even in the midst of their sufferings. But there is one thing we must always remember about the saints: they all started out just like each of us. What is more, each of us is called to be a saint, too.

Many a saint, writing or speaking about his life, remembered being unhappy for years while he ignored God and followed the ways of the world. He might have forgotten his unhappiness for awhile in seeking pleasure, but when the pleasure ended he was sadder than before. Then he had a change of heart, turned to God, and began a new life. This new beginning in God is called a conversion. Through prayer and the Sacraments he practiced loving God, and he practiced loving his neighbors by doing good works. His old life of sin was over and his new life with Christ gave him joy.

The great Saint Augustine wrote: "You have made us for yourself, O Lord, and our hearts are restless until they rest in you."

We can only be happy if we are in harmony with the will of God, which means we are doing what God wants. Any distance from God, great or small, caused by sin, means that much unhappiness. The key to happiness, then, is "friendship with God," which means doing God's will. The saints are close friends of God. This friendship brings them great joy, for we were made for friendship with God and nothing else can make up for that if we do not have it.

There is only one cure for the unhappy man: he must turn to God with all his heart. Nothing else can satisfy him.

Jesus relates **sanctity**, or happiness and holiness, to the "Kingdom of God." He compares true happiness to a merchant's search for fine pearls: "The kingdom of heaven is like a merchant in search of fine pearls, who, on finding one pearl of great value, went and sold all that he had and bought it" (Mt 13:45–46).

25

26

Saint Charles Lwanga   Saint John Bosco   Saint Maximilian Kolbe

"To the saints honor must be paid as friends of Christ, as sons and heirs of God."

—Saint John of Damascus

This is what the saints have done. In many cases they have completely changed their lives in order to obey God and be at peace with him. Now, after a happy life on earth, they enjoy the full and tremendous happiness of seeing God in heaven.

Saints Victorious

We call the saints in heaven the **Church Triumphant** because they have grasped the final prize which is God himself. God has given himself to them; he is theirs for all eternity. "Eternal life" doesn't just mean living forever; it means living *God's* life forever.

Intercessors

We should take advantage of the great power of the saints to intercede for us. "Intercede" means to speak up for someone, to pray for someone. We should pray to the saints and ask them to do this. They are called "intercessors"—those who intercede. When we pray to the saints we are honoring them, and in honoring them we honor God because we acknowledge that through God's grace they have been victo-

rious over sin. We ask other people on earth to pray to God for us. We can also ask the saints in heaven to intercede for us. Their prayers are very powerful because they are dear friends of God. Each of us should pray, particularly, to his **patron saint**, the saint for whom he was named. We should pray especially to the Blessed Virgin Mary, who is the greatest of all the saints, given to us as our Mother by Jesus himself. We have many special prayers to Mary, but the best known is the "Hail Mary." We should also pray to the good angels, although we know the names of only three of them: Saint Michael the Archangel, Saint Gabriel, whom God sent to the Blessed Virgin to ask her to become the Mother of his Son, and Saint Raphael. We should pray every day to our own guardian angel, for he is always with us to help us. In addition, we should pray to our favorite saints, those for whom we feel a special attraction.

Besides asking the saints to intercede for us, we should study their lives so that we may learn from them how to attain our goal of heaven. By imitating their virtuous lives we will find it easier to know and fulfill the will of God.

27

Preview

In the next lesson, the students will learn about the Saints Victorious.

41

CHAPTER FOUR: SAINTS—THEY MADE THE MOST OF IT
LESSON TWO: SAINTS VICTORIOUS

Aims

The students will learn that the saints in heaven are called the Church Triumphant because their eternal reward is union with God.

They will learn that, as Catholics, we believe in eternal life: not that we will live forever on earth, but that we will share in God's eternal life through grace.

Materials

- *Activity Book*, p. 14

- Lives of saints books

Optional:
- "For all the saints," *Adoremus Hymnal*, #590

Begin

You may distinguish between saints, who are holy souls united with God in heaven, and canonized saints, holy souls united with God in heaven whom the Church has infallibly defined to be saints and venerates as saints in her liturgical calendar.

Examples may include:
saints: Grandpa, Great Uncle Bob, Fr. Jones
canonized saints: Saint Mary, Saint Joseph, Saint Thérèse

Develop

1. Have the students read paragraph 8 in the text.

2. Review the Communion of Saints. The Communion of Saints includes all those who share in God's friendship. This includes the faithful souls on earth striving to get to heaven (The Church Militant), the holy souls in purgatory, who are assured of heaven but are being purified and prepared for their entry into heaven (The Church Suffering), and the souls in heaven with the angels. This includes the saints, the canonized saints, and the angels (The Church Triumphant). Have the students depict the Communion of Saints, or how we all share in the treasure of the Mass.

3. Today, the students will learn about the highlighted saints in their texts: Saint Charles Lwanga, Saint John Bosco, and Saint Maximilian Kolbe. Have the students research these saints. They may dramatize significant events from their

lives, make holy cards for these saints, write prayers asking these saints for their intercession, etc. Each student should research and know well one of these saints. Add these three saints to your litany of saints.

4. Angels are also in the Church Triumphant. Angels, too, had to choose to serve and be faithful to God. You may review the battle and fall of the angels with the students.

5. Can we pray to small *s* saints? Scripture tells us that we should not try to communicate with the dead. We can however, be united with them through the Mystical Body of Christ, and ask Jesus to let our loved ones know how much we love and miss them. We should only venerate the saints who are defined by the Church. We may pray for souls in purgatory and ask that souls in heaven and purgatory pray for us.

Reinforce

1. Have the students work on *Activity Book* p. 14 (see *Teacher's Manual*, p. 49).

2. The students should complete their patron saint reports.

3. Have the students demonstrate their knowledge on the saints they studied today.

4. You may wish to give the students time to work on their Memorization Questions and Words to Know.

Conclude

1. Lead the students in singing "For all the saints," *Adoremus Hymnal*, #590.

2. End class by leading the students in praying a litany of saints, using patron saints of students.

Saint Charles Lwanga

Saint John Bosco

Saint Maximilian Kolbe

> "To the saints honor must be paid as friends of Christ, as sons and heirs of God."
> —Saint John of Damascus

This is what the saints have done. In many cases they have completely changed their lives in order to obey God and be at peace with him. Now, after a happy life on earth, they enjoy the full and tremendous happiness of seeing God in heaven.

Saints Victorious

We call the saints in heaven the **Church Triumphant** because they have grasped the final prize which is God himself. God has given himself to them; he is theirs for all eternity. "Eternal life" doesn't just mean living forever; it means living *God's* life forever.

Intercessors

We should take advantage of the great power of the saints to intercede for us. "Intercede" means to speak up for someone, to pray for someone. We should pray to the saints and ask them to do this. They are called "**intercessors**"—those who intercede. When we pray to the saints we are honoring them, and in honoring them we honor God because we acknowledge that through God's grace they have been victo-

rious over sin. We ask other people on earth to pray to God for us. We can also ask the saints in heaven to intercede for us. Their prayers are very powerful because they are dear friends of God. Each of us should pray, particularly, to his **patron saint**, the saint for whom he was named. We should pray especially to the Blessed Virgin Mary, who is the greatest of all the saints, given to us as our Mother by Jesus himself. We have many special prayers to Mary, but the best known is the "Hail Mary." We should also pray to the good angels, although we know the names of only three of them: Saint Michael the Archangel, Saint Gabriel, whom God sent to the Blessed Virgin to ask her to become the Mother of his Son, and Saint Raphael. We should pray every day to our own guardian angel, for he is always with us to help us. In addition, we should pray to our favorite saints, those for whom we feel a special attraction.

Besides asking the saints to intercede for us, we should study their lives so that we may learn from them how to attain our goal of heaven. By imitating their virtuous lives we will find it easier to know and fulfill the will of God.

27

We should keep in mind that the saints are real people who are now with Jesus in heaven. If we make friends with them today, they will remember us when we need them most. They will help us grow closer to Jesus.

The Blessed in Heaven

Those whom we honor by name as saints are those whom the Church has determined with complete certainty to be now in heaven. There are many, many others in heaven unknown to us whom we will meet when we get there.

How many saints are there, including all those of whom we do not now know?

Saint John, in the Book of Revelation, tells us of a vision of heaven: "After this I looked, and behold, a great multitude which no man could number, from every nation, from all tribes and peoples and tongues" (Rev 7:9).

This is comforting, but we should never take heaven for granted. With Saint Paul we must "finish the race;" we must "fight the good fight" (see 2 Tim 4:7). We must follow Jesus in order to be with him one day in heaven; the saints can help us do this.

Words to Know:
    saints   sanctity   Church Triumphant
       intercessor   patron saint

28

Q. 15	*Who are the saints?*
	The saints are those who, by practicing the virtues to a heroic degree according to the teachings and example of Jesus Christ, have merited special glory in heaven and also on earth, where, by the authority of the Church, they are publicly honored and called upon (CCC 828, 927).
Q. 16	*Why should we pray to the saints in addition to God?*
	We should pray to the saints in addition to God because God wills to help us through the prayers of others, including the saints, who are very holy and close to God (CCC 956).
Q. 17	*Why are the angels, the saints, and our Lady powerful intercessors with God?*
	The angels and saints are powerful intercessors with God because they are his faithful servants and his beloved friends. Our Lady is the most powerful intercessor of all because she is the Mother of God. She is also a model for all who pray (CCC 956, 2679).
Q. 18	*What is the prayer that we use in a special way to invoke the intercession of our Lady?*
	We invoke the intercession of our Lady especially with the Hail Mary (CCC 2676–77).

29

THE COMMUNION OF SAINTS

Using the Apostles' Creed as its source, the *Catechism of the Catholic Church* defines the Communion of Saints as the entire Church:

CCC 946: After confessing "the holy catholic Church," the Apostles' Creed adds "the communion of saints." In a certain sense this article is a further explanation of the preceding: "What is the Church if not the assembly of all the saints?" The communion of saints is the Church.

The Church, and therefore the Communion of Saints, is composed of souls glorified in heaven, suffering in purgatory, and toiling on earth.

Preview

In the next lesson, the students will learn about intercessors and begin presenting their patron saints to the class.

Chapter Four: Saints—They Made the Most of It
Lesson Three: Intercessors

Aims

The students will learn that intercession is prayer on behalf of another.

They will learn that we can ask others on earth, those in purgatory, and those in heaven to pray for us. We often ask the saints to intercede for us. Their prayers are powerful before the throne of God.

Materials

- *Activity Book*, p. 15

Optional:
- "For all the saints," *Adoremus Hymnal*, #590

Begin

Often, people who are not Catholic misunderstand and think that Catholics worship the saints, especially Mary. Catholics worship God alone. Worship of God is called "Latria." However, we venerate the saints. This means we honor them because they are friends and heirs of God. This kind of veneration is called "Dulia." We have a special honor for Mary, as she is the most perfect saint, being the Mother of God and without sin. She is the highest honored saint, and the veneration reserved for Mary alone is called "Hyperdulia."

Develop

1. Read paragraphs 9–11 from the student text.

2. Catholics often say that they pray to the saints. We pray to Saint Anthony to find something, we pray to Saint Jude for a lost cause. However, we really are asking the saints to pray with us and for us, just as we would any other friend or family member. We pray with Saint Joseph to help us find a job or sell our house, we pray with Saint Anne to find a husband or wife. We pray with Mary for all our needs and for her special love and protection to lead us to Jesus most perfectly. We know that by asking a saint for help, that saint will take our prayer to God. God alone is the one who answers our prayers.

3. Some people wonder why we have pictures and statues of our favorite saints. Some think this is like having the golden calf at Mount Sinai. Rather, this is like having family portraits on the wall, or in a purse/wallet. The saints are our family in Christ. We love them and honor them, just as we do our natural family members.

4. Intercessory prayer is a form of supplication. We ask for things of God on behalf of another. We are often intercessors, for example, at Mass during the Prayers of the Faithful. We often ask people to pray for our needs, as well. So, too, the saints can pray for us, and we know that they are powerful intercessors before God. They are united with him for all eternity, in his friendship. We know that their intercession has already worked miracles!

5. How do we choose which saint to turn to? Well, they are real people; they too had struggles. We can learn about their lives and see which saints struggled as we do. Also, the Church has named saints as patrons of various peoples and for various needs. See the list to the right for some examples.

Reinforce

1. Have the students work on *Activity Book* p. 15 (see *Teacher's Manual*, p. 49).

2. Have the students begin presenting their patron saints to the class.

3. Have the students work on the Memorization Questions and Words to Know.

4. Allow the students to add various patrons to their prayer books.

Conclude

1. Lead the students in singing "For all the saints," *Adoremus Hymnal*, #590.

2. End class by leading the students in praying a litany of saints, using the patron saints of students.

Saint Charles Lwanga   Saint John Bosco   Saint Maximilian Kolbe

---

"To the saints honor must be paid as friends of Christ, as sons and heirs of God."

—Saint John of Damascus

This is what the saints have done. In many cases they have completely changed their lives in order to obey God and be at peace with him. Now, after a happy life on earth, they enjoy the full and tremendous happiness of seeing God in heaven.

Saints Victorious

We call the saints in heaven the **Church Triumphant** because they have grasped the final prize which is God himself. God has given himself to them; he is theirs for all eternity. "Eternal life" doesn't just mean living forever; it means living *God's* life forever.

Intercessors

We should take advantage of the great power of the saints to intercede for us. "Intercede" means to speak up for someone, to pray for someone. We should pray to the saints and ask them to do this. They are called "intercessors"—those who intercede. When we pray to the saints we are honoring them, and in honoring them we honor God because we acknowledge that through God's grace they have been victorious over sin. We ask other people on earth to pray to God for us. We can also ask the saints in heaven to intercede for us. Their prayers are very powerful because they are dear friends of God. Each of us should pray, particularly, to his **patron saint**, the saint for whom he was named. We should pray especially to the Blessed Virgin Mary, who is the greatest of all the saints, given to us as our Mother by Jesus himself. We have many special prayers to Mary, but the best known is the "Hail Mary." We should also pray to the good angels, although we know the names of only three of them: Saint Michael the Archangel, Saint Gabriel, whom God sent to the Blessed Virgin to ask her to become the Mother of his Son, and Saint Raphael. We should pray every day to our own guardian angel, for he is always with us to help us. In addition, we should pray to our favorite saints, those for whom we feel a special attraction.

Besides asking the saints to intercede for us, we should study their lives so that we may learn from them how to attain our goal of heaven. By imitating their virtuous lives we will find it easier to know and fulfill the will of God.

27

We should keep in mind that the saints are real people who are now with Jesus in heaven. If we make friends with them today, they will remember us when we need them most. They will help us grow closer to Jesus.

The Blessed in Heaven

Those whom we honor by name as saints are those whom the Church has determined with complete certainty to be now in heaven. There are many, many others in heaven unknown to us whom we will meet when we get there.

How many saints are there, including all those of whom we do not now know?

Saint John, in the Book of Revelation, tells us of a vision of heaven: "After this I looked, and behold, a great multitude which no man could number, from every nation, from all tribes and peoples and tongues" (Rev 7:9).

This is comforting, but we should never take heaven for granted. With Saint Paul we must "finish the race;" we must "fight the good fight" (see 2 Tim 4:7). We must follow Jesus in order to be with him one day in heaven; the saints can help us do this.

Words to Know:
saints   sanctity   Church Triumphant   intercessor   patron saint

28

PATRON SAINTS

Of Places:

- Africa: Mary, Queen of Africa
- The Americas: Our Lady of Guadalupe
- United States: Our Lady of the Immaculate Conception
- California: Our Lady of the Wayside
- Diocese of Richmond, VA: Saint Vincent de Paul
- Canada: Saint Joseph; Saint Isaac Jogues
- England: Saint George
- Ireland: Saint Patrick
- Rome: Saint Peter the Apostle; Saint Paul the Apostle

For Specific Intentions:

- Abandoned People: Saint Flora of Cordoba
- Against Cancer: Saint Peregrine Laziosi
- Against Poison: Saint Benedict
- Against Floods: Saint Columba
- Athletes and Sports: Saint Sebastian
- The Falsely Accused: Saint Elizabeth of Hungary
- Hopeless Causes: Saint Jude Thaddeus
- Lost Objects: Saint Anthony of Padua
- Music and Musicians: Saint Cecilia
- Safety for Travelers: Saint Christopher
- Students: Saint Thomas Aquinas

INTERCESSION

The word *intercede* comes from the Latin words *inter*, which means "between" and *cedere*, a verb that means "to go." So *intercede* literally means "to go between."

Preview

In the next lesson, the students will learn more about the blessed in heaven and the canonization process.

For the next class each student may bring in his favorite image of Mary. Every student should know the title by which Mary is called in that particular image.

CHAPTER FOUR: SAINTS—THEY MADE THE MOST OF IT
LESSON FOUR: MAKING SAINTS

Aims

The students will learn that the Church has canonized many saints and assures us that they are in heaven. Additionally, there are many saints in heaven who are unknown to us.

Materials

- *Activity Book*, p. 16

- Litany of Loreto (to be added to the prayer books), *Teacher's Manual*, p. 396

- Images of Mary

Optional:
- "For all the saints," *Adoremus Hymnal*, #590

Begin

Review that Mary has a special role among all the saints. She is the most honored and has many titles and images. Share the many titles and images of Mary. You may use books or images, and discuss what the various titles from the Litany of Loreto mean. Often we become confused because Mary has so many titles. Use yourself as an example. The students call you _____, while your family and friends call you by your first name. You may be known by your job, or by where you were seen, but all the names refer to you.

Develop

1. Finish reading the chapter with the students.

2. You may review the canonization process with the students. When the Church defines someone as a saint, she is infallible in this declaration—absolutely certain and without error that that person is a saint.

First, a person lives a life of heroic virtue in following Christ and living a life of sanctity. Then after their death, an investigation occurs. Information is gathered about the person. Their friends and family and people who knew them are interviewed. All their writings are gathered and read. A huge file is created and the bishop and promoter of this person's "cause," or case, then submits this case to the Vatican. The clergy at the Vatican then go through all the findings and may declare that this person has lived a life of heroic virtue and may be called Venerable. This person may be honored as a good example, and the promoter of the cause then prints prayer cards, asking people to pray for miracles through this saint's intercession.

When a miracle occurs a new phase is entered. The miracle must be scientifically unexplained (such as a healing of a blind person, or of a person with inoperable cancer, etc.), the miracle must occur instantaneously, and be attributed only to the intercession of this particular saint. If this miracle is accepted by the Vatican, then the person is declared Blessed. Upon the acceptance of a second miracle, the person can be canonized a saint by the Pope and added to the liturgical calendar for veneration by the faithful all over the world.

3. Trace the canonization process of a particular saint. Recommended saints are: Saint Edith Stein, Saint Elizabeth Ann Seton, Saint Padre Pio. Pick a saint, do the research and create a summary for the students to read.

Reinforce

1. Have the students work on *Activity Book* p. 16 (see *Teacher's Manual*, p. 49).

2. The students should finish presenting their patron saints to the class.

3. Have the students research the process through which a saint is canonized.

4. Have the students work on the Memorization Questions and Words to Know and prepare for the chapter quiz and unit test.

Conclude

1. Lead the students in singing "For all the saints," *Adoremus Hymnal*, #590.

2. Review for the Chapter 4 Quiz.

3. End class by leading the students in praying a litany of saints, using the patron saints of students.

Saint Charles Lwanga

Saint John Bosco

Saint Maximilian Kolbe

"To the saints honor must be paid as friends of Christ, as sons and heirs of God."
—Saint John of Damascus

This is what the saints have done. In many cases they have completely changed their lives in order to obey God and be at peace with him. Now, after a happy life on earth, they enjoy the full and tremendous happiness of seeing God in heaven.

Saints Victorious

We call the saints in heaven the **Church Triumphant** because they have grasped the final prize which is God himself. God has given himself to them; he is theirs for all eternity. "Eternal life" doesn't just mean living forever; it means living *God's* life forever.

Intercessors

We should take advantage of the great power of the saints to intercede for us. "Intercede" means to speak up for someone, to pray for someone. We should pray to the saints and ask them to do this. They are called "**intercessors**"—those who intercede. When we pray to the saints we are honoring them, and in honoring them we honor God because we acknowledge that through God's grace they have been victorious over sin. We ask other people on earth to pray to God for us. We can also ask the saints in heaven to intercede for us. Their prayers are very powerful because they are dear friends of God. Each of us should pray, particularly, to his **patron saint**, the saint for whom he was named. We should pray especially to the Blessed Virgin Mary, who is the greatest of all the saints, given to us as our Mother by Jesus himself. We have many special prayers to Mary, but the best known is the "Hail Mary." We should also pray to the good angels, although we know the names of only three of them: Saint Michael the Archangel, Saint Gabriel, whom God sent to the Blessed Virgin to ask her to become the Mother of his Son, and Saint Raphael. We should pray every day to our own guardian angel, for he is always with us to help us. In addition, we should pray to our favorite saints, those for whom we feel a special attraction.

Besides asking the saints to intercede for us, we should study their lives so that we may learn from them how to attain our goal of heaven. By imitating their virtuous lives we will find it easier to know and fulfill the will of God.

27

We should keep in mind that the saints are real people who are now with Jesus in heaven. If we make friends with them today, they will remember us when we need them most. They will help us grow closer to Jesus.

The Blessed in Heaven

Those whom we honor by name as saints are those whom the Church has determined with complete certainty to be now in heaven. There are many, many others in heaven unknown to us whom we will meet when we get there.

How many saints are there, including all those of whom we do not now know?

Saint John, in the Book of Revelation, tells us of a vision of heaven: "After this I looked, and behold, a great multitude which no man could number, from every nation, from all tribes and peoples and tongues" (Rev 7:9).

This is comforting, but we should never take heaven for granted. With Saint Paul we must "finish the race;" we must "fight the good fight" (see 2 Tim 4:7). We must follow Jesus in order to be with him one day in heaven; the saints can help us do this.

Words to Know:
saints   sanctity   Church Triumphant
intercessor   patron saint

28

Q. 15   *Who are the saints?*
The saints are those who, by practicing the virtues to a heroic degree according to the teachings and example of Jesus Christ, have merited special glory in heaven and also on earth, where, by the authority of the Church, they are publicly honored and called upon (CCC 828, 927).

Q. 16   *Why should we pray to the saints in addition to God?*
We should pray to the saints in addition to God because God wills to help us through the prayers of others, including the saints, who are very holy and close to God (CCC 956).

Q. 17   *Why are the angels, the saints, and our Lady powerful intercessors with God?*
The angels and saints are powerful intercessors with God because they are his faithful servants and his beloved friends. Our Lady is the most powerful intercessor of all because she is the Mother of God. She is also a model for all who pray (CCC 956, 2679).

Q. 18   *What is the prayer that we use in a special way to invoke the intercession of our Lady?*
We invoke the intercession of our Lady especially with the Hail Mary (CCC 2676–77).

29

CANONIZATION

Why does the Church canonize, or recognize officially, some of its members as saints?

CCC 828: By *canonizing* some of the faithful, i.e., by solemnly proclaiming that they practiced heroic virtue and lived in fidelity to God's grace, the Church recognizes the power of the Spirit of holiness within her and sustains the hope of believers by proposing the saints to them as models and intercessors. . . .

In addition to serving as powerful intercessors for us, the saints are our models in faith. It is for these reasons that the Church has a formal process of canonization.

Preview

In the next lesson, the students' understanding of the material covered in this chapter will be reviewed and assessed. There will be a quiz and unit test.

Chapter Four: Saints—They Made the Most of It
Review and Assessment

Aims

The students' understanding of the material covered in this chapter will be reviewed and assessed.

Materials

- Quiz 4, Appendix, p. A-4

Optional:
- "For all the saints," *Adoremus Hymnal*, #590

Review and Enrichment

1. The students should know the difference between saints and canonized saints.

2. The students should understand the concept of conversion and that man is designed to be happy when he is in union with God. We are all called to this union, which is called sanctity.

3. The students should understand the Communion of Saints, including the Church Militant, Suffering, and Triumphant.

4. The students should be familiar with one of the following saints: Saint Charles Lwanga, Saint John Bosco, or Saint Maximilian Kolbe, as well as their patron saints.

5. The students should understand the concept of intercessory prayer, that it is a form of supplication.

6. The students should understand that when the Church canonizes a saint, this is an infallible statement.

Name: _____

Saints—They Made the Most of It **Quiz 4**

Part I: Define the following:

conversion   Church Triumphant   intercede   patron saint

1. Conversion is the turning away from sin and toward God.
2. The Church Triumphant is the saints in heaven.
3. To intercede is to speak up for or pray for another person.
4. A patron saint is a special saint chosen to intercede for a particular person or group.

Part II: Answer in complete sentences.

1. What role does Mary have in heaven?
   Mary is the greatest of all the saints and our Mother. She is a powerful intercessor.

2. What is the only way to be happy?
   The only way to be happy is to be in friendship with God and to do what God wants.

3. What is the only cure for the unhappy man?
   The only cure for the unhappy man is to turn to God with all his heart.

Part III: Yes or No.

1. Yes Is each of us called to be a saint?
2. Yes Are the saints close friends of God?
3. No   Can our hearts rest in anything besides God?
4. Yes Should we pray to our patron saint and to our guardian angel?
5. Yes Are the saints powerful intercessors?
6. No   Is there any happiness more wonderful than heaven?

A-4   *Faith and Life Series • Grade 6 • Appendix A*

Assess

1. Distribute the quizzes and read through them with the students to be sure they understand the questions.

2. Administer the quiz. As they hand in their work, you may orally quiz the students on the Memorization Questions from this chapter.

3. After all the quizzes have been handed in, you may wish to review the correct answers with the class.

Conclude

1. Lead the students in singing "For all the saints," *Adoremus Hymnal*, #590.

2. End class by praying a litany of saints using patron saints.

Name:_____

Saints—They Made the Most of It

Can you find all thirty-five saints in the puzzle below?

Agnes	Dominic	Joan	Stephen	Matthew
Clare	James	Mary	Timothy	Philip
Ignatius	Margaret	Peter	Elizabeth Seton	Monica
Luke	Paul	Thomas	Frances Cabrini	Basil
Patrick	Therese	Anthony	Augustine	Mark
Lucy	Andrew	Gabriel	Catherine	Joseph
Anne	Francis	John	Rose of Lima	Michael

```
C C P P H I L I P R Z L U C E
I I H A H U U P E I G N N F R
N E I U L K K T T L L A R G W
I U L U C Y E H U E R A M R A
M I S I P P P E I E N C A A L
O S S Y Z E B R O C L A R M M
D A O T Z A B E E U Y T K A O
M M M E A B S I M O H K M N I
A O A R G C C E P A U E C I C
T H R A B A H H T R E R A L A
T T Y B U E G U N P S R C F A
H T R U L Y G N P E N R O J
E A E N N A U E E Q E O H
W N A M O E K A O S L H T S
I N H S C T I M O T H Y O L
M E T A I S E M A J B I B N
A N D R E W B D O O O A N A N
A C T O L E A H C I M A S E R
B A S S I C N A R F R A N I I
P A T S I I G N A T I U S S L
```

Faith and Life Series • Grade 6 • Chapter 4 • Lesson 1   13

Name:_____

Conversion

Answer the following questions in complete sentences.

1. From your text, name a saint who had a conversion.
   Answers will vary.

2. How was this saint unhappy before his conversion?
   He ignored God and followed the ways of the world.

3. How might he have forgotten his unhappiness for a while?
   He might have forgotten his unhappiness in seeking pleasure.

4. How did he practice loving God and neighbor?
   He practiced loving God through prayer and the Sacraments, and loving his neighbor by doing good works.

5. What does Saint Augustine mean when he writes, "You have made us for yourself, O Lord, and our hearts are restless until they rest in you"? Following this statement, what is the key to happiness?
   Answers will vary.

6. How are the saints close friends with God? What did they do?
   Answers will vary.

7. What is their reward?
   Their reward is friendship with God which brings them great joy. Ultimately, their reward is eternal life with God in heaven.

14   *Faith and Life Series • Grade 6 • Chapter 4 • Lesson 2*

Name:_____

Intercession

Answer the following questions in complete sentences.

1. What does "intercession" mean?
   Intercession means to speak up for or pray for another.

2. Who can intercede for us?
   The saints in heaven and people on earth can intercede for us.

3. In asking the saints to intercede for us, are we honoring God? How?
   We honor God because we acknowledge that through God's grace they have been victorious over sin.

4. Why are the angels, the saints, and our Lady powerful intercessors with God?
   They are powerful intercessors because they are his faithful servants and his beloved friends.

5. How can we know which saints to ask for intercessory prayers?
   We can ask our own patron saint or other saints to whom we feel a special attraction.

6. Why do we have statues of the saints? Do we worship saints?
   Answer is not in text but should be similar to: We have statues of the saints to remind us of them. We do not worship saints.

Faith and Life Series • Grade 6 • Chapter 4 • Lesson 3   15

Name:_____

Patron Saints

Answer the following questions in complete sentences.

Blessed Kateri Tekakwitha

1. Who is your patron saint?
   Answers to all of the following will vary.

2. What special virtue did this saint have? What special works did he do?

3. Of what (other than you) is your patron saint a patron?

4. When and where did your saint live?

5. Find a prayer that specifically asks for your saint's intercession and write it below.

16   *Faith and Life Series • Grade 6 • Chapter 4 • Lesson 4*

TEACHER'S NOTES

UNIT ONE TEST
CHAPTERS 1–4

CHAPTER ONE: GOD GIVES US THE LAW

CHAPTER TWO: THE FIRST COMMANDMENT IN OUR OWN DAY

CHAPTER THREE: PRAYER—HIDDEN TREASURE

CHAPTER FOUR: SAINTS—THEY MADE THE MOST OF IT

Aims

The students' understanding of the material covered in this unit will be reviewed and assessed.

Materials

• Unit 1 Test, Appendix, pp. A-5 and A-6

Assess

1. Distribute the unit tests and read through them with the students to be sure they understand the questions.

2. Administer the test.

3. After all the tests have been handed in, you may wish to review the correct answers with the class.

Name: _____

Unit 1 Test   **Chapters 1–4**

Part I: Fill in the blanks with the correct words from the Word Bank.

Word Bank:

good	evil	Decalogue
law	free will	judge
image	conscience	Ten Commandments

God created man in his _image_. It is written upon man's heart to do _good_ and avoid _evil_. Man's _conscience_ helps him to _judge_ right from wrong. To help us form our conscience, God revealed himself and gave us his _law_. He also gave us _free_ _will_ so that we can love and obey him and live in his friendship. God's law is summarized in the _Decalogue_, also known as the _Ten Commandments_.

Part II: Answer the following questions.

1. What kind of sin is the result of deliberately breaking a commandment in a serious way? _mortal sin_

2. Besides doing something seriously wrong, what two other things are necessary for a sin to be a mortal sin? _Knowing that what you are doing is seriously wrong and freely choosing to do what is seriously wrong._

3. Does the First Commandment require all men to acknowledge God as the one true God, Creator and Lord of all things and to worship and adore him as our God? _Yes_

Part III: Matching.

1. _b_ being irreverent or irreligious
2. _e_ worshipping a false god
3. _c_ believing in an error or denying a truth
4. _a_ placing faith or trust in something other than God
5. _d_ being able to let go of things

a. superstition
b. impiety
c. heresy
d. detachment
e. idolatry

Name: _____

Unit 1 Test (continued)

Part IV: Answer in complete sentences.

1. What are we required to do by the First Commandment. _The First Commandment requires us to believe in God, to hope in him, and to love him above all else; to worship and adore only God._

2. What does the First Commandment forbid? _The First Commandment forbids heresy, apostasy, voluntary doubt, deliberate ignorance of God's truth, despair, presumption, idolatry, indifference to God, hatred of God, superstition, and irreligious behavior._

3. What is prayer and how should we pray? _Prayer is the raising of the mind and heart to God. We should pray humbly, attentively, and devoutly._

4. What are the two forms of prayer? _The two forms of prayer are vocal and mental prayer._

5. What is a saint? _A saint is someone who loved God totally during his life on earth and is now with God in the perfect happiness of heaven._

6. What is the Church Triumphant? _The Church Triumphant is all the saints in heaven._

Part V: Write the Ten Commandments in order.

1. _I am the Lord your God; you shall not have other gods before me._
2. _You shall not take the name of the Lord your God in vain._
3. _Remember to keep holy the Lord's Day._
4. _Honor your father and mother._
5. _You shall not kill._
6. _You shall not commit adultery._
7. _You shall not steal._
8. _You shall not bear false witness against your neighbor._
9. _You shall not covet your neighbor's wife._
10. _You shall not covet your neighbor's goods._

TEACHER'S NOTES

TEACHER'S NOTES

CHAPTER FIVE
THE HOLY NAME

Catechism of the Catholic Church References

God Reveals His Name: 203–13, 231
Sacramentals: 1667–78
Second Commandment: 2142–59, 2160–67

The Lord's Name Is Holy: 2142–49, 2160–61, 2166
Taking the Lord's Name in Vain: 2150–55, 2162–64
The Christian Name: 2156–59, 2165, 2167

Scripture References

Called By Name:
    Abraham: Gen 17:1–8
    Jacob: Gen 32:24–30
    Moses: Ex 3:1–10

Samuel: 1 Sam 3:1–10
Zacchaeus: Lk 19:2–6
Reverence for the Name of Jesus: Phil 2:9–11
Abraham Offering Isaac; God's Oath: Gen 22:1–18

Summary of Lesson Content

Lesson 1

The Second Commandment forbids disrespect to God's name or to anything holy.

God revealed his name to Moses: "I AM WHO I AM" (Ex 3:14).

Lesson 2

Violations of the Second Commandment include blasphemy, false oaths, and swearing upon God's name unnecessarily.

Lesson 3

Vows are promises made before God. Vows are binding. A vow is a solemn declaration committing oneself to do something. A religious vow is made for a religious reason.

Religious vows include poverty, chastity, and obedience. These are called the three evangelical counsels.

Married couples vow fidelity in marriage.

Lesson 4

Respect is due not only to God, but also to holy things.

The church structure and objects used for Mass, as well as blessed objects, are holy and must be treated reverently.

We honor and respect priests and people consecrated to God because they belong to God in a special way.

CHAPTER FIVE: THE HOLY NAME
LESSON ONE: GOD'S NAME

Aims

The students will learn that the Second Commandment forbids disrespect to God's name or to anything holy.

They will learn that God revealed his name to Moses: "I AM WHO I AM" (Ex 3:14).

Materials

- *Activity Book*, p. 17

- Bible

Optional:
- "Holy God, we praise thy name!" *Adoremus Hymnal*, #461

Begin

Begin the class with a discussion. Why do we ask famous people for their autographs? When we call someone's house, why do we ask for him by name? Why do we write our names on our work? Should we take care and pride in work that has our name on it? When our mothers and fathers call out our names in public, why do we respond (and not another person)?

Our names identify us and bring to mind who we are. A name is an important thing—so important that God calls us by name.

Develop

1. Read paragraphs 1–3 with the students.

2. Read from the Bible, and dramatize God telling Moses the divine name (Ex 3:13 ff.). Discuss the reverence the Jews have for the divine name, for example, praying for a long time before writing the word "Yahweh" into their manuscripts of the Bible.

3. Read from the Bible various times when God has called someone by name:
Abraham: Gen 17:1–8; Israel: Gen 32:24–30; Moses: Ex 3:1–10; Samuel: 1 Sam 3:1–10; Zacchaeus: Lk 19:2–6.
The students may dramatize these stories.

4. God has called us by name as well. We are all baptized with a specific name, "(___, I baptize you in the name of the Father and of the Son and of the Holy Spirit.") We are called by name and God has a loving plan for each of us. At Baptism,

we receive an indelible mark on our souls, identifying us as Christians, members of God's family, the Church. We must take pride in the name "Christian" and in the name that has been bestowed upon us at Baptism, usually the name of a saint. As God has called us by name, we must listen to his plan for us.

5. Discuss reverence: it is respect and honor given to someone or something. We reverence the altar, we act with reverence in church, we speak reverently when using God's name or the names of the saints.

6. Taking God's name in vain is an offense against the Second Commandment. If I call out your name, you give me your attention. So, too, if you call upon God's name, it invokes his presence. Read from Philippians 2:9–11. We shall see what reverence we should have for the name of God.

Reinforce

1. Have the students work on *Activity Book* p. 17 (see *Teacher's Manual*, p. 63).

2. Have the students begin working on the Memorization Questions and Words to Know from this chapter.

3. Teach the students the Jesus Prayer used by monastics. This reverent prayer acknowledges the power that is present in Jesus' name. It is: Lord Jesus Christ, Son of God, have mercy upon me, a sinner.

Conclude

1. Teach the children to sing "Holy God, we praise thy name!" *Adoremus Hymnal*, #461.

2. End class by leading the students in the Divine Praises prayer (see facing page).

CHAPTER 5

The Holy Name

"You shall not take the name of the LORD your God in vain; for the LORD will not hold him guiltless who takes his name in vain."

Exodus 20:7

The Second Commandment forbids any lack of respect, or due **reverence**, toward God in the use of his most Holy Name, or toward any holy person or thing. Anyone who offends God by breaking this commandment is usually spiritually unwell, since no one who truly loves God would think of purposely misusing his name. On the contrary, someone who loves God goes out of his way to bless God's name and to make up for the times when others misuse his name.

When Moses asked God for his name, God said, "I AM WHO I AM." (Ex 3:14) For the Jewish people this name was so great and holy because it was the name that God personally revealed out of love.

What terrible foolishness, therefore, to misuse so great a Name!

* * *

There are different ways in which people violate the Second Commandment.

One way is called **blasphemy**. This is verbal abuse or scorn toward God himself or, by extension, toward the Blessed Virgin, the other saints, or holy things.

Another violation is swearing false oaths. A false **oath** calls on God to witness to the truth of what we are saying when in fact we are lying. An oath in itself is not wrong. We may be involved in a legal proceeding which requires one. This is a good enough reason to take an oath; however, we should not take oaths invoking the divine name without serious reason.

Obviously, a false oath is a very serious sin, since we are calling God, who is all Truth and all Justice, to witness to a lie.

Aside from the formality of a legal proceeding, it is common for people to use expressions like, "As God is my witness," or, "Honest to God." Spoken seriously, these are oaths and should not be used lightly. Said thoughtlessly or for unimportant reasons, they are swearing and should be avoided. (We must not confuse swearing with using bad language or cursing; using impure language is against the Sixth Commandment and cursing against the Fifth.)

The Second Commandment also requires us to fulfill the vows and promises we have made. A vow is a solemn declaration committing oneself to do something. A **vow** in religion is a vow by which someone promises something for a religious reason. Religious brothers and sisters make vows of poverty, chastity, and obedience. A married couple makes a vow of fidelity.

30

Holy Things

We must not only respect God but must extend that respect to all those things that belong to God in a special way. We refer to our church as the house of God and a place of worship. It is a building consecrated to the glorification of God, and our behavior in church ought to express that.

All of the objects used for Mass, such as the altar, chalice, and paten, are holy because they are used in the highest form of worship. It is easy to see why we revere the Holy Bible, since it is the Word of God. Just as we treasure pictures and mementos of those we love, we also cherish crucifixes, religious medals, and holy images as reminders of God and his saints.

Certain people within the Church (the Pope, bishops, priests, deacons, religious brothers and sisters) have consecrated their entire lives to God. Because they belong to God in a special way, we honor and respect them.

We express our love and reverence for God in the way we treat those things and people that belong to God.

Remember what God said to Moses from the burning bush: "Moses, Moses! . . . Do not come near; put off your shoes from your feet, for the place on which you are standing is holy ground" (Ex 3:4–5). The ground was holy because God was present.

Words to Know:
reverence blasphemy
oath vow

Holy Name Society

Some parishes have an organization called the Holy Name Society. This society goes back to the thirteenth century. Its aim is to bring about due love and reverence for the Holy Name of God and Jesus Christ.

"O LORD, our Lord, how majestic is your name in all the earth!"

Psalm 8:1

"From the rising of the sun to its setting the name of the LORD is to be praised!"

Psalm 113:3

31

"Young men and maidens together, old men and children! Let them praise the name of the LORD, for his name alone is exalted."

Psalm 148:12–13

Q. 19 *What does the Second Commandment require us to do?*
The Second Commandment requires us to respect and revere the Holy Name of God and to fulfill the vows and promises to which we have bound ourselves (CCC 2142, 2150).

Q. 20 *What does the Second Commandment forbid?*
The Second Commandment forbids us from dishonoring the name of God. To dishonor the name of God means to use his name without respect; to blaspheme God, the Holy Virgin, the saints, or holy things; or to swear oaths that are false, unnecessary, or wrong in any way (CCC 2146–49).

Q. 21 *What is an oath?*
An oath is calling upon God as witness for what is declared or promised. A person who swears falsely offends God seriously, for God is holiness and truth itself (CCC 2149–50).

Q. 22 *Is blasphemy a serious sin?*
Yes, blasphemy is a serious sin because it is injury and scorn toward God and his saints (CCC 2148).

Q. 23 *What is a vow?*
A vow is a promise made to God of some good that is pleasing to him (CCC 2102).

HALLOWED BE THY NAME

32

THE DIVINE PRAISES

Blessed be God.
Blessed be his Holy Name.
Blessed be Jesus Christ, true God and true Man.
Blessed be the Name of Jesus.
Blessed be his Most Sacred Heart.
Blessed be his Most Precious Blood.
Blessed be Jesus in the Most Holy Sacrament of the Altar.
Blessed be the Holy Spirit, the Paraclete.
Blessed be the great Mother of God, Mary most holy.
Blessed be her holy and Immaculate Conception.
Blessed be her Glorious Assumption.
Blessed be the name of Mary, Virgin and Mother.
Blessed be Saint Joseph, her most chaste spouse.
Blessed be God in his angels and in his saints.

Preview

In the next lesson, the students will learn about using God as our witness.

CHAPTER FIVE: THE HOLY NAME
LESSON TWO: GOD AS WITNESS

Aims

The students will learn that violations of the Second Commandment include blasphemy, false oaths, and swearing upon God's name unnecessarily.

Materials

- *Activity Book*, p. 18

- Bible

Optional:
- "Holy God, we praise thy name!" *Adoremus Hymnal*, #461

Begin

From the Bible, read the account of Abraham offering his son Isaac, and of the oath God makes by his own authority (Gen 22:1–18). Why does God swear by himself? Because there is no greater authority. When we swear oaths, we call down the highest authority as our witness. So with a legal proceeding, it is common for people to say "As God is my witness" or they swear to tell the truth with their hand on the Holy Bible.

Develop

1. Read paragraphs 4–8 with the students.

2. Define blasphemy. It is the verbal abuse or scorn of God's name or the names of the saints or holy things. We often hear phrases that use blasphemy. For some, blaspheming is a very bad habit, which must be stopped. It is important to recognize that our words are an expression of ourselves. We speak what we think. We communicate part of who we are with our words. People who speak blasphemy show that they are spiritually sick.

3. In making an oath, we call a higher authority to witness to a truth. This is not a bad thing, unless it is done lightly. It is a testimony, or gives witness or weight to a truth so that we can take a person's word as the very truth he proclaims. In the Bible, the gospel was preached in the name of Jesus. Read the following passages: Acts 2:38; 3:6, 16; 9:27; 1 Jn 3:23; Mt 28:18–20.

4. False oaths, however, are sinful. They call upon God to witness to a falsehood. Jesus said, "I am...the truth" (Jn 14:6); God can neither deceive nor be deceived.

5. We must have a grave reason for taking an oath, such as participating in a legal proceeding.

6. Oaths have consequences. We swear by something of great value to us, so we would not jeopardize its loss by breaking the oath. Covenants are entered by oaths. If we swore a false oath in court, we would commit the crime of perjury and would be sent to prison. Our words have very great value and we must always speak the truth responsibly.

7. Often, when we hear the word "swearing" we think of using bad language. This, too, is sinful, but using angry words breaks the Fifth Commandment and impure words violates the Sixth Commandment.

Reinforce

1. Have the students work on *Activity Book* p. 18 (see *Teacher's Manual*, p. 63).

2. Have the students work on the Memorization Questions and Words to Know from this chapter.

3. Have the students write prayers honoring God's Holy Name.

4. Have the students listen for God's Holy Name. Teach them to bow their heads when the name of Jesus is spoken.

Conclude

1. Lead the children in singing "Holy God, we praise thy name!" *Adoremus Hymnal*, #461.

2. End class by leading the students in praying the Divine Praises (see *Teacher's Manual*, p. 55).

CHAPTER 5

The Holy Name

"You shall not take the name of the LORD your God in vain; for the LORD will not hold him guiltless who takes his name in vain."

Exodus 20:7

The Second Commandment forbids any lack of respect, or due **reverence**, toward God in the use of his most Holy Name, or toward any holy person or thing. Anyone who offends God by breaking this commandment is usually spiritually unwell, since no one who truly loves God would think of purposely misusing his name. On the contrary, someone who loves God goes out of his way to bless God's name and to make up for the times when others misuse his name.

When Moses asked God for his name, God said, "I AM WHO I AM." (Ex 3:14) For the Jewish people this name was so great and holy because it was the name that God personally revealed out of love.

What terrible foolishness, therefore, to misuse so great a Name!

* * *

There are different ways in which people violate the Second Commandment.

One way is called **blasphemy**. This is verbal abuse or scorn toward God himself or, by extension, toward the Blessed Virgin, the other saints, or holy things.

Another violation is swearing false oaths. A false **oath** calls on God to witness to the truth of what we are saying when in fact we are

lying. An oath in itself is not wrong. We may be involved in a legal proceeding which requires one. This is a good enough reason to take an oath; however, we should not take oaths invoking the divine name without serious reason.

Obviously, a false oath is a very serious sin, since we are calling God, who is all Truth and all Justice, to witness to a lie.

Aside from the formality of a legal proceeding, it is common for people to use expressions like, "As God is my witness," or, "Honest to God." Spoken seriously, these are oaths and should not be used lightly. Said thoughtlessly or for unimportant reasons, they are swearing and should be avoided. (We must not confuse swearing with using bad language or cursing; using impure language is against the Sixth Commandment and cursing against the Fifth.)

The Second Commandment also requires us to fulfill the vows and promises we have made. A vow is a solemn declaration committing oneself to do something. A **vow** in religion is a vow by which someone promises something for a religious reason. Religious brothers and sisters make vows of poverty, chastity, and obedience. A married couple makes a vow of fidelity.

30

Holy Things

We must not only respect God but must extend that respect to all those things that belong to God in a special way. We refer to our church as the house of God and a place of worship. It is a building consecrated to the glorification of God, and our behavior in church ought to express that.

All of the objects used for Mass, such as the altar, chalice, and paten, are holy because they are used in the highest form of worship. It is easy to see why we revere the Holy Bible, since it is the Word of God. Just as we treasure pictures and mementos of those we love, we also cherish crucifixes, religious medals, and holy images as reminders of God and his saints.

Certain people within the Church (the Pope, bishops, priests, deacons, religious brothers and sisters) have consecrated their entire lives to God. Because they belong to God in a special way, we honor and respect them.

We express our love and reverence for God in the way we treat those things and people that belong to God.

Remember what God said to Moses from the burning bush: "Moses, Moses! . . . Do not come near; put off your shoes from your feet, for the place on which you are standing is holy ground" (Ex 3:4–5). The ground was holy because God was present.

Words to Know:
    reverence   blasphemy
    oath   vow

Holy Name Society

Some parishes have an organization called the Holy Name Society. This society goes back to the thirteenth century. Its aim is to bring about due love and reverence for the Holy Name of God and Jesus Christ.

"O LORD, our Lord, how majestic is your name in all the earth!"

Psalm 8:1

"From the rising of the sun to its setting the name of the LORD is to be praised!"

Psalm 113:3

31

"Young men and maidens together, old men and children! Let them praise the name of the LORD, for his name alone is exalted."

Psalm 148:12–13

> **Q. 19** *What does the Second Commandment require us to do?*
> The Second Commandment requires us to respect and revere the Holy Name of God and to fulfill the vows and promises to which we have bound ourselves (CCC 2142, 2150).
>
> **Q. 20** *What does the Second Commandment forbid?*
> The Second Commandment forbids us from dishonoring the name of God. To dishonor the name of God means to use his name without respect; to blaspheme God, the Holy Virgin, the saints, or holy things; or to swear oaths that are false, unnecessary, or wrong in any way (CCC 2146–49).
>
> **Q. 21** *What is an oath?*
> An oath is calling upon God as witness for what is declared or promised. A person who swears falsely offends God seriously, for God is holiness and truth itself (CCC 2149–50).
>
> **Q. 22** *Is blasphemy a serious sin?*
> Yes, blasphemy is a serious sin because it is injury and scorn toward God and his saints (CCC 2148).
>
> **Q. 23** *What is a vow?*
> A vow is a promise made to God of some good that is pleasing to him (CCC 2102).

HALLOWED BE THY NAME

32

SOCIETY OF THE HOLY NAME

Officially known as the Confraternity of the Most Holy Name of God and Jesus, the Society of the Holy Name is an ancient, holy organization within the Church. This Society originated in the thirteenth century. Still in existence today, the members of the Society are sworn to preserve and protect the Holy Name of God from blasphemy, misuse, and disrespect, and from abuse in oaths and profanity. Carried on chiefly by the Order of Preachers (the Dominicans), the Society began by combatting heretics, such as the Cathars, who were abusing God's name. Through the centuries, the need for the Society has clearly remained with us.

Preview

In the next lesson, the students will learn about vows.

CHAPTER FIVE: THE HOLY NAME
LESSON THREE: VOWS

Aims

The students will learn that vows are promises made before God. Vows are binding. A vow is a solemn declaration committing oneself to do something. A religious vow is made for a religious reason.

They will learn that religious vows include poverty, chastity, and obedience. These are called the three evangelical counsels.

They will learn that married couples vow fidelity in marriage.

Materials

- *Activity Book*, p. 19

- Rite of Marriage, Appendix, pp. B-3 and B-4

Optional:
- "Holy God, we praise thy name!" *Adoremus Hymnal*, #461

Begin

Have the students look up the definitions of oaths and vows. How are they similar? How are they different? Have the students give examples of each.

Read 1 Samuel 1. It is the story of Hannah begging God for a child and her vow to give him to God, should she have him. This is an example of a vow made to the Lord and of the fulfillment of that vow.

Develop

1. Read paragraph 9 with the students.

2. Explain and discuss promises and vows and their obligations: promises are made to people; vows are made to God. Vows are made to do something good and pleasing to God. We must never promise or vow to do evil things. If we do, we do wrong in fulfilling these evil promises; for example, certain people hated Saint Paul so much that they swore they would neither eat nor drink until they had killed him (Acts 23:12). However, there are good vows, such as the vows of marriage and the evangelical counsels of poverty, chastity, and obedience, which are so good that they are meant to last as long as we live.

3. Use the Chalk Talk, at right, to explain the vows of matrimony and of religious life.

4. Read through the Rite of Marriage with the students.

Explain that to enter into marriage, they must be mature, free to marry, and freely consenting to the vows that are made.

5. Diocesan clergy make different vows/promises than religious. They promise to say the Divine Office every day, to be obedient to their bishop and his successors, and to live a life of chastity. (They do not take the vow of poverty.)

6. If religious vows (marriage, religious, or diocesan) are broken, this is a mortal sin. So, for example, if a priest fails to pray his Divine Office, then he is in mortal sin and must confess this in the Sacrament of Penance.

7. Vows are binding, but it is through them that we find true freedom—the freedom to love and follow God all the days of our lives. For example, because of obedience, we never have to question God's will. When acting in obedience we please God.

Reinforce

1. Have the students work on *Activity Book* p. 19 (see *Teacher's Manual*, p. 63).

2. If possible, have a married person, a religious, and a member of the diocesan clergy visit the class to discuss their vocations. Engage the students in a dialogue about their own vocations. Be sure the guests share their stories of how they felt called to their particular vocations.

3. Have the students work on the Memorization Questions and Words to Know from this chapter.

Conclude

1. Lead the children in singing "Holy God, we praise thy name!" *Adoremus Hymnal*, #461.

2. End class by leading the students in praying the Divine Praises (see *Teacher's Manual*, p. 55).

CHAPTER 5

The Holy Name

"You shall not take the name of the Lord your God in vain; for the Lord will not hold him guiltless who takes his name in vain."

Exodus 20:7

The Second Commandment forbids any lack of respect, or due **reverence**, toward God in the use of his most Holy Name, or toward any holy person or thing. Anyone who offends God by breaking this commandment is usually spiritually unwell, since no one who truly loves God would think of purposely misusing his name. On the contrary, someone who loves God goes out of his way to bless God's name and to make up for the times when others misuse his name.

When Moses asked God for his name, God said, "I AM WHO I AM." (Ex 3:14) For the Jewish people this name was so great and holy because it was the name that God personally revealed out of love.

What terrible foolishness, therefore, to misuse so great a Name!

* * *

There are different ways in which people violate the Second Commandment.

One way is called **blasphemy**. This is verbal abuse or scorn toward God himself or, by extension, toward the Blessed Virgin, the other saints, or holy things.

Another violation is swearing false oaths. A false **oath** calls on God to witness to the truth of what we are saying when in fact we are lying. An oath in itself is not wrong. We may be involved in a legal proceeding which requires one. This is a good enough reason to take an oath; however, we should not take oaths invoking the divine name without serious reason.

Obviously, a false oath is a very serious sin, since we are calling God, who is all Truth and all Justice, to witness to a lie.

Aside from the formality of a legal proceeding, it is common for people to use expressions like, "As God is my witness," or, "Honest to God." Spoken seriously, these are oaths and should not be used lightly. Said thoughtlessly or for unimportant reasons, they are swearing and should be avoided. (We must not confuse swearing with using bad language or cursing; using impure language is against the Sixth Commandment and cursing against the Fifth.)

The Second Commandment also requires us to fulfill the vows and promises we have made. A vow is a solemn declaration committing oneself to do something. A **vow** in religion is a vow by which someone promises something for a religious reason. Religious brothers and sisters make vows of poverty, chastity, and obedience. A married couple makes a vow of fidelity.

Holy Things

We must not only respect God but must extend that respect to all those things that belong to God in a special way. We refer to our church as the house of God and a place of worship. It is a building consecrated to the glorification of God, and our behavior in church ought to express that.

All of the objects used for Mass, such as the altar, chalice, and paten, are holy because they are used in the highest form of worship. It is easy to see why we revere the Holy Bible, since it is the Word of God. Just as we treasure pictures and mementos of those we love, we also cherish crucifixes, religious medals, and holy images as reminders of God and his saints.

Certain people within the Church (the Pope, bishops, priests, deacons, religious brothers and sisters) have consecrated their entire lives to God. Because they belong to God in a special way, we honor and respect them.

We express our love and reverence for God in the way we treat those things and people that belong to God.

Remember what God said to Moses from the burning bush: "Moses, Moses! . . . Do not come near; put off your shoes from your feet, for the place on which you are standing is holy ground" (Ex 3:4–5). The ground was holy because God was present.

Words to Know:
reverence   blasphemy
oath   vow

Holy Name Society

Some parishes have an organization called the Holy Name Society. This society goes back to the thirteenth century. Its aim is to bring about due love and reverence for the Holy Name of God and Jesus Christ.

"O Lord, our Lord, how majestic is your name in all the earth!"

Psalm 8:1

"From the rising of the sun to its setting the name of the Lord is to be praised!"

Psalm 113:3

"Young men and maidens together, old men and children! Let them praise the name of the Lord, for his name alone is exalted."

Psalm 148:12–13

Q. 19   What does the Second Commandment require us to do?
The Second Commandment requires us to respect and revere the Holy Name of God and to fulfill the vows and promises to which we have bound ourselves (CCC 2142, 2150).

Q. 20   What does the Second Commandment forbid?
The Second Commandment forbids us from dishonoring the name of God. To dishonor the name of God means to use his name without respect; to blaspheme God, the Holy Virgin, the saints, or holy things; or to swear oaths that are false, unnecessary, or wrong in any way (CCC 2146–49).

Q. 21   What is an oath?
An oath is calling upon God as witness for what is declared or promised. A person who swears falsely offends God seriously, for God is holiness and truth itself (CCC 2149–50).

Q. 22   Is blasphemy a serious sin?
Yes, blasphemy is a serious sin because it is injury and scorn toward God and his saints (CCC 2148).

Q. 23   What is a vow?
A vow is a promise made to God of some good that is pleasing to him (CCC 2102).

HALLOWED BE THY NAME

CHALK TALK: CHRISTIAN VOWS

Chalk Talk
The vows of Matrimony and Religious Life:

Matrimony	Religious Life
Fidelity to one's spouse until death; giving up marrying anyone else.	Chastity: giving up marriage for the sake of God's Kingdom. Poverty: giving up the right to use property without permission and without necessity in order to be more like Jesus. Obedience: giving up one's own will to be more like Jesus.

Preview

In the next lesson, the students will learn about holy things.

- Poverty- live a simple life, share resources + time and talents, w/community
- dependent on God's gifts
- money earned or recieved are for good of the whole
- Chastity- love of God only
- listening and responding to pray

CHAPTER FIVE: THE HOLY NAME
LESSON FOUR: HOLY THINGS

Aims

The students will learn that respect is due, not only to God, but also to holy things.

They will learn that the church structure and objects used for Mass, as well as blessed objects, are holy and must be treated reverently.

They will learn that we honor and respect priests and people consecrated to God because they belong to God in a special way.

Materials

- *Activity Book*, p. 20

- Arrange for church tour and presentation of vessels used for worship

- Paper, pencils, and photocopied images of vessels to be labeled

- Appendix, pp. B-5–B-6

Optional:
- Holy God, we praise thy name!" *Adoremus Hymnal*, #461

Begin

Today, begin the class by reading the rest of the chapter with the students. Help the students to understand that certain people, places, and things are holy because of their relationship to God and his Church.

Develop

1. If needed, review paragraphs 10–14 with the students.

2. Distribute floor plans of your church. Have the students draw on the floor plan:
   - Tabernacle (where Jesus in the Eucharist is reserved)
   - Altar (where the Sacrifice of the Mass occurs)
   - Ambo (where the Word of God is proclaimed)
   - Presider's chair (where the priest sits during the Mass)
   - Choir (the place for the musicians)
   - Congregation (the place of the lay faithful)
   - Crucifix (a reminder of Christ's saving sacrifice)
   - Shrines ([if any] places for particular saints/devotions)
   - Baptismal font (where we become members of the Church)

Tour these places and explain the significance of each (you may wish to expand upon the brief notes beside each item listed above).

3. Provide a photocopy of the vessels and items used at church (see Appendix, pp. B-5 and B-6). Have the priest/presenter explain each of the vessels, what it is called, for what it is used, and the way it should be handled. Include in this presentation:
   - Chalice and paten
   - Ciborium
   - Linens
   - Cruets and basin
   - Monstrance

(Optional: Lectionary, book of Gospels, sacramentary, vestments)

4. The students may make posters explaining the various vestments, vessels, and spaces in the church (including the furnishings). Have each student make a poster on one item. Each should draw it (e.g., tabernacle), write what it is used for, where it is found in the church, and the specifics about it that make it unique to the parish.

Reinforce

1. Have the students work on *Activity Book* p. 20 (see *Teacher's Manual*, p. 63).

2. Have the students work on their posters.

3. Have the students work on the Memorization Questions and Words to Know from this chapter (see *Teacher's Manual*, p. 59). You may wish to provide class time for the students to review for the quiz.

Conclude

1. Lead the children in singing "Holy God, we praise thy name!" *Adoremus Hymnal*, #461.

2. End class by leading the students in praying the Divine Praises (see *Teacher's Manual*, p. 55).

CHAPTER 5

The Holy Name

"You shall not take the name of the Lord your God in vain; for the Lord will not hold him guiltless who takes his name in vain."

Exodus 20:7

The Second Commandment forbids any lack of respect, or due **reverence**, toward God in the use of his most Holy Name, or toward any holy person or thing. Anyone who offends God by breaking this commandment is usually spiritually unwell, since no one who truly loves God would think of purposely misusing his name. On the contrary, someone who loves God goes out of his way to bless God's name and to make up for the times when others misuse his name.

When Moses asked God for his name, God said, "I AM WHO I AM." (Ex 3:14) For the Jewish people this name was so great and holy because it was the name that God personally revealed out of love.

What terrible foolishness, therefore, to misuse so great a Name!

* * *

There are different ways in which people violate the Second Commandment.

One way is called **blasphemy**. This is verbal abuse or scorn toward God himself or, by extension, toward the Blessed Virgin, the other saints, or holy things.

Another violation is swearing false oaths. A false **oath** calls on God to witness to the truth of what we are saying when in fact we are lying. An oath in itself is not wrong. We may be involved in a legal proceeding which requires one. This is a good enough reason to take an oath; however, we should not take oaths invoking the divine name without serious reason.

Obviously, a false oath is a very serious sin, since we are calling God, who is all Truth and all Justice, to witness to a lie.

Aside from the formality of a legal proceeding, it is common for people to use expressions like, "As God is my witness," or, "Honest to God." Spoken seriously, these are oaths and should not be used lightly. Said thoughtlessly or for unimportant reasons, they are swearing and should be avoided. (We must not confuse swearing with using bad language or cursing; using impure language is against the Sixth Commandment and cursing against the Fifth.)

The Second Commandment also requires us to fulfill the vows and promises we have made. A vow is a solemn declaration committing oneself to do something. A **vow** in religion is a vow by which someone promises something for a religious reason. Religious brothers and sisters make vows of poverty, chastity, and obedience. A married couple makes a vow of fidelity.

30

Holy Things

We must not only respect God but must extend that respect to all those things that belong to God in a special way. We refer to our church as the house of God and a place of worship. It is a building consecrated to the glorification of God, and our behavior in church ought to express that.

All of the objects used for Mass, such as the altar, chalice, and paten, are holy because they are used in the highest form of worship. It is easy to see why we revere the Holy Bible, since it is the Word of God. Just as we treasure pictures and mementos of those we love, we also cherish crucifixes, religious medals, and holy images as reminders of God and his saints.

Certain people within the Church (the Pope, bishops, priests, deacons, religious brothers and sisters) have consecrated their entire lives to God. Because they belong to God in a special way, we honor and respect them.

We express our love and reverence for God in the way we treat those things and people that belong to God.

Remember what God said to Moses from the burning bush: "Moses, Moses! . . . Do not come near; put off your shoes from your feet, for the place on which you are standing is holy ground" (Ex 3:4–5). The ground was holy because God was present.

Words to Know:
    reverence blasphemy
    oath vow

Holy Name Society

Some parishes have an organization called the Holy Name Society. This society goes back to the thirteenth century. Its aim is to bring about due love and reverence for the Holy Name of God and Jesus Christ.

"O Lord, our Lord, how majestic is your name in all the earth!"

Psalm 8:1

"From the rising of the sun to its setting the name of the Lord is to be praised!"

Psalm 113:3

31

SAINT JOHN CHRYSOSTOM

Author of a liturgy still used in the Eastern rite of the Catholic Church, Saint John Chrysostom is venerated throughout the Church for his contributions to the understanding and expression of the Faith. Beginning his spiritual life as a contemplative, Saint John Chrysostom was soon named bishop and patriarch in the politically volatile diocese of Constantinople. As a bishop, Saint John became famous for his preaching and reform. He worked hard to encourage priestly sanctity and his title Chrysostom means "golden-tongued," a testament to his preaching. Unfortunately for him, his fiery preaching got him into trouble. When preaching about vanity, he often brought up the Byzantine Empress Eudoxia who ruled from Constantinople. She did not take kindly to his condemnations and had Saint John exiled. However, he was so popular with the common people of Constantinople that they protested and nearly rioted at his exile. In order to keep the peace, Empress Eudoxia allowed Saint John to return to the city. Although able to defy the Empress, Saint John lived a simple, humble life. He sold the treasure and furnishings of his house and gave the money to the poor. Nonetheless, he taught that furnishings within the churches must be respected. His teachings later proved a support against iconoclasts who wrongly believed that holy images were blasphemous.

VESSELS

Some other sacred vessels include a pyx and luna. A pyx is a small vessel used to carry the Blessed Sacrament to the sick or homebound. A luna is the vessel that holds the Blessed Sacrament upright in a monstrance.

Preview

In the next lesson, the students' understanding of the material covered in this chapter will be reviewed and assessed.

Chapter Five: The Holy Name
Review and Assessment

Aims

The students' understanding of the material covered in this chapter will be reviewed and assessed.

Materials

- Quiz 5, Appendix, p. A-7

Optional:
- "Holy God, we praise thy name!" *Adoremus Hymnal*, #461

Name: _____

The Holy Name   Quiz 5

Part I: Fill in the blanks.

1. The Second Commandment forbids any lack of respect, or <u>reverence</u>, toward God in the use of his most Holy Name.

2. When Moses asked God for his name, God said, "I <u>AM</u> WHO I <u>AM</u>."

3. <u>Blasphemy</u> is the verbal abuse or scorn toward God himself or to the Blessed Virgin, the other saints, or holy things.

4. An <u>oath</u> calls on God to witness to the truth of what we are saying.

5. A <u>vow</u> is a solemn declaration committing oneself to do something.

Part II: Yes or No.

1. <u>Yes</u> Is it permissible for someone to take an oath when he is involved in a legal proceeding that requires it?

2. <u>No</u> Should we ever take an oath lightly or falsely?

Part III: Answer in complete sentences.

1. What vows do religious brothers and sisters make?
   <u>Religious brothers and sisters make the vows of poverty, chastity and obedience.</u>

2. What kind of vow does a married couple make?
   <u>A married couple makes the vow of fidelity.</u>

3. Are the objects used for Mass, such as the altar, chalice, and paten considered to be holy? Why or why not?
   <u>Yes, the objects used for Mass are holy because they are used in the highest form of worship.</u>

4. How should we treat the people, places, and things consecrated to God?
   <u>We should show special respect for the people, places and things consecrated to God.</u>

Faith and Life Series • Grade 6 • Appendix A   A-7

Review and Enrichment

1. The students should understand what the Second Commandment requires of us, and what it forbids.

2. The students should know and understand what these words mean: reverence, blasphemy, oaths, vows, promises, evangelical counsels (poverty, chastity, and obedience), fidelity.

3. The students should know that they have been called by name by God as members of his family. God has a plan for each of them.

4. The students should be familiar with their church building, its furnishings, the vessels, and vestments used for Mass.

Assess

1. Distribute the quizzes and read through them with the students to be sure they understand the questions.

2. Administer the quiz. As they hand in their work, you may orally quiz the students on the Memorization Questions from this chapter.

3. After all the quizzes have been handed in, you may wish to review the correct answers with the class.

Conclude

1. Lead the children in singing "Holy God, we praise thy name!" *Adoremus Hymnal*, #461.

2. End class by leading the students in praying the Divine Praises (see *Teacher's Manual*, p. 55).

CHAPTER FIVE: THE HOLY NAME
ACTIVITY BOOK ANSWER KEYS

God's Name

Answer the following questions in complete sentences.

1. What is God's name as he revealed it in Exodus?
   <u>God's name is "I am who I am," or "Yahweh."</u>
2. To whom did God reveal his name?
   <u>God revealed his name to Moses.</u>
3. How can God's name be misused?
   <u>God's name can be misused by blasphemy and swearing false oaths.</u>
4. How should we use God's name?
   <u>We should use God's name with reverence and respect.</u>
5. What is the Second Commandment?
   <u>The Second Commandment is: You shall not take the name of the Lord your God in vain.</u>
6. Write a poem, song, or prayer blessing the name of the Lord.

<u>Answers will vary.</u>

God as Witness

Find the following words in your textbook or the glossary in the back of your textbook and define them using complete sentences.

Blasphemy: <u>The sin of speaking about or to God in a scornful or disrespectful way.</u>

Oath: <u>A declaration calling on God as a witness to the truth of what is being said.</u>

Vow: <u>A solemn promise made to God of something good and pleasing to him.</u>

Reverence: <u>Honor and respect.</u>

Cursing: <u>The sin of expressing hope that evil or harm will happen to someone or something.</u>

Impiety: <u>The sin of lacking reverence or proper respect for God.</u>

Scandal: <u>The sin of giving bad example which leads another into sin.</u>

Make Satisfaction For: <u>Making up for some wrong-doing.</u>

Swear: <u>To make an oath.</u>

False Oath: <u>An oath that calls on God to witness to the truth of what is said although we are lying.</u>

Sacred Objects: <u>Objects that are set apart for the worship of God.</u>

fering of man alone, no matter how valu-
le, can make up for it.

Man's helplessness was no obstacle to God
o wanted to save man. God himself became
n and offered himself on the Cross as a
ting sacrifice, which was far more than
ough to make up for all sins of all men. This
crifice is renewed daily in every Mass
und the world. The sacrifice of Jesus on the
oss is the greatest gift we can offer to God.
The sacrifice we offer in the Mass is the
hest possible act of worship. It contains all
t is necessary for giving due worship to
d. In the Mass we acknowledge God as

Creator, our Lord and Master. We thank hir
gratitude for all he has given us. And, in rec
nition that we are dependent on him, we ask
all we need and for what will help oth
Finally, we offer in the Mass the only thing
can make up for our sins and offenses. We o
the sacrifice of Jesus Christ on the Cross.

We can give God the love and wors
we owe him when we participate in H
Mass. Let's do so often!

Words to Know:
worship　adore　superstition　impiety
heresy　idolatry　sacrifice　apostasy

Bless the Lord, all works of the Lord, sing praise to im and highly exalt him for ever."

Daniel 3:.

Holy People and Things

Anything blessed or consecrated to God is holy. Make a list of some holy things and people, and explain the use of each in God's service. Some examples are given to help you. <u>Answers will vary</u>

Priest: _____

Church: _____

Holy Water: _____

Advent Wreath: _____

Rosary: _____

Chalice: _____

_____ : _____

_____ : _____

_____ : _____

_____ : _____

TEACHER'S NOTES

CHAPTER SIX
THE LORD'S DAY

Catechism of the Catholic Church References

Third Commandment: 2168–88, 2189–95
Sabbath Day: 2168–73, 2189–90
Sunday: The Lord's Day:
    Day of the Resurrection: the New Creation:
    2174, 2191
    Sunday, Fulfillment of the Sabbath: 2175–76, 2190

Sunday Mass: 2177–79
Sunday Obligation: 2180–83, 2192
Day of Grace and Rest from Work: 2184–88,
2193–95
Worship: 2096–97, 2135–36

Scripture References

God Rested from His Work: Gen 2:2
Resurrection on the First Day of the Week: Mk 16:2

Easter Sunday Remembered in the Mass: Acts 20:7

Summary of Lesson Content

Lesson 1

The Third Commandment sets aside the Lord's Day for worship and rest. It is a time that should be dedicated to God.

God made the world in six days; on the seventh he rested.

Jewish people observe the Lord's Day on the Sabbath (Saturday). Christians observe the Lord's Day on Sunday, the day of the Resurrection of Jesus Christ.

Lesson 2

Sunday is a day of rest. All unnecessary work must be avoided.

Some jobs require people to work on Sunday, but most jobs can and should be set aside.

Catholics are also obliged not to make others work unnecessarily on Sundays.

Lesson 3

The Third Commandment demands an external form of worship. Therefore, we are obliged to worship at Mass on Sundays (and Holy Days of Obligation). Private devotion does not replace the Sunday duty.

Missing Sunday Mass without a just reason is a mortal sin.

Lesson 4

Sunday is also to be a day of joy and rejuvenation. It is a time for spiritual reading, prayer, and private devotions.

Sunday is an opportunity to spend time with family and to do works of charity.

CHAPTER SIX: THE LORD'S DAY
LESSON ONE: HOLY TIME

Aims

The students will learn that the Third Commandment sets aside the Lord's Day for worship and rest. It is a time that should be dedicated to God.

They will learn that God made the world in six days; on the seventh he rested.

They will learn that Jewish people observe the Lord's Day on the Sabbath (Saturday). Christians observe the Lord's Day on Sunday, the day of the Resurrection of Jesus Christ.

Materials

- *Activity Book*, p. 21

- Appendix, p. B-7

Optional:
- "On this day, the first of days," *Adoremus Hymnal*, #610

Begin

Discuss what it means for God to be eternal. He is outside of time. He created the world, the sun, moon, stars—all that is used to measure time. So, if God made time, he is bigger than, or outside of time. This is important to understand because God is not bound to time. God has made time holy.

In the fullness of time, God became man in the Divine Person of Jesus Christ. Jesus' time on earth has changed how we measure time (BC and AD), and given us holy days (Sundays, and feast days) and devotional hours.

Develop

1. Read paragraphs 1–4 with the students.

2. We may be familiar with the phrase "time is money." It is another way of saying that time is precious. Some people think this means that there is never enough time, or that we must fill our time with work. Either way, how we spend our time is a measure of what is important to us. If God is more important to us than anything else, we should want to share our time with him, use our time to learn about him, and serve him through his Church.

3. God made the Sabbath (the seventh day of the week) holy. We see this in Creation, when God rested on the seventh day (Gen 2:2). This is the day the Jewish people honor and set aside for rest and worship of God. You may discuss with the students how the Jewish people honor the Sabbath.

4. As Christians, we honor Sunday, the Lord's Day, because it is the day of the Resurrection (the first day of the week, see

Mk 16:2). We honor Sunday and celebrate the Resurrection of Jesus by participating in the Mass (see Acts 20:7).

5. Discuss how we can give our time to God and honor him throughout the day. Discuss how much time we actually do spend with God, and how we may increase this time.

6. You may discuss various devotions for the different days of the week, or hours of the day.

7. Teach the students about the liturgical calendar. Begin with the season of Advent and work through the Church year, ending on the feast of Christ the King. Review the liturgical colors of the different seasons, and show the parallel between the Church year and the life of Christ (Advent preparing for the birth of Jesus, through Christmas, the life of Jesus in Ordinary Time, his Passion, death, Resurrection, and Ascension in Lent and Easter).

Reinforce

1. Have the students work on *Activity Book* p. 21 (see *Teacher's Manual*, p. 75).

2. Have the students create liturgical calendars. They may add the Holy Days of Obligation and the feasts of their patron saints to this calendar. You may wish to use Appendix p. B-7 for this.

3. Have the students begin working on the Memorization Questions and Words to Know from this chapter (see *Teacher's Manual*, p. 71).

Conclude

1. Teach the students to sing "On this day, the first of days," *Adoremus Hymnal*, #610.

2. End class by leading the students in praying a Morning Offering (see box on p. 69 or p. 396).

CHAPTER 6

The Lord's Day

"Remember the sabbath day, to keep it holy."

Exodus 20:8

Time is precious. Most people would agree on that. But this does not mean the same thing to everyone. Most people think that they never have enough time to do what *they* want to do.

So when God asks for some of our time for himself, people react differently. Some are so happy to give time to God that they are grateful for every opportunity. Others can't be bothered. They are shortsighted, for all men eventually run out of time, while God alone possesses a world without end which he wants to share with us. As we say in the prayer:

Glory be to the Father and to the Son and to the Holy Spirit; as it was in the beginning, is now, and ever shall be, *world without end. Amen.*

The Third Commandment tells us to give one day a week to God. It is written: "Six days you shall labor, and do all your work; but the seventh day is a sabbath to the LORD your God" (Ex 20:9–10). The **Sabbath** is a *holy* day, which, like anything holy, is consecrated or dedicated to God, set aside for him. God himself says that in six days he made the world and on the seventh he rested.

The Jewish people observe the Sabbath on Saturday, the last day of the week and the day on which God rested. But Christians observe Sunday instead, the day Jesus Christ, our Savior, rose from the dead. We give him this day, this entire day, to show that we recognize who he is and to honor and glorify him. Each Sunday is like Easter; we are celebrating the Resurrection of the Lord and his triumph over death.

Making Sunday a Holy Day

We owe God a double debt as Creator and Redeemer, and we make some repayment—at least a small amount—by making Sunday a really holy day.

First of all, we put aside our work, which has had our attention all week long, and we turn our eyes to God, because although work is very good and necessary, it is nevertheless a concern with what God has made—creation—and not with God who made it.

For this reason we are commanded not to do any unnecessary work on Sundays and Holy Days. Our jobs and unnecessary schoolwork should be set aside. There are some jobs which make it necessary for some people to work on Sunday, such as doctors and nurses, policemen, bus drivers, farmers, and others who must work because of economic necessity;

33

34

LITURGICAL CLOCK

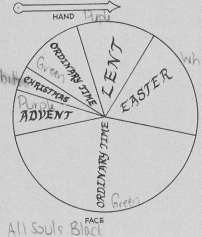

1. Color each season with its liturgical color.

2. Cut out face and hand.

3. Attach hand to face with a brad.

THE LITURGICAL CALENDAR

The liturgical year parallels the life of Christ:
- Advent: preparing for the birth of Christ
- Christmas: the birth of Christ
- Ordinary Time: the preaching and public ministry of Jesus
- Lent: preparing for the Passion and death of Christ
- Triduum (Holy Thursday, Good Friday, and Holy Saturday): the Passion and death of Christ
- Easter: the Resurrection

DEVOTIONS

Some examples of devotions for the different days of the week are to remember the institution of the Eucharist and to pray for priests on Thursdays, to worship the Sacred Heart of Jesus on Fridays, and to honor Mary on Saturdays.

Preview

In the next lesson, the students will learn about making Sunday holy.

Chapter Six: The Lord's Day
Lesson Two: Holy Day

Aims

The students will learn that Sunday is a day of rest. All unnecessary work must be avoided.

They will learn that some jobs require people to work on Sunday, but most jobs can and should be set aside.

They will learn that Catholics are also obliged not to make others work unnecessarily on Sundays.

Materials

- *Activity Book*, p. 22

- Copies of your parish bulletin with Mass times

Optional:
- "On this day, the first of days," *Adoremus Hymnal*, #610

Begin

We know that Sunday is a day dedicated to God. How should we prepare for Sunday? Have the students plan to make the next Sunday a day fully dedicated to God: When does your parish celebrate Mass? When will you go to church? What else will you do? Family breakfast or dinner? Prayer time?

Help the students plan a holy Sunday, and allow them to make choices with parameters: e.g., they must include Sunday Mass, but they may perhaps choose a different Mass time or decide to return after Mass to visit the Blessed Sacrament.

Develop

1. Read paragraphs 5–7.

2. Making Sunday a holy day is a sacrifice of love for God. We must choose not to work and to set aside this day for God. Sometimes this is difficult because we want to save our homework until Sunday, we may not want to get up early for Mass, or perhaps our parents cannot bring us to Mass this week. We must decide how we will make Sunday holy every week.

3. Discuss how the students can get to Mass, even if their parents cannot bring them. Are they old enough to go by themselves? Can they go by bus or taxi? Perhaps they can ask to go with a friend?

4. Why must we refrain from work on Sunday? We must make God our top priority on Sunday (instead of our work). We need a day of rest to refresh us for the rest of the week. What about homework? What about a part-time job? What

kind of work can and should be done on Sunday? Some people must work on Sunday. Discuss the Sunday Vigil Mass option.

5. Discuss how we should prepare for Sunday, especially for Mass. How would we prepare for the coming of a famous person to our house? We would clean, prepare a good meal, and dress well. How should we prepare for Mass, wherein we will meet God? Before we go to the church, we should prepare. We should pray, so that we can participate fully at Mass. We should begin our Eucharistic fast. We should dress appropriately—modestly. We should enter the church reverently, and be prepared to pay close attention at Mass.

6. What ways can the students most fully participate in the Mass? They should listen attentively, participate in the responses, sing along at the appropriate times, and prayerfully follow along.

Reinforce

1. Have the students work on *Activity Book* p. 22 (see *Teacher's Manual*, p. 75).

2. Have the students work on the Memorization Questions and Words to Know from this chapter (see *Teacher's Manual*, p. 71).

3. Have the students write prayers to help them prepare for Mass and to recognize Sunday as the Lord's Day.

Conclude

1. Lead the children in singing "On this day, the first of days," *Adoremus Hymnal*, #610.

2. End class by leading the students in praying the Morning Offering (see the facing page or *Teacher's Manual*, p. 396).

CHAPTER 6

The Lord's Day

"Remember the sabbath day, to keep it holy."

Exodus 20:8

Time is precious. Most people would agree on that. But this does not mean the same thing to everyone. Most people think that they never have enough time to do what *they* want to do.

So when God asks for some of our time for himself, people react differently. Some are so happy to give time to God that they are grateful for every opportunity. Others can't be bothered. They are shortsighted, for all men eventually run out of time, while God alone possesses a world without end which he wants to share with us. As we say in the prayer:

Glory be to the Father and to the Son and to the Holy Spirit; as it was in the beginning, is now, and ever shall be, *world without end. Amen.*

The Third Commandment tells us to give one day a week to God. It is written: "Six days you shall labor, and do all your work; but the seventh day is a sabbath to the LORD your God" (Ex 20:9–10). The **Sabbath** is a *holy* day, which, like anything holy, is consecrated or dedicated to God, set aside for him. God himself says that in six days he made the world and on the seventh he rested.

The Jewish people observe the Sabbath on Saturday, the last day of the week and the day on which God rested. But Christians observe Sunday instead, the day Jesus Christ, our Savior, rose from the dead. We give him this day, this entire day, to show that we recognize who he is and to honor and glorify him. Each Sunday is like Easter; we are celebrating the Resurrection of the Lord and his triumph over death.

Making Sunday a Holy Day

We owe God a double debt as Creator and Redeemer, and we make some repayment—at least a small amount—by making Sunday a really holy day.

First of all, we put aside our work, which has had our attention all week long, and we turn our eyes to God, because although work is very good and necessary, it is nevertheless a concern with what God has made—creation—and not with God who made it.

For this reason we are commanded not to do any unnecessary work on Sundays and Holy Days. Our jobs and unnecessary schoolwork should be set aside. There are some jobs which make it necessary for some people to work on Sunday, such as doctors and nurses, policemen, bus drivers, farmers, and others who must work because of economic necessity;

33

34

but most jobs can and should be put aside on Sunday.

The Third Commandment demands of us some form of external worship, not just internal or private worship. This is because our entire being is subject to God, both body and soul. We need to demonstrate this external worship publicly as a witness to the whole community that God has first place in our lives. God desires that our devotion be visible; he wants to be worshipped in broad daylight for all the world to see. Private devotion cannot take the place of this. If we omit outward worship together as a community, our faith will weaken and we may fall away from God.

The main way we worship God on the Lord's Day is by taking part in the Holy Sacrifice of the Mass because it is the greatest act of worship. For a Catholic, Sunday without Holy Mass is not a holy day. To miss Mass on Sunday is a mortal sin—unless, of course, there is a serious reason, such as sickness.

Mass on Sunday is an obligation we are bound to, but it is also a blessed opportunity for us. Anyone making a sincere effort to live the gospel will go not only to Holy Mass but to Holy Communion, as well, if he is prepared and worthy. Not to go to Sunday Mass is to cut ourselves off from the Sacraments and the grace which flows through them from Jesus to us. For Jesus says: "I am the vine, you are the branches. He who abides in me, and I in him, he it is that bears much fruit, for apart from me you can do nothing" (Jn 15:5).

Missing Mass on Sunday without a good reason is seriously wrong. It is also a great pity to go to Mass regularly but stay away from the Sacraments of Penance and Holy Communion. This would be a sign that Sunday Mass is just a duty, that there is no life in our observance, and that we do not understand much about the life of the Spirit or taste much of the goodness of the Lord.

* * *

There is great disrespect for the Lord's Day in our society, and it is growing all the time. It has always been understood that certain stores and certain services, such as hospitals and the police, have to be available on Sunday. Now we see people buying all sorts of unnecessary things in department stores that hum with business on this day, as if it were a day like any other. It is a sign that many people have lost touch with the spiritual side of life. We would not have such abuses of the Lord's Day if people realized that Sunday is a time to become like Jesus.

Day of Rest

Besides being a day to attend Mass, Sunday is supposed to be a day of joy and refreshment. Wholesome fun is a wonderful ingredient of holiness. We may take time for reading good books, more personal prayer and private devotions, works of charity, sports, hobbies, and real rest.

Let's use our imagination! As Mother Teresa of Calcutta said, let's do "something beautiful for God!" Let's really make Sunday a holy day.

"This is the day which the LORD has made; let us rejoice and be glad in it."

Psalm 118:24

35

MORNING OFFERING

O Jesus, through the Immaculate Heart of Mary, I offer thee all my prayers, works, joys, and sufferings of this day in union with the Holy Sacrifice of the Mass throughout the world.

I offer them for all the intentions of thy Sacred Heart: the salvation of souls, reparation for sin, the reunion of all Christians.

I offer them for the intentions of our Bishops and of all Apostles of Prayer, and in particular for those recommended by our Holy Father this month. *Amen.*

Preview

In the next lesson, the students will learn about our obligation to attend Sunday Mass.

CHAPTER SIX: THE LORD'S DAY
LESSON THREE: MASS DUTY

Aims

The students will learn that the Third Commandment demands an external form of worship. Therefore, we are obliged to worship at Mass on Sundays (and Holy Days of Obligation). Private devotion does not replace the Sunday duty.

They will learn that missing Sunday Mass without a just reason is a mortal sin.

Materials

- *Activity Book*, p. 23

Optional:
- "On this day, the first of days," *Adoremus Hymnal*, #610

Begin

The Third Commandment demands an external form of worship. As Catholics, we are obliged to attend Mass every Sunday and Holy Day of Obligation. Have the students memorize the Holy Days of Obligation.

Develop

1. Have the students read paragraphs 8–11.

2. Discuss the need for external worship. We are composed of a body and a soul, and so we must worship God with our bodies and souls. We need external worship to pray as true humans, as a community of believers. We need the witness of our fellow Catholics and to serve as witnesses to others. We worship publicly (liturgically) as witnesses that God has the first place in our lives.

3. Private devotion does not replace external worship. We have been commanded to attend Mass on Sundays; the requirement does not eliminate the necessity: we need communal worship, because God has redeemed us as a community.

4. Participation in the Holy Sacrifice of the Mass is the greatest act of worship. Why? It is the perfect sacrifice by Christ the high priest, of the perfect victim, Jesus the Lamb of God.

Through the Mass, we share in the sacred events of Jesus' life (remember, with God all things are possible; God is not bound by time). When we are at Mass, we are at the Last Supper with Jesus; we are under his Cross as he dies for our sins, at the empty tomb as he rises from the dead, on the road to Emmaus as he explains the Scriptures to us, and with him in the breaking of the bread. We are perfectly united with Jesus in Communion, as we receive him—Body, Blood, Soul, and Divinity—in the Holy Eucharist.

5. It is a great gift for us to receive Jesus in the Eucharist. Just as we must prepare to receive special guests into our homes, we must prepare to receive Jesus worthily by being free from mortal sin, fasting for one hour, and knowing whom we are about to receive.

6. Reminder: missing our Mass duty through our own fault is a mortal sin.

Reinforce

1. Have the students work on *Activity Book* p. 23 (see *Teacher's Manual*, p. 75).

2. Have the students work on the Memorization Questions and Words to Know from this chapter.

3. Discuss the obligation of attending Sunday Mass. We should fulfill this obligation not only in our actions, but with love in our hearts. If the students are having a hard time actively participating at Mass (or "getting something out of it"), help them identify ways they can participate more in the Mass. Understanding the Mass will help the students to maintain interest and increase their appreciation of this central event.

4. You may review all the Mass responses. Often students confuse words or do not understand what they are saying.

Conclude

1. Lead the children in singing "On this day, the first of days," *Adoremus Hymnal*, #610.

2. End class by leading the students in praying the Morning Offering (see *Teacher's Manual*, p. 69 or p. 396).

but most jobs can and should be put aside on Sunday.

The Third Commandment demands of us some form of external worship, not just internal or private worship. This is because our entire being is subject to God, both body and soul. We need to demonstrate this external worship publicly as a witness to the whole community that God has first place in our lives. God desires that our devotion be visible; he wants to be worshipped in broad daylight for all the world to see. Private devotion cannot take the place of this. If we omit outward worship together as a community, our faith will weaken and we may fall away from God.

The main way we worship God on the Lord's Day is by taking part in the Holy Sacrifice of the Mass because it is the greatest act of worship. For a Catholic, Sunday without Holy Mass is not a holy day. To miss Mass on Sunday is a mortal sin—unless, of course, there is a serious reason, such as sickness.

Mass on Sunday is an obligation we are bound to, but it is also a blessed opportunity for us. Anyone making a sincere effort to live the gospel will go not only to Holy Mass but to Holy Communion, as well, if he is prepared and worthy. Not to go to Sunday Mass is to cut ourselves off from the Sacraments and the grace which flows through them from Jesus to us. For Jesus says: "I am the vine, you are the branches. He who abides in me, and I in him, he it is that bears much fruit, for apart from me you can do nothing" (Jn 15:5).

Missing Mass on Sunday without a good reason is seriously wrong. It is also a great pity to go to Mass regularly but stay away from the Sacraments of Penance and Holy Communion. This would be a sign that Sunday Mass is just a duty, that there is no life in our observance, and that we do not understand much about the life of the Spirit or taste much of the goodness of the Lord.

* * *

There is great disrespect for the Lord's Day in our society, and it is growing all the time. It has always been understood that certain stores and certain services, such as hospitals and the police, have to be available on Sunday. Now we see people buying all sorts of unnecessary things in department stores that hum with business on this day, as if it were a day like any other. It is a sign that many people have lost touch with the spiritual side of life. We would not have such abuses of the Lord's Day if people realized that Sunday is a time to become like Jesus.

Day of Rest

Besides being a day to attend Mass, Sunday is supposed to be a day of joy and refreshment. Wholesome fun is a wonderful ingredient of holiness. We may take time for reading good books, more personal prayer and private devotions, works of charity, sports, hobbies, and real rest.

Let's use our imagination! As Mother Teresa of Calcutta said, let's do "something beautiful for God!" Let's really make Sunday a holy day.

"This is the day which the LORD has made; let us rejoice and be glad in it."

Psalm 118:24

35

Holy Days of Obligation

In addition to the obligation of Sunday Mass, there are **Holy Days of Obligation**, days which have the same obligation as Sundays.

The universal Church has ten Holy Days of Obligation. In certain countries attendance at Mass is not obligatory on all these Holy Days.

In the United States some of these are celebrated on Sunday and only six are considered Holy Days of Obligation. These six are the Solemnity of Mary Mother of God, Ascension, the Assumption of Mary, All Saints' Day, the Immaculate Conception of Mary, and Christmas.

- January 1, the Solemnity of Mary, Mother of God
- The Solemnity of the Ascension, forty days after Easter
- August 15, the Solemnity of the Assumption of the Blessed Virgin Mary
- November 1, the Solemnity of All Saints
- December 8, the Solemnity of the Immaculate Conception
- December 25, the Solemnity of the Nativity of Our Lord Jesus Christ

Words to Know:
Sabbath Holy Days of Obligation

36

Q. 24 *What does the Third Commandment require us to do?*
The Third Commandment requires us to honor God on Sundays and Holy Days by acts of public worship. We do this most perfectly by taking part in Holy Mass (CCC 2180).

Q. 25 *Why must we do acts of external worship?*
It is not sufficient to adore God internally in the heart. We must also give him external worship because we are subject to God in our entire being—body and soul. We are also bound to give good examples. If we were to omit external worship we might lose our religious spirit.

Q. 26 *Are we required to take part in Mass?*
We are required to take part in Mass on Sunday and on the Holy Days of Obligation (CCC 2180).

Q. 27 *What does the Third Commandment forbid?*
The Third Commandment forbids unnecessary work or other activity that hinders worship of God and proper relaxation of the mind and body on Sunday and other Holy Days (CCC 2185).

Q. 28 *Which days are the Holy Days of Obligation?*
In the United States, the Holy Days of Obligation include the Solemnity of Mary, Mother of God, the Ascension, the Assumption of Mary, All Saints Day, the Immaculate Conception of Mary, and Christmas (CCC 2042, 2177).

Q. 29 *Why do Christians worship on Sunday?*
Christians worship on Sunday, the first day of the week, because Jesus rose from the dead on Easter Sunday (CCC 2169, 2174).

37

HOLY DAYS OF OBLIGATION

These are special feast days on which the Church requires us to go to Mass. We celebrate six Holy Days of Obligation in the United States:

- The Immaculate Conception—December 8
- Christmas—December 25
- Mary, Mother of God—January 1
- The Ascension of Jesus—Forty days after Easter*
- The Assumption of Mary—August 15
- The Solemnity of All Saints—November 1

* The bishops' conference may transfer this feast to the following Sunday.

Preview

In the next lesson, the students will learn about Sunday as a day of rest.

CHAPTER SIX: THE LORD'S DAY
LESSON FOUR: DAY OF REST

Aims

The students will learn that Sunday is to be a day of joy and rejuvenation. It is a time for spiritual reading, prayer, and private devotions.

They will learn that Sunday is an opportunity to spend time with family and to do works of charity.

Materials

- *Activity Book*, p. 24

- Missals for the class

- Poster board, markers, video camera, audio recorder, or other creative resources you have available

Optional:
- "On this day, the first of days," *Adoremus Hymnal*, #610

Begin

Review the Mass responses with the students and be sure they also know the proper gestures for the Mass. It may be helpful for the students to follow along in missals.

Develop

1. Finish reading the text of this chapter with the students.

2. Discuss the need for a day of rest. It is good that we rest; God himself rested on the seventh day. Our bodies and minds need sufficient rest, so that we can serve God well the other six days of the week.

3. You may review when stores became open for business on Sundays. Why did this happen? What were the effects? In what other way(s) is Sunday no longer honored as the Lord's Day in our society?

4. You may have a discussion on Sunday shopping:
- Why is it wrong to shop on Sunday?
- Is it wrong to shop for all things on Sunday? What about food? Toys? Clothes?
- By unnecessarily shopping on Sundays, do we make other people have to work? Is this fair? Will they be able to attend Mass if they must work?

5. Have the students work on an advertising campaign, reminding people to keep Sunday holy. They may use various media and present their campaigns to the class. In their campaigns, the students should suggest ways to make Sunday holy, and reasons why we should. What are the benefits?

6. You may discuss how to keep Holy Days of Obligation holy. How can we fulfill our duty to attend Mass on these days? You may discuss whether any of these days are moved to Sundays, and why. Can you go to Mass at school? Can your parents attend Mass on their lunch hour? At what time does your parish have Mass on Holy Days?

7. Discuss ways that the students can enjoy Sunday with their families.

Reinforce

1. Have the students work on *Activity Book* p. 24 (see *Teacher's Manual*, p. 75).

2. Have the students work the Memorization Questions, Words to Know, and Holy Days of Obligation.

3. Have the students write commitment cards to attend Mass and make every Sunday holy.

Conclude

1. Lead the children in singing "On this day, the first of days," *Adoremus Hymnal*, #610.

2. End class by leading the students in praying the Morning Offering (see *Teacher's Manual*, p. 69 or p. 396).

but most jobs can and should be put aside on Sunday.

The Third Commandment demands of us some form of external worship, not just internal or private worship. This is because our entire being is subject to God, both body and soul. We need to demonstrate this external worship publicly as a witness to the whole community that God has first place in our lives. God desires that our devotion be visible; he wants to be worshipped in broad daylight for all the world to see. Private devotion cannot take the place of this. If we omit outward worship together as a community, our faith will weaken and we may fall away from God.

The main way we worship God on the Lord's Day is by taking part in the Holy Sacrifice of the Mass because it is the greatest act of worship. For a Catholic, Sunday without Holy Mass is not a holy day. To miss Mass on Sunday is a mortal sin—unless, of course, there is a serious reason, such as sickness.

Mass on Sunday is an obligation we are bound to, but it is also a blessed opportunity for us. Anyone making a sincere effort to live the gospel will go not only to Holy Mass but to Holy Communion, as well, if he is prepared and worthy. Not to go to Sunday Mass is to cut ourselves off from the Sacraments and the grace which flows through them from Jesus to us. For Jesus says: "I am the vine, you are the branches. He who abides in me, and I in him, he it is that bears much fruit, for apart from me you can do nothing" (Jn 15:5).

Missing Mass on Sunday without a good reason is seriously wrong. It is also a great pity to go to Mass regularly but stay away from the Sacraments of Penance and Holy Communion. This would be a sign that Sunday Mass is just a duty, that there is no life in our observance, and that we do not understand much about the life of the Spirit or taste much of the goodness of the Lord.

* * *

There is great disrespect for the Lord's Day in our society, and it is growing all the time. It has always been understood that certain stores and certain services, such as hospitals and the police, have to be available on Sunday. Now we see people buying all sorts of unnecessary things in department stores that hum with business on this day, as if it were a day like any other. It is a sign that many people have lost touch with the spiritual side of life. We would not have such abuses of the Lord's Day if people realized that Sunday is a time to become like Jesus.

Day of Rest

Besides being a day to attend Mass, Sunday is supposed to be a day of joy and refreshment. Wholesome fun is a wonderful ingredient of holiness. We may take time for reading good books, more personal prayer and private devotions, works of charity, sports, hobbies, and real rest.

Let's use our imagination! As Mother Teresa of Calcutta said, let's do "something beautiful for God!" Let's really make Sunday a holy day.

"This is the day which the LORD has made; let us rejoice and be glad in it."

Psalm 118:24

35

Holy Days of Obligation

In addition to the obligation of Sunday Mass, there are **Holy Days of Obligation**, days which have the same obligation as Sundays.

The universal Church has ten Holy Days of Obligation. In certain countries attendance at Mass is not obligatory on all these Holy Days.

In the United States some of these are celebrated on Sunday and only six are considered Holy Days of Obligation. These six are the Solemnity of Mary Mother of God, Ascension, the Assumption of Mary, All Saints' Day, the Immaculate Conception of Mary, and Christmas.

- January 1, the Solemnity of Mary, Mother of God
- The Solemnity of the Ascension, forty days after Easter
- August 15, the Solemnity of the Assumption of the Blessed Virgin Mary
- November 1, the Solemnity of All Saints
- December 8, the Solemnity of the Immaculate Conception
- December 25, the Solemnity of the Nativity of Our Lord Jesus Christ

Words to Know:
Sabbath   Holy Days of Obligation

36

Q. 24   *What does the Third Commandment require us to do?*
The Third Commandment requires us to honor God on Sundays and Holy Days by acts of public worship. We do this most perfectly by taking part in Holy Mass (CCC 2180).

Q. 25   *Why must we do acts of external worship?*
It is not sufficient to adore God internally in the heart. We must also give him external worship because we are subject to God in our entire being—body and soul. We are also bound to give good examples. If we were to omit external worship we might lose our religious spirit.

Q. 26   *Are we required to take part in Mass?*
We are required to take part in Mass on Sunday and on the Holy Days of Obligation (CCC 2180).

Q. 27   *What does the Third Commandment forbid?*
The Third Commandment forbids unnecessary work or other activity that hinders worship of God and proper relaxation of the mind and body on Sunday and other Holy Days (CCC 2185).

Q. 28   *Which days are the Holy Days of Obligation?*
In the United States, the Holy Days of Obligation include the Solemnity of Mary, Mother of God, the Ascension, the Assumption of Mary, All Saints Day, the Immaculate Conception of Mary, and Christmas (CCC 2042, 2177).

Q. 29   *Why do Christians worship on Sunday?*
Christians worship on Sunday, the first day of the week, because Jesus rose from the dead on Easter Sunday (CCC 2169, 2174).

37

DIES DOMINI: POPE JOHN PAUL II ON THE LORD'S DAY

Pope John Paul II made a point of teaching specifically on the Christian duty to make Sunday the Lord's Day. In his apostolic letter *Dies Domini* (*The Day of the Lord*), issued on Pentecost 1998, the Holy Father clearly defines the history of the Sunday obligation as a tradition stemming from the earliest days of the Church (both the Resurrection and Pentecost occurred on Sundays); further, he reiterates the necessity for assembly and worship in the Mass as well as abstaining from work in order to keep holy the Lord's Day. Most importantly, he explains that Sunday is joyfully the most important day of the week for Catholics. He says, "It is crucially important that all the faithful should be convinced that they cannot live their faith or share fully of the Christian community unless they take part regularly (every Sunday) in the Eucharistic assembly."

Preview

In the next lesson, the students' understanding of the material covered in this chapter will be reviewed and assessed.

CHAPTER SIX: THE LORD'S DAY
REVIEW AND ASSESSMENT

Aims

The students' understanding of the material covered in this chapter will be reviewed and assessed.

Materials

- Quiz 6, Appendix, p. A-8

Optional:
- "On this day, the first of days," *Adoremus Hymnal*, #610

Review and Enrichment

1. The students should know what the Third Commandment requires of us, and what it forbids.

2. The students should understand why Sunday is the Lord's Day.

3. The students should understand why we need both external worship and communal worship.

4. The students should understand the great events that happen at Mass. With God all things are possible, so, through the Mass, we share in the events of Jesus' life—especially the Last Supper, Crucifixion, Resurrection, and breaking of the bread. We must understand the reality of this to know why it is so grave a sin not to attend Mass on Sunday.

5. The students should know the steps to a worthy reception of Holy Communion. They are united with Jesus—Body, Blood, Soul, and Divinity—in the Holy Eucharist.

6. The students should know that Sunday is to be a day of rest and refreshment.

Name: _____

The Lord's Day   Quiz 6

Part I: Answer in complete sentences.

1. Which commandment requires us to give one day a week to God?
   The Third Commandment requires us to give one day a week to God.

2. Why do the Jewish people observe the Sabbath on Saturday?
   The Jewish people observe the Sabbath on Saturday because it is the day on which God rested.

3. Why do Christians celebrate the Lord's Day on Sunday?
   Christians celebrate the Lord's Day on Sunday because Jesus rose from the dead on a Sunday.

4. What is the main way that we worship God on the Lord's Day.
   The main way we worship God on the Lord's Day is by taking part in the Holy Sacrifice of the Mass.

5. Since Sunday is supposed to be a day of joy and refreshment, what sorts of things can we do on Sundays?
   Answers will vary: On Sundays we can rest, read good books, spend time with family, spend more time in personal prayer and private devotions, do works of charity, and enjoy sports, hobbies, or outdoor recreation.

Part II: Fill in the blanks.

1. The Sabbath (or Lord's Day) is a Holy Day, which is consecrated or dedicated to God.

2. We are commanded not to do any unnecessary work on Sundays and Holy Days.

3. To miss Mass on Sunday is a mortal sin unless there is a serious reason.

Part III: Match the date with the corresponding Holy Day of Obligation.

d All Saints	a. January 1
f Christmas	b. forty days after Easter
c Assumption	c. August 15
e Immaculate Conception	d. November 1
b Ascension	e. December 8
a Mary, Mother of God	f. December 25

A-8   *Faith and Life Series • Grade 6 • Appendix A*

Assess

1. Distribute the quizzes and read through them with the students to be sure they understand the questions.

2. Administer the quiz. As they hand in their work, you may orally quiz the students on the Memorization Questions from this chapter.

3. After all the quizzes have been handed in, you may wish to review the correct answers with the class.

Conclude

1. Lead the children in singing "On this day, the first of days," *Adoremus Hymnal*, #610.

2. End class by leading the students in praying the Morning Offering (see *Teacher's Manual*, p. 69 or p. 396).

CHAPTER SIX: THE LORD'S DAY
ACTIVITY BOOK ANSWER KEYS

Name:_____

Holy Time

Fill in this chart, blocking in the time you spend with God. Do you spend time with him every day? Do you make Sunday holy?

	SUN	MON	TUES	WED	THURS	FRI	SAT
7:00							
8:00							
9:00							
10:00							
11:00							
12:00							
1:00							
2:00							
3:00							
4:00							
5:00							
6:00							
7:00							
8:00							
9:00							
10:00							
11:00							

Name:_____

Making Sunday Holy

Answer the following questions in complete sentences.

1. What must you do on Sunday?
   On Sunday, we must go to Mass and rest from unnecessary work.

2. Why do we honor the Lord's Day on Sunday instead of Saturday?
   That is the day Jesus rose from the dead.

3. Should we do unnecessary work on Sunday?
   No.

4. Why must we have external worship?
   We must have external worship because our entire being, body and soul, is subject to God.

5. Why do we worship in a community?
   We worship in a community because we must witness publicly that God has first place in our lives.

6. What things can you do, both on your own and with your family and friends, to make Sunday holy?
   Answers will vary.

Name:_____

The Lord's Day

Answer the following questions in complete sentences.

1. What is the principal tribute we offer to God on the Lord's Day?
   The principal tribute we offer to God on the Lord's Day is to go to Mass.

2. If you miss Mass on Sunday without a serious reason, is it a mortal sin?
   Yes.

3. When should you not receive Holy Communion?
   One should not receive Holy Communion if he is not properly prepared.

4. With what attitude should we go to Mass?
   Answers will vary.

Name:_____

Holy Days of Obligation

Answer the following questions in complete sentences.

1. What are Holy Days of Obligation?
   A Holy Day of Obligation is a certain day, besides Sundays, when Catholics are required to take part in Holy Mass.

2. If you miss Mass on a Holy Day of Obligation without a serious reason, is it a mortal sin?
   Yes.

3. List the names and dates of the Holy Days on which Catholics in the United States are obliged to attend Mass.

NAME	DATE
Solemnity of Mary, Mother of God	January 1
Solemnity of the Ascension	Forty days after Easter
Solemnity of the Assumption of the Blessed Virgin Mary	August 15
Solemnity of All Saints	November 1
Solemnity of the Immaculate Conception	December 8
Solemnity of the Nativity of Our Lord Jesus Christ	December 25

TEACHER'S NOTES

TEACHER'S NOTES

CHAPTER SEVEN
THE CROSS AND TRUE RICHES

Catechism of the Catholic Church References

Advent: 524, 1095
Christ's Whole Life as a Self-Offering: 606–18, 621–23
Cross: 312, 599, 620, 622
Fasting as Church Precept: 2043
Forms of Penance in Christian Life: 1434–39
Jesus as Our Teacher and Model of Holiness: 468–69, 516, 519–21, 561

Lent: 538–40, 1095, 1438
Liturgical Seasons: 1163–65
Liturgical Year: 1168–71, 1194
Penance: 1430, 1460
Sacrifice: 2099–2100
Self-Control: 2339–42

Scripture References

Example of Crucified Christ: Phil 2:1–16

Running the Race of Faith: 1 Cor 9:24–27

Summary of Lesson Content

Lesson 1

Self-denial means sacrificing our own will, or something we desire, for the sake of the Kingdom of God.

Lesson 3

Fasting and abstinence are forms of penance. Penance is a form of sacrifice and purification to help us grow closer to Christ. Penance strengthens us to do his will.

Fasting is giving up food. The Church defines fasting as eating one regular meal and two small meals that do not exceed the one regular meal in any given day.

Abstinence is refraining from eating meat.

Lesson 2

The doctrine of the Cross calls us to die to our sinful ways, so that we may live in Christ.

In Baptism, Original Sin is washed away and the new life of grace is poured into the soul.

Bearing the crosses (trials and difficulties) that come our way is a kind of self-denial and is pleasing to God.

Lesson 4

Advent and Lent are the penitential seasons of the liturgical year.

Penance can make up for past sins and help prevent future sins.

The primary forms of penance include fasting, abstinence, almsgiving, and works of charity.

Chapter Seven: The Cross and True Riches

Lesson One: Self-Denial

Aims

The students will learn that self-denial means sacrificing our will, or something we desire, for the sake of the Kingdom of God.

Materials

- *Activity Book*, p. 25

- Crucifix

Optional:
- "Lift high the cross," *Adoremus Hymnal*, #606

Begin

Hold up a crucifix and read Philippians 2:1–16. Explain that Jesus' death on the Cross is the greatest act of love. Love is not just an emotion, but a gift of self. Jesus gave of himself completely, even unto death. The Cross, for Catholics, is a sign of our salvation, of God's great love for us, and of our hope.

Through our trials and sufferings, we share in the promise of the Resurrection. Pass the crucifix around to the students and allow each of them to silently look at the wounds of Christ and reverence the Cross.

Develop

1. Read paragraphs 1–3.

2. Have the students name some of their trials, or crosses. These will vary from student to student (e.g., math, my brother, parents' divorce, etc.).

3. Tell the story of a man who prayed to Jesus telling him that his cross was too heavy. Jesus heard his prayer and agreed to exchange his cross for another. The man entered a room, and Jesus took his cross away. This man started looking at all the other crosses. Some were huge, made of concrete, some were made of lead, others were covered with thorns, and some were too awful even to view. Then, in the corner, this man saw a small cross; it looked light in comparison with the others, and about his size. He went over, and could pick it up, and saw that it was a good fit. He told Jesus that this was the cross that he wanted. It was, of course, the cross he had originally carried.

4. Self-denial is very important because often we become focused only on ourselves. We become proud and fail to see the needs and sufferings of others. We should sacrifice in true love and concern for others (as Jesus did). To have true joy, we should do things in this order: Jesus, others, me.

5. The students may make collages in the shape of a cross, reflecting the various "crosses" in their daily lives, or in our society.

6. Teach the students the Stations of the Cross (see *Teacher's Manual*, p. 81 or p. 396). This is a means of uniting ourselves with Jesus' suffering, and meditating upon his greatest act of love for us. Pray the Stations with the students. You may wish to have the class make a set of Stations for your classroom. (These can be used during Lent.)

Reinforce

1. Have the students work on *Activity Book* p. 25 (see *Teacher's Manual*, p. 87).

2. Have the students make a set of Stations of the Cross for the classroom or to take home.

3. Have the students share ways of making sacrifices as acts of penance and love.

4. Have the students work on the Memorization Questions and Words to Know from this chapter (see *Teacher's Manual*, p. 83).

Conclude

1. Teach the students to sing "Lift high the cross," *Adoremus Hymnal*, #606.

2. End class by leading the students in praying the Prayer before a Crucifix (on the facing page).

The Cross and True Riches

"Then Jesus told his disciples, 'If any man would come after me, let him deny himself and take up his cross and follow me.'"

Matthew 16:24

The path through life to heaven is often compared to climbing a mountain, and the mountain-top is heaven, God's holy mountain. In Psalm 43, the pilgrim on life's journey cries out to God:

Oh, send out your light and your truth;
let them lead me,
let them bring me to your holy hill,
and to your dwelling! (Ps 43:3)

Christ our Savior offers us a way that will lead to peace, joy, and our final goal of total happiness with God. The way that leads to this wonderful state of perfection, or holiness, is based on Jesus' words: "If any man would come after me, let him deny himself and take up his cross daily and follow me" (Lk 9:23).

Self-denial means doing something we would rather not do or refusing some pleasure we would like for the sake of some greater good, for example, taking time to help your brother with his fractions or giving up dessert sometimes. Another example is giving your schoolwork your best effort, although it may not be easy and you may have to give up much of your free time to do it. Your schoolwork (or perhaps a particular subject) may take on the nature of a cross, especially if it is difficult.

Now we have come to a great mystery—the doctrine of the Cross. It is the principal sign of Christianity. As a result of Original Sin, it is necessary for us to put to death in ourselves a certain way of living which Saint Paul calls "the old man" and to put on "the new man," Jesus.

The old man is Adam, who misused the gifts of God and so brought sin and disorder into the world. As you know, this sin is passed on to all of us as Adam's children. We are born in the state of Original Sin. Through Baptism, Original Sin is washed away and we are given the life of grace. However, Original Sin has left in us many wounds and disorders. These wounds can only be healed by God's grace through a lifetime of right living, prayer, and self-denial.

This is not always easy. When Jesus asks us to love our enemy and to do good to those who hurt us, he is not asking us to do something that comes naturally or easily. But, by the power of God, it is not impossible. For with God "all things are possible" (Mt 19:26).

Our daily cross is all the things which, naturally speaking, we dislike. Our cross may be a penance we choose for ourselves or suffering that God allows in our life—perhaps an enemy at school or some sickness. Such sufferings are permitted for our good or the good of others,

"God loves a cheerful giver."
2 Corinthians 9:7

though we may not be able to see it at the time.

Bearing the crosses (that is, trials and difficulties) which we do not choose but which come to us anyhow in the course of life is a most perfect kind of self-denial, more pleasing to God than the acts of self-denial we choose for ourselves. For in all things it is most perfect to accept the will of God, even when we do not like it very much. Jesus' entire life was one of obedience to the will of the Father, no matter how hard it was or what it required of him, even his death. "Father, if you are willing, remove this chalice from me; nevertheless not my will, but yours, be done" (Lk 22:42).

And why are we willing to set out on such a way of life? In following the example of Jesus we are showing our love for God by willingly and, yes, even cheerfully accepting whatever he permits.

Fast and Abstinence

We are encouraged to choose some **penance** for ourselves. To help us, the Church requires **fasting** and **abstinence** from certain foods on penitential days. To abstain, in this case, means not to eat meat. If we are fourteen years old or more, we must abstain from meat on Ash Wednesday and Good Friday.

In the United States, the bishops have declared abstinence from meat on all Fridays of Lent. In other seasons, Friday remains a day of penance on which we are supposed to practice some kind of self-denial, and the Church advises us to make Friday a day of abstinence all year round.

Fasting, in general, means not eating at all. When the Church requires us to fast, however, it means that only one full meal a day should be eaten. In addition, two smaller meals may be taken, but those taken together should not equal another full meal. In the Church, there are two days of required fasting: Ash Wednesday and Good Friday. This applies to anyone eighteen to sixty years old.

Penitential Seasons

Advent and **Lent** are special seasons in the Church year in which we are reminded to renew our spirit. They are called penitential seasons.

Advent begins four Sundays before Christmas and is a season of special preparation for celebrating the birth of Christ. The Church suggests that we do some form of penance as part of this preparation.

The season of Lent begins six and a half weeks before Easter and is a season of preparation for the Passion, death, and Resurrection

"And when you fast, do not look dismal, like the hypocrites, for they disfigure their faces that their fasting may be seen by men. Truly, I say to you, they have received their reward. But when you fast, anoint your head and wash your face, that your fasting may not be seen by men but by your Father who is in secret; and your Father who sees in secret will reward you."

(Matthew 6:16–18)

PRAYER BEFORE A CRUCIFIX

Behold, O kind and most sweet Jesus,
I cast myself upon my knees in your sight,
and with the most fervent desire of my soul
I pray and beseech you to impress upon my heart
lively sentiments of faith, hope, and charity,
with true contrition for my sins, and a firm purpose of amendment,
while with deep affection and grief of soul
I ponder within myself and mentally contemplate your five wounds,
having before my eyes that which David, your prophet, spoke of you, my Jesus:
"They have pierced my hands and my feet; they have numbered all my bones."

Preview

In the next lesson, the students will learn more about their daily crosses.

CHAPTER SEVEN: THE CROSS AND TRUE RICHES
LESSON TWO: DAILY CROSSES

Aims

The students will learn that the doctrine of the Cross calls us to die to our sinful ways, so that we may live in Christ.

They will learn that, in Baptism, Original Sin is washed away and the new life of grace is poured into the soul.

They will learn that bearing the crosses (trials and difficulties) which come our way is a kind of self-denial and is pleasing to God.

Materials

• *Activity Book*, p. 26

Optional:
• "Lift high the cross," *Adoremus Hymnal*, #606

Begin

Review the doctrine of Original Sin. Because of the sin of Adam and Eve, we are all born with Original Sin. Its effects are absence of grace, suffering, death, and concupiscence (tendency to sin). In Baptism, Original Sin is washed away and we are filled with grace, but the wounds of this sin remain—we still suffer and die, and we still have a tendency to sin. Through accepting our sufferings and offering them to God, and uniting our sufferings with those of Christ, we can overcome our tendency to sin with the help of God and his grace.

Develop

1. Read paragraphs 4–9.

2. God gives us free will. Often, the sufferings we have, we have brought upon ourselves by our choices. For example, is Sunday night and we want to enjoy ourselves, but we still have homework to do because, by our own choice, we did not do it earlier. We can do penance by working diligently and making a good choice in the beginning (such as doing our homework as soon as we get home on Friday night). By making good choices, we can sometimes avoid suffering (e.g., not fighting with an enemy at school). By making good choices and sacrificing our immediate pleasures for a greater good, we bear our crosses well.

3. Some sufferings we do not choose; they are given to us (e.g., an illness). Some people often think that such suffering is pure evil or unnecessary. Seeing someone we love suffer is often harder than suffering ourselves. However, from such a suffering, a greater good can come about if we unite ourselves with Jesus and his sufferings. In suffering with Christ, we share in his great love, and we enter deeply into the mystery of redemption. We can also use this opportunity to suffer on behalf of another (i.e., offer our cross for another person's good). For example, I could offer my suffering to God as a penance or act of love for the conversion of a sinner or for a prayer request.

4. Jesus himself suffered greatly. He accepted the Father's will in his life, and was obedient unto death on the Cross. So, too, we must accept God's will. Accepting God's will in suffering is of greater value than our own self-imposed sufferings. However, in choosing our own, we are made ready and able to accept God's will because we are used to denying ourselves. Have the students list some self-imposed sufferings and some which are given to us by God's will.

Reinforce

1. Have the students work on *Activity Book* p. 26 (see *Teacher's Manual*, p. 87).

2. Have the students work on the Memorization Questions and Words to Know from this chapter (see *Teacher's Manual*, p. 83).

3. Have the students pray the Stations of the Cross or write their own prayers for each of the stations (see facing page).

Conclude

1. Lead the children in singing "Lift high the cross," *Adoremus Hymnal*, #606.

2. End class by leading the students in praying the Prayer before a Crucifix (see *Teacher's Manual*, p. 79).

CHAPTER 7

The Cross and True Riches

"Then Jesus told his disciples, 'If any man would come after me, let him deny himself and take up his cross and follow me.'"

Matthew 16:24

The path through life to heaven is often compared to climbing a mountain, and the mountain-top is heaven, God's holy mountain. In Psalm 43, the pilgrim on life's journey cries out to God:

Oh, send out your light and your truth;
let them lead me,
let them bring me to your holy hill,
and to your dwelling! (Ps 43:3)

Christ our Savior offers us a way that will lead to peace, joy, and our final goal of total happiness with God. The way that leads to this wonderful state of perfection, or holiness, is based on Jesus' words: "If any man would come after me, let him deny himself and take up his cross daily and follow me" (Lk 9:23).

Self-denial means doing something we would rather not do or refusing some pleasure we would like for the sake of some greater good, for example, taking time to help your brother with his fractions or giving up dessert sometimes. Another example is giving your schoolwork your best effort, although it may not be easy and you may have to give up much of your free time to do it. Your schoolwork (or perhaps a particular subject) may take on the nature of a cross, especially if it is difficult.

Now we have come to a great mystery—the doctrine of the Cross. It is the principal sign of

Christianity. As a result of Original Sin, it is necessary for us to put to death in ourselves a certain way of living which Saint Paul calls "the old man" and to put on "the new man," Jesus.

The old man is Adam, who misused the gifts of God and so brought sin and disorder into the world. As you know, this sin is passed on to all of us as Adam's children. We are born in the state of Original Sin. Through Baptism, Original Sin is washed away and we are given the life of grace. However, Original Sin has left in us many wounds and disorders. These wounds can only be healed by God's grace through a lifetime of right living, prayer, and self-denial.

This is not always easy. When Jesus asks us to love our enemy and to do good to those who hurt us, he is not asking us to do something that comes naturally or easily. But, by the power of God, it is not impossible. For with God "all things are possible" (Mt 19:26).

Our daily cross is all the things which, naturally speaking, we dislike. Our cross may be a penance we choose for ourselves or suffering that God allows in our life—perhaps an enemy at school or some sickness. Such sufferings are permitted for our good or the good of others,

"God loves a cheerful giver."
2 Corinthians 9:7

39

---

though we may not be able to see it at the time.

Bearing the crosses (that is, trials and difficulties) which we do not choose but which come to us anyhow in the course of life is a most perfect kind of self-denial, more pleasing to God than the acts of self-denial we choose for ourselves. For in all things it is most perfect to accept the will of God, even when we do not like it very much. Jesus' entire life was one of obedience to the will of the Father, no matter how hard it was or what it required of him, even his death. "Father, if you are willing, remove this chalice from me; nevertheless not my will, but yours, be done" (Lk 22:42).

And why are we willing to set out on such a way of life? In following the example of Jesus we are showing our love for God by willingly and, yes, even cheerfully accepting whatever he permits.

Fast and Abstinence

We are encouraged to choose some **penance** for ourselves. To help us, the Church requires **fasting** and **abstinence** from certain foods on penitential days. To abstain, in this case, means not to eat meat. If we are fourteen years old or more, we must abstain from meat on Ash Wednesday and Good Friday.

In the United States, the bishops have declared abstinence from meat on all Fridays of Lent. In other seasons, Friday remains a day of penance on which we are supposed to practice some kind of self-denial, and the Church advises us to make Friday a day of abstinence all year round.

Fasting, in general, means not eating at all. When the Church requires us to fast, however, it means that only one full meal a day should be eaten. In addition, two smaller meals may be taken, but those taken together should not equal another full meal. In the Church, there are two days of required fasting: Ash Wednesday and Good Friday. This applies to anyone eighteen to sixty years old.

Penitential Seasons

Advent and **Lent** are special seasons in the Church year in which we are reminded to renew our spirit. They are called penitential seasons.

Advent begins four Sundays before Christmas and is a season of special preparation for celebrating the birth of Christ. The Church suggests that we do some form of penance as part of this preparation.

The season of Lent begins six and a half weeks before Easter and is a season of preparation for the Passion, death, and Resurrection

"And when you fast, do not look dismal, like the hypocrites, for they disfigure their faces that their fasting may be seen by men. Truly, I say to you, they have received their reward. But when you fast, anoint your head and wash your face, that your fasting may not be seen by men but by your Father who is in secret; and your Father who sees in secret will reward you."

(Matthew 6:16–18)

40

---

of the Lord. Just as Jesus fasted for forty days, we too take on some penance during Lent to make up for our sins and to prepare our hearts to celebrate the great Easter feast.

Saint Paul compares the spiritual life to a race and the Christian to an athlete. Like an athlete, the Christian is asked to practice certain spiritual exercises. If an athlete will give up a great deal just to train for a race, how much more should we Christians be ready to practice self-denial for the sake of the Kingdom of God!

Besides, what the athlete gives up in training is not always so great, and his self-discipline is often very satisfying, invigorating, and enjoyable. His muscle tone, increased skill, and sense of well-being make it all worthwhile.

It is the same way with the Kingdom of God. The crosses we bear can include the many little things which make up our daily

lives, such as not always having our own way, forgiving an unkind word, turning from fun to duties at the proper time, not overeating, and the like. We are not expected to make life one big penance with no pleasures. After all, it is God who created the things in which we find pleasure. But, like a good athlete, we must keep an eye on the coach—Jesus—and not forget ourselves and break training.

By God's grace, penance can make up for past sin and help prevent future sin. It helps eliminate those things that take us away from God or are obstacles to our final goal—union with God in his Kingdom.

Words to Know:

self-denial penance fasting
abstinence Advent Lent

Rules of Fast and Abstinence in the United States

— The days and times of penance for the universal Church are each Friday of the whole year and the whole season of Lent.
— Abstinence and fasting are to be observed on Ash Wednesday and Good Friday. Abstinence is to be observed on all the Fridays during Lent.
— The law of abstinence binds those who have completed their fourteenth year. The law of fasting binds those eighteen years old to sixty years old.

Dearest Lord, teach me to be generous;
teach me to serve you as you deserve to be served—
to give and not to count the cost,
to fight and not to heed the wounds,
to toil and not to seek for rest,
to labor and not to ask any reward
except that of knowing that I do your holy will.
—Saint Ignatius Loyola

41

THE STATIONS OF THE CROSS

1. Jesus is condemned to death.
2. Jesus carries his Cross.
3. Jesus falls the first time.
4. Jesus meets his Mother.
5. Jesus is helped by Simon of Cyrene.
6. Veronica wipes the face of Jesus.
7. Jesus falls a second time.
8. Jesus speaks to the women.
9. Jesus falls a third time.
10. Jesus is stripped of his clothes.
11. Jesus is nailed to the Cross.
12. Jesus dies on the Cross.
13. Jesus is taken down from the Cross.
14. Jesus is placed in the tomb.

Preview

In the next lesson, the students will learn about fasting and abstinence.

CHAPTER SEVEN. THE CROSS AND TRUE RICHES
LESSON THREE: PENANCES

Aims

The students will learn that fasting and abstinence are forms of penance. Penance is a form of sacrifice and purification to help us grow closer to Christ. Penance strengthens us to do his will.

They will learn that fasting is giving up food. The Church defines fasting as eating one regular meal and two small meals that do not exceed the one regular meal in any given day. Abstinence is refraining from eating meat.

Materials

- *Activity Book*, p. 27
- Optional:
  - "Lift high the cross," *Adoremus Hymnal*, #606

Begin

Many Catholics are familiar with the phrase "offer it up." This is a reminder to accept a daily cross and to give it as a gift to God. Offering up a suffering is a great act of love, recognizing our dependence upon God's will. By offering up our sufferings we unite ourselves to God's will and live for his greater glory.

Develop

1. Read paragraphs 10–12.

2. Review the words *penance*, *fasting*, and *abstinence*, as defined in the glossary of the student text (see *Teacher's Manual*, p. 395).

3. Thoroughly explain the laws on fasting and abstinence and the obligation to do some kind of penance or self-denial every Friday. Abstinence means to avoid eating meat. Fasting, in general, means not eating at all. When the Church requires us to fast, however, it means that only one full meal a day should be eaten. In addition, two smaller meals may be eaten, but those taken together should not equal another full meal. Discuss the rules of fast and abstinence found in the student text.

4. There are three ways to live in the spirit of penance:
   - Doing Penance (self-denial)—The greatest penance is receiving the Sacrament of Penance in renouncing our sins and uniting ourselves with Jesus. Another is the acceptance of the daily cross (whatever sufferings God allows for our own good). We should also offer up additional prayers for our own good and the good of others.
   - Fasting and abstinence on the days prescribed by the Church—We may do more than the prescribed law, such as not eating meat and desserts on Fridays.
   - Almsgiving—Almsgiving is giving of our resources to those in need. Usually, this means giving of our money, but it can also mean giving of our time and talents to help others in need. We may do almsgiving by collecting clothes or food for people. We may help an elderly neighbor with yard work or spend time volunteering in a nursing home.

5. You may review the Spiritual and Corporal Works of Mercy with the students (see the facing page).

6. Arrange for a class project to exemplify this lesson.

Reinforce

1. Have the students work on *Activity Book* p. 27 (see *Teacher's Manual*, p. 87).

2. Have the students work on the Memorization Questions and Words to Know from this chapter.

3. Have the students do a class project, such as:
   - Doing penance by offering additional prayers
   - Fasting for a day or abstaining from desserts
   - Collecting goods for the poor

Conclude

1. Lead the children in singing "Lift high the cross," *Adoremus Hymnal*, #606.

2. End class by leading the students in praying the Prayer before a Crucifix (see *Teacher's Manual*, p. 79).

though we may not be able to see it at the time.

Bearing the crosses (that is, trials and difficulties) which we do not choose but which come to us anyhow in the course of life is a most perfect kind of self-denial, more pleasing to God than the acts of self-denial we choose for ourselves. For in all things it is most perfect to accept the will of God, even when we do not like it very much. Jesus' entire life was one of obedience to the will of the Father, no matter how hard it was or what it required of him, even his death. "Father, if you are willing, remove this chalice from me; nevertheless not my will, but yours, be done" (Lk 22:42).

And why are we willing to set out on such a way of life? In following the example of Jesus we are showing our love for God by willingly and, yes, even cheerfully accepting whatever he permits.

Fast and Abstinence

We are encouraged to choose some **penance** for ourselves. To help us, the Church requires **fasting** and **abstinence** from certain foods on penitential days. To abstain, in this case, means not to eat meat. If we are fourteen years old or more, we must abstain from meat on Ash Wednesday and Good Friday.

In the United States, the bishops have declared abstinence from meat on all Fridays of Lent. In other seasons, Friday remains a day of penance on which we are supposed to practice some kind of self-denial, and the Church advises us to make Friday a day of abstinence all year round.

Fasting, in general, means not eating at all. When the Church requires us to fast, however, it means that only one full meal a day should be eaten. In addition, two smaller meals may be taken, but those taken together should not equal another full meal. In the Church, there are two days of required fasting: Ash Wednesday and Good Friday. This applies to anyone eighteen to sixty years old.

Penitential Seasons

Advent and **Lent** are special seasons in the Church year in which we are reminded to renew our spirit. They are called penitential seasons.

Advent begins four Sundays before Christmas and is a season of special preparation for celebrating the birth of Christ. The Church suggests that we do some form of penance as part of this preparation.

The season of Lent begins six and a half weeks before Easter and is a season of preparation for the Passion, death, and Resurrection of the Lord. Just as Jesus fasted for forty days, we too take on some penance during Lent to make up for our sins and to prepare our hearts to celebrate the great Easter feast.

Saint Paul compares the spiritual life to a race and the Christian to an athlete. Like an athlete, the Christian is asked to practice certain spiritual exercises. If an athlete will give up a great deal just to train for a race, how much more should we Christians be ready to practice self-denial for the sake of the Kingdom of God!

Besides, what the athlete gives up in training is not always so great, and his self-discipline is often very satisfying, invigorating, and enjoyable. His muscle tone, increased skill, and sense of well-being make it all worthwhile.

It is the same way with the Kingdom of God. The crosses we bear can include the many little things which make up our daily lives, such as not always having our own way, forgiving an unkind word, turning from fun to duties at the proper time, not overeating, and the like. We are not expected to make life one big penance with no pleasures. After all, it is God who created the things in which we find pleasure. But, like a good athlete, we must keep an eye on the coach—Jesus—and not forget ourselves and break training.

By God's grace, penance can make up for past sin and help prevent future sin. It helps eliminate those things that take us away from God or are obstacles to our final goal—union with God in his Kingdom.

Words to Know:

> self-denial penance fasting
> abstinence Advent Lent

Rules of Fast and Abstinence in the United States

— The days and times of penance for the universal Church are each Friday of the whole year and the whole season of Lent.

— Abstinence and fasting are to be observed on Ash Wednesday and Good Friday. Abstinence is to be observed on all the Fridays during Lent.

— The law of abstinence binds those who have completed their fourteenth year. The law of fasting binds those eighteen years old to sixty years old.

Dearest Lord, teach me to be generous;
teach me to serve you as you deserve to be served—
to give and not to count the cost,
to fight and not to heed the wounds,
to toil and not to seek for rest,
to labor and not to ask any reward
except that of knowing that I do your holy will.

—Saint Ignatius Loyola

> "And when you fast, do not look dismal, like the hypocrites, for they disfigure their faces that their fasting may be seen by men. Truly, I say to you, they have received their reward. But when you fast, anoint your head and wash your face, that your fasting may not be seen by men but by your Father who is in secret; and your Father who sees in secret will reward you."
>
> (Matthew 6:16–18)

Q. 30 *What is abstinence?*

To abstain from something is to give it up voluntarily. A day of abstinence in the Church is one during which we abstain from eating meat (CIC, Canon 1251).

Q. 31 *What is penance?*

Penance is an act of self-denial or prayer that helps strengthen us to do God's will and, by his grace, to make up for sin (CCC 1434, 2043).

Q. 32 *When are the days and times for penance for the universal Church?*

All Fridays of the year and the time of Lent are days and times of penance for the universal Church (CCC 1438).

Q. 33 *What are the days when both fasting and abstinence are required in the universal Church?*

The days when both fasting and abstinence are required in the universal Church are Ash Wednesday and Good Friday (CIC, Canon 1251).

Q. 34 *In the United States what other days are days of required abstinence?*

Other days of required abstinence in the United States are all Fridays during Lent (CCC 1438).

SPIRITUAL AND CORPORAL WORKS OF MERCY

Spiritual:
- ✓ Instruct the ignorant
- ✓ Counsel the doubtful
- ✓ Admonish sinners
- Bear wrongs patiently
- ✓ Forgive offenses willingly
- ✓ Comfort the afflicted
- ✓ Pray for the living and the dead

Corporal:
- ✓ Feed the hungry
- ✓ Give drink to the thirsty
- ✓ Clothe the naked
- ✓ Harbor the harborless
- ✓ Visit the sick
- ✓ Ransom the captive
- ✓ Bury the dead

Preview

In the next lesson, the students will review the penitential seasons.

CHAPTER SEVEN: THE CROSS AND TRUE RICHES
LESSON FOUR: PENITENTIAL SEASONS

Aims

The students will learn that Advent and Lent are the penitential seasons of the liturgical year.

They will learn that penance can make up for past sins and help us prevent future sins.

They will learn that the primary forms of penance include fasting, abstinence, almsgiving, and works of charity.

Materials

- *Activity Book*, p. 28
- Appendix, pp. B-7– B-10

Optional:
- Lift high the cross," *Adoremus Hymnal*, #606

Begin

Review the liturgical calendar with the students using Appendix, pp. B-7–B-10.

Review that the liturgical color of purple should remind us of penance. The seasons of Advent and Lent are the penitential seasons of the Church. During these seasons, the vestments and cloths used in the Mass are primarily purple.

Develop

1. Finish reading the chapter from the student text.

2. Discuss some penitential practices done during Lent and Advent. (See box on facing page for ideas.)

3. Read and discuss 1 Corinthians 9:24–27 with the students. Use examples from modern day sports, such as football, to help put this lesson in context. For example, in football, to play the game you must first know the rules (like our Creed). You must exercise and practice (virtues) and give up things in order to be dedicated to this sport: players must diet, give up some relaxation time for practice, etc. (this is like penance). You must actively participate in the game and not be a bench warmer (Sacraments) and you must want to win in order to play well (prayer). In the game, the object is to get the ball (grace) and when you reach the end zone (death), you must have the ball in order to get a touchdown (enter heaven). You

may fumble the ball or have it intercepted (sin), but you can get it back through an interception (Sacrament of Penance). The challenge is to work together as a team (in the Church) to score some points and win the game (the joy of heaven for all of eternity with the Communion of Saints). Our sure guide in this game of life is the coach (Jesus) and his umpires call the shots (Magisterium).

4. You may review some of our reasons for doing penance:
- Overcome our sinfulness
- Atone for sins (unite ourselves with the suffering of Jesus, who paid the price for our sins)
- Offer our sufferings for others—for their conversion or intentions, for souls in purgatory
- For love of God and neighbor
- To grow in virtue
- Out of obedience, in accord with the liturgical season

Reinforce

1. Have the students work on *Activity Book* p. 28 (see *Teacher's Manual*, p. 87).

2. Have the students work on the Memorization Questions and Words to Know from this chapter. You may wish to provide the students class time to prepare for the quiz.

3. Have the students review Advent and Lenten penitential practices.

4. Lead the students in praying the Stations of the Cross (see *Teacher's Manual*, p. 81).

Conclude

1. Lead the children in singing "Lift high the cross," *Adoremus Hymnal*, #606.

2. Lead the students in praying the Prayer before a Crucifix (see *Teacher's Manual*, p. 79).

though we may not be able to see it at the time.

Bearing the crosses (that is, trials and difficulties) which we do not choose but which come to us anyhow in the course of life is a most perfect kind of self-denial, more pleasing to God than the acts of self-denial we choose for ourselves. For in all things it is most perfect to accept the will of God, even when we do not like it very much. Jesus' entire life was one of obedience to the will of the Father, no matter how hard it was or what it required of him, even his death. "Father, if you are willing, remove this chalice from me; nevertheless not my will, but yours, be done" (Lk 22:42).

And why are we willing to set out on such a way of life? In following the example of Jesus we are showing our love for God by willingly and, yes, even cheerfully accepting whatever he permits.

Fast and Abstinence

We are encouraged to choose some **penance** for ourselves. To help us, the Church requires **fasting** and **abstinence** from certain foods on penitential days. To abstain, in this case, means not to eat meat. If we are fourteen years old or more, we must abstain from meat on Ash Wednesday and Good Friday.

In the United States, the bishops have declared abstinence from meat on all Fridays of Lent. In other seasons, Friday remains a day of penance on which we are supposed to practice some kind of self-denial, and the Church advises us to make Friday a day of abstinence all year round.

Fasting, in general, means not eating at all. When the Church requires us to fast, however, it means that only one full meal a day should be eaten. In addition, two smaller meals may be taken, but those taken together should not equal another full meal. In the Church, there are two days of required fasting: Ash Wednesday and Good Friday. This applies to anyone eighteen to sixty years old.

Penitential Seasons

Advent and **Lent** are special seasons in the Church year in which we are reminded to renew our spirit. They are called penitential seasons.

Advent begins four Sundays before Christmas and is a season of special preparation for celebrating the birth of Christ. The Church suggests that we do some form of penance as part of this preparation.

The season of Lent begins six and a half weeks before Easter and is a season of preparation for the Passion, death, and Resurrection

> "And when you fast, do not look dismal, like the hypocrites, for they disfigure their faces that their fasting may be seen by men. Truly, I say to you, they have received their reward. But when you fast, anoint your head and wash your face, that your fasting may not be seen by men but by your Father who is in secret; and your Father who sees in secret will reward you."
>
> (Matthew 6:16–18)

40

of the Lord. Just as Jesus fasted for forty days, we too take on some penance during Lent to make up for our sins and to prepare our hearts to celebrate the great Easter feast.

Saint Paul compares the spiritual life to a race and the Christian to an athlete. Like an athlete, the Christian is asked to practice certain spiritual exercises. If an athlete will give up a great deal just to train for a race, how much more should we Christians be ready to practice self-denial for the sake of the Kingdom of God!

Besides, what the athlete gives up in training is not always so great, and his self-discipline is often very satisfying, invigorating, and enjoyable. His muscle tone, increased skill, and sense of well-being make it all worthwhile.

It is the same way with the Kingdom of God. The crosses we bear can include the many little things which make up our daily

lives, such as not always having our own way, forgiving an unkind word, turning from fun to duties at the proper time, not overeating, and the like. We are not expected to make life one big penance with no pleasures. After all, it is God who created the things in which we find pleasure. But, like a good athlete, we must keep an eye on the coach—Jesus—and not forget ourselves and break training.

By God's grace, penance can make up for past sin and help prevent future sin. It helps eliminate those things that take us away from God or are obstacles to our final goal—union with God in his Kingdom.

Words to Know:

self-denial penance fasting
abstinence Advent Lent

Rules of Fast and Abstinence in the United States

— The days and times of penance for the universal Church are each Friday of the whole year and the whole season of Lent.
— Abstinence and fasting are to be observed on Ash Wednesday and Good Friday. Abstinence is to be observed on all the Fridays during Lent.
— The law of abstinence binds those who have completed their fourteenth year. The law of fasting binds those eighteen years old to sixty years old.

Dearest Lord, teach me to be generous;
teach me to serve you as you deserve to be served—
to give and not to count the cost,
to fight and not to heed the wounds,
to toil and not to seek for rest,
to labor and not to ask any reward
except that of knowing that I do your holy will.

—Saint Ignatius Loyola

41

Q. 30 *What is abstinence?*
To abstain from something is to give it up voluntarily. A day of abstinence in the Church is one during which we abstain from eating meat (CIC, Canon 1251).

Q. 31 *What is penance?*
Penance is an act of self-denial or prayer that helps strengthen us to do God's will and, by his grace, to make up for sin (CCC 1434, 2043).

Q. 32 *When are the days and times for penance for the universal Church?*
All Fridays of the year and the time of Lent are days and times of penance for the universal Church (CCC 1438).

Q. 33 *What are the days when both fasting and abstinence are required in the universal Church?*
The days when both fasting and abstinence are required in the universal Church are Ash Wednesday and Good Friday (CIC, Canon 1251).

Q. 34 *In the United States what other days are days of required abstinence?*
Other days of required abstinence in the United States are all Fridays during Lent (CCC 1438).

42

Lent and Advent are the two penitential seasons of the liturgical year. The penances we practice should demonstrate and deepen our love for God above all worldly goods, specifically those which we are sacrificing. Traditionally, there are three forms of penance (see Mt 6:3, 6, 16):

- Prayer: We place a special emphasis on prayer, as we repent of our sins and pray to become closer to God.
- Fasting: We refrain from specific foods or activities, which may be hindering our relationship with God or causing us to sin (e.g., eating too much at meals, watching television, or spending time on the computer).
- Almsgiving: Even if we cannot give much (see Lk 21:1–4), giving something of our own to others is an important practice during these seasons.

The heart of our penance should be to increase our fervor and love for God and neighbor. Our practices during Advent and Lent should therefore bring us closer to God and enable to fully celebrate Christmas and Easter.

Preview

In the next lesson, the students' understanding of the material covered in this chapter will be reviewed and assessed.

85

CHAPTER SEVEN: THE CROSS AND TRUE RICHES
REVIEW AND ASSESSMENT

Aims

The students' understanding of the material covered in this chapter will be reviewed and assessed.

Materials

- Quiz 7, Appendix, p. A-9

Optional:
- "Lift high the cross," *Adoremus Hymnal*, #606

Review and Enrichment

1. The students should understand the glory of the Cross of Christ. They should know what our individual crosses are. They should understand that we have self-imposed sufferings and those given by God for our greater good.

2. The students should understand that self-denial means putting others first: God, others, and then one's self.

3. The students should know that penance includes sacrifices, prayer, fasting, abstinence, and almsgiving.

4. The students should know the rules of fasting and abstinence, according to the Church.

5. The students should know that the penitential seasons of the liturgical calendar are Advent and Lent. They should be aware of some of our penitential practices during these liturgical seasons.

6. The students should be able to fill in a liturgical calendar.

7. The students should understand how our Faith, like a sport, requires penances and discipline.

Name: _____

The Cross and True Riches   Quiz 7

Part I: Answer in complete sentences.

1. Why should we practice self-denial?
   We should practice self-denial to heal the wounds left by Original Sin, to do penance for our sins or the sins of others, to strengthen our ability to do good, to show our love for God.

2. Give three examples of acts of self-denial. Answers will vary.

3. What is the most perfect kind of self-denial?
   The most perfect kind of self-denial is bearing the crosses which we do not choose.

4. On days the Church requires abstinence, what are we not to do?
   On days the Church requires abstinence, we are not to eat meat.

5. On days the Church requires us to fast, what are we to do?
   On days the Church requires us to fast, we are to eat only one full meal a day; two smaller meals may be eaten, but those taken together should not equal another full meal.

6. What is the penitential season in the Church year that prepares us to celebrate the birth of Christ?
   Advent is the penitential season in the Church year that prepares us to celebrate the birth of Christ.

7. What is the penitential season in the Church year that prepares us to celebrate the Passion, death, and Resurrection of the Lord?
   Lent is the penitential season in the Church year that prepares us to celebrate the Passion, death and Resurrection of the Lord.

Part II: Yes or No.

1. No Is it always easy to do good?
2. Yes With the power of God is it possible to do good and even love our enemy?
3. Yes Can practicing self-denial strengthen our ability to do good with the help of God?
4. Yes Can our cross be a penance we choose for ourselves or suffering that God allows in our life?
5. Yes Can penance make up for past sin and help prevent future sin?
6. Yes Is it good to practice self-denial on Fridays?

Faith and Life Series • Grade 6 • Appendix A   *A-9*

Assess

1. Distribute the quizzes and read through them with the students to be sure they understand the questions.

2. Administer the quiz. As they hand in their work, you may orally quiz the students on the Memorization Questions from this chapter.

3. After all the quizzes have been handed in, you may wish to review the correct answers with the class.

Conclude

1. Lead the children in singing "Lift high the cross," *Adoremus Hymnal*, #606.

2. End class by leading the students in praying the Prayer before a Crucifix (see *Teacher's Manual*, p. 79).

CHAPTER SEVEN: THE CROSS AND TRUE RICHES
ACTIVITY BOOK ANSWER KEYS

Name:_____

The Cross and True Riches

Penance is an important part of being a follower of Christ. List ten penances that you could do and tell how each would help you become more like Christ. Some examples are given to start you off.

1. Keeping silence for one hour: <u>Answers will vary</u>

2. Doing an extra chore: _____

3. Giving up a dessert: _____

4. Kneeling while praying: _____

5. _____ : _____

6. _____ : _____

7. _____ : _____

8. _____ : _____

9. _____ : _____

10. _____ : _____

Faith and Life Series • Grade 6 • Chapter 7 • Lesson 1   25

Name:_____

The Cross

Answer the following questions in complete sentences.

1. What does Jesus mean when he says "If any man would come after me, let him deny himself and take up his cross daily and follow me"?
   <u>Answers will vary.</u>

2. What value is there in self-denial?
   <u>Answers will vary.</u>

3. What does Saint Paul mean when he tells us to put on the "new man"?
   <u>Saint Paul means that we should put to death in ourselves our life of sin and live a life of grace.</u>

4. Can we bear little crosses daily?
   <u>Yes</u>

5. How can we accept God's will?
   <u>We can accept the suffering that comes our way.</u>

6. What do we show by following the example of Jesus?
   <u>Answers will vary: love, obedience, etc.</u>

7. List some of your daily crosses.
   <u>Answers will vary.</u>

26   *Faith and Life Series • Grade 6 • Chapter 7 • Lesson 2*

Name:_____

Fast and Abstinence

Answer the following questions in complete sentences.

1. What is penance?
   <u>Penance is an act of self-denial or prayer that helps strengthen us to do God's will and, by his grace, to make up for sin.</u>

2. Why does the Church require certain days of fasting and abstinence?
   <u>The Church requires certain days of fasting and abstinence to help us see the importance of fasting.</u>

3. What does "to abstain" mean?
   <u>To abstain means not to eat meat.</u>

4. What does "to fast" mean?
   <u>To fast generally means not to eat anything, but when the Church requires it, is means that only one full meal and two smaller meals may be eaten in a day.</u>

5. On what days must we abstain?
   <u>We must abstain on Ash Wednesday, Good Friday, and every Friday of Lent.</u>

6. On what days must we fast?
   <u>We must fast on Ash Wednesday and Good Friday.</u>

7. What does Matthew 6:16–18 teach us about fasting?
   <u>Matthew 6:16-18 teaches that we should not show off when we fast. We should fast for God in secret.</u>

Faith and Life Series • Grade 6 • Chapter 7 • Lesson 3   27

Name:_____

The Penitential Seasons: Advent and Lent

Answer the following questions in complete sentences.

1. When is Advent?
   <u>Advent begins four Sundays before Christmas and ends on Christmas Eve.</u>

2. What are we preparing for during Advent?
   <u>During Advent, we prepare to celebrate the birth of Christ.</u>

3. Why do we do penance during Advent?
   <u>We do penance to help us to prepare.</u>

4. How does Advent prepare us for the coming of our Lord?
   <u>Answers will vary.</u>

5. When is Lent?
   <u>Lent is the forty days before Easter.</u>

6. What are we preparing for during Lent?
   <u>During Lent, we prepare to celebrate the Passion, death, and Resurrection of Jesus.</u>

7. Why do we do penance during Lent?
   <u>Just as Jesus fasted for forty days, we do penance to help us prepare and to make up for our sins.</u>

28   *Faith and Life Series • Grade 6 • Chapter 7 • Lesson 4*

TEACHER'S NOTES

TEACHER'S NOTES

CHAPTER EIGHT
IN THE HEART OF THE FAMILY

Catechism of the Catholic Church References

Authorities in Civil Society: 2234–46, 2254–57
Duties of Children: 2214–20, 2251
Duties of Parents: 2221–31, 2252–53
Fourth Commandment: 2197–2246, 2247–57
Family in God's Plan: 2201–6, 2249

Family and Society: 1655–58, 2207–33, 2250
Holy Family as Model of the Domestic Church: 2634–36, 2647
Prayer of Intercession: 2634–36, 2647
Sacrifice: 2099–2100

Scripture References

Honor Your Father and Your Mother: Ex 20:12

The Finding in the Temple: Lk 2:41–52

Summary of Lesson Content

Lesson 1

The Fourth Commandment teaches that we have obligations to our families.

Parents/married couples are obliged to raise children in the Faith, maintain good order in the home, provide necessities, educate, and (ultimately) to lead all members of the family toward God.

Lesson 2

To honor is to hold in high regard, respect, and love.

Children are to respect the authority of their parents and legitimate authorities. Obedience is an exercise of this respect.

Children can be a source of good and blessing for their parents. Children should pray for their parents.

Lesson 3

As the parent-child relationship changes, obedience gives way to respect.

Children are obliged to care for their parents' needs as they age.

Lesson 4

The Holy Family is the model for all families.

Society questions the role and definition of the family; however, the Church teaches that strong love among all members must unite every family and make it holy.

CHAPTER EIGHT: IN THE HEART OF THE FAMILY
LESSON ONE: DUTIES

Aims

The students will learn that the Fourth Commandment teaches that we have obligations to our families.

They will learn that parents are obliged to raise children in the Faith, maintain good order in the home, provide necessities, educate, and (ultimately) to lead all members of the family toward God.

Materials

- *Activity Book*, p. 29

- Text of Rite of Marriage and Rite of Baptism, Appendix, pp. B-3–B-4 and pp. B-11–B-12

Optional:
- "Now thank we all our God," *Adoremus Hymnal*, #607

Begin

Begin the class by discussing the family. In today's society, a "family" can mean many different things. We have families of mixed faiths, nuclear families, adoptive families, extended families, foster families, church families—the word family has been broadened to simply mean a community of people living together. Traditionally and more precisely, the word family refers to parents and children. A mother and father cooperate with God to bring new life into the world. They raise the child in the Faith and share in the rearing of God's family. Children are a gift from God and parents have the duty to raise God's children properly.

Develop

1. Read paragraphs 1–4 with the students.

2. Review the Blessed Trinity. Show how the Blessed Trinity is one God in three Divine Persons. The Persons are distinct; they are distinguished by their relationship with one another. Teach the students that the Father and the Son together sent the Holy Spirit.

3. Discuss how the family is an image of the Blessed Trinity. The Holy Spirit proceeds from the mutual love of the Father and the Son. The love of husband and wife may bring forth, with God, a third person, a child.

4. Discuss the love of a father, mother, and child. What distinguishes these relationships? What is expected of each person?

5. Using the Rites of Marriage and Baptism, show how parents view children as a gift from God and promise to raise their children in the Faith. This means to educate them in the teachings of the Church and help them to live sacramental lives.

6. Discuss the duties of parents: to care for their children, entrusted to them by God; to provide a home, food and clothing, education, health, moral example, and authority to form them and give them a safe, secure, and loving environment in which to grow.

7. Discuss how our parents exemplify God's attributes: his love, truth, generosity, care, goodness, etc. Help the students to recognize the goodness of their parents and to be thankful for them. The students may make thank you cards, letters, or do another project of their choosing to show their love and appreciation for their parents.

Reinforce

1. Have the students work on *Activity Book* p. 29 (see *Teacher's Manual*, p. 99).

2. Have the students work on a project to show their appreciation for their parents.

3. The students should begin working on the Memorization Questions and Word to Know from this chapter (see the facing page).

4. The students may write a psalm adoring God and his attributes.

Conclude

1. Teach the students to sing "Now thank we all our God," *Adoremus Hymnal*, #607.

2. End class by leading the students in praying the Hail, Holy Queen (see *Teacher's Manual*, p. 93).

CHAPTER 8

In the Heart of the Family

"Honor your father and your mother, that your days may be long in the land which the LORD your God gives you."

Exodus 20:12

We sometimes see elderly people with their children who are themselves approaching old age. No matter how old the parents are, no matter how old the children, the law of the Lord remains: "Honor your father and your mother."

Even without the Fourth Commandment we would be able to see that we have certain obligations toward our parents, for we would never have existed without them. They are special; they have given us life. This gift is so great that there is no way to repay them completely.

To see what is required of us by the Fourth Commandment, we need to look at family relations. Without children, husband and wife make a marriage; with a child, they make a family. The child is an extension of their love for each other and is included in their love. The relation of parent to child is a lasting one, no matter how old one is. It is from his parents that a child learns what love is. In that love the child is able to learn that God is also his loving Father.

Each child is a precious gift from God. But along with the blessing of a child there are many duties and responsibilities that parents must take on. God gives them the authority and duty to maintain good order in the home, to provide food and clothing, to educate, and to tend to the welfare of each of their children.

Now, the commandment tells us to **honor** our parents. To honor means to hold in high regard, to respect, and to love. A child honors his parents when he respects their authority over him. This also includes respecting and obeying government authorities, clergy, and those whom our parents place in authority over us, such as a teacher or scout leader.

God provides for the well-being and development of children by placing them under the loving authority of their parents, and so obedience to that authority is required.

With the years, children may discover faults and weaknesses in their parents, but they must still honor them. Children can sometimes be a powerful force for good and a source of grace for their parents. Prayer and sacrifice for the welfare of one's parents are always blessed by God.

As children get older they need less care and direction until they reach a point at which they are able to order their own lives. It is only reasonable, then, that the relationship between parent and child should gradually change. Obedience turns into respect for the wisdom of

43

our parents until we reach an age at which we are no longer bound by obedience but still gratefully accept our parents' advice.

Anyone who honors his parents will, when he grows older, look after their needs. In this regard, life is like a seesaw with the heavier end holding up the other. As a youngster, the child sits at the end upraised, with mother and father holding down the other. Many years later, the child holds the seesaw down while the elderly parents

44

receive the care and attention. They cared for us; now we care for them.

The Bible teaches: "O son, help your father in his old age, and do not grieve him as long as he lives" (Sir 3:12).

And God promises to bless those who keep the Fourth Commandment:

"Honor your father and your mother, that your days may be long in the land which the LORD your God gives you" (Ex 20:12).

The Family Today

In his Apostolic Exhortation *Familiaris Consortio*, "The Role of the Christian Family in the Modern World," Pope John Paul II singled out the family as the main means for the renewal of modern society. The family is so important that we cannot hope to survive as a society unless family life is healthy and strong. This means that strong love among all the members must unite the whole family and make it holy.

The Holy Family, Jesus, Mary, and Joseph, was united with that holy love. We should look to them as our model for family life.

There are many forces in our society that weaken the bonds of family life and even threaten to destroy it. The Christian family will survive only with renewed love for God and neighbor. We must pray together for our own families and for the family in general. Where there is no prayer, there will be no family unity and no peace. With prayer, we can hope for the blessings of family happiness on earth and reunion in our heavenly home.

Word to Know:
honor

> **Q. 35** *What does the Fourth Commandment require us to do?*
> The Fourth Commandment commands us to love, respect, and obey our parents and others who have authority over us (CCC 2199).

> **Q. 36** *What does the Fourth Commandment forbid?*
> The Fourth Commandment forbids us to disobey our parents and others in legitimate authority over us (CCC 2197).

Father, it is your commandment that we should honor our father and mother; hear the prayers I offer you for my parents. Grant them many years on earth, and keep them healthy in mind and body. Bless their work and all they do. Give them back a hundredfold whatever they have done for me. Inspire them with your love, and help them to fulfill your holy law. One day, may I be their comfort and support, so that, having enjoyed their affection on earth, I may have the joy of being with them forever in your home in heaven. Through Christ our Lord. *Amen.*

45

CHALK TALK: THE BLESSED TRINITY AND THE DOMESTIC CHURCH

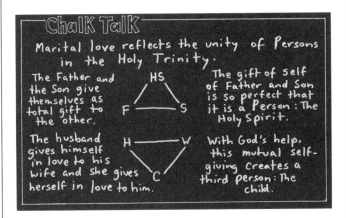

Chalk Talk

Marital love reflects the unity of Persons in the Holy Trinity.

The Father and the Son give themselves as total gift to the other.

The gift of self of Father and Son is so perfect that it is a Person: The Holy Spirit.

The husband gives himself in love to his wife and she gives herself in love to him.

With God's help, this mutual self-giving creates a third person: The child.

Preview

In the next lesson, the students will learn about the duty of children toward their parents.

CHAPTER EIGHT: IN THE HEART OF THE FAMILY
LESSON TWO: HONOR AND OBEY

Aims

The students will learn that to honor is to hold in high regard, respect, and love.

They will learn that children are to respect the authority of their parents and legitimate authorities. Obedience is an exercise of this respect.

They will learn that children can be a source of good and blessing for their parents. Children should pray for their parents.

Materials

- *Activity Book*, p. 30

Optional:
- "Now thank we all our God," *Adoremus Hymnal*, #607

Begin

Discuss the sacrifices, responsibilities and obligations involved in being a parent. This is a grave responsibility, and hard work! Sometimes we do not agree with our parents or think about them before ourselves. How should we treat our parents? How should we respond to their authority?

Develop

1. Read paragraphs 5–7.

2. Have the students look up *honor* and *obey* in the glossary (see *Teacher's Manual*, p. 395). Have the students give examples of each.

3. What is authority? To whom did God give authority over us? How should we respond to those in legitimate authority? How should those in roles of authority use it? Who else has authority over us? Discuss their roles:
   - Clergy (authority given by God)
   - Government authorities (authority given by election)
   - Those to whom our parents give authority over us (teachers, coaches, babysitters, etc.)

Further discussion questions: How should we honor and obey these authorities? How can these authorities seek our well-being? How can these authorities uphold God's law and true authority over all men?

4. How can the students be a powerful force for good and source of grace for their parents? By:
   - Loving their parents
   - Obeying them
   - Living with the love that their parents instill in them
   - Keeping a good name/reputation
   - Praying and sacrificing for their parents

5. Discuss how we can imitate the Christ Child. Read about the finding in the temple found in Luke 2:41–52.
   - How did Jesus respond to Mary and Joseph?
   - Was Jesus bound to the authority of Mary and Joseph (even though he is God)?
   - How can we follow Jesus' example?

6. Discuss what Jesus' life would have been like during the hidden years. How can the students follow his example?

Reinforce

1. Have the students work on *Activity Book* p. 30 (see *Teacher's Manual*, p. 99).

2. Have the students work on the Memorization Questions and Word to Know from this chapter (see *Teacher's Manual*, p. 97).

3. Have the students research what life would have been like in the time of Jesus. The students may do projects to demonstrate daily-life events for each other (e.g., portraying attire, cooking, shopping, and making necessary items).

Conclude

1. Lead the children in singing "Now thank we all our God," *Adoremus Hymnal*, #607.

2. End class by leading the students in praying the Hail, Holy Queen (see facing page).

CHAPTER 8

In the Heart of the Family

"Honor your father and your mother, that your days may be long in the land which the LORD your God gives you."

Exodus 20:12

We sometimes see elderly people with their children who are themselves approaching old age. No matter how old the parents are, no matter how old the children, the law of the Lord remains: "Honor your father and your mother."

Even without the Fourth Commandment we would be able to see that we have certain obligations toward our parents, for we would never have existed without them. They are special; they have given us life. This gift is so great that there is no way to repay them completely.

To see what is required of us by the Fourth Commandment, we need to look at family relations. Without children, husband and wife make a marriage; with a child, they make a family. The child is an extension of their love for each other and is included in their love. The relation of parent to child is a lasting one, no matter how old one is. It is from his parents that a child learns what love is. In that love the child is able to learn that God is also his loving Father.

Each child is a precious gift from God. But along with the blessing of a child there are many duties and responsibilities that parents must take on. God gives them the authority and duty to maintain good order in the home, to provide food and clothing, to educate, and to tend to the welfare of each of their children.

Now, the commandment tells us to **honor** our parents. To honor means to hold in high regard, to respect, and to love. A child honors his parents when he respects their authority over him. This also includes respecting and obeying government authorities, clergy, and those whom our parents place in authority over us, such as a teacher or scout leader.

God provides for the well-being and development of children by placing them under the loving authority of their parents, and so obedience to that authority is required.

With the years, children may discover faults and weaknesses in their parents, but they must still honor them. Children can sometimes be a powerful force for good and a source of grace for their parents. Prayer and sacrifice for the welfare of one's parents are always blessed by God.

As children get older they need less care and direction until they reach a point at which they are able to order their own lives. It is only reasonable, then, that the relationship between parent and child should gradually change. Obedience turns into respect for the wisdom of

43

our parents until we reach an age at which we are no longer bound by obedience but still gratefully accept our parents' advice.

Anyone who honors his parents will, when he grows older, look after their needs. In this regard, life is like a seesaw with the heavier end holding up the other. As a youngster, the child sits at the end upraised, with mother and father holding down the other. Many years later, the child holds the seesaw down while the elderly parents receive the care and attention. They cared for us; now we care for them.

The Bible teaches: "O son, help your father in his old age, and do not grieve him as long as he lives" (Sir 3:12).

And God promises to bless those who keep the Fourth Commandment:

"Honor your father and your mother, that your days may be long in the land which the LORD your God gives you" (Ex 20:12).

44

ROLES IN THE HOLY FAMILY

Though we cannot know exactly what life was like for the Holy Family, through Scripture and knowledge of Jewish families of the time, we can make a fairly good inference. We know that Joseph was a craftsman—a carpenter. In order to provide for his family, Joseph would have had to work a great deal, but he would have made time to lead his family in prayer and to take them to worship at the proper times (see Lk 2:22, 41). Mary would have tended to the house and looked after Jesus. She would have been a comfort and a help to Joseph and would have helped to instruct Jesus in the Jewish faith. Jesus would have been obedient to his parents and humbly received instruction from them.

HAIL, HOLY QUEEN

Hail, holy Queen, Mother of mercy,
our life, our sweetness, and our hope.
To you do we cry,
poor banished children of Eve.
To you do we send up our sighs
mourning and weeping in this
vale of tears.
Turn then, most gracious advocate,
your eyes of mercy toward us,
and after this exile
show to us the blessed fruit of
your womb, Jesus.
O clement, O loving,
O sweet Virgin Mary.

Children, obey your parents in the Lord, for this is right. "Honor your father and mother . . . that it may be well with you and that you may live long on the earth." Fathers, do not provoke your children to anger, but bring them up in the discipline and instruction of the Lord.
—Ephesians 6:1–4

Preview

In the next lesson, the students will learn about keeping the Fourth Commandment as society attempts to change roles in the family.

CHAPTER EIGHT: IN THE HEART OF THE FAMILY
LESSON THREE: ROLE CHANGES

Aims

The students will learn that, as the parent-child relationship changes, obedience gives way to respect.

They will learn that children are obliged to care for their parents' needs as they age.

Materials

• *Activity Book*, p. 31

Optional:
• "Now thank we all our God," *Adoremus Hymnal*, #607

Begin

Discuss ways that, as the students have grown, their parents' duties and care for their children have changed. For example:
• Changing diapers and feeding with a bottle
• Teaching to walk and speak
• Getting them dressed in the morning
• Helping with homework
• Taking them to sports practices
• Making dinner, but not feeding them
• Providing for their education
• Helping children to make good choices

Develop

1. Read paragraphs 8–11.

2. Discuss how, where once we were merely obedient, we may now see wisdom in our parents choices and do as they wish out of love and respect. Give examples of obedience and ask the students to find the wisdom in these decisions:
• Parent tells a child not to play in the street
• Parent tells a child to do his homework
• Parent tells a child to have proper manners at the dinner table
• Parent takes his child to Mass on Sundays
• Parent needs to know where the child is at all times
Have the students think of other examples.

3. As our parents get older, what do we notice is different about them? What about when they are the age of our grandparents or great-grandparents? What kind of additional needs will they have? What should we do to care for our aging parents?

4. Discuss the qualities we need in order to work with and care for the aged. Some seniors are very independent and active. We need to help them to maintain their activity and independence. Some, however need help getting around and do not drive anymore. Some need to change their diets. Some have physical demands that must be met, such as nursing care. What virtues should we develop to help them?
• Patience
• Long-suffering
• Forgiveness, etc.

You may note that these are the same virtues our parents need in order to raise us to be the adults we ought to be and that we are called to be as good Catholics.

Reinforce

1. Have the students work on *Activity Book* p. 31 (see *Teacher's Manual*, p. 99).

2. The students may work on their projects begun in Lesson 1 to thank their parents for their loving care.

3. You may assign the students to work on a project to share with their grandparents, or with senior citizens of the parish. For instance, they may host a seniors' tea. The children may entertain and spend time interviewing the seniors, asking them about their childhood.

4. Have the students work on the Memorization Questions and Word to Know from this chapter (see *Teacher's Manual*, p. 97).

Conclude

1. Lead the children in singing "Now thank we all our God," *Adoremus Hymnal*, #607.

2. End class by leading the students in praying the Hail, Holy Queen (see *Teacher's Manual*, p. 93).

CHAPTER 8

In the Heart of the Family

"Honor your father and your mother, that your days may be long in the land which the LORD your God gives you."

Exodus 20:12

We sometimes see elderly people with their children who are themselves approaching old age. No matter how old the parents are, no matter how old the children, the law of the Lord remains: "Honor your father and your mother."

Even without the Fourth Commandment we would be able to see that we have certain obligations toward our parents, for we would never have existed without them. They are special; they have given us life. This gift is so great that there is no way to repay them completely.

To see what is required of us by the Fourth Commandment, we need to look at family relations. Without children, husband and wife make a marriage; with a child, they make a family. The child is an extension of their love for each other and is included in their love. The relation of parent to child is a lasting one, no matter how old one is. It is from his parents that a child learns what love is. In that love the child is able to learn that God is also his loving Father.

Each child is a precious gift from God. But along with the blessing of a child there are many duties and responsibilities that parents must take on. God gives them the authority and duty to maintain good order in the home, to provide food and clothing, to educate, and to tend to the welfare of each of their children.

Now, the commandment tells us to **honor** our parents. To honor means to hold in high regard, to respect, and to love. A child honors his parents when he respects their authority over him. This also includes respecting and obeying government authorities, clergy, and those whom our parents place in authority over us, such as a teacher or scout leader.

God provides for the well-being and development of children by placing them under the loving authority of their parents, and so obedience to that authority is required.

With the years, children may discover faults and weaknesses in their parents, but they must still honor them. Children can sometimes be a powerful force for good and a source of grace for their parents. Prayer and sacrifice for the welfare of one's parents are always blessed by God.

As children get older they need less care and direction until they reach a point at which they are able to order their own lives. It is only reasonable, then, that the relationship between parent and child should gradually change. Obedience turns into respect for the wisdom of

43

our parents until we reach an age at which we are no longer bound by obedience but still gratefully accept our parents' advice.

Anyone who honors his parents will, when he grows older, look after their needs. In this regard, life is like a seesaw with the heavier end holding up the other. As a youngster, the child sits at the end upraised, with mother and father holding down the other. Many years later, the child holds the seesaw down while the elderly parents receive the care and attention. They cared for us; now we care for them.

The Bible teaches: "O son, help your father in his old age, and do not grieve him as long as he lives" (Sir 3:12).

And God promises to bless those who keep the Fourth Commandment:

"Honor your father and your mother, that your days may be long in the land which the LORD your God gives you" (Ex 20:12).

44

THE DIGNITY OF THE HUMAN PERSON

Human life is sacred from the moment of conception until the time of natural death. Every human life has immeasurable dignity because man is created in the image and likeness of God. According to the *Catechism of the Catholic Church:* "Endowed with 'a spiritual and immortal' soul, the human person is 'the only creature on earth that God has willed for its own sake.' From his conception, he is destined for eternal beatitude" (CCC 1703).

What does it mean to say the human person is "willed for its own sake"? Unlike the rest of material creation, mankind was created to spend eternity with God. That is the purpose of our existence. We exist for God but also for ourselves, because we will be perfectly happy and fulfilled living with God. A consequence of this fact is that we can never use another person merely as a means to an end. We must respect every human person as one who exists "for his own sake" and was created by, for, and in the image of God. "*Human life is sacred* because from its beginning it involves the creative action of God and it remains for ever in a special relationship with the Creator, who is its sole end. God alone is the Lord of life from its beginning until its end: no one can under any circumstance claim for himself the right directly to destroy an innocent human being" (CCC 2258).

Wisdom is with the aged, and understanding in length of days.

—Job 12:12

Listen to your father you begot you, and do not despise your mother when she is old.

—Proverbs 23:22

Preview

In the next lesson, the students will learn about the family.

CHAPTER EIGHT: IN THE HEART OF THE FAMILY
LESSON FOUR: FAMILY TODAY

Aims

The students will learn that the Holy Family is the model for all families.

They will learn that society questions the role and definition of family; however, the Church teaches that strong love among all members must unite every family and make it holy.

Materials

- *Activity Book*, p. 32

Optional:
- "Now thank we all our God," *Adoremus Hymnal*, #607

Begin

Discuss the ideal of the family: a father and mother who love each other and whose love overflows for their children. The model of this family is the Holy Family. The Holy Family had trials and sufferings (Joseph had to take Mary and Jesus to Egypt to escape certain death for Jesus at the hand of Herod). They had to work hard (we know that Joseph was a carpenter and Mary had to maintain a household). They laughed together, prayed together, and celebrated and practiced their faith together. How else is the Holy Family an excellent model for all families?

Develop

1. Finish reading the chapter.

2. Discuss why Pope John Paul II said that society cannot hope to survive without family life that is healthy and strong. Where do we learn about morality? Where do we safely grow? How do we learn to communicate and solve problems together? How do we learn to love? All good things are rooted in our families. From these many blessings, we bring gifts into society. For example, we learn to resolve our problems instead of fighting with our brothers and sisters. We must do this in society, too, so that we can avoid wars. Have the students find other examples.

3. There are many threats against the family in today's society. Have the students name some:
- Cost of living (a parent may not be able to spend much-needed time with the children because of work)
- Unclear definition of family (we see children with same-sex parents, etc.)
- Divorce
- Life issues (abortion and euthanasia)
- Crime (drugs, abuse)

4. The students have probably heard the saying, "The family that prays together stays together." What does this mean? Every family should be focused on God. The role of the husband and wife is to lead each other to God. The role of parents is to raise their children in the Faith and help them to be good Catholics. The role of children is to follow the example of their parents, to pray for them, and to love them as Jesus loves us. The family is a "domestic Church" (a Church in the home). God should be the center of the family's domestic Church. The family should pray and worship him together with each other's help. They should follow Jesus all the days of their lives.

Reinforce

1. Have the students work on *Activity Book* p. 32 (see *Teacher's Manual*, p. 99).

2. Have the students work on the Memorization Questions and Word to Know. You may wish to provide them class time to study for the chapter quiz and unit test.

3. The students can do a project in support of life issues (e.g., they may collect goods for a crisis pregnancy center).

4. The students can write prayers for their families.

Conclude

1. Lead the children in singing "Now thank we all our God," *Adoremus Hymnal*, #607.

2. End class by leading the students in praying the Hail, Holy Queen (see *Teacher's Manual*, p. 93).

our parents until we reach an age at which we are no longer bound by obedience but still gratefully accept our parents' advice.

Anyone who honors his parents will, when he grows older, look after their needs. In this regard, life is like a seesaw with the heavier end holding up the other. As a youngster, the child sits at the end upraised, with mother and father holding down the other. Many years later, the child holds the seesaw down while the elderly parents receive the care and attention. They cared for us; now we care for them.

The Bible teaches: "O son, help your father in his old age, and do not grieve him as long as he lives" (Sir 3:12).

And God promises to bless those who keep the Fourth Commandment:

"Honor your father and your mother, that your days may be long in the land which the LORD your God gives you" (Ex 20:12).

44

The Family Today

In his Apostolic Exhortation *Familiaris Consortio*, "The Role of the Christian Family in the Modern World," Pope John Paul II singled out the family as the main means for the renewal of modern society. The family is so important that we cannot hope to survive as a society unless family life is healthy and strong. This means that strong love among all the members must unite the whole family and make it holy.

The Holy Family, Jesus, Mary, and Joseph, was united with that holy love. We should look to them as our model for family life.

There are many forces in our society that weaken the bonds of family life and even threaten to destroy it. The Christian family will survive only with renewed love for God and neighbor. We must pray together for our own families and for the family in general. Where there is no prayer, there will be no family unity and no peace. With prayer, we can hope for the blessings of family happiness on earth and reunion in our heavenly home.

Word to Know:

honor

Q. 35 *What does the Fourth Commandment require us to do?*
The Fourth Commandment commands us to love, respect, and obey our parents and others who have authority over us (CCC 2199).

Q. 36 *What does the Fourth Commandment forbid?*
The Fourth Commandment forbids us to disobey our parents and others in legitimate authority over us (CCC 2197).

Father, it is your commandment that we should honor our father and mother; hear the prayers I offer you for my parents. Grant them many years on earth, and keep them healthy in mind and body. Bless their work and all they do. Give them back a hundredfold whatever they have done for me. Inspire them with your love, and help them to fulfill your holy law. One day, may I be their comfort and support, so that, having enjoyed their affection on earth, I may have the joy of being with them forever in your home in heaven. Through Christ our Lord. *Amen.*

45

SAINT GIANNA MOLLA

Gianna was born into a loving Catholic family on October 4, 1922 in Milan, Italy. Every morning the family attended Mass together, and every night they prayed the Rosary. When Gianna was twenty, her mother died and her father followed less than five months later. Soon after, Gianna began studies at the University of Milan to became a doctor and graduated in 1949. She opened a clinic in Mesero, a small city near Milan, in 1950 and, in 1955, married Pietro Molla. They lived together happily. In 1961 Gianna became pregnant with their fourth child. At the same time, they found that she had an ovarian cyst. The only way to save Gianna's life was an operation that would result in the death of her unborn child. Being a doctor, Gianna knew what would happen if she accepted the surgery. If she did not have the surgery, however, she would sacrifice her own life. Her words at this time were: "I trust in God, but now it is up to me to fulfill my duty as a mother. I renew the offering of my life to the Lord. I am ready for anything as long as my baby is saved." She refused the surgery—knowing that she would die, but her baby would live. Their daughter, Gianna Emanuela, was born on Holy Saturday, April 21, 1962. One week later, Gianna Molla died. Pietro relates that, as she lay on her death bed, Gianna repeated many times "Jesus, I love you. Jesus, I love you." On May 15, 2004, Pope John Paul II canonized Gianna in the presence of her husband and children.

Following the example of Christ, who "having loved his own . . . loved them to the end" (Jn 13:1), this holy mother of a family remained heroically faithful to the commitment she made on the day of her marriage. The extreme sacrifice she sealed with her life testifies that only those who have the courage to give of themselves totally to God and to others are able to fulfill themselves.

—Pope John Paul II
From the canonization Mass
for Saint Gianna Molla

Preview

In the next lesson, the students' understanding of the material covered in this chapter and unit will be reviewed and assessed. There will be a quiz and unit test.

Chapter Eight: In the Heart of the Family
Review and Assessment

Aims

The students' understanding of the material covered in this chapter will be reviewed and assessed.

Materials

- Quiz 8, Appendix, p. A-10

Optional:
- "Now thank we all our God," *Adoremus Hymnal*, #607

Review and Enrichment

1. The students should be able to explain how the family is an image of the Blessed Trinity.

2. The students should understand the duties of children and parents.

3. The students should know that husbands and wives vow to be open to children and to raise them in the Faith. At Baptism, parents again promise to raise their children in the Faith.

4. The students should understand (be able to define and give examples of) the following words: authority, honor, obey, respect, duties, responsibility.

5. The students should understand how roles change as the children get older and as parents age.

6. The students should understand the importance of the family in society.

7. The students should be able to discuss why the Holy Family is a model for all families.

Name: _____

In the Heart of the Family   **Quiz 8**

Part I: Answer the following in complete sentences.

1. What duties do parents have?
   Parents have the duty to maintain good order in the home, to provide food and clothing, to educate, and to tend to the welfare of each of their children.

2. What does it mean to honor?
   To honor means to hold in high regard, to respect, and to love.

3. How do the roles of care giving change as parents and children get older?
   Those who honor their parents will look after the needs of their parents as they grow old.

4. What must unite a family and make it holy?
   A strong love among all the members must unite the whole family and make it holy.

5. Who should we look to as our model for family life?
   We should look to the Holy Family as our model for family life.

Part II: Yes or No.

1. No If a child is disrespectful of his parents, is he honoring his parents?

2. Yes Does the Fourth Commandment require us to respect and obey government authorities and teachers?

3. Yes Should we pray and sacrifice for our parents?

4. Yes Do grown-ups have to respect their parents?

5. No Can a society survive if family life is not strong and healthy?

6. No Can the Christian family survive without love for God and neighbor?

7. Yes Is prayer necessary for family unity and peace?

Assess

1. Distribute the quizzes and read through them with the students to be sure they understand the questions.

2. Administer the quiz. As they hand in their work, you may orally quiz the students on the Memorization Questions from this chapter.

3. After all the quizzes have been handed in, you may wish to review the correct answers with the class.

Conclude

1. Lead the children in singing "Now thank we all our God," *Adoremus Hymnal*, #607.

2. End class by leading the students in prayer.

CHAPTER EIGHT: IN THE HEART OF THE FAMILY
ACTIVITY BOOK ANSWER KEYS

Name:_____

God's Plan for the Family

Fill in the chart below.

PARENTS' DUTIES	CHILDREN'S DUTIES
Answers will vary. Some examples: – maintain good order in the home – provide food and clothing – educate children	Answers will vary. Some examples: – love, honor, obey, and respect parents

Faith and Life Series • Grade 6 • Chapter 8 • Lesson 1   29

Name:_____

In the Heart of the Family

The Fourth Commandment tells us that our parents deserve our honor, love, and obedience. Write a brief essay on your parents or on parents in general, explaining why they deserve respect. You may want to mention some of the trials, sacrifices, responsibilities, and obligations involved in being a parent.

Answers will vary. _____

_____

_____

_____

_____

_____

_____

_____

_____

_____

_____

_____

_____

_____

30   *Faith and Life Series • Grade 6 • Chapter 8 • Lesson 2*

Name:_____

Honor Thy Father and Thy Mother

Answer the following questions in complete sentences.

1. Write out the Fourth Commandment.
   Honor your father and mother.

2. What does the Fourth Commandment require us to do?
   The Fourth Commandment requires us to love, respect, and obey our parents and others who have authority over us.

3. What does the Fourth Commandment forbid?
   The Fourth Commandment forbids us to disobey our parents and others in legitimate authority over us.

4. Do we need the Fourth Commandment to know we have obligations toward our parents and families? Why/why not?
   No. We would not even exist without our parents, so even without the commandment we should see that we have certain obligations toward them.

5. What does a child receive from his parents?
   Answers will vary. Most importantly, a child receives life from his parents.

6. What does "honor" mean?
   Honor means to hold in high regard, to respect, and to love.

7. Does this commandment also require you to honor other people?
   Yes. The commandment requires us to honor those in legitimate authority over us.

8. Can children be a source of grace for their parents? How?
   Yes. Answers will vary as to how.

Faith and Life Series • Grade 6 • Chapter 8 • Lesson 3   31

Name:_____

The Holy Family

Answer the following questions in complete sentences.

1. Name the three members of the Holy Family.
   Mary, Joseph and Jesus.

2. Can they be models for today's families?
   Yes.

3. What did Mary do for the Holy Family?
   Answers will vary.

4. What can today's mothers do to follow Mary's example?
   Answers will vary.

5. What did Joseph do for the Holy Family?
   Answers will vary.

6. What can today's fathers do to follow Joseph's example?
   Answers will vary.

7. What did Jesus do in the Holy Family?
   Answers will vary.

8. How can you follow Jesus' example in your family life?
   Answers will vary.

32   *Faith and Life Series • Grade 6 • Chapter 8 • Lesson 4*

TEACHER'S NOTES

UNIT TWO TEST
CHAPTERS 5–8

> ### CHAPTER FIVE: THE HOLY NAME
> ### CHAPTER SIX: THE LORD'S DAY
> ### CHAPTER SEVEN: THE CROSS AND TRUE RICHES
> ### CHAPTER EIGHT: IN THE HEART OF THE FAMILY

Aims

The students' understanding of the material covered in this unit will be reviewed and assessed.

Materials

• Unit 2 Test, Appendix, pp. A-11 and A-12

Assess

1. Distribute the unit tests and read through them with the students to be sure they understand the questions.

2. Administer the test.

3. After all the tests have been handed in, you may wish to review the correct answers with the class.

Name: _____

Unit 2 Test   **Chapters 5–8**

Part I: Yes or No.

1. <u>Yes</u> Must we be reverent toward God's most Holy Name?

2. <u>Yes</u> Is God's name "I AM WHO I AM"?

3. <u>Yes</u> Is blasphemy the verbal abuse or scorn toward God or by extension to the Blessed Virgin Mary or the saints?

4. <u>No</u> Are cursing and blasphemy the same thing?

5. <u>Yes</u> Must we be respectful while we are in a church?

6. <u>No</u> Is it permissible to take an oath without serious reason?

7. <u>Yes</u> Does an oath call on God to witness to the truth of what we are saying?

8. <u>Yes</u> Is a vow in religion a promise made for a religious reason?

9. <u>Yes</u> Do religious brothers and sisters vow poverty, chastity, and obedience?

10. <u>Yes</u> Do married people make a vow of fidelity to each other?

Part II: Answer in complete sentences.

1. What is the Second Commandment and what does it mean?
   <u>The Second Commandment is "You shall not take the name of the Lord your God in vain." This means that we must not disrespect the Holy Name of God or the saints or holy things.</u>

2. What is an oath?
   <u>An oath calls on God to witness to the truth of what we are saying. (Or, An oath is calling upon God as witness for what is declared or promised.)</u>

3. Why do Christians celebrate the Lord's Day on Sunday?
   <u>Christians celebrate the Lord's Day on Sunday because Jesus rose from the dead on Sunday.</u>

4. List five ways to keep the Lord's Day holy.
   <u>Answers will vary, but should include going to Mass and resting from unnecessary work.</u>

Name: _____

Unit 2 Test (continued)

5. Which commandment requires us to give one day a week to God? Write out this commandment.
   <u>The Third Commandment requires us to give one day a week to God. "Remember to keep holy the Lord's Day."</u>

6. What are we commanded not to do on Sundays and Holy Days?
   <u>We are commanded not to do any unnecessary work on Sundays and Holy Days.</u>

7. What are three ways of practicing self-denial?
   <u>Answers will vary.</u>

8. What are the two penitential seasons of the Church?
   <u>The two penitential seasons of the Church are Advent and Lent.</u>

9. On which days does the Church require us to fast?
   <u>The Church requires us to fast on Ash Wednesday and Good Friday.</u>

10. What does it mean when the Church requires us to fast?
    <u>On days the Church requires us to fast, we are to eat only one full meal a day; two smaller meals may be eaten, but those taken together should not equal another full meal.</u>

11. What age group is bound to fasting?
    <u>Those who are eighteen to sixty years old are bound to fasting.</u>

Part III: Match the date with the corresponding Holy Day of Obligation.

<u>d</u> All Saints   a. January 1
<u>f</u> Christmas   b. forty days after Easter
<u>c</u> Assumption   c. August 15
<u>e</u> Immaculate Conception   d. November 1
<u>b</u> Ascension   e. December 8
<u>a</u> Mary, Mother of God   f. December 25

TEACHER'S NOTES

CHAPTER NINE
CITIZENSHIP—RIGHTS AND DUTIES

Catechism of the Catholic Church References

Abortion: 2270–75, 2319, 2322–23
Authorities in Civil Society: 2234–46, 2254–57
Duties of Civil Authorities: 2235–37, 2254
Duties of Citizens: 2238–43, 2255–56
Social Justice: 2420–25

Society and State: 1897, 1899, 1918–21, 2338
The Political Community and the Church: 2244–46, 2257
Justice and Solidarity among Nations: 2437–42, 2461
Martyrdom: 2473–74, 2506
Taxes: 2436

Scripture References

Jesus' Respect for Civil Authority: Mt 22:17–21; 28:18–20;
Mk 10:2–9; Jn 19:1–8

Summary of Lesson Content

Lesson 1

Man is bound to the legitimate authority of the state, whose authority comes from God.

The state has the authority to make just laws for its citizens, in accordance with divine law.

Lesson 2

The state should never demand something that is against God's law.

Man is always obliged to follow God's law.

There are different kinds of governments and there can be several legitimate and good ways to govern a nation.

Lesson 3

Citizens have rights and duties. We must obey all just laws and regulations, pay taxes, support the government, and, when necessary, defend our nation.

Patriotism is the virtue of love for one's country. It is dedication to the welfare of the whole country and its citizens.

"Legal" and "moral" are not interchangeable terms.

Lesson 4

As Christians, we must be concerned for all of God's children. Many people and nations are in need of aid.

Wealthier and stronger countries have a responsibility to help the poorer and weaker nations and to uphold the dignity of all people.

We should pray for our country and its leaders.

CHAPTER NINE: CITIZENSHIP—RIGHTS AND DUTIES
LESSON ONE: THE STATE

Aims

The students will learn that man is bound to the legitimate authority of the state, whose authority comes from God.

The students will learn that the state has the authority to make just laws for its citizens, in accordance with divine law.

Materials

- *Activity Book*, p. 33

Optional:
- "Christ is made the sure foundation," *Adoremus Hymnal*, #561

Begin

As Catholics, we are members of God's family. We are also members of our parents' families. We are members of other communities: schools, clubs, teams, organizations, and the state. By the state, we mean a community gathered under civil authority or a common government. We must respect the authority of the state over us, as all authority comes from God. We must, therefore, keep just laws and be good citizens.

Develop

1. Read paragraphs 1 and 2 from the student text.

2. Review the Pledge of Allegiance. We are "under God." God's authority is supreme. He is the Creator and we the creatures. His law is written on our hearts (this is natural law). His law, however, is upheld and interpreted in different communities. The Church has authority to uphold the law (which we will learn about in the next chapter). Civil governments also create and uphold laws. For governments to use their authority well, their laws and authority should correspond to God's law. When they deviate from God's law, governments abuse their authority. Have the students give examples of this principle.

3. Though Jesus is God, he was bound to the authority of Mary and Joseph. Jesus also submitted himself to civil authority. Look up the following texts: Mt 22:17–21; 28:18–20; Mk 10:2–9; Jn 19:1–8.

4. Discuss the virtue of patriotism. True patriotism is the love of one's country and willingness to serve the common good. We should all have pride in the good qualities of our country. What are some of the good things that we have in our country? Freedom of religion, laws to protect the innocent, etc. How is patriotism expressed? (We show patriotism by honoring our flag and national anthem, serving in the armed forces, etc.) You may also think of ways that our country acknowledges God as its authority (e.g., "In God we trust," "under God" in the Pledge of Allegiance).

5. You may discuss various ways of selecting a government and governing a nation. The Church has taught that there are several good ways to govern. You may discuss how our government is elected. We have a Christian duty to vote for candidates who will support God's law.

Reinforce

1. Have the students work on *Activity Book* p. 33 (see *Teacher's Manual*, p. 113).

2. Provide the students time to work on the Memorization Questions from this chapter.

3. Have the students research political candidates, and discuss their good qualities and the qualities we should want to support with our votes.

Conclude

1. Teach the students to sing "Christ is made the sure foundation," *Adoremus Hymnal*, #561.

2. End class by leading the students in a prayer for our country.

CHAPTER 9

Citizenship–
Rights and Duties

"So then you are no longer strangers and sojourners, but you are
fellow citizens with the saints and members of the household of God."

Ephesians 2:19

As members of a family, we depend on others and they depend on us. This dependence of people on each other exists in society too. We are members of a state as well as a family. A state is a society of people united under a common government or authority. Our parents exercise a certain rightful authority over us, and so does the state. It is part of human nature for men to live together and to form societies with governments that exercise authority. Like our parents' authority, the state's authority comes from God. Saint Paul tells us: "Let every person be subject to the governing authorities. For there is no authority except from God.... Therefore he who resists the authorities resists what God has appointed" (Rom 13:1–2).

The state has the authority to make just laws for its citizens. The purpose of the state is to promote what is truly good for all members of its society. We call this the common good. The common good includes all the things in a society that allow people as individuals or in groups to have what they need in order to be truly happy. Jesus never denied the role of the government. When he was asked if people should pay taxes to the emperor Caesar, Jesus

said, "Render therefore to Caesar the things that are Caesar's, and to God the things that are God's" (Mt 22:21). In this way, Jesus taught that we have things we owe to God and things we owe to the state (Caesar).

The state should never demand something of us that is against God's law. If it does, it is denying its own authority, since that authority comes from God. The state is supposed to use its authority as God intends. This use of authority includes respecting God's law, encouraging virtue, and allowing people to be free to live according to that law.

As you probably already know, there are different kinds of government. God has never told us that one particular type of government is better than another. There can be several legitimate and good ways to govern a nation. The important thing is that the government respects and promotes the rights and well-being of all the people for the sake of the common good.

Good Citizens

Just as the state has certain rights and duties, so do we as citizens. As Christians we must be

46

good citizens, obeying all just laws and regulations, paying taxes to support the government, and when necessary defending our nation from attack.

Patriotism is the virtue of love of one's country. This virtue is in keeping with Christianity because it is natural and good for us to love our country. But patriotism is more than flag-waving. It is dedication to the promotion of the true welfare of the whole country and its citizens.

As citizens, we should be concerned about the health and well-being of our society. We should work to establish just conditions that allow all people to have what they have a right to have. If there is an unjust practice or an immoral law, then we must do all we can to overturn it. We must work within the structure of our government to establish justice for all and to make that justice secure.

Just because the state declares an action to be legal does not mean the action is morally good. Sometimes things that the state declares "legal" really violate natural law and the rights of others. It was once "legal" to enslave people

of a certain race, but that did not make it right or just. It is wrong to buy and sell people as if they were property. All human beings have the same basic dignity as persons. This means that they have rights, which the state is supposed to protect, and which it may not take away.

We have today the grave evil of "legalized" abortion. The state has declared a seriously immoral and unjust act to be acceptable and "within the law." It has declared it "legal" to take the life of an unborn child, even though the innocent child has the same basic God-given right to life as every other human being. We may not support such a declaration of the state because it is contrary to God's law and the state's duty to protect the rights of all people. We should do all in our power to change such a law or other laws that violate people's basic rights. "We must obey God rather than men" (Acts 5:29).

Across Boundaries

As followers of Christ we must not think only of our own nation. We must be concerned about the needs of all people. Many people and

47

nations are oppressed and deprived of basic human rights by severe poverty or by lack of freedom. Just as there are different forms of good governments, so there are governments that are bad and threaten the well-being of their citizens. Wealthier and stronger

countries have a responsibility to help these oppressed nations. As citizens we must encourage our government to do what is possible to help people in need.

Above all we must remember to pray for our country and its leaders.

> **Q. 37** *Why must we obey those in authority?*
> We must obey those in authority because this authority comes from God. To oppose it is to oppose the authority of God (CCC 2197, 2234).
>
> **Q. 38** *What must we do if men in authority command us to violate God's law?*
> If men in authority command us to violate God's law, we must obey God rather than men (CCC 2242).
>
> **Q. 39** *What is the duty of a citizen?*
> The duty of a citizen is to contribute to the good of society by obeying all just laws, paying taxes, voting, and defending one's own country (CCC 2239–40).

48

Preview

In the next lesson, the students will learn about obeying God's authority always.

CHAPTER NINE: CITIZENSHIP—RIGHTS AND DUTIES
LESSON TWO: SERVING GOD FIRST

Aims

The students will learn that the state should never demand something that is against God's law.

They will learn that man is always obliged to follow God's law.

They will learn that there are different kinds of governments and there can be several legitimate and good ways to govern a nation.

Materials

- *Activity Book*, p. 34

Optional:
- "Christ is made the sure foundation," *Adoremus Hymnal*, #561

Begin

Review various levels of authority: the authority of our parents, teachers, school, city, state, nation, and God. Review that all authority comes from God. To be used well, authority should never demand something that is against God's laws. We must know God's laws in order to be good citizens and to respect the true authority of our government. We must know God's laws in order to establish good governments which follow God's laws.

Develop

1. Read paragraphs 3 and 4 and page 49 (see *Teacher's Manual*, p. 111) from the student text.

2. The government can impose laws upon man. It should impose just laws that respect the good of the people. Laws should encourage virtues, allowing people to live in true freedom and order. There is often confusion as to what is meant by true freedom. Let us consider the definitions of freedom and free will. Free will is the ability to choose to do good or evil. Freedom is the assent to God's will in doing the true and the good. We are only free when we act in justice and work for the good. Even though we have the ability to choose to do evil things, we will not be truly free unless we choose good actions.

3. Next, explain that if the government established laws contrary to God's laws, it would be an abuse of power and authority, since God's laws and authority are the basis of all authority. Can the students think of an example where this is the case? In the United States, abortion is an example. It is legal to kill an innocent baby before it is born. This is contrary to God's laws, so this law should not be enforced. In Holland, legal euthanasia allows the sick and elderly to be killed. God's law demands that these people receive care.

4. Discuss things that are necessary for political freedom. For instance, are they willing to give up:
- Speech
- Religion
- Property
- Equality of the sexes under law
- Equality of races
- Right to keep and bear arms

5. Have the students write prayers, thanking God for their freedom and asking God to uphold these freedoms.

Reinforce

1. Have the students work on *Activity Book* p. 34 (see *Teacher's Manual*, p. 113).

2. The students may study other governments and various struggles for political freedom. Further, they should become familiar with Church teaching regarding various freedoms and human dignity throughout the world (see *Teacher's Manual*, p. 103 for references).

3. The students should work on the Memorization Questions from this chapter (see *Teacher's Manual*, p. 109).

Conclude

1. Lead the students in singing "Christ is made the sure foundation," *Adoremus Hymnal*, #561.

2. End class by leading the students in a prayer for our nation.

Citizenship–
Rights and Duties

"So then you are no longer strangers and sojourners, but you are fellow citizens with the saints and members of the household of God."

Ephesians 2:19

As members of a family, we depend on others and they depend on us. This dependence of people on each other exists in society too. We are members of a state as well as a family. A state is a society of people united under a common government or authority. Our parents exercise a certain rightful authority over us, and so does the state. It is part of human nature for men to live together and to form societies with governments that exercise authority. Like our parents' authority, the state's authority comes from God. Saint Paul tells us: "Let every person be subject to the governing authorities. For there is no authority except from God.... Therefore he who resists the authorities resists what God has appointed" (Rom 13:1–2).

The state has the authority to make just laws for its citizens. The purpose of the state is to promote what is truly good for all members of its society. We call this the common good. The common good includes all the things in a society that allow people as individuals or in groups to have what they need in order to be truly happy. Jesus never denied the role of the government. When he was asked if people should pay taxes to the emperor Caesar, Jesus said, "Render therefore to Caesar the things that are Caesar's, and to God the things that are God's" (Mt 22:21). In this way, Jesus taught that we have things we owe to God and things we owe to the state (Caesar).

The state should never demand something of us that is against God's law. If it does, it is denying its own authority, since that authority comes from God. The state is supposed to use its authority as God intends. This use of authority includes respecting God's law, encouraging virtue, and allowing people to be free to live according to that law.

As you probably already know, there are different kinds of government. God has never told us that one particular type of government is better than another. There can be several legitimate and good ways to govern a nation. The important thing is that the government respects and promotes the rights and well-being of all the people for the sake of the common good.

Good Citizens

Just as the state has certain rights and duties, so do we as citizens. As Christians we must be good citizens, obeying all just laws and regulations, paying taxes to support the government, and when necessary defending our nation from attack.

Patriotism is the virtue of love of one's country. This virtue is in keeping with Christianity because it is natural and good for us to love our country. But patriotism is more than flag-waving. It is dedication to the promotion of the true welfare of the whole country and its citizens.

As citizens, we should be concerned about the health and well-being of our society. We should work to establish just conditions that allow all people to have what they have a right to have. If there is an unjust practice or an immoral law, then we must do all we can to overturn it. We must work within the structure of our government to establish justice for all and to make that justice secure.

Just because the state declares an action to be legal does not mean the action is morally good. Sometimes things that the state declares "legal" really violate natural law and the rights of others. It was once "legal" to enslave people of a certain race, but that did not make it right or just. It is wrong to buy and sell people as if they were property. All human beings have the same basic dignity as persons. This means that they have rights, which the state is supposed to protect, and which it may not take away.

We have today the grave evil of "legalized" abortion. The state has declared a seriously immoral and unjust act to be acceptable and "within the law." It has declared it "legal" to take the life of an unborn child, even though the innocent child has the same basic God-given right to life as every other human being. We may not support such a declaration of the state because it is contrary to God's law and the state's duty to protect the rights of all people. We should do all in our power to change such a law or other laws that violate people's basic rights. "We must obey God rather than men" (Acts 5:29).

Across Boundaries

As followers of Christ we must not think only of our own nation. We must be concerned about the needs of all people. Many people and

SAINT THOMAS MORE

Some saints had lives of quiet devotion, monastic industry, or great leadership within the Church. Saint Thomas More was a saint who served in the public life of his country, England. After studying for many years at Oxford, gaining a reputation as a respected attorney, and authoring widely popular works of political literature, such as his classic, *Utopia*, Saint Thomas More was appointed Lord Chancellor of England by King Henry VIII. As long as the king recognized his duty to God and his Church, Saint Thomas was able to serve both God and country with steadfast loyalty. However, in 1531 King Henry VIII began to split with Rome. He attempted to have himself named "Protector and Supreme Head of the Church of England." In doing so, King Henry broke with the Holy Father and the true Church and demanded that Saint Thomas More do the same. For several years, Saint Thomas More openly opposed the King's move and finally Henry had him imprisoned in the Tower of London where he stayed for fifteen months. On July 6, 1535, Saint Thomas More was condemned to death for refusing to recognize the king as head of the Church of England. Before losing his head, Saint Thomas declared: "I die the king's good servant, but God's first."

Let every person be subject to the governing authorities. For there is no authority except from God, and those that exist have been instituted by God.

—Romans 13:1

Preview

In the next lesson, the students will learn what it means to be a good citizen.

CHAPTER NINE: CITIZENSHIP—RIGHTS AND DUTIES
LESSON THREE: GOOD CITIZENS

Aims

The students will learn that citizens have rights and duties. We must obey all just laws and regulations, pay taxes, support the government, and, when necessary, defend our nation.

They will learn that patriotism is the virtue of love for one's country. It is dedication to the welfare of the whole country and its citizens.

They will learn that "legal" and "moral" are not interchangeable terms.

Materials

- *Activity Book*, p. 35

Optional:
- "Christ is made the sure foundation," *Adoremus Hymnal*, #561

Begin

Lead the students in a discussion about citizenship. The following questions may facilitate the discussion:
- What is a citizen?
- What are we citizens of?
- How do we become citizens?
- Can we lose our citizenship?
- What should we be concerned about as good citizens? How should we act?

Develop

1. Read paragraphs 5–9 from the student text.

2. Review what the state's duties are and what a citizen's duties are. (See box on the facing page for assistance.)

3. Review the virtue of patriotism. There are extreme exercises of patriotism that exaggerate one's duty to country and place it before our duty to God. This is a false form of patriotism. True patriotism compels citizens to work for the true welfare of the whole country and its citizens and to concern themselves with the rights and welfare of other countries.

4. As good citizens, we must obey just laws. We are always to follow God's laws; therefore, if the state has a law that is unjust, we must instead follow God's Laws. Christians must use their influence to make a just state. If there is an unjust law, Christians have the duty to work to change it. For

example, at one time, it was legal to have slaves. This is unjust, and the law was changed. Nonetheless, there are still many ways that injustice exists today. What can we do to change these things?

5. Review the difference between legal and moral. *Legal* means "permitted by law." *Moral* means "good in the eyes of God." Legal and moral are not the same thing. For example, abortion is legal, but it is not moral. We must, as Christians, strive to overturn this unjust law.

6. Have the students learn about true love of neighbor. Though we are not all the same, we are all made in the image of God and deserve love and respect of other people. Jesus said, "Love one another as I have loved you." Help the students to foster love for people who are different. Some behaviors to address might include bullying and teasing those who are different.

Reinforce

1. Have the students work on *Activity Book* p. 35 (see *Teacher's Manual*, p. 113).

2. Have the students work on the Memorization Questions from this chapter.

3. Have the students learn about differences in people. They should know that all people are our neighbors and we are called to love them (e.g., those of a different race, religion, ability, those who are poor).

Conclude

1. Lead the students in singing "Christ is made the sure foundation," *Adoremus Hymnal*, #561.

2. End class by leading the students in a prayer for our nation.

CHAPTER 9

Citizenship–
Rights and Duties

"So then you are no longer strangers and sojourners, but you are fellow citizens with the saints and members of the household of God."

Ephesians 2:19

As members of a family, we depend on others and they depend on us. This dependence of people on each other exists in society too. We are members of a state as well as a family. A state is a society of people united under a common government or authority. Our parents exercise a certain rightful authority over us, and so does the state. It is part of human nature for men to live together and to form societies with governments that exercise authority. Like our parents' authority, the state's authority comes from God. Saint Paul tells us: "Let every person be subject to the governing authorities. For there is no authority except from God.... Therefore he who resists the authorities resists what God has appointed" (Rom 13:1–2).

The state has the authority to make just laws for its citizens. The purpose of the state is to promote what is truly good for all members of its society. We call this the common good. The common good includes all the things in a society that allow people as individuals or in groups to have what they need in order to be truly happy. Jesus never denied the role of the government. When he was asked if people should pay taxes to the emperor Caesar, Jesus

said, "Render therefore to Caesar the things that are Caesar's, and to God the things that are God's" (Mt 22:21). In this way, Jesus taught that we have things we owe to God and things we owe to the state (Caesar).

The state should never demand something of us that is against God's law. If it does, it is denying its own authority, since that authority comes from God. The state is supposed to use its authority as God intends. This use of authority includes respecting God's law, encouraging virtue, and allowing people to be free to live according to that law.

As you probably already know, there are different kinds of government. God has never told us that one particular type of government is better than another. There can be several legitimate and good ways to govern a nation. The important thing is that the government respects and promotes the rights and well-being of all the people for the sake of the common good.

Good Citizens

Just as the state has certain rights and duties, so do we as citizens. As Christians we must be

46

good citizens, obeying all just laws and regulations, paying taxes to support the government, and when necessary defending our nation from attack.

Patriotism is the virtue of love of one's country. This virtue is in keeping with Christianity because it is natural and good for us to love our country. But patriotism is more than flag-waving. It is dedication to the promotion of the true welfare of the whole country and its citizens.

As citizens, we should be concerned about the health and well-being of our society. We should work to establish just conditions that allow all people to have what they have a right to have. If there is an unjust practice or an immoral law, then we must do all we can to overturn it. We must work within the structure of our government to establish justice for all and to make that justice secure.

Just because the state declares an action to be legal does not mean the action is morally good. Sometimes things that the state declares "legal" really violate natural law and the rights of others. It was once "legal" to enslave people

of a certain race, but that did not make it right or just. It is wrong to buy and sell people as if they were property. All human beings have the same basic dignity as persons. This means that they have rights, which the state is supposed to protect, and which it may not take away.

We have today the grave evil of "legalized" abortion. The state has declared a seriously immoral and unjust act to be acceptable and "within the law." It has declared it "legal" to take the life of an unborn child, even though the innocent child has the same basic God-given right to life as every other human being. We may not support such a declaration of the state because it is contrary to God's law and the state's duty to protect the rights of all people. We should do all in our power to change such a law or other laws that violate people's basic rights. "We must obey God rather than men" (Acts 5:29).

Across Boundaries

As followers of Christ we must not think only of our own nation. We must be concerned about the needs of all people. Many people and

47

---

nations are oppressed and deprived of basic human rights by severe poverty or by lack of freedom. Just as there are different forms of good governments, so there are governments that are bad and threaten the well-being of their citizens. Wealthier and stronger

countries have a responsibility to help these oppressed nations. As citizens we must encourage our government to do what is possible to help people in need.

Above all we must remember to pray for our country and its leaders.

Q. 37 *Why must we obey those in authority?*
We must obey those in authority because this authority comes from God. To oppose it is to oppose the authority of God (CCC 2197, 2234).

Q. 38 *What must we do if men in authority command us to violate God's law?*
If men in authority command us to violate God's law, we must obey God rather than men (CCC 2242).

Q. 39 *What is the duty of a citizen?*
The duty of a citizen is to contribute to the good of society by obeying all just laws, paying taxes, voting, and defending one's own country (CCC 2239–40).

48

DUTIES OF CITIZEN AND STATE

The *Catechism of the Catholic Church* helps us to define the duties of the citizen and of the state:

State:
- Make laws that accord with natural law (2235)
- Preserve the welfare of the community (2236)
- Promote justice (2236)
- Serve the common good (2237)
- Uphold human dignity of citizens (2237)

Citizen:
- Respect state officials (2238)
- Serve the country for common good (2239)
- Pay taxes, vote, defend country (2240)
- Welcome foreigners (2241)
- Refuse obedience to the state in directives that violate the moral law (2242)

Preview

In the next lesson, the students will learn about their Christian responsibilities throughout the world.

CHAPTER NINE. CITIZENSHIP—RIGHTS AND DUTIES
LESSON FOUR: CHRIST'S FAMILY

Aims

The students will learn that, as Christians, we must be concerned for all of God's children. Many people and nations are in need of aid.

They will learn that wealthier and stronger countries have a responsibility to help the poorer and weaker nations and to uphold the dignity of all people.

They will learn that we should pray for our country and its leaders.

Materials

• *Activity Book*, p. 36

• Newspapers/selected articles

Optional:
• "Christ is made the sure foundation," *Adoremus Hymnal*, #561

Begin

Begin class by having the students select an article from a newspaper. The article chosen should address the needs of people from around the world. You may choose to select articles in advance for the children to read. Give the students time to read these articles.

Develop

1. Have the students finish reading the chapter.

2. Discuss the obligation of wealthier and stronger nations to help, support, and defend poor and needy nations. We must do this because we are all God's children. The blessings that we have are from God and are to be shared with others (this sharing is called stewardship). Ask how we can help people around the world who:
   • Do not have food, water, clothes
   • Are dying from diseases for which we have cures or vaccines
   • Are poor and have no means of income
   • Are being unjustly invaded by another nation
   • Do not yet have knowledge of the Faith

3. As Catholics, we belong to a culture that goes far beyond the borders of our own country. We are united in faith with people from every part of the world. Because we are Catholic, we should be concerned with the well-being of all people, no matter what their country. Have the students list ways that they can help other peoples or have them give reports on the Church in other countries.

4. Have the students read their articles, and work on Activity Book, p. 36 (see *Teacher's Manual*, p. 113). The students should make presentations on their articles for the other students in the class.

5. Have the students work on a social justice project. They may do a fundraiser or a collection for a developing country. They should pray for people in need. The students may write letters to pen pals, children in another church or in a different country.

7. The students should study missionaries in the world.

Reinforce

1. Have the students work on *Activity Book* p. 36 (see *Teacher's Manual*, p. 113).

2. The students should work on the Memorization Questions from this chapter and study for the quiz.

3. The students may study the Church's missionary work in a developing nation.

4. The students should do a project to support the missions, such as a collection of necessary items.

Conclude

1. Lead the students in singing "Christ is made the sure foundation," *Adoremus Hymnal*, #561.

2. End class by leading the students in praying for our nation.

good citizens, obeying all just laws and regulations, paying taxes to support the government, and when necessary defending our nation from attack.

Patriotism is the virtue of love of one's country. This virtue is in keeping with Christianity because it is natural and good for us to love our country. But patriotism is more than flag-waving. It is dedication to the promotion of the true welfare of the whole country and its citizens.

As citizens, we should be concerned about the health and well-being of our society. We should work to establish just conditions that allow all people to have what they have a right to have. If there is an unjust practice or an immoral law, then we must do all we can to overturn it. We must work within the structure of our government to establish justice for all and to make that justice secure.

Just because the state declares an action to be legal does not mean the action is morally good. Sometimes things that the state declares "legal" really violate natural law and the rights of others. It was once "legal" to enslave people

of a certain race, but that did not make it right or just. It is wrong to buy and sell people as if they were property. All human beings have the same basic dignity as persons. This means that they have rights, which the state is supposed to protect, and which it may not take away.

We have today the grave evil of "legalized" abortion. The state has declared a seriously immoral and unjust act to be acceptable and "within the law." It has declared it "legal" to take the life of an unborn child, even though the innocent child has the same basic God-given right to life as every other human being. We may not support such a declaration of the state because it is contrary to God's law and the state's duty to protect the rights of all people. We should do all in our power to change such a law or other laws that violate people's basic rights. "We must obey God rather than men" (Acts 5:29).

Across Boundaries

As followers of Christ we must not think only of our own nation. We must be concerned about the needs of all people. Many people and nations are oppressed and deprived of basic human rights by severe poverty or by lack of freedom. Just as there are different forms of good governments, so there are governments that are bad and threaten the well-being of their citizens. Wealthier and stronger countries have a responsibility to help these oppressed nations. As citizens we must encourage our government to do what is possible to help people in need.

Above all we must remember to pray for our country and its leaders.

47

Q. 37 *Why must we obey those in authority?*
We must obey those in authority because this authority comes from God. To oppose it is to oppose the authority of God (CCC 2197, 2234).

Q. 38 *What must we do if men in authority command us to violate God's law?*
If men in authority command us to violate God's law, we must obey God rather than men (CCC 2242).

Q. 39 *What is the duty of a citizen?*
The duty of a citizen is to contribute to the good of society by obeying all just laws, paying taxes, voting, and defending one's own country (CCC 2239–40).

Saint Thomas More

In the year 1535 Sir Thomas More was beheaded by order of the king of England and his court of law. Thomas More had been a friend to King Henry the Eighth and had even held the office of Lord Chancellor, second in power to the king. What had Sir Thomas More done that caused his one-time friend and ruler to have him put to death? He had chosen to obey God's law rather than man's. King Henry the Eighth had declared himself to be the supreme head of the Church in England. Thomas More knew that such a declaration was a violation of the law of God, and so he would not accept it, even if his refusal meant death.

Saint Thomas More had been a great statesman and had dedicated himself to the service of his king and country. But he knew that God's law was above the King's, and so he was willing to die "the King's good servant, but God's first." For suffering this martyrdom, Thomas More has been declared a saint by the Church.

49

HELPING OTHER NATIONS

According to the *Catechism of the Catholic Church*, wealthier, developed nations have a duty to the developing world. This duty can be realized through solidarity demonstrated through direct aid in cases of disaster or emergency, and through political assistance when developing nations struggle to attain civil and religious freedom.

CCC 2439: *Rich nations* have a grave moral responsibility toward those which are unable to ensure the means of their development by themselves or have been prevented from doing so by tragic historical events. It is a duty in solidarity and charity; it is also an obligation of justice. . . .

Preview

In the next lesson, the students' understanding of the material covered in this chapter will be reviewed and assessed.

CHAPTER NINE: CITIZENSHIP—RIGHTS AND DUTIES
REVIEW AND ASSESSMENT

Aims

The students' understanding of the material covered in this chapter will be reviewed and assessed.

Materials

- Quiz 9, Appendix, p. A-13

Optional:
- "Christ is made the sure foundation," *Adoremus Hymnal*, #561

Review and Enrichment

1. The students should understand the duties of the state and of its citizens.

2. The students should be familiar with Saint Thomas More.

3. The difference between legal and moral should be understood. The students should know that man must follow just laws, in accordance with God's teachings.

4. The students should understand that we are responsible for people all over the world. We must exercise good stewardship. They should understand the principles of social justice, which call us to stand against oppression, poverty, and injustice in the world.

5. The students should be familiar with the missionary works of the Church throughout the world.

Name: _____

Citizenship—Rights and Duties   Quiz 9

Part I: Fill in the blanks.

1. A <u>state</u> is a society of people united under a common government or authority.
2. The <u>common</u> <u>good</u> includes all the things in a society that allow people to have what they need in order to be truly happy.
3. <u>Patriotism</u> is the virtue of love of one's country.
4. Saint Paul says, "There is no authority except from <u>God</u>."
5. The government is supposed to use its <u>authority</u> as God intends.

Part II: Yes or No.

1. <u>Yes</u> Does the government exercise a rightful authority over us?
2. <u>Yes</u> Does the government's authority come from God?
3. <u>No</u> Is it acceptable for the government to demand something of us that is against God's law?
4. <u>Yes</u> Should the government respect God's law?
5. <u>Yes</u> Is there more than one kind of legitimate government?
6. <u>Yes</u> Is it important for the government to respect and promote the rights and well-being of all the people?
7. <u>Yes</u> Is patriotism in keeping with Christianity?
8. <u>Yes</u> Does patriotism include the promotion of the true welfare of the whole country and its citizens?
9. <u>No</u> If the government declares an action to be legal, does that mean that the action is moral?
10. <u>No</u> Is it permissible to support immoral laws?

Part III: Compare the duties of the government with those of citizens.

DUTIES OF THE GOVERNMENT	DUTIES OF CITIZENS
— Promote what is truly good for its citizens (the common good) allowing people to have what they need in order to be truly happy	— Obey all just laws and regulations
— Make just laws	— Be concerned for the health and well-being of society
— Encourage virtues and sound values	— Pay taxes
— Allow people to live according to God's laws	— Defend the nation from attack when necessary
	— Work to have unjust laws or laws that violate people's rights changed

Faith and Life Series • Grade 6 • Appendix A   A-13

Assess

1. Distribute the quizzes and read through them with the students to be sure they understand the questions.

2. Administer the quiz. As they hand in their work, you may orally quiz the students on the Memorization Questions from this chapter.

3. After all the quizzes have been handed in, you may wish to review the correct answers with the class.

Conclude

1. Lead the students in singing "Christ is made the sure foundation," *Adoremus Hymnal*, #561.

2. End class by leading the students in a prayer for our nation.

CHAPTER NINE: CITIZENSHIP—RIGHTS AND DUTIES
ACTIVITY BOOK ANSWER KEYS

Name:_____

The State

Answer the following questions in complete sentences.

1. Is it good to be a member of a community?
   Yes.

2. Do people in communities have to work together?
   Yes.

3. Who has authority over us?
   Our parents and the state have authority over us.

4. From whom does the state receive its authority?
   The state receives its authority from God.

5. What did Saint Paul teach about this?
   Saint Paul says that if we resist the authorities we resist what God has appointed.

6. What is the purpose of the state?
   The purpose of the state is to promote what is truly good for all its members.

7. Should the state ever demand something that is contrary to God's law?
   No.

8. If it did, what would the state be doing?
   It would deny its own authority because that authority comes from God.

Faith and Life Series • Grade 6 • Chapter 9 • Lesson 1

33

Name:_____

Saint Thomas More

Answer the following questions in complete sentences.

1. When did Sir Thomas More live?
   More lived in the sixteenth century (or 1535, 1500's, etc.).

2. Describe the office Sir Thomas More held.
   Sir Thomas More was Lord Chancellor. He was second in power only to the king.

3. Name the king who reigned in England at the time of Sir Thomas More.
   King Henry the Eighth reigned in England.

4. What decision did Sir Thomas More have to make?
   He had to choose whether to obey God's law or man's.

5. What did the king want Sir Thomas More to declare?
   The king wanted Sir Thomas More to declare that the king was the supreme head of the Church in England.

6. Was this right or wrong? Why?
   This was wrong because the king cannot declare himself head of the Church.

7. Whom did Sir Thomas More serve first?
   Sir Thomas More served God first.

8. What happened to him because of his decision?
   Because of his decision, he was beheaded.

9. What is it called when one lays down his life as a witness to the truth?
   This is called martyrdom.

10. What title has the Church given to Thomas More?
    The Church has given him the title of saint.

34   *Faith and Life Series • Grade 6 • Chapter 9 • Lesson 2*

Name:_____

Good Citizens

Answer the following questions in complete sentences.

1. What responsibilities do we have as citizens?
   We must be good citizens, obey all just laws and regulations, pay taxes, and defend our country when necessary.

2. What is patriotism?
   Patriotism is the virtue of love of one's country.

3. Is this virtue in keeping with Christianity?
   Yes.

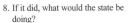

4. As citizens, what is our concern?
   We should be concerned about the health and well-being of our society.

5. Is everything that is legal also morally good?
   No.

6. Should we support immoral laws?
   No.

7. What are we to do when the government legalizes an immoral action?
   We must do all we can to overturn any decision that legalizes an immoral action.

8. Give some examples of immoral things that governments have declared legal.
   Answers will vary. Two examples given in the text are slavery and abortion.

Faith and Life Series • Grade 6 • Chapter 9 • Lesson 3   35

Name:_____

Christ's Family

Using a newspaper or magazine, answer the following questions in complete sentences.

1. As Christians, we must be concerned about the needs of all people. Find an article about a group of people in need. Write the name of that group (name of country, ethnic group, etc.).
   Answers will vary.

2. Why do these people need help?

3. What kind of help do they most need?

4. What can our country do for these people?

5. What can you do for these people?

36   *Faith and Life Series • Grade 6 • Chapter 9 • Lesson 4*

TEACHER'S NOTES

CHAPTER TEN
CHURCH AUTHORITY—OUR FATHERS IN FAITH

Catechism of the Catholic Church References

Apostolic: 857–65, 869
Apostolic Succession: 77–79, 861–62, 869
Attributes: 750, 811, 822, 825–26, 865, 875, 876, 891, 936
Catholic: 830–35, 868
Church's Hierarchical Constitution: 871–96, 934–39
Ecclesial Ministry: 874–79
Episcopal College and Its Head, the Pope: 880–87
Task of Teaching: 888–92
Task of Sanctifying: 893
Task of Governing: 894–96
Church's Origin, Foundation, and Mission: 758–69, 778
Holy: 823–29, 866
Infallible: 889–92, 2035

Mission of the Apostles: 858–60, 869
One: 813–22, 866
Pope and Bishops: Successors of Peter and the Apostles: 861–62, 880–87, 935–38
Precepts of the Church: 2041–43
Sacraments: 1113, 1131–34
Sacraments of Christ: 1114–16
Sacraments of the Church: 1117–21
Sacraments of Faith: 1122–26
Sacraments of Salvation: 1127–29
Sacraments of Eternal Life: 1130
Vicar of Christ: 424, 834

Scripture References

Peter Made Pope: Mt 16:13–20; Jn 21:14–19
Guiding Spirit of Truth: Jn 14:16–17; 15:26–27; 16:13; 1 Jn 4:6
Baptism: Mt 28:18–20
Eucharist: Mk 14:22–25

Confirmation: Jn 7:37–39; 14:26; 20:22; Acts 1:8; 2:4
Penance: Jn 20:21–23
Anointing of the Sick: Mk 6:13; Jas 5:14
Matrimony: Mt 19:4–6; Jn 2:1–11
Holy Orders: Lk 22:19; Jn 13:1–15; Acts 6:6

Summary of Lesson Content

Lesson 1

The Catholic Church was founded by Jesus Christ. The mission of the Church is to save souls and to teach all men the truths of the Faith.

Jesus is the head of the Church and has given his authority to the Pope. The Pope and the bishops in union with him govern the Church.

The Church governs her people, as seen in the precepts of the Church.

Lesson 3

It is through the Sacraments that the Church sanctifies her members.

The Church governs the manner in which a Sacrament should be celebrated and ensures universality in all times and places of celebration.

The doctrines of the Church always will remain the same, but the disciplines may develop and change throughout the ages.

Lesson 2

To ensure that the Faith is taught without error, the Pope has the authority to declare what must be taught. He is given the aid of the Holy Spirit.

The Pope teaches through his encyclicals, letters, declarations, and speeches.

Bishops teach through preaching and pastoral letters in their dioceses.

Lesson 4

The Church is our Holy Mother. Through her we receive the life of grace.

We should have respect for the Church and her ministers.

Jesus Christ gave us the Church as a sign of his love for us.

CHAPTER TEN: CHURCH AUTHORITY—OUR FATHERS IN FAITH
LESSON ONE: THE CHURCH

Aims

The students will learn that the Catholic Church was founded by Jesus Christ. The mission of the Church is to save souls and to teach all men the truths of the Faith.

They will learn that Jesus is the head of the Church and has given his authority to the Pope. The Pope and the bishops in union with him govern the Church.

Materials

- *Activity Book*, p. 37
- Bible
- Diocesan map
- List of Popes from Peter to present, Appendix, pp. B-13 and B-14

Optional:
- "The Church's one foundation," *Adoremus Hymnal*, #560

Begin

Read Matthew 16:13–20. This is an important reading, because here we see that Jesus founded a Church (at the moment of the revelation of who Jesus is) and that he chose Peter to be her head and to have her keys. A master who gave his keys to a steward made the steward his representative, bearing his authority until his return. You may also read John 21:14–19: Jesus commands Peter to feed his sheep and care for his flock, the Church.

Develop

1. Read paragraphs 1–7 from the student text.

2. Jesus founded the Church to continue his work on earth, until his return in glory. Jesus is the head of his Church and gives life to the Church. The Holy Spirit guides the Church and Jesus works through the Church in her Sacraments. Jesus made the Pope to be his representative—his steward—until his return.

3. Have the students dramatize one of the Bible readings from the Begin section, or an encounter of today's Pope with Saint Peter. What might Peter say to the Pope?

4. How is the Church the Kingdom of God? Jesus reigns through the Church. He brings us into his family and guides us through his Church, under the teaching authority of the Magisterium (exercising its authority in union with God). Christ, then is the King and we are heirs to the Kingdom!

5. With the students, make a chart or timeline of all the Popes until present (see Appendix, pp. B-13 and B-14, with list of Popes and their dates). You may trace out the timeline on butcher paper, or using a Pope chart, have the students research various significant papacies with the *Catholic Encyclopedia*.

6. Review that the Pope is the Vicar of Christ and successor of Peter. The bishops are also successors of the Apostles and bring Christ to the Church. They, too, can trace their ordinations back to one of the Apostles. Priests are helpers of the bishops and share their ministry within their dioceses.

7. The role of the bishops is to teach, sanctify, and govern the Church (in union with the Pope). The bishop is given jurisdiction over a diocese (usually a geographical area). Have the students trace out their diocesan boundaries on a map. They may also trace out their parish boundaries within their diocese.

Reinforce

1. Have the students work on *Activity Book* p. 37 (see *Teacher's Manual*, p. 125).

2. Have the students prepare a timeline of the Popes, from Peter to the present (see Develop 5 above).

3. Have the students research the current Pope and significant events in his papacy.

4. Have the students research their bishop and parish priests. They may write letters of support to their bishop and priests.

Conclude

1. Teach the students to sing "The Church's one foundation," *Adoremus Hymnal*, #560.

2. End class by leading the students in praying the Anima Christi (see *Teacher's Manual*, p. 397).

CHAPTER 10

Church Authority— Our Fathers in Faith

"He who hears you hears me, and he who rejects you rejects me, and he who rejects me rejects him who sent me."

Luke 10:16

Besides our parents and the state there is another authority over us that demands our obedience. That is the Catholic Church as founded on earth by Jesus.

Jesus gave to the Church its mission to save souls and to teach all men the truths of the Faith. He chose his Apostles to govern the Church as a body. Establishing the Church was the means Jesus chose to remain with us always and to lead us to his heavenly Kingdom, our final goal.

The Vicar of Christ

Jesus is the head or ruler of his Church, which is his Body. He is the one who has given the authority to the Pope to rule the Church on his behalf. It was to Saint Peter, the first Pope, that Jesus said: "I will give you the keys of the kingdom of heaven, and whatever you bind on earth shall be bound in heaven, and whatever you loose on earth shall be loosed in heaven" (Mt 16:19).

Including our present Pope, there have been more than 260 Popes. The authority of Saint Peter has been passed on to each one down to our own day.

The mission of the Church is to preach the gospel and lead all people to holiness. The Pope is chiefly responsible for seeing that this mission is accomplished. It is for this purpose that the Pope and bishops, as successors of the Apostles, have the authority to make the **precepts** or rules and disciplines of the Church.

A bishop is the chief authority in his own diocese. (A diocese is the part of the Church led by a bishop.) The bishop has this authority as long as he remains in union with the Pope. The bishop shares some of his authority with the priests and deacons of his diocese. In this way, Christ governs his people, the Church, through the Pope, the other bishops, and the priests and deacons under the bishops. These ordained ministers share in Jesus' authority in order to help the whole Church, the Body of Christ, to be holy and to spread the message of Jesus to others.

The Church is carefully governed so that it may be clearly recognized by the unity of its faith and worship.

50

51

HIERARCHY OF THE CHURCH

- Pope: The Pope is the Vicar of Christ, the head of the Church on earth. He shepherds and guides the Church on earth and is protected by the gift of infallibility when he teaches on matters of faith and morals.

- Cardinal: Cardinals are bishops and priests who have a special service in the Church. They usually work at the Vatican or take care of a very large diocese. They choose and elect the Holy Father.

- Bishop: Bishops are the direct successors of the Apostles. They shepherd a diocese with their preaching, teaching, and example, and by administering the Sacraments. They also are responsible for assigning priests to the parishes and supporting them in their ministry.

- Priest: Priests work in parishes, preach, teach, and minister with the Sacraments. They bring Jesus into the lives of the laity and help them to lead Christian lives.

- Deacon: Deacons serve the laity and assist priests in their ministry.

- Laity: The laity serve God in the world. They are called to holiness in their daily lives and to bring Jesus into the world.

Who then is the faithful and wise servant, whom his master has set over his household, to give them their food at the proper time? Blessed is that servant whom his master when he comes will find so doing.

—Matthew 24:45–46

Preview

In the next lesson, the students will learn about the unity of the Faith.

CHAPTER TEN: CHURCH AUTHORITY—OUR FATHERS IN FAITH
LESSON TWO: UNITY OF FAITH

Aims

The students will learn that to ensure that the Faith is taught without error, the Pope has the authority to declare what must be taught. He is given the aid of the Holy Spirit.

They will learn that the Pope teaches through his encyclicals, letters, declarations, and speeches. Bishops teach through preaching and pastoral letters in their dioceses.

Materials

• *Activity Book*, p. 38

Optional:
• "The Church's one foundation," *Adoremus Hymnal*, #560

Begin

Review the marks of the true Church:
One: Unified in faith/teaching, one Pope
Holy: Christ offered holy sacrifice and works through the Sacraments

Catholic: The Church is all over the world and throughout time (universal)
Apostolic: Founded upon the teachings of the Apostles as taught by Christ

Develop

1. Read paragraph 8 from the student text.

2. The teaching Church is called the Magisterium. The Magisterium is responsible for interpreting and correctly passing on Sacred Scripture and Sacred Tradition. These are defined as:
   • Sacred Scripture: the Word of God as written down under the inspiration of the Holy Spirit
   • Sacred Tradition: the entirety of the Word of God (including oral tradition and the development of doctrine through the ages)

3. Read the following passages from the Bible: Jn 14:16–17; 15:26–27; 16:13; and 1 Jn 4:6 to show how the Holy Spirit guides the Church in the truth and protects it from error.

4. The Magisterium is comprised of the Pope and the bishops in union with him. The Magisterium is protected from error in teaching on matters of faith and morals. This protection from error is called infallibility. There are two ways to teach infallibly: through the ordinary and extraordinary Magisterium. Ordinary Magisterium is exercised when the bishops teach on matters of faith and morals in union with the Pope, and with each other (union throughout time, and geographically). Extraordinary Magisterium is exercised when the Pope calls an ecumenical council of all the bishops from around the world. When the bishops gather with sufficient representation to teach on matters of faith and morals, in union with the Pope, their teaching is protected by infallibility. Also, the Pope by himself is infallible when teaching on matters of faith in morals, when he teaches universally and authoritatively, "ex cathedra" (from the chair of Peter).

5. Have the students research a council or papal teaching.

Reinforce

1. Have the students work on *Activity Book* p. 38 (see *Teacher's Manual*, p. 125).

2. Have the students research a specific Catholic teaching, demonstrating the ways it is supported by Sacred Scripture and Sacred Tradition. The students may research a council or an authoritative papal teaching to see how the Church has taught infallibly.

3. The students may work on the Memorization Questions and Words to Know from this chapter.

Conclude

1. Lead the students in singing "The Church's one foundation," *Adoremus Hymnal*, #560.

2. End class by leading the students in praying the Anima Christi (see *Teacher's Manual*, p. 397).

CHAPTER 10

Church Authority– Our Fathers in Faith

"He who hears you hears me, and he who rejects you rejects me, and he who rejects me rejects him who sent me."

Luke 10:16

Besides our parents and the state there is another authority over us that demands our obedience. That is the Catholic Church as founded on earth by Jesus.

Jesus gave to the Church its mission to save souls and to teach all men the truths of the Faith. He chose his Apostles to govern the Church as a body. Establishing the Church was the means Jesus chose to remain with us always and to lead us to his heavenly Kingdom, our final goal.

The Vicar of Christ

Jesus is the head or ruler of his Church, which is his Body. He is the one who has given the authority to the Pope to rule the Church on his behalf. It was to Saint Peter, the first Pope, that Jesus said: "I will give you the keys of the kingdom of heaven, and whatever you bind on earth shall be bound in heaven, and whatever you loose on earth shall be loosed in heaven" (Mt 16:19).

Including our present Pope, there have been more than 260 Popes. The authority of Saint Peter has been passed on to each one down to our own day.

The mission of the Church is to preach the gospel and lead all people to holiness. The Pope is chiefly responsible for seeing that this mission is accomplished. It is for this purpose that the Pope and bishops, as successors of the Apostles, have the authority to make the **precepts** or rules and disciplines of the Church.

A bishop is the chief authority in his own diocese. (A diocese is the part of the Church led by a bishop.) The bishop has this authority as long as he remains in union with the Pope. The bishop shares some of his authority with the priests and deacons of his diocese. In this way, Christ governs his people, the Church, through the Pope, the other bishops, and the priests and deacons under the bishops. These ordained ministers share in Jesus' authority in order to help the whole Church, the Body of Christ, to be holy and to spread the message of Jesus to others.

The Church is carefully governed so that it may be clearly recognized by the unity of its faith and worship.

51

Unity of Faith

To make sure that the Faith is taught correctly and the gospel preached to all without error, the Pope has the authority to declare what is to be taught. He answers moral questions and addresses himself to any current problem which affects the lives of Christians. The Pope does this in his speeches, encyclicals, letters, and declarations. The bishops do the same in their dioceses, usually through pastoral letters that are made available to everyone in the world by the Church.

One in the Sacraments

Since it is through the Sacraments that the Church fulfills her role in sanctifying men, it is necessary that they be administered in a consistent way in all times and places. The Church determines what is required to receive each Sacrament: for example, how old a person must be and what the accompanying ceremony should include. The Church also sets the requirements for becoming and remaining a member of the Church. The Pope and the other bishops make judgments about moral

---

Precepts of the Church

1. "You shall attend Mass on Sundays and on Holy Days of Obligation and rest from servile labor." The first precept requires us to keep holy the day of the Lord's Resurrection; to worship God by participating in Mass every Sunday and Holy Day of Obligation; to avoid those activities that would hinder renewal of soul and body on the Lord's day.
2. "You shall confess your sins at least once a year." The second precept requires us to lead a sacramental life; to receive the Sacrament of Penance regularly—minimally, to receive the Sacrament of Penance at least once a year (annual confession is obligatory only if serious sin is involved) in preparation to receive Holy Communion.
3. "You shall receive the Sacrament of the Eucharist at least during the Easter season." The third precept requires us to receive Holy Communion frequently; minimally, to receive Holy Communion once during the Easter season.
4. "You shall observe the days of fasting and abstinence established by the Church." The fourth precept requires us to do penance, including abstaining from meat and fasting from food on the appointed days.
5. "You shall help to provide for the needs of the Church." The fifth precept requires us to strengthen and support the Church—one's own parish community and parish priests, the worldwide Church, and the Pope.

(CCC 2042–43)

52

---

and social issues when these things affect people's basic rights or their salvation.

Holy Mother Church

The Church is often referred to as our Holy Mother Church. This shows the attitude we should have toward the Church and her leaders. Like all mothers, the Church exists to give us life and to provide for our well-being and development until we reach our final goal. We should have great reverence and love for the Church because Jesus gave us the Church as a sign of his love for us.

Words to Know:

Vicar of Christ   precepts

Q. 40   *Why does the Church have the authority to make laws and precepts?*
The Church has the authority to make laws and precepts because she has received this authority from Jesus Christ through his Apostles. Thus he who disobeys the Church disobeys God himself (CCC 2035–37).

Q. 41   *Who can make laws and precepts in the Church?*
The bishops in union with the Pope, as successors of the Apostles, can make laws and precepts in the Church. Jesus Christ said to them: "He who hears you hears me, and he who rejects you rejects me, and he who rejects me rejects him who sent me" (CCC 2041, Lk 10:16).

Q. 42   *Must members of the Church obey the precepts of the Church?*
Yes, members of the Church must obey the precepts of the Church (CCC 2037).

53

CHURCH DOCUMENTS

Many official documents are written by the Church. Some appear very rarely, such as a Motu Proprio; others, such as apostolic letters, appear more often. Here are a few examples:

- Encyclical: This is a pastoral letter written by the Pope to the Church and the whole world. It expresses Church teaching on an important matter.
- Motu Proprio: Meaning "of his own will," it is a rarely used direct instruction from the Pope regarding a particular question.
- Bull: This is an extremely formal document expressing a teaching of the Pope (so named for its large round leaden seal, nicknamed a *bullae,* or bubble).

Preview

In the next lesson, the students will learn about the Sacraments.

CHAPTER TEN: CHURCH AUTHORITY—OUR FATHERS IN FAITH
LESSON THREE: SACRAMENTS

Aims

The students will learn that it is through the Sacraments that the Church sanctifies her members.

They will learn that the Church governs the manner in which a Sacrament should be celebrated and ensures universality in all times and places of celebration.

They will learn that the doctrines of the Church always remain the same, though the particular disciplines may develop throughout the ages.

Materials

- *Activity Book*, p. 39

Optional:
- "The Church's one foundation," *Adoremus Hymnal*, #560

Begin

Begin this class by reviewing the definition of a Sacrament. A Sacrament is an outward sign that effects grace. A sign points to a reality, such as a road sign (e.g., Washington, 10 miles). A Sacrament is different in that it is a sign that works a change in us.

This would be like a stop sign that actually brings your car to a complete stop. There are seven Sacraments in the Catholic Church: Baptism, Eucharist, Confirmation, Penance, Anointing of the Sick, Matrimony, and Holy Orders.

Develop

1. Read paragraph 9 from the student text.

2. The students should know that Christ himself instituted the seven Sacraments to continue his work of sanctifying men through the Church that he founded. You may find examples in Scripture:
- Baptism: Mt 28:18–20
- Eucharist: Mk 14:22–25
- Confirmation: Jn 7:37–39; 14:26; 20:22; Acts 1:8; 2:4
- Penance: Jn 20:21–23
- Anointing of the Sick: Mk 6:13; Jas 5:14
- Matrimony: Mt 19:4–6; Jn 2:1–11
- Holy Orders: Lk 22:19; Jn 13:1–15; Acts 6:6

3. Review that every Sacrament works *ex opere operato*. This means "from the work worked." This means that when the minister uses the correct matter and form and acts with the intention of the Church, the Sacrament is effective (it does not depend upon the minister's sanctity), for it is Jesus who works through the minister to effect the Sacrament. It is Jesus who baptizes, forgives in the Sacrament of Penance, etc.

4. It is important to understand that the effectiveness of grace received from the Sacrament is partially determined by our internal disposition (the *opus operantis*).

5. The Church has the duty to safeguard the Sacraments and determine the discipline necessary for each Sacrament. Additionally, the Church determines the rites to assist the faithful in worthy reception. The Sacrament itself never changes, but the ceremony may, so that we can better understand and more fully participate with our minds and hearts in the Sacraments.

Reinforce

1. Have the students work on *Activity Book* p. 39 (see *Teacher's Manual*, p. 125). Assign each student a Sacrament, have him research the teachings of the Church on that Sacrament, and prepare a presentation to show his findings.

2. Have the students work on the Memorization Questions and Words to Know from this chapter.

3. You may teach the students how there is a continuity in the celebration of the Sacrament from the time of the early Church up to the present time.

Conclude

1. Lead the students in singing "The Church's one foundation," *Adoremus Hymnal*, #560.

2. End class by leading the students in praying the Anima Christi (see *Teacher's Manual*, p. 397).

CHAPTER 10

Church Authority— Our Fathers in Faith

"He who hears you hears me, and he who rejects you rejects me, and he who rejects me rejects him who sent me."

Luke 10:16

Besides our parents and the state there is another authority over us that demands our obedience. That is the Catholic Church as founded on earth by Jesus.

Jesus gave to the Church its mission to save souls and to teach all men the truths of the Faith. He chose his Apostles to govern the Church as a body. Establishing the Church was the means Jesus chose to remain with us always and to lead us to his heavenly Kingdom, our final goal.

The Vicar of Christ

Jesus is the head or ruler of his Church, which is his Body. He is the one who has given the authority to the Pope to rule the Church on his behalf. It was to Saint Peter, the first Pope, that Jesus said: "I will give you the keys of the kingdom of heaven, and whatever you bind on earth shall be bound in heaven, and whatever you loose on earth shall be loosed in heaven" (Mt 16:19).

Including our present Pope, there have been more than 260 Popes. The authority of Saint Peter has been passed on to each one down to our own day.

The mission of the Church is to preach the gospel and lead all people to holiness. The Pope is chiefly responsible for seeing that this mission is accomplished. It is for this purpose that the Pope and bishops, as successors of the Apostles, have the authority to make the **precepts** or rules and disciplines of the Church.

A bishop is the chief authority in his own diocese. (A diocese is the part of the Church led by a bishop.) The bishop has this authority as long as he remains in union with the Pope. The bishop shares some of his authority with the priests and deacons of his diocese. In this way, Christ governs his people, the Church, through the Pope, the other bishops, and the priests and deacons under the bishops. These ordained ministers share in Jesus' authority in order to help the whole Church, the Body of Christ, to be holy and to spread the message of Jesus to others.

The Church is carefully governed so that it may be clearly recognized by the unity of its faith and worship.

51

Unity of Faith

To make sure that the Faith is taught correctly and the gospel preached to all without error, the Pope has the authority to declare what is to be taught. He answers moral questions and addresses himself to any current problem which affects the lives of Christians. The Pope does this in his speeches, encyclicals, letters, and declarations. The bishops do the same in their dioceses, usually through pastoral letters that are made available to everyone in the world by the Church.

One in the Sacraments

Since it is through the Sacraments that the Church fulfills her role in sanctifying men, it is necessary that they be administered in a consistent way in all times and places. The Church determines what is required to receive each Sacrament: for example, how old a person must be and what the accompanying ceremony should include. The Church also sets the requirements for becoming and remaining a member of the Church. The Pope and the other bishops make judgments about moral

---

Precepts of the Church

1. "You shall attend Mass on Sundays and on Holy Days of Obligation and rest from servile labor." The first precept requires us to keep holy the day of the Lord's Resurrection; to worship God by participating in Mass every Sunday and Holy Day of Obligation; to avoid those activities that would hinder renewal of soul and body on the Lord's day.
2. "You shall confess your sins at least once a year." The second precept requires us to lead a sacramental life; to receive the Sacrament of Penance regularly—minimally, to receive the Sacrament of Penance at least once a year (annual confession is obligatory only if serious sin is involved) in preparation to receive Holy Communion.
3. "You shall receive the Sacrament of the Eucharist at least during the Easter season." The third precept requires us to receive Holy Communion frequently; minimally, to receive Holy Communion once during the Easter season.
4. "You shall observe the days of fasting and abstinence established by the Church." The fourth precept requires us to do penance, including abstaining from meat and fasting from food on the appointed days.
5. "You shall help to provide for the needs of the Church." The fifth precept requires us to strengthen and support the Church—one's own parish community and parish priests, the worldwide Church, and the Pope.

(CCC 2042–43)

52

---

and social issues when these things affect people's basic rights or their salvation.

Holy Mother Church

The Church is often referred to as our Holy Mother Church. This shows the attitude we should have toward the Church and her leaders. Like all mothers, the Church exists to give us life and to provide for our well-being and development until we reach our final goal. We should have great reverence and love for the Church because Jesus gave us the Church as a sign of his love for us.

Words to Know:

Vicar of Christ   precepts

Q. 40 *Why does the Church have the authority to make laws and precepts?*

The Church has the authority to make laws and precepts because she has received this authority from Jesus Christ through his Apostles. Thus he who disobeys the Church disobeys God himself (CCC 2035–37).

Q. 41 *Who can make laws and precepts in the Church?*

The bishops in union with the Pope, as successors of the Apostles, can make laws and precepts in the Church. Jesus Christ said to them: "He who hears you hears me, and he who rejects you rejects me, and he who rejects me rejects him who sent me" (CCC 2041, Lk 10:16).

Q. 42 *Must members of the Church obey the precepts of the Church?*

Yes, members of the Church must obey the precepts of the Church (CCC 2037).

53

THE SACRAMENT OF THE EUCHARIST FACTS

- Matter: bread and wine
- Form: "This is my Body" and "This is the chalice of my Blood"
- Minister: priest

Names: Eucharist, Blessed Sacrament, Holy Communion (when received)

Effects: see index p. 788 of the CCC, 2nd ed.

Preview

In the next lesson, the students will learn about the image of the Church as mother and the precepts of the Church.

Chapter Ten: Church Authority—Our Fathers in Faith
Lesson Four: Mother Church

Aims

The students will learn that the Church is our Holy Mother. Through her we receive the life of grace.

They will learn that we should have respect for the Church and her ministers.

They will learn that Jesus Christ gave us the Church as a sign of his love for us.

Materials

- *Activity Book*, p. 40

Optional:
- The Church's one foundation," *Adoremus Hymnal*, #560

Begin

Discuss the roles in a traditional family: a father and mother who give life; a mother who brings the child to life in conception and birth. We are reared by our parents: fed, kept healthy, brought to maturity. We are guided in our vocations and eventually we pass from this life into the next. So too,

God has provided for our spiritual life. We know that God is our Father, and he gives us a Mother who can rear us in the Faith: the Church. You may parallel the natural life with the spiritual life in a chart on the board. (See box, "The Spiritual Life and the Natural Life.")

Develop

1. Finish reading the chapter.

2. Discuss how the Church is like a mother. This should teach us the attitude we should have toward the Church and her leaders. The Church gives us life and provides for us until we reach our final goal of heaven. How is the Church motherly?
   - She gives us the life of grace through the Sacraments.
   - She guides us in the moral life.
   - She tends to the needs of our senses (images, scents, etc.).

3. We may wonder why priests may not marry. A priest consecrates himself to the ministry of the Church. We call him father, since he acts in the Person of Christ (who is God) and who is the minister of the Sacraments. The priest, through the Church, confers the life of grace upon us. A priest must serve the Church single-heartedly and does so by giving himself entirely to the Church. We can say that

the priest "weds" the Church, our Mother, so that we can share in Gods' life.

4. Review the precepts of the Church with the students. Be sure that the students understand these precepts and know that they are morally binding. The students should memorize the precepts of the Church. The students may make posters, one for each precept, to be displayed in the classroom.

5. The Church has the authority to make laws and precepts in order to protect her members and safeguard her treasures (i.e., her Sacraments). For example, the Church binds her members to be married in the Catholic Church to ensure that marriages are valid and entered into according to Church law. We must learn these precepts and laws, so that we may be protected from grievous error. Free from error, we may worthily receive the Sacraments and the fullness of grace they offer.

Reinforce

1. Have the students work on *Activity Book* p. 40 (see *Teacher's Manual*, p. 125).

2. Have the students continue to work on their precepts of the Church posters.

3. You may wish to provide the students with time to work on their Memorization Questions, Words to Know, precepts of the Church, and to prepare for the quiz.

Conclude

1. Lead the students in singing "The Church's one foundation," *Adoremus Hymnal*, #560.

2. End class by leading the students in praying the Anima Christi (see *Teacher's Manual*, p. 397).

CHAPTER 10

Church Authority—
Our Fathers in Faith

"He who hears you hears me, and he who rejects you rejects me, and he who rejects me rejects him who sent me."

Luke 10:16

Besides our parents and the state there is another authority over us that demands our obedience. That is the Catholic Church as founded on earth by Jesus.

Jesus gave to the Church its mission to save souls and to teach all men the truths of the Faith. He chose his Apostles to govern the Church as a body. Establishing the Church was the means Jesus chose to remain with us always and to lead us to his heavenly Kingdom, our final goal.

The Vicar of Christ

Jesus is the head or ruler of his Church, which is his Body. He is the one who has given the authority to the Pope to rule the Church on his behalf. It was to Saint Peter, the first Pope, that Jesus said: "I will give you the keys of the kingdom of heaven, and whatever you bind on earth shall be bound in heaven, and whatever you loose on earth shall be loosed in heaven" (Mt 16:19).

Including our present Pope, there have been more than 260 Popes. The authority of Saint Peter has been passed on to each one down to our own day.

The mission of the Church is to preach the gospel and lead all people to holiness. The Pope is chiefly responsible for seeing that this mission is accomplished. It is for this purpose that the Pope and bishops, as successors of the Apostles, have the authority to make the **precepts** or rules and disciplines of the Church.

A bishop is the chief authority in his own diocese. (A diocese is the part of the Church led by a bishop.) The bishop has this authority as long as he remains in union with the Pope. The bishop shares some of his authority with the priests and deacons of his diocese. In this way, Christ governs his people, the Church, through the Pope, the other bishops, and the priests and deacons under the bishops. These ordained ministers share in Jesus' authority in order to help the whole Church, the Body of Christ, to be holy and to spread the message of Jesus to others.

The Church is carefully governed so that it may be clearly recognized by the unity of its faith and worship.

Unity of Faith

To make sure that the Faith is taught correctly and the gospel preached to all without error, the Pope has the authority to declare what is to be taught. He answers moral questions and addresses himself to any current problem which affects the lives of Christians. The Pope does this in his speeches, encyclicals, letters, and declarations. The bishops do the same in their dioceses, usually through pastoral letters that are made available to everyone in the world by the Church.

One in the Sacraments

Since it is through the Sacraments that the Church fulfills her role in sanctifying men, it is necessary that they be administered in a consistent way in all times and places. The Church determines what is required to receive each Sacrament: for example, how old a person must be and what the accompanying ceremony should include. The Church also sets the requirements for becoming and remaining a member of the Church. The Pope and the other bishops make judgments about moral

---

Precepts of the Church

1. "You shall attend Mass on Sundays and on Holy Days of Obligation and rest from servile labor." The first precept requires us to keep holy the day of the Lord's Resurrection; to worship God by participating in Mass every Sunday and Holy Day of Obligation; to avoid those activities that would hinder renewal of soul and body on the Lord's day.

2. "You shall confess your sins at least once a year." The second precept requires us to lead a sacramental life; to receive the Sacrament of Penance regularly—minimally, to receive the Sacrament of Penance at least once a year (annual confession is obligatory only if serious sin is involved) in preparation to receive Holy Communion.

3. "You shall receive the Sacrament of the Eucharist at least during the Easter season." The third precept requires us to receive Holy Communion frequently; minimally, to receive Holy Communion once during the Easter season.

4. "You shall observe the days of fasting and abstinence established by the Church." The fourth precept requires us to do penance, including abstaining from meat and fasting from food on the appointed days.

5. "You shall help to provide for the needs of the Church." The fifth precept requires us to strengthen and support the Church—one's own parish community and parish priests, the worldwide Church, and the Pope.

(CCC 2042–43)

---

and social issues when these things affect people's basic rights or their salvation.

Holy Mother Church

The Church is often referred to as our Holy Mother Church. This shows the attitude we should have toward the Church and her leaders. Like all mothers, the Church exists to give us life and to provide for our well-being and development until we reach our final goal. We should have great reverence and love for the Church because Jesus gave us the Church as a sign of his love for us.

Words to Know:
Vicar of Christ   precepts

Q. 40   Why does the Church have the authority to make laws and precepts?
The Church has the authority to make laws and precepts because she has received this authority from Jesus Christ through his Apostles. Thus he who disobeys the Church disobeys God himself (CCC 2035–37).

Q. 41   Who can make laws and precepts in the Church?
The bishops in union with the Pope, as successors of the Apostles, can make laws and precepts in the Church. Jesus Christ said to them: "He who hears you hears me, and he who rejects you rejects me, and he who rejects me rejects him who sent me" (CCC 2041, Lk 10:16).

Q. 42   Must members of the Church obey the precepts of the Church?
Yes, members of the Church must obey the precepts of the Church (CCC 2037).

THE SUPERNATURAL LIFE AND THE NATURAL LIFE

NATURAL	SUPERNATURAL
Birth	Baptism
Food	Eucharist
Healing	Penance
Adulthood	Confirmation
Family	Matrimony
Service	Holy Orders
Death	Anointing of the Sick

Preview

In the next lesson, the students' understanding of the material covered in this chapter will be reviewed and assessed.

CHAPTER TEN: CHURCH AUTHORITY—OUR FATHERS IN FAITH
REVIEW AND ASSESSMENT

Aims

The students' understanding of the material covered in this chapter will be reviewed and assessed.

Materials

- Quiz 10, Appendix, p. A-14

Optional:
- "The Church's one foundation," *Adoremus Hymnal,* #560

Review and Enrichment

1. The students should understand that Jesus founded the Church to continue his ministry of sanctification on earth until his glorious return.

2. The Pope is the Vicar of Christ—Christ's representative on earth.

3. The Magisterium is the teaching authority of the Church. The Magisterium has the duty of interpreting Sacred Scripture and Sacred Tradition. The Magisterium is made up of the Pope and the bishops in union with him. The teaching Church is protected from error in matters of faith and morals. This protection is called infallibility.

4. The students should understand that the true Church is one, holy, catholic, and apostolic. These are the marks of the true Church.

5. The students should know what a Sacrament is, the names of the seven Sacraments, and the matter, form, minister, and effects of the Sacraments. They should be familiar with the terms *ex opere operato* and *opus operantis.* They should understand these concepts.

6. The Church is our Mother in faith.

7. The students should know the precepts of the Church.

Assess

1. Distribute the quizzes and read through them with the students to be sure they understand the questions.

2. Administer the quiz. As they hand in their work, you may orally quiz the students on the Memorization Questions from this chapter.

3. After all the quizzes have been handed in, you may wish to review the correct answers with the class.

Conclude

1. Lead the students in singing "The Church's one foundation," *Adoremus Hymnal,* #560.

2. End class by leading the students in praying the Anima Christi (see *Teacher's Manual,* p. 397).

CHAPTER TEN: CHURCH AUTHORITY—OUR FATHERS IN FAITH
ACTIVITY BOOK ANSWER KEYS

Name:_____

The Pope, the Vicar of Christ

Answer the following questions in complete sentences.

1. Who founded the Catholic Church?
   <u>Jesus founded the Catholic Church.</u>

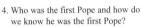

2. What mission does the Church have?
   <u>Her mission is to save souls and teach all men the truths of the Faith.</u>

3. Who is the head of the Church?
   <u>Jesus is the head of the Church.</u>

4. Who was the first Pope and how do we know he was the first Pope?
   <u>Peter was the first Pope. We know this because Jesus gave him the keys of the Kingdom and the power to bind and loose.</u>

5. Who is our present Pope?
   <u>Students should give the name of the current Pope.</u>

6. What does the Pope do? What is his responsibility?
   <u>The Pope is responsible for making sure that the Church accomplishes her mission.</u>

7. Is the Pope a bishop?
   <u>Yes.</u>

Faith and Life Series • Grade 6 • Chapter 10 • Lesson 1   37

Name:_____

Unity of Faith

Answer the following questions in complete sentences.

1. How do we know that the Faith is taught correctly and the gospel is preached without error?
   <u>Answers will vary.</u>

2. What does the Pope do to ensure the truth is taught?
   <u>The Pope answers moral questions and addresses himself to any current problem which affects the lives of Christians.</u>

3. How does the Pope address people to teach the truth?
   <u>The Pope addresses people through speeches, encyclicals, letters, and declarations.</u>

4. How do bishops teach the truth?
   <u>The text only mentions pastoral letters, but students should understand that they can use other methods such as preaching too.</u>

5. Why does the Church have the authority to make laws and precepts?
   <u>The Church has the authority to make laws and precepts because she has received this authority from Jesus Christ through his Apostles. Thus, he who disobeys the Church disobeys God himself.</u>

6. The Pope is given a gift called infallibility. Read John 14:15–16, 25–26 and write what Jesus teaches us about maintaining the truth in his Church.
   <u>The Holy Spirit helps us to maintain the truth.</u>

38   *Faith and Life Series • Grade 6 • Chapter 10 • Lesson 2*

Name:_____

One in Sacraments

Answer the following questions in complete sentences.

1. What do the Sacraments do?
   <u>The Sacraments sanctify the members of the Church.</u>

2. Who determines what is required to receive the Sacraments?
   <u>The Church determines what is required to receive the Sacraments.</u>

3. Who determines the requirements for becoming and remaining a Church member?
   <u>The Church also determines the requirements for becoming and remaining a Church member.</u>

4. How many of the precepts of the Church concern the Sacraments?
   <u>Three of the precepts concern the Sacraments.</u>

Faith and Life Series • Grade 6 • Chapter 10 • Lesson 3   39

Name:_____

Precepts of the Church

Answer the following questions in complete sentences.

1. Who can make the laws and precepts of the Church?
   <u>The Pope and the bishops in union with him can make the laws and precepts of the Church.</u>

2. What does the first precept require?
   <u>The first precept requires us to attend Mass and avoid unnecessary work every Sunday and Holy Day of Obligation</u>

3. What does the second precept require?
   <u>The second precept requires us to confess our sins once a year if serious sin is involved.</u>

4. What does the third precept require?
   <u>The third precept requires us to receive Holy Communion frequently, and at least to receive it once a year.</u>

5. What does the fourth precept require?
   <u>The fourth precept requires us to do penance on the appointed days.</u>

6. What does the fifth precept require?
   <u>The fifth precept requires us to strengthen and support the Church.</u>

40   *Faith and Life Series • Grade 6 • Chapter 10 • Lesson 4*

TEACHER'S NOTES

TEACHER'S NOTES

CHAPTER ELEVEN
RESPECT LIFE

Catechism of the Catholic Church References

Fifth Commandment: 2258–2317, 2318–30
Respect for Human Life: 2259–83, 2319–25
Respect for the Dignity of Persons: 2284–2301, 2326

Safeguarding Peace and Avoiding War: 2302–17, 2327–30
Man as Body and Soul: 362–68, 382

Scripture References

Creation of Man: Gen 1:26–31; 2:4–25.

Summary of Lesson Content

Lesson 1

Man is composed of a body and a soul.

At death, the body and the soul are separated; however, on the Last Day they will be reunited in their eternal reward.

We must care for both our physical and spiritual lives.

Lesson 2

God is the giver of life. No man has the right to take innocent human life.

Murder is a grave sin—it is the taking of an innocent life. Abortion and euthanasia are examples of murder.

Lesson 3

The Fifth Commandment forbids taking innocent life or causing physical harm to another.

There are times when killing is not forbidden, such as in self-defense (for it is not the taking of innocent life).

Suicide is killing one's self and is seriously wrong. If someone commits suicide without full knowledge and consent, his responsibility before God is lessened.

Lesson 4

The Fifth Commandment demands that we care for ourselves with a proper diet, hygiene, exercise, and rest. We should protect ourselves from disease and receive appropriate medical treatment.

We must avoid foolish and dangerous stunts. We must avoid carelessness that may lead to accident or injury.

Gluttony and improper use of medicine, drugs, or alcohol that harm the body are sinful.

CHAPTER ELEVEN: RESPECT LIFE
LESSON ONE: BODY AND SOUL

Aims

The students will learn that man is composed of a body and a soul.

They will learn that, at death, the body and the soul are separated; however, on the Last Day they will be reunited in their eternal reward. We must care for both our physical and spiritual lives.

Materials

- *Activity Book*, p. 41

- Bible

Optional:
- "O Lord, the Giver of all life," *Adoremus Hymnal*, #609

Begin

Read the story of God's Creation of Man and Woman: Gen 1:26–31; 2:4–15.

The students may discuss the similarities and the differences between these two accounts. The most important aspect is the recognition that man is made in God's image (that we are persons and are spiritual). The second Creation account clearly shows that man is made of matter (body) and spirit (soul). The students may write about the gifts of body and soul.

Develop

1. Read paragraphs 1–3 from the student text.

2. Discuss how our soul differs from that of an animal or an angel. (Man, animals, and angels are all creatures created by God.)
   - Angel soul: An angel is a pure spirit. It is a person and it is rational. Because angels are immaterial, they have great knowledge given to them directly by God, and they are immortal.
   - Human soul: A human has a rational, incarnate soul (it is the form of the body). Our soul determines who we are, and it allows us to learn, to love, and to choose things. It is, however, limited by the body (it learns through the senses and experience, it can only go where the body goes, etc.). When we die, our soul will continue to exist, but it will be incomplete (without the body) until the General Judgment when our bodies and souls will be reunited in the resurrection of the body.
   - Animal soul: An animal is animate—it can move around. It can be trained, but it is not rational. It cannot learn or love. When an animal dies, it does not go to heaven.

3. Discuss how man is a body-soul unity. Man without a soul is a corpse. Man without a body is a soul. The body and the soul are both essential to the human being. They are separated at death; however, the body and soul will be reunited at the resurrection on the Last Day.

4. Knowing that we believe in the resurrection of the body, how should we treat the body? Good health, proper exercise, nutrition, hygiene, (no drugs or voluntary harm to the body) are very important.

5. Knowing that we have a soul and that our souls are going to live forever, how should we treat them? We should avoid sin, seek to be filled with grace, learn about God, grow in virtue, pray, etc.

6. Because man is a body-soul unity, what must we do to respect both our body and soul? How should we treat other people? (We must respect their bodies and souls.)

Reinforce

1. Have the students work on *Activity Book* p. 41 (see *Teacher's Manual*, p. 137).

2. Have the students work on the Memorization Questions and Words to Know from this chapter (see *Teacher's Manual*, p. 135).

3. Have the students discuss how they know that they have souls. You may use balloons or bubbles as examples of things which are made of matter, but are changed with the addition of something not visible to the eyes or senses. The soul is to the body what air is to a balloon or bubble.

Conclude

1. Teach the students to sing "O Lord, the Giver of all life," *Adoremus Hymnal*, #609.

2. End class by leading the students in a prayer for life.

CHAPTER 11

Respect Life

"You shall not kill."

Exodus 20:13

Man is a creature composed of body and soul. Some people go about their business as if they had never heard of the soul. The truth is that both body and soul are essential to the human being. Though separated by death, the body and the soul are destined to be reunited at the resurrection on the Last Day.

Because we have souls made in the image of God we can share in God's life. We call this supernatural life because it is above our natural life here on earth. We can possess it only as God's gift.

The Fifth Commandment, "You shall not kill," gives us the responsibility to care for both the natural and supernatural life that God has given to us and all men.

Right to Life

Since God is the giver of life, no man or group of men has the right to take innocent human life. To do so is **murder**. And murder is a serious crime and a very serious sin, a mortal sin. Murder violates the God-given right to life of the one who is murdered. Many people today think they can take the matter of life and death into their own hands. For example, many people ignore or accept the murder of millions of unborn babies in our own nation and around the world. An estimated fifty million unborn babies are killed every year by abortion.

Another area where there is a weakening of respect for human life is euthanasia, or "mercy killing." It is never justified. A sick or elderly person must be given the normal or ordinary treatment to keep him alive. To do otherwise would be murder. Extraordinary treatment is another matter—it is not required.

These days there is more and more pressure for euthanasia. Men are taking the beginning and the end of life into their own hands.

The Fifth Commandment makes it clear that it is wrong to take innocent life. Some people maintain that all killing is wrong and never allowable, no matter what the reasons. But there are certain situations in which killing is not the same thing as murder. The most obvious examples of this are the taking of life in self-defense, capital punishment, and just wars. The Church has never condemned these acts as murder. But since every act of taking human life is a serious matter, we must always look to the Church for guidance in these areas.

Murder is not the only violation of the Fifth Commandment. It would be a mortal sin to injure someone seriously by careless driving. It is wrong *not to care* whether our actions may injure others.

Suicide, the act of killing oneself, is always seriously wrong. God alone is the master of our lives, and we are too precious in his sight

54

to toss our lives away. If someone commits suicide without full knowledge and consent, his responsibility before God is lessened. But even if a man is not blameworthy, his action is still wrong.

It is also wrong not to take proper care of ourselves, with proper diet, exercise, and rest. We should avoid risking our lives by doing foolish stunts when we are encouraged by a dare or a desire to show off. We should protect ourselves from disease by sensible habits of cleanliness and dress. We should avoid impatience and carelessness that may lead to accident or injury.

The sin of eating and drinking too much is a

sin that can harm the body; so can the improper use of medicines and other drugs. Taking a little less food and drink than we want is a small but sensible restraint on our bodies and an excellent form of self-denial. As we have seen, some self-denial is a necessary part of Christian living. We have considered acts against the Fifth Commandment that harm people's physical well-being, such as murder, suicide, and not taking care of your health. In the next chapter, we will consider acts that cause other kinds of harm.

Words to Know:
murder   suicide

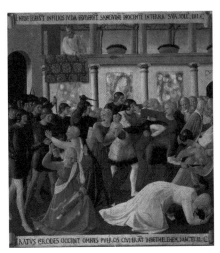

55

HIERARCHY OF CREATION

There are various levels of life or existence in God's creation. There is a certain order or hierarchy among them.

SPIRITUAL
Divine Life
Angelic Life
Human Life*
MATERIAL
Human Life*
Animal Life (sensitive)
Plant Life (vegetative)
Non-life (inanimate)

PRAYER FOR LIFE
BY POPE JOHN PAUL II

O Mary, bright dawn of the new world, Mother of the living, to you do we entrust the cause of life: Look down, O Mother, upon the vast numbers of babies not allowed to be born, of the poor whose lives are made difficult, of men and women who are victims of brutal violence, of the elderly and the sick killed by indifference or out of misguided mercy. Grant that all who believe in your Son may proclaim the Gospel of life with honesty and love to the people of our time. Obtain for them the grace to accept that Gospel as a gift ever new, the joy of celebrating it with gratitude throughout their lives, and the courage to bear witness to it resolutely, in order to build, together with all people of goodwill, the civilization of truth and love, to the praise and glory of God, the Creator and lover of life.

It belongs to the notion of man to be composed of soul, flesh, and bones.
—Saint Thomas Aquinas

Preview

In the next lesson, the students will learn about the grave sin of taking innocent life.

CHAPTER ELEVEN: RESPECT LIFE
LESSON TWO: RIGHT TO LIFE

Aims

The students will learn that God is the giver of life. No man has the right to take innocent human life.

They will learn that murder is a grave sin—it is the taking of an innocent life. Abortion and euthanasia are examples of murder.

Materials

- *Activity Book*, p. 42

Optional:
- "O Lord, the Giver of all life," *Adoremus Hymnal*, #609

- Video of an ultrasound (Note: there is one available through most pro-life ministries)

Begin

We read in Genesis how life is a blessing from God (Gen 1:28). We cannot create life. We can simply cooperate with God who gives life to man through the soul. Man and woman can provide the matter (e.g., DNA, cells) for the body, but they cannot create a soul.

God's gift of life is precious. He has directly given life to every person and he holds us in existence at every moment. God has great love for us. Because of this great dignity, we must always respect life and see every person as created in the image of God.

Develop

1. Have the students read paragraphs 4–6.

2. If you can obtain a video of an ultrasound, show this to the children. Let the children see the beauty of life in the womb. The students should understand that all life is precious. You may discuss the stages of development of a baby in the womb.

3. Review that, because God is the author of all life, no man or group of men has the right to take away innocent human life. To do so is murder. Murder is a mortal sin. It violates the God-given right to life of the one who is murdered.

4. We often hear of murder on the news at night. It is a very sad thing. Murders are often related to theft and gang violence. Murder is a crime and a grave sin. Murder is especially sad when the life taken is particularly innocent, such as that of a child.

5. Another type of murder is abortion. It is particularly evil, since the innocent life that is killed is an unborn baby who has no voice in society. Many people think that abortion is a matter of choice, since it is legal. Though it is legal, it is not morally good. Many people in today's society ignore or accept the millions of abortions that are procured. There are two major movements to bring awareness of abortion in this country: Pro-Life (anti-abortion) and Pro-Choice (pro-abortion). Have the students discuss adoption as a loving choice for a baby who is not "expected."

6. Another type of murder is euthanasia. It is the taking of the life of a sick or elderly person. It is sometimes called "mercy killing." We must give our sick and elderly people the ordinary treatment to keep them alive. Every person, including the aged and the suffering, has great value. God, who gives us life, has a special plan for each and every person. Have the students discuss God's plan for them.

Reinforce

1. Have the students work on *Activity Book* p. 42 (see *Teacher's Manual*, p. 137).

2. Have the students work on the Memorization Questions and Words to Know from this chapter (see *Teacher's Manual*, p. 135).

3. Have the students work on a pro-life project.

4. The students should discuss how God has a plan for each of them. They can see God working in their lives and in the lives of all other people.

Conclude

1. Lead the students in singing "O Lord, the Giver of all life," *Adoremus Hymnal*, #609.

2. End class by leading the students in a prayer for life.

CHAPTER 11

Respect Life

"You shall not kill."

Exodus 20:13

Man is a creature composed of body and soul. Some people go about their business as if they had never heard of the soul. The truth is that both body and soul are essential to the human being. Though separated by death, the body and the soul are destined to be reunited at the resurrection on the Last Day.

Because we have souls made in the image of God we can share in God's life. We call this supernatural life because it is above our natural life here on earth. We can possess it only as God's gift.

The Fifth Commandment, "You shall not kill," gives us the responsibility to care for both the natural and supernatural life that God has given to us and all men.

Right to Life

Since God is the giver of life, no man or group of men has the right to take innocent human life. To do so is **murder**. And murder is a serious crime and a very serious sin, a mortal sin. Murder violates the God-given right to life of the one who is murdered. Many people today think they can take the matter of life and death into their own hands. For example, many people ignore or accept the murder of millions of unborn babies in our own nation and around the world. An estimated fifty million unborn babies are killed every year by abortion.

Another area where there is a weakening of respect for human life is euthanasia, or "mercy killing." It is never justified. A sick or elderly person must be given the normal or ordinary treatment to keep him alive. To do otherwise would be murder. Extraordinary treatment is another matter—it is not required.

These days there is more and more pressure for euthanasia. Men are taking the beginning and the end of life into their own hands.

The Fifth Commandment makes it clear that it is wrong to take innocent life. Some people maintain that all killing is wrong and never allowable, no matter what the reasons. But there are certain situations in which killing is not the same thing as murder. The most obvious examples of this are the taking of life in self-defense, capital punishment, and just wars. The Church has never condemned these acts as murder. But since every act of taking human life is a serious matter, we must always look to the Church for guidance in these areas.

Murder is not the only violation of the Fifth Commandment. It would be a mortal sin to injure someone seriously by careless driving. It is wrong *not to care* whether our actions may injure others.

Suicide, the act of killing oneself, is always seriously wrong. God alone is the master of our lives, and we are too precious in his sight

to toss our lives away. If someone commits suicide without full knowledge and consent, his responsibility before God is lessened. But even if a man is not blameworthy, his action is still wrong.

It is also wrong not to take proper care of ourselves, with proper diet, exercise, and rest. We should avoid risking our lives by doing foolish stunts when we are encouraged by a dare or a desire to show off. We should protect ourselves from disease by sensible habits of cleanliness and dress. We should avoid impatience and carelessness that may lead to accident or injury.

The sin of eating and drinking too much is a sin that can harm the body; so can the improper use of medicines and other drugs. Taking a little less food and drink than we want is a small but sensible restraint on our bodies and an excellent form of self-denial. As we have seen, some self-denial is a necessary part of Christian living. We have considered acts against the Fifth Commandment that harm people's physical well-being, such as murder, suicide, and not taking care of your health. In the next chapter, we will consider acts that cause other kinds of harm.

Words to Know:
        murder   suicide

54

55

PRO-LIFE ACTIVITIES

Many communities offer opportunities, in which the students may participate, to assist the pro-life movement. The cause of pro-life in our nation goes well beyond public opposition to abortion and may be supported through "behind the scenes" charities that assist needy mothers and babies. Some activities to suggest to the students include:

- The March for Life and Walk for Life
- Collections of goods for crisis pregnancy centers
- Prayers for the unborn and their parents
- Writing letters to politicians

EUTHANASIA

There are certain terms the students must understand in order to have a mature understanding of exactly what euthanasia is. See CCC 2276–2279.

- Ordinary treatment: care given to a patient such as providing them with food, water, and medication. If this care is taken away, it may cause the death of the patient. E.g., if a patient is not given food, the cause of death would be starvation. To remove ordinary treatment and so end the life of a patient is euthanasia.

- Extraordinary treatment: medical care that is "burdensome, dangerous, extraordinary, or disproportionate to the expected outcome" (CCC 2278). To end such care can be legitimate. This is not an example of euthanasia because use of such treatment is more a matter of delaying death than preserving life.

Before I formed you in the womb I knew you.

—Jeremiah 1:5

For you formed my inward parts, you knitted me together in my mother's womb. I praise you, for I am wondrously made. Wonderful are your works!

—Psalm 139:13–14

Preview

In the next lesson, the students will learn about more life issues.

Chapter Eleven: Respect Life
Lesson Three: Killing

Aims

The students will learn that the Fifth Commandment forbids taking innocent life or causing physical harm to another.

They will earn that there are times when killing is not forbidden, such as in self-defense (for this is not the taking of innocent life).

They will learn that suicide is killing one's self and is seriously wrong. If, however, someone commits suicide without full knowledge and consent, his responsibility before God is lessened.

Materials

• *Activity Book*, p. 43

Optional:
• "O Lord, the Giver of all life," *Adoremus Hymnal*, #609

Begin

Review that murder is the taking of innocent life, and that it is never permissible and is always a grave and mortal sin. Review the types of murder that the students have already discussed (murder, abortion, euthanasia) and why such acts of violence are never a "good choice" for anyone involved.

Develop

1. Read paragraphs 7–8 from the student text.

2. Is killing always the same thing as murder? No. Murder is the taking of innocent life. Killing is the taking of any life. There are some instances of killing that are not the same as murder and we must receive guidance from the Church to understand their gravity. The Fifth Commandment forbids murder, the intentional killing of innocent life.

3. Self-defense may end in the killing of a person. The slain attacker, however, is not an innocent person. He is a perpetrator or someone who is threatening harm to you or a loved one. In such a case, proportionate action may be taken, in order to defend the innocent life. Ideally, self-defense would not end in the taking of a life, but should it be a secondary effect of defending oneself it would not be a grave offense.

4. Capital punishment occurs when the state determines that a criminal's actions are so dangerous to society that his life is taken as a punishment and a protection to society. In the United States, capital punishment is limited to extreme circumstances. Pope John Paul II, however, has said in non-magisterial teaching that if a criminal can be incarcerated and/or rehabilitated, we must do this, and capital punishment is not justifiable because imprisonment can protect the state from the threat of the criminal.

5. War is an awful thing. Loss of life occurs and often civilians are devastated by a military strike. However, the Church has guidelines for just wars. This means that sometimes a war is permitted in order to protect a people and bring about a good for them. See the principles at right. Note that in just war, there is not intentional or indiscriminate killing (e.g., of innocent civilians).

Reinforce

1. Have the students work on *Activity Book* p. 43 (see *Teacher's Manual*, p. 137).

2. The students should work on the Memorization Questions and Words to Know from this chapter (see *Teacher's Manual*, p. 135).

3. The students may discuss articles from a current newspaper to apply some of the principles they have learned in the last few classes regarding life issues. Answer as many questions as you can. Invite a priest or your Director of Religious Education to visit the class to answer difficult questions.

Conclude

1. Lead the students in singing "O Lord, the Giver of all life," *Adoremus Hymnal*, #609.

2. End class by leading the students in a prayer for life.

CHAPTER 11

Respect Life

"You shall not kill."

Exodus 20:13

Man is a creature composed of body and soul. Some people go about their business as if they had never heard of the soul. The truth is that both body and soul are essential to the human being. Though separated by death, the body and the soul are destined to be reunited at the resurrection on the Last Day.

Because we have souls made in the image of God we can share in God's life. We call this supernatural life because it is above our natural life here on earth. We can possess it only as God's gift.

The Fifth Commandment, "You shall not kill," gives us the responsibility to care for both the natural and supernatural life that God has given to us and all men.

Right to Life

Since God is the giver of life, no man or group of men has the right to take innocent human life. To do so is **murder**. And murder is a serious crime and a very serious sin, a mortal sin. Murder violates the God-given right to life of the one who is murdered. Many people today think they can take the matter of life and death into their own hands. For example, many people ignore or accept the murder of millions of unborn babies in our own nation and around the world. An estimated fifty million unborn babies are killed every year by abortion.

Another area where there is a weakening of respect for human life is euthanasia, or "mercy killing." It is never justified. A sick or elderly person must be given the normal or ordinary treatment to keep him alive. To do otherwise would be murder. Extraordinary treatment is another matter—it is not required.

These days there is more and more pressure for euthanasia. Men are taking the beginning and the end of life into their own hands.

The Fifth Commandment makes it clear that it is wrong to take innocent life. Some people maintain that all killing is wrong and never allowable, no matter what the reasons. But there are certain situations in which killing is not the same thing as murder. The most obvious examples of this are the taking of life in self-defense, capital punishment, and just wars. The Church has never condemned these acts as murder. But since every act of taking human life is a serious matter, we must always look to the Church for guidance in these areas.

Murder is not the only violation of the Fifth Commandment. It would be a mortal sin to injure someone seriously by careless driving. It is wrong *not to care* whether our actions may injure others.

Suicide, the act of killing oneself, is always seriously wrong. God alone is the master of our lives, and we are too precious in his sight

54

to toss our lives away. If someone commits suicide without full knowledge and consent, his responsibility before God is lessened. But even if a man is not blameworthy, his action is still wrong.

It is also wrong not to take proper care of ourselves, with proper diet, exercise, and rest. We should avoid risking our lives by doing foolish stunts when we are encouraged by a dare or a desire to show off. We should protect ourselves from disease by sensible habits of cleanliness and dress. We should avoid impatience and carelessness that may lead to accident or injury.

The sin of eating and drinking too much is a

sin that can harm the body; so can the improper use of medicines and other drugs. Taking a little less food and drink than we want is a small but sensible restraint on our bodies and an excellent form of self-denial. As we have seen, some self-denial is a necessary part of Christian living. We have considered acts against the Fifth Commandment that harm people's physical well-being, such as murder, suicide, and not taking care of your health. In the next chapter, we will consider acts that cause other kinds of harm.

Words to Know:

murder   suicide

55

SELF-DEFENSE AND CAPITAL PUNISHMENT

When attacked, we have a duty to defend ourselves and others. The *Catechism* teaches that "Someone who defends his life is not guilty of murder even if he is forced to deal his aggressor a lethal blow" (CCC 2264). If, in defending ourselves, we are forced to kill the other, that is not murder. CCC 2263 says: "The act of self defense can have a double effect: the preservation of one's own life; and the killing of the aggressor. . . . The one is intended, the other is not."

The Church has always permitted the death penalty, provided it is the "only possible way" to defend human life against a criminal. However, she warns us that cases in which we must resort to the death penalty are now "very rare, if not practically non-existent" (CCC 2267).

JUST WAR

The *Catechism of the Catholic Church* defines the very strict requirements in order for an armed military action against an aggressor nation to be termed a just act of war by the Church:

- The aggressor nation must inflict "lasting, grave, and certain" damage against the defender

- There must be no other remaining means besides war to end the damage of the aggressor

- A serious chance of success must exist

- The evils produced by armed conflict must not exceed the evil of the aggressor

—See CCC 2307–2317

Human life is sacred because from its beginning it involves the creative action of God and it remains forever in a special relationship with the Creator, who is its sole end. God alone is the Lord of life from its beginning until its end: no one can under any circumstance claim for himself the right directly to destroy an innocent human being.

—Joseph Cardinal Ratzinger
Donum Vitae

Preview

In the next lesson, the students will learn about the duty to care for their own lives.

Chapter Eleven: Respect Life
Lesson Four: Our Lives

Aims

The students will learn that the Fifth Commandment demands that we care for ourselves with proper diet, hygiene, exercise, and rest. We should protect ourselves from disease and receive appropriate medical treatment.

They will learn that we must avoid foolish and dangerous stunts. We must avoid carelessness that may lead to accident or injury. Gluttony and improper use of medicines, drugs, or alcohol that harm the body are sinful.

Materials

• *Activity Book*, p. 44

Optional:
• "O Lord, the Giver of all life," *Adoremus Hymnal*, #609

Begin

There is one other form of taking life/killing. This is suicide. Suicide is the taking of one's own life. It is a grave sin, and is always seriously wrong. Sometimes, people who kill themselves do not have full knowledge or consent; if this is the case, their responsibility before God is lessened. However, even if their guilt is lessened, their actions are still wrong.

Develop

1. Finish reading the chapter with the students, paragraphs 9–11.

2. Discuss the great value of every student in God's eyes. We must strive to care for ourselves as God desires. We must not be reckless, doing foolish and dangerous stunts. We must avoid occasions that can cause grave harm to ourselves. We must properly take medicines for our well-being and to restore health.

3. We are called to care for our bodies, as well as our souls. We should enjoy a healthy diet. Review the American Dietary Guide, and our need to eat fruits/vegetables, starches, meats/proteins, and dairy products. We should not have too many unhealthy snacks (such as soda, chips, or candy). We should also strive to eat at regular times. We must strive to be healthy (not too thin or overweight). We must not be gluttonous by eating or drinking too much.

4. We should strive to get proper exercise. It is important to be active and to exercise. In school, this is often easy with organized physical education classes and sports teams. As adults, we must make time to exercise. It helps to have an active hobby.

5. We must also get sufficient rest. Sundays are a day dedicated to worshipping God and to resting. So too, on all the other days of the week, we must still worship God and get sufficient rest.

6. We must also respect our bodies' needs and avoid things that are harmful to our health, such as drugs, smoking, and abuse of alcohol. Have the students research these harmful substances, write a report, and present their findings on them.

Reinforce

1. Have the students work on *Activity Book* p. 44 (see *Teacher's Manual*, p. 137).

2. Have the students complete their research on common harmful substances (drugs, alcohol, cigarettes) and present their findings to the class.

3. For more Church teaching on human life have the students look up the *Catechism of the Catholic Church* 2270, Jeremiah 1:5, and Psalm 139:15–16.

4. Have the students work on the Memorization Questions and Words to Know from this chapter and prepare for their quiz.

Conclude

1. Lead the students in singing "O Lord, the Giver of all life," *Adoremus Hymnal*, #609.

2. End class by leading the students in a prayer for life.

CHAPTER 11

Respect Life

"You shall not kill."

Exodus 20:13

Man is a creature composed of body and soul. Some people go about their business as if they had never heard of the soul. The truth is that both body and soul are essential to the human being. Though separated by death, the body and the soul are destined to be reunited at the resurrection on the Last Day.

Because we have souls made in the image of God we can share in God's life. We call this supernatural life because it is above our natural life here on earth. We can possess it only as God's gift.

The Fifth Commandment, "You shall not kill," gives us the responsibility to care for both the natural and supernatural life that God has given to us and all men.

Right to Life

Since God is the giver of life, no man or group of men has the right to take innocent human life. To do so is **murder**. And murder is a serious crime and a very serious sin, a mortal sin. Murder violates the God-given right to life of the one who is murdered. Many people today think they can take the matter of life and death into their own hands. For example, many people ignore or accept the murder of millions of unborn babies in our own nation and around the world. An estimated fifty million unborn babies are killed every year by abortion.

Another area where there is a weakening of respect for human life is euthanasia, or "mercy killing." It is never justified. A sick or elderly person must be given the normal or ordinary treatment to keep him alive. To do otherwise would be murder. Extraordinary treatment is another matter—it is not required.

These days there is more and more pressure for euthanasia. Men are taking the beginning and the end of life into their own hands.

The Fifth Commandment makes it clear that it is wrong to take innocent life. Some people maintain that all killing is wrong and never allowable, no matter what the reasons. But there are certain situations in which killing is not the same thing as murder. The most obvious examples of this are the taking of life in self-defense, capital punishment, and just wars. The Church has never condemned these acts as murder. But since every act of taking human life is a serious matter, we must always look to the Church for guidance in these areas.

Murder is not the only violation of the Fifth Commandment. It would be a mortal sin to injure someone seriously by careless driving. It is wrong *not to care* whether our actions may injure others.

Suicide, the act of killing oneself, is always seriously wrong. God alone is the master of our lives, and we are too precious in his sight

54

to toss our lives away. If someone commits suicide without full knowledge and consent, his responsibility before God is lessened. But even if a man is not blameworthy, his action is still wrong.

It is also wrong not to take proper care of ourselves, with proper diet, exercise, and rest. We should avoid risking our lives by doing foolish stunts when we are encouraged by a dare or a desire to show off. We should protect ourselves from disease by sensible habits of cleanliness and dress. We should avoid impatience and carelessness that may lead to accident or injury.

The sin of eating and drinking too much is a sin that can harm the body; so can the improper use of medicines and other drugs. Taking a little less food and drink than we want is a small but sensible restraint on our bodies and an excellent form of self-denial. As we have seen, some self-denial is a necessary part of Christian living. We have considered acts against the Fifth Commandment that harm people's physical well-being, such as murder, suicide, and not taking care of your health. In the next chapter, we will consider acts that cause other kinds of harm.

Words to Know:
    murder   suicide

55

"Any one who hates his brother is a murderer, and you know that no murderer has eternal life abiding in him."

1 John 3:15

> **Q. 43** *What does the Fifth Commandment require?*
> The Fifth Commandment requires that we respect all human life from the moment of conception to natural death, as well as the spiritual life of grace in human beings (CCC 2258, 2287).
>
> **Q. 44** *What does the Fifth Commandment forbid?*
> The Fifth Commandment forbids *direct and intentional killing*. This includes murder, the taking of innocent life, curses, and scandal (CCC 2268, 2284).

56

SAINT RAPHAEL

An archangel whose name means "God heals," Raphael is the patron of doctors and the blind. He is an example for us of caring for the health and well-being of others. In the Old Testament book of Tobit, Raphael appears as Azariah to assist blind Tobit and his son Tobias. Betrothed to Sarah, a woman whose last seven husbands all died on their wedding nights, Tobias needed all the help he could get. Raphael intervened, instructed Tobias in how he could survive his wedding night with Sarah, drove a demon from her house, and cured Tobit's blindness. It was this intervention of the archangel in the trials of the weak that identified Raphael as a powerful patron. (See Tob 5:1–6; 6:9–17; 8:1–3; 11:1–14; 12:1–21.)

Preview

In the next lesson, the students' understanding of the material covered in this chapter will be reviewed and assessed.

CHAPTER ELEVEN: RESPECT LIFE
REVIEW AND ASSESSMENT

Aims

The students' understanding of the material covered in this chapter will be reviewed and assessed.

Materials

- Quiz 11, Appendix, p. A-15

Optional:
- "O Lord, the Giver of all life," *Adoremus Hymnal*, #609

Review and Enrichment

1. The students should understand that man is a body-soul unity, made in the image and likeness of God.

2. Life is a precious gift from God. We must protect life from the moment of conception to natural death.

3. The taking of an innocent life is murder. This is always seriously wrong and sinful. The students have learned about murder, abortion, and euthanasia.

4. The students should understand the difference between killing and murder and the extraordinary circumstances of self-defense, capital punishment, and just war. The students should know that we are forbidden to directly and intentionally kill.

5. The students should know that we must care for our own lives. Suicide is a grave sin and is seriously wrong. We must care for our bodies. We must have proper diet, exercise, and rest. We must not be reckless with our activities or in abuse of drugs or alcohol.

Name: _____

Respect Life   **Quiz 11**

Part I: Yes or No.

1. <u>Yes</u> Are the body and soul essential to the human being?
2. <u>Yes</u> Is murder a mortal sin?
3. <u>Yes</u> Does murder violate the God-given right to life of the one who is murdered?
4. <u>Yes</u> Is abortion the killing of an unborn baby?
5. <u>Yes</u> Is abortion murder?
6. <u>Yes</u> Is euthanasia the killing of the elderly or the sick?
7. <u>Yes</u> Is euthanasia murder?
8. <u>Yes</u> Must sick or elderly people be given normal or ordinary treatment to be kept alive?
9. <u>Yes</u> Is careless driving a sin against the Fifth Commandment?
10. <u>No</u> Is it acceptable to risk our lives by doing foolish stunts when we are encouraged by a dare or a desire to show off?
11. <u>Yes</u> Is it a sin to eat and drink too much?
12. <u>Yes</u> Is the improper use of medicines and other drugs wrong?

Part II: Answer in complete sentences.

1. What is the Fifth Commandment?
   <u>The Fifth Commandment is "You shall not kill."</u>

2. What are three examples of situations when killing is not the same as murder?
   <u>Killing is not the same as murder in situations of self-defense, capital punishment, and just wars.</u>

3. What sorts of things should you do to take care of yourself?
   <u>To take care of yourself you should have a proper diet, exercise, and rest.</u>

Part III: Fill in the blanks.

1. To take an innocent human life is called <u>murder</u>.

2. The <u>Fifth</u> Commandment makes it clear that it is wrong to take innocent life.

3. <u>Suicide</u>, the act of killing oneself, is always wrong.

Faith and Life Series • Grade 6 • Appendix A   *A-15*

Assess

1. Distribute the quizzes and read through them with the students to be sure they understand the questions.

2. Administer the quiz. As they hand in their work, you may orally quiz the students on the Memorization Questions from this chapter.

3. After all the quizzes have been handed in, you may wish to review the correct answers with the class.

Conclude

1. Lead the students in singing "O Lord, the Giver of all life," *Adoremus Hymnal*, #609.

2. End class by leading the students in a prayer for life.

Chapter Eleven: Respect Life
Activity Book Answer Keys

Name:_____

Respect Life

Answer the following questions in complete sentences.

1. What is the Fifth Commandment?
   The Fifth Commandment is "You shall not kill."

2. What does the Fifth Commandment forbid?
   The Fifth Commandment forbids direct and intentional killing, including murder, curses, and scandal.

3. What two things is man made up of?
   Man is made up of body and soul.

4. After death, will they be reunited? When?
   Yes. They will be reunited at the resurrection on the Last Day.

5. What does the Fifth Commandment give us the responsibility to do?
   The Fifth Commandment requires that we respect all human life from the moment of conception to natural death, as well as the spiritual life of grace in human beings.

6. Who is the giver of life?
   God is the giver of life.

7. If someone other than God takes away innocent life, is it a sin? Why or why not?
   It is a sin because God is the giver of life.

Name:_____

Right to Life

Fill in the two charts below.

List some reasons people have for abortion and why these reasons are wrong.

REASON	REBUTTAL
Answers will vary.	

List some reasons people have for euthanasia and why these reasons are wrong.

REASON	REBUTTAL

Name:_____

More Right to Life

Answer the following questions in complete sentences.

1. What is abortion?
   Abortion is the killing of an unborn baby.

2. Is abortion a sin? Why?
   Yes, because unborn children also have the right to life.

3. Is abortion legal in the United States?
   Yes.

4. What can we do to stop abortion?
   Answers will vary.

5. What is euthanasia?
   Euthanasia is the killing of a sick or elderly person.

6. Is euthanasia a sin? Why?
   Yes, because it is always a sin to take the life of an innocent person deliberately.

7. How should we care for the elderly?
   We must give the elderly the normal or ordinary treatment to keep them alive.

8. Is it a sin to take the life of another in self-defense? Why or why not?
   No. The Church has never condemned these acts as murder.

Name:_____

Caring for Life

Answer the following questions in complete sentences.

1. Is it a mortal sin to injure someone seriously by accident?
   No.

2. Must we respect our own lives?
   Yes.

3. Are our lives precious to God?
   Yes.

4. Must we care for our bodies as well as our souls? How?
   Yes. We can care for our bodies with proper diet, exercise, and rest. We should avoid unnecessarily risking our lives through foolish stunts, and protect ourselves from disease by sensible habits of cleanliness and dress.

5. Why is abusing drugs and alcohol wrong?
   Abusing drugs and alcohol is wrong because it can cause great harm to our bodies.

TEACHER'S NOTES

CHAPTER TWELVE
CHARITY TOWARD ALL

Catechism of the Catholic Church References

Anger: 2302
Charity: 743, 815, 864, 1813, 1822–39, 1844, 2055, 2086, 2093–94, 2197
Forgiveness: 2842–45, 2862
Hatred: 2303

Jesus as Our Teacher and Model of Holiness: 468–69, 516, 519–21, 561
Respect for the Souls of Others:
Scandal: 2284–87, 2326

Scripture References

Love Enemies: Lk 6:27–35
Good Samaritan: Lk 10:30–37
Reconciliation: Mt 5:22–25; 18:15–17

Self-Affliction: Rom 7:14–25
Cleansing of the Temple: Jn 2:13–17
Scandal: Mt 18:6

Summary of Lesson Content

Lesson 1

Christians must have goodwill toward their neighbors. We are called to "love our enemies." Goodwill is a willed love, rather than emotional love.

Lesson 2

The Fifth Commandment forbids unrighteous anger and hatred. We must not say or do things to hurt others (or take revenge for injuries we have received).

Lesson 3

When someone hurts us, we must forgive him and have goodwill toward him.

We can offer to God our pain and sufferings for the salvation of those who hurt us.

We must show respect and consideration for our enemies.

Just anger helps us to do good and to protect the good.

Lesson 4

Scandal is conscious and deliberate encouragement of others to sin. It is serious as it endangers the eternal reward of other people. There is no greater lack of charity to our neighbor.

The person who gives scandal is responsible for the sins into which others are led.

Following the example of Jesus Christ, we must be willing to forgive those who hurt us.

Chapter Twelve: Charity toward All
Lesson One: Goodwill

Aims

The students will learn that Christians must have goodwill toward their neighbors. We are called to "love our enemies." Goodwill is a willed love, rather than emotional love.

Materials

- *Activity Book*, p. 45

- Bibles

Optional:
- "Love divine, all loves excelling," *Adoremus Hymnal*, #470

Begin

Read Jesus' teaching on loving our enemies from Luke 6:27–35. Discuss this passage:
- Is Jesus talking about an emotional love? (As we have for friends and family?)
- Is Jesus talking about romantic love? (As our parents have?)

- What is Jesus talking about?
- Do we have to like our enemies or the way that they treat us?
- Do we have to mind our thoughts about them?
This discussion should lead to goodwill.

Develop

1. Read paragraphs 1–4.

2. Discuss charity with the students. Charity is the virtue by which we love God and love our neighbors for the sake of our love of God. This means that, because we love God and he is our Father, we must love all of his children (because they are his children). We are all family through God. How may we treat our enemies with charity?
- Pray for them, that they will know God's love and follow his ways.
- Do not wish them harm.
- Be obedient to them if they are our legitimate superiors.

3. Discuss that we must love all our neighbors, including our enemies. How do we know our enemies? Sometimes they are harmful strangers. Sometimes they were once friends. Often, we know our "enemy" because of stereotypes and labels. (E.g., we may be at war with a country

and therefore its people are our enemies. This does not mean that their citizens have necessarily done anything to harm us, nor that they want to be involved in the conflict.) Often, it is because of our own fears that we think of people as our enemies (e.g., a known bully at school, someone from a different background). Read the story of the Good Samaritan, and discuss this passage: Lk 10:30–37. (Note: Jews and Samaritans were enemies, and would not speak to each other during this time.)

4. Sometimes we have fights with people. It is always good to make-up. To do this, we must admit our wrong and apologize. Usually when there is a disagreement, both people are at fault. Discuss ways to make amends and to avoid conflicts.

5. Discuss goodwill. We are obliged to want good things for all people, even people we dislike or do not even know.

Reinforce

1. Have the students work on *Activity Book* p. 45 (see *Teacher's Manual*, p. 149).

2. Have the students dramatize the story of the Good Samaritan. Have them place this story in a modern day setting and discuss the reasons they should have goodwill.

3. Have the students begin working on the Memorization Questions and Words to Know from this chapter (see *Teacher's Manual*, p. 147).

4. Have the students discuss conflict resolution and practical applications.

Conclude

1. Teach the students to sing "Love divine, all loves excelling," *Adoremus Hymnal*, #470.

2. End class by leading the students in praying the Our Father (see *Teacher's Manual*, p. 396).

CHAPTER 12

Charity toward All

"If you love those who love you, what credit is that to you? For even sinners love those who love them. . . . But love your enemies, and do good, and lend, expecting nothing in return; and your reward will be great, and you will be sons of the Most High; for he is kind to the ungrateful and the selfish."

Luke 6:32, 35

The law of love—"Love your neighbor as yourself"—is closely connected to the Fifth Commandment. We have seen many striking and violent offenses against this commandment. There are other more common offenses in which persons are not hurt physically but harm is done. Such actions are far from Christian.

Goodwill

Christ preached goodwill toward all, friends and enemies alike. This is what he meant when he said, "Love your enemies." It is hard enough not to strike back when we are hurt; it is even harder to respond with love.

But how do we know if we love our enemies? Do we have to love them with our feelings? Do I have to *feel* this love for my enemy? Not necessarily. We will not be held accountable for the absence of such feeling, but we are responsible for *goodwill*.

I will know whether I love my enemy if I want what is good for him regardless of how I may feel. We must willingly want what is good for others; the will is the center of love. I may not *like* my enemy, but if I wish him well and treat him well, I am fulfilling Christ's words, "Love your enemies" (Mt 5:44).

One thing that can get in the way of goodwill is anger. When we lose our tempers, we say things and do things to get back at others, to *hurt* them. How terrible, then, the gift of speech can be! We can make it a weapon by yelling at someone, calling someone names, or **cursing**. All these things come under the Fifth Commandment, which prohibits deliberate injury to another human being in any way.

Closely linked to anger is hatred. To hate someone is to wish evil to someone, or even to wish that he did not exist! It may be conceived in the heat of anger but persist even when the feelings have cooled down because, like love, it is willed, although it is the very opposite of love. This is ill will, a wish that another person be hurt and suffer, perhaps even be killed.

Saint John wrote: "Any one who hates his brother is a murderer" (1 Jn 3:15). Indeed, we can have our neighbor dead and buried in our minds without ever doing anything to him, but because of our hatred we are like murderers!

All this can start, perhaps, because we lost our tempers and began to nurture ill will. The

57

danger of anger is that we do things blindly, unaware of the evil in our thoughts, careless of the bitter enmity we may provoke with our stinging words, perhaps stirred even to the point of physical violence.

Jesus left no doubt about the sinfulness of anger when he said in the Sermon on the Mount:

You have heard that it was said to the men of old, "You shall not kill; and whoever kills shall be liable to judgment." But I say to you that every one who is angry with his brother shall be liable to judgment; whoever insults his brother shall be liable to the council. . . (Mt 5:21–22).

When someone has hurt us in some way, we are required to refrain not only from striking back but also from harboring ill will toward him. We must do something positive. Jesus says: "Love your enemies, do good to those who hate you, bless those who curse you, pray for those who abuse you" (Lk 6:27–28).

And Saint Paul wrote: "Bless those who persecute you; bless and do not curse them. . . . Repay no one evil for evil, but take thought for what is noble in the sight of all" (Rom 12:14, 17).

Here is a thought which can take a lot of the sting out of harsh words and ill treatment: try offering the pain to God for the salvation of the one who hurts you. No matter how you feel, surely you would like to see your enemy in heaven someday.

In addition, if you get the opportunity, show respect and consideration to your enemy. Suddenly you may see things through the eyes of Jesus. How many times he was insulted! No

58

SAINT ELIZABETH ANN SETON

The Church's first American-born saint, Elizabeth Ann Seton was shunned by New York society and even by some parts of her family when she converted to the Catholic Church. Raised by her father in the Anglican church, Elizabeth was drawn to the true Church while her husband was convalescing in Italy. After his death in 1803, Elizabeth returned to New York and was received into the Catholic Church on Ash Wednesday, 1805. Soon after her conversion, Elizabeth made efforts to promote Catholic education in the United States. She was banned from contact with some of her family, and the state legislature considered banishing her from the state. Despite these early trials, Elizabeth succeeded in converting much of her family to Catholicism and established a successful religious order and school in Maryland. This school was the first free Catholic school in America. In 1821, Saint Elizabeth Ann Seton died at the age of forty-six. She had only been a Catholic for sixteen years. On September 14, 1975, she became the first native-born American to be canonized.

CHARITY

The word *charity* comes from the Latin word *caritas*, which originally was used to refer to things that were precious, dear, or costly. It later came to be used to mean "affection, love, or esteem."

Preview

In the next lesson, the students will learn about anger.

CHAPTER TWELVE: CHARITY TOWARD ALL
LESSON TWO: ANGER

Aims

The students will learn that the Fifth Commandment forbids unrighteous anger and hatred. We must not say or do things to hurt others (or take revenge for injuries we have received).

Materials

- *Activity Book*, p. 46
- Bible

Optional:
- "Love divine, all loves excelling," *Adoremus Hymnal*, #470

Begin

Discuss ways that we can hurt someone. We can physically harm someone. We can also hurt people with our words. Words can be particularly cruel. We can use them to fight with a person or to turn others against a person, to harm a reputation, or spread lies. Words are more powerful than we might think: they spread quickly, and we cannot take them back. How many times can we think of something we said that we did not really mean, or that we said in anger and later regretted? We will learn more about this today.

Develop

1. Read paragraphs 5–9 from the student text.

2. Paragraph 5 teaches us about revenge. Sometimes, when we feel that we have not been treated fairly, or we are angry because someone has hurt us, we want to "get even" and hurt them as we are hurt. Read what Jesus said about this: Mt 5:39.

3. What is cursing? Cursing is wishing harm upon another. It is evil and it violates the Fifth Commandment.

4. Hatred is linked to anger. It is the chosen ill will we have for another or even ourselves. It is wrong to wish harm for another. Saint John tells us that hatred is like murder.

5. Jesus teaches us to be reconciled with those with whom we are fighting. Read Matthew 5:22–25. We must not have unrighteous anger and hatred in our hearts when we come before the Lord. We must try to reconcile our differences.

Jesus gives us an example of how to reconcile with one who has sinned against us: read Matthew 18:15–17. If you cannot reconcile, how then should you treat this person? (Jesus says to treat the person like a Gentile or a tax collector. What does this mean?) We must treat them as we would anyone we do not know (or hate/are angry with), namely:
- We can pray that we will one day be reconciled.
- We must stop harboring anger or hatred.
- We must avoid talking about this person with unjust anger.
- We must strive to set our feelings aside and be good to this person.
- We must be just in our encounters with him.

6. Sometimes we are very cruel to ourselves. We are frustrated with the ways we do things, or dislike the way we are (or look). Saint Paul reminds us that we must love God in ourselves too! (See Rom 7:14–25.) Self-hate and despair are bad for our souls.

Reinforce

1. Have the students work on *Activity Book* p. 46 (see *Teacher's Manual*, p. 149).

2. Have the students work on a project that enhances their true self-esteem by emphasizing that they are made in God's image. They should reflect on their good qualities while acknowledging their imperfection. They should think about the times that they have received God's forgiveness as well as areas in which they are in need of his forgiveness.

3. Have the students work on the Memorization Questions and Words to Know from this chapter (see *Teacher's Manual*, p. 147).

4. Have the students pray for their enemies.

Conclude

1. Lead the students in singing "Love divine, all loves excelling," *Adoremus Hymnal*, #470.

2. End class by leading the students in praying the Our Father (see *Teacher's Manual*, p. 396).

CHAPTER 12

Charity toward All

"If you love those who love you, what credit is that to you? For even sinners love those who love them. . . . But love your enemies, and do good, and lend, expecting nothing in return; and your reward will be great, and you will be sons of the Most High; for he is kind to the ungrateful and the selfish."

Luke 6:32, 35

The law of love—"Love your neighbor as yourself"—is closely connected to the Fifth Commandment. We have seen many striking and violent offenses against this commandment. There are other more common offenses in which persons are not hurt physically but harm is done. Such actions are far from Christian.

Goodwill

Christ preached goodwill toward all, friends and enemies alike. This is what he meant when he said, "Love your enemies." It is hard enough not to strike back when we are hurt; it is even harder to respond with love.

But how do we know if we love our enemies? Do we have to love them with our feelings? Do I have to *feel* this love for my enemy? Not necessarily. We will not be held accountable for the absence of such feeling, but we are responsible for *goodwill*.

I will know whether I love my enemy if I want what is good for him regardless of how I may feel. We must willingly want what is good for others; the will is the center of love. I may not *like* my enemy, but if I wish him

well and treat him well, I am fulfilling Christ's words, "Love your enemies" (Mt 5:44).

One thing that can get in the way of goodwill is anger. When we lose our tempers, we say things and do things to get back at others, to *hurt* them. How terrible, then, the gift of speech can be! We can make it a weapon by yelling at someone, calling someone names, or **cursing**. All these things come under the Fifth Commandment, which prohibits deliberate injury to another human being in any way.

Closely linked to anger is hatred. To hate someone is to wish evil to someone, or even to wish that he did not exist! It may be conceived in the heat of anger but persist even when the feelings have cooled down because, like love, it is willed, although it is the very opposite of love. This is ill will, a wish that another person be hurt and suffer, perhaps even be killed.

Saint John wrote: "Any one who hates his brother is a murderer" (1 Jn 3:15). Indeed, we can have our neighbor dead and buried in our minds without ever doing anything to him, but because of our hatred we are like murderers!

All this can start, perhaps, because we lost our tempers and began to nurture ill will. The

57

danger of anger is that we do things blindly, unaware of the evil in our thoughts, careless of the bitter enmity we may provoke with our stinging words, perhaps stirred even to the point of physical violence.

Jesus left no doubt about the sinfulness of anger when he said in the Sermon on the Mount:

You have heard that it was said to the men of old, "You shall not kill; and whoever kills shall be liable to judgment." But I say to you that every one who is angry with his brother shall be liable to judgment; whoever insults his brother shall be liable to the council. . . (Mt 5:21–22).

When someone has hurt us in some way, we are required to refrain not only from striking back but also from harboring ill will toward

him. We must do something positive. Jesus says: "Love your enemies, do good to those who hate you, bless those who curse you, pray for those who abuse you" (Lk 6:27–28).

And Saint Paul wrote: "Bless those who persecute you; bless and do not curse them. . . . Repay no one evil for evil, but take thought for what is noble in the sight of all" (Rom 12:14, 17).

Here is a thought which can take a lot of the sting out of harsh words and ill treatment: try offering the pain to God for the salvation of the one who hurts you. No matter how you feel, surely you would like to see your enemy in heaven someday.

In addition, if you get the opportunity, show respect and consideration to your enemy. Suddenly you may see things through the eyes of Jesus. How many times he was insulted! No

58

doubt he felt the pain, like every other man—perhaps even more—but he knew that the men who insulted him were wonderful creations and that no matter how bad they were, they were continually being called to a new life of grace.

Not all anger is wrong. There is such a thing as *just anger*; for instance, when Jesus chased the money-changers from the temple or when he rebuked hypocrites. Righteous anger can help us to stand up for the rights of oppressed persons or come to the defense of those suffering unjust aggression. It may help us to speak up for someone who isn't getting his rights —ourselves or others. Finally, a holy anger may motivate us to fight for a very important cause —like working in the pro-life movement to end the evil of abortion or against other injustices.

Scandal

There is a special case of bad will which Jesus condemned with utmost severity: **scandal**. It is a fully conscious and deliberate bad example or encouragement that could lead another person into sin. This sin endangers someone else's eternal destiny. There can be no greater lack of charity to our neighbor.

Any sinful act could lead another into sin, but anything said or done with the knowledge that it may weaken the faith or destroy the spiritual life of another is scandal. The person who gives scandal is responsible for all the sins into which others are led. Jesus said:

Whoever receives one such child in my name receives me; but whoever causes one of these little ones who believe in me to sin, it would be better for him to have a great millstone fastened round his neck and to be drowned in the depth of the sea (Mt 18:5–6).

Forgive Us, as We Forgive Others

On the Cross Jesus prayed to his Father, "Father, forgive them; for they know not what they do" (Lk 23:34). As followers of Christ we must be willing to forgive those who hurt us. And we must also govern our thoughts and actions so that we do not injure other people physically or spiritually.

Words to Know:

cursing   scandal

"Let all bitterness and wrath and anger and clamor and slander be put away from you, with all malice, and be kind to one another, tenderhearted, forgiving one another, as God in Christ forgave you."

Ephesians 4:31–32

59

DEFINITIONS

- **Anger** is a desire for revenge. When unjust and unrestrained, it is a violation of the Fifth Commandment. If it causes one to desire to kill or seriously injure another, it is a grave sin (see CCC 2302).
- **Hatred** is the sin of deliberately wishing evil upon another. It is a grave sin when one desires grave harm to another (see CCC 2303).
- **Revenge** is the sinful desire to "get even" and hurt others as they have hurt us (see CCC 2302).
- **Cursing** is wishing harm upon another. It violates the Fifth Commandment.
- **Evil** is the result of man's decision to sin, it harms the evildoer as well as those victimized.
- **Hurtful** means anything that harms one's self or others.

Preview

In the next lesson, the students will learn about just anger and forgiveness.

CHAPTER TWELVE: CHARITY TOWARD ALL
LESSON THREE: JUST ANGER AND FORGIVENESS

Aims

The students will learn that when someone hurts us, we must forgive him and have goodwill toward him.

They will learn that we can offer our pain and sufferings to God for the salvation of those who hurt us. We must show respect and consideration for our enemies.

The students will learn that just anger helps us to do good and to protect the good.

Materials

- *Activity Book*, p. 47

- Bible

Optional:
- "Love divine, all loves excelling," *Adoremus Hymnal*, #470

Begin

We have been praying the Our Father this week. The words: "Forgive us our trespasses as we forgive those who trespass against us," should make us think. We will be forgiven as much as we forgive. Forgiveness is important for healing and moving past anger. We should forgive our offenders when they ask for our forgiveness, and even if they cannot. It is important for us to let go of any anger we have, for ultimately it is hurtful to us.

Develop

1. Read paragraphs 10–14 from the student text.

2. In paragraph 12, we see the concept of offering our pain to God for the salvation of the ones who hurt us. How do we "offer up" our pain? We should be willing to suffer the pain we have and unite it to Christ, who suffered for us. We, therefore, give our sufferings to God, knowing that there is great value in suffering (for through Jesus' suffering and death, he won eternal life for mankind). We should pray that God will accept the gift of our suffering for our intention.

3. You may lead the students in meditation on the sufferings of Jesus at the hand of his enemies and how he responded to this suffering: Lk 23:34. Have the students write psalms on the sufferings of Christ and his mercy and forgiveness.

4. Have the students find references to forgiveness of enemies in the Gospels. Have them make a poster or banner of their favorite passage. Suggested passages include: Mt 18:21–22; 11:25; Lk 6:37; 17:3–4.

5. Read about the cleansing of the temple, found in John 2:13–17. Although Jesus was angry, was he sinning? No. Some anger is just anger. Just, or righteous, anger can help us stand up for the rights of ourselves and others. It might commit us to serving a worthy cause, such as the Pro-Life movement. However, in this anger, we do not wish ill of our enemies. We want the good that is just and holy. A good test to see if anger is just or unjust is to ask the question, "is God offended or is my pride offended?" Draw or dramatize the cleansing of the temple.

6. Have the class work on a cause that deserves righteous anger, such as the Pro-Life movement. They may do a project to advance this movement, such as praying, creating posters, or spreading awareness with a fundraiser (e.g., bakesale).

Reinforce

1. Have the students work on *Activity Book* p. 47 (see *Teacher's Manual*, p. 149).

2. Have the students complete their work on a poster project in support of a worthy cause.

3. Have the students create posters/banners based on Scripture verses that address forgiveness (see Develop 4).

4. Have the students work on the Memorization Questions and Words to Know from this chapter (see *Teacher's Manual*, p. 147).

Conclude

1. Lead the students in singing "Love divine, all loves excelling," *Adoremus Hymnal*, #470.

2. End class by leading the students in praying the Our Father (see *Teacher's Manual*, p. 396).

danger of anger is that we do things blindly, unaware of the evil in our thoughts, careless of the bitter enmity we may provoke with our stinging words, perhaps stirred even to the point of physical violence.

Jesus left no doubt about the sinfulness of anger when he said in the Sermon on the Mount:

> You have heard that it was said to the men of old, "You shall not kill; and whoever kills shall be liable to judgment." But I say to you that every one who is angry with his brother shall be liable to judgment; whoever insults his brother shall be liable to the council. . . (Mt 5:21–22).

When someone has hurt us in some way, we are required to refrain not only from striking back but also from harboring ill will toward

him. We must do something positive. Jesus says: "Love your enemies, do good to those who hate you, bless those who curse you, pray for those who abuse you" (Lk 6:27–28).

And Saint Paul wrote: "Bless those who persecute you; bless and do not curse them. . . . Repay no one evil for evil, but take thought for what is noble in the sight of all" (Rom 12:14, 17).

Here is a thought which can take a lot of the sting out of harsh words and ill treatment: try offering the pain to God for the salvation of the one who hurts you. No matter how you feel, surely you would like to see your enemy in heaven someday.

In addition, if you get the opportunity, show respect and consideration to your enemy. Suddenly you may see things through the eyes of Jesus. How many times he was insulted! No

doubt he felt the pain, like every other man— perhaps even more—but he knew that the men who insulted him were wonderful creations and that no matter how bad they were, they were continually being called to a new life of grace.

Not all anger is wrong. There is such a thing as *just anger*; for instance, when Jesus chased the money-changers from the temple or when he rebuked hypocrites. Righteous anger can help us to stand up for the rights of oppressed persons or come to the defense of those suffering unjust aggression. It may help us to speak up for someone who isn't getting his rights —ourselves or others. Finally, a holy anger may motivate us to fight for a very important cause —like working in the pro-life movement to end the evil of abortion or against other injustices.

Scandal

There is a special case of bad will which Jesus condemned with utmost severity: **scandal**. It is a fully conscious and deliberate bad example or encouragement that could lead another person into sin. This sin endangers someone else's eternal destiny. There can be no greater lack of charity to our neighbor.

Any sinful act could lead another into sin, but anything said or done with the knowledge that it may weaken the faith or destroy the spiritual life of another is scandal. The person who gives scandal is responsible for all the sins into which others are led. Jesus said:

> Whoever receives one such child in my name receives me; but whoever causes one of these little ones who believe in me to sin, it would be better for him to have a great millstone fastened round his neck and to be drowned in the depth of the sea (Mt 18:5–6).

Forgive Us, as We Forgive Others

On the Cross Jesus prayed to his Father, "Father, forgive them; for they know not what they do" (Lk 23:34). As followers of Christ we must be willing to forgive those who hurt us. And we must also govern our thoughts and actions so that we do not injure other people physically or spiritually.

Words to Know:
  cursing   scandal

"Let all bitterness and wrath and anger and clamor and slander be put away from you, with all malice, and be kind to one another, tenderhearted, forgiving one another, as God in Christ forgave you."

Ephesians 4:31–32

58

59

USING JUST ANGER

As Jesus was just in his anger against the money changers in the temple, there are many evils in the world today that should inspire just anger. Evils such as poverty, starvation, ignorance, abortion, and euthanasia should move us to action. The students may use their just anger to benefit the world through productive action against evil and injustice. Some opportunities include volunteering to assist in:

• The Pro-Life Movement

• Catholic charities and societies benefitting the poor

• A local soup kitchen

• A local nursing home

JUDGING JUST ANGER

Even when acting with just anger, we must always remember charity. It is possible to get overzealous and to believe we are acting in just anger when we are not. A good way to judge is to remember Jesus' law of love (Mt 22:39; Jn 13:34). Although I am angry at the injustice, do I love those with whom I disagree? Do I pray for them and would I be willing to forgive them if they repented? Do I hate the sin, but love the sinner? The students should remember the advice of Saint Augustine of Hippo: "Love and do what you will."

Learn to do good; seek justice, correct oppression; defend the fatherless, plead for the widow.

—Isaiah 1:17

Preview

In the next lesson, the students will learn about scandal.

CHAPTER TWELVE: CHARITY TOWARD ALL
LESSON FOUR: SCANDAL

Aims

The students will learn that scandal is conscious and deliberate encouragement of others to sin. It is serious as it endangers the eternal reward of other people. There is no greater lack of charity.

They will learn that the person who gives scandal is responsible for the sins into which others are led.

The students will learn that by the example of Jesus Christ, we must be willing to forgive those who hurt us.

Materials

• *Activity Book*, p. 48

Optional:
• "Love divine, all loves excelling," *Adoremus Hymnal*, #470

Begin

Review that, as humans, we must protect the life of our body and soul. We protect the life of our body with good health, proper diet, exercise and sufficient rest. We care for the life of our soul by reception of the Sacraments, prayer, living the moral life, and reading the Scriptures and spiritual readings.

We are bound to protect the lives of others. We care for them bodily through Corporal Works of Mercy and spiritually through Spiritual Works of Mercy. We must never lead a person to spiritual death.

Develop

1. Finish reading the chapter (paragraphs 15–17).

2. Review the Corporal Works of Mercy with the students. The students may do projects as acts of mercy (suggestions are in parentheses). Corporal Works of Mercy: feed the hungry (collect food for the poor); give drink to the thirsty (collect drinks for the poor, such as juice and milk); clothe the naked (have a clothes-drive); visit the sick (make get-well cards); visit the imprisoned (write letters of Christian encouragement to be taken to prisons by the prison ministry of your diocese); shelter the homeless (collect blankets and toiletries for a homeless shelter); bury the dead (visit a cemetery and pray for these souls).

3. Review the Spiritual Works of Mercy with the students. The students may do projects as acts of mercy (suggestions are in parentheses). Spiritual Works of Mercy: admonish the sinner (examine conscience and receive Sacrament of

Penance); instruct the ignorant (visit a class of young students and share the posters/banners that you made in the last lesson); counsel the doubtful (have them share stories of faith or Bible stories with a younger class or with their families); comfort the sorrowful (make sympathy cards for parishioners who recently had a loved one die); bear wrongs patiently (have the students write prayers offering up their sufferings to God); forgive all injuries (have the students meditate on injuries and people they need to forgive); pray for the living and the dead (as a class pray for others, including the holy souls in purgatory).

4. Discuss scandal. Read Matthew 18:6. Jesus tells us that it is better to be cast into the sea with a millstone around our neck than to scandalize anyone. Scandal is providing a bad example that leads someone else to sin or lose his faith. We should never encourage anyone to sin.

Reinforce

1. Have the students work on *Activity Book* p. 48 (see *Teacher's Manual*, p. 149).

2. Have the students review the Memorization Questions and Words to Know from this chapter and review for the chapter quiz and unit test.

Conclude

1. Lead the students in singing "Love divine, all loves excelling," *Adoremus Hymnal*, #470.

2. End class by leading the students in praying the Our Father (see *Teacher's Manual*, p. 396).

danger of anger is that we do things blindly, unaware of the evil in our thoughts, careless of the bitter enmity we may provoke with our stinging words, perhaps stirred even to the point of physical violence.

Jesus left no doubt about the sinfulness of anger when he said in the Sermon on the Mount:

> You have heard that it was said to the men of old, "You shall not kill; and whoever kills shall be liable to judgment." But I say to you that every one who is angry with his brother shall be liable to judgment; whoever insults his brother shall be liable to the council. . . (Mt 5:21–22).

When someone has hurt us in some way, we are required to refrain not only from striking back but also from harboring ill will toward

him. We must do something positive. Jesus says: "Love your enemies, do good to those who hate you, bless those who curse you, pray for those who abuse you" (Lk 6:27–28).

And Saint Paul wrote: "Bless those who persecute you; bless and do not curse them. . . . Repay no one evil for evil, but take thought for what is noble in the sight of all" (Rom 12:14, 17).

Here is a thought which can take a lot of the sting out of harsh words and ill treatment: try offering the pain to God for the salvation of the one who hurts you. No matter how you feel, surely you would like to see your enemy in heaven someday.

In addition, if you get the opportunity, show respect and consideration to your enemy. Suddenly you may see things through the eyes of Jesus. How many times he was insulted! No

---

doubt he felt the pain, like every other man—perhaps even more—but he knew that the men who insulted him were wonderful creations and that no matter how bad they were, they were continually being called to a new life of grace.

Not all anger is wrong. There is such a thing as *just anger*; for instance, when Jesus chased the money-changers from the temple or when he rebuked hypocrites. Righteous anger can help us to stand up for the rights of oppressed persons or come to the defense of those suffering unjust aggression. It may help us to speak up for someone who isn't getting his rights —ourselves or others. Finally, a holy anger may motivate us to fight for a very important cause —like working in the pro-life movement to end the evil of abortion or against other injustices.

Scandal

There is a special case of bad will which Jesus condemned with utmost severity: **scandal**. It is a fully conscious and deliberate bad example or encouragement that could lead another person into sin. This sin endangers someone else's eternal destiny. There can be no greater lack of charity to our neighbor.

Any sinful act could lead another into sin, but anything said or done with the knowledge that it may weaken the faith or destroy the spiritual life of another is scandal. The person who gives scandal is responsible for all the sins into which others are led. Jesus said:

> Whoever receives one such child in my name receives me; but whoever causes one of these little ones who believe in me to sin, it would be better for him to have a great millstone fastened round his neck and to be drowned in the depth of the sea (Mt 18:5–6).

Forgive Us, as We Forgive Others

On the Cross Jesus prayed to his Father, "Father, forgive them; for they know not what they do" (Lk 23:34). As followers of Christ we must be willing to forgive those who hurt us. And we must also govern our thoughts and actions so that we do not injure other people physically or spiritually.

Words to Know:
cursing   scandal

"Let all bitterness and wrath and anger and clamor and slander be put away from you, with all malice, and be kind to one another, tenderhearted, forgiving one another, as God in Christ forgave you."

Ephesians 4:31–32

Q. 45   *What is scandal?*
Scandal is the sin of leading others into sin by the example of our action (CCC 2284).

Q. 46   *Does the Fifth Commandment require us to have goodwill toward all, even our enemies?*
Yes, the Fifth Commandment requires us to have goodwill toward all, even our enemies (CCC 2262).

BEING A GOOD EXAMPLE

Have the students list:

Ways to give bad example:
- Cursing or swearing
- Skipping Mass
- Speaking ill of others
- Speaking ill of holy things

Ways to give good example:
- Practice the Corporal Works of Mercy (see p. 83)
- Practice the Spiritual Works of Mercy (see p. 83)
- Pray
- Pay attention at Mass
- Pay attention in religion class

Preview

In the next lesson, the students' understanding of the material covered in this chapter and unit will be reviewed and assessed. There will be a quiz and unit test.

CHAPTER TWELVE: CHARITY TOWARD ALL
REVIEW AND ASSESSMENT

Aims

The students' understanding of the material covered in this chapter will be reviewed and assessed.

Materials

- Quiz 12, Appendix, p. A-16

Optional:
- "Love divine, all loves excelling," *Adoremus Hymnal*, #470

Review and Enrichment

1. The students should know that they must have goodwill toward all people, including their enemies.

2. The students should know the definitions of anger, vengeance, cursing, hatred, scandal.

3. Forgiveness and reconciliation with those whom we offend, and who offend us, is of great importance to our souls.

4. The students should understand what just anger is and how it differs from sinful anger.

5. The students should understand the need to care for the life of our bodies and souls. Examples of this are found in the Corporal and Spiritual Works of Mercy. The students should know both the Corporal Works of Mercy and the Spiritual Works of Mercy.

Name:

Charity toward All   **Quiz 12**

Part I: Yes or No.

1. <u>Yes</u> Must we have goodwill toward everyone?
2. <u>No</u> Must we have good feelings about everyone?
3. <u>Yes</u> Can we love our enemies by wishing them well and treating them justly?
4. <u>No</u> Must we like our enemies?
5. <u>Yes</u> It is wrong to wish that another person be hurt and suffer, or perhaps be killed?
6. <u>Yes</u> Should we show respect and consideration for our enemies?
7. <u>Yes</u> When we suffer the sting of harsh words or ill treatment from others can we offer the pain to God for the one who hurts us?
8. <u>No</u> Is all anger wrong?
9. <u>Yes</u> Can just anger help us to stand up for the rights of the oppressed or come to the defense of someone?

Part II: Answer the following in complete sentences.

1. What other actions does the Fifth Commandment prohibit besides murder?
   <u>Answers will vary: Besides murder, the Fifth Commandment prohibits yelling at someone, calling someone names, and cursing.</u>

2. What are some of the dangers of anger?
   <u>Answers will vary: Some of the dangers of anger are that we do things blindly, unaware of the evil in our thoughts, careless of the bitter enmity we may provoke with our stinging words, perhaps stirred even to the point of physical violence.</u>

3. What is the sin of scandal?
   <u>The sin of scandal is setting a bad example that could lead others into sin.</u>

Part III: Fill in the blanks.

1. The <u>Fifth</u> Commandment prohibits actions that cause deliberate injury to another human being.

2. To <u>hate</u> someone is to wish evil to someone.

3. Jesus says: "<u>Love</u> your enemies, do good to those who hate you, bless those who curse you, pray for those who abuse you" (Lk 6:27–28).

4. Saint Paul wrote: "<u>Bless</u> those who persecute you; bless and do not curse them ... Repay no one evil for evil, but take thought for what is noble in the sight of all" (Rom 12:14–17).

Assess

1. Distribute the quizzes and read through them with the students to be sure they understand the questions.

2. Administer the quiz. As they hand in their work, you may orally quiz the students on the Memorization Questions from this chapter.

3. After all the quizzes have been handed in, you may wish to review the correct answers with the class.

Conclude

1. Lead the students in singing "Love divine, all loves excelling," *Adoremus Hymnal*, #470.

2. End class by leading the students in the Our Father (see *Teacher's Manual*, p. 396).

CHAPTER TWELVE: CHARITY TOWARD ALL
ACTIVITY BOOK ANSWER KEYS

Name:_____

Charity toward All

Answer the following questions in complete sentences.

1. Is charity in our will or our emotions?
   <u>Charity is in our will.</u>

2. To whom must you be charitable?
   <u>We must be charitable to everyone.</u>

3. Must you be charitable to your enemies as well?
   <u>Yes.</u>

4. Who gave us the best example of charity?
   <u>Jesus gave us the best example of charity.</u>

5. What kind of love did Jesus give?
   <u>Answers will vary. Something to the effect of unconditional love.</u>

6. How can we follow Jesus' example?
   <u>Answers will vary. See p. 58 of the student text for many examples.</u>

Faith and Life Series • Grade 6 • Chapter 12 • Lesson 1   45

Name:_____

Love Your Enemies

Answer the following questions in complete sentences.

1. Jesus told us to love our enemies. What does this mean?
   <u>To love our enemies means to have goodwill toward them. That is, to wish him well and treat him well.</u>

2. What can get in the way of goodwill?
   <u>Anger can get in the way of goodwill.</u>

3. What happens when we lose our tempers?
   <u>When we lose our tempers, we say and do things to hurt others.</u>

4. What is ill will?
   <u>Ill will comes from hatred. It is a wish that another person be hurt and suffer, perhaps even be killed.</u>

5. What did Saint John teach us about ill will?
   <u>Saint John taught that "any one who hates his brother is a murderer."</u>

46   *Faith and Life Series • Grade 6 • Chapter 12 • Lesson 2*

Name:_____

Forgiveness

Answer the following questions in complete sentences.

1. What prayer of forgiveness did Jesus say upon the Cross?
   <u>Jesus prayed "Father, forgive them; for they know not what they do."</u>

2. What should we learn about forgiveness from Jesus' example?
   <u>We must always be willing to forgive others.</u>

3. What is the condition for our forgiveness according to the Our Father? (What must we do to be forgiven?)
   <u>According the the Our Father, we must forgive others in order to be forgiven.</u>

4. If we offend God, how can we seek his forgiveness?
   <u>Answer is not in text, but students should know: the Sacrament of Penance.</u>

Faith and Life Series • Grade 6 • Chapter 12 • Lesson 3   47

Name:_____

Scandal

Answer the following questions in complete sentences.

1. What is scandal?
   <u>Scandal is the sin of leading others into sin by the example of our action.</u>

2. What does scandal endanger?
   <u>Scandal endangers someone else's eternal destiny.</u>

3. For what is the person who gives scandal responsible?
   <u>The person who gives scandal is responsible for all the sins into which others are led.</u>

4. Write out Matthew 18:6. What does this verse mean?
   <u>"Whoever causes one of these little ones who believe in me to sin, it would be better for him to have a great millstone fastened round his neck and to be drowned in the depth of the sea." This verse teaches us how serious the sin of scandal is.</u>

6. What should you do if you are a cause of scandal for someone else?
   <u>Answers will vary.</u>

7. Why is there no greater lack of charity toward our neighbor than scandal?
   <u>There is no greater lack of charity than scandal because scandal endangers someone else's eternal destiny.</u>

48   *Faith and Life Series • Grade 6 • Chapter 12 • Lesson 4*

TEACHER'S NOTES

TEACHER'S NOTES

UNIT THREE TEST
CHAPTERS 9–12

> **CHAPTER NINE: CITIZENSHIP—RIGHTS AND DUTIES**
>
> **CHAPTER TEN: CHURCH AUTHORITY—OUR FATHERS IN FAITH**
>
> **CHAPTER ELEVEN: RESPECT LIFE**
>
> **CHAPTER TWELVE: CHARITY TOWARD ALL**

Aims

The students' understanding of the material covered in this unit will be reviewed and assessed.

Materials

• Unit 3 Test, Appendix, pp. A-17 and A-18

Assess

1. Distribute the unit tests and read through them with the students to be sure they understand the questions.

2. Administer the test.

3. After all the tests have been handed in, you may wish to review the correct answers with the class.

Name: _____

Unit 3 Test   **Chapters 9–12**

Part I: Fill in the blanks.

1. <u>Scandal</u> is giving a fully conscious and deliberate bad example or encouragement meant to lead another person into sin.

2. To take an innocent human life is <u>murder</u>.

3. Murder is a <u>mortal (or serious)</u> sin.

4. <u>Suicide</u>, the act of killing oneself, is always wrong.

Part II: Yes or No.

1. <u>No</u> Just because the government decides something is legal, does that mean that it is moral?

2. <u>Yes</u> Are abortion and euthanasia murder?

3. <u>Yes</u> Must sick or elderly people be given normal or ordinary treatment to be kept alive?

4. <u>No</u> Is it morally acceptable to risk our lives by doing foolish stunts when we are encouraged by a dare or a desire to show off?

5. <u>Yes</u> Is it a sin to eat and drink too much?

6. <u>Yes</u> Must we wish well to everyone?

7. <u>No</u> Must we feel good about everyone?

8. <u>Yes</u> Does Jesus ask us to forgive those who hurt us?

9. <u>Yes</u> Should we care about the well-being of people in other countries?

Name: _____

Unit 3 Test (continued)

Part III: Answer the following in complete sentences.

1. What should the government do for its citizens?
   <u>The government should make just laws for its citizens and promote what is truly good for all members of the society (the common good).</u>

2. What does a good citizen do?
   <u>A good citizen obeys all just laws and regulations, pays taxes, and when necessary defends his nation from attack.</u>

3. Whose authority is greater, the government's or God's? <u>God's authority is greater than the government's.</u>

4. How should we treat our enemies?
   <u>We must love and forgive them. We do not have to like them, but we must wish them well and treat them well.</u>

5. Why is scandal wrong?
   <u>Scandal is wrong because it endangers someone's eternal destiny.</u>

6. What is hatred?
   <u>Hatred is wishing someone evil or even that he did not exist.</u>

Part IV: Matching.

1. <u>f</u> a successor of the Apostles	a. Vicar of Christ
2. <u>c</u> the first Pope	b. Church
3. <u>a</u> rules the Church on earth on behalf of Christ	c. Saint Peter
4. <u>b</u> the Body of Christ	d. diocese
5. <u>e</u> rules of the Church	e. precepts of the Church
6. <u>d</u> geographic area governed by a bishop	f. bishop

TEACHER'S NOTES

CHAPTER THIRTEEN
THE SACRED FLAME

Catechism of the Catholic Church References

Dignity of the Human Person: 1700–9, 1710–12
Equality and Differences among Men: 1934–38, 1944–46
Man Created in the Image of God: 355–57, 380–81
Man's Freedom: 1730–42, 1743–48
Ninth Commandment: 2514–27, 2528–33
Purity of Heart: 2517–19, 2531

Struggle for Purity: 2520–27, 2530, 2532–33
Respect for the Dignity of Persons: 2284–2301, 2326
Sixth Commandment: 2331–91, 2392–2400
Vocation to Chastity: 2337–59, 2394–95
Love and Fidelity of Spouses: 2360–65, 2397

Scripture References

Creation of Man: Gen 1:26—2:25

Temples of the Holy Spirit: 1 Cor 6:19

Summary of Lesson Content

Lesson 1

All men were made in the image and likeness of God. All men are loved by God.

Everyone is worthy of respect, for everyone was made by God to be loved by God and to share in his life.

We must have self-respect and respect for others. To maintain this, we must do what is right and avoid doing what is wrong.

Lesson 2

Man is fruitful and multiplies. Reproduction is a blessing from God.

Man is free and must use the power of reproduction according to God's will and design.

God's commandments are not mere restrictions, but the way to true freedom.

Lesson 3

The Sixth Commandment guides our actions. The Ninth Commandment guides our thoughts.

God reserves the good of human sexuality for marriage. Any use of human sexuality outside of marriage is seriously sinful.

In marriage, we share in God's creative powers. The love between a man and a woman in marriage, made fruitful and blessed by God, lovingly brings a child into the family.

Lesson 4

The proper use of our sexual powers is called chastity. Chastity requires self-denial and self-control.

To be chaste, we must avoid occasions for sin and temptations. We must be modest in our appearance and in our observation.

Impurity is a sexual thought or action that violates the Sixth and Ninth Commandments.

Chapter Thirteen: The Sacred Flame
Lesson One: Respect

Aims

The students will learn that all men were made in the image and likeness of God. All men are loved by God.

They will learn that everyone is worthy of respect, for everyone was made by God to be loved by God and to share in his life.

They will learn that we must have self-respect and respect for others. We must do what is right and avoid doing what is wrong.

Materials

- *Activity Book*, p. 49

- Bibles

Optional:
- "All you who seek a comfort sure," *Adoremus Hymnal*, #472

Begin

Review the accounts of the Creation of Man: Gen 1:26—2:25. The students should be able to discuss the origin of man and his distinct dignity as a creature of God.
- Man is created in relationship with himself and with God.

- Man is created naked and without shame.
- Man is in God's image and likeness.
- Man has a special dignity because of his relationship with God and because he is a rational body-soul unity.

Develop

1. Read paragraphs 1–4 from the student text.

2. Men are unique and distinct from other creatures, since they were created to live in life-long, loving relationships. Man is capable of commitment and sacrificial love. He is drawn toward the unity found in relationship. Man is first given love by God and his parents. He is able to return this love and share it with others. This love becomes fruitful when it is committed in the life-long, faithful relationship of marriage. Marriage is a sacred bond—a covenant—in which a man and woman freely give themselves in love to one another. Men and women marry to help each other get to heaven and to share their love with children, if they are so blessed to have them.

3. At Baptism, we become temples of the Holy Spirit (1 Cor 6:19). This means that the indwelling of the Blessed Trinity, and the life of grace, resides within each of us, and brings eternal life to our souls. This is a great gift from God. We must, therefore, love ourselves and all men as God's own.

4. We must have respect for ourselves and others. This means that we must do good and avoid evil. We love ourselves and others. We strive for the good that God intends for us. To do this we need self-control and virtue (to overcome our weaknesses). To help us, at Baptism the Holy Spirit gives us his gifts. If we are using these gifts well, we can see the fruits of the Holy Spirit in our lives. If we exhibit the fruits, we are living the gifts!

5. God has a special call for each of us—for many it is marriage. We must always act in a way that will prepare us for our vocations—respecting ourselves as someone's future husband or wife, and others as someone's future husband or wife. Also, some people are called to be priests and religious. We must treat people with respect for who they are, and for who they are called to be.

Reinforce

1. Have the students work on *Activity Book* p. 49 (see *Teacher's Manual*, p. 163).

2. You may review the vocations to married life, religious life, and Holy Orders. We will examine these in greater detail later as we discuss chastity appropriate to our vocations.

3. The students should begin working on the Memorization Questions and Words to Know from this chapter (see *Teacher's Manual*, p. 159).

4. You may wish to discuss respect further, in thought, word, deed, and omission.

Conclude

1. Teach the students to sing "All you who seek a comfort sure," *Adoremus Hymnal*, #472.

2. End class by leading the students in a Prayer for Purity (on the facing page).

CHAPTER 13

The Sacred Flame

"You shall not commit adultery. . . . You shall not covet your neighbor's house; you shall not covet your neighbor's wife, or his manservant, or his maidservant, or his ox, or his donkey, or anything that is your neighbor's."

Exodus 20:14, 17

All men were made by God in his image and likeness. And all of us are known and loved by God as distinct individuals. It is this special relation each of us has to God that is the foundation of our dignity as persons and the source of our rights as human beings.

Everyone has this dignity as a child of God, and so every individual is worthy of our respect, for each person is made by God to be loved by him and to have God's life within. We ourselves have this dignity, of course, and so we must also have respect for ourselves—self-respect.

To maintain our self-respect and respect for others we have to do what we know is right and avoid what we know is wrong. To do this we need to develop our self-control and overcome our weaknesses.

The Sixth and Ninth Commandments, "You shall not commit adultery" and "You shall not covet your neighbor's wife," demand from us that respect which we are to have for ourselves and for others, and in a special way for those things that belong to married life and the family.

Be Fruitful

When a seed is planted in the earth there are certain laws that govern its development, and if the conditions are right it grows into a specific plant, whether it is a sunflower or an olive tree. Then it will produce seeds after its own kind which will propagate the species—that is, reproduce or multiply. God finds this very good; it is the way he designed things.

Animals propagate as well. Like the flowers, when conditions are right everything happens according to certain laws and there is no misuse of these powers. We don't have to preach self-control to plants and animals because they act through instinct.

But man is different. Like plants and animals, he reproduces and multiplies and fills the earth. This is what God wants, for Scripture says:

So God created man in his own image, in the image of God he created him; male and female he created them. And God blessed them, and God said to them, "Be fruitful and multiply, and fill the earth. . ." (Gen 1:27–28).

61

But, unlike the rest of visible creation, man does not multiply blindly, following the seasons, like plants, or by instinct, like animals. These creatures are not free to make decisions about their reproductive powers. Man *is* free. This is an aspect of man's dignity. It is also a possible source of abuse.

Man may have very powerful urges, but he is not led blindly by his instincts. Man is called to cooperate with God in a plan that is not recorded in his genes or in his blood but is revealed by God in his commandments—specifically, the Sixth and Ninth Commandments.

Many people look upon these two commandments as restrictions, but we can think about them in the following way. The seed that becomes a sunflower is guided to this fulfillment by a biochemical blueprint invented by God. Though we do not see it, God, who holds the sacred flame of *all* life, has a blueprint for our fulfillment too. Man should thus follow God's plan in the use of his reproductive powers. If God can lead the sunflower to full beauty from a seed, then he can lead a man to fullness of life by the laws he has given us, though we may see only a little of his plan.

When you are about to plant a seed and water it, you do not have to remind it to trust God; the seed knows all that, so to speak. It is *man* who needs to be reminded to trust God!

Laws of Life

All this is said to point out the proper beauty and nature of the human reproductive powers. The Sixth Commandment guides us in our actions, the Ninth in our thoughts and desires. It is important to remember that all our actions start in our mind, and so we should see the importance of properly directing our thoughts and desires.

Put simply, God reserved the pleasures and joys of human sexuality for marriage. Any use of these powers outside of marriage is a serious sin. God plans to give those who marry an actual share in the creation of a new human being; God creates the soul and the human parents help fashion the body. Does it seem

62

Preview

In the next lesson, the students will learn about God's blessing of fruitfulness.

CHAPTER THIRTEEN: THE SACRED FLAME
LESSON TWO: BE FRUITFUL!

Aims

The students will learn that man is fruitful and multiplies. Reproduction is a blessing from God.

They will learn that man is free and must use the power of reproduction according to God's will and design. God's commandments are not mere restrictions, but the way to true freedom.

Materials

• *Activity Book*, p. 50

Optional:
• "All you who seek a comfort sure," *Adoremus Hymnal*, #472

Begin

Man has free will. He can make choices that have consequences. For example, man can choose to use his gift of intellect to make tools that simplify his work and make him more productive. He may choose to love, to give to others, and to help others. He can choose not to learn or train his brain. Man must live with the consequences of whatever he chooses. Intellect is not man's only power. He has many different gifts from God, one of which is his power of sexuality. God has a design for this gift.

Develop

1. Read paragraphs 5–11 from the student text.

2. It is God's will that the created, visible world is fruitful and multiplies. We see that it is good when a tree grows and gives fruit to eat; from the seeds of this fruit, other trees can grow. We see it is good that animals have babies, so we may benefit from them (e.g., milk and meat from cows). God provides a structure for the cycle of life. Plants produce fruit and grow in different seasons (new life in spring, dormant in the winter). Animals mate through instinct and have their babies; the babies grow and eventually they, too, mate. God provides a structure in which it is good for all species to procreate.

3. Man is good and God blessed man to be fruitful and to multiply. Man, however, is different from plants and animals because he has free will. God provides the best structure possible for the procreation of new life in humans: marriage. Man is also unique from animals in that he does not mate blindly, and is not driven solely by his urges. He is called to use his sexual powers according to God's plan. Man, however, has free will and can abuse these powers and deviate from God's plan. This deviation is seriously wrong. God knows what is best for us and gives us the strength to do what is right. We must trust in God.

4. Celibacy means to possess one's self and save the sacred powers of fruitfulness for God. As children and youths, we are all celibate. As our powers mature and we are called to give of ourselves, we are to live chaste lives. Chastity is a self-gift, according to one's state in life and God's plan. For married people, this means faithful love for a spouse. For single people, this means reserving sexual powers until marriage. For priests, religious, and consecrated single people, this means sacrificing these powers and gifts to God for the life of the Church.

Reinforce

1. Have the students work on *Activity Book* p. 50 (see *Teacher's Manual*, p. 163).

2. Explain the life cycles of various plants or animals. Let the students see plant and animal life are dependent upon God and the structure he provides for life to exist (e.g., plants need nutrients, water, and sunlight; animals need plants and other animals).

Conclude

1. Lead the class in singing "All you who seek a comfort sure," *Adoremus Hymnal*, #472.

2. End class by leading the students in a Prayer for Purity (see *Teacher's Manual*, p. 155).

CHAPTER 13

The Sacred Flame

"You shall not commit adultery. . . . You shall not covet your neighbor's house; you shall not covet your neighbor's wife, or his manservant, or his maidservant, or his ox, or his donkey, or anything that is your neighbor's."

Exodus 20:14, 17

All men were made by God in his image and likeness. And all of us are known and loved by God as distinct individuals. It is this special relation each of us has to God that is the foundation of our dignity as persons and the source of our rights as human beings.

Everyone has this dignity as a child of God, and so every individual is worthy of our respect, for each person is made by God to be loved by him and to have God's life within. We ourselves have this dignity, of course, and so we must also have respect for ourselves—self-respect.

To maintain our self-respect and respect for others we have to do what we know is right and avoid what we know is wrong. To do this we need to develop our self-control and overcome our weaknesses.

The Sixth and Ninth Commandments, "You shall not commit adultery" and "You shall not covet your neighbor's wife," demand from us that respect which we are to have for ourselves and for others, and in a special way for those things that belong to married life and the family.

Be Fruitful

When a seed is planted in the earth there are certain laws that govern its development, and if the conditions are right it grows into a specific plant, whether it is a sunflower or an olive tree. Then it will produce seeds after its own kind which will propagate the species—that is, reproduce or multiply. God finds this very good; it is the way he designed things.

Animals propagate as well. Like the flowers, when conditions are right everything happens according to certain laws and there is no misuse of these powers. We don't have to preach self-control to plants and animals because they act through instinct.

But man is different. Like plants and animals, he reproduces and multiplies and fills the earth. This is what God wants, for Scripture says:

So God created man in his own image, in the image of God he created him; male and female he created them. And God blessed them, and God said to them, "Be fruitful and multiply, and fill the earth. . ." (Gen 1:27–28).

61

But, unlike the rest of visible creation, man does not multiply blindly, following the seasons, like plants, or by instinct, like animals. These creatures are not free to make decisions about their reproductive powers. Man *is* free. This is an aspect of man's dignity. It is also a possible source of abuse.

Man may have very powerful urges, but he is not led blindly by his instincts. Man is called to cooperate with God in a plan that is not recorded in his genes or in his blood but is revealed by God in his commandments—specifically, the Sixth and Ninth Commandments.

Many people look upon these two commandments as restrictions, but we can think about them in the following way. The seed that becomes a sunflower is guided to this fulfillment by a biochemical blueprint invented by God. Though we do not see it, God, who holds the sacred flame of *all* life, has a blueprint for our fulfillment too. Man should thus follow God's plan in the use of his reproductive powers. If God can lead the sunflower to full beauty from a seed, then he can lead a man to fullness of life by the laws he has given us, though we may see only a little of his plan.

When you are about to plant a seed and water it, you do not have to remind it to trust God; the seed knows all that, so to speak. It is *man* who needs to be reminded to trust God!

Laws of Life

All this is said to point out the proper beauty and nature of the human reproductive powers. The Sixth Commandment guides us in our actions, the Ninth in our thoughts and desires. It is important to remember that all our actions start in our mind, and so we should see the importance of properly directing our thoughts and desires.

Put simply, God reserved the pleasures and joys of these powers outside of marriage is a serious sin. God plans to give those who marry an actual share in the creation of a new human being; God creates the soul and the human parents help fashion the body. Does it seem

62

THEOLOGICAL DEFINITIONS

The *Catechism of the Catholic Church* defines:

- Chastity: This is the moral virtue that, under the cardinal virtue of temperance, provides for the successful integration of sexuality within the person, leading to the inner unity of bodily and spiritual being (2337). Chastity is called one of the fruits of the Holy Spirit.

- Celibacy: This is the state or condition of those who have chosen to remain unmarried for the sake of the kingdom of heaven in order to give themselves entirely to God and to the service of his people. In the Latin Church, celibacy is obligatory for bishops and priests. In some Eastern Churches, celibacy is a prerequisite for ordination only of bishops; priests may not marry after they have been ordained.

—Glossary, CCC, Second Edition

The disciples said to [Jesus], "If such is the case of a man with his wife, it is not expedient to marry." But he said to them, "Not all men can receive this precept, both only those to whom it is given. For there are eunuchs who have been so from birth, and there are eunuchs who have been made eunuchs by men, and there are eunuchs who have made themselves eunuchs for the sake of the kingdom of heaven. He who is able to receive this, let him receive it."

—Matthew 19:10–12

Preview

In the next lesson, the students will learn about the laws of life.

CHAPTER THIRTEEN: THE SACRED FLAME
LESSON THREE: LAWS OF LIFE

Aims

The students will learn that the Sixth Commandment guides our actions. The Ninth Commandment guides our thoughts.

They will learn that God reserves the good of human sexuality for marriage. Any use of human sexuality outside of marriage is seriously sinful.

They will learn that, in marriage, we share in God's creative powers. The love between a husband and wife, made fruitful and blessed by God, lovingly brings a child into the family.

Materials

- *Activity Book*, p. 51

Optional:
- "All you who seek a comfort sure," *Adoremus Hymnal*, #472

Begin

God knows that human babies deserve the very best care. To be conceived and to nurture their growth, they need a mother and a father. God knows that the sexual love of a man and a woman can (with God) bring forth new life. Man can choose not to follow God's plan, but he will suffer the consequences of his actions. God, knowing the needs of babies, designed sexual love to be reserved for marriage. Man can choose this good and has the power to live up to this choice with God's help.

Develop

1. Read paragraphs 12–14 from the student text.

2. The goods and joys of sexuality are reserved for marriage. (Sex is like God's wedding gift to a couple who vow fidelity to one another for the rest of their lives.) All sexual love is to be unitive (generous self-gift of the husband and wife to one another) and procreative (open to life if God should bless the married couple with a baby). If these three conditions are not met—in marriage, unitive, procreative—then the use of sexual powers is a serious sin. Any abuse of the sexual powers given to man by God is a sin.

3. Using the Chalk Talk on the facing page, show how marital love reflects the unity of Persons in the Blessed Trinity. What a beautiful gift to reflect this love to the world—what a vocation with awesome responsibility.

4. Discuss the responsibilities of having a family (this is review from the lessons on the Fourth Commandment). You must provide for the needs of the child, both physical and spiritual.

5. Review the respect due to other people—in thoughts, words, deeds, and omissions. Review that it is God's plan that a husband and wife should give themselves entirely to one another. Should they give themselves to other people before marriage? No. What about in marriage—should they give themselves to someone other than their spouse? No. What about divorce? If marital love is unitive, is divorce a good action? No.

6. You may review what is necessary for marriage: maturity, freedom, and vows between a man and a woman. Maturity means we can live out the vows that we make and that we understand our actions and their consequences before we act.

Reinforce

1. Have the students work on *Activity Book* p. 51 (see *Teacher's Manual*, p. 163).

2. Have the students work on the Memorization Questions and Words to Know from this chapter.

3. You may discuss the pressures and evils in today's society that are contrary to God's plans for marriage. Explain the proper use of man's sexual powers.

Conclude

1. Lead the class in singing "All you who seek a comfort sure," *Adoremus Hymnal*, #472.

2. End class by leading the students in a Prayer for Purity (see *Teacher's Manual*, p. 155).

But, unlike the rest of visible creation, man does not multiply blindly, following the seasons, like plants, or by instinct, like animals. These creatures are not free to make decisions about their reproductive powers. Man *is* free. This is an aspect of man's dignity. It is also a possible source of abuse.

Man may have very powerful urges, but he is not led blindly by his instincts. Man is called to cooperate with God in a plan that is not recorded in his genes or in his blood but is revealed by God in his commandments—specifically, the Sixth and Ninth Commandments.

Many people look upon these two commandments as restrictions, but we can think about them in the following way. The seed that becomes a sunflower is guided to this fulfillment by a biochemical blueprint invented by God. Though we do not see it, God, who holds the sacred flame of *all* life, has a blueprint for our fulfillment too. Man should thus follow God's plan in the use of his reproductive powers. If God can lead the sunflower to full beauty from a seed, then he can lead a man

to fullness of life by the laws he has given us, though we may see only a little of his plan.

When you are about to plant a seed and water it, you do not have to remind it to trust God; the seed knows all that, so to speak. It is *man* who needs to be reminded to trust God!

Laws of Life

All this is said to point out the proper beauty and nature of the human reproductive powers. The Sixth Commandment guides us in our actions, the Ninth in our thoughts and desires. It is important to remember that all our actions start in our mind, and so we should see the importance of properly directing our thoughts and desires.

Put simply, God reserved the pleasures and joys of human sexuality for marriage. Any use of these powers outside of marriage is a serious sin. God plans to give those who marry an actual share in the creation of a new human being; God creates the soul and the human parents help fashion the body. Does it seem

62

unreasonable, then, for God to require that men use these powers in the right way? God created us male or female. Being male or female is important to who we are as human beings. It is important to use our sexuality according to the will of God, who created and loves us.

The love between a man and a woman, made fruitful and blessed by God in marriage, lovingly brings a new child into a family, where he will have the attention and devotion of both father and mother. It is to assure such conditions for children that God has designed human sexuality to be enjoyed only in marriage, and then only in the proper way. Society is filled to overflowing with the problems, evils, and afflictions caused by disregard for God's wise guidance and authority.

The proper use or control of our sexual powers is called **chastity**, which is a virtue or good habit. Chastity requires that we practice self-denial and self-control. A person who has

the virtue of chastity is chaste. A chaste person will avoid anything that might be a temptation to sin against purity, such as indecent books, magazines, video games, and movies. Our purity is something to be protected. To safeguard it we are forbidden to commit any act in thought or deed that is impure and shameful. **Impurity** is sexual thought or action that is against the Sixth or Ninth Commandments.

What God requires of us is purity of heart and soul, all in keeping with our dignity as his children.

Saint Maria Goretti

In 1950, at Rome, a girl who had died at the age of twelve was declared a saint. She had been stabbed to death because she refused to commit an act of impurity. Her name is Maria Goretti.

63

Maria was born in Ancona, Italy, in 1890. Her father was a tenant farmer; his family moved around a lot as he looked for work. He died when Maria was ten.

Maria never had the chance to go to school; she never learned to read or write. But she was carefully instructed in the Catholic Faith by her mother, Assunta. She received her first Holy Communion when she was twelve.

Assunta had advised her daughter Maria as she had all her children: "Never, at any cost, never must you sin!" Maria never forgot.

Shortly after her first Communion, a nine-

teen-year-old boy who worked with Maria's family wanted her to be unchaste and threatened her with a knife. When she would not give in, he stabbed her to death.

Many years later, the man who had killed her repented and turned to a life devoted to God. He joined those who sought her canonization.

Maria is the great saint of purity for our difficult age.

Words to Know:
　　　　chastity　impurity

> Purity prepares the soul for love, and love confirms the soul in purity.
> —Blessed Cardinal Newman

Q. 47　What does the Sixth Commandment require?
The Sixth Commandment requires us to be chaste in our actions and words (CCC 2331, 2336).

Q. 48　What does the Sixth Commandment forbid?
The Sixth Commandment forbids unchastity, or impurity, of any kind, including looking at immoral pictures, movies, games, and shows (CCC 2351, 2354, 2396, 2523).

Q. 49　What does the Ninth Commandment require?
The Ninth Commandment requires us to be chaste in our thoughts and desires (CCC 2517, 2532–33).

Q. 50　What does the Ninth Commandment forbid?
The Ninth Commandment forbids unchaste or impure thoughts and desires (CCC 2520, 2528–30).

64

CHALK TALK: THE BLESSED TRINITY AND THE DOMESTIC CHURCH

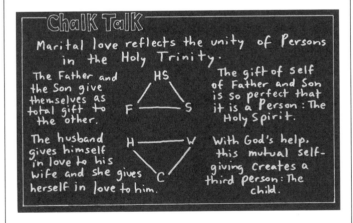

Preview

In the next lesson, the students will learn about chastity.

CHAPTER THIRTEEN: THE SACRED FLAME
LESSON FOUR: CHASTITY

Aims

The students will learn that the proper use of our sexual powers is called chastity. Chastity requires self-denial and self-control.

They will learn that to be chaste, we must avoid occasions for sin. We must be modest in our appearance and in our observation. Impurity is a sexual thought or action that violates the Sixth and Ninth Commandments.

Materials

- *Activity Book*, p. 52

Optional:
- "All you who seek a comfort sure," *Adoremus Hymnal*, #472

Begin

Review the definitions of chastity and celibacy from Lesson 2. Review that chastity is a fruit of the Holy Spirit, a virtue acquired through discipline and practice. We must be chaste in what we think, in what we see, in what we say, and in what we do. We must protect our own purity and the purity of those we love.

Develop

1. Finish reading the chapter.

2. Go through the "One step leads to another" Chalk Talk at right with the students. Explain that, to be pure, we must strive to be pure in our senses, imagination, thoughts, desires and actions so that one sin does not lead to another. We do not suddenly commit impure acts, but we are led into temptation, through occasions of sin, and into bad choices, by which we commit impure acts.

Step 1: Senses. As humans, our senses are very powerful. If we watch something on television or listen to a song we will remember the image, or the words and tune of the song. We must guard what we see, listen to, and read. We must be especially careful with the internet—for sometimes things we do not expect will appear on the screen. We must immediately close any disrespectful images and adjust the settings to block such images. We should also pray for purity and avoid feeding curiosity through images.

Step 2: Imagination. Sometimes we cannot help that we see something or hear something impure. However, we should never ponder these things and encourage our imaginations to take them to the next level or to expand upon them.

Step 3: Thoughts. We must not purposely think about impurities. If an impure thought comes to mind, we should pray that it goes away, or replace it with another thought, such as a prayer, something funny, a wholesome memory, etc.

Step 4: Desires. We must harness our desires. It is normal for us to have desires to love someone and to be loved. It is natural to have feelings and to want to feel them, but we must be disciplined and keep them according to God's law—reserved for marriage. When we are dating, we must not compromise ourselves and give in to our desires.

Step 5: Actions. We must not place ourselves in occasions of sin (being alone late at night or in a private place, etc.). We must not be impure by ourselves or with another person.

Reinforce

1. Have the students work on *Activity Book* p. 52 (see *Teacher's Manual*, p. 163).

2. Read about Saint Maria Goretti. Explain why she is a model of purity for our young people. The students may write prayers, asking Saint Maria Goretti to intercede for them and help them preserve their purity.

3. Have the students work on the Memorization Questions and Words to Know from this chapter. You may wish to provide class time to prepare for the quiz.

Conclude

1. Lead the class in singing "All you who seek a comfort sure," *Adoremus Hymnal*, #472.

2. End class by leading the students in a Prayer for Purity (see *Teacher's Manual*, p. 155).

But, unlike the rest of visible creation, man does not multiply blindly, following the seasons, like plants, or by instinct, like animals. These creatures are not free to make decisions about their reproductive powers. Man *is* free. This is an aspect of man's dignity. It is also a possible source of abuse.

Man may have very powerful urges, but he is not led blindly by his instincts. Man is called to cooperate with God in a plan that is not recorded in his genes or in his blood but is revealed by God in his commandments—specifically, the Sixth and Ninth Commandments.

Many people look upon these two commandments as restrictions, but we can think about them in the following way. The seed that becomes a sunflower is guided to this fulfillment by a biochemical blueprint invented by God. Though we do not see it, God, who holds the sacred flame of *all* life, has a blueprint for our fulfillment too. Man should thus follow God's plan in the use of his reproductive powers. If God can lead the sunflower to full beauty from a seed, then he can lead a man to fullness of life by the laws he has given us, though we may see only a little of his plan.

When you are about to plant a seed and water it, you do not have to remind it to trust God; the seed knows all that, so to speak. It is *man* who needs to be reminded to trust God!

Laws of Life

All this is said to point out the proper beauty and nature of the human reproductive powers. The Sixth Commandment guides us in our actions, the Ninth in our thoughts and desires. It is important to remember that all our actions start in our mind, and so we should see the importance of properly directing our thoughts and desires.

Put simply, God reserved the pleasures and joys of human sexuality for marriage. Any use of these powers outside of marriage is a serious sin. God plans to give those who marry an actual share in the creation of a new human being; God creates the soul and the human parents help fashion the body. Does it seem

unreasonable, then, for God to require that men use these powers in the right way? God created us male or female. Being male or female is important to who we are as human beings. It is important to use our sexuality according to the will of God, who created and loves us.

The love between a man and a woman, made fruitful and blessed by God in marriage, lovingly brings a new child into a family, where he will have the attention and devotion of both father and mother. It is to assure such conditions for children that God has designed human sexuality to be enjoyed only in marriage, and then only in the proper way. Society is filled to overflowing with the problems, evils, and afflictions caused by disregard for God's wise guidance and authority.

The proper use or control of our sexual powers is called **chastity**, which is a virtue or good habit. Chastity requires that we practice self-denial and self-control. A person who has the virtue of chastity is chaste. A chaste person will avoid anything that might be a temptation to sin against purity, such as indecent books, magazines, video games, and movies. Our purity is something to be protected. To safeguard it we are forbidden to commit any act in thought or deed that is impure and shameful. **Impurity** is sexual thought or action that is against the Sixth or Ninth Commandments.

What God requires of us is purity of heart and soul, all in keeping with our dignity as his children.

Saint Maria Goretti

In 1950, at Rome, a girl who had died at the age of twelve was declared a saint. She had been stabbed to death because she refused to commit an act of impurity. Her name is Maria Goretti.

Maria was born in Ancona, Italy, in 1890. Her father was a tenant farmer; his family moved around a lot as he looked for work. He died when Maria was ten.

Maria never had the chance to go to school; she never learned to read or write. But she was carefully instructed in the Catholic Faith by her mother, Assunta. She received her first Holy Communion when she was twelve.

Assunta had advised her daughter Maria as she had all her children: "Never, at any cost, never must you sin!" Maria never forgot.

Shortly after her first Communion, a nineteen-year-old boy who worked with Maria's family wanted her to be unchaste and threatened her with a knife. When she would not give in, he stabbed her to death.

Many years later, the man who had killed her repented and turned to a life devoted to God. He joined those who sought her canonization.

Maria is the great saint of purity for our difficult age.

Words to Know:

chastity   impurity

> Purity prepares the soul for love, and love confirms the soul in purity.
> —Blessed Cardinal Newman

Q. 47 *What does the Sixth Commandment require?*
The Sixth Commandment requires us to be chaste in our actions and words (CCC 2331, 2336).

Q. 48 *What does the Sixth Commandment forbid?*
The Sixth Commandment forbids unchastity, or impurity, of any kind, including looking at immoral pictures, movies, games, and shows (CCC 2351, 2354, 2396, 2523).

Q. 49 *What does the Ninth Commandment require?*
The Ninth Commandment requires us to be chaste in our thoughts and desires (CCC 2517, 2532–33).

Q. 50 *What does the Ninth Commandment forbid?*
The Ninth Commandment forbids unchaste or impure thoughts and desires (CCC 2520, 2528–30).

CHALK TALK: ONE STEP LEADS TO ANOTHER

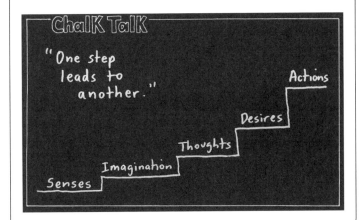

Preview

In the next lesson, the students' understanding of the material covered in this chapter will be reviewed and assessed.

Chapter Thirteen: The Sacred Flame
Review and Assessment

Aims

The students' understanding of the material covered in this chapter will be reviewed and assessed.

Materials

• Quiz 13, Appendix, p. A-19

Optional:
• "All you who seek a comfort sure," *Adoremus Hymnal*, #472

Review and Enrichment

1. The students should know that they are made in the image and likeness of God. Men share a great dignity.

2. The students should know about man's sexual powers and that these powers should be used according to God's plan. We have free will in using these powers. Abuse of these powers is a serious sin.

3. Sexual love is reserved for marriage and is to be unitive and procreative. Outside of these requirements, it is sinful.

4. Marital love reflects the unity of Persons in the Holy Trinity.

5. To enter into marriage, man must be mature and free to vow fidelity until death. Fruitfulness in marriage (procreation) is God's blessing.

6. The students should understand celibacy and chastity.

7. The students should know that, in regard to purity, "One step leads to another" through senses, imagination, thoughts, desires, and actions.

Name: _____

The Sacred Flame   **Quiz 13**

Part I: Fill in the blanks.

1. To maintain our self-respect and respect for others we have to do what we know is right and avoid what we know is <u>wrong</u>.

2. The <u>Sixth</u> and <u>Ninth</u> Commandments require us to respect ourselves and others, and especially married life and the family.

3. All our actions start in our <u>mind</u>, so we should see the importance of properly directing our thoughts and desires.

4. God has designed human sexuality to be enjoyed only in <u>marriage</u> and only in the proper way.

5. The proper use or control of our sexual powers is called <u>chastity</u>.

6. A chaste person will avoid anything that might be a <u>temptation</u> against purity.

7. <u>Impurity</u> is sexual thought or action that is against the Sixth or Ninth Commandments.

8. Chastity requires that we practice self-<u>denial</u> and self-<u>control</u>.

Part II: Answer the following.

1. Write out the two commandments that pertain to chastity.
   <u>You shall not commit adultery. You shall not covet your neighbor's wife.</u>

2. How do these two commandments guide us?
   <u>These two commandments guide us in our actions, thoughts and desires.</u>

3. Why has God designed human sexuality to be enjoyed only in marriage?
   <u>God has designed human sexuality to be enjoyed only in marriage so that children will have the attention and devotion of both father and mother.</u>

4. What sorts of things does a chaste person avoid?
   <u>Answers will vary. A chaste person avoids indecent books, magazines, video games, and movies.</u>

Part III: Yes or No.

1. <u>Yes</u> Has God reserved the joys of human sexuality for marriage?

2. <u>Yes</u> Is it a serious sin to use sexual powers outside of marriage?

3. <u>Yes</u> Does God want to give those who marry an actual share in the creation of a new human being?

Faith and Life Series • Grade 6 • Appendix A   *A-19*

Assess

1. Distribute the quizzes and read through them with the students to be sure they understand the questions.

2. Administer the quiz. As they hand in their work, you may orally quiz the students on the Memorization Questions from this chapter.

3. After all the quizzes have been handed in, you may wish to review the correct answers with the class.

Conclude

1. Lead the class in singing "All you who seek a comfort sure," *Adoremus Hymnal*, #472.

2. End class by leading the students in a Prayer for Purity (see *Teacher's Manual*, p. 155).

Name:_____

The Dignity of People

Answer the following questions in complete sentences.

1. How was man made by God?
   Man was made in the image and likeness of God.

2. Describe the special relationship each of us has with God?
   All of us are known and loved by God as distinct individuals.

3. What is each person worthy of as a child of God?
   Each person is worthy of dignity and respect.

4. Why must we have self-respect? Why do all people have dignity?
   We must have self-respect because we are made by God to be loved by him and to have his life within us. All people have dignity because all were made in God's image and likeness, and are known and loved by him.

5. What do we have to do in order to maintain self-respect?
   We have to do what we know is right and avoid what we know is wrong.

6. Which commandments demand respect for ourselves and others?
   The Sixth and Ninth Commandments demand respect for ourselves and others.

7. Which commandments demand respect for things that belong to married life and the family?
   The Sixth and Ninth Commandments again.

Faith and Life Series • Grade 6 • Chapter 13 • Lesson 1　　49

Name:_____

Be Fruitful . . .

Answer the following questions in complete sentences.

1. Why do we not have to preach to plants and animals about self-control?
   We do not have to preach to plants and animals about self-control because they act through instinct.

2. Did God want man to reproduce? How do we know?
   Yes. We know this because God said "Be fruitful and multiply, and fill the earth."

3. Does man reproduce blindly (by instinct) like plants and animals?
   No. Man is free.

4. What does it mean for man to cooperate with God?
   To cooperate with God means to follow his commandments—specifically the Sixth and Ninth Commandments.

5. Who holds man's sacred flame? Whose plan should man follow in using his reproductive powers?
   God holds man's sacred flame and man should follow God's plan in using his reproductive powers.

6. Can man's reproductive powers be abused?
   Yes.

7. Why should man trust God's plan for his reproductive powers?
   We should trust God's plan because God's laws lead us to fullness of life.

50　　*Faith and Life Series • Grade 6 • Chapter 13 • Lesson 2*

Name:_____

God's Wedding Gift

Answer the following questions in complete sentences.

1. What gift does God give to married people?
   God gives married people the gift of sharing in the creation of a new human being.

2. What does this gift tell us about the pleasures and joys of human sexuality?
   The gift tells us that God reserved the pleasure and joys of human sexuality for marriage.

3. If we use these powers outside of marriage, is it a serious sin?
   Yes.

4. God creates the soul. The husband and wife cooperate with God to bring what into being?
   The husband and wife cooperate with God to bring the body into being.

5. Why is it important that we use our sexuality according to God's will?
   Sexuality is central to our human nature, so it is important that we use it as God intends.

6. What conditions should be given to every child?
   Every child should have the attention and devotion of both father and mother.

7. What is chastity?
   Chastity is the virtue of ordering sexual pleasures according to the Sixth and Ninth Commandments.

Faith and Life Series • Grade 6 • Chapter 13 • Lesson 3　　51

Name:_____

God Blessed Them . . .

Answer the following questions in complete sentences.

1. What is the Sixth Commandment?
   The Sixth Commandment is "You shall not commit adultery."

2. What does the Sixth Commandment forbid?
   The Sixth Commandment forbids unchastity, or impurity, of any kind, including looking at immoral pictures, movies, games, and shows.

3. What does the Sixth Commandment require?
   The Sixth Commandment requires us to be chaste in our action and words.

4. What is the Ninth Commandment?
   The Ninth Commandment is "You shall not covet your neighbor's wife."

5. What does the Ninth Commandment forbid?
   The Ninth Commandment forbids unchaste or impure thoughts and desires.

6. What does the Ninth Commandment require?
   The Ninth Commandment requires us to be chaste in our thoughts and desires.

7. For what do these two commandments demand respect?
   Answers will vary. Something to the effect of: These two commandments demand respect for human sexuality.

8. Are these two commandments restrictions? Why?
   Answers will vary.

52　　*Faith and Life Series • Grade 6 • Chapter 13 • Lesson 4*

TEACHER'S NOTES

TEACHER'S NOTES

CHAPTER FOURTEEN
OWNERSHIP

Catechism of the Catholic Church References

Charity: 1822–29, 1844
Justice: 1805, 2411
Seventh Commandment: 2401–49, 2450–63
Respect for Persons and Their Goods: 2407–18, 2453–57
Love for the Poor: 2443–49, 2462–63
Tenth Commandment: 2534–50, 2551–57

Disorder of Covetous Desires: 2535–40, 2552–53
Desire of the Spirit: 2541–43, 2554–55
Poverty of Heart: 2544–47, 2556
Desire to See God: 2548–50, 2557

Scripture References

Final Judgment and Works of Mercy: Mt 25:34–40

Summary of Lesson Content

Lesson 1

God gave man the earth and its resources to use, enjoy, appreciate, and share freely with one another. This is called stewardship.

Individuals or groups of people may own property. Every person has the right to own property. Property requires respect for ownership.

The Seventh Commandment teaches us not to steal or damage the property of others.

Lesson 2

We have obligations when we use another's property by permission. We must return it in the same condition in which we received it. If we damage or lose it, we must make restitution.

The Seventh Commandment forbids fraud and usury.

We must be just in payment for goods and services we receive.

Lesson 3

The Tenth Commandment governs our desire for possessions.

Two ways this commandment is broken are through envy and avarice. Envy is being resentful of another's success. Avarice is greed.

Lesson 4

Stealing is wrong because it is unjust. The Seventh Commandment governs wages: just wages must be paid, and just work must be done for wages.

Charity requires us to share what we have with those in need. Almsgiving is a work of justice and charity. If someone cannot provide for his needs by his labor, others are required to share of their excess.

CHAPTER FOURTEEN: OWNERSHIP
LESSON ONE: PROPERTY

Aims

The students will learn that God gave man the earth and its resources to use, enjoy, appreciate, and share freely with one another. This is called stewardship.

They will learn that individuals or groups of people may own property. Every person has the right to own property. Property requires respect for ownership.

The Seventh Commandment teaches us not to steal or damage the property of others.

Materials

- *Activity Book*, p. 53

Optional:
- "As with gladness men of old," *Adoremus Hymnal*, #353

Begin

Begin the class by having the students write lists of ten things that they own and ten things that their parents own. They may write lists of things that the church, school, city, state, and nation own. Help the students categorize property. Also, list things that they might see in their community, and ask them who owns them—they will find that most everything belongs to someone. "Property" is something that belongs to someone.

Develop

1. Read paragraphs 1–6 from the student text.

2. Review stewardship with the students. God created all things for the proper use of men. Therefore, we must use created things well, according to God's plan. Review ways that we practice good stewardship in society; e.g., recycling.

3. Define theft. Theft is the taking of something that belongs to someone else without his permission. We can steal big things or little things. We can also steal things which are not material (such as ideas or intellectual property, e.g., by cheating on a test).

4. Borrowing something is asking permission to use what belongs to another. Lending is an act of charity and of good stewardship. What are some things we have borrowed? When must we return them? In what condition? Why must we return them?

5. Discuss damaging or purposely destroying something, e.g., vandalism. Can the students think of an example of vandalism? Why is this wrong?

6. Discuss the cardinal virtues: prudence, temperance, justice, and fortitude. These are habits that we must practice in order to grow in them. How should we use these virtues when it comes to other people's property?

7. Discuss justice explicitly. Justice demands that we give to others what is due to them. We must, therefore, return borrowed goods in the same condition as we borrowed them. We must make restitution when we steal or damage another's property.

8. We must not keep something that someone else has stolen. This is contrary to justice, for the rightful owner deserves his property.

Reinforce

1. Have the students work on *Activity Book* p. 53 (see *Teacher's Manual*, p. 175). Have the students look up the definitions of all the words in the puzzle.

2. Have the students work on the Memorization Questions and Words to Know from this chapter (see *Teacher's Manual*, p. 173).

3. The students should memorize the cardinal virtues.

Conclude

1. Teach the students to sing "As with gladness men of old," *Adoremus Hymnal*, #353.

2. End class by leading the students in the Prayer of Saint Francis (see *Teacher's Manual*, p. 169).

CHAPTER 14

Ownership

"You shall not steal."

Exodus 20:15

God gave to the human race the earth and its resources, to use, to enjoy, to appreciate, and to share freely with one another. People use these goods of creation to keep themselves from poverty and to meet other basic human needs.

You will find very few things around you that someone does not own. The things around us may be owned by a group of people like a company, or by a larger community such as a city, state, or nation, or by a single person. Every person has the right to own property; groups have the same right. This requires respect for the right of ownership; all have the right to have their possessions safe from theft, damage, and destruction.

These rights are protected by the Seventh Commandment: "You shall not **steal**".

This commandment tells us how to treat other peoples' belongings. God commands us not to take what belongs to another. If I take your shoes without asking you, I am guilty of theft. To be free from guilt I must return what I have stolen or replace it if I can, as well as confess my sin if the matter is serious. If I purposely damage or destroy property, justice demands that I make restitution—that is, pay for the damage.

We must have nothing to do with stolen property, even if we didn't steal it ourselves.

Neither can we claim to own something that belongs to someone else—for example, when one student copies another's homework. Such a student is guilty of both stealing and lying, since he presents the work as his own.

On Loan

We have duties and obligations when we make rightful use of another's property by permission. Perhaps we have borrowed a CD to see how we like it before buying one of our own. Then we must return it in the same condition in which we received it. If we have damaged it, we must replace it. So too, in a store, we must handle merchandise with care and be

65

honest if we damage something. We must always pay back in full all loans and debts; if we don't we are stealing.

The Seventh Commandment also forbids any kind of deception or breach of contract in our dealings with others' property. This is called **fraud**. There is another evil practice called **usury** in which someone lends money at an excessively high rate of interest. This is a very bad thing. Someone who practices usury is making money out of another person's great need.

We are also required to be just in payment for services or goods bought. We must always pay a worker what he has earned.

The Seventh Commandment also requires respect for creation. This includes mineral resources, plants, and animals. We should respect and appreciate such gifts and use them according to God's laws. We should also take care to make sure future generations can appreciate and use these gifts.

The Tenth Commandment, "You shall not covet your neighbor's goods," is meant to direct our desire for possessions.

There are two very common ways in which people break this commandment: **envy** and **avarice**. Both reveal that something is wrong with the way a person looks upon material goods. Envy is being resentful of another's success. The envious man is unhappy because he wants what another man has. Avarice is like greed. The avaricious man has an excessive desire for wealth. He always wants more, no matter how much he already has.

Justice and Charity

There are certain societies in which the right to own private property is denied. However, the right to private property is acknowledged by God in the Ten Commandments. He would not condemn stealing if no one were to own anything.

66

> Be not anxious about what you have, but about what you are.
>
> —Pope Saint Gregory

Stealing is wrong because it is unjust. Thus, justice is the virtue that protects personal possessions. Justice obliges me to make restitution if I steal. It obliges my employer to pay me my due wage and obliges me to earn it with honest labor.

But the right to private property, protected by justice, is not enough for the happy life of a society; charity is needed.

For instance, the right to property may be acknowledged by everyone, while at the same time some persons have more than they need —even much more—and others do not have even a minimum required by human dignity.

If I have many possessions should they be taken away and given to the poor? No, but should I forget the poor? Charity requires me to share what I have with those who need decent food, clothing, and shelter. Such almsgiving is a work of justice as well as charity, and it is pleasing to God. One reason God allows us to have possessions is in order for us to share them with others.

Every human being is made in God's image and deserves respect as a person. This is where justice comes in. Justice involves giving everyone his due, what he has a right to receive. Every human being has a right to food, clothing, and shelter. Of course the ordinary way we should obtain these things is through our work. But if circumstances do not make it possible for someone to obtain these things through his labor, then other people are obliged to help him from their excess.

If people are in extreme need and they have no choice, then the taking of what is necessary to maintain life is not stealing. In that case, it is unreasonable and unjust for

THE CARDINAL VIRTUES

- *Prudence* is the virtue of recognizing the good and the best way of attaining it. One with the virtue of prudence will use reason to discern the best way to act in a given circumstance.

- *Justice* is the virtue of giving God and neighbor what they deserve. One with the virtue of justice respects the rights of others.

- *Fortitude*, or courage, consists in persevering toward the good in the face of difficulties. One with the virtue of fortitude will overcome temptations and obstacles in order to do good.

- *Temperance* is the virtue of moderating pleasures. One with temperance has self-discipline and does not abuse food, alcohol, and other created goods.

—See the *Catechism of the Catholic Church*, paragraphs 1806–1809.

REPARATION

When Zacchaeus repented saying, "If I have defrauded any one of anything, I restore it fourfold," Jesus said, "Today salvation has come to this house" (Lk 19:8–9). In seeking forgiveness for theft one must return or make restitution for the stolen goods.

Preview

In the next lesson, the students will learn about loans and debts.

CHAPTER FOURTEEN: OWNERSHIP
LESSON TWO: LOANS AND DEBTS

Aims

The students will learn that we have obligations when we use another's property by permission. We must return it in the same condition in which we received it. If we damage or lose it, we must make restitution.

They will learn that the Seventh Commandment forbids fraud and usury. We must be just in payment for goods and services we receive.

Materials

- *Activity Book*, p. 54

Optional:
- "As with gladness men of old," *Adoremus Hymnal*, #353

Begin

Review the definitions of all the words found in the word search from the *Activity Book* (see *Teacher's Manual*, p. 175 and p. 395). Have the students use the vocabulary words in sentences relevant to this chapter.

Develop

1. Read paragraphs 7–10 from the student text.

2. Discuss the need to return in a timely manner things that are borrowed. Borrowed items should be returned in the same condition as that in which they were borrowed. You may give the students various scenarios that they can discuss.

3. Discuss how to handle merchandise in a store. What should we do if we break something? To whom does that property belong? Must we make restitution for items we damage in a store? What is shop-lifting? It is another word for stealing from a store.

4. What is a loan? What is a debt? A loan is money given to someone with the expectation that he will pay it back. A debt is owed to another. We must repay our debts and any interest that we may have agreed to pay. If we do not, we commit theft.

5. What is a contract? It is a promise in writing that must be upheld. For example, a bank loans me money for a house, and the contract says I will repay it at a certain rate of interest over a given period of time. Breaking a contract is called fraud. When we violate the terms of a contract we deceive and commit theft. We must honor employment contracts by working for our wages and by paying our workers a just wage.

6. Usury—lending money to someone at a very high rate of interest—is another form of evil. This abuses another by exploiting him in his need.

7. The Seventh Commandment demands respect for all created goods, including our environment. Have the students work on an environmental project, such as a recycling project, trash-collection, planting trees/flowers, etc.

Reinforce

1. Have the students work on *Activity Book* p. 54 (see *Teacher's Manual*, p. 175).

2. Have the students work on their environmental projects.

3. Have the students work on the Memorization Questions and Words to Know from this chapter (see *Teacher's Manual*, p. 173).

Conclude

1. Lead the class in singing "As with gladness men of old," *Adoremus Hymnal*, #353.

2. End class by leading the students in the Prayer of Saint Francis (on the facing page).

CHAPTER 14

Ownership

"You shall not steal."

Exodus 20:15

God gave to the human race the earth and its resources, to use, to enjoy, to appreciate, and to share freely with one another. People use these goods of creation to keep themselves from poverty and to meet other basic human needs.

You will find very few things around you that someone does not own. The things around us may be owned by a group of people like a company, or by a larger community such as a city, state, or nation, or by a single person. Every person has the right to own property; groups have the same right. This requires respect for the right of ownership; all have the right to have their possessions safe from theft, damage, and destruction.

These rights are protected by the Seventh Commandment: "You shall not **steal**".

This commandment tells us how to treat other peoples' belongings. God commands us not to take what belongs to another. If I take your shoes without asking you, I am guilty of theft. To be free from guilt I must return what I have stolen or replace it if I can, as well as confess my sin if the matter is serious. If I purposely damage or destroy property, justice demands that I make restitution—that is, pay for the damage.

We must have nothing to do with stolen property, even if we didn't steal it ourselves.

Neither can we claim to own something that belongs to someone else—for example, when one student copies another's homework. Such a student is guilty of both stealing and lying, since he presents the work as his own.

On Loan

We have duties and obligations when we make rightful use of another's property by permission. Perhaps we have borrowed a CD to see how we like it before buying one of our own. Then we must return it in the same condition in which we received it. If we have damaged it, we must replace it. So too, in a store, we must handle merchandise with care and be

65

honest if we damage something. We must always pay back in full all loans and debts; if we don't we are stealing.

The Seventh Commandment also forbids any kind of deception or breach of contract in our dealings with others' property. This is called **fraud**. There is another evil practice called **usury** in which someone lends money at an excessively high rate of interest. This is a very bad thing. Someone who practices usury is making money out of another person's great need.

We are also required to be just in payment for services or goods bought. We must always pay a worker what he has earned.

The Seventh Commandment also requires respect for creation. This includes mineral resources, plants, and animals. We should respect and appreciate such gifts and use them according to God's laws. We should also take care to make sure future generations can appreciate and use these gifts.

The Tenth Commandment, "You shall not covet your neighbor's goods," is meant to direct our desire for possessions.

There are two very common ways in which people break this commandment: **envy** and **avarice**. Both reveal that something is wrong with the way a person looks upon material goods. Envy is being resentful of another's success. The envious man is unhappy because he wants what another man has. Avarice is like greed. The avaricious man has an excessive desire for wealth. He always wants more, no matter how much he already has.

Justice and Charity

There are certain societies in which the right to own private property is denied. However, the right to private property is acknowledged by God in the Ten Commandments. He would not condemn stealing if no one were to own anything.

66

> Be not anxious about what you have, but about what you are.
>
> —Pope Saint Gregory

Stealing is wrong because it is unjust. Thus, justice is the virtue that protects personal possessions. Justice obliges me to make restitution if I steal. It obliges my employer to pay me my due wage and obliges me to earn it with honest labor.

But the right to private property, protected by justice, is not enough for the happy life of a society; charity is needed.

For instance, the right to property may be acknowledged by everyone, while at the same time some persons have more than they need —even much more—and others do not have even a minimum required by human dignity.

If I have many possessions should they be taken away and given to the poor? No, but should I forget the poor? Charity requires me to share what I have with those who need decent food, clothing, and shelter. Such alms-giving is a work of justice as well as charity, and it is pleasing to God. One reason God allows us to have possessions is in order for us to share them with others.

Every human being is made in God's image and deserves respect as a person. This is where justice comes in. Justice involves giving everyone his due, what he has a right to receive. Every human being has a right to food, clothing, and shelter. Of course the ordinary way we should obtain these things is through our work. But if circumstances do not make it possible for someone to obtain these things through his labor, then other people are obliged to help him from their excess.

If people are in extreme need and they have no choice, then the taking of what is necessary to maintain life is not stealing. In that case, it is unreasonable and unjust for

---

ZACCHAEUS

Whenever we think of loans and debts in the Gospel, one name that immediately comes to mind is Zacchaeus. A scorned tax collector, Zacchaeus nonetheless desired to see Jesus when he heard that Jesus was passing through Jericho. Zacchaeus climbed a tree to get a good view (and probably to stay clear of the crowds who hated him as well), but when Jesus came by, he called to Zacchaeus and told him to come down from the tree and host him. The crowd grumbled at Jesus' choice of accommodation, but Zaccheus said aloud to Jesus, "Behold, Lord, the half of my goods I give to the poor; and if I have defrauded any one of anything, I restore it fourfold" (Lk 19:8).

PRAYER OF SAINT FRANCIS

Lord, make me an instrument of thy peace;
where there is hatred, let me sow love;
where there is injury, pardon;
where there is doubt, faith;
where there is despair, hope;
where there is darkness, light;
and where there is sadness, joy.

O Divine Master,
grant that I may not so much seek
to be consoled as to console;
to be understood, as to understand;
to be loved, as to love;
for it is in giving that we receive,
it is in pardoning that we are pardoned,
and it is in dying that we are born
to eternal life. *Amen.*

> The wicked borrows, and cannot pay back,
> but the righteous is generous and gives.
>
> —Psalm 37:21

Preview

In the next lesson, the students will learn about covetousness.

CHAPTER FOURTEEN: OWNERSHIP
LESSON THREE: COVETING

Aims

The students will learn that the Tenth Commandment governs our desire for possessions.

They will learn two ways this commandment is broken are through envy and avarice. Envy is being resentful of another's success. Avarice is greed.

Materials

• *Activity Book*, p. 55

Optional:
• "As with gladness men of old," *Adoremus Hymnal*, #353

Begin

Review ways that we can steal or abuse another's property:
• Theft
• Vandalism
• Destruction/damaging another's property
• Fraud
• Usury

Review ways we can respect property:
• Stewardship
• Borrowing/lending in charity
• Working hard for wages

Develop

1. Read paragraphs 11–12 from the student text.

2. The Tenth Commandment is about coveting—it has more to do with our thoughts than our actions—but remember that "One step leads to another" and our sinful thoughts can lead to sinful actions. Apply the Chalk Talk from Chapter 13, Lesson 4 to property:
Step One (Senses): We see something we are attracted to (e.g., a video game).
Step Two (Imagination): We can imagine how much fun it would be and how great it would be to have the video game.
Step Three (Thoughts): We start thinking of ways we can get the video game.
Step Four (Desires): We really want the game (maybe even so much that we decide that the rightful owner doesn't need his possession).
Step Five (Actions): We steal the video game.

3. Discuss jealousy. It is a desire to have something that someone else has. It is disordered, for we should be happy for others in their good fortune, rather than unhappy for ourselves.

4. Discuss envy. Envy is being resentful of another person's success or possessions. Instead of just being jealous that someone has a car, we decide that if we can't have it, neither can he, so we destroy or damage his property. We may also dislike a person because of his possessions.

5. Discuss avarice. Avarice is like greed. It is an excessive desire for wealth and possessions—no matter the cost to ourselves or others.

6. Discuss how material things cannot make us truly happy; we become enslaved to our desire for them.

Reinforce

1. Have the students work on *Activity Book* p. 55 (see *Teacher's Manual*, p. 175).

2. Have the students play "You Be the Judge" from the box on the facing page.

3. Have the students work on the Memorization Questions and Words to Know from this chapter (see *Teacher's Manual*, p. 173).

Conclude

1. Lead the class in singing "As with gladness men of old," *Adoremus Hymnal*, #353.

2. End class by leading the students in the Prayer of Saint Francis (see *Teacher's Manual*, p. 169).

honest if we damage something. We must always pay back in full all loans and debts; if we don't we are stealing.

The Seventh Commandment also forbids any kind of deception or breach of contract in our dealings with others' property. This is called **fraud**. There is another evil practice called **usury** in which someone lends money at an excessively high rate of interest. This is a very bad thing. Someone who practices usury is making money out of another person's great need.

We are also required to be just in payment for services or goods bought. We must always pay a worker what he has earned.

The Seventh Commandment also requires respect for creation. This includes mineral resources, plants, and animals. We should respect and appreciate such gifts and use them according to God's laws. We should also take care to make sure future generations can appreciate and use these gifts.

The Tenth Commandment, "You shall not covet your neighbor's goods," is meant to direct our desire for possessions.

There are two very common ways in which people break this commandment: **envy** and **avarice**. Both reveal that something is wrong with the way a person looks upon material goods. Envy is being resentful of another's success. The envious man is unhappy because he wants what another man has. Avarice is like greed. The avaricious man has an excessive desire for wealth. He always wants more, no matter how much he already has.

Justice and Charity

There are certain societies in which the right to own private property is denied. However, the right to private property is acknowledged by God in the Ten Commandments. He would not condemn stealing if no one were to own anything.

> Be not anxious about what you have, but about what you are.
> —Pope Saint Gregory

Stealing is wrong because it is unjust. Thus, justice is the virtue that protects personal possessions. Justice obliges me to make restitution if I steal. It obliges my employer to pay me my due wage and obliges me to earn it with honest labor.

But the right to private property, protected by justice, is not enough for the happy life of a society; charity is needed.

For instance, the right to property may be acknowledged by everyone, while at the same time some persons have more than they need —even much more—and others do not have even a minimum required by human dignity.

If I have many possessions should they be taken away and given to the poor? No, but should I forget the poor? Charity requires me to share what I have with those who need decent food, clothing, and shelter. Such almsgiving is a work of justice as well as charity, and it is pleasing to God. One reason God allows us to have possessions is in order for us to share them with others.

Every human being is made in God's image and deserves respect as a person. This is where justice comes in. Justice involves giving everyone his due, what he has a right to receive. Every human being has a right to food, clothing, and shelter. Of course the ordinary way we should obtain these things is through our work. But if circumstances do not make it possible for someone to obtain these things through his labor, then other people are obliged to help him from their excess.

If people are in extreme need and they have no choice, then the taking of what is necessary to maintain life is not stealing. In that case, it is unreasonable and unjust for

66

Spirit of Poverty

someone to refuse to provide such people with what they need to live.

Jesus identifies himself with the poor when he says:

"Come, O blessed of my Father, inherit the kingdom prepared for you from the foundation of the world; for I was hungry and you gave me food, I was thirsty and you gave me drink, I was a stranger and you welcomed me, I was naked and you clothed me, I was sick and you visited me, I was in prison and you came to me." Then the righteous will answer him, "Lord, when did we see you hungry and feed you, or thirsty and give you drink? And when did we see you a stranger and welcome you, or naked and clothe you? And when did we see you sick or in prison and visit you?" And the King will answer them, "Truly, I say to you, as you did it to one of the least of these my brethren, you did it to me" (Mt 25:34–40).

In this way, Jesus shows how God blesses those who help the poor. When we help the poor, we show our love for them and for Jesus himself. We should do what we can to see to it that everyone has what he needs to live a decent human life.

Saint Francis of Assisi was known as "the poor man." He won this title by owning little more than the shirt on his back. If he was asked about his circumstances he would often reply that he was married to Lady Poverty. Francis meant that he loved poverty and never wanted to own anything.

This was a great shock to his father, who was a rich cloth merchant and had great plans for his son. But God had other plans. Francis' father, Pietro Bernardone, did not accept God's plans gracefully. The result was that father and son parted company. Pietro's plans were ruined, but a whole new world opened up for Francis. He roamed the hillsides of Assisi; he walked the byways praising God; he lived in the open; he prayed long hours; he begged; and he rebuilt a mountain chapel that had fallen into disrepair. Soon others began following him, until finally a great religious order grew up around Francis' example.

Saint Francis is set before us as one who had the right attitude toward material possessions. We should not set our hearts on riches. Few of us are called to be as poor as Francis, but our Lord addressed the following words to all men:

67

YOU BE THE JUDGE

Divide the class into groups of two or three and have them look through recent newspapers for articles about crimes against property: stealing, vandalizing, cheating, embezzling, etc. Once a group has found a suitable article, have them highlight important details (the nature of the crime, the person who committed it, his age, the value of the property involved, etc.) that would be considered in the sentencing of the guilty party.

When all the groups have finished their research, have one group present the facts of the case to a second group who will serve as the judging panel. After the panel has heard the details of the crime, they are to sentence the guilty party. The rest of the class may then comment on the sentence. Continue this procedure until all of the groups have had a chance to present and sentence a case.

Remind the students to temper their desire for retribution with a measure of hope for the criminal's recovery remembering that they are seeking a *just* sentence. Help them to come up with creative sentences, such as making restitution to the community or to the offended party, rather than simply prison terms. Ask the judging panel to consider whether their sentence will help the criminal take responsibility for his actions and make amends for the harm he has caused.

Students may find that it is difficult to know how to sentence justly someone who has committed the crimes that were discussed in the above paragraph. While we or our judicial system must make judgments for the flourishing of our society and country, we also can recognize how perfect judgment is nevertheless lacking. Christians place their hope in Jesus to be both entirely just and entirely merciful. We pray in the Psalms, "Righteousness and peace will kiss each other" (Ps 85:10).

Preview

In the next lesson, the students will learn about justice.

CHAPTER FOURTEEN: OWNERSHIP
LESSON FOUR: JUSTICE

Aims

The students will learn that stealing is wrong because it is unjust. The Seventh Commandment also governs wages: just wages must be paid and just work must be done for wages.

They will learn that charity requires us to share what we have with those in need. Almsgiving is a work of justice and charity. If someone cannot provide for his needs by his labor, others are required to share out of their excess.

Materials

• *Activity Book*, p. 56

Optional:
• "As with gladness men of old," *Adoremus Hymnal*, #353

• A video about Saint Francis of Assisi; see www.faithandlifeseries. com and click the downloads tab for audio-visual resource suggestions

Begin

Discuss again the virtue of justice. It is justice that states we have the right to own property. It is justice that states it is wrong to steal. It is justice that demands restitution for damaged goods and obliges one to labor for wages and to pay a laborer for his work. Justice is about giving everyone his due. Ask the students to give examples of justice.

Develop

1. Have the students read paragraphs 13–21, Justice and Charity.

2. Discuss almsgiving. How is almsgiving an act of justice? Are we obliged to give to others out of our excess or out of our substance? Which is more noble and loving? Must we provide for the necessities of life for other people?

3. Discuss the Bible passage, Matthew 25:34–40. What good works are listed here? (the Corporal Works of Mercy). How do we serve Jesus in serving the poor? Does Jesus bless those who help the poor? Is there a blessing in being poor? Is there a blessing in receiving charity?

4. Read the section in the student text, Spirit of Poverty. If possible, watch a video about Saint Francis of Assisi. Discuss Francis and his spirit of poverty:

• Why would Saint Francis reject the good of property?
• Why did Saint Francis beg?
• Was Saint Francis a burden on society?
• What does Matthew 6:24 mean?
• Why might material things distract us from the Kingdom of God?
• Who provides for all our needs?
• Is owning property bad?
• How should we use our possessions and money?
• How do we know if we are choosing riches instead of God's plan?
• Why do you think that Saint Francis had many followers?

5. Discuss how justice and charity should work together. We should give what is due to someone because we love him.

Reinforce

1. Have the students work on *Activity Book* p. 56 (see *Teacher's Manual*, p. 175).

2. Have the students watch a video about Saint Francis of Assisi if you have not already done so.

3. Have the students read and dramatize parables on charity: Mt 25:31–46; Lk 10:29–37; 16:19–31.

4. Have the students work on the Memorization Questions and Words to Know from this chapter.

Conclude

1. Lead the class in singing "As with gladness men of old," *Adoremus Hymnal*, #353.

2. End class by leading the students in the Prayer of Saint Francis (see *Teacher's Manual*, p. 169).

honest if we damage something. We must always pay back in full all loans and debts; if we don't we are stealing.

The Seventh Commandment also forbids any kind of deception or breach of contract in our dealings with others' property. This is called **fraud**. There is another evil practice called **usury** in which someone lends money at an excessively high rate of interest. This is a very bad thing. Someone who practices usury is making money out of another person's great need.

We are also required to be just in payment for services or goods bought. We must always pay a worker what he has earned.

The Seventh Commandment also requires respect for creation. This includes mineral resources, plants, and animals. We should respect and appreciate such gifts and use them according to God's laws. We should also take care to make sure future generations can appreciate and use these gifts.

The Tenth Commandment, "You shall not covet your neighbor's goods," is meant to direct our desire for possessions.

There are two very common ways in which people break this commandment: **envy** and **avarice**. Both reveal that something is wrong with the way a person looks upon material goods. Envy is being resentful of another's success. The envious man is unhappy because he wants what another man has. Avarice is like greed. The avaricious man has an excessive desire for wealth. He always wants more, no matter how much he already has.

Justice and Charity

There are certain societies in which the right to own private property is denied. However, the right to private property is acknowledged by God in the Ten Commandments. He would not condemn stealing if no one were to own anything.

> Be not anxious about what you have, but about what you are.
> —Pope Saint Gregory

Stealing is wrong because it is unjust. Thus, justice is the virtue that protects personal possessions. Justice obliges me to make restitution if I steal. It obliges my employer to pay me my due wage and obliges me to earn it with honest labor.

But the right to private property, protected by justice, is not enough for the happy life of a society; charity is needed.

For instance, the right to property may be acknowledged by everyone, while at the same time some persons have more than they need —even much more—and others do not have even a minimum required by human dignity.

If I have many possessions should they be taken away and given to the poor? No, but should I forget the poor? Charity requires me to share what I have with those who need decent food, clothing, and shelter. Such almsgiving is a work of justice as well as charity, and it is pleasing to God. One reason God allows us to have possessions is in order for us to share them with others.

Every human being is made in God's image and deserves respect as a person. This is where justice comes in. Justice involves giving everyone his due, what he has a right to receive. Every human being has a right to food, clothing, and shelter. Of course the ordinary way we should obtain these things is through our work. But if circumstances do not make it possible for someone to obtain these things through his labor, then other people are obliged to help him from their excess.

If people are in extreme need and they have no choice, then the taking of what is necessary to maintain life is not stealing. In that case, it is unreasonable and unjust for

66

Spirit of Poverty

someone to refuse to provide such people with what they need to live.

Jesus identifies himself with the poor when he says:

> "Come, O blessed of my Father, inherit the kingdom prepared for you from the foundation of the world; for I was hungry and you gave me food, I was thirsty and you gave me drink, I was a stranger and you welcomed me, I was naked and you clothed me, I was sick and you visited me, I was in prison and you came to me." Then the righteous will answer him, "Lord, when did we see you hungry and feed you, or thirsty and give you drink? And when did we see you a stranger and welcome you, or naked and clothe you? And when did we see you sick or in prison and visit you?" And the King will answer them, "Truly, I say to you, as you did it to one of the least of these my brethren, you did it to me" (Mt 25:34–40).

In this way, Jesus shows how God blesses those who help the poor. When we help the poor, we show our love for them and for Jesus himself. We should do what we can to see to it that everyone has what he needs to live a decent human life.

Saint Francis of Assisi was known as "the poor man." He won this title by owning little more than the shirt on his back. If he was asked about his circumstances he would often reply that he was married to Lady Poverty. Francis meant that he loved poverty and never wanted to own anything.

This was a great shock to his father, who was a rich cloth merchant and had great plans for his son. But God had other plans. Francis' father, Pietro Bernardone, did not accept God's plans gracefully. The result was that father and son parted company. Pietro's plans were ruined, but a whole new world opened up for Francis. He roamed the hillsides of Assisi; he walked the byways praising God; he lived in the open; he prayed long hours; he begged; and he rebuilt a mountain chapel that had fallen into disrepair. Soon others began following him, until finally a great religious order grew up around Francis' example.

Saint Francis is set before us as one who had the right attitude toward material possessions. We should not set our hearts on riches. Few of us are called to be as poor as Francis, but our Lord addressed the following words to all men:

67

"No one can serve two masters; for either he will hate the one and love the other, or he will be devoted to the one and despise the other. You cannot serve God and mammon" (Mt 6:24).

Jesus means that a person who has his heart set on material possessions will not be able to pay attention to the Kingdom of God. Instead of looking for chances to serve God, to pray, or to study our Lord's words and example, such a person will be looking for chances to collect more riches. (This may mean piling up much more than one needs.) One cannot have one's mind on both things—God and money. It must be one or the other.

Serving God wholeheartedly, of course, need not mean choosing Lady Poverty, like Francis; but it cannot mean choosing riches instead of God's plan, like his father. We should try to be content with what we have and take reasonable care of our interests.

Words to Know:
steal   fraud   usury   envy   avarice

"Keep your life free from love of money, and be content with what you have."   *Hebrews 13:5*

> **Q. 51 What does the Seventh Commandment require us to do?**
> The Seventh Commandment requires us to respect the property of others, to return anything we have stolen or borrowed, to repair damages for which we are responsible, to pay our debts, and to pay a just wage to those who work for us (CCC 2411–12).
>
> **Q. 52 What does the Seventh Commandment forbid?**
> The Seventh Commandment forbids unjustly taking or keeping our neighbor's property. Sins against the Seventh Commandment include theft, damage of property, usury, and fraud (CCC 2408–9).
>
> **Q. 53 What does the Tenth Commandment require us to do?**
> The Tenth Commandment requires us to be just and moderate in the desire to improve our own condition of life. We are called to suffer with patience the hardships and other difficulties permitted by the Lord for our good (CCC 2545).
>
> **Q. 54 What does the Tenth Commandment forbid?**
> The Tenth Commandment forbids wrongly desiring what others have and excessively desiring riches and power (CCC 2536, 2538).

68

DETACHMENT

The Ten Commandments clearly protect the right of individuals to own property. How then are we to understand Jesus' call to renounce the things of this world? Behind Jesus' teaching is the call to detach ourselves from the things of this world so that we might live beyond them. We can own and use things, but we must use them only as means to an end (heaven). "Jesus enjoins his disciples to prefer him to everything and everyone, and bids them 'renounce all that [they have]' for his sake and that of the Gospel. . . . The precept of detachment from riches is obligatory for entrance into the Kingdom of Heaven" (CCC 2544). We must be willing to do anything for love of God, and to place our highest hope in him. The command, "sell what you have, and give to the poor" is always followed by the invitation: "come, follow me" (see Mk 10:17–21).

Preview

In the next lesson, the students' understanding of the material covered in this chapter will be reviewed and assessed.

CHAPTER FOURTEEN: OWNERSHIP
REVIEW AND ASSESSMENT

Aims

The students' understanding of the material covered in this chapter will be reviewed and assessed.

Materials

- Quiz 14, Appendix, p. A-20

Optional:
- "As with gladness men of old," *Adoremus Hymnal*, #353

Review and Enrichment

1. The students should know what property is, and that man has the right to own property. This right is protected by justice.

2. The Seventh and Tenth Commandments protect man's property.

3. The students should understand the definitions of:
- Theft
- Vandalism
- Restitution
- Damage/destruction
- Loans/debts
- Breach of contract/fraud
- Jealousy
- Usury
- Envy
- Avarice
- Stewardship

They should be able to give examples of each of these.

4. The students should know the cardinal virtues.

5. The students should know how justice and charity work together. Almsgiving is an act both of justice and of charity.

6. The students should understand the spirit of poverty.

7. The students should be able to apply the idea of "one step leads to another" to property.

Name: _____

Ownership   Quiz 14

Part I: Define each term.

1. stealing (theft): <u>taking something that belongs to someone else without his permission</u>

2. restitution: <u>making up for the damage of destroyed or stolen property</u>

3. fraud: <u>deceiving another in order to deprive him of his property</u>

4. usury: <u>lending money at an excessive interest rate</u>

5. envy: <u>being resentful or saddened by the success or good fortune of another</u>

6. avarice: <u>excessive desire for things or wealth; greed</u>

7. justice: <u>giving everyone what he is due, what he has a right to receive</u>

Part II: Write a paragraph about Saint Francis of Assisi and his spirit of poverty.

_____
_____
_____
_____
_____
_____
_____
_____
_____
_____
_____
_____
_____

A-20   *Faith and Life Series • Grade 6 • Appendix A*

Assess

1. Distribute the quizzes and read through them with the students to be sure they understand the questions.

2. Administer the quiz. As they hand in their work, you may orally quiz the students on the Memorization Questions from this chapter.

3. After all the quizzes have been handed in, you may wish to review the correct answers with the class.

Conclude

1. Lead the class in singing "As with gladness men of old," *Adoremus Hymnal*, #353.

2. End class by leading the students in the Prayer of Saint Francis (see *Teacher's Manual*, p. 169).

CHAPTER FOURTEEN: OWNERSHIP
ACTIVITY BOOK ANSWER KEYS

Name:_____

Ownership

The Seventh Commandment speaks of respecting the property of others. Find the following words that have to do with respecting property in the puzzle.

damage	bribe	underpay	borrow	possess
justice	destroy	honesty	loan	wages
deceive	cheat	fairness	property	envy
steal	protect	repair	return	promise
injustice	dishonesty	restitution	ownership	agreement

```
B  B  R  I  B  E  E  W  D  E  N  R  U  T  E  R
R  R  A  N  N  P  R  A  P  R  O  P  E  R  T  Y
I  I  N  B  O  J  R  G  D  R  I  A  P  E  R  T
B  O  P  A  D  A  U  E  D  I  A  E  P  N
W  O  R  R  O  B  M  S  C  C  H  R  E  C  O  E
D  L  O  D  L  L  A  E  T  S  D  I  S  I  S  M
D  A  M  A  G  E  N  T  R  I  C  I  T  T  S  E
D  I  I  P  R  O  T  E  C  T  C  U  S  S  E  E
Y  U  S  A  M  W  N  G  V  I  T  E  S  U  S  R
T  N  E  H  B  W  I  N  G  I  A  R  E  J  S  G
S  D  S  S  O  U  N  D  T  H  E  B  G  N  N  A
E  F  A  I  R  N  E  S  S  E  H  C  C  N  V  V
N  A  Y  O  R  D  E  L  O  A  C  A  E  O  L  Y
O  I  Y  Y  O  R  T  S  E  D  W  A  G  D  S  O
H  R  G  A  J  U  S  T  T  C  E  T  A  R  P  O
E  N  U  N  D  E  R  P  A  Y  R  U  S  S  E  E
```

Name:_____

Using Another's Property

Answer the following questions in complete sentences.

1. If we borrow something from someone, how should we return it?
   We should return something in the same condition we borrowed it.

2. If we damage another person's property, what must we do?
   If we have damaged another's property, we must replace it.

3. If we borrow money from someone, must we repay it?
   Yes.

4. What does justice require of me if I steal something?
   Justice requires us to make restitution if we steal.

5. If I receive an honest day's pay, what must I give?
   If we receive an honest day's pay, we must give an honest day's work.

6. If I steal some bread because I have no food to eat and I might die, do I commit a sin? Why or why not?
   No. If people are in extreme need and have no choice, taking what is necessary to maintain life is not stealing.

7. Is taking another person's ideas or work a form of stealing?
   Yes.

8. What does it mean to say "you cannot serve God and mammon"?
   This means that a person who has his heart set on material possessions will not be able to pay attention to the Kingdom of God.

Name:_____

Ownership

Answer the following questions in complete sentences.

1. Does everyone have the right to own property?
   Yes.

2. Does property need to be owned by one single person?
   No.

3. What is the Seventh Commandment?
   The Seventh Commandment is "You shall not steal."

4. What does the Seventh Commandment forbid?
   The Seventh Commandment forbids unjustly taking or keeping our neighbor's property. Sins against this commandment include theft, damage of property, usury, and fraud.

5. What is the Tenth Commandment?
   The Tenth Commandment is "You shall not covet your neighbor's goods."

6. What does the Tenth Commandment require us to do?
   The Tenth Commandment requires us to be just and moderate in the desire to improve our own condition of life. We are called to suffer with patience the hardships and other difficulties permitted by the Lord for our good.

7. What is restitution?
   Restitution is paying for damage or making recompense for some wrong we have done.

8. What is justice?
   Justice is the virtue that protects personal possessions. It involves giving everyone his due.

Name:_____

Charity

Answer the following questions in complete sentences.

1. Does everyone have all that they need?
   No.

2. Do some people have more than they need?
   Yes.

3. What does charity oblige us to do?
   Charity obliges us to share what we have with those in need.

4. How did Jesus identify himself with the poor?
   Jesus identifies himself with the poor when he says, "As you did it to one of the least of these my brethren, you did it to me."

5. What is almsgiving?
   Almsgiving is sharing what we have with those in need.

TEACHER'S NOTES

CHAPTER FIFTEEN
BACKED BY TRUTH

Catechism of the Catholic Church References

Eighth Commandment: 2464–2503, 2504–13
Living in the Truth: 2465–70, 2505
Bearing Witness to the Truth: 2471–74, 2506

Offenses against Truth: 2475–87, 2507–9
Respect for the Truth: 2488–92, 2510–11

Scripture References

Truth: Jn 1:14, 17; 4:24; 8:31–32; 14:6; 15:26; 16:7, 13; 18:37
Jesus is the Truth: Jn 1:1–14

Careless Words: Mt 12:36–37
Controlling Our Words: Mt 12:36–37; 5:10–11, 18–19; 1 Cor 13:6–7; Eph 4:29; Jas 3:2–12

Summary of Lesson Content

Lesson 1

The Eighth Commandment requires that we speak the truth. It governs our powers of communication.

Jesus is the Truth.

We must not intend to deceive another or bear false witness.

Lesson 2

Lying is a deliberate attempt to mislead others. We must not lie, even if what we want is good.

Hypocrisy is pretending to be better than one really is.

It is important to keep promises and oaths. A promise kept is truth in action. Lying under oath is called perjury.

Lesson 3

Speaking the truth in order to harm another is a sin. We must speak the truth if we speak. However, sometimes it is more prudent and charitable not to speak at all.

We must not harm another's name or reputation.

We should take care to be worthy of a good reputation.

Malicious or irresponsible use of truth to harm another is detraction; the use of lies to hurt another is slander.

Lesson 4

We must also be careful of what we think of others. The sin of rash judgment is to judge another person's character on flimsy evidence.

Gossip is talking of another's faults or exaggerating them.

If we are told a secret or discover something that must be kept secret for another's good, then we must be silent about what we have learned.

CHAPTER FIFTEEN: BACKED BY TRUTH
LESSON ONE: THE TRUTH

Aims

The students will learn that the Eighth Commandment requires us to speak the truth. It governs our powers of communication.

They will learn that Jesus is the Truth.

They will learn that we must not intend to deceive another or bear false witness.

Materials

• *Activity Book*, p. 57

• Appendix, p. B-15

Optional
• "I bind unto myself today," *Adoremus Hymnal*, #463

Begin

What is the truth? Have two students stand in different spots in the room and then stage an "accident." Have each student give his testimony as to what happened. Is all the testimony the same or different? Why might it be different? (They are seeing it from different angles). What are they saying the same? (Facts—the truth). Do their testimonies contradict one another? They should not, for the truth is objective.

Develop

1. Read paragraphs 1–4 from the student text.

2. Discuss why the truth is so important to us. How would society function if we never knew what was true and what was not? We would have to question everything. We could not trust one another—and it would be impossible to have relationships. Business could not function. We would doubt everything said. Is the sky blue or is it red? How do we know that what we see as blue really is not red—we have been mistaken all this time in what we call it!

3. What did Jesus teach us about truth? Read the following verses from the Gospel of John: 1:14, 17; 4:24; 8:31–32; 14:6; 15:26; 16:7, 13; 18:37.
Have the students explain these sayings, and make bumper-stickers with these texts.

4. What are some of the ways we communicate?

We communicate through speech (face-to-face), telephone, internet, fax, body language, sign language, etc.
Truth must be told no matter what way we communicate. It governs all our communications.

5. Ask the students to think about whether they have ever told a lie. If so, did they tell another lie to cover-up their first lie? What kind of damage can be done by a single lie? What if we lied and said someone was guilty of something he did not do? What if we lied and took credit for another's work? What if we lied to prevent someone from getting in trouble?

6. The Eighth Commandment tells us to speak the truth responsibly. We must never intend to deceive another when he has the right to the truth. Bearing false witness is not just about lying, but about any kind of deception or abuse of the truth.

Reinforce

1. Have the students work on *Activity Book* p. 57 (see *Teacher's Manual*, p. 187).

2. Have the students begin working on the Memorization Questions and Words to Know from this chapter (see *Teacher's Manual*, p. 185).

3. Have the students discuss how Pilate agreed to a lie. Did he recognize the truth? How did Pilate deny the truth?

Conclude

1. Lead the class in singing "I bind unto myself today," *Adoremus Hymnal*, #463.

2. End class by leading the students in the Prayer of Saint Patrick's Breastplate, Appendix, p. B-15.

CHAPTER 15

Backed by Truth

"You shall not bear false witness against your neighbor."

Exodus 20:16

The Eighth Commandment requires that we speak the truth always, but especially in matters involving the good name and honor of others. Truth is very important to us. If men were not truthful it would be impossible for us to live together.

When he was on trial before Pilate, Jesus said: "For this I was born, and for this I have come into the world, to bear witness to the truth. Every one who is of the truth hears my voice" (Jn 18:37). Pilate said to him, "What is truth?" (Jn 18:38). Evidently Pilate, who may at one time have been concerned about truth, about the meaning of life, about right and wrong, no longer cared, or had given up on it and decided there was no such thing.

But our Lord had come as a witness to the truth. And Pilate could not help being impressed. This is perhaps what led him to make a few weak attempts to save our Lord's life; but, as we know, Pilate gave in under pressure and agreed to a lie by condemning Jesus.

We all know what harm can be done just by one lie. The Eighth Commandment tells us we must never tell even a single lie. But it also directs all our powers of communication. We are obliged to speak the truth and must never intend to deceive another when he has the right to the truth. We must not bear **false witness**.

Lying

A lie is a deliberate attempt to mislead others. It is always sinful. We may not lie to get out of trouble, to cover up for a friend, or to get into a movie. Even if what we want is good, we may not lie to get it.

We can be strongly tempted to lie sometimes—it can seem so simple and so harmless. But we must always tell the truth to those who have a right to know.

Hypocrisy

One kind of untruthfulness is hypocrisy, which is when someone pretends to be better than he really is or pretends to believe something he really denies just to impress people. Jesus condemned this sin many times. However, it is not wrong to be on one's best behavior with those on whom one wishes to make a good impression.

Promises and Oaths

An important aspect of honesty is keeping one's word. One makes one's word true by living up to it. Keeping one's word means telling the truth about one's future actions.

69

In taking an oath in a courtroom one promises to tell the truth with God as one's witness. This is very serious. It is always a serious sin to lie in an important matter, but to lie under oath before God is much worse. Such a lie is called perjury.

Another's Good Name

There are times when we may be telling the truth and still sin. We must always speak the truth if we speak at all, but sometimes it is more prudent or charitable for us to remain silent. There are even times when we must not tell what we know to be true, for to do so would be wrong.

We have a precious possession that we may take for granted: our good name or reputation. We may hardly think of it, unless it is endangered. But if it is hurt or lost we see how precious it is to us. "A good name is to be chosen rather than great riches" (Prov 22:1). Regaining a good name once it is lost is very difficult; just think how hard it must be for an ex-convict to find a job. To damage a person's reputation is a serious matter. Therefore, one must have a very good reason for revealing anything about a person which would hurt his good name.

As for ourselves, we should take care to be worthy of a good reputation—not by seeking fame and renown, but by loving God and our neighbor and by being known as faithful followers of Christ.

There may be times when we are called upon to reveal what we know about someone—for instance, in legal proceedings—but we must be very careful about what we do with damaging facts, even if they are true.

How much worse, then, is a damaging story which is not true! Irresponsible or malicious use of the truth to harm another is called

70

detraction and is a serious sin. The use of lies to hurt someone is called calumny or **slander** and is an even greater sin. There is a grave obligation to repair the damage done by any of these sins.

Rash Judgment

Besides being careful in what we say about someone, we must also be careful in what we think. There is a sin called **rash judgment**, which is to judge another person's character without enough evidence. This does not mean that we may never make a judgment, but that we must be very careful about it. Otherwise someone may lose our esteem without a good reason. We should be very slow to judge another.

Gossip

As a rule, we should not talk about the faults of others unless there is a good and important reason to do so. **Gossip** usually consists of talking about the faults of others or exaggerating them. People who gossip may deal with facts, but they destroy another person's good name to satisfy idle curiosity. We must not be willing even to listen to people who gossip about others.

Secrets

We must keep any promise we have made, including the promise to keep a secret. If someone tells us a secret, or if we find out something that must be kept secret for another person's good, then we must be silent about what we have learned.

Our power of speech is a precious gift, a gift that must not be used to hurt others! Jesus says:

I tell you, on the day of judgment men will render account for every careless word they utter; for by your words you will be justified, and by your words you will be condemned (Mt 12:36–37).

Words to Know:
false witness   detraction   slander
rash judgment   gossip

"Let no evil talk come out of your mouths, but only such as is good for edifying, as fits the occasion, that it may impart grace to those who hear."

Ephesians 4:29

71

OBJECTIVE TRUTH

In our present era of the twenty-first century, attacks upon the very idea of truth that began early in the last century are still alive and well. Such products of modernism as relativism, nominalism, and subjectivism are dangerous errors that deny the existence of one truth, placing the emphasis on the subjective conceptions of men, rather than on a universal objective reality. Christianity is utterly dependent upon the existence of objective truth; without objective truth, belief in God (and logic) is impossible. Without objective truth, everyone is lost at sea with no solid foundation on which to base our lives. This is one of the greatest evils of our time.

Preview

In the next lesson, the students will learn about the importance of our words.

Chapter Fifteen: Backed by Truth
Lesson Two: Speaking Truth

Aims

The students will learn that lying is a deliberate attempt to mislead others. We must not lie, even if what we want is good.

They will learn that hypocrisy is pretending to be better than one really is.

They will learn that it is important to keep promises and oaths. A promise kept is truth in action. Lying under oath is called perjury.

Materials

- *Activity Book*, p. 58

- Appendix, p. B-15

Optional:
- "I bind unto myself today," *Adoremus Hymnal*, #463

Begin

Discuss the question: Do we have to speak to lie? What do the students think? No. Lying is the deliberate misleading of another. We can directly speak a falsehood, or we can imply one. We can also give the impression that a lie is the truth by not speaking the truth or by misleading another through trickery. The students should come to understand that the truth must be kept in word and in action and that we must watch what we say and do not say.

Develop

1. Read paragraphs 5–9 from the student text.

2. Words are very important. Words communicate what we are thinking and share who we are with others. We can say that our words are self-communication. The perfect self-communicator is God, the Word made flesh in the Divine Person of Jesus. Read John 1:1–14.

3. If our words communicate who we are, what does it say about us when we lie, use bad language, speak impurities, scream, shout, whisper, etc.?

4. Is lying ever a good thing? What if we tell a lie not to hurt someone's feelings? (e.g., Mary asks if you like her new haircut and you think it looks awful.) What should we do? What if we want something really badly—is it okay to lie to get it? How about to protect someone (such as you are hiding a person who is being chased by a bully)? Should you lie to con-

ceal his location? How can you work around this? Lying is always wrong and we are never permitted to lie.

5. What is hypocrisy? Can the students give an example of hypocrisy? Why is it wrong? Is it hypocrisy to be on our best behavior? What about to be proud of our accomplishments?

6. We discussed the importance of words; now we must address the importance of keeping our word. To keep our word means that when we say something, we mean it—we live up to it. It is telling the truth about our future actions. Have the students give examples.

7. An oath is when we call upon God's witness to the truth. We learned about false oaths and how wrong these are (in fact, this is a sin called perjury). Not all oaths are bad. An oath should only be sworn to in grave matters, e.g., in court.

Reinforce

1. Have the students work on *Activity Book* p. 58 (see *Teacher's Manual*, p. 187).

2. Have the students work on the Memorization Questions and Words to Know from this chapter (see *Teacher's Manual*, p. 185).

3. Have the students write a poem on the importance of words and of truth. The students may share their poems with the class.

Conclude

1. Lead the class in singing "I bind unto myself today," *Adoremus Hymnal*, #463.

2. End class by leading the students in the Prayer of Saint Patrick's Breastplate, Appendix, p. B-15.

CHAPTER 15

Backed by Truth

"You shall not bear false witness against your neighbor."

Exodus 20:16

The Eighth Commandment requires that we speak the truth always, but especially in matters involving the good name and honor of others. Truth is very important to us. If men were not truthful it would be impossible for us to live together.

When he was on trial before Pilate, Jesus said: "For this I was born, and for this I have come into the world, to bear witness to the truth. Every one who is of the truth hears my voice" (Jn 18:37). Pilate said to him, "What is truth?" (Jn 18:38). Evidently Pilate, who may at one time have been concerned about truth, about the meaning of life, about right and wrong, no longer cared, or had given up on it and decided there was no such thing.

But our Lord had come as a witness to the truth. And Pilate could not help being impressed. This is perhaps what led him to make a few weak attempts to save our Lord's life; but, as we know, Pilate gave in under pressure and agreed to a lie by condemning Jesus.

We all know what harm can be done just by one lie. The Eighth Commandment tells us we must never tell even a single lie. But it also directs all our powers of communication. We are obliged to speak the truth and must never intend to deceive another when he has the right to the truth. We must not bear **false witness**.

Lying

A lie is a deliberate attempt to mislead others. It is always sinful. We may not lie to get out of trouble, to cover up for a friend, or to get into a movie. Even if what we want is good, we may not lie to get it.

We can be strongly tempted to lie sometimes—it can seem so simple and so harmless. But we must always tell the truth to those who have a right to know.

Hypocrisy

One kind of untruthfulness is hypocrisy, which is when someone pretends to be better than he really is or pretends to believe something he really denies just to impress people. Jesus condemned this sin many times. However, it is not wrong to be on one's best behavior with those on whom one wishes to make a good impression.

Promises and Oaths

An important aspect of honesty is keeping one's word. One makes one's word true by living up to it. Keeping one's word means telling the truth about one's future actions.

69

In taking an oath in a courtroom one promises to tell the truth with God as one's witness. This is very serious. It is always a serious sin to lie in an important matter, but to lie under oath before God is much worse. Such a lie is called perjury.

Another's Good Name

There are times when we may be telling the truth and still sin. We must always speak the truth if we speak at all, but sometimes it is more prudent or charitable for us to remain silent. There are even times when we must not tell what we know to be true, for to do so would be wrong.

We have a precious possession that we may take for granted: our good name or reputation. We may hardly think of it, unless it is endangered. But if it is hurt or lost we see how precious it is to us. "A good name is to be chosen rather than great riches" (Prov 22:1). Regaining a good name once it is lost is very difficult; just think how hard it must be for an ex-convict to find a job. To damage a person's reputation is a serious matter. Therefore, one must have a very good reason for revealing anything about a person which would hurt his good name.

As for ourselves, we should take care to be worthy of a good reputation—not by seeking fame and renown, but by loving God and our neighbor and by being known as faithful followers of Christ.

There may be times when we are called upon to reveal what we know about someone—for instance, in legal proceedings—but we must be very careful about what we do with damaging facts, even if they are true.

How much worse, then, is a damaging story which is not true! Irresponsible or malicious use of the truth to harm another is called

70

---

detraction and is a serious sin. The use of lies to hurt someone is called calumny or **slander** and is an even greater sin. There is a grave obligation to repair the damage done by any of these sins.

Rash Judgment

Besides being careful in what we say about someone, we must also be careful in what we think. There is a sin called **rash judgment**, which is to judge another person's character without enough evidence. This does not mean that we may never make a judgment, but that we must be very careful about it. Otherwise someone may lose our esteem without a good reason. We should be very slow to judge another.

Gossip

As a rule, we should not talk about the faults of others unless there is a good and important reason to do so. **Gossip** usually consists of talking about the faults of others or exaggerating them. People who gossip may deal with facts, but they destroy another person's good name to satisfy idle curiosity. We must not be willing even to listen to people who gossip about others.

Secrets

We must keep any promise we have made, including the promise to keep a secret. If someone tells us a secret, or if we find out something that must be kept secret for another person's good, then we must be silent about what we have learned.

Our power of speech is a precious gift, a gift that must not be used to hurt others! Jesus says:

I tell you, on the day of judgment men will render account for every careless word they utter; for by your words you will be justified, and by your words you will be condemned (Mt 12:36–37).

Words to Know:
false witness   detraction   slander
rash judgment   gossip

"Let no evil talk come out of your mouths, but only such as is good for edifying, as fits the occasion, that it may impart grace to those who hear."

Ephesians 4:29

71

Oaths, vows, and promises are serious commitments to the truth. We must treat these words with the greatest respect, and we must be careful when we make them.

CCC 2150: The second commandment *forbids false oaths*. Taking an oath or swearing is to take God as witness to what one affirms. It is to invoke the divine truthfulness as a pledge of one's own truthfulness. An oath engages the Lord's name. "You shall fear the Lord your God; you shall serve him, and swear by his name" [Deut 6:13].

Preview

In the next lesson, the students will learn about the importance of another's good name.

CHAPTER FIFTEEN: BACKED BY TRUTH
LESSON THREE: A GOOD NAME

Aims

The students will learn that speaking the truth in order to harm another is a sin. We must speak the truth if we speak. However, sometimes it is more prudent and charitable not to speak at all.

They will learn that we must not harm another's name or reputation. We should take care to be worthy of a good reputation. Malicious or irresponsible use of truth to harm another is called detraction. The use of lies to hurt another is slander.

Materials

- *Activity Book*, p. 59

- Appendix, p. B-15

Optional:
- "I bind unto myself today," *Adoremus Hymnal*, #463

Begin

Why is our good name or reputation one of our greatest treasures? It speaks to people about who we are. It is our honor. We see people taking pride in their family name (they may name their business after it). Often a family takes pride in its traits and claims them with their family name: "He has that Bradshaw intelligence" or "She has the MacDonald grin!" We know how horrible it is to call someone a bad name or to make fun of someone's name. This is because our name and reputation are important.

Develop

1. Read paragraphs 10–14 from the student text.

2. Explain to the students that we must speak the truth responsibly. Sometimes it is better to be silent than to speak the truth (for we should never lie)! For example, we may know someone's fault, but it is not necessary to reveal it to others. We do not need to speak that particular truth. It is more charitable to be silent.

3. We should not harm another's reputation. What must we avoid doing? We must not reveal the faults of others unnecessarily, through gossip, lying about them, etc.

4. We must strive to keep a good reputation for ourselves. What should we do? We should be honest, virtuous, etc.

5. Review definitions and examples of detraction and slander, or calumny.

6. Discuss that when we harm another's reputation, we can never fully reverse the effects of our sinful deed. We must, however, repair the damage we have done as far as it is possible. If you spread a lie about someone, you must tell everyone who heard this lie that you told this lie. You should also apologize to the person about whom you lied.

7. Discuss rash judgment with the students. We must be careful not to judge another harshly. Why? We do not know the whole truth about other people—why they are the way they are. Rash judgment is judging someone upon flimsy evidence. This, however, does not mean that we cannot make judgments. For example, if a person consistently shows themselves to do bad things, then we can judge his actions. We should be very slow to judge.

8. Review the vocabulary for this chapter in the box on the facing page.

Reinforce

1. Have the students work on *Activity Book* p. 59 (see *Teacher's Manual*, p. 187).

2. Each student may create a banner with his family name on it, decorating it according to his interpretation of the value of his "good name."

3. Have the students work on the Memorization Questions and Words to Know from this chapter (see *Teacher's Manual*, p. 185).

Conclude

1. Lead the class in singing "I bind unto myself today," *Adoremus Hymnal*, #463.

2. End class by leading the students in the Prayer of Saint Patrick's Breastplate, Appendix, p. B-15.

In taking an oath in a courtroom one promises to tell the truth with God as one's witness. This is very serious. It is always a serious sin to lie in an important matter, but to lie under oath before God is much worse. Such a lie is called perjury.

Another's Good Name

There are times when we may be telling the truth and still sin. We must always speak the truth if we speak at all, but sometimes it is more prudent or charitable for us to remain silent. There are even times when we must not tell what we know to be true, for to do so would be wrong.

We have a precious possession that we may take for granted: our good name or reputation. We may hardly think of it, unless it is endangered. But if it is hurt or lost we see how precious it is to us. "A good name is to be

chosen rather than great riches" (Prov 22:1). Regaining a good name once it is lost is very difficult; just think how hard it must be for an ex-convict to find a job. To damage a person's reputation is a serious matter. Therefore, one must have a very good reason for revealing anything about a person which would hurt his good name.

As for ourselves, we should take care to be worthy of a good reputation—not by seeking fame and renown, but by loving God and our neighbor and by being known as faithful followers of Christ.

There may be times when we are called upon to reveal what we know about someone—for instance, in legal proceedings—but we must be very careful about what we do with damaging facts, even if they are true.

How much worse, then, is a damaging story which is not true! Irresponsible or malicious use of the truth to harm another is called

detraction and is a serious sin. The use of lies to hurt someone is called calumny or **slander** and is an even greater sin. There is a grave obligation to repair the damage done by any of these sins.

Rash Judgment

Besides being careful in what we say about someone, we must also be careful in what we think. There is a sin called **rash judgment**, which is to judge another person's character without enough evidence. This does not mean that we may never make a judgment, but that we must be very careful about it. Otherwise someone may lose our esteem without a good reason. We should be very slow to judge another.

Gossip

As a rule, we should not talk about the faults of others unless there is a good and important reason to do so. **Gossip** usually consists of talking about the faults of others or exaggerating them. People who gossip may deal with facts, but they destroy another person's

good name to satisfy idle curiosity. We must not be willing even to listen to people who gossip about others.

Secrets

We must keep any promise we have made, including the promise to keep a secret. If someone tells us a secret, or if we find out something that must be kept secret for another person's good, then we must be silent about what we have learned.

Our power of speech is a precious gift, a gift that must not be used to hurt others! Jesus says:

I tell you, on the day of judgment men will render account for every careless word they utter; for by your words you will be justified, and by your words you will be condemned (Mt 12:36–37).

Words to Know:
false witness   detraction   slander
rash judgment   gossip

"Let no evil talk come out of your mouths, but only such as is good for edifying, as fits the occasion, that it may impart grace to those who hear."

Ephesians 4:29

70

71

VOCABULARY LIST—STUDENTS SHOULD BE ABLE TO DEFINE ALL THESE WORDS

- *Slander* is the sin of saying something false about another—harming his good name.
- *Flattery* is false or exaggerated praise.
- *Detraction* is the sin of using the truth irresponsibly or maliciously to harm another's reputation.
- *Rash judgment* is the sin of judging another's behavior as wrong without enough evidence.
- *Gossip* is the sin of idle or malicious talk about others.
- *False witness* is the sin of giving untrue testimony—lying about another.
- *Hypocrisy* is the sin of pretending to be better than you really are or pretending to believe something you know is not true in order to impress people.
- *Perjury* is the sin of lying under oath before God.
- *Calumny* is the use of lies to hurt someone's reputation (synonym of slander).
- *Oath* is a declaration calling on God as witness to the truth of what is being said.
- *Truth* is the conformity of the mind (or intellect) to reality; in accordance with reality; to "say it like it is."

Slander is a poison which extinguishes charity, both in the slanderer and in the persons who listen to it.

—Saint Bernard of Clairvaux

Preview

In the next lesson, the students will learn about the danger of idle talk.

CHAPTER FIFTEEN: BACKED BY TRUTH
LESSON FOUR: CARELESS TALK

Aims

The students will learn that we must be careful of what we think of others. The sin of rash judgment is to judge another person's character on flimsy evidence. Gossip is talking of or exaggerating another's faults.

They will learn that if we are told a secret or discover something that must be kept secret for another's good, then we must be silent about what we have learned.

Materials

- *Activity Book*, p. 60

- Appendix, p. B-15

Optional:
- "I bind unto myself today," *Adoremus Hymnal*, #463

Begin

Together read Matthew 12:36–37 as found at the end of the text of this chapter. What does "careless words" mean? How often do we talk with friends and even strangers without thinking about what we are saying? We waste our words when we do not give them meaning. "How are you?" "Fine." Really?

Are you actually great because you won a game, or sad because you have a lot of homework, or are you tired because you got up too early this morning? Do we really think about what we say?

Develop

1. Finish reading the chapter from the student text.

2. Gossip is talking about the faults of others or exaggerating their faults. It is wrong to gossip and talk about a person behind his back.

3. Often when we gossip, we tell rumors. Telling a rumor is spreading a story that we do not know to be true. It is dangerous to spread rumors because we do not know if they are true or not and they often harm the reputations of others.

4. Flattery is false or exaggerated praise, which is also sinful, since it is not based in truth. Have the students give examples of flattery.

5. Read the story of Saint Philip Neri and the Gossip of Rome from the box on p. 185. Have the students cut out feathers from construction paper and write a vocabulary word and its definition on each feather. Then have all the students place these "feathers" in a bag and release them into the wind. Have the students then try to find their own feathers.

6. Discuss secrets with the students. We are obliged to keep the secrets that we make. We must only make secrets we can keep. If there is a secret that we should not keep, we must ask to be released from the secret. If we find out something that should be kept a secret for another person's good, we must then keep silent about what we have learned.

7. Read and discuss Scripture quotes on the control of our speech in Matthew 12:36–37; 5:10–11, 18–19; 1 Corinthians 13:6–7; Ephesians 4:29; and James 3:2–12.

Reinforce

1. Have the students work on *Activity Book* p. 60 (see *Teacher's Manual*, p. 187).

2. Have the students work on the Memorization Questions and Words to Know from this chapter and review for the quiz.

Conclude

1. Lead the class in singing "I bind unto myself today," *Adoremus Hymnal*, #463.

2. End class by leading the students in the Prayer of Saint Patrick's Breastplate, Appendix, p. B-15.

detraction and is a serious sin. The use of lies to hurt someone is called calumny or **slander** and is an even greater sin. There is a grave obligation to repair the damage done by any of these sins.

Rash Judgment

Besides being careful in what we say about someone, we must also be careful in what we think. There is a sin called **rash judgment**, which is to judge another person's character without enough evidence. This does not mean that we may never make a judgment, but that we must be very careful about it. Otherwise someone may lose our esteem without a good reason. We should be very slow to judge another.

Gossip

As a rule, we should not talk about the faults of others unless there is a good and important reason to do so. **Gossip** usually consists of talking about the faults of others or exaggerating them. People who gossip may deal with facts, but they destroy another person's good name to satisfy idle curiosity. We must not be willing even to listen to people who gossip about others.

Secrets

We must keep any promise we have made, including the promise to keep a secret. If someone tells us a secret, or if we find out something that must be kept secret for another person's good, then we must be silent about what we have learned.

Our power of speech is a precious gift, a gift that must not be used to hurt others! Jesus says:

I tell you, on the day of judgment men will render account for every careless word they utter; for by your words you will be justified, and by your words you will be condemned (Mt 12:36–37).

Words to Know:
false witness detraction slander
rash judgment gossip

"*Let no evil talk come out of your mouths, but only such as is good for edifying, as fits the occasion, that it may impart grace to those who hear.*"

Ephesians 4:29

71

72

SAINT PHILIP NERI AND THE GOSSIP OF ROME

Saint Philip Neri lived in Italy in the early sixteenth century. After many years as a lay apostle, caring for the sick and teaching young people, especially boys in street gangs, about the love of Jesus, Philip became a priest. One day, a woman who was notorious in all of Rome for being a gossip went to confession to Father Philip. For her penance, Philip told her to carry her feather pillow to the windiest hill of Rome, cut it open and shake out all the feathers, and then return to him. The penitent did as she was told. When she returned, Philip told the woman to go back to the hill and collect all the feathers that she had shaken out. "But Father!" she exclaimed, "The wind has carried away all the feathers by now! It would be impossible for me to collect them again." Saint Philip replied, "That is what has happened to all the rumors and gossip you have spread around Rome. You can never take back all those idle words you have spoken."

Every kind of beast and bird, of reptile and sea creature, can be tamed and has been tamed by mankind, but no human being can tame the tongue—a restless evil, full of deadly poison.

—James 3:7–9

Preview

In the next lesson, the students' understanding of the material covered in this chapter will be reviewed and assessed.

CHAPTER FIFTEEN: BACKED BY TRUTH
REVIEW AND ASSESSMENT

Aims

The students' understanding of the material covered in this chapter will be reviewed and assessed.

Materials

- Quiz 15, Appendix, p. A-21

Optional:
- "I bind unto myself today," *Adoremus Hymnal*, #463

Review and Enrichment

1. The students should know the Eighth Commandment and what it requires and forbids.

2. The students should know all of the Words to Know from this chapter. They should be able to give examples of the actions described by these words.

3. The students should understand the importance of words and of a good name.

4. The students should understand the need to speak the truth responsibly. It is always wrong to tell a lie.

Name: _____

Backed by Truth   **Quiz 15**

Part I: Matching.

1. _d_ idle talk about the faults of others
2. _g_ lying under oath
3. _a_ saying something false about another
4. _f_ pretending to be better than you are
5. _c_ judging another's character without enough evidence
6. _e_ giving untrue testimony about another
7. _h_ deliberately deceiving someone
8. _b_ using the truth to harm another

a. slander/calumny
b. detraction
c. rash judgment
d. gossip
e. false witness
f. hypocrisy
g. perjury
h. lying

Part II: Write a paragraph about what you should do when you are tempted to gossip or listen to gossip. Be sure to explain what gossip is and why it is wrong.

_____
_____
_____
_____
_____
_____
_____
_____
_____
_____
_____
_____
_____
_____
_____
_____

Faith and Life Series • Grade 6 • Appendix A   *A-21*

Assess

1. Distribute the quizzes and read through them with the students to be sure they understand the questions.

2. Administer the quiz. As they hand in their work, you may orally quiz the students on the Memorization Questions from this chapter.

3. After all the quizzes have been handed in, you may wish to review the correct answers with the class.

Conclude

1. Lead the class in singing "I bind unto myself today," *Adoremus Hymnal*, #463.

2. End class by leading the students in the Prayer of Saint Patrick's Breastplate, Appendix, p. B-15.

CHAPTER FIFTEEN: BACKED BY TRUTH
ACTIVITY BOOK ANSWER KEYS

Name:_____

Backed by the Truth

Answer the following questions in complete sentences.

1. What is the Eighth Commandment?
   The Eighth Commandment is "You shall not bear false witness against your neighbor."

2. What does the Eighth Commandment forbid?
   The Eighth Commandment forbids all deliberate falsehood and unjust damage to another person's reputation. E.g. bearing false witness, slander, lying, detraction, flattery, unfounded suspicion, and rash judgment.

3. What does the Eighth Commandment require?
   The Eighth Commandment requires us to speak the truth responsibly and to avoid rash judgment of our neighbors' actions.

4. Why is telling the truth important?
   Telling the truth is important, in part, because if men were not truthful it would be impossible to live together.

5. Why did Jesus say he was born into the world?
   Jesus said he was born into the world "to bear witness to the truth."

6. Did Pilate recognize the truth?
   Yes.

7. How did Pilate agree to a lie?
   Pilate gave in under pressure and condemned Jesus.

Faith and Life Series • Grade 6 • Chapter 15 • Lesson 1   57

Name:_____

The Value of Words

Answer the following questions in complete sentences.

1. What value do words have? Why do we use them?
   Answers will vary.

2. What would happen if everyone said things they did not mean?
   Answers will vary.

3. Why is lying a sin?
   Answers will vary.

4. Should we lie to get out of trouble?
   No.

5. Should we lie to make someone else feel better?
   No.

6. What is hypocrisy?
   Hypocrisy is pretending to be better than we really are or pretending to believe in something we do not believe just to impress people.

7. Is it wrong (a sin of hypocrisy) to be on your best behavior to make a good impression?
   No.

8. Why must we keep our word?
   We must keep our word because it would be dishonest not to do so.

58   *Faith and Life Series • Grade 6 • Chapter 15 • Lesson 2*

Name:_____

Another's Good Name

Answer the following questions in complete sentences.

1. How can speaking the truth be sinful? What would be more prudent and charitable in this situation?
   If speaking the truth will hurt someone's good name (damage their reputation), it is sinful to do so if done without sufficient reason. It would be better to remain silent.

2. Why is a good name hard to regain once it is lost?
   Answers will vary. E.g., it is hard to get others to trust you and give you another chance once you have lost it.

3. How can we take care to be worthy of a good reputation?
   To be worthy of a good reputation, we should not seek fame and renown. We should simply love God and our neighbor and be known as a faithful follower of Christ.

4. What is calumny (slander)?
   Calumny or slander is the use of lies to hurt someone.

5. If you commit the sin of slander, what is your grave obligation?
   There is a grave obligation to repair the damage done by sins such as slander.

Faith and Life Series • Grade 6 • Chapter 15 • Lesson 3   59

Name:_____

Gossip and Secrets

Answer the following questions in complete sentences.

1. What is rash judgment?
   Rash judgment is to judge another person's character on flimsy evidence.

2. What is gossip?
   Gossip is talking about the faults of others or exaggerating them.

3. What does gossiping do to another's good name?
   Gossiping destroys another's good name.

4. Should we be willing to listen to gossip?
   No.

5. What is a secret?
   Definitions will vary.

6. Must we keep a promise of keeping a secret?
   Yes.

7. Can speech be a weapon? How?
   Yes. It can cause great harm to others.

8. Is it okay to discuss difficult situations with other people when it involves a third party? For example, if Mary and Jane have a fight, can Mary talk about it with her mother for advice?
   Yes.

60   *Faith and Life Series • Grade 6 • Chapter 15 • Lesson 4*

TEACHER'S NOTES

CHAPTER SIXTEEN
THE BEATITUDES

Catechism of the Catholic Church References

Baptism of Jesus: 535–37, 565
Beatitudes: 1716–19, 1726–28, 1820
Christian Beatitude: 1720–24, 1728–29
Desire for Happiness: 1718–19, 1726–27
Forgiveness: 2842–45, 2862
Good News: God Sent His Son: 422–29
Heaven: 1023–29, 1052–53
Jesus: the Only Son of God: 441–45, 454
Jesus and the Law: 574–82, 592, 2051–55, 2075

Jesus' Mission of Salvation: 456–60
Jesus' Temptation: 538–40, 566
John: Forerunner, Prophet, Baptizer: 523, 717–20
"The Kingdom of God is Very Near": 541–42, 567
Old Law: 1961–64, 1975, 1980–82
Peace: 2302–6, 2330
Poverty of Spirit: 2544–47, 2556
Proclamation of the Kingdom of God: 543–46
Purity of Heart: 2517–19, 2531–33

Scripture References

Jesus' Baptism in the Jordan: Mt 3:4–17
Beatitudes: Mt 5:3–12; Lk 6:20–23

Sermon on the Mount: Mt 5–7

Summary of Lesson Content

Lesson 1

At age thirty, Jesus was baptized by John the Baptist. Following his baptism, Jesus was led into the desert and prepared for his public ministry.

After forty days in the desert, Jesus preached the Good News of God's Kingdom. He was a teacher and miracle worker.

Jesus taught the Beatitudes, which tell us of the blessings of following Jesus.

Lesson 2

The poor in spirit value their heavenly treasure and are ready to make sacrifices for it. They need not be without material goods.

Mourners have sorrow for sin and separation from their brethren. They are comforted and strengthened in faith.

The meek are the truly humble and kind.

Those whose wills correspond with God's will are blessed.

Lesson 3

The merciful love others and forgive in compassion.

The pure of heart live chaste lives and are free of excessive love of earthly things.

Peacemakers remove obstacles that keep men apart or in disagreement with one another.

Those persecuted for Jesus' sake embrace the Cross of Christ and will share in his Resurrection.

Lesson 4

The Beatitudes are the counsels of the New Testament. They are positive exhortations to live in a way that keeps us close to Jesus Christ. The Beatitudes have a promise of reward.

To live the Beatitudes we must live the Ten Commandments, receive sacramental grace, and be prayerful people.

CHAPTER SIXTEEN: THE BEATITUDES
LESSON ONE: NEW LAW

Aims

The students will learn that at age thirty, Jesus was baptized by John the Baptist. Following his baptism, Jesus went into the desert and prepared for his public ministry.

They will learn that after forty days in the desert, Jesus preached the Good News of God's Kingdom. He was a teacher and miracle worker. Jesus taught the Beatitudes, which tell us of the blessings of heaven.

Materials

- *Activity Book*, p. 61

- Bibles

Optional:
- "Be thou my vision," *Adoremus Hymnal*, #623

Begin

From the Bible, read the account of Jesus' baptism in the Jordan: Mt 3:4–17. The students may dramatize this event. Discussion questions may include:
- Why was Jesus baptized if he is sinless? (He was baptized to unite himself to all people, the sinners.)

- When Jesus came out of the water, what happened? What doctrine does this teach? (Blessed Trinity)
- After Jesus was anointed with the Spirit what happened?
- Why did Jesus fast in the desert for forty days?
- How was Jesus prepared to speak the gospel?

Develop

1. Read paragraphs 1–5 from the student text.

2. If the Good News is the Kingdom of God, who then is the King? Where is the Kingdom? How can we enter the Kingdom? Under whose reign do we live?

3. How do we know that Jesus is God the Son? He taught and preached about God and his Kingdom, he challenged people to see things as God wants us to, he worked miracles and was our perfect example. Have the students research the various miracles Jesus works in the Gospels. They should each write a report on a miracle of Jesus or create a presentation (a poster, animated presentation, dramatization, newspaper article, etc.) on this miracle.

4. Where did Jesus teach? How was Jesus a witness? Where was Jesus a witness? How can we be his witnesses? Where can we teach what he taught us?

5. Have the students research various parables. Have the students write modern-day parables.

6. Jesus taught the Beatitudes, which are an exhortation of the fulfillment of the Old Law with the New Law. This teaching is part of the "Sermon on the Mount" or the "Sermon on the Plain." It is recorded in Matthew 5:1–12 and Luke 6:20–23. Have the students compare these two sets of Beatitudes.

7. Discuss how the Old Law commands with prohibitions. One could follow the Ten Commandments out of duty, but in his heart not embrace the spirit of the Law. The Beatitudes show us how to love and live the law of God.

8. Review that for each beatitude, there is a promise. Have the students make a chart comparing who is blessed and the promises given to the blessed. The students should start memorizing the Beatitudes.

Reinforce

1. Have the students work on *Activity Book* p. 61 (see *Teacher's Manual*, p. 199).

2. Have the students begin working on their Memorization Questions, Word to Know (see *Teacher's Manual*, p. 195) and study of the Beatitudes.

Conclude

1. Lead the class in singing "Be thou my vision," *Adoremus Hymnal*, #623.

2. End class by leading the students in reciting the Beatitudes (Mt 5:3–12).

CHAPTER 16

The Beatitudes

"O LORD of hosts, blessed is the man who trusts in you!"

Psalm 84:12

When he was about thirty years old, Jesus began his public life with his baptism by Saint John the Baptist in the Jordan River. When he was baptized, the Holy Spirit descended like a dove and rested upon Jesus. A voice from the heavens said: "This is my beloved Son, with whom I am well pleased" (Mt 3:17).

Following his baptism, Jesus was led by the Spirit into the wilderness, where he prayed and fasted for forty days and overcame the devil's temptations.

After this, Jesus set out to preach the Good News of God's Kingdom. He was a teacher, a reformer, and a miracle worker, and he was the perfect living example of everything he taught. He even raised the dead to life. He taught everywhere: in the fields, on the roads, on the hillsides, in the synagogues, by lakes, and even from a boat. He often taught in parables, using for examples things people used and saw every day, from the lilies of the field to the sparrows of the air.

Jesus didn't come to abolish the Old Law but to fulfill it in the New. He built on the Ten Commandments and the "you shall not" prohibitions by giving positive exhortations to live the Christian life. Among these exhortations are those called the Beatitudes. They sum up the blessings and joys in store for people who follow Jesus and his way of life. A **beatitude** is a blessing or special happiness of a spiritual nature.

Jesus emphasized that these blessings are open to everyone, no matter how poor or uneducated or sick or seemingly unwanted a person may be. This contradicted the Scribes and Pharisees, who taught that poverty or bad health was a punishment and a sign of God's disfavor.

The Beatitudes

"Blessed are the poor in spirit, for theirs is the kingdom of heaven" (Mt 5:3).

The poor in spirit are those who may have material possessions but who are ready to give them up when self-sacrifice is called for. They value heavenly treasure above everything else and never lose sight of it.

You may remember the rich young man who turned away from following Jesus because this man was attached to his many possessions. The poor in spirit do just the opposite: when Jesus calls, they leave all things to follow him. Because their hearts are not filled with things of earth, God fills their hearts with himself.

"Blessed are those who mourn, for they shall be comforted" (Mt 5:4).

73

Mourning, in this beatitude, means sorrow for sin and sorrow over the loss, by separation or by death, of someone dear to us.

Jesus promises the sorrowful that they will get the strength they need to stand firm in their trials and troubles and even to grow through their sorrows in their friendship with God.

"Blessed are the meek, for they shall inherit the earth" (Mt 5:5).

The meek are those who are truly humble and kind. They don't think of themselves as being better than other people. They accept and recognize the gifts God has given them with gratitude and patience and without complaint.

"Blessed are those who hunger and thirst for righteousness, for they shall be satisfied" (Mt 5:6).

Blessed is the heart that wants what God wants! If we desire to be righteous and holy, Jesus will help us and our desire will be fulfilled. Jesus promises joy to those who do God's will.

"Blessed are the merciful, for they shall obtain mercy" (Mt 5:7).

Mercy is love shown to those in need as well as those who have been unjust and ungrateful. The merciful provide for the needs of others, forgive others their offenses, and show kindness and compassion toward the sinner. They, in turn, will receive mercy from God. Jesus said: "If you forgive men their trespasses, your heavenly Father also will forgive you" (Mt 6:14).

"Blessed are the pure in heart, for they shall see God" (Mt 5:8).

The pure in heart are those who live chaste lives and are free of all excessive love of earthly things. They have put God first in their lives. Because they are single-hearted, they can feel God's presence in this life and will see him face to face in the next.

"Blessed are the peacemakers, for they shall be called sons of God" (Mt 5:9).

Psalm 133 begins: "Behold, how good and how pleasant it is when brothers dwell together in unity!"

Peacemakers go out of their way to remove the obstacles that keep men apart. They work especially hard to bring sinners back to God. Jesus promises that peacemakers will be God's special children here on earth and will enjoy heavenly glory in the family of the saints.

"Blessed are those who are persecuted for righteousness' sake, for theirs is the kingdom of heaven" (Mt 5:10).

"Blessed are you when men revile you and persecute you and utter all kinds of evil against you falsely on my account" (Mt 5:11).

Jesus suffered everything to witness to the truth. If we are persecuted because we are loyal to Jesus and his Church, we will know a little of what he suffered on the Cross to free us from sin and death. But we will also share in the joy of his Resurrection, his gift of eternal life with God.

* * *

The Beatitudes are the counsels of the New Testament; instead of being prohibitions, they are positive exhortations to live in a way that keeps us close to Jesus Christ. Each beatitude has attached to it a promise of great rewards.

Perhaps you have been thinking how difficult this is—how impossible, even, for human strength alone to live up to. You're right—it *is* hard!

74

PARABLES

- Sower and the Seed: Mk 4:3–8
- Weeds and Wheat: Mt 13:24–30
- Unmerciful Servant: Mt 18:24–35
- Workers in the Vineyard: Mt 20:1–16
- The Ten Maidens: Mt 25:1–12
- The Talents: Mt 25:14–30
- Sheep and Goats: Mt 25:31–46
- The Good Samaritan: Lk 10:30–37
- Rich Farmer: Lk 12:16–21
- Great Feast: Lk 14:15–24
- Lost Sheep: Lk 15:3–7
- Prodigal Son: Lk 15:11–32
- Rich Man and Lazarus: Lk 16:19–31
- Persistent Widow: Luke 18:1–8

MIRACLES

Nature Miracles:
- Water to Wine: Jn 2:1–11
- Miraculous Catch of Fish: Lk 5:1–11
- Calming of Storm: Mt 8:23–27
- Multiplication of Loaves and Fish: Mt 14:13–21
- Walking on Water: Mt 14:22–33
- Coin in Fish's Mouth: Mt 17:24–27

Healings:
- Leper: Lk 17:11–19
- Paralytic: Lk 5:17–26
- Withered Hand: Mt 12:9–13
- Centurion's Servant: Lk 7:1–10
- Woman with Hemorrhage: Mt 9:20–22
- Eyes of Blind: Mk 8:22–26
- Man Born Blind: Jn 9:1–4
- Malchus' Ear: Lk 22:49–51

MORE MIRACLES

Deliverances:
- Demoniac at Capernaum: Mk 1:23–28
- Mute Demoniac: Mt 9:32–33
- Demoniac at Gerasenes: Lk 8:26–33

Raisings from the Dead:
- Jairus' Daughter: Mt 9:18–19, 23–26
- Son of Widow: Lk 7:11–17
- Lazarus: Jn 11:1–44

Preview

In the next lesson, the students will learn about the first four Beatitudes.

CHAPTER SIXTEEN: THE BEATITUDES
LESSON TWO: BLESSED ARE THE . . .

Aims

The students will learn that the poor in spirit value their heavenly treasure and are ready to make sacrifices for it. They need not be without material goods. Mourners have sorrow for sin and separation from their brethren. They are comforted and strengthened in faith. The meek are the truly humble and kind.

They will learn that those whose wills correspond with God's will are blessed.

Materials

- *Activity Book*, p. 62
- Saints books

Optional:
- "Be thou my vision," *Adoremus Hymnal*, #623

Begin

Review that the Beatitudes are ways that we can live in God's spirit and love greatly, as God has loved us. Anyone can follow the Beatitudes as a path to holiness. Have the students give examples of people they know (or saints) who lived the Beatitudes well, and how God has blessed them.

Today we will study the first four Beatitudes.

Develop

1. Read paragraphs 6–15 (up to "Blessed are the merciful").

2. Who are the poor in spirit? How are they different from the poor? Why is spiritual poverty important? You may review the Scripture: Mt 6:24. We cannot serve two masters. Spiritual poverty means that we place God above all things, even our material possessions. We must trust in God completely, listen to his words in our lives, and follow his call. Have the students think of an empty pail. Imagine two large items that could go in this pail, but only one will fit at a time. This is how it is with God and worldly treasures. We can only truly fit one of them in our hearts. If we fill our hearts with worldly treasures, then we cannot fill our heart with God. Our hearts were made to be filled with God and we will be most happy (and blessed) when we empty ourselves of material things and become filled with God.

3. Who are those who mourn? The mourners are those who have sorrow for sin. We should mourn sin, for in sin we offend God and hurt ourselves.

4. Who are the meek? The meek are people who bear offenses patiently, humbly accepting God's will. They are temperate and restrain their anger and do not harbor ill will toward those who offend them.

5. Who are those who hunger and thirst for righteousness? These are the people who want what God wants (note: the Our Father, "Thy will be done"). God will help us to do his will, and if we cooperate with his grace, his will shall be done!

6. Have the students find examples of these Beatitudes among the saints and make presentations on their findings.

Reinforce

1. Have the students work on *Activity Book* p. 62 (see *Teacher's Manual*, p. 199).

2. The students should continue to research saints who lived the Beati-tudes, and make presentations for the class on the lives of these saints.

3. The students should discuss how they can live the Beatitudes every day.

4. The students should work on their Memorization Questions, Word to Know (see *Teacher's Manual*, p. 195) and memorization of the Beatitudes.

Conclude

1. Lead the class in singing "Be thou my vision," *Adoremus Hymnal*, #623.

2. End class by leading the students in reciting the Beatitudes (Mt 5:3–12).

CHAPTER 16

The Beatitudes

"O LORD of hosts, blessed is the man who trusts in you!"

Psalm 84:12

When he was about thirty years old, Jesus began his public life with his baptism by Saint John the Baptist in the Jordan River. When he was baptized, the Holy Spirit descended like a dove and rested upon Jesus. A voice from the heavens said: "This is my beloved Son, with whom I am well pleased" (Mt 3:17).

Following his baptism, Jesus was led by the Spirit into the wilderness, where he prayed and fasted for forty days and overcame the devil's temptations.

After this, Jesus set out to preach the Good News of God's Kingdom. He was a teacher, a reformer, and a miracle worker, and he was the perfect living example of everything he taught. He even raised the dead to life. He taught everywhere: in the fields, on the roads, on the hillsides, in the synagogues, by lakes, and even from a boat. He often taught in parables, using for examples things people used and saw every day, from the lilies of the field to the sparrows of the air.

Jesus didn't come to abolish the Old Law but to fulfill it in the New. He built on the Ten Commandments and the "you shall not" prohibitions by giving positive exhortations to live the Christian life. Among these exhortations are those called the Beatitudes. They sum up the blessings and joys in store for people who follow Jesus and his way of life. A **beatitude** is a blessing or special happiness of a spiritual nature.

Jesus emphasized that these blessings are open to everyone, no matter how poor or uneducated or sick or seemingly unwanted a person may be. This contradicted the Scribes and Pharisees, who taught that poverty or bad health was a punishment and a sign of God's disfavor.

The Beatitudes

"Blessed are the poor in spirit, for theirs is the kingdom of heaven" (Mt 5:3).

The poor in spirit are those who may have material possessions but who are ready to give them up when self-sacrifice is called for. They value heavenly treasure above everything else and never lose sight of it.

You may remember the rich young man who turned away from following Jesus because this man was attached to his many possessions. The poor in spirit do just the opposite: when Jesus calls, they leave all things to follow him. Because their hearts are not filled with things of earth, God fills their hearts with himself.

"Blessed are those who mourn, for they shall be comforted" (Mt 5:4).

73

Mourning, in this beatitude, means sorrow for sin and sorrow over the loss, by separation or by death, of someone dear to us.

Jesus promises the sorrowful that they will get the strength they need to stand firm in their trials and troubles and even to grow through their sorrows in their friendship with God.

"Blessed are the meek, for they shall inherit the earth" (Mt 5:5).

The meek are those who are truly humble and kind. They don't think of themselves as being better than other people. They accept and recognize the gifts God has given them with gratitude and patience and without complaint.

"Blessed are those who hunger and thirst for righteousness, for they shall be satisfied" (Mt 5:6).

Blessed is the heart that wants what God wants! If we desire to be righteous and holy, Jesus will help us and our desire will be fulfilled. Jesus promises joy to those who do God's will.

"Blessed are the merciful, for they shall obtain mercy" (Mt 5:7).

Mercy is love shown to those in need as well as those who have been unjust and ungrateful. The merciful provide for the needs of others, forgive others their offenses, and show kindness and compassion toward the sinner. They, in turn, will receive mercy from God. Jesus said: "If you forgive men their trespasses, your heavenly Father also will forgive you" (Mt 6:14).

"Blessed are the pure in heart, for they shall see God" (Mt 5:8).

The pure in heart are those who live chaste lives and are free of all excessive love of earthly things. They have put God first in their lives. Because they are single-hearted, they can feel God's presence in this life and will see him face to face in the next.

"Blessed are the peacemakers, for they shall be called sons of God" (Mt 5:9).

Psalm 133 begins: "Behold, how good and how pleasant it is when brothers dwell together in unity!"

Peacemakers go out of their way to remove the obstacles that keep men apart. They work especially hard to bring sinners back to God. Jesus promises that peacemakers will be God's special children here on earth and will enjoy heavenly glory in the family of the saints.

"Blessed are those who are persecuted for righteousness' sake, for theirs is the kingdom of heaven" (Mt 5:10).

"Blessed are you when men revile you and persecute you and utter all kinds of evil against you falsely on my account" (Mt 5:11).

Jesus suffered everything to witness to the truth. If we are persecuted because we are loyal to Jesus and his Church, we will know a little of what he suffered on the Cross to free us from sin and death. But we will also share in the joy of his Resurrection, his gift of eternal life with God.

* * *

The Beatitudes are the counsels of the New Testament; instead of being prohibitions, they are positive exhortations to live in a way that keeps us close to Jesus Christ. Each beatitude has attached to it a promise of great rewards.

Perhaps you have been thinking how difficult this is—how impossible, even, for human strength alone to live up to. You're right—it *is* hard!

74

That is why Christ has left us a great source of divine power in the Holy Eucharist. If we take the Ten Commandments and the Beatitudes seriously and desire to live up to them, we will feel the call to unite ourselves to Christ by receiving the Holy Eucharist often—perhaps even daily. And we will be well on our way to living the authentic Christian life.

Word to Know:

beatitude

75

THE BLESSINGS OF THE FIRST FOUR BEATITUDES (MT 5:3–6)

Theirs is the Kingdom of Heaven: We will be so full of the love and life of God (grace) that we will continue to live in his love for all of eternity.

They shall be comforted: The Holy Spirit is known as the "Comforter" or "Consoler." In our times of sadness, we are never alone, for God is with us.

They shall inherit the earth: We will live in the reign of God here on earth and will not be controlled by power, self-importance, or money.

They shall be satisfied: God will be our satisfaction and will fulfill our desires, if we desire his will in our lives.

Preview

In the next lesson, the students will learn about the rest of the Beatitudes.

Chapter Sixteen: The Beatitudes
Lesson Three: Sons of God

Aims

The students will learn that they should mercifully love others and forgive in compassion. The pure of heart live chaste lives and are free of excessive love of earthly things. Peacemakers remove obstacles that keep men apart or in disagreement with one another. Those persecuted for Jesus' sake embrace the Cross of Christ and will share in his Resurrection.

Materials

- *Activity Book*, p. 63

- Saints books

Optional:
- "Be thou my vision," *Adoremus Hymnal*, #623

Begin

The students should review ways the first four Beatitudes can be lived in their daily lives. How were various saints able to live these Beatitudes and grow in holiness?

Today, the students will study the rest of the Beatitudes.

Develop

1. Read paragraphs 16–26 from the student text.

2. Who are the merciful? The merciful exercise the Corporal and Spiritual Works of Mercy out of love for God. What is mercy? Mercy is the gift of loving someone who may be difficult to love (and often includes forgiveness). It is the ability to love the ungrateful or unjust (like criminals or sinners). Who is all merciful? We should imitate Jesus' merciful love for us. (This may be a great opportunity to learn about Saint Faustina and the feast of Divine Mercy.)

3. Who are the pure in heart? Purity means being singular (like pure sugar, or pure olive oil). Often when we speak of purity, we speak of chastity (review the Sixth and Ninth Commandments). To be pure of heart is to reserve your whole heart for God and his ways and to live in a way that is pleasing to him. We must be single-hearted and disciplined in our love of God above all things, not allowing sin and earthly desires to enter into our thoughts, hearts, or actions.

4. Who are the peacemakers? We are not simply speaking of those who end wars, although that is a clear example. A peacemaker wants unity between both parties. Peacemakers go out of their way to remove obstacles that keep men apart. They work hard at bringing sinners back to God (review the Spiritual Works of Mercy of "admonish the sinner," and "instruct the ignorant.") How can we do this in our daily lives? (E.g., invite someone to receive the Sacrament of Penance when you are going.) Have the students think of ways they can be peacemakers even within their families.

5. Who are those persecuted for righteousness sake? Sometimes people do not want to hear the truth, and the truth-teller is persecuted, punished, or disliked. We must always speak the truth, and not compromise—even when it becomes difficult. God will give us courage and strength. Can the students think of examples? (E.g., to stand against abortion, euthanasia.)

Reinforce

1. Have the students work on *Activity Book* p. 63 (see *Teacher's Manual*, p. 199).

2. The students should research saints who lived the Beatitudes and make presentations for the class on the lives of these saints.

3. The students should discuss how they can live the last four Beatitudes in their own lives.

4. The students should work on the Memorization Questions and Word to Know from this chapter. They should memorize the Beatitudes.

Conclude

1. Lead the class in singing "Be thou my vision," *Adoremus Hymnal*, #623.

2. End class by leading the students in reciting the Beatitudes (Mt 5:3–12).

Mourning, in this beatitude, means sorrow for sin and sorrow over the loss, by separation or by death, of someone dear to us.

Jesus promises the sorrowful that they will get the strength they need to stand firm in their trials and troubles and even to grow through their sorrows in their friendship with God.

"Blessed are the meek, for they shall inherit the earth" (Mt 5:5).

The meek are those who are truly humble and kind. They don't think of themselves as being better than other people. They accept and recognize the gifts God has given them with gratitude and patience and without complaint.

"Blessed are those who hunger and thirst for righteousness, for they shall be satisfied" (Mt 5:6).

Blessed is the heart that wants what God wants! If we desire to be righteous and holy, Jesus will help us and our desire will be fulfilled. Jesus promises joy to those who do God's will.

"Blessed are the merciful, for they shall obtain mercy" (Mt 5:7).

Mercy is love shown to those in need as well as those who have been unjust and ungrateful. The merciful provide for the needs of others, forgive others their offenses, and show kindness and compassion toward the sinner. They, in turn, will receive mercy from God. Jesus said: "If you forgive men their trespasses, your heavenly Father also will forgive you" (Mt 6:14).

"Blessed are the pure in heart, for they shall see God" (Mt 5:8).

The pure in heart are those who live chaste lives and are free of all excessive love of earthly things. They have put God first in their lives. Because they are single-hearted, they can feel God's presence in this life and will see him face to face in the next.

"Blessed are the peacemakers, for they shall be called sons of God" (Mt 5:9).

Psalm 133 begins: "Behold, how good and how pleasant it is when brothers dwell together in unity!"

Peacemakers go out of their way to remove the obstacles that keep men apart. They work especially hard to bring sinners back to God.

Jesus promises that peacemakers will be God's special children here on earth and will enjoy heavenly glory in the family of the saints.

"Blessed are those who are persecuted for righteousness' sake, for theirs is the kingdom of heaven" (Mt 5:10).

"Blessed are you when men revile you and persecute you and utter all kinds of evil against you falsely on my account" (Mt 5:11).

Jesus suffered everything to witness to the truth. If we are persecuted because we are loyal to Jesus and his Church, we will know a little of what he suffered on the Cross to free us from sin and death. But we will also share in the joy of his Resurrection, his gift of eternal life with God.

* * *

The Beatitudes are the counsels of the New Testament; instead of being prohibitions, they are positive exhortations to live in a way that keeps us close to Jesus Christ. Each beatitude has attached to it a promise of great rewards.

Perhaps you have been thinking how difficult this is—how impossible, even, for human strength alone to live up to. You're right—it *is* hard!

74

That is why Christ has left us a great source of divine power in the Holy Eucharist. If we take the Ten Commandments and the Beatitudes seriously and desire to live up to them, we will feel the call to unite ourselves to Christ by receiving the Holy Eucharist often—perhaps even daily. And we will be well on our way to living the authentic Christian life.

Word to Know:

beatitude

75

Q. 59 *How are the Beatitudes related to the Ten Commandments?*
The Beatitudes are the fulfillment of the Ten Commandments and reveal the goal of human existence. The Beatitudes promise the reign of the Kingdom of God, which is at the heart of Jesus' teaching (CCC 1716, 1727).

Q. 60 *How do the Beatitudes call us to moral choices?*
The Beatitudes call us to moral choices by inviting us to purify our hearts and seek the love of God above all else (CCC 1723).

76

THE BLESSINGS OF THE LAST FOUR BEATITUDES (MT 5:7–10)

They shall obtain mercy: In giving mercy, we too understand how we are unjust and ungrateful to God, and we seek his love and mercy, which he readily offers to us.

They shall see God: When we always seek God and his ways, he will reveal himself to us.

They shall be called sons of God: We will be part of God's family in the Communion of Saints for we have shared God's love with others in the world.

Theirs is the Kingdom of Heaven: In uniting ourselves with the sufferings of Christ, we share in his glory.

Preview

In the next lesson, the students will learn about the Beatitudes as a moral guide.

Chapter Sixteen: The Beatitudes
Lesson Four: Christian Living

Aims

The students will learn that the Beatitudes are the counsels of the New Testament. They are positive exhortations to live in a way that keeps us close to Jesus Christ. The Beatitudes have a promise of reward.

They will learn that to live the Beatitudes we must live the Ten Commandments, receive sacramental grace, and be prayerful people.

Materials

- *Activity Book*, p. 64

  Optional:
  - "Be thou my vision," *Adoremus Hymnal*, #623

Begin

Review the eight Beatitudes and how they are moral guides for all Christians. Have the students give examples of different saints and how they have lived each of the Beatitudes.

Develop

1. Finish reading the chapter.

2. Review how, by our own strength, we cannot be perfect, as the Beatitudes call us to be. Review our fallen nature and concupiscence. We need God's grace so that we can live according to his laws. How can we stay in the state of grace? Keep God's commandments, pray for grace, receive the Sacraments, grow in virtue, etc. You may wish to have the students provide examples.

3. In addition to grace, which is a share of God's life in us, God has given us a very special gift to help us on our journey to become saints: the Sacraments. We can encounter Christ in his Sacraments. Review the seven Sacraments, and how each Sacrament is an encounter with Christ:
   - Baptism: Christ baptizes us into God's family.
   - Penance: Christ forgives our sins and reconciles us to God and his Church.
   - Confirmation: Christ anoints us with the Holy Spirit, making us his soldiers and witnesses to carry on his ministry.
   - Holy Orders: Christ ordains those in Holy Orders to be his ministers, so that they may bring Christ to the world in the Sacraments.
   - Matrimony: Christ unites a man and a woman together as models of his love for the Church.
   - Anointing of the Sick: Christ anoints the sick, preparing them for their entrance to heaven to be united with him forever.
   - Eucharist: Christ makes himself present on the altar and gives us himself so that we can be united with him in Communion. This is the greatest Sacrament, for it is Christ himself. We should adore our Eucharistic Lord and visit him daily.

Reinforce

1. Have the students work on *Activity Book* p. 64 (see *Teacher's Manual*, p. 199).

2. The students should visit Jesus in the Blessed Sacrament. Ideally the students should have the opportunity to attend an Adoration and Benediction service; however, they should at least visit Jesus in the tabernacle.

3. The students should discuss how a sacramental life helps them keep the commandments, live the Beatitudes, and grow in grace. We need both the moral life and the Sacraments in order to grow in holiness.

4. Have the students work on their Memorization Questions and Word to Know. They should memorize the Beatitudes and prepare for their chapter quiz and unit test.

Conclude

1. Lead the class in singing "Be thou my vision," *Adoremus Hymnal*, #623.

2. End class by leading the students in reciting the Beatitudes (Mt 5:3–12).

Mourning, in this beatitude, means sorrow for sin and sorrow over the loss, by separation or by death, of someone dear to us.

Jesus promises the sorrowful that they will get the strength they need to stand firm in their trials and troubles and even to grow through their sorrows in their friendship with God.

"Blessed are the meek, for they shall inherit the earth" (Mt 5:5).

The meek are those who are truly humble and kind. They don't think of themselves as being better than other people. They accept and recognize the gifts God has given them with gratitude and patience and without complaint.

"Blessed are those who hunger and thirst for righteousness, for they shall be satisfied" (Mt 5:6).

Blessed is the heart that wants what God wants! If we desire to be righteous and holy, Jesus will help us and our desire will be fulfilled. Jesus promises joy to those who do God's will.

"Blessed are the merciful, for they shall obtain mercy" (Mt 5:7).

Mercy is love shown to those in need as well as those who have been unjust and ungrateful. The merciful provide for the needs of others, forgive others their offenses, and show kindness and compassion toward the sinner. They, in turn, will receive mercy from God. Jesus said: "If you forgive men their trespasses, your heavenly Father also will forgive you" (Mt 6:14).

"Blessed are the pure in heart, for they shall see God" (Mt 5:8).

The pure in heart are those who live chaste lives and are free of all excessive love of earthly things. They have put God first in their lives. Because they are single-hearted, they can feel God's presence in this life and will see him face to face in the next.

"Blessed are the peacemakers, for they shall be called sons of God" (Mt 5:9).

Psalm 133 begins: "Behold, how good and how pleasant it is when brothers dwell together in unity!"

Peacemakers go out of their way to remove the obstacles that keep men apart. They work especially hard to bring sinners back to God.

Jesus promises that peacemakers will be God's special children here on earth and will enjoy heavenly glory in the family of the saints.

"Blessed are those who are persecuted for righteousness' sake, for theirs is the kingdom of heaven" (Mt 5:10).

"Blessed are you when men revile you and persecute you and utter all kinds of evil against you falsely on my account" (Mt 5:11).

Jesus suffered everything to witness to the truth. If we are persecuted because we are loyal to Jesus and his Church, we will know a little of what he suffered on the Cross to free us from sin and death. But we will also share in the joy of his Resurrection, his gift of eternal life with God.

* * *

The Beatitudes are the counsels of the New Testament; instead of being prohibitions, they are positive exhortations to live in a way that keeps us close to Jesus Christ. Each beatitude has attached to it a promise of great rewards.

Perhaps you have been thinking how difficult this is—how impossible, even, for human strength alone to live up to. You're right—it *is* hard!

74

That is why Christ has left us a great source of divine power in the Holy Eucharist. If we take the Ten Commandments and the Beatitudes seriously and desire to live up to them, we will feel the call to unite ourselves to Christ by receiving the Holy Eucharist often—perhaps even daily. And we will be well on our way to living the authentic Christian life.

Word to Know:

beatitude

75

> **Q. 59** *How are the Beatitudes related to the Ten Commandments?*
> The Beatitudes are the fulfillment of the Ten Commandments and reveal the goal of human existence. The Beatitudes promise the reign of the Kingdom of God, which is at the heart of Jesus' teaching (CCC 1716, 1727).
>
> **Q. 60** *How do the Beatitudes call us to moral choices?*
> The Beatitudes call us to moral choices by inviting us to purify our hearts and seek the love of God above all else (CCC 1723).

76

BEATITUDE SAINT: PIER GIORGIO

Known as "The Man of the Beatitudes," Blessed Pier Giorgio never swerved in his devotion and love for the poor and the sick. Born in 1901 in Turin, Italy, the son of a newspaper publisher and Italian ambassador to Germany, Pier Giorgio was a robust, good-humored man whose favorite pastime was mountain climbing. Despite the privileges he was born to, Pier Giorgio found his greatest joy in the Eucharist and sought to share his love of God with the poor, often giving money or even the coat off his back to people he met on the street. His life was a catalog of the Beatitudes brought to life. In 1925, at the age of 24, he died of an illness caught while tending to the sick. To the surprise of his family, huge crowds filled the streets for his funeral procession.

Preview

In the next lesson, the students' understanding of the material covered in this chapter and unit will be reviewed and assessed. There will be a quiz and unit test.

CHAPTER SIXTEEN: THE BEATITUDES
REVIEW AND ASSESSMENT

Aims

The students' understanding of the material covered in this chapter will be reviewed and assessed.

Materials

- Quiz 16, Appendix, p. A-22

Optional:
- "Be thou my vision," *Adoremus Hymnal*, #623

Review and Enrichment

1. The students should know that the Beatitudes are an exhortation of the fulfillment of the Old Law.

2. The students should know all eight Beatitudes and be able to give examples of how to live them. They should know of saints who bore witness to the Beatitudes in their lives of holiness.

3. The students should understand that to live a Christian life, they must keep the moral law and receive the Sacraments. They must receive the Sacraments in order to grow in holiness.

Name:

The Beatitudes   Quiz 16

Part I: Match the two parts of each beatitude and give an example of how to practice each one (either in your own life or from the life of a saint).

1. _e/g_ Blessed are the poor in spirit,	a. for they shall be satisfied.
2. _d_ Blessed are those who mourn,	b. for they shall obtain mercy.
3. _f_ Blessed are the meek,	c. for they shall be called sons of God.
4. _a_ Blessed are those who hunger and thirst for righteousness,	d. for they shall be comforted.
5. _b_ Blessed are the merciful,	e. for theirs is the Kingdom of Heaven.
6. _h_ Blessed are the pure in heart,	f. for they shall inherit the earth.
7. _c_ Blessed are the peacemakers,	g. for theirs is the Kingdom of Heaven.
8. _e/g_ Blessed are those who are persecuted for righteousness' sake,	h. for they shall see God.

1. _Examples will vary._

2. _____

3. _____

4. _____

5. _____

6. _____

7. _____

8. _____

_A-22_   *Faith and Life Series • Grade 6 • Appendix A*

Assess

1. Distribute the quizzes and read through them with the students to be sure they understand the questions.

2. Administer the quiz. As they hand in their work, you may orally quiz the students on the Memorization Questions from this chapter.

3. After all the quizzes have been handed in, you may wish to review the correct answers with the class.

Conclude

1. Lead the class in singing "Be thou my vision," *Adoremus Hymnal*, #623.

2. End class by leading the students in the Beatitudes (Mt 5:3–12).

Chapter Sixteen: The Beatitudes
Activity Book Answer Keys

Name:_____

The Fulfillment of the Law

Answer the following questions in complete sentences.

1. When did Jesus begin his public ministry?
   Jesus began his public ministry when he was about thirty years old.

2. With what preparatory rite did Jesus begin his public ministry?
   Jesus began his public ministry with baptism.

3. What happened at Jesus' baptism?
   At Jesus' baptism, the Holy Spirit descended like a dove and rested upon Jesus, and a voice from heaven said "this is my beloved son with whom I am well pleased."

4. What did Jesus do for forty days and nights after his baptism?
   For forty days and nights after his baptism, Jesus went to the desert where he fasted, prayed, and overcame the devil's temptation.

5. What did Jesus preach and do during his public ministry?
   Jesus preached the Good News of God's Kingdom and did many miracles.

6. Where did Jesus teach?
   He taught all over the country, in the fields, on the roads, on the hillsides, in synagogues, by lakes, and even from a boat.

7. Did Jesus abolish the Old Law?
   No.

8. What are the Beatitudes?
   The Beatitudes are exhortations that sum up the blessings and joys in store for those who follow Jesus.

Name:_____

The First Four Beatitudes

Write who is being blessed and why underneath each beatitude.

1. Blessed are the poor in spirit, for theirs is the Kingdom of Heaven.
   Those who have material possessions but are ready to give them up when self-sacrifice is called for. They value heavenly treasure above everything else.

2. Blessed are those who mourn, for they shall be comforted.
   Those who feel sorrow over the loss, by separation or death, of someone dear to them. They will get the strength to stand firm and even to grow closer to God.

3. Blessed are the meek, for they shall inherit the earth.
   Those who are truly humble and kind. They accept and recognize the gifts God has given them with gratitude and patience and without complaint.

4. Blessed are those who hunger and thirst for righteousness, for they shall be satisfied.
   Those who want what God wants. If we desire to be righteous and holy, our desire will be fulfilled.

Name:_____

The Last Four Beatitudes

Write who is being blessed and why underneath each beatitude.

1. Blessed are the merciful, for they shall obtain mercy.
   Those who forgive others and show kindness and compassion toward the sinner. Jesus said, "If you forgive men their trespasses, your heavenly Father will also forgive you."

2. Blessed are the pure in heart, for they shall see God.
   Those who live chaste lives and are free of excessive love of earthly things. They have put God first in their lives and so will see him in the next.

3. Blessed are the peacemakers, for they shall be called sons of God.
   Those who go out of their way to remove obstacles that keep men apart. They are God's special children and will enjoy heavenly glory in the family of the saints.

4. Blessed are those who are persecuted for righteousness' sake, for theirs is the Kingdom of Heaven.
   Those who are persecuted for loyalty to Jesus and his Church. If we suffer with Christ, we will share in his Resurrection.

Name:_____

More on the Beatitudes

Match the two parts of each beatitude and give an example of how you can practice each one in your daily life.

1. _e/g_ Blessed are the poor in spirit,
2. _d_ Blessed are those who mourn,
3. _f_ Blessed are the meek,
4. _a_ Blessed are those who hunger and thirst for righteousness,
5. _b_ Blessed are the merciful,
6. _h_ Blessed are the pure in heart,
7. _c_ Blessed are the peacemakers,
8. _e/g_ Blessed are those who are persecuted for righteousness' sake,

a. for they shall be satisfied.
b. for they shall obtain mercy.
c. for they shall be called sons of God.
d. for they shall be comforted.
e. for theirs is the Kingdom of Heaven.
f. for they shall inherit the earth.
g. for theirs is the Kingdom of Heaven.
h. for they shall see God.

1. Answers will vary.
2.
3.
4.
5.
6.
7.
8.

TEACHER'S NOTES

UNIT FOUR TEST
CHAPTERS 13–16

> ## CHAPTER THIRTEEN: THE SACRED FLAME
>
> ## CHAPTER FOURTEEN: OWNERSHIP
>
> ## CHAPTER FIFTEEN: BACKED BY TRUTH
>
> ## CHAPTER SIXTEEN: THE BEATITUDES

Aims

The students' understanding of the material covered in this unit will be reviewed and assessed.

Materials

- Unit 4 Test, Appendix, pp. A-23 and A-24

Assess

1. Distribute the unit tests and read through them with the students to be sure they understand the questions.

2. Administer the test.

3. After all the tests have been handed in, you may wish to review the correct answers with the class.

Name: _____

Unit 4 Test   **Chapters 13–16**

Part I: Yes or No.

1. <u>Yes</u> Do the Sixth and Ninth Commandments command us to be pure?
2. <u>Yes</u> Does the Seventh Commandment require us to respect the property of others?
3. <u>No</u> Are we allowed to own stolen property, even if we didn't steal it ourselves?
4. <u>No</u> Are we allowed to claim as our own something that belongs to someone else?
5. <u>Yes</u> Is copying someone else's homework considered stealing?
6. <u>Yes</u> When we borrow something, must we return it in the same condition in which we received it?
7. <u>No</u> Can a person who has his heart set on material possessions pay attention to the Kingdom of God?
8. <u>No</u> Are we ever allowed to tell a lie?
9. <u>No</u> Should we listen to people who gossip?

Part II: Fill in the blanks.

1. All have the right to have their possessions safe from <u>theft</u> , damage, and destruction.
2. If I have taken something that does not belong to me, I must return what I have <u>stolen</u> or replace it if I can, and confess my sin if the matter is serious.
3. If I purposely damage or destroy property, justice demands that I make restitution, that is, <u>pay</u> for the damage.
4. <u>Charity (or justice)</u> requires me to share what I have with those who need decent food, clothing, and shelter.
5. <u>Justice</u> involves giving everyone his due, what he has a right to receive.
6. Every human being has a right to <u>food</u> , <u>clothing</u> , and <u>shelter</u> .
7. A <u>beatitude</u> is a blessing or special happiness promised by Jesus to those who follow him.

Part III: Answer the following.

1. What is the Seventh Commandment?
   <u>You shall not steal.</u>

2. What is the Tenth Commandment?
   <u>You shall not covet your neighbor's goods.</u>

Name: _____

Unit 4 Test (continued)

Part IV: Matching.

1. <u>d</u> idle talk about the faults of others
2. <u>g</u> lying under oath
3. <u>a</u> saying something false about another
4. <u>f</u> pretending to be better than you are
5. <u>c</u> judging another's character without enough evidence
6. <u>e</u> giving untrue testimony about another
7. <u>h</u> deliberately deceiving someone
8. <u>b</u> using the truth to harm another

a. slander/calumny
b. detraction
c. rash judgment
d. gossip
e. false witness
f. hypocrisy
g. perjury
h. lying

1. <u>e/g</u> Blessed are the poor in spirit,
2. <u>d</u> Blessed are those who mourn,
3. <u>f</u> Blessed are the meek,
4. <u>a</u> Blessed are those who hunger and thirst for righteousness,
5. <u>b</u> Blessed are the merciful,
6. <u>h</u> Blessed are the pure in heart,
7. <u>c</u> Blessed are the peacemakers,
8. <u>e/g</u> Blessed are those who are persecuted for righteousness' sake,

a. for they shall be satisfied.
b. for they shall obtain mercy.
c. for they shall be called sons of God.
d. for they shall be comforted.
e. for theirs is the Kingdom of Heaven.
f. for they shall inherit the earth.
g. for theirs is the Kingdom of Heaven.
h. for they shall see God.

TEACHER'S NOTES

CHAPTER SEVENTEEN
AT THE LAST SUPPER

Catechism of the Catholic Church References

Apostolic Succession: 77–79, 861–62, 869
Christ as a Self-Offering to the Father: 606–18, 621–23
Jesus Freely Embraces the Father's Redemptive Love: 609
Incarnation: 359, 456–60, 470–473, 522–23, 606–11, 653–54, 1612
Last Supper: 610–11, 621
Agony at Gethsemani: 612
Death of Christ as the Unique and Definitive Sacrifice: 613–14
Jesus Substitutes His Obedience for Our Disobedience: 615
Jesus Consummates His Sacrifice on the Cross: 616–17
Our Participation in Christ's Sacrifice: 618
"Do This in Memory of Me": 1341–44, 1409

Fruits of Communion: 1391–1401, 1416
Holy Communion: 1355, 1382–90, 1415, 1417
Institution of the Eucharist: 1337–40
Jesus as True God and True Man: 464–70, 480–83
Paschal Mystery of Christ: 571–1067
Passover: 1164
Passover in Relation to the Holy Eucharist: 1334, 1362–65, 1409
Presence of Christ in the Eucharist: 1373–81, 1410, 1418
Sacrifice: 2099–2100
Signs of Bread and Wine in the Eucharist: 1333–36, 1412
Typology and the Unity of the Old and New Testaments: 128–30, 140

Scripture References

Miracle of Loaves and Fish and Walk on Water: John 6:1–34
Bread of Life Discourse: Jn 6:35–54
Last Supper: Mt 26:17–30; Mk 14:13–26; Lk 22:11–22; 1 Cor 11:23–26

Passover: Ex 12:1–14
Jesus as Passover Lamb: Jn 1:29
Sacrifices: Cain and Abel: Gen 4:1–12; Noah: Gen 8:15–22; Abraham: Gen 22: 1–18; Moses: Ex 24:1–12

Summary of Lesson Content

Lesson 1

Jesus gives us his Body and Blood in the Eucharist.

Jesus foreshadowed the Eucharist with the multiplication of loaves and fish.

Jesus instituted the Eucharist at the Last Supper, which was a celebration of the Passover meal. Jesus established the New Covenant with this meal. He is the sacrifice and meal of the New Covenant.

Lesson 2

The Passover is a celebration of God's mercy in leading the Israelites to freedom from slavery in Egypt. The first Passover meal required the slaughter of a lamb to be eaten. The blood of the lamb, sprinkled on their doorposts, saved the Israelites from the angel of death.

In the sacrifice of himself, in the Eucharist and on the Cross, Jesus frees us from sin and, through grace, gives us a share in his life. Jesus is the Passover Lamb. We share in this gift through Holy Communion at Mass.

Lesson 3

In the Old Testament, people offered sacrifices to adore God, thank God, make up for sins, and ask God's help.

Every Old Testament sacrifice required a victim, a priest, and an altar. Jesus, the perfect priest, offered himself as the perfect victim at the Last Supper and died upon the Cross, which was his altar. This same sacrifice is made present on the altar at Mass.

Lesson 4

Jesus told the Apostles "Do this in memory of me." This gave them the power as priests to consecrate the Eucharist.

The power of the priesthood has been passed on through Holy Orders to bishops and priests. They celebrate the Eucharist at Mass, making Christ present and allowing us to share in his Holy Communion.

Chapter Seventeen: At the Last Supper
Lesson One: Bread of Life

Aims

The students will learn that Jesus gives us his Body and Blood in the Eucharist.

They will learn that Jesus foreshadowed the Eucharist with the multiplication of loaves and fish. He instituted the Eucharist at the Last Supper, which was a celebration of the Passover meal. Jesus established the New Covenant with this meal. He is the sacrifice and meal of the New Covenant.

Materials

- *Activity Book*, p. 65
- Bible
- Grape juice and bread

Optional:
- "Jesus, my Lord, my God, my all!" *Adoremus Hymnal*, #516

Begin

Read John 6:35–54 with the students. Jesus shocked some of his followers so much that they stopped following him. Yet, when they started to leave, Jesus did not say, "Wait a minute, you misunderstood me." Rather, he made the statement even stronger and more clear. As usual, it was Peter who spoke for all the disciples when he said, "Lord, to whom shall we go? You have the words of eternal life." In the Eucharist, we receive all of Christ: his Body, Blood, Soul, and Divinity.

Develop

1. Read paragraphs 1–5 from the student text.

2. Read John 6:1–34 from your Bible. Discuss these events with the students.
   - The multiplication of loaves and fish: Jesus gave thanks (Greek word for thanksgiving is eucharistia) and multiplied loaves and fish, everyone had their fill.
   - Walking on water: Jesus went to pray by himself, then walked on water to join his disciples. He told them not to be afraid, for he was coming to them.
   - People seeking Christ: The people who had their fill of bread and fish came seeking Christ. To do the works of God, we must believe in Jesus.
   - Bread of Life discourse: Jesus is the Bread come down from heaven. This Bread is for the life of the world. It is his Body and Blood.

3. Have the students dramatize the various parts of John 6.

4. Review that the Last Supper was a celebration of the Passover meal, a memorial of God's saving actions of the Exodus. You may review the account of the Exodus using your Bible: Ex 12:1–14. A memorial is more than just remembering an event in the past, it makes it present—it re-presents it.

5. Read the Last Supper accounts: Mt 26:17–30; Mk 14:13–26; Lk 22:11–22; 1 Cor 11:23–26. Have the students gather around a large table and, with a glass of grape juice and a loaf of bread, dramatize the Last Supper as a narrator reads the account from the Bible. Have the students share in your "Last Supper." (See Reinforce 2.)

6. If the Last Supper was a Passover meal, we should know that Jesus is the Passover Lamb (see Jn 1:29). He is to be slain and, by his blood, we shall have life. The Last Supper and the Crucifixion of Jesus are one saving event.

Reinforce

1. Have the students work on *Activity Book* p. 65 (see *Teacher's Manual*, p. 213).

2. The students should research the twelve Apostles. When they dramatize the Last Supper, they should all be in character, ready to share information about the Apostles.

3. Have the students begin working on the Memorization Questions and Words to Know from this chapter (see *Teacher's Manual*, p. 209).

Conclude

1. Teach the students to sing "Jesus, my Lord, my God, my all!" *Adoremus Hymnal*, #516.

2. End class by leading the students in the Prayer before Communion (on the facing page).

At the Last Supper

"Truly, truly, I say to you, unless you eat the flesh of the Son of man and drink his blood, you have no life in you."

John 6:53

Let us begin by reading chapter six of Saint John's Gospel.

Jesus shocked many of his followers by saying that he would give them his Body to eat and his Blood to drink, and that they would not have life in them unless they accepted it. At this many of his followers left him. Peter answered for those who remained faithful. When Jesus asked them, "Will you also go away?" Peter said, "Lord, to whom shall we go? You have the words of eternal life" (Jn 6:67–68).

Peter and the faithful disciples did not foresee how Jesus was going to do what he said; they did not have the slightest idea how it could be possible. But they had come to know and love Jesus; they had come to hunger for the words of eternal life that came from him; and they believed.

Just before he told them this, Jesus had demonstrated his power by feeding a crowd of about five thousand people with a few loaves and fish, and he had announced greater things to come. But he did not explain. When the time came for him to leave his Apostles, Jesus gave them a treasure of immeasurable richness—his own Self in the **Eucharist**. With the utmost simplicity he found a way to give them his Body and Blood to eat and drink: he changed bread into his Body and wine into his Blood.

This wonderful event took place at Jesus' **Last Supper** with his Apostles the night before he died. They were celebrating one of the great festivals of the Jewish people, the Passover. With Jesus' action the sacrifice of the Old Covenant was ended and the sacrifice of the New Covenant established.

The Passover

The **Passover** commemorated God's rescue of his chosen people from slavery in Egypt. He worked great signs and wonders through his servant Moses to strike the fear of God into the hearts of the Egyptians so that Pharaoh would free the Hebrews and allow them to depart and worship the true God.

Pharaoh was very stubborn about keeping the Hebrews captive until one night the angel of death passed through Egypt, striking down the firstborn sons of the Egyptians.

The Hebrews had been instructed by God through Moses to offer a special sacrifice that night: a spotless lamb, one for each family. Every Hebrew dwelling was to be marked on the doorpost with the blood of the lamb so that

79

THE SYMBOLISM OF THE FISH

The symbol of the fish in Christian art may have been suggested by the miraculous multiplication of the loaves and fish, or by the Apostles' breakfast of fish on the shore of the Sea of Galilee after the Resurrection (Jn 21:9–14). However, the fish's popularity among Christians is likely the result of the acrostic forming the Greek word for fish (*ichthys*), which briefly but clearly describes the character and divinity of Christ: *Iesous Christos Theou Yios Soter*, i.e., *Jesus Christ, Son of God, Savior*. This word, as well as the representation of the fish, was a brief profession of faith. Tertullian called Christians, "little fishes," who, after the image of the Ichthys, are born in the water.

PRAYER BEFORE COMMUNION OF SAINT FRANCIS DE SALES

Divine Savior, we come to your sacred table to nourish ourselves, not with bread but with yourself, true Bread of eternal life. Help us daily to make a good and perfect meal of this divine food. Let us be continually refreshed by the perfume of your kindness and goodness. May the Holy Spirit fill us with his love. Meanwhile, let us prepare a place for this holy food by emptying our hearts. *Amen.*

Jesus said to them, "I am the bread of life; he who comes to me shall not hunger, and he who believes in me shall never thirst."

—John 6:35

Preview

In the next lesson, the students will learn more about the Passover.

Chapter Seventeen: At the Last Supper
Lesson Two: Passover

Aims

The students will learn that the Passover is a celebration of God's mercy in leading the Israelites to freedom from slavery in Egypt. The first Passover meal required the slaughter of a lamb to be eaten. The blood of the lamb, sprinkled on their doorposts, saved the Israelites from the angel of death.

They will learn that, in sacrificing himself on the Cross and in the Eucharist, Jesus frees us from sin and, through grace, gives us a share in his life. Jesus is the Passover Lamb. We share in this gift through Holy Communion at Mass.

Materials

- *Activity Book*, p. 66

- Appendix, pp. B-16–B-20

Optional:
- "Jesus, my Lord, my God, my all!" *Adoremus Hymnal*, #516

Begin

Before the students come in, have the seder meal set up. See Appendix, pp. B-16–B-20.

As the students come in, have them wash their hands and take a seat at the table. When they are seated, explain the preparation of this meal to them. Explain each food and what it represents, and why the table is set in the manner it is.

Develop

1. Read paragraphs 6–12 from the student text.

2. Share a seder meal with the students, using the script on Appendix, pp. B-16–B-20.

3. After your meal, discuss the Passover. How is it a sacrifice? How is it a meal? Why did Jesus celebrate this feast with his Apostles?

4. Review that during the Passover meal, Jesus consecrated the Eucharist. Review (from the study of the Sacraments) that the matter of the Eucharist is unleavened bread and wine. The form is the very words of Jesus at the Last Supper: "This is my Body," and "This is the chalice of my Blood." With this, as promised in the Bread of Life discourse, Jesus changed the bread and wine into his Body and Blood, so that when we eat his Flesh and drink his Blood, we may have eternal life.

5. It is important to review the Church's teaching on transubstantiation. The species, or appearance, remains the same: it looks, tastes, and smells like bread and wine. But the substance—what it is—changes. It is no longer bread and wine, but truly Jesus—wholly present: Body, Blood, Soul, and Divinity in the Eucharist. He is entirely present in the consecrated Bread (Sacred Host) and he is entirely present in the consecrated wine (Precious Blood). He is entirely and wholly present in each of their parts (if the Host is broken, Christ is not broken).

6. Review from the first lesson of this chapter that Jesus is the Passover Lamb. He was sacrificed on the Cross for our sins. He anticipated this by the Last Supper—he said, "This is the chalice of my Blood…which WILL be poured out for you . . ." Just as Jesus gave his Body and Blood for us on the Cross, the same gift of his Body and Blood is present in the Eucharist.

Reinforce

1. Have the students work on *Activity Book* p. 66 (see *Teacher's Manual*, p. 213).

2. Take the students to visit Jesus in the Blessed Sacrament. They should spend some quiet time in prayer before the tabernacle.

Conclude

1. Lead the students in singing "Jesus, my Lord, my God, my all!" *Adoremus Hymnal*, #516.

2. End class by leading the students in the Prayer before Communion (see *Teacher's Manual*, p. 205).

CHAPTER 17

At the Last Supper

"Truly, truly, I say to you, unless you eat the flesh of the Son of man and drink his blood, you have no life in you."

John 6:53

Let us begin by reading chapter six of Saint John's Gospel.

Jesus shocked many of his followers by saying that he would give them his Body to eat and his Blood to drink, and that they would not have life in them unless they accepted it. At this many of his followers left him. Peter answered for those who remained faithful. When Jesus asked them, "Will you also go away?" Peter said, "Lord, to whom shall we go? You have the words of eternal life" (Jn 6:67–68).

Peter and the faithful disciples did not foresee how Jesus was going to do what he said; they did not have the slightest idea how it could be possible. But they had come to know and love Jesus; they had come to hunger for the words of eternal life that came from him; and they believed.

Just before he told them this, Jesus had demonstrated his power by feeding a crowd of about five thousand people with a few loaves and fish, and he had announced greater things to come. But he did not explain. When the time came for him to leave his Apostles, Jesus gave them a treasure of immeasurable richness—his own Self in the **Eucharist**. With the utmost simplicity he found a way to give them his Body and Blood to eat and drink:

he changed bread into his Body and wine into his Blood.

This wonderful event took place at Jesus' **Last Supper** with his Apostles the night before he died. They were celebrating one of the great festivals of the Jewish people, the Passover. With Jesus' action the sacrifice of the Old Covenant was ended and the sacrifice of the New Covenant established.

The Passover

The **Passover** commemorated God's rescue of his chosen people from slavery in Egypt. He worked great signs and wonders through his servant Moses to strike the fear of God into the hearts of the Egyptians so that Pharaoh would free the Hebrews and allow them to depart and worship the true God.

Pharaoh was very stubborn about keeping the Hebrews captive until one night the angel of death passed through Egypt, striking down the firstborn sons of the Egyptians.

The Hebrews had been instructed by God through Moses to offer a special sacrifice that night: a spotless lamb, one for each family. Every Hebrew dwelling was to be marked on the doorpost with the blood of the lamb so that

79

the angel of death would pass over without harming those within.

After this event the Egyptians finally let the Hebrews go, for the fear of God had fallen on them.

All of this is important if we are to understand what Jesus did at the Last Supper. We can see the slavery of the Hebrew people as an image of the slavery of all people to sin. And just as God freed the Hebrews, he frees us. The sacrifice that frees man from sin is the Crucifixion and death of our Lord Jesus Christ. He is the Passover Lamb.

Each year the Hebrew people observed the anniversary of the Passover—and the mighty events that led to their freedom—with a special meal. Each family would offer a Paschal lamb in sacrifice and would eat it with unleavened bread and bitter herbs. These were symbols that recalled the original Passover. To this day the Jewish people observe the Passover.

Jesus and his Apostles were celebrating this special meal when Jesus "took bread, and blessed, and broke it, and gave it to the disciples and said, 'Take, eat; this is my body.' And he took a chalice, and when he had given thanks he gave it to them, saying, 'Drink of it, all of you; for this is my blood of the covenant, which is poured out for many for the forgiveness of sins' " (Mt 26:26–28).

The Perfect Sacrifice

From the time of Adam's Fall, men have felt the need to make a public offering to God to make up for their sins and ask for mercy. The firstfruits of a harvest, a lamb or a goat—something needed for life—would be offered on an altar by a priest to indicate that, like everything that exists, they belong to God. Men desired to be restored to that friendship with God which sin had broken. Their sacrifices were an attempt to do this.

80

Offering a sacrifice has four distinct purposes: to adore God, to thank him, to make up for sin, and to ask his help.

Before the coming of Christ a great many sacrifices were offered to God, but not one of them offered a **victim** that could atone for men's sins. Alone, men were unable to offer to God anything so fitting and precious that it could make up for such a grave offense against God. But God loves us so much and so much desired our reconciliation to him that he gave us an acceptable victim that would satisfy our debt.

Jesus, given to us by the Father, was that acceptable victim. This divine victim was sacrificed upon the Cross to make peace between heaven and earth once and for all.

The word **oblation** is used to indicate the total offering of a victim or gift in a sacrifice. In the oblation of Jesus Christ, he was both priest and victim. For he was held on the Cross by his love alone; at any moment he could have come down from the Cross, but he would not. He truly offered himself. To all appearances he died like a criminal, but, unlike anyone else who was ever crucified, he freely laid down his life and offered himself for the sins of the world.

Being God and Man

When Jesus took the bread at the Last Supper and said, "This is my Body," he made himself present on the table as the gift of the sacrifice. He stood over the gift and looked down upon it, but the gift was no longer bread; it was his Body, it was himself. He did the same thing with the wine; it became his Precious Blood. Jesus could do this because he was God as well as man.

At the Last Supper, the Apostles received the first Holy Communion, and each Apostle received Jesus complete and entire—not part

of Jesus but the whole Jesus—Body, Blood, Soul, and Divinity, God and man. The whole Jesus went to Andrew, to Peter, to John, to Philip, to each one. And so he comes to us, too, when we receive Holy Communion. The Apostles were united with Christ and filled with grace. So are we.

But what did the Apostles see when Jesus said, "This is my Body. . . . This is my Blood"? What they saw still looked like bread and wine. What had been bread still had the same weight, color, and taste; what had been wine still had the same taste, odor, and color. But its *substance*, the underlying reality that makes it what it is, had been changed. The looks and other properties known by the senses are called the *appearances*; the Body and Blood of Jesus kept the *appearances* of bread and wine. The **mystery** of this change in the bread and wine is called "**transubstantiation**," which means change of substance.

The substance of bread and wine have been changed into the substance of the Body and Blood of Christ. We cannot see the change but it has happened.

Why does Jesus change bread and wine into his Body and Blood but leave the appearances of bread and wine? The Eucharist is a Sacrament, a sign instituted by Christ to give us grace. The appearances of bread and wine remain as signs that Jesus is true spiritual food and drink for our souls given to us in a special way in the Eucharist. He is the source of our life as Christians.

We call Jesus' presence in the Eucharist the Real Presence. It is called "real" because Jesus is really and truly with us. The Eucharist is no mere symbol of Jesus; it truly is Jesus, under the appearances of bread and wine.

The Everlasting Sacrifice

After the Apostles had each received Holy Communion, Jesus said to them, "Do this in remembrance of me" (Lk 22:19). When he said this he made them priests; for by telling them to do what he had just done—to change bread and wine into his Body and Blood—he gave them the power to do it.

The greatest power of the priesthood is the power to offer this sacrifice of Jesus' Body

81

CHALK TALK: TRANSUBSTANTIATION

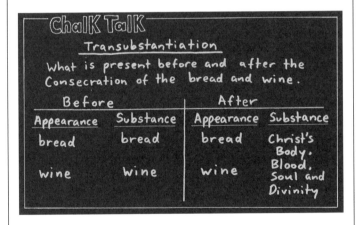

ChalK TalK

Transubstantiation

What is present before and after the Consecration of the bread and wine.

Before		After	
Appearance	Substance	Appearance	Substance
bread	bread	bread	Christ's Body, Blood, Soul and Divinity
wine	wine	wine	

Preview

In the next lesson, the students will better understand Jesus as the perfect sacrifice.

CHAPTER SEVENTEEN: AT THE LAST SUPPER
LESSON THREE: THE SACRIFICE

Aims

The students will learn that, in the Old Testament, people offered sacrifices to adore God, thank God, make up for sins, and ask God's help. Every Old Testament sacrifice required a victim, a priest, and an altar.

They will learn that Jesus, the perfect priest, offered himself as the perfect victim at the Last Supper and died upon the Cross, which was his altar. This same sacrifice is made present on the altar at Mass.

Materials

• *Activity Book*, p. 67

Optional:
• "Jesus, my Lord, my God, my all!" *Adoremus Hymnal*, #516

Begin

Teach the students what a sacrifice is. A sacrifice is a total offering to God of something precious. This may be done as an act of love, an act of contrition, a sign of repentance, a sign of thanksgiving to God for his goodness, and to make a petition to God (ask God for our needs).

Every Old Testament sacrifice had a priest: person who offered the sacrifice (may be a mediator); a victim (the best of something, like crops, animals, etc.); and an altar.

Develop

1. Read paragraphs 13–23 from the student text.

2. Review the need for sacrifice. With the Fall of Adam and Eve, through Original Sin, a great chasm was cleft between God and man. Man's sin was so grave and man so imperfect that he could not make up for his sin. Man offered the very best things he had, but they too were imperfect. To offer the perfect sacrifice, a perfect priest with pure intent and a perfect victim would be needed. You may want to review:
   • Atonement is the act of reconciliation (literally, to make at one with). This is why a perfect priest with pure intention had to offer the perfect sacrifice.
   • Redemption is the act of buying something back, or paying the price. This is why a perfect victim was needed.

3. Review some of the Old Testament sacrifices (for example, those of Cain and Abel: Gen 4:1–12; Noah: Gen 8:15–22; Abraham: Gen 22:1–18; Moses: Ex 24:1–12). Have the stu-

dents explain why each of these sacrifices could not reconcile man with God and pay the price for man's sin.

4. Discuss paragraphs 16–17 with the students. How is the sacrifice of Jesus different from the sacrifices of the Old Testament? Who is the priest of this sacrifice? Who is the victim? What is the altar? Was this a worthy sacrifice that could gain atonement and redemption? How do we know?

5. You may discuss what happens at the Mass. The ordained minister acts in the Person of Christ; as we already discussed, it is Christ who works through the Sacraments. It is Christ who speaks his own words at the Consecration (this is why the words of Consecration are in the first person). Jesus is the priest acting through the ordained minister. He is the victim (it is Christ's Body and Blood upon the altar). It is the same sacrifice, offered in an unbloody manner.

Reinforce

1. Have the students work on *Activity Book* p. 67 (see *Teacher's Manual*, p. 213).

2. Take the students to visit Jesus in the Blessed Sacrament. They should pray before the tabernacle.

3. Have the students make charts/posters comparing the Sacrifices of the Last Supper, the Cross, and Mass.

4. The students should work on the Memorization Questions and Words to Know from this chapter.

Conclude

1. Lead the students in singing "Jesus, my Lord, my God, my all!" *Adoremus Hymnal*, #516.

2. End class by leading the students in the Prayer before Communion (see *Teacher's Manual*, p. 205).

the angel of death would pass over without harming those within.

After this event the Egyptians finally let the Hebrews go, for the fear of God had fallen on them.

All of this is important if we are to understand what Jesus did at the Last Supper. We can see the slavery of the Hebrew people as an image of the slavery of all people to sin. And just as God freed the Hebrews, he frees us. The sacrifice that frees man from sin is the Crucifixion and death of our Lord Jesus Christ. He is the Passover Lamb.

Each year the Hebrew people observed the anniversary of the Passover—and the mighty events that led to their freedom—with a special meal. Each family would offer a Paschal lamb in sacrifice and would eat it with unleavened bread and bitter herbs. These were symbols that recalled the original Passover. To this day the Jewish people observe the Passover.

Jesus and his Apostles were celebrating this special meal when Jesus "took bread, and blessed, and broke it, and gave it to the disciples and said, 'Take, eat; this is my body.' And he took a chalice, and when he had given thanks he gave it to them, saying, 'Drink of it, all of you; for this is my blood of the covenant, which is poured out for many for the forgiveness of sins' " (Mt 26:26–28).

The Perfect Sacrifice

From the time of Adam's Fall, men have felt the need to make a public offering to God to make up for their sins and ask for mercy. The firstfruits of a harvest, a lamb or a goat—something needed for life—would be offered on an altar by a priest to indicate that, like everything that exists, they belong to God. Men desired to be restored to that friendship with God which sin had broken. Their sacrifices were an attempt to do this.

Offering a sacrifice has four distinct purposes: to adore God, to thank him, to make up for sin, and to ask his help.

Before the coming of Christ a great many sacrifices were offered to God, but not one of them offered a **victim** that could atone for men's sins. Alone, men were unable to offer to God anything so fitting and precious that it could make up for such a grave offense against God. But God loves us so much and so much desired our reconciliation to him that he gave us an acceptable victim that would satisfy our debt.

Jesus, given to us by the Father, was that acceptable victim. This divine victim was sacrificed upon the Cross to make peace between heaven and earth once and for all.

The word **oblation** is used to indicate the total offering of a victim or gift in a sacrifice. In the oblation of Jesus Christ, he was both priest and victim. For he was held on the Cross by his love alone; at any moment he could have come down from the Cross, but he would not. He truly offered himself. To all appearances he died like a criminal, but, unlike anyone else who was ever crucified, he freely laid down his life and offered himself for the sins of the world.

Being God and Man

When Jesus took the bread at the Last Supper and said, "This is my Body," he made himself present on the table as the gift of the sacrifice. He stood over the gift and looked down upon it, but the gift was no longer bread; it was his Body, it was himself. He did the same thing with the wine; it became his Precious Blood. Jesus could do this because he was God as well as man.

At the Last Supper, the Apostles received the first Holy Communion, and each Apostle received Jesus complete and entire—not part

80

---

of Jesus but the whole Jesus—Body, Blood, Soul, and Divinity, God and man. The whole Jesus went to Andrew, to Peter, to John, to Philip, to each one. And so he comes to us, too, when we receive Holy Communion. The Apostles were united with Christ and filled with grace. So are we.

But what did the Apostles see when Jesus said, "This is my Body. . . . This is my Blood"? What they saw still looked like bread and wine. What had been bread still had the same weight, color, and taste; what had been wine still had the same taste, odor, and color. But its *substance*, the underlying reality which makes it what it is, had been changed. The looks and other properties known by the senses are called the *appearances*; the Body and Blood of Jesus kept the *appearances* of bread and wine. The **mystery** of this change in the bread and wine is called "**transubstantiation**," which means change of substance.

The substance of bread and wine have been changed into the substance of the Body and Blood of Christ. We cannot see the change but it has happened.

Why does Jesus change bread and wine into his Body and Blood but leave the appearances of bread and wine? The Eucharist is a Sacrament, a sign instituted by Christ to give us grace. The appearances of bread and wine remain as signs that Jesus is true spiritual food and drink for our souls given to us in the Eucharist. He is the source of our life as Christians.

We call Jesus' presence in the Eucharist the Real Presence. It is called "real" because Jesus is really and truly with us. The Eucharist is no mere symbol of Jesus; it truly is Jesus, under the appearances of bread and wine.

The Everlasting Sacrifice

After the Apostles had each received Holy Communion, Jesus said to them, "Do this in remembrance of me" (Lk 22:19). When he said this he made them priests; for by telling them to do what he had just done—to change bread and wine into his Body and Blood—he gave them the power to do it.

The greatest power of the priesthood is the power to offer this sacrifice of Jesus' Body

81

---

and Blood. It is the same sacrifice that Jesus offered at the Last Supper and the next day on the Cross. Through this power the Body and Blood of Jesus continue to be offered to God under the appearances of bread and wine whenever the Mass is celebrated.

So God left us an everlasting sacrifice of such richness and power that nothing else can be compared to it.

The Apostles used their powers to feed the new Church of Christ with the Bread from heaven: the Eucharist. They shared their power with other men, co-workers and their successors, so that the Church could continue from generation to generation to offer the great sacrifice, making it present to all who seek it, until the end of time.

Words to Know:
Eucharist   Last Supper   Passover   victim
   oblation   mystery   transubstantiation

Q. 61 ***What is the Eucharist?***
The Eucharist is the Sacrament of the Body, Blood, Soul, and Divinity of Christ, really and truly present under the appearances of bread and wine (CCC 1333).

Q. 62 ***What does it mean to say that the whole Christ is contained in the Eucharist under the appearances of bread and wine?***
To say that the whole Christ is contained in the Eucharist under the appearances of bread and wine means that the Body, Blood, Soul, and Divinity of Jesus are present (CCC 1374).

Q. 63 ***When did Jesus Christ institute the Eucharist?***
Jesus Christ instituted the Eucharist at the Last Supper when he changed bread and wine into his Body and Blood and commanded the Apostles to do the same in his memory (CCC 1323, 1337).

Q. 64 ***Why did Jesus Christ institute the Eucharist?***
Jesus Christ instituted the Eucharist in order to leave his Church a visible sacrifice by which the Sacrifice of the Cross would be re-presented and recalled. In the Eucharist, the benefits of the Cross are applied and spiritual food is given to our souls in Holy Communion (CCC 1366, 1382).

Q. 65 ***What is a sacrifice?***
A sacrifice is the public offering of something to God in order to profess that he is Creator and Supreme Ruler to whom everything belongs (CCC 1366, 2099).

82

THE ONE SACRIFICE OF CHRIST

	LAST SUPPER	CROSS	MASS
PRIEST	Jesus	Jesus	Jesus
VICTIM	Jesus	Jesus	Jesus
ALTAR	Table	Cross	Altar

Preview

In the next lesson, the students will learn about Jesus as the mediator.

CHAPTER SEVENTEEN: AT THE LAST SUPPER
LESSON FOUR: ETERNAL PRIEST

Aims

The students will learn that Jesus told the Apostles, "Do this in remembrance of me." This gave them the power as priests to consecrate the Eucharist.

They will learn that the power of the priesthood has been passed on, through Holy Orders, to bishops and priests. They celebrate the Eucharist at Mass, making Christ present and allowing us to share in his Holy Communion.

Materials

• *Activity Book*, p. 68

Optional:
• "Jesus, my Lord, my God, my all!" *Adoremus Hymnal*, #516

Begin

Discuss the priesthood with the students. Some men are called by God to this sacred vocation. They receive the Sacrament of Holy Orders and their souls are changed forever, marked with a holy seal. The first level of Holy Orders is the episcopate (bishops); the second level is the presbyterate (priests). Bishops and priests receive sacred powers from Christ to celebrate his Sacraments. They act in the Person of Christ (in persona Christi) any time they are celebrating the Liturgy or the Sacraments. Christ ministers to his Church through his ordained bishops and priests.

Develop

1. Finish reading the chapter from the student text, paragraphs 24–27.

2. Jesus instituted the Sacrament of Holy Orders at the Last Supper. You may re-read the Last Supper account if you wish. By saying, "Do this in memory of me," Jesus gave his power to the Apostles to consecrate the Eucharist. This power has been passed down to all bishops and priests through their ordination by the anointing with chrism and the laying on of hands of a bishop.

3. If possible, have a priest visit your class. He should share the beauty of his call to the priesthood and the wonder of the mystery he celebrates at the Mass daily. Allow the students to ask questions of the priest.

4. Jesus gives himself to the Church so that he can continue to be present to us and work through it. Read John 14:15–21.

Have the students silently reflect on this passage. The students can write a journal entry on this passage. Discuss how Jesus remains with us through the Eucharist. He does not leave us desolate.

5. You may discuss the Mass as a sacred meal and sacrifice. It is a meal because we receive our Lord in Holy Communion. It is a sacrifice because Jesus offers himself to the Father for our salvation. This sacrifice is not offered over and over again, as one might think. Review that, with God, there is no time. Just as with the Passover memorial, the sacred events are made present. When we are at Mass, we are at the Last Supper, beneath the Cross, at the empty tomb, and sharing in the Emmaus meal of the risen Lord. The Eucharistic sacrifice is a sacrifice once and for all with the same priest: Jesus; the same victim: Jesus; and the same offering of Jesus to the Father for the sins of men.

Reinforce

1. Have the students work on *Activity Book* p. 68 (see *Teacher's Manual*, p. 213).

2. The students may write thank you letters to the parish priests (for bringing Jesus to them through the Mass).

3. Give the students time to work on the Memorization Questions and Words to Know, and to review for the chapter quiz.

Conclude

1. Lead the students in singing "Jesus, my Lord, my God, my all!" *Adoremus Hymnal*, #516.

2. End class by leading the students in the Prayer before Communion (see *Teacher's Manual*, p. 205).

of Jesus but the whole Jesus—Body, Blood, Soul, and Divinity, God and man. The whole Jesus went to Andrew, to Peter, to John, to Philip, to each one. And so he comes to us, too, when we receive Holy Communion. The Apostles were united with Christ and filled with grace. So are we.

But what did the Apostles see when Jesus said, "This is my Body. . . . This is my Blood"? What they saw still looked like bread and wine. What had been bread still had the same weight, color, and taste; what had been wine still had the same taste, odor, and color. But its *substance*, the underlying reality which makes it what it is, had been changed. The looks and other properties known by the senses are called the *appearances*; the Body and Blood of Jesus kept the *appearances* of bread and wine. The **mystery** of this change in the bread and wine is called "**transubstantiation**," which means change of substance.

The substance of bread and wine have been changed into the substance of the Body and Blood of Christ. We cannot see the change but it has happened.

Why does Jesus change bread and wine into his Body and Blood but leave the appearances of bread and wine? The Eucharist is a Sacrament, a sign instituted by Christ to give us grace. The appearances of bread and wine remain as signs that Jesus is true spiritual food and drink for our souls given to us in a special way in the Eucharist. He is the source of our life as Christians.

We call Jesus' presence in the Eucharist the Real Presence. It is called "real" because Jesus is really and truly with us. The Eucharist is no mere symbol of Jesus; it is truly Jesus, under the appearances of bread and wine.

The Everlasting Sacrifice

After the Apostles had each received Holy Communion, Jesus said to them, "Do this in remembrance of me" (Lk 22:19). When he said this he made them priests; for by telling them to do what he had just done—to change bread and wine into his Body and Blood—he gave them the power to do it.

The greatest power of the priesthood is the power to offer this sacrifice of Jesus' Body

81

and Blood. It is the same sacrifice that Jesus offered at the Last Supper and the next day on the Cross. Through this power the Body and Blood of Jesus continue to be offered to God under the appearances of bread and wine whenever the Mass is celebrated.

So God left us an everlasting sacrifice of such richness and power that nothing else can be compared to it.

The Apostles used their powers to feed the new Church of Christ with the Bread from

heaven: the Eucharist. They shared their power with other men, co-workers and their successors, so that the Church could continue from generation to generation to offer the great sacrifice, making it present to all who seek it, until the end of time.

Words to Know:
Eucharist Last Supper Passover victim
oblation mystery transubstantiation

Q. 61 *What is the Eucharist?*
The Eucharist is the Sacrament of the Body, Blood, Soul, and Divinity of Christ, really and truly present under the appearances of bread and wine (CCC 1333).

Q. 62 *What does it mean to say that the whole Christ is contained in the Eucharist under the appearances of bread and wine?*
To say that the whole Christ is contained in the Eucharist under the appearances of bread and wine means that the Body, Blood, Soul, and Divinity of Jesus are present (CCC 1374).

Q. 63 *When did Jesus Christ institute the Eucharist?*
Jesus Christ instituted the Eucharist at the Last Supper when he changed bread and wine into his Body and Blood and commanded the Apostles to do the same in his memory (CCC 1323, 1337).

Q. 64 *Why did Jesus Christ institute the Eucharist?*
Jesus Christ instituted the Eucharist in order to leave his Church a visible sacrifice by which the Sacrifice of the Cross would be re-presented and recalled. In the Eucharist, the benefits of the Cross are applied and spiritual food is given to our souls in Holy Communion (CCC 1366, 1382).

Q. 65 *What is a sacrifice?*
A sacrifice is the public offering of something to God in order to profess that he is Creator and Supreme Ruler to whom everything belongs (CCC 1366, 2099).

82

SAINT JOHN MARY VIANNEY, PATRON OF PRIESTS

Saint John Vianney, the patron saint of priests and the first diocesan priest to be canonized, spent his life serving the small community of Ars, France, in the early nineteenth century. When he began to study for the priesthood he seemed like a hopeless cause. He was not very intelligent and had a lot of trouble with his studies, especially Latin, which was necessary for a priest at that time. Despite many setbacks, Saint John persevered and was finally ordained and sent to work in the small, remote hamlet of Ars. He lived a life of severe penance, living mostly on potatoes, and dedicatedly served his people. Soon he became known throughout France for his wisdom, sanctity, and charity. People came from all over the world to see this holy priest and to confess to him. He spent as many as sixteen hours a day in the confessional and was said to have the gift of knowing exactly what advice to give to sinners and exactly what their sins were—even if they did not confess them. Even bishops and cardinals came to see this priest who was barely able to pass his seminary exams. The life of Saint John Vianney shows us the most important role of a priest: to bring Jesus to the people he serves. Saint John used the graces God had given him, especially the ability to administer the Sacraments, and brought many people to Jesus.

Give us priests who are on fire, and who are true children of Mary, priests who will give Jesus to souls with the same tenderness and care with which Mary carried the Little Child of Bethlehem.

—Saint Thérèse of Lisieux

Preview

In the next lesson, the students' understanding of the material covered in this chapter will be reviewed and assessed.

CHAPTER SEVENTEEN: AT THE LAST SUPPER
REVIEW AND ASSESSMENT

Aims

The students' understanding of the material covered in this chapter will be reviewed and assessed.

Materials

- Quiz 17, Appendix, p. A-25

Optional:
- "Jesus, my Lord, my God, my all!" *Adoremus Hymnal*, #516

Review and Enrichment

1. The students should be familiar with the Bread of Life discourse. Jesus said that we must eat his Body and drink his Blood to have eternal life. This is a difficult teaching to accept, but Jesus, as Lord, has the words of everlasting life.

2. Jesus celebrated the Last Supper during a Passover meal. The students should be familiar with the Passover meal, a memorial (meaning it is made present in a re-presentation) of the saving actions of God during the Exodus.

3. The students should be familiar with the events of the Last Supper, at which Jesus instituted two Sacraments: Eucharist and Holy Orders.

4. The students should understand that the Last Supper, the Crucifixion, and the Mass are all the same sacrifice (one action—one sacrifice with Jesus as priest, victim, and offering). Only the manner of the sacrifice is different.

5. The students should understand transubstantiation, when the bread and wine are changed in substance (though the appearances, or species, remain the same) to the Body, Blood, Soul, and Divinity of Jesus, really and truly present in the Eucharist, in each species and in each of its parts.

6. The students should know the role of a priest.

212

At the Last Supper   Quiz 17

Part I: Yes or No.

1. No Did all of Jesus' followers accept his saying when he told them that he would give them his Body to eat and his Blood to drink?
2. Yes At the Last Supper, did the Apostles receive Jesus in Holy Communion?
3. No Is the Eucharist only a symbol?
4. Yes Is the Eucharist truly Jesus?
5. Yes Did Jesus make the Apostles priests at the Last Supper?
6. Yes Does the priest offer the same sacrifice that Jesus offered at the Last Supper and on the Cross?

Part II: Fill in the chart.

BEFORE THE WORDS "THIS IS MY BODY … THIS IS MY BLOOD"		AFTER THE WORDS "THIS IS MY BODY … THIS IS MY BLOOD"	
APPEARANCE	SUBSTANCE	APPEARANCE	SUBSTANCE
Bread	Bread	Bread	Jesus
Wine	Wine	Wine	Jesus
This change is called: Transubstantiation			

Part III: Fill in the blanks.

1. The Passover commemorated God's rescue of his chosen people from slavery in Egypt.
2. The sacrifice that frees man from sin is the Crucifixion and death of our Lord Jesus Christ.
3. The word oblation is used to indicate the total offering of a victim or gift in a sacrifice.
4. In the oblation of Jesus Christ, he was both priest and victim.
5. In Holy Communion we receive the Body, Blood, Soul, and Divinity of Jesus.
6. We call Jesus' presence in the Eucharist the Real Presence.

Part IV: Answer the following in complete sentences.

1. The slavery of the Hebrew people is an image of what other kind of slavery?
   The slavery of the Hebrew people is an image of the slavery of all people to sin.

2. What are the four purposes of offering a sacrifice?
   The four purposes of offering a sacrifice are to adore God, to thank him, to make up for sin, and to ask his help.

Faith and Life Series • Grade 6 • Appendix A   A-25

Assess

1. Distribute the quizzes and read through them with the students to be sure they understand the questions.

2. Administer the quiz. As they hand in their work, you may orally quiz the students on the Memorization Questions from this chapter.

3. After all the quizzes have been handed in, you may wish to review the correct answers with the class.

Conclude

1. Lead the students in singing "Jesus, my Lord, my God, my all!" *Adoremus Hymnal*, #516.

2. End class by leading the students in the Prayer before Communion (see *Teacher's Manual*, p. 205).

CHAPTER SEVENTEEN: AT THE LAST SUPPER
ACTIVITY BOOK ANSWER KEYS

Name:_____

The Eucharist

Put Jesus' actions and words from the Last Supper in the proper order.

<u>2</u> Jesus said, "Take this, all of you, and eat of it, for this is my Body."

<u>6</u> Jesus said, "[It] will be poured out…for the forgiveness of sin."

<u>8</u> Jesus gave the cup to his disciples.

<u>5</u> Jesus said, "This is the chalice of my Blood."

<u>1</u> Jesus took the bread, blessed it, and broke it.

<u>4</u> Jesus took the cup and gave thanks.

<u>3</u> Jesus gave the bread to his disciples.

<u>7</u> Jesus said, "Take this, all of you, and drink from it."

Read John 6:35–69 and answer the questions in complete sentences.

1. Who is the Bread of Life?
   <u>Jesus is the Bread of Life.</u>

2. Was Jesus speaking in riddles or metaphors when he said that we must eat his Body and drink his Blood in order to have eternal life?
   <u>No.</u>

3. Did everyone accept this teaching?
   <u>No.</u>

4. If you eat Jesus' Body and drink his Blood, what is promised to you?
   <u>Eternal life is promised to those who eat Jesus' Body and drink his Blood.</u>

5. Who left Jesus? Why did they no longer follow him?
   <u>Many of Jesus followers left Jesus because his teaching was too hard for them to accept.</u>

6. What did Peter say? What did the Apostles do?
   <u>Peter said, "Lord, to whom shall we go? You have the words of eternal life." The Apostles stayed with Jesus.</u>

Faith and Life Series • Grade 6 • Chapter 17 • Lesson 1   65

Name:_____

The Passover

Compare the Passover with Christ's Last Supper and sacrifice.

PASSOVER SACRIFICE	CHRIST'S SACRIFICE
• God's chosen people	<u>Answers will vary.</u>
• God worked great wonders and signs	
• Fear into hearts of Egyptians	
• To bring Hebrews to freedom	
• Striking down firstborn sons	
• Angel of death	
• Spotless lamb	
• Blood of lamb on doorpost	
• Eat lamb	
• Dressed, ready to follow God's command	
• Led to Mount Sinai to make (Old) Covenant	

66   *Faith and Life Series • Grade 6 • Chapter 17 • Lesson 2*

Name:_____

Jesus: True God and True Man

Answer the following questions in complete sentences.

1. What did Jesus do at the Last Supper?
   <u>Jesus changed bread and wine into his Body and Blood.</u>

2. Was Jesus present both visibly and in the Eucharist?
   <u>Yes.</u>

3. What did the bread and wine become?
   <u>They became Jesus—Body, Blood, Soul, and Divinity.</u>

4. Why do we say the bread and wine are Jesus' Body and Blood when it looks the same, tastes the same, and has the same color, odor, weight, etc.?
   <u>We say the bread and wine are Jesus' Body and Blood because the substance, what they are, has changed.</u>

5. What is this change called and what does it mean?
   <u>The change is called transubstantiation, which means change of substance.</u>

Faith and Life Series • Grade 6 • Chapter 17 • Lesson 3   67

Name:_____

Do This in Memory of Me

Answer the following questions in complete sentences.

1. What is the Eucharist?
   <u>The Eucharist is the Sacrament of the Body, Blood, Soul, and Divinity of Christ, really and truly present under the appearances of bread and wine.</u>

2. Why did Jesus Christ institute the Eucharist?
   <u>Jesus instituted the Eucharist in order to leave his Church a visible sign by which the Sacrifice of the Cross would be re-presented and recalled.</u>

3. When did Jesus institute the Eucharist?
   <u>Jesus instituted the Eucharist at the Last Supper when he changed bread and wine into his Body and Blood and commanded the Apostles to do the same in his memory.</u>

4. What did Jesus do when he said, "Do this in memory of me"?
   <u>Jesus made the Apostles his priests.</u>

5. What special power do priests have?
   <u>Priests have the power to offer the sacrifice of Jesus' Body and Blood.</u>

6. Where do priests get their powers?
   <u>Priests get their powers from Jesus.</u>

68   *Faith and Life Series • Grade 6 • Chapter 17 • Lesson 4*

TEACHER'S NOTES

CHAPTER EIGHTEEN
THE LIVING SACRIFICE

Catechism of the Catholic Church References

Christ's Whole Life as a Self-Offering to the Father: 606–18, 621–23

"Do This in Memory of Me": 1341–44, 1409

Eucharist as Sacrifice: 1356–81, 1414

Eucharist as Thanksgiving and Praise to the Father: 1359–61

Eucharist as Sacrificial Memorial of His Body, the Church: 1362–71, 1408, 1414

Mass as Memorial: 1356–57, 1409

Presence of Christ in the Eucharist: 1373–81, 1410, 1418

Sacrifice: 1330, 1359–61, 1643, 1365–72, 1410, 1414, 1366, 1369, 2099–2100

Satisfaction for Sin: 1459–60, 1494

Sunday Eucharist: 2177–79

Scripture References

Passion and Death of Christ: Jn 18:1—19:42

Summary of Lesson Content

Lesson 1

Jesus was crucified, died, was buried, and rose again.

Jesus saved mankind with his sacrifice and won grace for us through the Paschal Mystery.

The Eucharist allows us to share in his one sacrifice and to receive grace.

Mass is a sacred meal and a sacrifice.

Lesson 2

Jesus told his Apostles (and through them, all priests) to celebrate Mass as a memorial of his sacrifice.

Jesus' sacrifice on Calvary and his Resurrection are made present at Mass.

At every Mass, Jesus offers himself—Body, Blood, Soul, and Divinity—to the Father on our behalf. He is the priest and the victim. We can unite ourselves to him.

Lesson 3

Mass is the perfect prayer. It is the supreme act of worship.

Mass is Jesus' greatest gift to the Church. In the Mass we offer to God a pleasing sacrifice; through the Mass we are united with God.

We offer thanksgiving and receive grace through the Mass.

Lesson 4

At Mass, we can offer satisfaction for our sin.

The Sacrifice of the Mass does not offer Jesus as a new sacrifice over and over again. The Mass is a share in the one true sacrifice of Jesus on the Cross, made present by the power of Jesus Christ, who acts through the priest and offers himself in the Eucharist.

At Mass, we can petition God the Father for graces.

CHAPTER EIGHTEEN: THE LIVING SACRIFICE
LESSON ONE: MEDIATOR

Aims

The students will learn that Jesus was crucified, died, was buried, and rose again.

They will learn that Jesus saved mankind with his sacrifice and won grace for us through the Paschal Mystery. The Eucharist allows us to share in his one sacrifice and to receive grace.

They will learn that the Mass is a sacred meal and a sacrifice.

Materials

• *Activity Book*, p. 69

Optional:
• "O saving Victim," *Adoremus Hymnal*, #520

Begin

Review the chasm created by man's Original Sin, which separated God and man. Review the need for this chasm to be bridged. Today, we will learn more about Jesus as our mediator (or bridge) and his sacrifice.

Develop

1. Read paragraphs 1–4 from the student text.

2. Review the Blessed Trinity. We believe in one God in three Divine Persons: God the Father, God the Son, and God the Holy Spirit. Each Person is distinct, yet all are God. The Persons all have the same divine attributes (since they all are God—"consubstantial"—with the same substance). Each is all good, all loving, all knowing, all powerful, all merciful, etc. Have the students discuss and give examples of the divine attributes.

3. The Second Divine Person of the Blessed Trinity is the Son. In the fullness of time, the Son became man and took on human nature in what is called the Incarnation. By the power of the Holy Spirit, the Virgin Mary conceived and gave birth to Jesus the Christ, God the Son. In the Divine Person of Jesus, are two natures: human and divine. They are united in what is called the hypostatic union. Jesus has a body, soul, and will—he is like us in all things but sin. Jesus is also God with all of God's attributes. This is why he could do miracles, reveal the teachings of God, and reveal God, himself! Jesus, as true God and true man, is the perfect mediator—the "bridge" that reconciles God and man.

4. God the Father so loved the world, and so desired a new and everlasting covenant between God and man, that he sent his Son, Jesus, to establish this covenant. Jesus would, by his life, death, and Resurrection, give us the way to be united with God through this covenant. Jesus won grace for us and opened the gates of heaven by the Paschal Mystery. We enter this covenant through Baptism, when we receive grace. We maintain this covenant and in a way "renew" it every time we come to Mass, in which these saving mysteries are made present and we unite ourselves with the perfect sacrifice of Jesus (who is the perfect priest) in the Eucharist.

Reinforce

1. Have the students work on *Activity Book* p. 69 (see *Teacher's Manual*, p. 225).

2. The students should meditate upon Jesus as the mediator. They may write stories describing what it would have been like for them to meet the Son of God made man in the Divine Person of Jesus. What would their encounters have been like?

3. The students should begin working on the Memorization Questions and Words to Know from this chapter.

4. Tell the students that each of them should bring to the next class a picture depicting a special time in his life.

Conclude

1. Teach the students to sing "O saving Victim," *Adoremus Hymnal*, #520.

2. End class by leading the students in the Spiritual Communion prayer (see *Teacher's Manual*, p. 397).

3. Remind the students to bring pictures to the next class.

CHAPTER 18

The Living Sacrifice

"... for then he would have had to suffer repeatedly since the foundation of the world. But as it is, he has appeared once for all at the end of the age to put away sin by the sacrifice of himself."

Hebrews 9:26

Jesus Christ, through whom all good things come to us, died on Calvary and rose again from the dead. His sacrifice redeemed the human race. Every day that sacrifice is renewed in the Holy Mass. That is what the Mass is all about. The Mass is the same sacrifice as the sacrifice at Calvary; it not only recalls that sacrifice but continues it.

Jesus gave us the precious **Sacrament** of the Eucharist for two reasons: so that we might have eternal life and so that we might have an acceptable sacrifice to offer continually to the Father.

As Catholic writer Frank Sheed expressed it, "The Mass *is* Calvary, as Christ now offers it to his Father." The victim offered is the same—Jesus himself. He is present as he made himself present under the appearances of bread and wine at the Last Supper. The priest is one and the same; for the priest at our altar acts in the person of Jesus to change the bread and wine into the Body and Blood of the Lord.

On the altar Jesus offers himself through the words and actions of the priest, without shedding his blood or dying again. After his resurrection Jesus can no longer die. But he still offers his one sacrifice on the Cross to the Father for us. The Bible tells us that he is doing that right now in heaven, as our high priest there (Heb 7:24–25; 8:1–2; 9:11–14). At the Mass, Jesus makes the heavenly offering of his Body and Blood present on earth, under the appearances of bread and wine. We join with the priest and each other to offer Jesus to the Father, as well as offering ourselves to him with Jesus. In this way, we grow more deeply as the Church, the Body of Christ on earth.

A Memorial

A memorial is a recalling of a past event. Besides being a sacrifice, the Mass is a **memorial** by which until the end of time we call to mind the death of Christ. Christ said to his Apostles, "Do this in memory of me."

He did not mean, however, that the Mass would be *only* a memorial. In the Mass we not only remember Christ's death on the Cross, but Christ brings his sacrifice before us in a real and sacramental way.

Mass is a memorial of Christ's Resurrection as well. The Church teaches that it is "a memorial of his death and Resurrection." Here, too, the reality is more than a recollection. For the chief priest at Mass is the Risen Christ who is present in the Eucharist.

The Four Ends of the Mass

Holy Mass is the perfect prayer. So it has the same ends, or purposes, as prayer.

83

1. The Mass is an act of supreme worship; it is Christ's greatest gift to his Church. Men with nothing worthy to offer God have now been given a victim and a sacrifice of infinite value: Jesus Christ himself.

2. The Mass is a prayer of thanksgiving; the word "eucharist" actually means "thanksgiving." We have so much to thank God for: our lives, with all that they contain of family and friends, people, places, and things. Most of all, there is the supernatural life of grace given to us by Jesus Christ, our Savior. It is through the life of grace that we have hope of reaching heaven and can enjoy great happiness even now.

Through the Mass we have the chance to thank God for all his benefits, most of all for his generosity and mercy in sending us Jesus, his Son. And it is Jesus, his gift to us, whom we now offer back to him. God is infinitely pleased with this gift that he has put in our hands.

3. The Mass is a way to **make satisfaction for** (make up for) sins. We pray: "Lamb of God, you take away the sins of the world, have mercy on us . . . grant us peace."

Are we asking Jesus to do something that he has already done? Are we asking him to take away the sins of the world again and again, every time the Mass is offered?

No; there is really only one Mass, and it was offered on Calvary once for all. And it is this one sacrifice that is offered on all our altars at Mass. Through the gift of the Holy Eucharist, Jesus has extended his sacrifice in time and space. Our participation at Mass is our time to be with Christ at the Cross.

84

4. The Mass is our best means of petitioning the Father and obtaining the graces we ask for, both for ourselves and for others. In the Mass we are offering to God the perfect sacrifice, Jesus Christ, the most pleasing offering we have to give, and God will be pleased by our offering so great a gift.

Words to Know:
Sacrament   memorial
make satisfaction for

> **Q. 66** **What is the Holy Mass?**
> The Holy Mass is the sacrifice of the Body and Blood of Jesus Christ. This sacrifice is offered to God under the appearances of bread and wine through the ministry of a priest, in order to remember, renew, and re-present the Sacrifice of the Cross, and to be received in the sacred meal of Holy Communion (CCC 1367, 1382).
>
> **Q. 67** *Is the Sacrifice of the Mass the same as the Sacrifice of the Cross?*
> The Sacrifice of the Mass is the same sacrifice as the Sacrifice of the Cross; the only difference is in the manner of offering it (CCC 1364, 1367).
>
> **Q. 68** *Who is the priest and the victim in the Holy Sacrifice of the Mass?*
> In the Holy Sacrifice of the Mass Jesus Christ is the priest, acting through his ordained minister, and Christ is the victim, offered to the Father under the appearances of bread and wine (CCC 1367).
>
> **Q. 69** *What is the difference between the Sacrifice of the Cross and the Sacrifice of the Mass?*
> On the Cross, Christ shed his blood and died; in the Mass, he offers himself under the appearances of bread and wine by the ministry of a priest, in an unbloody manner and without dying; on the Cross he merited redemption for man; in the Mass, he applies the benefits of his sacrifice on the Cross (CCC 1367).
>
> **Q. 70** *Why is the Mass offered to God?*
> The Mass is offered to God to give him the supreme worship of adoration; to thank him for his blessings to us; to make satisfaction for our sins; and to obtain graces for the good of the faithful, living and dead (CCC 1365, 1368).

85

CHALK TALK: CALVARY AND THE MASS

ChalK TalK	Calvary	Mass
Victim	Jesus	Jesus
Priest	Jesus	Jesus (through the ministry of a priest)
Sacrifice	Bloody Manner	Unbloody Manner

THE PASCHAL MYSTERY

The word Pasch refers to the feast of Passover. By the blood of the Passover lamb, the Hebrew people were protected in Egypt. That event prefigured the blood of Jesus, which frees us from sin and death. The Paschal Mystery, then, is "Christ's work of redemption accomplished primarily by his Passion, death, Resurrection, and glorious Ascension" (Glossary, CCC second ed).

Preview

In the next lesson, the students will learn more about the memorial aspect of the Mass.

CHAPTER EIGHTEEN: THE LIVING SACRIFICE
LESSON TWO: MEMORIAL

Aims

The students will learn that Jesus told his Apostles (and through them, all priests) to celebrate Mass as a memorial of Jesus' sacrifice.

They will learn that Jesus' sacrifice on Calvary and his Resurrection are made present at Mass. At every Mass, Jesus offers himself—Body, Blood, Soul, and Divinity— to the Father on our behalf. He is the priest and the victim. We can unite ourselves to him.

Materials

• *Activity Book*, p. 70

• Students' photos

• Children's missals

Optional:
• O saving Victim,"
   Adoremus Hymnal, #520

Begin

If possible, have the students bring in pictures of a special time in their lives. Have each share the special memory that goes with the picture. Discuss how remembering is different from a memorial. In a memorial, past events are made present—in the today of the memorial. There is no time with God. The Mass is a porthole into the saving events of history. When we celebrated the Passover meal we were experiencing the saving actions of God through the Exodus. When we receive the Holy Eucharist, we experience firsthand the mysteries of Jesus' sacrifice.

Develop

1. Read paragraphs 5–7 from the student text.

2. Review the definition of a Sacrament—an outward sign that effects Christ's grace. The Sacrament points to and effects a hidden reality through the signs used in the Sacrament (e.g., the water of Baptism washes away sin and pours the life of grace into our souls).

3. The Mass is also an outward sign that effects grace. Through what theologians call "mystagogy," the events commemorated are made present. A greater reality is present— even if we cannot fully grasp it with our senses. We are able to understand these mysteries by the signs, symbols, and words said at Mass. To grasp the reality, we must have faith.

4. Using a set of children's missals, explain how the Word of God is being proclaimed directly to us—just as it was to the people in the Bible. We are inserted into the stories! It is as though we were hearing a reading about Noah's Ark, and being on the boat, too.

5. God's word is effective—it causes conversion. The more we hear, the more we love God and will "convert" or turn toward him. His word effected miracles. When Jesus said, "be healed" a person was healed. At Mass, the priest acts in the Person of Christ. When the priest says, "This is my Body," "This is the chalice of my Blood" a change in the bread and wine is truly effected by Jesus working through the priest. We are thus present with Christ at the Last Supper and the Crucifixion, and Resurrection. Like the disciples of Emmaus, we recognize Christ in the breaking of the bread. We know that the Eucharist is Jesus (even though it looks like bread and wine). By faith, we know these realities are made present in the Liturgy.

Reinforce

1. Have the students work on *Activity Book* p. 70 (see *Teacher's Manual*, p. 225).

2. The students may write stories of what it would have been like to witness the Last Supper, the Crucifixion, the Resurrection, and the appearance of Jesus on the road to Emmaus. After composing their story-meditations, the students should explain how these events are made present at the Mass.

3. Using missals, the students should read through the parts of the Mass, finding clues to better understand when the saving mysteries are made present.

4. Have the students work on the Memorization Questions and Words to Know from this chapter.

Conclude

1. Lead the students in singing "O saving Victim," *Adoremus Hymnal*, #520.

2. End class by leading the students in the Spiritual Communion prayer (see *Teacher's Manual*, p. 397).

CHAPTER 18

The Living Sacrifice

> ". . . for then he would have had to suffer repeatedly since the foundation of the world. But as it is, he has appeared once for all at the end of the age to put away sin by the sacrifice of himself."
>
> Hebrews 9:26

Jesus Christ, through whom all good things come to us, died on Calvary and rose again from the dead. His sacrifice redeemed the human race. Every day that sacrifice is renewed in the Holy Mass. That is what the Mass is all about. The Mass is the same sacrifice as the sacrifice at Calvary; it not only recalls that sacrifice but continues it.

Jesus gave us the precious **Sacrament** of the Eucharist for two reasons: so that we might have eternal life and so that we might have an acceptable sacrifice to offer continually to the Father.

As Catholic writer Frank Sheed expressed it, "The Mass *is* Calvary, as Christ now offers it to his Father." The victim offered is the same —Jesus himself. He is present as he made himself present under the appearances of bread and wine at the Last Supper. The priest is one and the same; for the priest at our altar acts in the person of Jesus to change the bread and wine into the Body and Blood of the Lord.

On the altar Jesus offers himself through the words and actions of the priest, without shedding his blood or dying again. After his resurrection Jesus can no longer die. But he still offers his one sacrifice on the Cross to the Father for us. The Bible tells us that he is doing that right now in heaven, as our high priest there (Heb 7:24–25; 8:1–2; 9:11–14). At the Mass, Jesus makes the heavenly offering of his Body and Blood present on earth, under the appearances of bread and wine. We join with the priest and each other to offer Jesus to the Father, as well as offering ourselves to him with Jesus. In this way, we grow more deeply as the Church, the Body of Christ on earth.

A Memorial

A memorial is a recalling of a past event. Besides being a sacrifice, the Mass is a **memorial** by which until the end of time we call to mind the death of Christ. Christ said to his Apostles, "Do this in memory of me."

He did not mean, however, that the Mass would be *only* a memorial. In the Mass we not only remember Christ's death on the Cross, but Christ brings his sacrifice before us in a real and sacramental way.

Mass is a memorial of Christ's Resurrection as well. The Church teaches that it is "a memorial of his death and Resurrection." Here, too, the reality is more than a recollection. For the chief priest at Mass is the Risen Christ who is present in the Eucharist.

The Four Ends of the Mass

Holy Mass is the perfect prayer. So it has the same ends, or purposes, as prayer.

83

1. The Mass is an act of supreme worship; it is Christ's greatest gift to his Church. Men with nothing worthy to offer God have now been given a victim and a sacrifice of infinite value: Jesus Christ himself.

2. The Mass is a prayer of thanksgiving; the word "eucharist" actually means "thanksgiving." We have so much to thank God for: our lives, with all that they contain of family and friends, people, places, and things. Most of all, there is the supernatural life of grace given to us by Jesus Christ, our Savior. It is through the life of grace that we have hope of reaching heaven and can enjoy great happiness even now.

Through the Mass we have the chance to thank God for all his benefits, most of all for his generosity and mercy in sending us Jesus, his Son. And it is Jesus, his gift to us, whom we now offer back to him. God is infinitely pleased with this gift that he has put in our hands.

3. The Mass is a way to **make satisfaction for** (make up for) sins. We pray: "Lamb of God, you take away the sins of the world, have mercy on us . . . grant us peace."

Are we asking Jesus to do something that he has already done? Are we asking him to take away the sins of the world again and again, every time the Mass is offered?

No; there is really only one Mass, and it was offered on Calvary once for all. And it is this one sacrifice that is offered on all our altars at Mass. Through the gift of the Holy Eucharist, Jesus has extended his sacrifice in time and space. Our participation at Mass is our time to be with Christ at the Cross.

84

4. The Mass is our best means of petitioning the Father and obtaining the graces we ask for, both for ourselves and for others. In the Mass we are offering to God the perfect sacrifice, Jesus Christ, the most pleasing offering we have to give, and God will be pleased by our offering so great a gift.

Words to Know:
Sacrament memorial
make satisfaction for

> **Q. 66** *What is the Holy Mass?*
> The Holy Mass is the sacrifice of the Body and Blood of Jesus Christ. This sacrifice is offered to God under the appearances of bread and wine through the ministry of a priest, in order to remember, renew, and re-present the Sacrifice of the Cross, and to be received in the sacred meal of Holy Communion (CCC 1367, 1382).
>
> **Q. 67** *Is the Sacrifice of the Mass the same as the Sacrifice of the Cross?*
> The Sacrifice of the Mass is the same sacrifice as the Sacrifice of the Cross; the only difference is in the manner of offering it (CCC 1364, 1367).
>
> **Q. 68** *Who is the priest and the victim in the Holy Sacrifice of the Mass?*
> In the Holy Sacrifice of the Mass Jesus Christ is the priest, acting through his ordained minister, and Christ is the victim, offered to the Father under the appearances of bread and wine (CCC 1367).
>
> **Q. 69** *What is the difference between the Sacrifice of the Cross and the Sacrifice of the Mass?*
> On the Cross, Christ shed his blood and died; in the Mass, he offers himself under the appearances of bread and wine by the ministry of a priest, in an unbloody manner and without dying; on the Cross he merited redemption for man; in the Mass, he applies the benefits of his sacrifice on the Cross (CCC 1367).
>
> **Q. 70** *Why is the Mass offered to God?*
> The Mass is offered to God to give him the supreme worship of adoration; to thank him for his blessings to us; to make satisfaction for our sins; and to obtain graces for the good of the faithful, living and dead (CCC 1365, 1368).

85

CHALK TALK: THE MASS

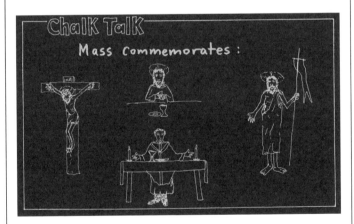

Preview

In the next lesson, the students will learn about the first two ends (purposes) of the Mass.

CHAPTER EIGHTEEN: THE LIVING SACRIFICE
LESSON THREE: WORSHIP AND THANKS

Aims

The students will learn that Mass is the perfect prayer. It is the supreme act of worship. The Mass is Jesus' greatest gift to the Church. In the Mass we offer to God a pleasing sacrifice; through the Mass we are united with God.

They will learn that we offer thanksgiving and receive grace through the Mass.

Materials

- *Activity Book*, p. 71

- Children's missals

Optional:
- "O saving Victim," *Adoremus Hymnal*, #520

Begin

Holy Mass is the perfect prayer, and thus Mass shares in the same ends as prayer:

A (adoration)
C (contrition)
T (thanksgiving)
S (supplication)

Today, we will begin studying the ends of the Mass. The students will find examples of these ends in their missals.

Develop

1. Read paragraphs 8–11.

2. Have the students compete to see who can find the most examples of adoration/worship and thanksgiving from the missals. The students may set up a chart with four columns titled: adoration, contrition, thanksgiving, and supplication.

3. What is worship/adoration? It is recognizing God and his divine attributes. It involves giving praise and loving God. In recognizing God as our Lord, we know that:
- We are not God.
- We are dependent upon God and his benevolence.
- God is all powerful.
Therefore, in our worship we should praise and bless God for his attributes and wondrous deeds. We can tell God how much we love him. We can tell God how we appreciate his good work. We should humble ourselves before God, and see,

in truth, that God's attributes are eternal and that we are unworthy of his love and generosity, though he gives them freely to us.

4. What is thanksgiving? It is recognizing the many gifts we have received, using them well, and appreciating the gifts, as well as the giver. When our parents give us gifts (like a birthday present) how do we respond? We say, "Thank you." We use the gift as it ought to be used (e.g., play with a toy, wear an outfit, put a beautiful item on display). We are grateful to the giver—for we know that he did not have to give us anything; he freely chose, out of love, to give us a gift. It is just this way with God. We should be thankful for his gifts and use them well, but we should also respond in love to God's generous love.

5. How do we see adoration and thanksgiving in the Mass?

Reinforce

1. Have the students work on *Activity Book* p. 71 (see *Teacher's Manual*, p. 225).

2. The students may continue their search through the missal to find examples of adoration and thanksgiving.

3. Have the students work on the Memorization Questions and Words to Know from this chapter (see *Teacher's Manual*, p. 223).

Conclude

1. Lead the students in singing "O saving Victim," *Adoremus Hymnal*, #520.

2. End class by leading the students in the Spiritual Communion prayer (see *Teacher's Manual*, p. 397).

CHAPTER 18

The Living Sacrifice

"... for then he would have had to suffer repeatedly since the foundation of the world. But as it is, he has appeared once for all at the end of the age to put away sin by the sacrifice of himself."

Hebrews 9:26

Jesus Christ, through whom all good things come to us, died on Calvary and rose again from the dead. His sacrifice redeemed the human race. Every day that sacrifice is renewed in the Holy Mass. That is what the Mass is all about. The Mass is the same sacrifice as the sacrifice at Calvary; it not only recalls that sacrifice but continues it.

Jesus gave us the precious **Sacrament** of the Eucharist for two reasons: so that we might have eternal life and so that we might have an acceptable sacrifice to offer continually to the Father.

As Catholic writer Frank Sheed expressed it, "The Mass *is* Calvary, as Christ now offers it to his Father." The victim offered is the same —Jesus himself. He is present as he made himself present under the appearances of bread and wine at the Last Supper. The priest is one and the same; for the priest at our altar acts in the person of Jesus to change the bread and wine into the Body and Blood of the Lord.

On the altar Jesus offers himself through the words and actions of the priest, without shedding his blood or dying again. After his resurrection Jesus can no longer die. But he still offers his one sacrifice on the Cross to the Father for us. The Bible tells us that he is doing that right now in heaven, as our high priest there (Heb 7:24–25; 8:1–2; 9:11–14). At the Mass, Jesus makes the heavenly offering of his Body and Blood present on earth, under the appearances of bread and wine. We join with the priest and each other to offer Jesus to the Father, as well as offering ourselves to him with Jesus. In this way, we grow more deeply as the Church, the Body of Christ on earth.

A Memorial

A memorial is a recalling of a past event. Besides being a sacrifice, the Mass is a **memorial** by which until the end of time we call to mind the death of Christ. Christ said to his Apostles, "Do this in memory of me."

He did not mean, however, that the Mass would be *only* a memorial. In the Mass we not only remember Christ's death on the Cross, but Christ brings his sacrifice before us in a real and sacramental way.

Mass is a memorial of Christ's Resurrection as well. The Church teaches that it is "a memorial of his death and Resurrection." Here, too, the reality is more than a recollection. For the chief priest at Mass is the Risen Christ who is present in the Eucharist.

The Four Ends of the Mass

Holy Mass is the perfect prayer. So it has the same ends, or purposes, as prayer.

83

1. The Mass is an act of supreme worship; it is Christ's greatest gift to his Church. Men with nothing worthy to offer God have now been given a victim and a sacrifice of infinite value: Jesus Christ himself.

2. The Mass is a prayer of thanksgiving; the word "eucharist" actually means "thanksgiving." We have so much to thank God for: our lives, with all that they contain of family and friends, people, places, and things. Most of all, there is the supernatural life of grace given to us by Jesus Christ, our Savior. It is through the life of grace that we have hope of reaching heaven and can enjoy great happiness even now.

Through the Mass we have the chance to thank God for all his benefits, most of all for his generosity and mercy in sending us Jesus, his Son. And it is Jesus, his gift to us, whom we now offer back to him. God is infinitely pleased with this gift that he has put in our hands.

3. The Mass is a way to **make satisfaction for** (make up for) sins. We pray: "Lamb of God, you take away the sins of the world, have mercy on us . . . grant us peace."

Are we asking Jesus to do something that he has already done? Are we asking him to take away the sins of the world again and again, every time the Mass is offered?

No; there is really only one Mass, and it was offered on Calvary once for all. And it is this one sacrifice that is offered on all our altars at Mass. Through the gift of the Holy Eucharist, Jesus has extended his sacrifice in time and space. Our participation at Mass is our time to be with Christ at the Cross.

84

SAINT PADRE PIO

Padre Pio was canonized in 2002 as Saint Pio of Pietrelcina. Padre Pio is a saint who truly suffered with Christ. He joined the Order of the Capuchins at the age of sixteen and was ordained a priest seven years later. In 1918, as Saint Pio was praying before a crucifix, he received the stigmata, the wounds of Christ, on his hands and feet. These wounds were very painful and Saint Pio lost huge amounts of blood every day. In humility, he tried to hide the wounds and is commonly pictured wearing gloves, but his stigmata was well known. Saint Pio's life was full of many other amazing mystical graces. There are many accounts of the saint bilocating and of healings attributed to his prayer, and he reportedly had visions of angels and demons. People came from all over the world to confess to the saint who spent as many as twelve hours in the confessional each day. It could be said that he was a modern day Saint John Vianney. Before Pope John Paul II became Pope, he visited Saint Pio's monastery and later said that he was struck by watching the saint celebrate Mass, particularily seeing the love and reverence with which he celebrated. Although it seemed that his stigmata became even more painful, Padre Pio celebrated every Mass reverently, knowing that he was present at Calvary. His Masses could go on for hours, but he endured the pain out of love for God.

Prayer is the best weapon we have; it is the key to God's heart. You must speak to Jesus not only with your lips, but with your heart. In fact on certain occasions you should only speak to Him with your heart.

—Saint Padre Pio

Preview

In the next lesson, the students will learn about the other ends of the Mass: contrition and supplication.

CHAPTER EIGHTEEN: THE LIVING SACRIFICE
LESSON FOUR: CONTRITION AND SUPPLICATION

Aims

The students will learn that, at Mass, we can offer satisfaction for our sin.

They will learn that the Sacrifice of the Mass does not offer Jesus as a new sacrifice over and over again. The Mass is a share in the one true sacrifice of Jesus on the Cross, made present by the power of Jesus Christ, who acts through the priest and offers himself in the Eucharist. At Mass, we can petition God the Father for graces.

Materials

- *Activity Book*, p. 72

- Children's missals

Optional:
- "O saving Victim," *Adoremus Hymnal*, #520

Begin

Recall that Holy Mass is the perfect prayer, and thus it shares in the same ends as ordinary prayer:

A (adoration)
C (contrition)
T (thanksgiving)
S (supplication)

Have the students give examples of adoration and thanksgiving as found in their missals. Today we will learn about contrition and supplication.

Develop

1. Finish reading the chapter.

2. Have the students compete to see who can find the most examples of contrition and supplication in the missals. The students may fill in the chart they started in the previous lesson with four columns titled: adoration, contrition, thanksgiving, and supplication.

3. What is contrition? It is sorrow for our sins. You will recall perfect contrition is when we are sorry that our sins offend God. Imperfect contrition (or attrition) is when we are sorry because we fear the just punishments due to our sin. At Mass, we have opportunities to express our sorrow for sin. The Mass also provides a way to make reparation for our sin by uniting our contrition to the sacrifice of reparation (Jesus upon the Cross). We are not asking Jesus to take away the sins of the world again, but we are uniting ourselves to his sacrifice, for his merciful love of the Eucharist extends his

sacrifice in time and space. By our participation we can ask Jesus to atone for our sins and bring sinners back to the flock to be reconciled. We can pray for the punishment for sin to be lessened (e.g., pray for the souls in purgatory) by applying the treasury of Jesus' sufferings to those in need.

4. What is petition? It is asking for something—either for ourselves or for others (intercession). At Mass, we have a great means to ask the Father for graces. At Mass we are offering the perfect sacrifice of Jesus Christ, the most pleasing offering to the Father. He will be pleased with so great a gift! In our petitions at Mass, we should remember those listed in the Prayers of the Faithful, the needs of our loved ones, the souls in purgatory, and all who are in need.

5. Have the students give examples of contrition and supplication from their missals.

Reinforce

1. Have the students work on *Activity Book* p. 72 (see *Teacher's Manual*, p. 225).

2. The students should continue their search through the missal to find examples of contrition and supplication in the Mass.

3. You may wish to give the students time to work on the Memorization Questions and Words to Know and to study for the quiz.

Conclude

1. Lead the students in singing "O Saving Victim," *Adoremus Hymnal*, #520.

2. End class by leading the students in the Spiritual Communion prayer (see *Teacher's Manual*, p. 397).

1. The Mass is an act of supreme worship; it is Christ's greatest gift to his Church. Men with nothing worthy to offer God have now been given a victim and a sacrifice of infinite value: Jesus Christ himself.

2. The Mass is a prayer of thanksgiving; the word "eucharist" actually means "thanksgiving." We have so much to thank God for: our lives, with all that they contain of family and friends, people, places, and things. Most of all, there is the supernatural life of grace given to us by Jesus Christ, our Savior. It is through the life of grace that we have hope of reaching heaven and can enjoy great happiness even now.

Through the Mass we have the chance to thank God for all his benefits, most of all for his generosity and mercy in sending us Jesus, his Son. And it is Jesus, his gift to us, whom we now offer back to him. God is infinitely pleased with this gift that he has put in our hands.

3. The Mass is a way to **make satisfaction for** (make up for) sins. We pray: "Lamb of God, you take away the sins of the world, have mercy on us . . . grant us peace."

Are we asking Jesus to do something that he has already done? Are we asking him to take away the sins of the world again and again, every time the Mass is offered?

No; there is really only one Mass, and it was offered on Calvary once for all. And it is this one sacrifice that is offered on all our altars at Mass. Through the gift of the Holy Eucharist, Jesus has extended his sacrifice in time and space. Our participation at Mass is our time to be with Christ at the Cross.

84

4. The Mass is our best means of petitioning the Father and obtaining the graces we ask for, both for ourselves and for others. In the Mass we are offering to God the perfect sacrifice, Jesus Christ, the most pleasing offering we have to give, and God will be pleased by our offering so great a gift.

Words to Know:
Sacrament   memorial
make satisfaction for

Q. 66   *What is the Holy Mass?*
The Holy Mass is the sacrifice of the Body and Blood of Jesus Christ. This sacrifice is offered to God under the appearances of bread and wine through the ministry of a priest, in order to remember, renew, and re-present the Sacrifice of the Cross, and to be received in the sacred meal of Holy Communion (CCC 1367, 1382).

Q. 67   *Is the Sacrifice of the Mass the same as the Sacrifice of the Cross?*
The Sacrifice of the Mass is the same sacrifice as the Sacrifice of the Cross; the only difference is in the manner of offering it (CCC 1364, 1367).

Q. 68   *Who is the priest and the victim in the Holy Sacrifice of the Mass?*
In the Holy Sacrifice of the Mass Jesus Christ is the priest, acting through his ordained minister, and Christ is the victim, offered to the Father under the appearances of bread and wine (CCC 1367).

Q. 69   *What is the difference between the Sacrifice of the Cross and the Sacrifice of the Mass?*
On the Cross, Christ shed his blood and died; in the Mass, he offers himself under the appearances of bread and wine by the ministry of a priest, in an unbloody manner and without dying; on the Cross he merited redemption for man; in the Mass, he applies the benefits of his sacrifice on the Cross (CCC 1367).

Q. 70   *Why is the Mass offered to God?*
The Mass is offered to God to give him the supreme worship of adoration; to thank him for his blessings to us; to make satisfaction for our sins; and to obtain graces for the good of the faithful, living and dead (CCC 1365, 1368).

85

WE ARE NOT ALONE

In the Mass, just before the *Sanctus*, the priest says, "…with the Angels and all the Saints, we declare your glory" (Preface VI). Eucharistic Prayer IV prays "…in your presence are countless hosts of Angels, who serve you day and night and, gazing upon the glory of your face, glorify you without ceasing. With them, we, too, confess your name in exultation, giving voice to every creature under heaven…" What does this mean? When we worship at Mass, we are not worshiping alone. We are in union with the entire Church: triumphant, suffering, and militant. We are worshipping with the saints and angels, the souls being purified in purgatory, and our brothers and sisters in the Catholic Church all over the world.

SAINTS AND LITURGY

In the earthly liturgy we share in a foretaste of that heavenly liturgy which is celebrated in the Holy City of Jerusalem toward which we journey as pilgrims, where Christ is sitting at the right hand of God, Minister of the sanctuary and of the true tabernacle. With all the warriors of the heavenly army we sing a hymn of glory to the Lord; venerating the memory of the saints, we hope for some part and fellowship with them; we eagerly await the Savior, our Lord Jesus Christ, until he, our life, shall appear and we too will appear with him in glory.
—CCC 1090 citing *Sacrosanctum Concilium*

"When Jesus is corporally present within us, the angels surround us as a guard of love."
—Saint Bernard

Preview

In the next lesson, the students' understanding of the material covered in this chapter will be reviewed and assessed.

CHAPTER EIGHTEEN: THE LIVING SACRIFICE
REVIEW AND ASSESSMENT

Aims

The students' understanding of the material covered in this chapter will be reviewed and assessed.

Materials

- Quiz 18, Appendix, p. A-26

Optional:
- "O saving Victim," *Adoremus Hymnal*, #520

Review and Enrichment

1. The students should understand that Jesus is the mediator. He is God the Son made man in the Incarnation. By his life, death, and Resurrection the chasm between God and man is bridged. Man is reconciled with God and Jesus has redeemed man.

2. The students should understand that the saving events of Christ are sacramentally made present in the Mass.

3. The students should know the four ends of the Mass:
- Adoration
- Contrition
- Thanksgiving
- Supplication

They should be able to explain these terms, giving examples from the text of the Mass which they have found in their missals.

Name: _____

The Living Sacrifice   Quiz 18

Part I: Yes or No.

1. <u>Yes</u> Is the victim offered at Mass the same victim offered on Calvary?
2. <u>No</u> Does Jesus die again at every Mass?
3. <u>Yes</u> Does Jesus make his Body and Blood present on earth under the appearances of bread and wine?
4. <u>Yes</u> Does Christ bring his sacrifice before us in a real way at Mass?

Part II: Answer in complete sentences.

1. What are two reasons Jesus gave us the Sacrament of the Eucharist?
   <u>Jesus gave us the Sacrament of the Eucharist so that we might have eternal life and so that we might have an acceptable sacrifice to offer continually to the Father.</u>

2. What is the most perfect prayer?
   <u>The most perfect prayer is the Holy Mass.</u>

3. What are the four ends of the Mass?
   <u>The four ends of the Mass are worship (adoration), thanksgiving, satisfaction for sins, petition.</u>

Part III: Write a paragraph explaining *one* of the four ends of the Mass.

_____
_____
_____
_____
_____
_____
_____
_____
_____
_____
_____
_____
_____
_____
_____

Assess

1. Distribute the quizzes and read through them with the students to be sure they understand the questions.

2. Administer the quiz. As they hand in their work, you may orally quiz the students on the Memorization Questions from this chapter.

3. After all the quizzes have been handed in, you may wish to review the correct answers with the class.

Conclude

1. Lead the students in singing "O saving Victim," *Adoremus Hymnal*, #520.

2. End class by leading the students in the Spiritual Communion prayer (see *Teacher's Manual*, p. 397).

CHAPTER EIGHTEEN: THE LIVING SACRIFICE
ACTIVITY BOOK ANSWER KEYS

Name:_____

The Living Sacrifice

Write the significance and meaning of each term in the Sacrifice of the Mass.

Answers will vary.

1. Sacrifice: _____

_____

2. Risen Christ: _____

_____

3. Celebration: _____

_____

4. Eucharist: _____

_____

5. People of God: _____

_____

6. Merits: _____

_____

7. Memorial: _____

_____

8. Priest: _____

_____

9. The Church: _____

_____

10. The Cross: _____

_____

Name:_____

A Memorial

Answer the following questions in complete sentences.

1. What did Jesus' sacrifice do?
   Jesus' sacrifice redeemed the human race.

2. What is the difference between the Sacrifice of the Cross and the Sacrifice of the Mass?
   On the Cross, Jesus shed his blood and died; in the Mass, he offers himself under the appearances of bread and wine in an unbloody manner and without dying.

3. What is a memorial?
   A memorial is the recalling or remembrance of a past event.

4. What are we remembering?
   We are remembering the death and Resurrection of Christ.

5. Is the Mass only a memorial?
   No.

Name:_____

The Mass: Worship and Thanksgiving

Answer the following questions in complete sentences.

1. How is the Mass an act of worship?
   Men with nothing worthy to offer God have now been given a victim and a sacrifice of infinite value.

2. What was Christ's greatest gift to his Church?
   The Mass is Christ's greatest gift to his Church.

3. What can we now offer to God the Father?
   We can now offer Jesus Christ himself to God the Father.

4. Is this offering better than anything we could humanly offer?
   Yes.

5. What does "eucharist" mean?
   Eucharist means thanksgiving.

6. What do we have for which we must thank God?
   Answers will vary. E.g. life, family, friends, etc.

7. What supernatural gift has God given to us? What does this gift do for us?
   God has given us the gift of grace. This gift gives us hope of reaching heaven.

Name:_____

The Mass: Atonement and Petitioning

Answer the following questions in complete sentences.

1. What does "making satisfaction" mean?
   Making satisfaction means making up for some wrongdoing.

2. What does it mean to say that Jesus has extended his sacrifice in time and space?
   This means that there is only one Mass and it was offered on Calvary. Our participation at Mass is our time to be with Christ at the Cross.

3. What does "petition" mean?
   Petition means to ask for something.

4. Does God give us everything we ask for? Why or why not?
   No. He gives us what is best for us.

6. Why is the Mass the best means for asking the Father for things?
   It is the best means of asking for things because we are offering God the most pleasing sacrifice we have to give.

TEACHER'S NOTES

TEACHER'S NOTES

CHAPTER NINETEEN
THE FEAST OF GOD

Catechism of the Catholic Church References

Church as the Body of Christ: 787–96, 805–8
Eucharist as our Daily Bread: 2837, 2861
Fruits of Communion: 1391–1401, 1416
Holy Communion: 1355, 1382–90, 1415, 1417

Names for the Eucharist: 1328–32
Presence of Christ in the Eucharist: 1373–81, 1410, 1418
Titles of the Mass: 1328–1332

Scripture References

Bread of Life Discourse: Jn 6:35–54

Last Supper: Mt 26:17–30; Mk 14:13–26; Lk 22:11–22;
1 Cor 11:23–26

Summary of Lesson Content

Lesson 1

At Mass, we celebrate in a sacred meal the death and Resurrection of Jesus.

Mass is time consecrated to God. It is sacred time.

Proper dress and gestures are signs of reverence.

Lesson 3

Mass is the sacrifice of Christ made present.

We give God our very best as a sacrificial offering. We eat the sacrifice to receive from God his wondrous gifts. We offer Christ, truly present, to the Father. We receive his Body, Blood, Soul, and Divinity in Holy Communion to share in this sacrifice, which is pleasing to God.

Lesson 2

Communion is a holy meal. It unites us with God and with our brothers and sisters in Christ.

Lesson 4

We should offer ourselves, in union with Jesus in the Eucharist, to the Father.

Jesus feeds us in the Eucharist.

We are united with God and the members of his Body, the Church, in Holy Communion.

CHAPTER NINETEEN: THE FEAST OF GOD
LESSON ONE: HOLY CELEBRATION

Aims

The students will learn that, at Mass, we celebrate with a sacred meal the death and Resurrection of Jesus.

They will learn that Mass is time consecrated to God. It is sacred time. Proper dress and gestures are signs of reverence.

Materials

- *Activity Book*, p. 73

- Missals

Optional:
- "O Lord, I am not worthy," *Adoremus Hymnal*, #512

Begin

Write on the board all the reasons why the students like going to Mass, and all the reasons they do not like going to Mass. (Hopefully today we will change all the negatives into positives).

Like:	*Don't Like:*
Music	Early in morning
Eucharist	Bored
Family Time	Dressing up

Develop

1. Read paragraphs 1 and 2.

2. Mass is to be a celebration: Christ has died, Christ is risen, Christ will come again! Often at Mass, we find ourselves caught in a routine—an unthoughtful habit. We just say the words without thinking about them. Read through the missals and find words of celebration (e.g., Alleluia!, Peace be with you, etc.). Have the students take the time to think about what they are saying.

3. At Mass, we see many of our friends and, usually, we attend with our families. It is a great way to reconnect with people we love. Rather than a mere social gathering, however, at Mass, we are all united in the one celebration and in one Communion with our Lord.

4. Often at Mass, we feel like we just sit through the readings; if, however, we use our imagination and remember that we are inserted into the stories, the Scriptures will take on a whole new meaning. For example, what would it have been like on Noah's Ark—what a smell! Would you have been seasick? Can you imagine all the rain and the hard work of tending the animals? What would you say to God in prayer?

5. With the mystery of mystagogy, the Mass is never just the "same old" Mass; it is always a new experience.

6. We should anticipate these great events, keeping in mind that they are sacred. How should we dress? (Emphasize modesty.) How should we act? Do our gestures at Mass have meaning? Review basic Mass gestures: genuflecting, bowing, standing, sitting, kneeling, praying, etc. What can we do to help us focus? (E.g., we should stand up straight, keep our hands folded in prayer when standing, not slouch when sitting, and follow along in a missal.)

Reinforce

1. Have the students work on *Activity Book* p. 73 (see *Teacher's Manual*, p. 237).

2. Arrange for a Mass to be said for the students, for the class' intention. Before the Mass have the priest explain what he will do and what will happen at each part of the Mass. The students may do the readings, choose the songs, etc.

3. The students may create invitations for a Mass. Let them be creative in designing them.

4. Have the students work on the Memorization Questions from this chapter (see *Teacher's Manual*, p. 231).

Conclude

1. Teach the students to sing "O Lord, I am not worthy," *Adoremus Hymnal*, #512.

2. End class by leading the students in praying an Our Father (see *Teacher's Manual*, p. 396).

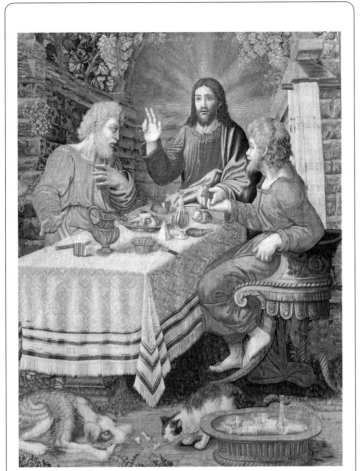

CHAPTER 19

The Feast of God

"For as often as you eat this bread and drink the chalice, you proclaim the Lord's death until he comes."

1 Corinthians 11:26

At Mass we celebrate the death and Resurrection of the Lord in a sacred banquet. These are truly matters for celebration. We should take time out for special activities to underline the significance of our redemption and to rejoice with our risen Lord.

However, this is no ordinary, casual celebration like a birthday party or a big family meal. This is a sacred celebration; it is *holy*. It is time consecrated to God, dedicated to him, and set aside for him alone. Therefore we should approach this celebration with an attitude of reverence and profound respect. We express reverence by our attitude and our actions: by proper dress, by silence, by genuflection, by prayerfulness. When we understand this, we are ready to consider Holy Mass as a celebration. The mysteries we celebrate are worthy of the deepest awe. With Jesus, as with anyone whom we love, friendship and respect must go together. But Jesus is more than just a friend; he is God. We must never forget who he is and who we are; he is the Creator, and we are his creatures.

Sacred Banquet

What is the special activity which makes the Mass a celebration? It is the sacred banquet, the holy meal—Communion. A common meal has always been a way of celebrating important occasions.

A big family meal is a good example of a celebration. We show that the cause for celebration is important to us, not only as individuals but as a family, a group, and a community. It is important enough, in fact, to take a group of individuals, each of whom could have gone his own way, and bring them together in a unifying action. Why do we all do something together? Because it is important to us. Those who participate become part of something greater than any one person.

Table of the Lord

We have seen that the Mass is the re-presentation of Christ's sacrifice on Calvary. We have watched and prayed with the priest. We now have the wonderful opportunity to go to Holy Communion, to receive Christ in the Eucharist, the Word made flesh.

In Old Testament sacrifices, the people offered God a gift, such as a lamb. The lamb was slaughtered to offer it up. But this was not all. To complete the religious ritual or celebration of the sacrifice, the people would eat the lamb. The gift that they offered was received back as a gift. The people were trying to be in closer union with God by partaking of something that had been offered to and accepted by God.

GESTURES OF THE MASS

Because we are composed of both body and soul, we can express our prayer through our bodies as we lift our hearts and minds to God.

- *Standing* is a sign of respect and honor. We stand when the priest enters and exits, during the Gospel and for certain prayers.
- *Kneeling* is a sign of homage and adoration. In the middle ages it signified homage toward a lord. That is why we kneel before our Lord in the Eucharist.
- *Sitting* is a posture of listening and meditation. We sit during the readings and the homily.
- The *Sign of the Cross* brings to mind the Cross of Christ and the Blessed Trinity. It marks the beginning and end of the Mass.
- *Bowing* shows respect, thanksgiving, and honor. We are to bow when we say the words "by the Holy Spirit he was incarnate of the Virgin Mary and became man" during the Nicene Creed; we also bow before receiving Holy Communion as a sign of our thankfulness for the great gift of the Eucharist, and when we receive special blessings.
- To *Genuflect* is a sign of worship and honor. We genuflect to Jesus in the tabernacle.

MYSTAGOGY

Mystagogy is the prayerful catechetical period following entrance into the Church. While formally it may be only a few weeks, it is an ongoing process by which the faithful enter ever more deeply into the mysteries of Christ and the Church.

Preview

In the next lesson, the students will learn about the Mass as a sacred banquet.

CHAPTER NINETEEN: THE FEAST OF GOD
LESSON TWO: SACRED BANQUET

Aims

The students will learn that Communion is a holy meal. It unites us with God and with our brothers and sisters in Christ.

Materials

- *Activity Book*, p. 74

Optional:
- "O Lord, I am not worthy," *Adoremus Hymnal*, #512

Begin

Discuss various family celebrations, such as Christmas or Easter, during which we have big meals. (Note: if we celebrate at home, how much more should we celebrate at Mass, wherein these events are made present!) Why do we share food? We are united in a common meal (e.g., if you and I both eat turkey and potatoes, then there is something the same in each of us). Certain foods are more common for celebration (e.g., wine and dessert). We might also set the table with nice dishes in order to honor the occasion and our guests.

Develop

1. Read paragraphs 3 and 4.

2. Have you ever heard the saying: "You are what you eat?" If you eat healthy food, you will be healthy. If you eat unhealthy food, you will be unhealthy. What if you eat the Eucharist? What is the Eucharist, but our Lord really and truly present under the sacramental signs of bread and wine? We do not just receive blessed bread. We receive Jesus Christ—Body, Blood, Soul, and Divinity! Therefore, when we receive Holy Communion, we receive God and his own life into us.

3. How should we prepare for such a gift?
- Be free from mortal sin
- Fast for one hour before receiving (except from water and medicine)
- Know whom we are about to receive

4. How should we receive our Lord? We should make a sign of reverence before we receive Communion, such as bowing. Then we may choose whether we receive on the hand or the tongue. Either way is acceptable, but we should know how to do both. The priest or extraordinary minister of Holy Communion will hold up our Lord in the Eucharistic Host and say: "The Body of Christ." We should reply, "Amen" and receive our Lord. If the Precious Blood is offered, he will say: "The Blood of Christ" and again we say, "Amen." We receive just a sip holding the chalice with both hands, and not letting go until the minister of the cup has a good hold on it. After receiving Jesus, we can make the Sign of the Cross and return to our pew to pray in thanksgiving.

Reinforce

1. Have the students work on *Activity Book* p. 74 (see *Teacher's Manual*, p. 237).

2. Review the reception of Holy Communion. The students should be familiar with receiving the Host in the hand and on the tongue, and in receiving from the chalice. Encourage the parents to participate in the lesson and review proper Communion procedure with them, as well.

3. Have the students work on the Memorization Questions from this chapter.

Conclude

1. Lead the students in singing "O Lord, I am not worthy," *Adoremus Hymnal*, #512.

2. End class by leading the students in praying the Our Father (see *Teacher's Manual*, p. 396).

CHAPTER 19

The Feast of God

"For as often as you eat this bread and drink the chalice, you proclaim the Lord's death until he comes."

1 Corinthians 11:26

At Mass we celebrate the death and Resurrection of the Lord in a sacred banquet. These are truly matters for celebration. We should take time out for special activities to underline the significance of our redemption and to rejoice with our risen Lord.

However, this is no ordinary, casual celebration like a birthday party or a big family meal. This is a sacred celebration; it is *holy*. It is time consecrated to God, dedicated to him, and set aside for him alone. Therefore we should approach this celebration with an attitude of reverence and profound respect. We express reverence by our attitude and our actions: by proper dress, by silence, by genuflection, by prayerfulness. When we understand this, we are ready to consider Holy Mass as a celebration. The mysteries we celebrate are worthy of the deepest awe. With Jesus, as with anyone whom we love, friendship and respect must go together. But Jesus is more than just a friend; he is God. We must never forget who he is and who we are; he is the Creator, and we are his creatures.

Sacred Banquet

What is the special activity which makes the Mass a celebration? It is the sacred banquet, the holy meal—Communion. A common meal has always been a way of celebrating important occasions.

A big family meal is a good example of a celebration. We show that the cause for celebration is important to us, not only as individuals but as a family, a group, and a community. It is important enough, in fact, to take a group of individuals, each of whom could have gone his own way, and bring them together in a unifying action. Why do we all do something together? Because it is important to us. Those who participate become part of something greater than any one person.

Table of the Lord

We have seen that the Mass is the re-presentation of Christ's sacrifice on Calvary. We have watched and prayed with the priest. We now have the wonderful opportunity to go to Holy Communion, to receive Christ in the Eucharist, the Word made flesh.

In Old Testament sacrifices, the people offered God a gift, such as a lamb. The lamb was slaughtered to offer it up. But this was not all. To complete the religious ritual or celebration of the sacrifice, the people would eat the lamb. The gift that they offered was received back as a gift. The people were trying to be in closer union with God by partaking of something that had been offered to and accepted by God.

As we have seen, the Mass is a sacrifice far greater than any other. It is the one and only perfect sacrifice because it is the sacrifice of Jesus himself. But here, too, the religious ritual is not really complete until we partake of the gift that has been offered.

We join the priest in offering Jesus to the Father; the Father accepts our gift and gives it back to us to eat. Therefore, the Mass is considered a feast, a meal, and a sacred banquet. It can be thought of as a big family meal as long as two points are kept in mind: the family consists of all those joined in the Church of Christ, and the food is the sacred Body and Blood of Christ. Holy Communion is normally meant to be received in the communal religious service which is the Mass.

We are to go forward as God's family—not alone but in company.

In the Our Father, we pray for our "daily bread," expressing our trust in God who provides for all our earthly needs. On another level, our "daily bread" is Christ, the spiritual bread in the Eucharistic banquet that we need in order to be made holy.

And we pray to "our" Father, not just "my" Father, because we are meant to grow into the perfect unity of a happy and glorious community—a family—in the Mystical Body of Christ.

In the sacred meal of Holy Mass, we come together as God's People to receive the Body of Christ in the Eucharist. As we do, we are spiritually fed by Jesus to be more truly his Body in the world.

O Sacred Banquet,
in which Christ is received,
the memory of his Passion is renewed,
the mind is filled with grace,
and a pledge of future glory is given us.
Alleluia.

Q. 71	**How is the Mass a sacrifice and a meal?** The Mass is a sacrifice because, on the altar, Jesus is offered to the Father in an unbloody re-presentation of the Sacrifice of the Cross. It is a meal because we are invited to receive Jesus, who has offered himself for us (CCC 1382).

Q. 72 *How can we most perfectly participate in the Mass?*
We can most perfectly participate in the Mass by listening to and meditating upon the Word of God, uniting ourselves in the sacrifice of Christ offered to the Father, and worthily receiving Holy Communion (CCC 1388–89)

Q. 73 *Is the same Jesus Christ, who was born of the Blessed Virgin Mary, truly present in the Eucharist?*
Yes, the same Jesus Christ, who was born of the Blessed Virgin Mary, is truly present in the Eucharist (CCC 1373).

Q. 74 *How is the Eucharist food for our souls?*
Just as normal food preserves and renews the body, the Eucharist preserves, renews, and increases the soul's life of grace we received at Baptism (CCC 1392).

Q. 75 *How does the Eucharist unite us in Christ?*
The Eucharist unites us in Christ by bringing all of the faithful into one body: the Mystical Body of Christ (CCC 1396).

OLD TESTAMENT SACRIFICES

The Old Testament is full of communion sacrifices. For example, see Leviticus 3 and 1 Samuel 1:1–8. The communion sacrifice is a ritual meal during which part of the victim was offered to God and part eaten by the worshippers, so that the sacrificial meal was "shared" with God. Discuss how the Mass is a communion sacrifice.

- What do we give to God?

- What does he give us in return?

Preview

In the next lesson, the students will learn about the table of the Lord.

Chapter Nineteen: The Feast of God
Lesson Three: Table of the Lord

Aims

The students will learn that Mass is the sacrifice of Christ made present.

They will learn that we give God our very best as a sacrificial offering. We eat the sacrifice to receive from God his wondrous gifts. We offer Christ, truly present, to the Father. We receive his Body, Blood, Soul, and Divinity in Holy Communion to share in this sacrifice, which is pleasing to God.

Materials

- *Activity Book*, p. 75

- Linens and vessels used at Mass

Optional:
- "O Lord, I am not worthy," *Adoremus Hymnal*, #512

Begin

On big family celebrations at special occasions, we might use our best dishes or set the table to honor our guests. What special things might we do?
- Set out our best table cloth
- Make a centerpiece

- Use good napkins
- Set out our best dishes and silverware

Today, we will learn how the table of the Lord is prepared.

Develop

1. Read paragraphs 5–7 from the student text.

2. Take the students to the church (or if this is not possible, arrange to do this activity in the classroom with a table). Show the students the vessels and linens used at Mass.
- Altar: It is the table of the Lord and altar of sacrifice. The altar is to be solid, immovable, made of solid material (preferably stone or precious wood). It is a symbol of Christ himself, who is the cornerstone of our faith. Show the students the altar stone and tell them which saint's relics are contained therein.
- Altar cloth: It reminds us of the holy shroud.
- Corporal: This is taken from the word for body. It is placed on the altar, upon which are placed the paten and chalice.
- Chalice: It is the cup used to contain wine, which will become the Precious Blood. It must be made of precious metal. It should be the very best, for it contains Christ.

- Paten: This is the plate upon which the host that will become the Sacred Body of Christ is placed. This, too, is made of precious metal.
- Purificator: It is a linen used to purify the vessels after the Consecration.
- Pall: It is a square to cover the chalice to protect the Precious Blood from outside elements.
- Cruets: These contain water and wine.
- Water basin (lavabo) and finger towel: These are there to wash the hands of the priest.

3. The vessels and linens used at Mass should be the very best for the sacred meal is for the Lord.

4. You may explain the vessels used in temple worship (see the facing page).

Reinforce

1. Have the students work on *Activity Book* p. 75 (see *Teacher's Manual*, p. 237).

2. Review the vessels and linens used during the Mass.

3. Have the students work on the Memorization Questions from this chapter (see *Teacher's Manual*, p. 235).

Conclude

1. Lead the students in singing "O Lord, I am not worthy," *Adoremus Hymnal*, #512.

2. End class by leading the students in praying the Our Father (see *Teacher's Manual*, p. 396).

CHAPTER 19

The Feast of God

"For as often as you eat this bread and drink the chalice, you proclaim the Lord's death until he comes."

1 Corinthians 11:26

At Mass we celebrate the death and Resurrection of the Lord in a sacred banquet. These are truly matters for celebration. We should take time out for special activities to underline the significance of our redemption and to rejoice with our risen Lord.

However, this is no ordinary, casual celebration like a birthday party or a big family meal. This is a sacred celebration; it is *holy*. It is time consecrated to God, dedicated to him, and set aside for him alone. Therefore we should approach this celebration with an attitude of reverence and profound respect. We express reverence by our attitude and our actions: by proper dress, by silence, by genuflection, by prayerfulness. When we understand this, we are ready to consider Holy Mass as a celebration. The mysteries we celebrate are worthy of the deepest awe. With Jesus, as with anyone whom we love, friendship and respect must go together. But Jesus is more than just a friend; he is God. We must never forget who he is and who we are; he is the Creator, and we are his creatures.

Sacred Banquet

What is the special activity which makes the Mass a celebration? It is the sacred banquet, the holy meal—Communion. A common meal has always been a way of celebrating important occasions.

A big family meal is a good example of a celebration. We show that the cause for celebration is important to us, not only as individuals but as a family, a group, and a community. It is important enough, in fact, to take a group of individuals, each of whom could have gone his own way, and bring them together in a unifying action. Why do we all do something together? Because it is important to us. Those who participate become part of something greater than any one person.

Table of the Lord

We have seen that the Mass is the re-presentation of Christ's sacrifice on Calvary. We have watched and prayed with the priest. We now have the wonderful opportunity to go to Holy Communion, to receive Christ in the Eucharist, the Word made flesh.

In Old Testament sacrifices, the people offered God a gift, such as a lamb. The lamb was slaughtered to offer it up. But this was not all. To complete the religious ritual or celebration of the sacrifice, the people would eat the lamb. The gift that they offered was received back as a gift. The people were trying to be in closer union with God by partaking of something that had been offered to and accepted by God.

87

As we have seen, the Mass is a sacrifice far greater than any other. It is the one and only perfect sacrifice because it is the sacrifice of Jesus himself. But here, too, the religious ritual is not really complete until we partake of the gift that has been offered.

We join the priest in offering Jesus to the Father; the Father accepts our gift and gives it back to us to eat. Therefore, the Mass is considered a feast, a meal, and a sacred banquet. It can be thought of as a big family meal as long as two points are kept in mind: the family consists of all those joined in the Church of Christ, and the food is the sacred Body and Blood of Christ. Holy Communion is normally meant to be received in the communal religious service which is the Mass.

We are to go forward as God's family—not alone but in company.

In the Our Father, we pray for our "daily bread," expressing our trust in God who provides for all our earthly needs. On another level, our "daily bread" is Christ, the spiritual bread in the Eucharistic banquet that we need in order to be made holy.

And we pray to "our" Father, not just "my" Father, because we are meant to grow into the perfect unity of a happy and glorious community—a family—in the Mystical Body of Christ.

In the sacred meal of Holy Mass, we come together as God's People to receive the Body of Christ in the Eucharist. As we do, we are spiritually fed by Jesus to be more truly his Body in the world.

O Sacred Banquet,
in which Christ is received,
the memory of his Passion is renewed,
the mind is filled with grace,
and a pledge of future glory is given us.
Alleluia.

88

VESSELS USED IN JERUSALEM TEMPLE WORSHIP

- Altar of Holocaust: This was a large altar located outside the temple proper. This is where the animal sacrifices were made. The animals were sacrificed and burnt.

- Altar of Incense: This was a small rectangular box of gold-covered cedar wood located inside the Holy Place before the entrance to the Holy of Holies. The use of incense was important in temple worship.

- Table of Proposition: This was a golden table located in the Holy Place. It held the loaves of proposition.

- Loaves of Proposition: This was the special bread that was offered to God. New loaves were placed on the table of proposition each Sabbath. When the new loaves arrived, the priests consumed the old ones in the Holy Place.

- Snuffers, bowls, knives, mortars, cups, censers: These were various articles used for worship in the temple. All were specially consecrated to God and made of gold.

I give you thanks, O LORD, with my whole heart; before the angels I sing your praise; I bow down toward your holy temple and give thanks to your name for your mercy and your faithfulness.

—Psalm 138:1–2

Preview

In the next lesson, the students will learn about the effects of Holy Communion.

CHAPTER NINETEEN: THE FEAST OF GOD
LESSON FOUR: EFFECTS OF HOLY COMMUNION

Aims

The students will learn that we should offer ourselves, in union with Jesus in the Eucharist, to the Father.

They will learn that Jesus feeds us in the Eucharist.

They will learn that we are united with God and the members of his Body, the Church, in Holy Communion.

Materials

- *Activity Book*, p. 76

Optional:
- "O Lord, I am not worthy," *Adoremus Hymnal*, #512

Begin

Holy Communion is the reception of the Eucharist—the Sacrifice of the Mass. At Mass, Jesus offers himself to the Father as a total sacrifice. God gives the Eucharist back to us so that we may share in this sacred meal. When we receive Holy Communion, we enter into union with God and his Church.

Develop

1. Finish reading the chapter with the students.

2. The Eucharist is food for the soul. Just as we need food to nourish our bodies, to keep us alive, and to make us strong, so, too, we need food for our souls to keep us alive spiritually and make us strong to overcome sin.

3. Just as Jesus is the Word made flesh in the Incarnation, so too he is the Word made flesh in the Eucharist. This divine gift for us is veiled from our eyes, so that we may not fear approaching our Lord in his wonder and awe. He feeds our souls and comes in this intimate union with man. This tremendous love is the greatest gift we could hope for. When we receive our Lord in Holy Communion, he physically remains in us as long as the species remains (about 10–15 minutes). We should spend this time in deep prayer and in union with him. Christ, in coming into us, in order to have a suitable host, forgives our venial sins.

4. In Holy Communion, we are all united in the one Christ. Christ is the head of the Church and we are the Body. He nourishes his entire Body through Holy Communion. We are closely bound to one another. We should grow in love for our neighbor, for in him is Christ our Lord. This union with Christ and the Church is referred to as the Mystical Body; we are members of this Mystical Body of Christ.

5. In receiving Communion, we receive an increase in grace. This grace makes us strong to overcome sin. It is an anticipation of the heavenly glory in which we will share in God's love and life forever.

6. When we pray the Our Father, we do not just pray "My Father." We should never be alone or selfish in our faith, for we should all be concerned about the good of our neighbor. We should help each other to get to heaven, with the assistance of the "daily bread" of the Eucharist.

Reinforce

1. Have the students work on *Activity Book* p. 76 (see *Teacher's Manual*, p. 237).

2. The students should work on a project to depict the Mystical Body of Christ.

3. Give the students time to work on the Memorization Questions and to review for the quiz.

Conclude

1. Lead the students in singing "O Lord, I am not worthy," *Adoremus Hymnal*, #512.

2. End class by leading the students in praying an Our Father (see *Teacher's Manual*, p. 396).

CHAPTER 19

The Feast of God

"For as often as you eat this bread and drink the chalice, you proclaim the Lord's death until he comes."

1 Corinthians 11:26

At Mass we celebrate the death and Resurrection of the Lord in a sacred banquet. These are truly matters for celebration. We should take time out for special activities to underline the significance of our redemption and to rejoice with our risen Lord.

However, this is no ordinary, casual celebration like a birthday party or a big family meal. This is a sacred celebration; it is *holy*. It is time consecrated to God, dedicated to him, and set aside for him alone. Therefore we should approach this celebration with an attitude of reverence and profound respect. We express reverence by our attitude and our actions: by proper dress, by silence, by genuflection, by prayerfulness. When we understand this, we are ready to consider Holy Mass as a celebration. The mysteries we celebrate are worthy of the deepest awe. With Jesus, as with anyone whom we love, friendship and respect must go together. But Jesus is more than just a friend; he is God. We must never forget who he is and who we are; he is the Creator, and we are his creatures.

Sacred Banquet

What is the special activity which makes the Mass a celebration? It is the sacred banquet, the holy meal—Communion. A common meal has always been a way of celebrating important occasions.

A big family meal is a good example of a celebration. We show that the cause for celebration is important to us, not only as individuals but as a family, a group, and a community. It is important enough, in fact, to take a group of individuals, each of whom could have gone his own way, and bring them together in a unifying action. Why do we all do something together? Because it is important to us. Those who participate become part of something greater than any one person.

Table of the Lord

We have seen that the Mass is the re-presentation of Christ's sacrifice on Calvary. We have watched and prayed with the priest. We now have the wonderful opportunity to go to Holy Communion, to receive Christ in the Eucharist, the Word made flesh.

In Old Testament sacrifices, the people offered God a gift, such as a lamb. The lamb was slaughtered to offer it up. But this was not all. To complete the religious ritual or celebration of the sacrifice, the people would eat the lamb. The gift that they offered was received back as a gift. The people were trying to be in closer union with God by partaking of something that had been offered to and accepted by God.

87

As we have seen, the Mass is a sacrifice far greater than any other. It is the one and only perfect sacrifice because it is the sacrifice of Jesus himself. But here, too, the religious ritual is not really complete until we partake of the gift that has been offered.

We join the priest in offering Jesus to the Father; the Father accepts our gift and gives it back to us to eat. Therefore, the Mass is considered a feast, a meal, and a sacred banquet. It can be thought of as a big family meal as long as two points are kept in mind: the family consists of all those joined in the Church of Christ, and the food is the sacred Body and Blood of Christ. Holy Communion is normally meant to be received in the communal religious service which is the Mass.

We are to go forward as God's family—not alone but in company.

In the Our Father, we pray for our "daily bread," expressing our trust in God who provides for all our earthly needs. On another level, our "daily bread" is Christ, the spiritual bread in the Eucharistic banquet that we need in order to be made holy.

And we pray to "our" Father, not just "my" Father, because we are meant to grow into the perfect unity of a happy and glorious community—a family—in the Mystical Body of Christ.

In the sacred meal of Holy Mass, we come together as God's People to receive the Body of Christ in the Eucharist. As we do, we are spiritually fed by Jesus to be more truly his Body in the world.

O Sacred Banquet,
in which Christ is received,
the memory of his Passion is renewed,
the mind is filled with grace,
and a pledge of future glory is given us.
Alleluia.

88

Q. 71 *How is the Mass a sacrifice and a meal?*
The Mass is a sacrifice because, on the altar, Jesus is offered to the Father in an unbloody re-presentation of the Sacrifice of the Cross. It is a meal because we are invited to receive Jesus, who has offered himself for us (CCC 1382).

Q. 72 *How can we most perfectly participate in the Mass?*
We can most perfectly participate in the Mass by listening to and meditating upon the Word of God, uniting ourselves in the sacrifice of Christ offered to the Father, and worthily receiving Holy Communion (CCC 1388–89)

Q. 73 *Is the same Jesus Christ, who was born of the Blessed Virgin Mary, truly present in the Eucharist?*
Yes, the same Jesus Christ, who was born of the Blessed Virgin Mary, is truly present in the Eucharist (CCC 1373).

Q. 74 *How is the Eucharist food for our souls?*
Just as normal food preserves and renews the body, the Eucharist preserves, renews, and increases the soul's life of grace we received at Baptism (CCC 1392).

Q. 75 *How does the Eucharist unite us in Christ?*
The Eucharist unites us in Christ by bringing all of the faithful into one body: the Mystical Body of Christ (CCC 1396).

89

SAINT TARCISIUS

Saint Tarcisius was a young boy and acolyte who died to protect Jesus in the Blessed Sacrament. During the persecution of Emperor Valerian (253–260), the Christians in Rome were forced to celebrated Mass in the catacombs—a network of tunnels many miles long that runs under the city of Rome. One day, Saint Tarcisius was assigned to take the Blessed Sacrament out of the catacombs and bring it to some Christian prisoners. Walking down the Appian Way, he was surrounded by a mob of pagan Romans who recognized him as a Christian and killed him. He was later buried in the same catacombs and is now the patron of altar boys and an example of the devotion we should have for the Blessed Sacrament.

Preview

In the next lesson, the students' understanding of the material covered in this chapter will be reviewed and assessed.

CHAPTER NINETEEN: THE FEAST OF GOD
REVIEW AND ASSESSMENT

Aims

The students' understanding of the material covered in this chapter will be reviewed and assessed.

Materials

- Quiz 19, Appendix, p. A-27

Optional:
- "O Lord, I am not worthy," *Adoremus Hymnal*, #512

Review and Enrichment

1. The students should understand that Mass is a holy celebration. We must be reverent at Mass. We are called to participate by listening and meditating upon the Word of God, uniting ourselves to Christ's sacrifice, and worthily receiving Communion.

2. The students should know how to prepare for Mass, including proper dress. They should also know the gestures of the Mass.

3. The students should understand that they are receiving Jesus Christ—Body, Blood, Soul, and Divinity—in the Eucharist.

4. The students should be familiar with the vessels and linens used at Mass.

5. The students should understand that the effects of the Eucharist include:
   - Nourishment for the soul
   - Union with the Mystical Body of Christ
   - An increase in grace
   - Strength to overcome sin
   - Anticipation of heaven
   - Forgiveness of venial sin

Name: _____

The Feast of God   Quiz 19

Part I: Yes or No.

1. <u>Yes</u> Is Mass a sacred banquet?

2. <u>Yes</u> Is Mass the re-presentation of Christ's sacrifice on Calvary?

3. <u>No</u> Is the Mass like any ordinary celebration?

4. <u>Yes</u> Is the Mass a sacred celebration?

5. <u>No</u> Can there be friendship without respect?

Part II: Answer in complete sentences.

1. What do we celebrate at Mass?
   <u>At Mass we celebrate the death and Resurrection of the Lord.</u>

2. With what kind of attitude should we approach the Mass?
   <u>We should approach the Mass with an attitude of reverence and profound respect.</u>

3. How can we express our reverence for the Mass?
   <u>We can express our reverence for the Mass by our attitude and our actions, such as proper dress, silence, genuflection, and prayerfulness.</u>

4. In the Old Testament sacrifices, what did the people have to do in order to complete the religious ritual?
   <u>In order to complete the religious ritual they would eat the lamb.</u>

5. Why is the Mass the one and only perfect sacrifice?
   <u>The Mass is the one and only perfect sacrifice because it is the sacrifice of Jesus himself.</u>

6. Why is the Mass considered a feast and a sacred banquet?
   <u>The Mass is considered a feast and a sacred banquet because we eat and drink the Body and Blood of Christ.</u>

7. What two things does "our daily bread" refer to in the Our Father?
   <u>"Our daily bread" refers to our earthly needs and to Christ, our spiritual bread in Holy Communion.</u>

Faith and Life Series • Grade 6 • Appendix A   *A-27*

Assess

1. Distribute the quizzes and read through them with the students to be sure they understand the questions.

2. Administer the quiz. As they hand in their work, you may orally quiz the students on the Memorization Questions from this chapter.

3. After all the quizzes have been handed in, you may wish to review the correct answers with the class.

Conclude

1. Lead the students in singing "O Lord, I am not worthy," *Adoremus Hymnal*, #512.

2. End class by leading the students in praying the Our Father (see *Teacher's Manual*, p. 396).

CHAPTER NINETEEN: THE FEAST OF GOD
ACTIVITY BOOK ANSWER KEYS

Name:_____

The Feast of God

Find these words about the sacred banquet in the puzzle below.

banquet	sacred meal	Real Presence	offer
Mass	Holy Communion	daily bread	receive
gift	Paschal Lamb	Eucharist	Jesus
mystery	spiritual food	Mystical Body	Host
bread			wine
Passover	Lamb of God	sacrifice	unite

```
Y L A B B B B O B O G O O D C U E
E M A S S R R E F F O O O Q N U
A Y E S E E M F O N A C D B
L S Y T L A M B O F G O D E A
A T D P I D M M L I S I R N I C
E E O A U N I A O A N N Q M L I
M R B E I N U L A A T U W Y Y F
D L A C I H T W L C S E M I I B
E L A C I H A O T M M S N R R I
R G C R N J E H M Y Y O P P E C
C G I E F J E C M U S C I A A A
A P T F O E E S E B T Y R S D S
S B S I T S M A U R I L I C A C
L O Y S A P A P A S S O V E R A
A D M E N T S I R A H C U E I
M R E R E A L P R E S E N C E L
```

Faith and Life Series • Grade 6 • Chapter 19 • Lesson 1 73

Name:_____

Sacred Banquet

Answer the following questions in complete sentences.

1. What is Communion?
   Communion is a sacred banquet or a holy meal.

2. What is one way of celebrating important occasions?
   A common meal is one way of celebrating important occasions.

3. Is community important when you celebrate together?
   Yes.

4. Does sharing a meal with your family bring you closer together?
   Answers will vary—hopefully, yes.

Fill in the table below to see how a family meal can be a sign that points to the sacred banquet, Holy Mass

FAMILY MEAL	HOLY MASS
• Do people come together?	Answers will vary.
• Do you celebrate special occasions together with a feast?	
• Do you gather to eat special foods?	
• Does sharing the meal bring you closer together?	
• Is there proper behavior to be used at the table?	
• Do you dress up for special occasions?	

74 *Faith and Life Series • Grade 6 • Chapter 19 • Lesson 2*

Name:_____

Table of the Lord

Answer the following questions in complete sentences.

1. What is the big "table" at the front of the church called?
   Altar

2. What is the "cup" that holds the Precious Blood called?
   Chalice

3. What is the little "plate" that holds the Hosts called?
   Paten

4. What is the "tablecloth" called?
   Altar Cloth

5. What are the little containers that hold the wine and water called?
   Cruets

6. What is the little white square that is put over the cup called?
   Pall

7. What is the white linen cloth used to purify the vessels after Communion called?
   Purificator

8. What kind of "lighting" is used at the Lord's table?
   Candles

9. What kind of "clothing" is worn by the priest at the Lord's table?
   Vestments

10. What is the big "book" on the Lord's table called?
    Sacramentary

11. What is the "smoke" sometimes used at Mass called?
    Incense

Faith and Life Series • Grade 6 • Chapter 19 • Lesson 3 75

Name:_____

The Mass

Explain how the Mass is:

1. A Sacrifice.
   Answers to all the following will vary, but should be based on pp. 87 and 88 of the student text.

2. The Passover Meal of Christians.

3. A Sacred Meal.

4. The Perfect Prayer and Act of Worship.

76 *Faith and Life Series • Grade 6 • Chapter 19 • Lesson 4*

TEACHER'S NOTES

CHAPTER TWENTY
PROMISE AND FULFILLMENT

Catechism of the Catholic Church References

Eucharist as Our Daily Bread: 2837, 2831
Fruits of Communion: 1391–1401, 1416
Holy Communion: 1355, 1382–90, 1415, 1417
Jesus: the Only Son of God: 441–45, 454
Man as Body and Soul: 362–68, 382

Miracles and Other Signs of the Kingdom: 547–50, 567
Mystery of Faith: 42, 50, 158, 206, 230, 234, 237, 1066
Presence of Christ in the Eucharist: 1373–81, 1410, 1418
Proclamation of the Kingdom of God: 543–46

Scripture References

Bread of Life Discourse: Jn 6:35–69
Last Supper: Mk 14:22–24
Sending of the Holy Spirit: Jn 14:15–21

Sending Forth of the Apostles at the Ascension: Mt 28:16–20
Unworthy Reception of Eucharist: 1 Cor 11:26–31

Summary of Lesson Content

Lesson 1

Jesus is the Bread of Life.

We must eat his Body and drink his Blood in the Eucharist. This is a mystery of faith.

Lesson 3

When Jesus speaks of the Eucharist being his Body and Blood, he is not speaking figuratively or symbolically. This is to be understood literally.

The Eucharist is spiritual food—food for our souls.

Lesson 2

If we believe in Jesus, we will do what he has commanded.

The Apostles came to believe in Jesus because of his teaching and miracles.

Lesson 4

The steps to a worthy reception of Holy Communion include being free from mortal sin, fasting for one hour, knowing whom we are to receive, reverently receiving, and offering thanksgiving.

The effects of a worthy reception of the Eucharist include an increase in grace, growth in holiness, pardon of venial sins, and strength to overcome sin.

CHAPTER TWENTY: PROMISE AND FULFILLMENT
LESSON ONE: DO YOU ALSO WISH TO GO AWAY

Aims

The students will learn that Jesus is the Bread of Life.

They will learn that we must eat his Body and drink his Blood in the Eucharist. This is a mystery of faith.

Materials

- *Activity Book*, p. 77
- Bible

Optional:
- "Godhead here in hiding," *Adoremus Hymnal*, #511

Begin

Read John 6:35–67. Ask some questions of the students to be sure they understand. *Causing general public outcry by Offense*
- What was so scandalous about Jesus' teaching? *Offense*
- Why couldn't some of the disciples accept this teaching?
- When they murmured against Jesus' teaching, did he make apologies for it?

- How did many of the followers of Jesus react?
- Why did they not follow Jesus anymore?
- How would you have reacted at that time?
- Knowing now how Jesus would fulfill this, do you believe?

Develop

1. Read paragraphs 1–4.

2. You may discuss two common arguments against the Eucharist:
- Cannibalism: Is receiving the Eucharist cannibalism? No, because the species remain the same. Although the substance changes, it still looks, tastes, feels, and smells like bread and wine.
- Symbolism: Is the Eucharist only a symbol of Jesus' Body and Blood? No. Jesus did not say at the Last Supper: "This is a symbol of my Body" and "This chalice is a symbol of my Blood." It truly is Jesus' Body and Blood—we know this because he said so!

3. Do all people believe in the Eucharist? Sadly, no. Most other Christian denominations do not believe in the Real Presence of the Eucharist and cannot have the Eucharist in their churches because they do not have valid Holy Orders

(they cannot trace their priesthood back to the Apostles and Christ as we can in the Catholic Church). Other Christian denominations often have communion services, during which they eat bread and drink wine or grape juice and recall Jesus' gift of himself, as in a spiritual communion.

4. You may review some of the heresies or teachings of non-Catholics. Because they do not believe in the Eucharist, they are not united in the Faith. This is why non-Catholics cannot receive Communion in a Catholic church—for in saying "Amen" they are saying that they believe (it would be a lie). Also, Catholics do not share in communion at non-Catholic churches, for we know that they do not share our Faith. The only exception to this is the Orthodox Church, which has valid Sacraments; however, because we are not in union with one another, we should only receive Communion from them under extraordinary circumstances.

Reinforce

1. Have the students work on *Activity Book* p. 77 (see *Teacher's Manual*, p. 249).

2. The students should begin working on the Memorization Questions from this chapter (see *Teacher's Manual*, p. 245).

Conclude

1. Teach the students to sing "Godhead here in hiding," *Adoremus Hymnal*, #511.

2. End class by leading the students in the Prayer after Communion (on the facing page).

CHAPTER 20

Promise and Fulfillment

"I am the living bread which came down from heaven; if any one eats of this bread, he will live for ever; and the bread which I shall give for the life of the world is my flesh."

John 6:51

In Saint John's Gospel we read the text,

"This is a hard saying" (Jn 6:60).

These were the words with which many of his followers greeted Jesus' announcement of the Holy Eucharist. If Jesus had been misunderstood he could have set things straight before they walked away from him. But Jesus did not stop them. In fact, the Gospel says: "But Jesus, knowing in himself that his disciples murmured at it, said to them, 'Do you take offense at this?'" (Jn 6:61). The Gospel goes on to say: "After this many of his disciples drew back and no longer walked with him" (Jn 6:66).

What had Jesus said, exactly, which they would not accept?

[H]e who eats my flesh and drinks my blood has eternal life, and I will raise him up at the last day. For my flesh is food indeed, and my blood is drink indeed (Jn 6:54–55).

And what did those who did not believe say?

"How can this man give us his flesh to eat?" (Jn 6:52).

We Have Come To Believe

The Gospel goes on to tell us:

Jesus said to the Twelve, "Will you also go away?" Simon Peter answered him, "Lord, to whom shall we go? You have the words of eternal life; and we have believed, and have come to know, that you are the Holy One of God" (Jn 6:67–69).

Jesus had not led his followers to this point to catch them unprepared. As Peter put it, they had "believed and come to know."

The Apostles believed not because they fully understood, but because they had faith in Jesus. This is what Jesus was looking for. The Gospel says: "Then they said to him, 'What must we do, to be doing the works of God?' Jesus answered them, 'This is the work of God, that you believe in him whom he has sent'" (Jn 6:28–29). Jesus had given them more than sufficient evidence to believe in him. He had been going about doing good, teaching and preaching the Good News of the Kingdom of God, and performing many miracles.

In every generation Jesus looks for generous people who really hear him, who really want to be his followers and really put their faith in him, who will not turn away because of the "hard saying" about the Eucharist, who will say with Saint Peter: "You have the words of eternal life; and we have believed, and have come to know, that you are the Holy One of God" (Jn 6:68–69).

My Flesh Is Food Indeed

Just what was Christ offering the crowds when he announced the Eucharist? He said that his "Flesh is food indeed" and his "Blood is real drink." We have seen that he meant this to be taken literally. However, he did not mean that the Eucharist would be food for our bodies. The Eucharist is spiritual food, nourishment for our souls, which comes to us through our bodies.

What happens when we receive the Eucharist worthily? Because the Eucharist truly is the Body and Blood of Jesus, it is the source of all grace. It can transform us by the increase of sanctifying grace, which is God's life in the soul. We grow in holiness, which means that we become more like Jesus. Receiving the Eucharist worthily pardons our venial sins. Because it is such "rich and nourishing" food

90

91

EUCHARISTIC BELIEFS

For 1500 years all Christians were united in their belief in the Real Presence of Jesus in the Eucharist, but with the Protestant Reformation, all sorts of new beliefs and heresies appeared. The following are three of the most common misunderstandings:

- Consubstantiation: This is the belief that the bread and wine remain bread and wine, but Jesus is somehow present *with* them; the bread and wine *coexist* with Jesus. This belief came from Martin Luther.

- Spiritual Presence: This is the belief that Jesus is *spiritually* present, but not *really* present. This was taught by John Calvin.

- Symbolism: This belief teaches that Jesus is not present at all. The bread and wine are just *symbols* of his Body and Blood. This was taught by Huldreich Zwingli and is probably the most common view in Protestant churches today.

PRAYER AFTER COMMUNION OF SAINT PIO OF PIETRELCINA

Stay with me, Lord, for you are my life, and without you, I am without fervor.

Stay with me, Lord, for you are my light, and without you, I am in darkness.

Stay with me, Lord, to show me your will.

Stay with me, Lord, so that I hear your voice and follow you.

Stay with me, Lord, for I desire to love you very much, and always be in your company.

Stay with me, Lord, if you wish me to be faithful to you.

Stay with me, Lord, for as poor as my soul is, I wish it to be a place of consolation for you, a nest of love.

Preview

In the next lesson, the students will learn more about why we can believe in the Eucharist.

Chapter Twenty: Promise and Fulfillment
Lesson Two: Yes, Lord, I Believe

Aims

The students will learn that if we believe in Jesus, we will do what he has commanded.

They will learn that the Apostles came to believe in Jesus because of his teaching and miracles.

Materials

- *Activity Book*, p. 78

- Bible

Optional:
- "Godhead here in hiding," *Adoremus Hymnal*, #511

Begin

Read the rest of the Bread of Life discourse with the students: Jn 6:67–69.

The students may dramatize the entire Bread of Life discourse, using the Bible as a script.

Develop

1. Read paragraphs 5–8.

2. You may choose to reinforce the teaching on the primacy of Peter, who again in this story answers on behalf of all the Apostles.

3. Why did the Apostles accept Jesus' teaching? They believed in Jesus. Why had the Apostles come to believe in Jesus?
  - They spent time with him.
  - They saw Jesus doing good, being a witness of God.
  - They heard his teachings and they made sense. (Jesus also explained his parables to the Apostles when they were alone so that they had a clear understanding of the teachings of Christ.)
  - They saw Jesus work many miracles, such as healing people, calming a storm, walking on water, forgiving sins.
  - They saw how, when people encountered Christ, their lives were changed for the better.
  - They knew the changes they saw in themselves (from being fishermen, tax collectors, etc. to becoming students of Christ, given the power to heal people in his name, to preach in his name, etc.).

4. At the time of the Bread of Life discourse, the Apostles did not know of the greatest miracle of Christ: his Resurrection. We know that Jesus is the Son of God—not just a great prophet—because he rose from the dead!

5. You may discuss the need to take God at his word (that is, believe what he tells us because he is God) even when we do not understand. We need faith to believe in the Eucharist and to give our lives fully to God. Many things in this world only make sense in light of faith. What a comfort we find in our faith in the teachings of Christ: e.g., our sins are forgiven, he is present with us.

Reinforce

1. Have the students work on *Activity Book* p. 78 (see *Teacher's Manual*, p. 249).

2. Review basic Christian apologetics concerning the Eucharist.

3. The students should work on the Memorization Questions from this chapter (see *Teacher's Manual*, p. 245).

Conclude

1. Lead the students in singing "Godhead here in hiding," *Adoremus Hymnal*, #511.

2. End class by leading the students in the Prayer after Communion (see *Teacher's Manual*, p. 241).

CHAPTER 20

Promise and Fulfillment

"I am the living bread which came down from heaven; if any one eats of this bread, he will live for ever; and the bread which I shall give for the life of the world is my flesh."

John 6:51

In Saint John's Gospel we read the text,

"This is a hard saying" (Jn 6:60).

These were the words with which many of his followers greeted Jesus' announcement of the Holy Eucharist. If Jesus had been misunderstood he could have set things straight before they walked away from him. But Jesus did not stop them. In fact, the Gospel says: "But Jesus, knowing in himself that his disciples murmured at it, said to them, 'Do you take offense at this?'" (Jn 6:61). The Gospel goes on to say: "After this many of his disciples drew back and no longer walked with him" (Jn 6:66).

What had Jesus said, exactly, which they would not accept?

[H]e who eats my flesh and drinks my blood has eternal life, and I will raise him up at the last day. For my flesh is food indeed, and my blood is drink indeed (Jn 6:54–55).

And what did those who did not believe say?

"How can this man give us his flesh to eat?" (Jn 6:52).

We Have Come To Believe

The Gospel goes on to tell us:

Jesus said to the Twelve, "Will you also go away?" Simon Peter answered him, "Lord, to whom shall we go? You have the words of eternal life; and we have believed, and have come to know, that you are the Holy One of God" (Jn 6:67–69).

Jesus had not led his followers to this point to catch them unprepared. As Peter put it, they had "believed and come to know."

The Apostles believed not because they fully understood, but because they had faith in Jesus. This is what Jesus was looking for. The Gospel says: "Then they said to him, 'What must we do, to be doing the works of God?' Jesus answered them, 'This is the work of God, that you believe in him whom he has sent'" (Jn 6:28–29). Jesus had given them more than sufficient evidence to believe in him. He had been going about doing good, teaching and preaching the Good News of the Kingdom of God, and performing many miracles.

In every generation Jesus looks for generous people who really hear him, who really want to be his followers and really put their faith in him, who will not turn away because of the "hard saying" about the Eucharist, who will say with Saint Peter: "You have the words of eternal life; and we have believed, and have come to know, that you are the Holy One of God" (Jn 6:68–69).

My Flesh Is Food Indeed

Just what was Christ offering the crowds when he announced the Eucharist? He said that his "Flesh is food indeed" and his "Blood is real drink." We have seen that he meant this to be taken literally. However, he did not mean that the Eucharist would be food for our bodies. The Eucharist is spiritual food, nourishment for our souls, which comes to us through our bodies.

What happens when we receive the Eucharist worthily? Because the Eucharist truly is the Body and Blood of Jesus, it is the source of all grace. It can transform us by the increase of sanctifying grace, which is God's life in the soul. We grow in holiness, which means that we become more like Jesus. Receiving the Eucharist worthily pardons our venial sins. Because it is such "rich and nourishing" food

90

91

SAINT JOHN THE BELOVED

Jesus loved all of his Apostles, but the Gospel of John tells us that Jesus was especially close to one of them. John 13:23 tells us that the disciple "whom Jesus loved" sat next to Jesus at the Last Supper and asked him who would betray him. This Apostle was the only one present at the Cross and it was to him that Jesus said "Behold, your mother" (Jn 19:26). On the day of the Resurrection, this disciple ran with Peter to the tomb and he first recognized Jesus while fishing with Peter (Jn 20:2–8; 21:7). It is not until the end of the Gospel of John that we discover the identity of this special Apostle. John 21:24 says "This is the disciple who is bearing witness to these things, and who has written these things; and we know that his testimony is true." Saint John dedicated the rest of his life to teaching people about Jesus. At one point, he was exiled to the prison island of Patmos in the Eastern Mediterranean for being a Christian. This disciple "whom Jesus loved" also had a great love for Jesus and his Church. In 1 John 4:7–11 we read, "Beloved, let us love one another; for love is of God and he who loves is born of God and knows God. He who does not love does not know God; for God is love. . . . In this is love, not that we loved God but that he loved us and sent his Son to be the expiation for our sins. Beloved, if God so loved us, we also ought to love one another."

Truly, truly, I say to you, he who believes in me will also do the works that I do; and greater works than these he will do, because I go to the Father. Whatever you ask in my name, I will do it, that the Father may be glorified in the Son; if you ask anything in my name, I will do it.
—John 14:12–14

Preview

In the next lesson, the students will learn about the Real Presence of Christ in the Eucharist.

CHAPTER TWENTY: PROMISE AND FULFILLMENT
LESSON THREE: REAL PRESENCE

Aims

The students will learn that when Jesus speaks of the Eucharist being his Body and Blood, he is not speaking figuratively or symbolically. This is to be understood literally.

They will learn that the Eucharist is spiritual food—food for our souls.

Materials

• *Activity Book*, p. 79

Optional:
• "Godhead here in hiding," *Adoremus Hymnal*, #511

Begin

Review the teaching of transubstantiation. Review that before Consecration, the host and wine are simply bread and wine. After Consecration (which effects transubstantiation), the species remains the same, but the substance is changed into the Body, Blood, Soul, and Divinity of Jesus Christ. He is wholly present in the Sacred Host. He is wholly present in the Precious Blood. If the Host is broken, Jesus is wholly present in each of its parts, including the tiniest piece. This is the Real Presence of Christ.

Develop

1. Read paragraph 9 from the student text.

2. In the Old Testament, it was forbidden to drink an animal's blood. (See Gen 9:3–4.) Blood was seen as its life. If one drank an animal's blood, it was a sign of sharing in the life of a mere animal. Man was allowed to eat the flesh of an animal. Often sacrificial meals included animal meat. It was offered to God in a burnt offering, and man ate some of its flesh as a sign of unity with the one he shared his meal with (God). From this, we know that eating flesh is a bond of unity. We also know that drinking blood is sharing in life.

3. At the Last Supper, Jesus instituted the Eucharist: read the account from Mark 14:22–24. Jesus clearly said: "This is my Body," and "This is my Blood," and he gave it to his disciples to eat and drink. Through the Eucharist, Jesus fulfilled the Bread of Life discourse. He also invited his faithful disciples, who believed, to receive the Eucharist.

4. In receiving Jesus' Body, we enter a unity with him and all who receive the Eucharist. In receiving Jesus' Blood, we share in his life—the divine and eternal life. Just as God became man, we become as God through this unity with the Son. Through our unity with the Son—being part of his Body, we call God "Father," and we share in his life and the promise of his eternal reward.

5. The Eucharist is nourishment for our souls. Its sacramental grace strengthens our souls, forgiving our venial sins and giving us the strength not to sin again.

6. Review and discuss the intimacy of Christ with the soul in Holy Communion. Our tongues become as patens, and our hearts as chalices. We should be living tabernacles.

Reinforce

1. Have the students work on *Activity Book* p. 79 (see *Teacher's Manual*, p. 249).

2. Have the students research what some of the saints have said about Holy Communion.

3. Have the students work on the Memorization Questions from this chapter.

Conclude

1. Lead the students in singing "Godhead here in hiding," *Adoremus Hymnal*, #511.

2. End class by leading the students in the Prayer after Communion (see *Teacher's Manual*, p. 241).

want to be his followers and really put their faith in him, who will not turn away because of the "hard saying" about the Eucharist, who will say with Saint Peter: "You have the words of eternal life; and we have believed, and have come to know, that you are the Holy One of God" (Jn 6:68–69).

My Flesh Is Food Indeed

Just what was Christ offering the crowds when he announced the Eucharist? He said that his "Flesh is food indeed" and his "Blood is real drink." We have seen that he meant this to be taken literally. However, he did not mean that the Eucharist would be food for our bodies. The Eucharist is spiritual food, nourishment for our souls, which comes to us through our bodies.

What happens when we receive the Eucharist worthily? Because the Eucharist truly is the Body and Blood of Jesus, it is the source of all grace. It can transform us by the increase of sanctifying grace, which is God's life in the soul. We grow in holiness, which means that we become more like Jesus. Receiving the Eucharist worthily pardons our venial sins. Because it is such "rich and nourishing" food

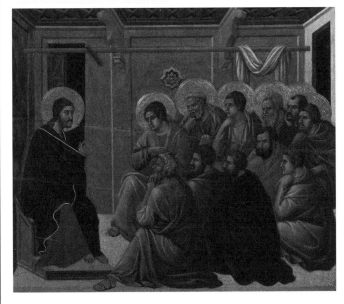

91

for our souls, it cancels out our lesser failings. It also strengthens us to overcome temptations and helps us to break bad habits.

Christ has a plan for extending his Kingdom to the whole world: he offers his followers the invitation to become other Christs. Those who feed on his Body and Blood have life in him—Christ's life, which does not destroy our personality, but perfects, enriches, and preserves it to life everlasting.

"I am the living bread which came down from heaven; if any one eats of this bread, he will live for ever."

John 6:51

Q. 76 *Why do you believe that Jesus Christ is truly present in the Eucharist?*
I believe that Jesus Christ is truly present in the Eucharist because he himself said that he would give us his Body to eat and his Blood to drink. At the Last Supper, he consecrated bread and wine and made them his Body and Blood, and commanded the Church to "Do this in memory of me" (CCC 1375).

Q. 77 *What effect does the Eucharist have on one who receives it worthily?*
In one who receives it worthily, the Holy Eucharist preserves and increases grace, which is the life of the soul. The Holy Eucharist takes away venial sin and strengthens us against mortal sin, and it gives spiritual joy and consolation by increasing charity and the hope of eternal life, of which it is the pledge (CCC 1392, 1394, 1402).

Q. 78 *How do we receive the Eucharist worthily?*
To receive the Eucharist worthily, we must be in a state of grace, we must recognize whom we are receiving in Communion, and we must participate in the Eucharistic fast (CCC 1385, 1387).

92

THE SAINTS ON COMMUNION

"The celebration of the Holy Mass is as valuable as the death of Jesus on the Cross."
—Saint Thomas Aquinas

"Man should tremble, the world should vibrate, all heaven should be deeply moved when the Son of God appears on the altar in the hands of the priest."
—Saint Francis of Assisi

"It would be easier for the earth to carry on without the sun than without the Holy Mass."
—Saint Pio of Pietrelcina

"If the angels could envy, they would envy us for Holy Communion."
—Saint Pope Pius X

"Put all the good works in the world against one Holy Mass; they will be as a grain of sand beside a mountain."
—Saint John Vianney

When you have received Him, stir up your heart to do Him homage; speak to Him about your spiritual life, gazing upon Him in your soul where He is present for your happiness; welcome Him as warmly as possible, and behave outwardly in such a way that your actions may give proof to all of His Presence.
—Saint Francis de Sales

Preview

In the next lesson, the students will learn about worthy reception of Holy Communion.

CHAPTER TWENTY: PROMISE AND FULFILLMENT
LESSON FOUR: LORD, I AM NOT WORTHY

Aims

The students will learn that the steps to a worthy reception of Holy Communion include being free from mortal sin, fasting for one hour, knowing whom we are to receive, reverently receiving, and offering thanksgiving.

They will learn that the effects of a worthy reception of the Eucharist include an increase in grace, growth in holiness, pardon of venial sins, and strength to overcome sin.

Materials

• *Activity Book*, p. 80

Optional:
• "Godhead here in hiding," *Adoremus Hymnal*, #511

Begin

Pose this question to the students: if you had a really beautiful treasure (such as a large diamond) of great value, what would you do with it?
• Would you store it in a trash can?
• Would you trade it for a toy worth much less?
• Would you care for it? How?

• Would you want to show it to others?
• Would you be protective of it?
• Would you handle it with care?

How much more should we value our Lord in the Eucharist?

Develop

1. Finish reading the chapter with the students.

2. The Church has the duty to protect her Sacraments and to ensure that they are received worthily. (E.g., only Catholics who are in the state of grace may receive Holy Communion.)

3. Review the steps to a worthy Communion:
• Be free from mortal sin (be in a state of grace)
• Fast for one hour (except from water and medicine)
• Know whom you are about to receive
• Receive reverently
• Offer prayers of thanksgiving

4. You may remind the students that the Sacraments are effective ex opere operato (by the work worked). That is, if the proper minister uses the right matter and form with the intention of doing what the Church intends, the Sacrament is effected (so if a priest uses bread and wine and says: "This is my Body" and "This is the chalice of my Blood" it becomes the Body, Blood, Soul, and Divinity of Jesus Christ, regardless of the priest's own holiness or failings). However, how much we benefit from the Sacraments is dependent upon our internal disposition. Are we in the state of grace? Do we believe? Have we fasted? Do we understand the great mystery before us? Do we desire the effects of the Sacrament?

5. Review the effects of worthy Holy Communion: union with Christ and his Church, increase of grace, forgiveness of venial sin, strengthening of the soul to overcome sin, anticipation of heaven.

6. Read from 1 Corinthians 11:26–31 about unworthy reception of Holy Communion. Unworthy reception of the Eucharist is a grave sin, called sacrilege.

Reinforce

1. Have the students work on *Activity Book* p. 80 (see *Teacher's Manual*, p. 249).

2. Give the students time to work on the Memorization Questions and to study for their chapter quiz.

Conclude

1. Lead the students in singing "Godhead here in hiding," *Adoremus Hymnal*, #511.

2. End class by leading the students in the Prayer after Communion (see *Teacher's Manual*, p. 245).

want to be his followers and really put their faith in him, who will not turn away because of the "hard saying" about the Eucharist, who will say with Saint Peter: "You have the words of eternal life; and we have believed, and have come to know, that you are the Holy One of God" (Jn 6:68–69).

My Flesh Is Food Indeed

Just what was Christ offering the crowds when he announced the Eucharist? He said that his "Flesh is food indeed" and his "Blood is real drink." We have seen that he meant this to be taken literally. However, he did not mean that the Eucharist would be food for our bodies. The Eucharist is spiritual food, nourishment for our souls, which comes to us through our bodies.

What happens when we receive the Eucharist worthily? Because the Eucharist truly is the Body and Blood of Jesus, it is the source of all grace. It can transform us by the increase of sanctifying grace, which is God's life in the soul. We grow in holiness, which means that we become more like Jesus. Receiving the Eucharist worthily pardons our venial sins. Because it is such "rich and nourishing" food for our souls, it cancels out our lesser failings. It also strengthens us to overcome temptations and helps us to break bad habits.

Christ has a plan for extending his Kingdom to the whole world: he offers his followers the invitation to become other Christs. Those who feed on his Body and Blood have life in him—Christ's life, which does not destroy our personality, but perfects, enriches, and preserves it to life everlasting.

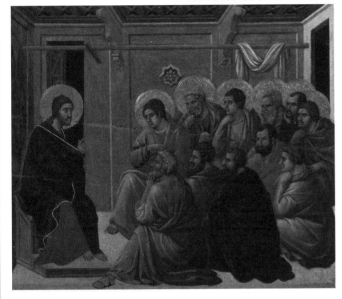

91

92

"I am the living bread which came down from heaven; if any one eats of this bread, he will live for ever."

John 6:51

Q. 76 *Why do you believe that Jesus Christ is truly present in the Eucharist?*

I believe that Jesus Christ is truly present in the Eucharist because he himself said that he would give us his Body to eat and his Blood to drink. At the Last Supper, he consecrated bread and wine and made them his Body and Blood, and commanded the Church to "Do this in memory of me" (CCC 1375).

Q. 77 *What effect does the Eucharist have on one who receives it worthily?*

In one who receives it worthily, the Holy Eucharist preserves and increases grace, which is the life of the soul. The Holy Eucharist takes away venial sin and strengthens us against mortal sin, and it gives spiritual joy and consolation by increasing charity and the hope of eternal life, of which it is the pledge (CCC 1392, 1394, 1402).

Q. 78 *How do we receive the Eucharist worthily?*

To receive the Eucharist worthily, we must be in a state of grace, we must recognize whom we are receiving in Communion, and we must participate in the Eucharistic fast (CCC 1385, 1387).

MORE SAINTS ON COMMUNION

"One single Mass gives more honor to God than all the penances of the saints, the labors of the apostles, the sufferings of the martyrs, and even the burning love of the Blessed Mother of God."

—Saint Alphonsus Liguori

"Do you realize that Jesus is there in the tabernacle expressly for you, for you alone? He burns with the desire to come into your heart."

—Saint Thérèse of Lisieux

"When you see [the body of Christ] set before you, say to yourself: 'Because of this Body I am no longer earth and ashes, no longer a prisoner, but free. . . . This body, nailed and scourged, was more than death could stand against. . . . This is even that Body, the bloodstained, the pierced, and that out of which gushed forth the saving fountains, the one of blood, the other of water, for all the world.' . . . This Body has he given to us both to hold and to eat; a thing appropriate to his intense love."

—Saint John Chrysostom

If Christ did not want to dismiss the Jews without food in the desert for fear that they would collapse on the way, it was to teach us that it is dangerous to try to get to heaven without the Bread of Heaven.

—Saint Jerome

Preview

In the next lesson, the students' understanding of the material covered in this chapter will be reviewed and assessed.

CHAPTER TWENTY: PROMISE AND FULFILLMENT
REVIEW AND ASSESSMENT

Aims

The students' understanding of the material covered in this chapter and unit will be reviewed and assessed.

Materials

- Quiz 20, Appendix, p. A-28

Optional:
- "Godhead here in hiding," *Adoremus Hymnal*, #511

Review and Enrichment

1. Have the students explain that not all people believe in the Eucharist. Why cannot non-Catholics receive the Eucharist? What are some heresies about the Eucharist?

2. Why can we believe in the Eucharist?

3. Why do we receive Jesus' Body and Blood in Holy Communion? Can we take this teaching literally?

4. The students should have received the teachings on the Eucharist:
   - Ex opere operato
   - Opus operantis
   - Effects of worthy Communion
   - Grave sin of unworthy Communion

Assess

1. Distribute the quizzes and read through them with the students to be sure they understand the questions.

2. Administer the quiz. As they hand in their work, you may orally quiz the students on the Memorization Questions from this chapter.

3. After all the quizzes have been handed in, you may wish to review the correct answers with the class.

Conclude

1. Lead the students in singing "Godhead here in hiding," *Adoremus Hymnal*, #511.

2. End class by leading the Prayer after Communion (see *Teacher's Manual*, p. 241).

CHAPTER TWENTY: PROMISE AND FULFILLMENT
ACTIVITY BOOK ANSWER KEYS

Name:_____

The Acceptance of the Father's Will

Answer the following questions in complete sentences.

1. What teaching of Jesus turned many people away?

   Jesus' teaching of the Holy Eucharist turned many people away.

2. What could they not believe?

   They could not believe that "[H]e who eats my flesh and drinks my blood has eternal life, and I will raise him up on the last day."

3. How did Jesus make this happen?

   Jesus made this happen because he is God.

4. When did Jesus make it happen?

   Jesus made it happen at the Last Supper.

5. How are we able to partake in this gift?

   We are able to partake in this gift when we go to Mass.

6. Why do we need to have faith?

   Answers will vary.

7. Do all people believe in the Real Presence in the Eucharist? Why or why not?

   No. Answers will vary as to why.

Name:_____

This is My Body, This is My Blood

Answer the following questions in complete sentences.

1. Is the same Jesus who was born on earth of the Virgin Mary present in the Eucharist?

   Yes.

2. Why do you believe that Jesus Christ is truly present in the Eucharist?

   Answers will vary. Student text answer is: I believe that Jesus Christ is truly present in the Eucharist because he himself said that he would give us his Body to eat and his Blood to drink. At the Last Supper, he consecrated bread and wine and made them his Body and Blood, and commanded the Church to "Do this in memory of me."

3. What effect does the Eucharist have on one who receives it worthily?

   In one who receives it worthily, the Holy Eucharist preserves and increases grace, which is the life of the soul. The Holy Eucharist takes away venial sin and strengthens us against mortal sin, and it gives spiritual joy and consolation by increasing charity and the hope of eternal life.

4. How do we worthily receive the Eucharist?

   To receive the Eucharist worthily, we must be in a state of grace, we must recognize whom we are receiving in Communion, and we must participate in the Eucharistic fast.

Name:_____

Transubstantiation

Answer the following questions in complete sentences.

1. What is present before the Consecration?

   Before the Consecration, bread and wine are present.

2. What is present after the Consecration?

   After the Consecration, Jesus is present, Body, Blood, Soul, and Divinity.

3. What is this change called?

   This change is called transubstantiation.

4. Why do we say the bread and wine have changed when they still look, taste, smell, and feel like bread and wine?

   Answers will vary.

This is my body which is given for you. Do this in remembrance of me.
Luke 22:19

This chalice which is poured out for you is the new covenant in my blood.
Luke 22:20

Name:_____

Worthy Reception

Answer the following questions in complete sentences.

1. Why is it important to receive the Eucharist worthily?

   Answers will vary.

2. What are the steps to receiving the Eucharist worthily?

   1. Be in a state of grace.
   2. Recognize whom we are receiving.
   3. Participate in the Eucharistic fast.

3. Can you receive Holy Communion in a state of mortal sin?

   No.

4. If you do, what is this called?

   This is called sacrilege.

5. If you are in the state of mortal sin, what must you do before you receive Holy Communion?

   You must have your mortal sin forgiven in the Sacrament of Penance.

6. What must you think about before you receive Holy Communion?

   We must think about whom we are about to receive, that is, Jesus.

7. Why must we fast before receiving Holy Communion?

   Answers will vary.

8. Explain the Eucharistic fast.

   We may not eat or drink anything but water or medications for one hour before we receive Communion.

TEACHER'S NOTES

TEACHER'S NOTES

CHAPTER TWENTY-ONE
NEW LIFE

Catechism of the Catholic Church References

Apparitions of the Risen One: 641–44
Ascension: 659–64, 665–67
Christ's Descent into Hell: 631–35, 637
Christ's Resurrection and Ours: 992–1004, 1015–17
Empty Tomb: 640, 657
Historical and Transcendent Event of the Resurrection: 638–39, 656

Jesus and the Holy Spirit: 727–30, 746
Resurrection as Transcendent Event: 647
Resurrection as a Work of the Holy Trinity: 648–50
Resurrection's Meaning and Consequences for Salvation: 651–55, 658
Resurrection of the Body: 652–8, 988
State of Christ's Risen Humanity: 645–46

Scripture References

Passion of Jesus: Lk 22:1—23:56
Jesus Appears to Mary Magdelene at the Tomb: Jn 20:1–18
Emmaus: Lk 24:13–35
Upper Room: Lk 24:36–48
Sea of Tiberius: Jn 21:3–18

Great Commission: Mt 28:1–20
Ascension: Acts 1:1–12
Pentecost: Acts 2:1–42
Conversion of Saint Paul: Acts 9:1–22
The Good News is Brought to the Gentiles: Acts 10:21—11:18

Summary of Lesson Content

Lesson 1

Before the Sabbath, Jesus was buried in a tomb in a garden.

The Apostles were dismayed at the death of Jesus.

Jesus rose from the dead.

The women found the tomb empty; an angel announced the Resurrection to them. The Apostles were told of the Resurrection and they also found the tomb empty.

Lesson 2

After the Resurrection, Jesus appeared to the Apostles in an upper room in Jerusalem.

The risen Jesus was not a ghost. He had a recognizable body. The Apostles could touch him. Jesus ate food with them.

Jesus breathed on the Apostles, giving them the Holy Spirit and the power to forgive sins.

Lesson 3

Jesus appeared to the Apostles on several occasions.

Jesus appointed Peter as the head of the Apostles and his Vicar on earth to lead the Church. Peter was the first Pope.

Forty days after the Resurrection, Jesus ascended, body and soul, into heaven. Jesus promised to remain with his Church until the end of time.

Lesson 4

Jesus' Resurrection proved his divinity and signified that the world had been redeemed. It also demonstrated that the powers and promises Jesus gave to the Apostles were real.

Jesus' Resurrection is a sign of hope that we too will rise from the dead. We believe in the resurrection of the body.

CHAPTER TWENTY-ONE: NEW LIFE
LESSON ONE: THE FIRST DAY

Aims

The students will learn that, before the Sabbath, Jesus was buried in a tomb in a garden. The Apostles were dismayed at the death of Jesus.

They will learn that Jesus rose from the dead.

They will learn that the women found the tomb empty and that an angel announced the Resurrection to them. The Apostles were told of the Resurrection and they, too, found the tomb empty.

Materials

- *Activity Book*, p. 81

- Bible

- Image of the Shroud of Turin (large, if possible)

Optional:
- "Good Christian men, rejoice and sing," *Adoremus Hymnal*, #419

Begin

From the Gospel of Luke 22:1—23:56, read the Passion and death of Jesus Christ up to the burial in the tomb. This reading includes the Last Supper. It is important to show the connection between the Last Supper and the death of Christ.

The students may dramatize this passage or write down their thoughts in a journal.

Develop

1. Read paragraphs 1–6 with the students.

2. Have the students discuss what the Apostles must have felt at the time of Jesus' death. The man they believed to be the Son of God, whom they followed for three years, who performed many miracles, and who ate the Passover meal with them, died on the Cross. They loved Jesus and must have felt tremendous sorrow at the time of his death. They also must have been disappointed with themselves for not staying with Jesus at the time of his persecution and Crucifixion. The Apostles must have been fearful for their own lives and confused about their belief in Jesus.

3. On the first day of the week (Sunday) the Apostles went to the tomb. We celebrate the Resurrection on each and every Sunday since it was on the first day of the week that Jesus rose from the dead. We must also make every effort to attend Mass on Sundays.

4. Review the Church's teaching about angels. They are pure spirits. There are nine choirs of angels. They are God's messengers. We should honor the angels, pray to our guardian angels, and thank them for watching over us. The students may do some research on angels by reading passages in the Bible.

5. Teach the students about the Shroud of Turin. It is believed to be the burial cloth of Christ. We read about Christ's garment being left after his Resurrection (Jn 20:6–7). The Shroud of Turin bears the image of a crucified man. This image was not painted on the cloth. It is said that the image is somehow impressed upon the garment in such a powerful way that it would resemble a nuclear blast! The Resurrection of Christ must have been a truly awesome event.

Reinforce

1. Have the students work on *Activity Book* p. 81 (see *Teacher's Manual*, p. 261).

2. Show the students a large image of the Shroud of Turin and ask them to point out details. Discuss the class' observations of the Shroud of Turin.

3. Have the students work on the Memorization Questions from this chapter (see *Teacher's Manual*, p. 257).

Conclude

1. Teach the students to sing "Good Christian men, rejoice and sing," *Adoremus Hymnal*, #419.

2. End class by praying the Apostles' Creed (see *Teacher's Manual*, p. 396).

CHAPTER 21

New Life

"Jesus said to her, 'I am the resurrection and the life; he who believes in me, though he die, yet shall he live, and whoever lives and believes in me shall never die. Do you believe this?'"

John 11:25–26

When Jesus died, his disciples, helped by Joseph of Arimathea, came and took his body and buried it in a tomb cut in rock in a garden. This was done in haste, because they had to prepare for the Sabbath (Lk 23:54).

What would happen next? Was it all over, the glorious dream, the visible evidence of the power of God? The Messiah was dead, their beloved Jesus. The Apostles were in hiding for fear of the Jewish leaders.

Then, on the first day of the week, some of the women who had travelled with Jesus and the Apostles set out for the tomb with spices to anoint the body of Jesus and to tend to the details of ceremonial burial which had not been observed the day he died. On the way they began to wonder who would open the tomb for them, since a great stone had been rolled into place to seal it.

But when they got there the stone had been rolled back and an angel from heaven was sitting on it. He informed them that Jesus, who had been crucified, had risen from the dead. He invited them into the tomb to see for themselves.

The women looked in and saw that the tomb was empty. Then the angel said: "Go quickly and tell his disciples that he has risen from the dead, and behold, he is going before you to Galilee; there you will see him" (Mt 28:7).

The women hurried back to the Apostles, filled with awe and great joy. But the Apostles did not believe their marvelous news. Peter and John set out to see for themselves; they found the empty tomb with nothing in it but the wrappings in which Jesus had been buried (Jn 20:6–7).

When the Apostles were gathered together Jesus suddenly appeared among them. "Peace be with you," he said.

The Apostles were in a panic, thinking they were seeing a ghost. Jesus reassured them, telling them that it was really he. He invited them to touch his flesh and asked for something to eat. They gave him a piece of cooked fish and he ate it to show that he was not a ghost (Lk 24:36–43).

In these and other ways Jesus helped them realize that he had risen from the dead and that he was really standing there before them. How they rejoiced!

Then Jesus breathed on them, strengthening them with the Holy Spirit and giving them the power to forgive sins: "Receive the Holy Spirit. If you forgive the sins of any, they are forgiven; if you retain the sins of any, they are

93

94

THE NINE CHOIRS OF ANGELS ACCORDING TO SAINT THOMAS AQUINAS

- Seraphim: The choir of angels closest to God's throne. They have the greatest intellect, love, and will. They perceive God in the richest way possible for a created being. Their only task is to worship and adore God.
- Cherubim: This choir is noted for its perfect vision of God and the beauty of creation, as well as its willingness to share that vision with others.
- Thrones: The Thrones are the choir through which God accomplishes his judgments.
- Dominions: This choir directs the Virtues and Powers in their duty of governing and ordering the laws of creation.
- Virtues: Virtues give the power to accomplish the ordering of nature.
- Powers: Powers are responsible for directing the remaining choirs to carry out what has been commanded.
- Principalities: These angels lead the last two orders in the direct implementation of God's will.
- Archangels: The Archangels serve God's saving plan, doing whatever is necessary.
- Angels: God's messengers and guardians to mankind.

When the Son of man comes in his glory, and all the angels with him, then he will sit on his glorious throne.

—Matthew 25:31

Preview

In the next lesson, the students will learn about the resurrected body of Christ.

Chapter Twenty-One: New Life
Lesson Two: He Is Risen

Aims

The students will learn that, after the Resurrection, Jesus appeared to the Apostles in an upper room in Jerusalem.

They will learn that the risen Jesus was not a ghost. He had a recognizable body. The Apostles could touch him. Jesus ate food with them.

They will learn that Jesus breathed on the Apostles, giving them the Holy Spirit and the power to forgive sins.

Materials

• *Activity Book*, p. 82

Optional:
• "Good Christian men, rejoice and sing," *Adoremus Hymnal*, #419

Begin

To prepare for this lesson, have the students read Luke 24:13–48 and John 20:22–23. The students may dramatize the following post-Resurrection accounts: the Road to Emmaus, Jesus with the Apostles in the upper room, and Jesus breathing the Holy Spirit upon the Apostles and giving them the power to forgive sins.

Develop

1. Read paragraphs 7–10 from the student text.

2. How did the Apostles know that Jesus was not a ghost? They touched him and ate with Jesus. Jesus explained the Scriptures to them so they would understand this mystery.

3. The resurrected body of Christ is different from a normal body as we know it. At the end of time, our own bodies will be resurrected from the dead; then our bodies will share the same qualities of Jesus' resurrected body:
   • Immortal: The body will not die again—it will be eternal. Jesus won eternal life and conquered death by his death, Resurrection, and Ascension into heaven.
   • Lucid: The body is beautiful and perfect. Jesus' body was made beautiful and radiantly illuminated (as with the Transfiguration of Christ). Jesus was not immediately recognized by the Apostles even though he still bore the wounds of the Crucifixion.

• Spiritual: The body is in accordance with the will (there will no longer be concupiscence). It will be made spiritual and subject to our souls.
• Impassible: It will be the same body, but it will not suffer. We know from the Resurrection of Jesus that the same body of the deceased is raised up and glorified. (Jesus' resurrected body still bore his wounds, although he did not suffer from them.)
• Agile: It will not be limited by time and space. Jesus was able to be in many places at once, he was able to enter a locked room, and he was able to disappear after breaking bread at the supper at Emmaus.

4. We see in John 20:22–23 that Jesus instituted the Sacrament of Penance after his Resurrection. You may review the steps to a good confession and the Rite of Penance.

Reinforce

1. Have the students work on *Activity Book* p. 82 (see *Teacher's Manual*, p. 261).

2. The students may work on the Memorization Questions from this chapter (see *Teacher's Manual*, p. 257).

3. Arrange for your students to receive the Sacrament of Penance.

4. Discuss how different people recognized the resurrected Christ. For example, when Jesus called Mary Magdelene by name, when Jesus broke bread with the Apostles at Emmaus, etc.

Conclude

1. Lead the students in singing "Good Christian men, rejoice and sing," *Adoremus Hymnal*, #419.

2. End the class by leading the students in praying the Apostles' Creed (see *Teacher's Manual*, p. 396).

CHAPTER 21

New Life

"Jesus said to her, 'I am the resurrection and the life; he who believes in me, though he die, yet shall he live, and whoever lives and believes in me shall never die. Do you believe this?'"

John 11:25–26

When Jesus died, his disciples, helped by Joseph of Arimathea, came and took his body and buried it in a tomb cut in rock in a garden. This was done in haste, because they had to prepare for the Sabbath (Lk 23:54).

What would happen next? Was it all over, the glorious dream, the visible evidence of the power of God? The Messiah was dead, their beloved Jesus. The Apostles were in hiding for fear of the Jewish leaders.

Then, on the first day of the week, some of the women who had travelled with Jesus and the Apostles set out for the tomb with spices to anoint the body of Jesus and to tend to the details of ceremonial burial which had not been observed the day he died. On the way they began to wonder who would open the tomb for them, since a great stone had been rolled into place to seal it.

But when they got there the stone had been rolled back and an angel from heaven was sitting on it. He informed them that Jesus, who had been crucified, had risen from the dead. He invited them into the tomb to see for themselves.

The women looked in and saw that the tomb was empty. Then the angel said: "Go quickly and tell his disciples that he has risen from the dead, and behold, he is going before you to Galilee; there you will see him" (Mt 28:7).

The women hurried back to the Apostles, filled with awe and great joy. But the Apostles did not believe their marvelous news. Peter and John set out to see for themselves; they found the empty tomb with nothing in it but the wrappings in which Jesus had been buried (Jn 20:6–7).

When the Apostles were gathered together Jesus suddenly appeared among them. "Peace be with you," he said.

The Apostles were in a panic, thinking they were seeing a ghost. Jesus reassured them, telling them that it was really he. He invited them to touch his flesh and asked for something to eat. They gave him a piece of cooked fish and he ate it to show that he was not a ghost (Lk 24:36–43).

In these and other ways Jesus helped them realize that he had risen from the dead and that he was really standing there before them. How they rejoiced!

Then Jesus breathed on them, strengthening them with the Holy Spirit and giving them the power to forgive sins: "Receive the Holy Spirit. If you forgive the sins of any, they are forgiven; if you retain the sins of any, they are

93

94

retained" (Jn 20:22–23). He told them that they were to be his witnesses to all nations, beginning at Jerusalem (Lk 24:47).

After that, Jesus did not remain with them, but he appeared to them on several occasions, putting the finishing touches to his work on earth. During one of his appearances by the Sea of Galilee, Jesus asked Peter. "Simon, son of John, do you love me more than these?" Peter answered "Yes, Lord; you know that I love you." Jesus said to him, "Feed my lambs." A second time he said to him, "Simon, son of John, do you love me?" Peter answered "Yes, Lord; you know that I love you." Jesus said to him, "Tend my sheep." Jesus said to Peter the third time, "Simon, son of John, do you love me?" Peter was grieved because he said to him the third time, "Do you love me?" And Peter said to him, "Lord, you know everything; you know that I love you" (Jn 21:15–17).

Jesus was giving Peter a chance to declare his love three times before witnesses because Peter had denied Jesus three times before witnesses when Jesus was on trial.

When Peter had answered his questions, Jesus instructed him, "Feed my lambs; feed my sheep." There Jesus made Peter the universal shepherd of all his followers, the first Pope. At last Jesus simply said to Peter: "Follow me" (Jn 21:19).

Forty days after his Resurrection, Jesus ascended to heaven in the presence of his followers. Before this he had instructed the Apostles not to go anywhere until he sent them the Holy Spirit, who would lead them in all truth and give them special power to extend Christ's Church to every part of the earth. He promised to remain with his Church always, even to the end of the world (Mt 28:20).

What happened next is recorded in the book of the Bible called the Acts of the Apostles. It tells of the coming of the Holy Spirit in the form of tongues of fire, of the conversion of Saint Paul and the works of the Apostles, and of the wonderful early days of the Church and the first Christian communities.

Resurrected Life

When Jesus rose from the dead on Easter Sunday he proved that he was truly the Son of God, as he had said. This meant that his death had not been in vain. He really had redeemed the world from sin. It also meant that the powers that he had given his Apostles were real, and so were his promises to send the Holy Spirit and to remain always with his Church.

But Jesus did more than just pay for our sins by his death on Calvary. His Resurrection on Easter Sunday was a sign that he had also brought us new life. This new life is the life of sanctifying grace, God's own life within us, which enables us to desire and to do what God wants and what will truly make us happy.

Jesus' Resurrection is also a sign of hope that we too will one day rise from the dead just as he did.

95

RITE OF PENANCE

1. Make the Sign of the Cross and say: *"Bless me father for I have sinned, it has been _____ (how long) since my last confession."*

2. Confess your sins.

3. Pray an Act of Contrition, such as the one found on p. 148 of the student text (see *Teacher's Manual*, p. 396).

4. Absolution. The priest prays the prayer of absolution.

5. Penance. The priest will assign a penance.

(See *Teacher's Manual* p. 41 for the Steps to a Good Confession.)

Preview

In the next lesson, the students will learn about Jesus' plan for his Church.

255

CHAPTER TWENTY-ONE: NEW LIFE
LESSON THREE: HIS CHURCH

Aims

The students will learn that Jesus appeared to the Apostles on several occasions.

They will learn that Jesus appointed Peter as the head of the Apostles and his Vicar on earth to lead the Church. Peter was the first Pope.

They will learn that, forty days after the Resurrection, Jesus ascended, body and soul, into heaven. Jesus promised to remain with his Church until the end of time.

Materials

- *Activity Book*, p. 83

Optional:
- "Good Christian men, rejoice and sing," *Adoremus Hymnal*, #419

Begin

Ask the students why we have the Church. Why couldn't we just meet as fellow Christians and guide each other in matters of faith and morals?
- We need the guidance of the Magisterium in our teaching of the Faith.

- We need to safeguard the Sacraments.
- Christ works through the Church he established.
- We need to come together as a community and the Church helps us to recognize others of the same Faith.
- We need governing in our geographical areas.

Develop

1. Read paragraphs 11–14 with the students.

2. After his Resurrection, Jesus appeared many times to his disciples. The students may read about some of these appearances:
- Jesus appeared to Mary Magdelene at the tomb: Jn 20:1–18
- Emmaus: Lk 24:13–35
- Upper room: Lk 24:36–48
- Sea of Tiberius: Jn 21:3–18
- Great Commission: Mt 28:1–20
- Ascension: Acts 1:1–12

The students may dramatize these passages or write about their reflections.

3. Go over the account of Jesus appearing to the disciples at the Sea of Tiberius. Discuss this passage (suggested questions follow):

- Who first recognized Jesus?
- How was Jesus recognized?
- How did Peter respond?
- What was waiting on the shoreline for the disciples? (Could a ghost make breakfast?)
- Why did Jesus ask Peter three times if he loved our Lord? (Peter had denied Jesus three times)
- Who are the lambs/sheep?
- What special role did Jesus give to Peter? (Pope)

4. Jesus stayed on earth for forty days after the Resurrection in order to further teach his Apostles. He would have explained to them how he fulfilled the Scriptures. He would have instructed them to preach the gospel and spread and govern his Church.

5. Jesus promised to remain with the Church until the end of time. Jesus then ascended into heaven. There were many witnesses of our Lord's Ascension.

Reinforce

1. Have the students work on *Activity Book* p. 83 (see *Teacher's Manual*, p. 261).

2. Have the students create a timeline of the Life of Christ. They may draw important events from his life along the timeline.

3. You may wish to give the students time to work on the Memorization Questions from this chapter.

Conclude

1. Lead the students in singing "Good Christian men, rejoice and sing," *Adoremus Hymnal*, #419.

2. End class by praying the Apostles' Creed (see *Teacher's Manual*, p. 396).

retained" (Jn 20:22–23). He told them that they were to be his witnesses to all nations, beginning at Jerusalem (Lk 24:47).

After that, Jesus did not remain with them, but he appeared to them on several occasions, putting the finishing touches to his work on earth. During one of his appearances by the Sea of Galilee, Jesus asked Peter. "Simon, son of John, do you love me more than these?" Peter answered "Yes, Lord; you know that I love you." Jesus said to him, "Feed my lambs." A second time he said to him, "Simon, son of John, do you love me?" Peter answered "Yes, Lord; you know that I love you." Jesus said to him, "Tend my sheep." Jesus said to Peter the third time, "Simon, son of John, do you love me?" Peter was grieved because he said to him the third time, "Do you love me?" And Peter said to him, "Lord, you know everything; you know that I love you" (Jn 21:15–17).

Jesus was giving Peter a chance to declare his love three times before witnesses because Peter had denied Jesus three times before witnesses when Jesus was on trial.

When Peter had answered his questions, Jesus instructed him, "Feed my lambs; feed my sheep." There Jesus made Peter the universal shepherd of all his followers, the first Pope. At last Jesus simply said to Peter: "Follow me" (Jn 21:19).

Forty days after his Resurrection, Jesus ascended to heaven in the presence of his followers. Before this he had instructed the Apostles not to go anywhere until he sent them the Holy Spirit, who would lead them in all truth and give them special power to extend Christ's Church to every part of the earth. He promised to remain with his Church always, even to the end of the world (Mt 28:20).

What happened next is recorded in the book of the Bible called the Acts of the Apostles. It tells of the coming of the Holy Spirit in the form of tongues of fire, of the conversion of Saint Paul and the works of the Apostles, and of the wonderful early days of the Church and the first Christian communities.

Resurrected Life

When Jesus rose from the dead on Easter Sunday he proved that he was truly the Son of God, as he had said. This meant that his death had not been in vain. He really had redeemed the world from sin. It also meant that the powers that he had given his Apostles were real, and so were his promises to send the Holy Spirit and to remain always with his Church.

But Jesus did more than just pay for our sins by his death on Calvary. His Resurrection on Easter Sunday was a sign that he had also brought us new life. This new life is the life of sanctifying grace, God's own life within us, which enables us to desire and to do what God wants and what will truly make us happy.

Jesus' Resurrection is also a sign of hope that we too will one day rise from the dead just as he did.

95

Q. 79 *After his death, what did Jesus Christ do?*
After his death, Jesus Christ descended into hell to take the souls of the just who had died before that time into paradise. Then he rose from the dead, taking up his body which had been buried (CCC 632, 638).

Q. 80 *What did Jesus Christ do after his Resurrection?*
After his Resurrection, Jesus Christ remained on earth forty days and taught his Apostles all they needed to know to continue his ministry through the Church. Then he ascended to heaven, where he sits at the right hand of God the Father almighty (CCC 642, 659).

Q. 81 *Why did Jesus Christ remain on earth forty days after his Resurrection?*
Jesus Christ remained on earth forty days after his Resurrection in order to show that he had truly risen from the dead, to confirm his disciples' faith in him, and to instruct them more profoundly in his teaching (CCC 642, 659).

Q. 82 *What is the significance of the Resurrection?*
The Resurrection proves that Jesus is God, and that all he taught and promised, including our share in the Resurrection, is true (CCC 651, 653–54).

"I am the resurrection and the life. . . ."
John 11:25

96

TIMELINE: THE LIFE OF JESUS

- 9 months before birth: Jesus is conceived in Mary's womb.
- Birth: Jesus is born in Bethlehem.
- Infancy: Jesus is presented in the temple; Simeon makes his prophecy; Holy Family flees to Egypt.
- 12 years: The Holy Family travels to Jerusalem for the feast of Passover; Jesus stays behind in the temple.
- Hidden years: Jesus lives with Mary and Joseph in Nazareth.
- 30 years: Jesus is baptized and begins public ministry. Transfiguration, healings, Sermon on the Mount, raising of Lazarus, etc. all take place in the next three years.
- 33 years: The Passion—Jesus celebrates the Last Supper, travels to the Garden of Olives and prays, is betrayed and arrested, tried by the Sanhedrin, taken before Pilate, sent to Herod, sent back to Pilate, scourged, crowned with thorns and mocked, condemned to death, carries the Cross to Calvary, is crucified, dies, and descends to the dead.
- 3 days later: Jesus rises from the dead and appears to some women and Apostles.
- For 40 days: He appears to the Apostles and teaches them; at the end of 40 days, he ascends into heaven.
- 10 days later: Jesus sends the Holy Spirit to the Apostles on Pentecost.

Go therefore and make disciples of all nations, baptizing them in the name of the Father and of the Son and of the Holy Spirit, teaching them to observe all that I have commanded you; and behold, I am with you always, to the close of the age.

—Matthew 28:19–20

Preview

In the next lesson, the students will learn about the early Church.

CHAPTER TWENTY-ONE: NEW LIFE
LESSON FOUR: EARLY CHURCH

Aims

The students will learn that Jesus' Resurrection proved his divinity and signified that the world had been redeemed. It also demonstrated that the powers and promises Jesus gave to the Apostles were real.

They will learn that Jesus' Resurrection is a sign of hope that we too will rise from the dead. We believe in the resurrection of the body.

Materials

• *Activity Book*, p. 84

• Bibles

Optional:
• "Good Christian men, rejoice and sing," *Adoremus Hymnal*, #419

Begin

When Jesus rose from the dead he proved that he is God the Son, the Second Person of the Blessed Trinity. His Resurrection showed that his suffering and death were not in vain. His death was accepted as the pleasing and atoning sacrifice to God, redeeming the world from sin. Furthermore, if Jesus is God, his powers are real, and:
• the powers he gave to his Apostles are real.
• the promises that Jesus made were true.

Develop

1. Finish reading the chapter (paragraphs 15–18).

2. Jesus promised to send the Holy Spirit to the Apostles. Read Acts 2:1–42. Discuss the events of Pentecost. (Suggested questions below):
   • Who was gathered in prayer for nine days in the upper room?
   • What were Mary and the Apostles doing when the Holy Spirit descended?
   • How was the Holy Spirit recognized?
   • Why did Peter have to say that they were not drunk?
   • What special gift did the Holy Spirit give to the Apostles? (the ability to speak in different languages)
   • Who spoke? Why do the students think Peter was the one to speak on Pentecost?
   • How many were baptized?
   • Why is Pentecost known as the "birthday of the Church"?

3. Have the students read from the Bible the story of the conversion of Saint Paul (Acts 9:1–22).
   • Why is Saint Paul important to the early Church?
   • Did Saint Paul always support the Christians?
   • Why then was Saint Paul such an effective witness?
   • Who appeared to Saint Paul to cause his conversion?
   • What miracle occurred?

4. Read how the early Church was opened to the Gentiles (since it started with just the Jewish people) from Acts 10:21—11:18.
   • How did the Holy Spirit descend upon Cornelius? (Note: the Holy Spirit descends upon us at our Confirmation.)
   • Who had the authority to permit Gentiles to join the Church of Christ?

5. Note: we participate in the joy of the Resurrection in two ways: at Baptism and at death.

Reinforce

1. Have the students work on *Activity Book* p. 84 (see *Teacher's Manual*, p. 261).

2. Using one of the events studied in this lesson, the students should consider and discuss how Jesus worked through the early Church and how he continues to work through his Church.

3. Have the students work on the Memorization Questions from this chapter. They should prepare for the chapter quiz and unit test.

Conclude

1. Lead the students in singing "Good Christian men, rejoice and sing," *Adoremus Hymnal*, #419.

2. End class by praying the Apostles' Creed (see *Teacher's Manual*, p. 396).

retained" (Jn 20:22–23). He told them that they were to be his witnesses to all nations, beginning at Jerusalem (Lk 24:47).

After that, Jesus did not remain with them, but he appeared to them on several occasions, putting the finishing touches to his work on earth. During one of his appearances by the Sea of Galilee, Jesus asked Peter. "Simon, son of John, do you love me more than these?" Peter answered "Yes, Lord; you know that I love you." Jesus said to him, "Feed my lambs." A second time he said to him, "Simon, son of John, do you love me?" Peter answered "Yes, Lord; you know that I love you." Jesus said to him, "Tend my sheep." Jesus said to Peter the third time, "Simon, son of John, do you love me?" Peter was grieved because he said to him the third time, "Do you love me?" And Peter said to him, "Lord, you know everything; you know that I love you" (Jn 21:15–17).

Jesus was giving Peter a chance to declare his love three times before witnesses because Peter had denied Jesus three times before witnesses when Jesus was on trial.

When Peter had answered his questions, Jesus instructed him, "Feed my lambs; feed my sheep." There Jesus made Peter the universal shepherd of all his followers, the first Pope. At last Jesus simply said to Peter: "Follow me" (Jn 21:19).

Forty days after his Resurrection, Jesus ascended to heaven in the presence of his followers. Before this he had instructed the Apostles not to go anywhere until he sent them the Holy Spirit, who would lead them in all truth and give them special power to extend Christ's Church to every part of the earth. He promised to remain with his Church always, even to the end of the world (Mt 28:20).

What happened next is recorded in the book of the Bible called the Acts of the Apostles. It tells of the coming of the Holy Spirit in the form of tongues of fire, of the conversion of

Saint Paul and the works of the Apostles, and of the wonderful early days of the Church and the first Christian communities.

Resurrected Life

When Jesus rose from the dead on Easter Sunday he proved that he was truly the Son of God, as he had said. This meant that his death had not been in vain. He really had redeemed the world from sin. It also meant that the powers that he had given his Apostles were real, and so were his promises to send the Holy Spirit and to remain always with his Church.

But Jesus did more than just pay for our sins by his death on Calvary. His Resurrection on Easter Sunday was a sign that he had also brought us new life. This new life is the life of sanctifying grace, God's own life within us, which enables us to desire and to do what God wants and what will truly make us happy.

Jesus' Resurrection is also a sign of hope that we too will one day rise from the dead just as he did.

95

96

Q. 79 *After his death, what did Jesus Christ do?*
After his death, Jesus Christ descended into hell to take the souls of the just who had died before that time into paradise. Then he rose from the dead, taking up his body which had been buried (CCC 632, 638).

Q. 80 *What did Jesus Christ do after his Resurrection?*
After his Resurrection, Jesus Christ remained on earth forty days and taught his Apostles all they needed to know to continue his ministry through the Church. Then he ascended to heaven, where he sits at the right hand of God the Father almighty (CCC 642, 659).

Q. 81 *Why did Jesus Christ remain on earth forty days after his Resurrection?*
Jesus Christ remained on earth forty days after his Resurrection in order to show that he had truly risen from the dead, to confirm his disciples' faith in him, and to instruct them more profoundly in his teaching (CCC 642, 659).

Q. 82 *What is the significance of the Resurrection?*
The Resurrection proves that Jesus is God, and that all he taught and promised, including our share in the Resurrection, is true (CCC 651, 653–54).

"I am the resurrection and the life. . . ."
John 11:25

SAINT THÉRÈSE OF LISIEUX

Saint Thérèse is one of the patron saints of missions. She entered a cloistered Carmelite convent when she was fifteen and died nine years later. She never once worked as a missionary. Why, then, is she a patron saint of missions? She always had a great love for the missions and wrote many letters to encourage missionaries. Most importantly, she prayed and offered sacrifices for them. The work missionaries do is very important, but evangelization can never succeed without prayer. The prayers of the missionaries and of people who stay behind and pray for them are essential. Many times in his letters, Saint Paul asked for prayers from the churches because he realized that his work would be fruitless without God's help.

NOVENAS

A novena is a special prayer, prayed over the course of nine days, in which we ask for a saint's intercession. There is a special tradition regarding novenas said to Saint Thérèse. She is often called the Little Flower and is pictured carrying a bouquet of roses. It is said that Saint Thérèse will send a rose to those who pray a novena to her as a sign that their prayers have been heard. Many people have received roses after praying novenas to this saint.

"We can never have too much confidence in the good God. He is so mighty and so merciful. As we hope in him so shall we receive."
—Saint Thérèse of Lisieux

Preview

In the next lesson, the students' understanding of the material covered in this chapter will be reviewed and assessed. There will be a quiz and unit test.

Chapter Twenty-One: New Life
Review and Assessment

Aims

The students' understanding of the material covered in this chapter will be reviewed and assessed.

Materials

- Quiz 21, Appendix, p. A-29

Optional:
- "Good Christian men, rejoice and sing," *Adoremus Hymnal*, #419

Review and Enrichment

1. The students should be familiar with the events of the Resurrection.

2. The students should know some of the various post-Resurrection stories.

3. The students should know the proofs that the resurrected Jesus was not a ghost. They should know the qualities of the resurrected body.

4. The students should know that Jesus affirmed the primacy of Peter on the shore of the Sea of Tiberias when he told him to feed his sheep.

5. The students should know the timeline of the life of Christ. They should at least know that Jesus remained on earth for forty days after his Resurrection. He then ascended into heaven. Ten days later, he and the Father sent the Holy Spirit.

6. The students should be familiar with some stories of the early Church, including Pentecost, the conversion of Saint Paul, and the acceptance of Gentiles into the Church.

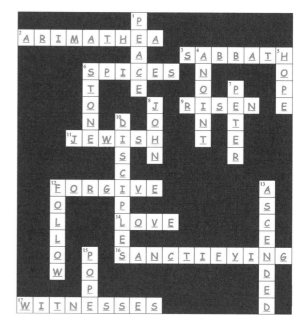

Name: _____

New Life   Quiz 21

Across
2. Joseph of <u>Arimathea</u> took the body of Jesus and buried it in a tomb.
3. Jesus was buried in haste because they had to prepare for the <u>Sabbath</u> .
6. On the first day of the week, some women set out for the tomb with <u>spices</u> .
9. An angel informed the women that Jesus had <u>risen</u> from the dead.
11. The Apostles were in hiding for fear of the <u>Jewish</u> leaders.
12. After the Resurrection, Jesus breathed on the Apostles and gave them the power to <u>forgive</u> sins.
14. Jesus asked Peter three times "Do you <u>love</u> me?"
16. Through his Resurrection Jesus brought us the new life of <u>sanctifying</u> grace.
17. Jesus told his Apostles that they were to be his <u>witnesses</u> to all nations.

Down
1. Jesus appeared among the Apostles and said "<u>Peace</u> be with you".
4. On the first day of the week some women went to <u>anoint</u> the body of Jesus.
5. Jesus' Resurrection is a sign of <u>hope</u> that we too will one day rise from the dead.
6. When the women arrived to the tomb the great <u>stone</u> had been rolled back.
7. The Apostle <u>Peter</u> set out to see for himself and found the empty tomb.
8. The Apostle <u>John</u> went along with Peter.
10. The angel told the women to go tell the news to Jesus' <u>disciples</u> .
12. Jesus said to Peter: "<u>Follow</u> me".
13. Forty days after his Resurrection, Jesus <u>ascended</u> to heaven.
15. Jesus made Peter the first <u>Pope</u> .

Faith and Life Series • Grade 6 • Appendix A   A-29

Assess

1. Distribute the quizzes and read through them with the students to be sure they understand the questions.

2. Administer the quiz. As the students hand in their work, you may orally quiz them on the Memorization Questions from this chapter.

3. After all the quizzes have been handed in, you may wish to review the correct answers with the class.

Conclude

1. Lead the students in singing "Good Christian men, rejoice and sing," *Adoremus Hymnal*, #419.

2. End class by praying the Apostles' Creed (see *Teacher's Manual*, p. 396).

Chapter Twenty-One: New Life
Activity Book Answer Keys

Name:_____

He Is Risen!

Answer the following questions in complete sentences.

1. What happened to Jesus' body after it was taken down from the Cross?
   The disciples buried Jesus' body in a tomb.

2. On the first day of the week, who went to Jesus' tomb and why did they go there?
   Some of the women who had travelled with Jesus went to the tomb to tend to the details of ceremonial burial.

3. What did they see when they got there?
   When they got there, they saw an open tomb and an angel.

4. What did this angel say?
   The angel said that Jesus had risen from the dead and then sent the women to tell the Apostles.

5. What did the women do?
   The women hurried back and told the Apostles.

Faith and Life Series • Grade 6 • Chapter 21 • Lesson 1   81

Name:_____

Receive the Holy Spirit

Answer the following questions in complete sentences.

1. Why did Jesus breathe on the Apostles?
   Jesus breathed on the Apostles to give them the Holy Spirit and the power to forgive sins.

2. What did Jesus say to his Apostle after breathing on them?
   Jesus said, "Receive the Holy Spirit. If you forgive the sins of any, they are forgiven; if you retain the sins of any, they are retained."

3. What Sacrament did Jesus institute by doing this?
   Jesus instituted the Sacrament of Penance.

4. Did Jesus remain with the Apostles?
   No, but he appeared to them on several occasions.

82   *Faith and Life Series • Grade 6 • Chapter 21 • Lesson 2*

Name:_____

The Ascension

Answer the following questions in complete sentences.

1. Why did Jesus ask Peter, "Do you love me"?
   Jesus asked Peter if he loved him to give Peter a chance to make up for his denial of Jesus.

2. What did Jesus instruct Peter to do?
   Jesus told Peter to "Tend my sheep."

3. What did Peter become?
   Peter became the first Pope.

4. What did Jesus do after his death?
   After his death, Jesus descended into hell to take the souls of the just who had died before that time into Paradise. Then he rose from the dead, taking up his body which had been buried.

5. Why did Jesus remain on earth for forty days after his Resurrection?
   Jesus Christ remained on earth for forty days after his Resurrection in order to show that he had truly risen from the dead, to confirm his disciples' faith in him, and to instruct them more profoundly in his teaching.

6. What did Jesus instruct the Apostles to do? Why? What is this event called?
   Jesus told the Apostles not to go anywhere because he was going to send them the Holy Spirit. This is called Pentecost.

Faith and Life Series • Grade 6 • Chapter 21 • Lesson 3   83

Name:_____

Resurrection of the Body

Answer the following questions in complete sentences.

1. When did Jesus rise from the dead and what did his Resurrection prove?
   Jesus rose on Easter Sunday. This proved that he truly is the Son of God.

2. What promises did Jesus make that were confirmed by his Resurrection?
   Jesus' promises to send the Holy Spirit and to remain always with his Church were confirmed.

3. Did Jesus simply pay for our sins by his death?
   No. He also brought us new life.

4. What life did Jesus win for us?
   Jesus won us sanctifying grace, God's own life within us.

5. What hope do we have because of Jesus' Resurrection?
   Because of Jesus' Resurrection, we have hope that we too will one day rise from the dead just as he did.

6. Will we have bodies like Jesus' some day?
   Yes.

84   *Faith and Life Series • Grade 6 • Chapter 21 • Lesson 4*

TEACHER'S NOTES

UNIT FIVE TEST
CHAPTERS 17–21

> CHAPTER SEVENTEEN: AT THE LAST SUPPER
>
> CHAPTER EIGHTEEN: THE LIVING SACRIFICE
>
> CHAPTER NINETEEN: THE FEAST OF GOD
>
> CHAPTER TWENTY: PROMISE AND FULFILLMENT
>
> CHAPTER TWENTY-ONE: NEW LIFE

Aims

The students' understanding of the material covered in this unit will be reviewed and assessed.

Materials

• Unit 5 Test, Appendix, pp. A-30 and A-31

Assess

1. Distribute the unit tests and read through them with the students to be sure they understand the questions.

2. Administer the test.

3. After all the tests have been handed in, you may wish to review the correct answers with the class.

Name: _____

Unit 5 Test   **Chapters 17–21**

Part I: Fill in the chart below comparing the Passover to Christ's Last Supper and Crucifixion.

PASSOVER SACRIFICE	CHRIST'S SACRIFICE
- slavery of the Hebrew people	- slavery of all to sin
- God frees the Hebrews	- God frees us from sin
- Passover lamb	- Jesus
- the lamb is slaughtered	- Crucifixion and death of Jesus
- eat the lamb	- eat and drink the Body and Blood of Jesus

Part II: Answer in complete sentences.

1. What is transubstantiation?
   Transubstantiation is the change of the substances of bread and wine into the substances of the Body and Blood of Christ.

2. What is an oblation?
   An oblation is the total offering of a victim or gift in a sacrifice.

3. What do we call the presence of Jesus in the Eucharist?
   We call the presence of Jesus in the Eucharist the Real Presence.

4. What is the greatest power of the priesthood?
   The greatest power of the priesthood is the power to offer the sacrifice of Jesus' Body and Blood.

5. What are two reasons Jesus gave us the Sacrament of the Eucharist?
   Jesus gave us the Sacrament of the Eucharist so that we might have eternal life and so that we might have an acceptable sacrifice to offer continually to the Father.

6. What are the four ends of the Mass?
   The four ends of the Mass are worship (adoration), thanksgiving, satisfaction for sins, and petition.

7. With what kind of attitude should we approach the Mass?
   We should approach the Mass with an attitude of reverence and profound respect.

Name: _____

Unit 5 Test (continued)

8. How can we express our reverence for the Mass?
   We can express our reverence for the Mass by our attitude and our actions, such as proper dress, silence, genuflection, and prayerfulness.

9. What happens when we receive the Eucharist worthily?
   When we receive the Eucharist worthily it increases sanctifying grace, it helps us to grow in holiness and become more like Jesus, it pardons our venial sins, strengthens us to overcome temptations and helps us to break bad habits. (See also Q. 77 on page 92 of the student text for other possible answers.)

Part III: Yes or No.

1. No   When the bread and wine are changed into the Body and Blood of Christ, can we see the change?

2. Yes Is the whole Jesus present in the Eucharist?

3. Yes Is Mass a sacred banquet?

4. Yes Is Mass the re-presentation of Christ's sacrifice on Calvary?

5. No   Does Jesus die again every time we go to Mass?

6. No   Was Jesus' teaching on the Eucharist readily accepted by all?

7. Yes Did Peter accept Jesus' teaching on the Eucharist?

8. Yes Did Jesus make Peter the first Pope?

9. No   Jesus truly died on the Cross, but is he still dead?

10. No Was the risen Jesus a ghost?

11. Yes After the Resurrection did Jesus give the Apostles the power to forgive sins?

12. Yes After forty days, did Jesus ascend into heaven?

13. Yes Did the Resurrection of Jesus bring new life?

14. Yes Does Jesus' Resurrection give us hope that we too will rise from the dead?

15. Yes Does the Resurrection of Jesus help us to believe that he is God?

TEACHER'S NOTES

CHAPTER TWENTY-TWO
COME INTO THE LORD'S PRESENCE SINGING FOR JOY

Catechism of the Catholic Church References

Altar: 1383
Celebration through the Ages: 1345–47
Forgiveness: 2842–45, 2862
Liturgy: 1348, 1351, 1401, 903, 1352–55, 1105–6, 1353–54, 1362–66, 1352

Liturgical Seasons: 1163–65
Liturgical Year: 1168–71, 1194
Movement of the Celebration: 1348–55, 1408
Sanctoral in the Liturgical Year: 1172–73, 1195

Scripture References

Mass in the Early Church: Acts 2:42, 46

Bread of Heaven and Cup of Salvation: Jn 6:51

Summary of Lesson Content

Lesson 1

The Mass is the re-presentation of the death and Resurrection of Jesus. We encounter Christ in the celebration of the Eucharist.

Reverence should be extended to all things holy, including church buildings.

Lesson 2

Liturgy is public, communal worship. It includes the Mass, the Sacraments, and the Liturgy of the Hours.

The two main parts of the Mass are the Liturgy of the Word and the Liturgy of the Eucharist.

The Introductory Rite prefaces the Liturgy of the Word.

Lesson 3

The priest enters the church with an entrance antiphon or hymn. The Sign of the Cross and the greeting follow the entrance antiphon or hymn.

The Penitential Rite calls to mind our sins, and we collectively ask for God's forgiveness. We pray the Confiteor and then the Kyrie Eleison. This does not replace the Sacrament of Penance.

Lesson 4

The Gloria is then said or sung, except during the seasons of Advent and Lent.

The Introductory Rites end with the Opening Prayer, or the Collect. These prayers are determined by the day of the liturgical year.

The color of the vestments changes according to the liturgical season and feast day.

Chapter Twenty-Two: Come into the Lord's Presence Singing for Joy
Lesson One: Coming to Mass

Aims

The students will learn that the Mass is the re-presentation of the death and Resurrection of Jesus. We encounter Christ in the celebration of the Eucharist.

They will learn that reverence should be extended to all things holy, including church buildings.

Materials

- *Activity Book*, p. 85

- Appendix, pp. B-21– B-29

Optional:
- "All people that on earth do dwell," *Adoremus Hymnal*, #622

Begin

Make copies of Appendix pp. B-21–B-29 on the parts of the Mass so that every student has a set. The students should assemble these booklets or use them as a guide/pattern for making their own booklet.

Be sure the students assemble these booklets in the correct order.

Develop

1. Read paragraphs 1 and 2.

2. Review the importance of participating in the Mass. The Mass is a memorial of the life, death, and Resurrection of our Lord. At Mass, we receive the Word of God in the reading of the Scriptures. We also receive the Word of God made flesh in the Holy Eucharist. It is a way for us to be intimately united with Jesus: Body, Blood, Soul, and Divinity.

3. If we really understand the reality of what occurs at Mass, how should we feel about going to Mass? How should we prepare?

4. Discuss attire appropriate for Mass. We should wear our best clothing and always dress modestly. We should recognize that our outward appearance is an expression of our inner being (just as our words express our thoughts).

5. To prepare inwardly, we should consider what occurs at the Mass. We should anticipate these events. We should be ready to participate actively in the Mass.

6. Have each student write a letter to a friend inviting him to Mass. The letter should explain what happens at Mass and how to prepare to go to Mass.

7. Discuss how to participate actively in the Mass. It is important that they learn to say the responses to the Mass. They should know the order of the Mass and become familiar with the sung responses in your parish. To participate most perfectly in the Mass, they should worthily receive Holy Communion and offer themselves to the Father as they are united to Christ in the Eucharist. They can be nourished with God's Word in the Scriptures and in the Eucharist. They may commit themselves more firmly to follow Christ.

Reinforce

1. Have the students work on *Activity Book* p. 85 (see *Teacher's Manual*, p. 275).

2. The students may complete work on their letters, inviting friends to Mass. Their letters should help to prepare their friends for what will happen at Mass.

3. Have the students work on the Memorization Questions and Word to Know from this chapter.

Conclude

1. Teach the students to sing "All people that on earth do dwell," *Adoremus Hymnal*, #622.

2. End the class by leading the students in praying the Confiteor (see *Teacher's Manual*, p. 271).

CHAPTER 22

Come into the Lord's Presence Singing for Joy

"And one called to another and said: 'Holy, holy, holy is the Lord of hosts; the whole earth is full of his glory.'"

Isaiah 6:3

We have been studying the death and Resurrection of our Lord Jesus Christ by which he redeemed all mankind. We have seen that the Mass is the re-presentation of this saving sacrifice. We have seen that through his ordained priest, Christ himself presides over every Mass. Now we will look at each part of the Mass.

We should approach not only Mass but the church building itself with the proper attitude. This means getting ready to take part in public worship of God. We get ready outwardly by wearing suitable clothes. We get ready inwardly by understanding our purpose in coming: to offer the Holy Sacrifice of the Mass with the priest and to be nourished by the Word of God and the precious Body and Blood of our Lord Jesus Christ. We will come eagerly if we have thought deeply about the meaning of all these things.

The Sacred Liturgy

The public worship of God is called the Sacred Liturgy. The word **liturgy** means "work of the people." It includes the worship we offer to God when we come together as his people, the Body of Christ, especially in the Mass. Through the Sacred Liturgy, we on earth take part in the worship of God that goes on in heaven with the angels and the saints.

The main parts of the Mass are the Liturgy of the Word and the Liturgy of the Eucharist. But before these two parts comes a smaller part called the Introductory Rites. The Introductory Rites prepare us to take part worthily and to focus our hearts and our minds on the Mass.

First there is the *Entrance Antiphon* or *Hymn* during which the priest and altar servers enter the church and go to the altar. It is accompanied

by signs of reverence, such as the carrying of candles, incense, and the Book of the Gospels.

After the entrance song, the priest and the people make the Sign of the Cross. The priest greets the people: "The Lord be with you;" and the people answer: "And with your spirit."

Next is the *Penitential Rite*. The priest invites the people to think of their sins and be sorry for them. Then we all acknowledge our sins together, using one of three possible prayers of confession. This is not the same thing as the Sacrament of Penance, but it helps to purify our hearts.

The prayer of confession usually used is called the *Confiteor*. It begins: "I confess to almighty God and to you, my brothers and sisters . . . ," and it is followed by the invocations: "Lord, have mercy. Christ, have mercy. Lord, have mercy." Or "Kyrie, eleison. Christe, eleison. Kyrie, eleison."

The Penitential Rite reminds us that we are sinners in need of God's mercy. It reminds us

that we are all in desperate need of God's forgiveness. Put another way, we must remember that almighty God is almighty God and that we are merely his creatures in need of forgiveness. Then we begin to see things in the right perspective.

After asking for forgiveness we are ready to praise God and to recall that his divine Son became man to redeem us from our sins and make us children of his heavenly Father. We do so in the *Gloria*, a prayer that was once a Christmas hymn and begins with the words with which the angels greeted the shepherds: "Glory to God in the highest, and on earth peace to people of good will" (see Lk 2:14). The Gloria is used at most Sunday Masses and on other special days.

In this prayer we offer God praise, honor, and adoration, addressing Father, Son, and Holy Spirit. We plead with the God-man Jesus Christ to hear our prayers and ask him to give us a share in his sacrifice and his victory over death as they are re-presented in the Mass.

The Introductory Rites are ended with the *Opening Prayer* or *Collect*. The priest invites the people to pray, and together they may spend some moments in silence so that they can realize that they are in God's presence and make their petitions. Then the priest says the prayer that expresses the theme of the particular Mass, whether it be, for example, a Sunday, the feast day of a saint, or a feast of the Blessed Virgin.

These prayers are determined by the day of the liturgical year. The liturgical year is the Church's calendar; it has its own seasons and special feast days. We know about Advent and Lent, the two penitential seasons, and there are other seasons in the liturgical year. The seasons are to remind us of the life and teachings of Jesus and to help us live as he wants us to.

Not only are certain prayers and the readings of the Mass determined by the liturgical

97

98

season; so are the church decorations and the priest's vestments. The color of the vestment is an indication of what season or feast day is being celebrated.

Word to Know:
> liturgy

> **Introductory Rites**
>
> **Entrance Antiphon (Hymn)**
> **Greeting of the People**
> **Penitential Rite**
> **Gloria**
> **Opening Prayer (Collect)**

> **Q. 83** *Who presides over every Mass?*
> Christ himself, through his ordained priest, presides over every Mass (CCC 1348).
>
> **Q. 84** *What are the two main parts of the Mass?*
> The two main parts of the Mass are the Liturgy of the Word and the Liturgy of the Eucharist (CCC 1346).

"Then I will go to the altar of God, to God my exceeding joy; and I will praise you with the lyre, O God, my God."

Psalm 43:4

99

TEACHER'S NOTES

Preview

In the next lesson, the students will begin learning about the Sacred Liturgy.

Chapter Twenty-Two: Come into the Lord's Presence Singing for Joy

Lesson Two: Sacred Liturgy

Aims

The students will learn that liturgy is public, communal worship. It includes the Mass, the Sacraments, and the Liturgy of the Hours.

They will learn that the two main parts of the Mass are the Liturgy of the Word and the Liturgy of the Eucharist.

They will learn that Introductory Rites preface the Liturgy of the Word.

Materials

- *Activity Book*, p. 86
- Missal
- Index cards with words from *Activity Book*, p. 86

Optional:
- "All people that on earth do dwell," *Adoremus Hymnal*, #622

Begin

Explain that *liturgy* is an ancient word for "public work" or "work of the people." Liturgy is the public worship of the People of God. It is not private devotion. It is communal by nature. We come together to worship God and serve him. We participate in the Liturgy with people in our parish, in the Catholic Church around the world, and with the holy souls in purgatory and the saints in heaven.

Develop

1. Read paragraphs 3 and 4 from the student text.

2. Give each of the students a set of cards upon which he can write the words from the lists on the Activity Book, p. 86. Using a missal, have each student write out all the words of the prayers of the Mass (in English). On the back of the same card, he should write the Latin/Greek names.
   - The students can quiz each other with the Latin/Greek name and respond with the prayer in English.
   - The students can then put these cards in the correct order for the Mass.
   - The students can create a second set of cards to make a matching game of English and Latin/Greek terms.
   - The students can have a "Latin Bee." Standing by their seats, the students are given the Latin, Greek, or English name of a part of the Mass. The students give the corresponding English, Latin, or Greek name. Students remain standing as long as they have answered correctly. The last student standing wins a prize.

3. Teach the basic structure of the Mass:
   - Introductory Rites: This includes everything up to the first reading. The Introductory Rites help us prepare to participate worthily and focus our hearts and our minds on the Mass.
   - Liturgy of the Word: This includes the first reading, the Psalm, the second reading, the Gospel, homily, profession of faith, and Prayers of the Faithful.
   - Liturgy of the Eucharist: This includes the Offertory, Eucharistic Prayer, and Communion Rite.
   - Concluding Rites: This includes the final blessing and dismissal.

4. The students should understand that Latin is the official language of the Church.

Reinforce

1. Have the students work on *Activity Book* p. 86 (see *Teacher's Manual*, p. 275).

2. Have the students work on the Memorization Questions and Word to Know from this chapter (see *Teacher's Manual*, p. 273).

Conclude

1. Lead the students in singing "All people that on earth do dwell," *Adoremus Hymnal*, #622.

2. End the class by leading the students in praying the Confiteor (see *Teacher's Manual*, p. 271).

CHAPTER 22

Come into the Lord's Presence Singing for Joy

"And one called to another and said: 'Holy, holy, holy is the Lord of hosts; the whole earth is full of his glory.'"

Isaiah 6:3

We have been studying the death and Resurrection of our Lord Jesus Christ by which he redeemed all mankind. We have seen that the Mass is the re-presentation of this saving sacrifice. We have seen that through his ordained priest, Christ himself presides over every Mass. Now we will look at each part of the Mass.

We should approach not only Mass but the church building itself with the proper attitude. This means getting ready to take part in public worship of God. We get ready outwardly by wearing suitable clothes. We get ready inwardly by understanding our purpose in coming: to offer the Holy Sacrifice of the Mass with the priest and to be nourished by the Word of God and the precious Body and Blood of our Lord Jesus Christ. We will come eagerly if we have thought deeply about the meaning of all these things.

The Sacred Liturgy

The public worship of God is called the Sacred Liturgy. The word **liturgy** means "work of the people." It includes the worship we offer to God when we come together as his people, the Body of Christ, especially in the Mass. Through the Sacred Liturgy, we on earth take part in the worship of God that goes on in heaven with the angels and the saints.

The main parts of the Mass are the Liturgy of the Word and the Liturgy of the Eucharist. But before these two parts comes a smaller part called the Introductory Rites. The Introductory Rites prepare us to take part worthily and to focus our hearts and our minds on the Mass.

First there is the *Entrance Antiphon* or *Hymn* during which the priest and altar servers enter the church and go to the altar. It is accompanied

97

by signs of reverence, such as the carrying of candles, incense, and the Book of the Gospels.

After the entrance song, the priest and the people make the Sign of the Cross. The priest greets the people: "The Lord be with you;" and the people answer: "And with your spirit."

Next is the *Penitential Rite*. The priest invites the people to think of their sins and be sorry for them. Then we all acknowledge our sins together, using one of three possible prayers of confession. This is not the same thing as the Sacrament of Penance, but it helps to purify our hearts.

The prayer of confession usually used is called the *Confiteor*. It begins: "I confess to almighty God and to you, my brothers and sisters . . . ," and it is followed by the invocations: "Lord, have mercy. Christ, have mercy. Lord, have mercy." Or "Kyrie, eleison. Christe, eleison. Kyrie, eleison."

The Penitential Rite reminds us that we are sinners in need of God's mercy. It reminds us

that we are all in desperate need of God's forgiveness. Put another way, we must remember that almighty God is almighty God and that we are merely his creatures in need of forgiveness. Then we begin to see things in the right perspective.

After asking for forgiveness we are ready to praise God and to recall that his divine Son became man to redeem us from our sins and make us children of his heavenly Father. We do so in the *Glôria*, a prayer that was once a Christmas hymn and begins with the words with which the angels greeted the shepherds: "Glory to God in the highest, and on earth peace to people of good will" (see Lk 2:14). The Gloria is used at most Sunday Masses and on other special days.

In this prayer we offer God praise, honor, and adoration, addressing Father, Son, and Holy Spirit. We plead with the God-man Jesus Christ to hear our prayers and ask him to give us a share in his sacrifice and his victory over death as they are re-presented in the Mass.

The Introductory Rites are ended with the *Opening Prayer* or *Collect*. The priest invites the people to pray, and together they may spend some moments in silence so that they can realize that they are in God's presence and make their petitions. Then the priest says the prayer that expresses the theme of the particular Mass, whether it be, for example, a Sunday, the feast day of a saint, or a feast of the Blessed Virgin.

These prayers are determined by the day of the liturgical year. The liturgical year is the Church's calendar; it has its own seasons and special feast days. We know about Advent and Lent, the two penitential seasons, and there are other seasons in the liturgical year. The seasons are to remind us of the life and teachings of Jesus and to help us live as he wants us to.

Not only are certain prayers and the readings of the Mass determined by the liturgical

98

LATIN: THE LANGUAGE OF THE CHURCH

For hundreds of years all of the Masses in the Western rite were said in Latin. Latin was, and still is, the official language of the Church. Even today official documents written at the Vatican, such as the *Catechism of the Catholic Church*, are written in Latin. At the Second Vatican Council (1962–1965), the fathers decided that the time had come to approve some use of vernacular language in the Liturgy. As the document *Sacrosanctum Concilium* states, "The use of the Latin language is to be preserved in the Latin rites. But since the use of the mother tongue, whether in the Mass, the administration of the Sacraments, or other parts of the liturgy, frequently may be of great advantage to the people, the limits of its employment may be extended. This will apply in the first place to the readings and directives, and to some of the prayers and chants" (36.1–2). It is important to remember that Latin is still the official language of the Church and even though the Church allows us to use the vernacular, we should still respect and use our own language—Latin.

On July 7, 2007 Pope Benedict issued an apostolic letter, which gives Catholics the permission "to celebrate the Sacrifice of the Mass following the typical edition of the Roman Missal promulgated by Bl. John XXIII in 1962 and never abrogated, as an extraordinary form of the Liturgy of the Church." This Mass is in Latin, and is sometimes referred to as the Tridentine Mass.

Preview

In the next lesson, the students will begin learning the Introductory Rites.

Chapter Twenty-Two: Come into the Lord's Presence Singing for Joy

Lesson Three: Introductory Rites—Part One

Aims

The students will learn that the priest enters the church with an entrance antiphon or hymn. The Sign of the Cross and the greeting follow the entrance antiphon or hymn.

They will learn that the Penitential Rite calls to mind our sins, and we collectively ask for God's forgiveness. We pray the Confiteor and then the Kyrie Eleison. This does not replace the Sacrament of Penance.

Materials

- *Activity Book*, p. 87

- Appendix, pp. B-21–B-29

Optional:
- "All people that on earth do dwell," *Adoremus Hymnal*, #622

Begin

Review the definition of liturgy—public work. Review how their participation in the Liturgy is important. Review that the entire Communion of Saints participates in the Liturgy.

You may play a review game with the English/ Latin/Greek words from the *Activity Book,* p. 86.

Develop

1. Read paragraphs 5–9 with the students.

2. Review each of the parts of the Introductory Rites with the students:
  - Entrance antiphon or hymn, during which the priest and altar servers enter the church and go to the altar: During this time, signs of reverence (such as candles, incense, processional Cross, and the book of the Gospels) are carried into the church. The candles are a sign of Christ the Light. The incense is a sign of holiness and our prayer rising to heaven. The Cross is the sign of our salvation. The book of the Gospels is the Word of God to be proclaimed during the Mass.
  - Sign of the Cross: We profess our faith in the Three Divine Persons of the Blessed Trinity and trace the Cross over ourselves as a sign of our salvation and of God's great love for us.

  - Penitential Rite: We recall our sins and our sorrow for them. We acknowledge our sins together with a prayer called the Confiteor. This is not the same as the Sacrament of Penance, through which our mortal sins are absolved. The Penitential Rite is to help purify us of our lesser, venial sins.
  - Kyrie Eleison: Following the Penitential Rite, we pray in humility for the Lord's mercy. The Penitential Rite and Kyrie Eleison remind us that we are a community of sinners, desperate for God's mercy and forgiveness.

3. Review these prayers with the students. They should have them memorized. They should know the Kyrie Eleison in Greek. Discuss how these prayers prepare our hearts for the Mass.

Reinforce

1. Have the students work on *Activity Book* p. 87 (see *Teacher's Manual*, p. 275).

2. Have the students begin assembling their "missal" (using Appendix, pp. B-21–B-29).

3. Have the students work on the Memorization Questions and Word to Know from this chapter (see *Teacher's Manual*, p. 273).

Conclude

1. Lead the students in singing "All people that on earth do dwell," *Adoremus Hymnal*, #622.

2. End the class by leading the students in praying the Confiteor (see *Teacher's Manual*, p. 271).

CHAPTER 22

Come into the Lord's Presence Singing for Joy

"And one called to another and said: 'Holy, holy, holy is the Lord of hosts; the whole earth is full of his glory.'"

Isaiah 6:3

We have been studying the death and Resurrection of our Lord Jesus Christ by which he redeemed all mankind. We have seen that the Mass is the re-presentation of this saving sacrifice. We have seen that through his ordained priest, Christ himself presides over every Mass. Now we will look at each part of the Mass.

We should approach not only Mass but the church building itself with the proper attitude. This means getting ready to take part in public worship of God. We get ready outwardly by wearing suitable clothes. We get ready inwardly by understanding our purpose in coming: to offer the Holy Sacrifice of the Mass with the priest and to be nourished by the Word of God and the precious Body and Blood of our Lord Jesus Christ. We will come eagerly if we have thought deeply about the meaning of all these things.

The Sacred Liturgy

The public worship of God is called the Sacred Liturgy. The word **liturgy** means "work of the people." It includes the worship we offer to God when we come together as his people, the Body of Christ, especially in the Mass. Through the Sacred Liturgy, we on earth take part in the worship of God that goes on in heaven with the angels and the saints.

The main parts of the Mass are the Liturgy of the Word and the Liturgy of the Eucharist. But before these two parts comes a smaller part called the Introductory Rites. The Introductory Rites prepare us to take part worthily and to focus our hearts and our minds on the Mass.

First there is the *Entrance Antiphon* or *Hymn* during which the priest and altar servers enter the church and go to the altar. It is accompanied

97

by signs of reverence, such as the carrying of candles, incense, and the Book of the Gospels.

After the entrance song, the priest and the people make the Sign of the Cross. The priest greets the people: "The Lord be with you;" and the people answer: "And with your spirit."

Next is the *Penitential Rite*. The priest invites the people to think of their sins and be sorry for them. Then we all acknowledge our sins together, using one of three possible prayers of confession. This is not the same thing as the Sacrament of Penance, but it helps to purify our hearts.

The prayer of confession usually used is called the *Confiteor*. It begins: "I confess to almighty God and to you, my brothers and sisters . . . ," and it is followed by the invocations: "Lord, have mercy. Christ, have mercy. Lord, have mercy." Or "Kyrie, eleison. Christe, eleison. Kyrie, eleison."

The Penitential Rite reminds us that we are sinners in need of God's mercy. It reminds us

98

that we are all in desperate need of God's forgiveness. Put another way, we must remember that almighty God is almighty God and that we are merely his creatures in need of forgiveness. Then we begin to see things in the right perspective.

After asking for forgiveness we are ready to praise God and to recall that his divine Son became man to redeem us from our sins and make us children of his heavenly Father. We do so in the *Gloria*, a prayer that was once a Christmas hymn and begins with the words with which the angels greeted the shepherds: "Glory to God in the highest, and on earth peace to people of good will" (see Lk 2:14). The Gloria is used at most Sunday Masses and on other special days.

In this prayer we offer God praise, honor, and adoration, addressing Father, Son, and Holy Spirit. We plead with the God-man Jesus Christ to hear our prayers and ask him to give us a share in his sacrifice and his victory over death as they are re-presented in the Mass.

The Introductory Rites are ended with the *Opening Prayer* or *Collect*. The priest invites the people to pray, and together they may spend some moments in silence so that they can realize that they are in God's presence and make their petitions. Then the priest says the prayer that expresses the theme of the particular Mass, whether it be, for example, a Sunday, the feast day of a saint, or a feast of the Blessed Virgin.

These prayers are determined by the day of the liturgical year. The liturgical year is the Church's calendar; it has its own seasons and special feast days. We know about Advent and Lent, the two penitential seasons, and there are other seasons in the liturgical year. The seasons are to remind us of the life and teachings of Jesus and to help us live as he wants us to.

Not only are certain prayers and the readings of the Mass determined by the liturgical

---

LATIN/GREEK/ENGLISH PRAYERS

SIGN OF THE CROSS
In nomine Patris et Filii, et Spiritus Sancti. *Amen.*
In the name of the Father, and of the Son, and of the Holy Spirit. *Amen.*

CONFITEOR
Confiteor Deo omnipotenti et vobis, fratres, quia peccavi nimis cogitatione, verbo, opere et omissione: mea culpa, mea culpa, mea maxima culpa. Ideo precor beatam Mariam semper Virginem, omnes Angelos et Sanctos, et vos, fratres, orare pro me ad Dominum Deum nostrum.
I confess to almighty God and to you, my brothers and sisters, that I have greatly sinned, in my thoughts and in my words, in what I have done and in what I have failed to do; through my fault, through my fault, through my most grievous fault; therefore I ask blessed Mary ever-Virgin, all the Angels and Saints, and you, my brothers and sisters, to pray for me to the Lord our God.

KYRIE ELEISON
Kyrie, eleison. Christe, eleison. Kyrie, eleison.
Lord, have mercy. Christ, have mercy. Lord, have mercy.

O come, let us worship and bow down, let us kneel before the LORD, our Maker!

—Psalm 95:6

Preview

In the next lesson, the students will learn the rest of the Introductory Rites.

Chapter Twenty-Two: Come into the Lord's Presence Singing for Joy

Lesson Four: Introductory Rites—Part Two

Aims

The students will learn that the Gloria is said or sung, except during the seasons of Advent and Lent.

They will learn that the Introductory Rites end with the Opening Prayer, or the Collect. These prayers are determined by the day of the liturgical year. Likewise, the color of the vestments changes according to the liturgical season and feast day.

Materials

- *Activity Book*, p. 88

Optional:
- "All people that on earth do dwell," *Adoremus Hymnal*, #622

Begin

Review the entrance antiphon or hymn, the items brought forward in the procession, and who participates in the procession.

Review the Sign of the Cross, the Penitential Rite, and the Kyrie Eleison.

Develop

1. Finish reading the chapter.

2. Continue explaining the Introductory Rites. After asking for God's forgiveness and mercy, we give him glory:

- GLORIA: The Gloria is used on most Sundays, except during Advent and Lent. It recalls how the Divine Son became man to redeem us from our sins and make us children of the heavenly Father.

- OPENING PRAYERS OR THE COLLECT: The prayers change each day. The priest invites the people to pray in silence to be in God's presence and offer their petitions. The priest says the prayer that expresses the theme of the Mass.

3. Review the liturgical year. The students should know all the different liturgical seasons and the current season.

4. Review the liturgical colors (see box at right). Where do we see the liturgical colors in the church? (In cloth decorations and vestments.) The students should be familiar with the penitential seasons (Advent and Lent) and know that in Lent, flowers are not used to decorate the church except for certain special days. You may want to show the students various decorations/sacramentals used to adorn the church in the various liturgical seasons; e.g., nativity scene, Advent wreath, etc.

5. If possible, have a priest show the students the different vestments used during the Mass throughout the liturgical year. They should see an amice, alb, cincture, stole, and chasuble.

Reinforce

1. Have the students work on *Activity Book* p. 88 (see *Teacher's Manual*, p. 275).

2. The students may discuss various family and Church traditions celebrated throughout the liturgical year; e.g., family Advent calendar/wreath, lenten disciplines, prayers.

3. Have the students work on the Memorization Questions and Word to Know from this chapter.

Conclude

1. Lead the students in singing "All people that on earth do dwell," *Adoremus Hymnal*, #622.

2. End the class by leading the students in praying the Confiteor (see *Teacher's Manual*, p. 271).

CHAPTER 22

Come into the Lord's Presence Singing for Joy

"And one called to another and said: 'Holy, holy, holy is the Lord of hosts; the whole earth is full of his glory.'"

Isaiah 6:3

We have been studying the death and Resurrection of our Lord Jesus Christ by which he redeemed all mankind. We have seen that the Mass is the re-presentation of this saving sacrifice. We have seen that through his ordained priest, Christ himself presides over every Mass. Now we will look at each part of the Mass.

We should approach not only Mass but the church building itself with the proper attitude. This means getting ready to take part in public worship of God. We get ready outwardly by wearing suitable clothes. We get ready inwardly by understanding our purpose in coming: to offer the Holy Sacrifice of the Mass with the priest and to be nourished by the Word of God and the precious Body and Blood of our Lord Jesus Christ. We will come eagerly if we have thought deeply about the meaning of all these things.

The Sacred Liturgy

The public worship of God is called the Sacred Liturgy. The word **liturgy** means "work of the people." It includes the worship we offer to God when we come together as his people, the Body of Christ, especially in the Mass. Through the Sacred Liturgy, we on earth take part in the worship of God that goes on in heaven with the angels and the saints.

The main parts of the Mass are the Liturgy of the Word and the Liturgy of the Eucharist. But before these two parts comes a smaller part called the Introductory Rites. The Introductory Rites prepare us to take part worthily and to focus our hearts and our minds on the Mass.

First there is the *Entrance Antiphon* or *Hymn* during which the priest and altar servers enter the church and go to the altar. It is accompanied

97

by signs of reverence, such as the carrying of candles, incense, and the Book of the Gospels.

After the entrance song, the priest and the people make the Sign of the Cross. The priest greets the people: "The Lord be with you;" and the people answer: "And with your spirit."

Next is the *Penitential Rite.* The priest invites the people to think of their sins and be sorry for them. Then we all acknowledge our sins together, using one of three possible prayers of confession. This is not the same thing as the Sacrament of Penance, but it helps to purify our hearts.

The prayer of confession usually used is called the *Confiteor.* It begins: "I confess to almighty God and to you, my brothers and sisters . . . ," and it is followed by the invocations: "Lord, have mercy. Christ, have mercy. Lord, have mercy." Or "Kyrie, eleison. Christe, eleison. Kyrie, eleison."

The Penitential Rite reminds us that we are sinners in need of God's mercy. It reminds us

98

that we are all in desperate need of God's forgiveness. Put another way, we must remember that almighty God is almighty God and that we are merely his creatures in need of forgiveness. Then we begin to see things in the right perspective.

After asking for forgiveness we are ready to praise God and to recall that his divine Son became man to redeem us from our sins and make us children of his heavenly Father. We do so in the *Gloria,* a prayer that was once a Christmas hymn and begins with the words with which the angels greeted the shepherds: "Glory to God in the highest, and on earth peace to people of good will" (see Lk 2:14). The Gloria is used at most Sunday Masses and on other special days.

In this prayer we offer God praise, honor, and adoration, addressing Father, Son, and Holy Spirit. We plead with the God-man Jesus Christ to hear our prayers and ask him to give us a share in his sacrifice and his victory over death as they are re-presented in the Mass.

The Introductory Rites are ended with the *Opening Prayer* or *Collect.* The priest invites the people to pray, and together they may spend some moments in silence so that they can realize that they are in God's presence and make their petitions. Then the priest says the prayer that expresses the theme of the particular Mass, whether it be, for example, a Sunday, the feast day of a saint, or a feast of the Blessed Virgin.

These prayers are determined by the day of the liturgical year. The liturgical year is the Church's calendar; it has its own seasons and special feast days. We know about Advent and Lent, the two penitential seasons, and there are other seasons in the liturgical year. The seasons are to remind us of the life and teachings of Jesus and to help us live as he wants us to.

Not only are certain prayers and the readings of the Mass determined by the liturgical

season; so are the church decorations and the priest's vestments. The color of the vestment is an indication of what season or feast day is being celebrated.

Word to Know:

liturgy

> **Introductory Rites**
>
> **Entrance Antiphon (Hymn)**
> **Greeting of the People**
> **Penitential Rite**
> **Gloria**
> **Opening Prayer (Collect)**

Q. 83 *Who presides over every Mass?*

Christ himself, through his ordained priest, presides over every Mass (CCC 1348).

Q. 84 *What are the two main parts of the Mass?*

The two main parts of the Mass are the Liturgy of the Word and the Liturgy of the Eucharist (CCC 1346).

"Then I will go to the altar of God, to God my exceeding joy; and I will praise you with the lyre, O God, my God."

Psalm 43:4

99

CHALK TALK: THE LITURGICAL COLORS

ChalK TalK	Liturgical Colors				
	Green	Red	White	Purple	Rose
Meaning	Life, Hope	Fire, Love	Purity, Joy	Sorrow Penitence	Joy
Use	Masses during Ordinary	Masses for Martyrs, Pentecost, Passion	Masses for Jesus, Mary, Virgins, Confessors, etc.	Masses during Advent and Lent / Masses for the Dead (white and black may also be used)	Gaudete Sunday in Advent, Laetare Sunday in Lent

Preview

In the next lesson, the students' understanding of the material covered in this chapter will be reviewed and assessed.

Chapter Twenty-Two: Come into the Lord's Presence Singing for Joy

Review and Assessment

Aims

The students' understanding of the material covered in this chapter will be reviewed and assessed.

Materials

- Quiz 22, Appendix, p. A-32

Optional:
- "All people that on earth do dwell," *Adoremus Hymnal*, #622

Review and Enrichment

1. The students should know how to prepare for Mass (inwardly and outwardly).

2. The students should know the basic structure of the Mass: Introductory Rites, Liturgy of the Word, Liturgy of the Eucharist, Concluding Rites.

3. The students should know the parts of the Introductory Rites:
   - Entrance antiphon or hymn and procession
   - Sign of the Cross
   - Penitential Rite
   - Confiteor
   - Kyrie Eleison
   - Gloria
   - Opening Prayer, or Collect

4. The students should know the seasons and colors of the liturgical year.

Name: _____

Come into the Lord's Presence Singing for Joy Quiz 22

Part I: Answer in complete sentences.

1. What do we do to be outwardly prepared to come to Mass?
   To be outwardly prepared to come to Mass we wear suitable clothes.

2. What do we do to be inwardly prepared to come to Mass?
   To be inwardly prepared to come to Mass we understand and think about our purpose in coming to Mass, which is to offer the Holy Sacrifice of the Mass with the priest and to be nourished by the Word of God and the precious Body and Blood of Jesus. (Other answers may be acceptable.)

3. In the Sacred Liturgy do we take part in the worship of God that goes on in heaven?
   Yes, in the Sacred Liturgy we take part in the worship of God that goes on in heaven.

4. What are the two main parts of the Mass?
   The two main parts of the Mass are the Liturgy of the Word and the Liturgy of the Eucharist.

5. Are we in need of forgiveness when we come to Mass?
   Yes, we are in need of forgiveness when we come to Mass.

6. From where do the words in the first part of the Gloria come?
   The words in the first part of the Gloria come from the words with which the angels greeted the shepherds at Christmas.

7. When we pray the Gloria what type of prayer are we offering to God?
   When we pray the Gloria we are offering God praise, honor, and adoration.

8. What is the liturgical year?
   The liturgical year is the Church's calendar.

Part II: What are the five parts of the Introductory Rites?

1. Entrance Antiphon or Hymn
2. Greeting of the People
3. Penitential Rite
4. Gloria
5. Opening Prayer or Collect

A-32   *Faith and Life Series • Grade 6 • Appendix A*

Assess

1. Distribute the quizzes, and read through them with the students to be sure they understand the questions.

2. Administer the quiz. As the students hand in their work, you may orally quiz them on the Memorization Questions from this chapter.

3. After all the quizzes have been handed in, you may wish to review the correct answers with the class.

Conclude

1. Lead the students in singing "All people that on earth do dwell," *Adoremus Hymnal*, #622.

2. End class by leading the students in praying the Confiteor (see *Teacher's Manual*, p. 271).

Chapter Twenty-Two: Come into the Lord's Presence Singing for Joy
Activity Book Answer Keys

Name:_____

Going to Mass

Answer the following questions in complete sentences.

1. How should we approach a church building?
   <u>Answers will vary; with reverence, respect, etc.</u>

2. How should we dress for Mass? Why?
   <u>We should dress well because Mass is very important.</u>

3. How do we get ready for Mass inwardly?
   <u>We should understand that we go to Mass to offer the</u>
   <u>Holy Sacrifice with the priest and to be nourished by the</u>
   <u>Word of God and the precious Body and Blood of our Lord.</u>

4. Write a short reflection to help you to prepare for Mass.
   <u>Answers will vary.</u>

Faith and Life Series • Grade 6 • Chapter 22 • Lesson 1   85

Name:_____

Divine Liturgy

Match the Greek or Latin names of the parts of the Mass with their English translation.

1. _h_ Greeting (Sign of the Cross)
2. _p_ I Confess
3. _k_ Lord, Have Mercy
4. _a_ Glory to God
5. _o_ Creed (I believe)
6. _c_ Washing of the Hands (I will wash)
7. _f_ Holy, Holy, Holy
8. _b_ Invocation of the Holy Spirit
9. _m_ Consecration of the Bread (This is my Body)
10. _j_ Consecration of the Wine (This is the chalice of my Blood)
11. _d_ Our Father
12. _g_ Rite of Peace (Peace of the Lord)
13. _e_ Lamb of God
14. _i_ Lord, I am not worthy
15. _l_ Communion (Body of Christ)
16. _n_ Final Blessing

a. Gloria in excelsis Deo
b. Epiclesis
c. Lava me
d. Pater Noster
e. Agnus Dei
f. Sanctus
g. Pax Domini
h. In Nomine Patris, et Filii, et Spiritus Sancti
i. Domine, non sum dignus
j. Hic est enim calix Sanguinis mei
k. Kyrie, Eleison
l. Corpus Christi
m. Hoc est enim Corpus meum
n. Benedicat vos
o. Credo
p. Confiteor

86   *Faith and Life Series • Grade 6 • Chapter 22 • Lesson 2*

Name:_____

Mass: Introductory Rites

Fill in the blanks to complete the prayer.

CONFITEOR

I <u>confess</u> to <u>almighty</u> <u>God</u> and to you, my
<u>brothers</u> and <u>sisters</u>, that I have greatly <u>sinned</u>,
in my <u>thoughts</u> and in my <u>words</u>, in what I have
<u>done</u> and in what I have <u>failed</u> to do, through my
<u>fault</u>, through my <u>fault</u>, through my most grievous
<u>fault</u>; therefore I ask blessed <u>Mary</u>
ever-<u>Virgin</u>, all the <u>Angels</u> and
<u>Saints</u>, and you, my brothers and sisters, to <u>pray</u> for
me to the <u>Lord</u> our <u>God</u>.

Answer the following questions in complete sentences.

1. What do the Introductory Rites do?
   <u>The Introductory Rites prepare us to take part worthily</u>
   <u>and to focus our hearts and our minds on the Mass.</u>

2. What happens as the priest enters the church?
   <u>As the priest enters the church, we sing the Entrance</u>
   <u>Antiphon or Hymn.</u>

3. Write out the invocations that follow the Confiteor (in English and Greek).
   <u>Kyrie, eleison; Christe, eleison; Kyrie, eleison.</u>
   <u>Lord, have mercy; Christ, have mercy; Lord, have mercy.</u>

4. Of what does the Penitential Rite remind us?
   <u>The Penitential Rite reminds us that we are sinners in need</u>
   <u>of God's mercy and forgiveness.</u>

5. What does the priest invite us to do during the Collect?
   <u>During the Collect, the priest invites us to pray and realize</u>
   <u>that we are in God's presence.</u>

Faith and Life Series • Grade 6 • Chapter 22 • Lesson 3   87

Name:_____

The Gloria

Fill in the blanks to complete the prayers.

GLORIA

Glory to <u>God</u> in the highest, and on earth <u>peace</u> to
<u>people</u> of good will. We <u>praise</u> you, we <u>bless</u> you, we
<u>adore</u> you, we glorify you, we give you <u>thanks</u> for your
great <u>glory</u>, Lord God, <u>heavenly</u> <u>King</u>, O
God, almighty Father. Lord Jesus Christ, <u>Only</u> Begotten
<u>Son</u>, Lord God, <u>Lamb</u> <u>of</u>
<u>God</u>, Son of the <u>Father</u>, you take away the
<u>sins</u> of the <u>world</u>, have <u>mercy</u> on us; you
take away the <u>sins</u> of the <u>world</u>, receive our
<u>prayer</u>; you are <u>seated</u> at the right <u>hand</u> of
the <u>Father</u>, have <u>mercy</u> on us. For you alone are the
<u>Holy One</u>, you alone are the <u>Lord</u>, you
alone are the <u>Most</u> <u>High</u>, Jesus Christ, with the
<u>Holy Spirit</u>, in the <u>glory</u> of God the
<u>Father</u>. Amen.

Answer the following questions in complete sentences.

1. After asking God's forgiveness, we praise him. Why?
   <u>We praise God because we recall that his Divine Son</u>
   <u>became man to redeem us from our sins.</u>

2. What does this prayer offer to God?
   <u>This prayer offers praise, honor, and</u>
   <u>adoration to God.</u>

3. What are we asking Jesus to do?
   <u>We are asking Jesus to hear</u>
   <u>our prayers and give us a</u>
   <u>share in his sacrifice.</u>

4. Where did this prayer originate?
   <u>This prayer originated with</u>
   <u>the song the angels sang to</u>
   <u>the shepherds.</u>

88   *Faith and Life Series • Grade 6 • Chapter 22 • Lesson 4*

TEACHER'S NOTES

CHAPTER TWENTY-THREE
SPEAK LORD, YOUR SERVANT IS LISTENING

Catechism of the Catholic Church References

Creeds: 185–97
Celebration through the Ages: 1345–47
Liturgical Celebration of the Eucharist:
Movement of the Celebration: 1348–55, 1408
New Testament: 124–27, 139, 515

Old Testament: 121–23
Scriptures in the Life of the Church: 131–33, 141
Typology and the Unity of the Old and New Testaments:
128–30, 140

Scripture References

Mass in the Early Church: Acts 2:42, 46

Bread of Heaven and Cup of Salvation: Jn 6:51

Summary of Lesson Content

Lesson 1

During the Liturgy of the Word, we listen to God.

The first reading is usually from the Old Testament (during the Easter season it is from the Acts of the Apostles). We learn how God formed his people for the coming of Jesus.

The Responsorial Psalm follows the first reading.

The second reading comes from the Epistles or Revelation, which discuss the Christian life.

Lesson 3

In the homily, the priest explains and expands upon the Word of God in light of Church teaching.

Lesson 2

The four Gospels are those according to Matthew, Mark, Luke, and John. Out of reverence, we stand when they are read. The Gospels are a record of what Jesus said and did on earth.

Lesson 4

At Sunday Mass and on special feasts we recite the Creed. The Creed is a summary of our Faith and a statement of what we believe as Catholics.

Following the Creed are the intercessions, or Prayers of the Faithful. These prayers are for the Church, public authorities, and the salvation of the world.

Chapter Twenty-Three: Speak Lord, Your Servant Is Listening
Lesson One: We Listen to God

Aims

The students will learn that, during the Liturgy of the Word, we listen to God.

They will learn that the first reading is usually from the Old Testament (during Easter it is from the Acts of the Apostles). We learn how God formed his people for the coming of Jesus.
The Responsorial Psalm follows the first reading.
The second reading comes from the Epistles or Revelation, which discuss the Christian life.

Materials

• *Activity Book*, p. 89

• Missals, Bibles

Optional:
• "Glorious things of thee are spoken," *Adoremus Hymnal*, #563

Begin

Discuss the difference between hearing and listening. Listening is an active role. To listen, we must engage ourselves and try to understand what is being said. To listen, we should be comfortable (but not too comfortable) in a position of sitting. We should be facing the reader. We may follow along in a missal or in a worship sheet/program. It is important to listen to the readings of the Church, for the first readings help us better to understand the Gospel.

Develop

1. Read paragraphs 1–4 from the student text.

2. Review the basic structure of the Liturgy of the Word: first reading, Psalm, second reading, Gospel, homily, Creed, intercessions/Prayers of the Faithful. You may play a game to memorize these in the correct order.

3. Review the responses to be said at the appropriate times of the Liturgy of the Word; e.g., Thanks be to God; Glory to You, O Lord; Praise to You, Lord Jesus Christ.

4. For the first reading, Responsorial Psalm, and second reading, the appropriate posture is to sit attentively.

5. Review that the readings at Mass are the Word of God, taken from the Bible. You may have the students find Mass readings from the Bible.
 • FIRST READING: It is usually from the Old Testament. During the Easter season it is from the Acts of the

Apostles. From the Old Testament, we learn the history of creation and God's chosen people. We hear the prophecies of the coming of Jesus. Many Old Testament events foreshadow the Gospel (e.g., Moses giving the Ten Commandments, Jesus giving the Beatitudes—have the students think of other examples). The readings from the Acts of the Apostles tell us about the early Church.
 • RESPONSORIAL PSALM: It may be read or sung. The Responsorial Psalm is taken from the Book of Psalms, composed in part by David.
 • SECOND READING: It is from the Epistles. The Epistles are divinely inspired letters from the Apostles to the first Christian Churches. We can learn from them and apply their wisdom to the Church today.

6. Using missals, show how the readings are thematically connected.

Reinforce

1. Have the students work on *Activity Book* p. 89 (see *Teacher's Manual*, p. 287).

2. Give the class the chapters and verses of this Sunday's readings. Tell the students to find the readings in the Bible, read and discuss the common theme, and review how these readings can be applied to our lives today.

3. Have the students work on the Memorization Questions from this chapter (see *Teacher's Manual*, p. 281).

Conclude

1. Teach the students to sing "Glorious things of thee are spoken," *Adoremus Hymnal*, #563.

2. End the class by leading the students in praying the Gloria (on the facing page).

CHAPTER 23

Speak Lord,
Your Servant Is Listening

"We are of God. Whoever knows God listens to us, and he who is not of God does not listen to us. By this we know the spirit of truth and the spirit of error."

1 John 4:6

As we have seen, the Introductory Rites involve our speaking to God. We pray for God's forgiveness in the Penitential Rite, praise his goodness in the Gloria, and pray the Opening Prayer or Collect. In the next part of the Mass, the LITURGY OF THE WORD, God speaks to us.

At Sunday Mass there are three readings from the Bible. The *First Reading* is usually from the Old Testament. (During the Easter season it is from the Acts of the Apostles.) From the Old Testament we learn the history of creation and of God's chosen people, the Hebrews. Sometimes we hear prophecies of the coming of the Savior. And many Old Testament events foreshadow the Gospel. For example, the Passover lamb foretells, or prefigures, Jesus' sacrifice on the Cross and the Holy Eucharist.

The First Reading is followed by the *Responsorial Psalm*, the reading or singing of a Psalm with a refrain that we repeat. The Psalms express every kind of prayer: praise, thanksgiving, reparation for sin, and petition.

The *Second Reading* comes from the Epistles (letters) that the Apostles wrote to the first Christian Churches. Some of the letters explained what to do with collection money or how to deal with troublemakers. For the most part, the letters discuss how to grow in holiness, how to pray, and how to treat the people around us with true Christian charity.

Next we stand for the *Gospel*, to show our reverence for the words of Jesus. After we recite or sing the Alleluia verse, the priest says: "The Lord be with you." The people answer: "And with your spirit." The priest goes on to say: "A reading from the holy Gospel according to Matthew" (or Mark, Luke, or John). Then the priest makes the Sign of the Cross on the Lectionary (or the book of the Gospels), and then on his forehead, lips, and heart. The people do the same as they answer: "Glory to you, Lord." The little crosses indicate that the word of our Lord is to be in our thoughts, on our lips, and in our hearts.

We hear the Gospel readings again and again, and we may be quite familiar with them. Why go over them so many times?

The Gospels are the record of what Jesus said and did on earth. Listening again and again to the teachings of Jesus or the stories about his miracles is a way to spend time with

100

him, to know and love him better. The more we think about Jesus' life and words, the more we learn about him. We can never go over the Gospels too many times; for every word and action is the word and action of God himself as he lived and walked among men.

We must pay attention during the readings. We must try not to drift off into daydreams during a familiar reading. God gives us special graces if we listen when he speaks to us.

In fact, we share the privilege of the disciples, to whom Jesus said: "Blessed are the eyes which see what you see! For I tell you that many prophets and kings desired to see what you see, and did not see it, and to hear what you hear, and did not hear it" (Lk 10:23–24). Our Lord was talking about his own words and actions. He included in this privilege not only those who lived with him but all the people down through the ages who would do their best to get to know him by studying the accounts of his life, guided by the teaching and Tradition of the Church.

Next comes the *Homily*. The readings and Psalm we have heard have been chosen to illustrate a theme. This theme may be explained by the priest in his homily. Jesus' words and actions, which are sometimes hard to understand, are explained in light of the Church's teaching. The priest may talk about how we can apply what Jesus said and did to our own lives, and how understanding the Gospel can help us decide how to think and act.

At Sunday Mass, and on Holy Days or solemn (special) feasts, the sermon, or homily, is followed by the *Creed*, recited by everyone together. The Creed is a statement of what all

Catholics believe. We have listened to Sacred Scripture, and the priest has explained it and applied it to practical cases; now it is time to express our faith in what God has revealed and taught us. In reciting the Creed, we testify that we believe what God has revealed to men. We worship God, the author of all truth, with our minds.

The Creed is followed by the *General Intercessions* or *Prayers of the Faithful*. These prayers are for the needs of the Church, for our public authorities, for the salvation of the world, for those oppressed by any need, and for our local community and families.

This concludes the Liturgy of the Word.

"Man shall not live by bread alone, but by every word that proceeds from the mouth of God."

Matthew 4:4

101

SAINT DOMINIC

Saint Dominic lived during a time of crisis in the Church. A heresy called Albigensianism was rampant in southern France. The Albigensians believed that all spirit was good and all matter was, by nature, evil. Because of this, they denied the Incarnation and all of the Sacraments. As a sheltered priest in Spain, Saint Dominic knew nothing of these people until he travelled through southern France with his bishop. They lodged with an Albigensian and Dominic stayed up all night talking with him. By morning, Saint Dominic had convinced the Albigensian of the truths of Catholicism. After that meeting, Saint Dominic dedicated the rest of his life to spreading the truths of the Catholic Faith. He founded an order called the Order of Preachers whose members were to live lives of poverty and sanctity, and to be contemplative, intellectual, and pastoral. They were to come to know God through their contemplation and study, and then to share the fruits of that contemplation through their preaching. Saint Dominic also taught his friars the importance of living what they preached. He said that all their work must be motivated by charity and that life must follow preaching. By the end of Saint Dominic's life, the Albigensians had been converted and the Order of Preachers had spread across Europe. He was canonized in 1234 by his friend, Pope Gregory IX.

Glory to God in the highest, and on earth peace to people of good will. We praise you, we bless you, we adore you, we glorify you, we give you thanks for your great glory, Lord God, heavenly King, O God, almighty Father. Lord Jesus Christ, Only Begotten Son, Lord God, Lamb of God, Son of the Father, you take away the sins of the world, have mercy on us; you take away the sins of the world, receive our prayer; you are seated at the right hand of the Father, have mercy on us. For you alone are the Holy One, you alone are the Lord, you alone are the Most High, Jesus Christ, with the Holy Spirit, in the glory of God the Father. Amen.

Preview

In the next lesson, the students will learn about the Gospel.

Chapter Twenty-Three: Speak Lord, Your Servant Is Listening
Lesson Two: Gospel

Aims

The students will learn that the four Gospels are those according to Matthew, Mark, Luke, and John. Out of reverence, we stand when they are read. The Gospels are a record of what Jesus said and did on earth.

Materials

• *Activity Book*, p. 90

• Missals, Bibles

• Art supplies

Optional:
• "Glorious things of thee are spoken," *Adoremus Hymnal*, #563

Begin

Review how to find the Gospels in the Bible. If the students open the Bible half way, then take the second half and divide it in two, they should be in the Gospels. The students should know the names of the four Gospels: Matthew, Mark, Luke, and John. Have the students learn the symbols for each (see box at right). Have the students draw, paint, or otherwise render these symbols as an art project.

Develop

1. Read paragraphs 5–10 from the student text.

2. For the Gospel, we stand out of reverence for the words of Jesus.

3. We begin the Gospel with the alleluia verse (or, during Lent, "Praise and honor to You, Lord Jesus Christ"). The priest says: "A reading from the holy Gospel according to ____ (Matthew, Mark, Luke, or John)." The priest traces a cross on the book of the Gospels and then on his forehead, lips and heart. The people cross their forehead, lips, and heart as they say: "Glory to you, Lord." As we trace the little cross on our forehead we silently pray: "May the Lord be in my thoughts," as we trace a little cross on our lips, we silently pray "on my lips" and as we trace a little cross over our heart we silently pray: "and in my heart." We stand attentively and listen to the Gospel.

4. The Gospels are a record of what Jesus said and did. They include the stories of his teachings and parables, as well as records of his miracles. We should become familiar with these accounts, for in them, we may learn the source of faith, hope, and love of God.

5. You may explain that each writer of the Gospels wrote for a different audience and, therefore, they often wrote of the same things. There are three Gospels called the synoptic Gospels (Matthew, Mark, and Luke) for they are very similar—with the same stories. E.g., Matthew wrote of the birth of Christ for a primarily learned Jewish audience, emphasizing the fulfillment of the Hebrew Scriptures; Luke wrote of the same event for a Gentile audience.

6. The word *gospel* means "good news." What is the good news? The Kingdom of God is at hand, Jesus is the King, and we can live under the reign of Christ.

Reinforce

1. Have the students work on *Activity Book* p. 90 (see *Teacher's Manual*, p. 287).

2. The students may work on a craft to depict the symbols used for the four evangelists.

3. Have the students work on the Memorization Questions from this chapter.

Conclude

1. Lead the students in singing "Glorious things of thee are spoken," *Adoremus Hymnal*, #563.

2. End class by leading the students in praying the Gloria (see *Teacher's Manual*, p. 279).

CHAPTER 23

Speak Lord,
Your Servant Is Listening

"We are of God. Whoever knows God listens to us, and he who is not of God does not listen to us. By this we know the spirit of truth and the spirit of error."

1 John 4:6

As we have seen, the Introductory Rites involve our speaking to God. We pray for God's forgiveness in the Penitential Rite, praise his goodness in the Gloria, and pray the Opening Prayer or Collect. In the next part of the Mass, the LITURGY OF THE WORD, God speaks to us.

At Sunday Mass there are three readings from the Bible. The *First Reading* is usually from the Old Testament. (During the Easter season it is from the Acts of the Apostles.) From the Old Testament we learn the history of creation and of God's chosen people, the Hebrews. Sometimes we hear prophecies of the coming of the Savior. And many Old Testament events foreshadow the Gospel. For example, the Passover lamb foretells, or prefigures, Jesus' sacrifice on the Cross and the Holy Eucharist.

The First Reading is followed by the *Responsorial Psalm*, the reading or singing of a Psalm with a refrain that we repeat. The Psalms express every kind of prayer: praise, thanksgiving, reparation for sin, and petition.

The *Second Reading* comes from the Epistles (letters) that the Apostles wrote to the first Christian Churches. Some of the letters explained what to do with collection money or how to deal with troublemakers. For the most part, the letters discuss how to grow in holiness, how to pray, and how to treat the people around us with true Christian charity.

Next we stand for the *Gospel*, to show our reverence for the words of Jesus. After we recite or sing the Alleluia verse, the priest says: "The Lord be with you." The people answer: "And with your spirit." The priest goes on to say: "A reading from the holy Gospel according to Matthew" (or Mark, Luke, or John). Then the priest makes the Sign of the Cross on the Lectionary (or the book of the Gospels), and then on his forehead, lips, and heart. The people do the same as they answer: "Glory to you, Lord." The little crosses indicate that the word of our Lord is to be in our thoughts, on our lips, and in our hearts.

We hear the Gospel readings again and again, and we may be quite familiar with them. Why go over them so many times?

The Gospels are the record of what Jesus said and did on earth. Listening again and again to the teachings of Jesus or the stories about his miracles is a way to spend time with him, to know and love him better. The more we think about Jesus' life and words, the more we learn about him. We can never go over the Gospels too many times; for every word and action is the word and action of God himself as he lived and walked among men.

We must pay attention during the readings. We must try not to drift off into daydreams during a familiar reading. God gives us special graces if we listen when he speaks to us.

In fact, we share the privilege of the disciples, to whom Jesus said: "Blessed are the eyes which see what you see! For I tell you that many prophets and kings desired to see what you see, and did not see it, and to hear what you hear, and did not hear it" (Lk 10:23–24).

Our Lord was talking about his own words and actions. He included in this privilege not only those who lived with him but all the people down through the ages who would do their best to get to know him by studying the accounts of his life, guided by the teaching and Tradition of the Church.

Next comes the *Homily*. The readings and Psalm we have heard have been chosen to illustrate a theme. This theme may be explained by the priest in his homily. Jesus' words and actions, which are sometimes hard to understand, are explained in light of the Church's teaching. The priest may talk about how we can apply what Jesus said and did to our own lives, and how understanding the Gospel can help us decide how to think and act.

At Sunday Mass, and on Holy Days or solemn (special) feasts, the sermon, or homily, is followed by the *Creed*, recited by everyone together. The Creed is a statement of what all

Catholics believe. We have listened to Sacred Scripture, and the priest has explained it and applied it to practical cases; now it is time to express our faith in what God has revealed and taught us. In reciting the Creed, we testify that we believe what God has revealed to men. We worship God, the author of all truth, with our minds.

The Creed is followed by the *General Intercessions* or *Prayers of the Faithful*. These prayers are for the needs of the Church, for our public authorities, for the salvation of the world, for those oppressed by any need, and for our local community and families.

This concludes the Liturgy of the Word.

"Man shall not live by bread alone, but by every word that proceeds from the mouth of God."

Matthew 4:4

"Speak, for your servant hears."

1 Samuel 3:10

Liturgy of the Word
First Reading
Responsorial Psalm
Second Reading
Gospel
Homily
Profession of Faith (Creed)
Prayers of the Faithful

Q. 85 *What does the Liturgy of the Word include?*
The Liturgy of the Word includes readings from the Old Testament, Psalms, Epistles, and the Gospel, a homily, the profession of faith, and the Prayers of the Faithful (CCC 1349).

Q. 86 *What is the homily?*
The homily is an exhortation to accept the Word of God proclaimed in the readings, and to put the Word of God into practice (CCC 1349).

MATTHEW, MARK, LUKE, AND JOHN

Matthew teaches about Jesus' nature and uses his paternal genealogy. His symbol is a winged man.

Mark informs us of Jesus' royal dignity. His symbol is a winged lion.

Luke ends with the sacrificial aspects of Jesus' life. His symbol is a winged ox.

John pierces into the mysteries of heaven. His symbol is a rising eagle.

—See Ezekiel 1:10–11

Preview

In the next lesson, the students will learn about the homily.

CHAPTER TWENTY-THREE: SPEAK LORD, YOUR SERVANT IS LISTENING
LESSON THREE: HOMILY

Aims

The students will learn that, in the homily, the priest explains and expands upon the Word of God, in light of Church teaching.

Materials

- *Activity Book*, p. 91

- Missals the students started assembling in Lesson 3 of Chapter 22

Optional:
- "Glorious things of thee are spoken," *Adoremus Hymnal*, #563

Begin

Years ago, there were many great and holy preachers who would preach for hours! Can you imagine a three-hour homily? We have many of the homilies of the saints and Church Fathers written down and we can read them for our spiritual formation and enjoyment. Homilies must be given on Sundays and Holy Days of Obligation, and should be given at daily Masses, when there is a congregation. If a priest is saying a private Mass, he does not need to give a homily.

Develop

1. Read paragraph 11 from the student text.

2. As an exercise, assign the students to write a summary of the priest's homily from a recent Mass. This will encourage them to listen carefully and to ask questions of their parents. They must understand the homily in order to write their summaries.

3. Have the students look up the reading for their saint day, or their birthday. Lead a class discussion about the meaning of the readings and how their lessons can be applied to our lives today.

4. If the students have not already finished the missals they were making, they may work on these today.

5. Have the students write a letter to a parish priest saying what they like about his homilies. The students should give concrete examples. This letter should be written using proper letter-writing format. It should be written neatly. They may include a picture if they wish. This can be done as a thank you card.

6. Discuss how the students should behave during the homily. What should they do if they find their minds wandering or if they become distracted?

Reinforce

1. Have the students work on *Activity Book* p. 91 (see *Teacher's Manual*, p. 287).

2. The students may continue to work on their missals.

3. Have the students work on the Memorization Questions from this chapter.

4. The students should write letters to their parish priest.

Conclude

1. Lead the students in singing "Glorious things of thee are spoken," *Adoremus Hymnal*, #563.

2. End class by leading the students in praying the Gloria (see *Teacher's Manual*, p. 279).

CHAPTER 23

Speak Lord, Your Servant Is Listening

"We are of God. Whoever knows God listens to us, and he who is not of God does not listen to us. By this we know the spirit of truth and the spirit of error."

1 John 4:6

As we have seen, the Introductory Rites involve our speaking to God. We pray for God's forgiveness in the Penitential Rite, praise his goodness in the Gloria, and pray the Opening Prayer or Collect. In the next part of the Mass, the LITURGY OF THE WORD, God speaks to us.

At Sunday Mass there are three readings from the Bible. The *First Reading* is usually from the Old Testament. (During the Easter season it is from the Acts of the Apostles.) From the Old Testament we learn the history of creation and of God's chosen people, the Hebrews. Sometimes we hear prophecies of the coming of the Savior. And many Old Testament events foreshadow the Gospel. For example, the Passover lamb foretells, or prefigures, Jesus' sacrifice on the Cross and the Holy Eucharist.

The First Reading is followed by the *Responsorial Psalm*, the reading or singing of a Psalm with a refrain that we repeat. The Psalms express every kind of prayer: praise, thanksgiving, reparation for sin, and petition.

The *Second Reading* comes from the Epistles (letters) that the Apostles wrote to the first Christian Churches. Some of the letters explained what to do with collection money or how to deal with troublemakers. For the most part, the letters discuss how to grow in holiness, how to pray, and how to treat the people around us with true Christian charity.

Next we stand for the *Gospel*, to show our reverence for the words of Jesus. After we recite or sing the Alleluia verse, the priest says: "The Lord be with you." The people answer: "And with your spirit." The priest goes on to say: "A reading from the holy Gospel according to Matthew" (or Mark, Luke, or John). Then the priest makes the Sign of the Cross on the Lectionary (or the book of the Gospels), and then on his forehead, lips, and heart. The people do the same as they answer: "Glory to you, Lord." The little crosses indicate that the word of our Lord is to be in our thoughts, on our lips, and in our hearts.

We hear the Gospel readings again and again, and we may be quite familiar with them. Why go over them so many times?

The Gospels are the record of what Jesus said and did on earth. Listening again and again to the teachings of Jesus or the stories about his miracles is a way to spend time with him, to know and love him better. The more we think about Jesus' life and words, the more we learn about him. We can never go over the Gospels too many times; for every word and action is the word and action of God himself as he lived and walked among men.

We must pay attention during the readings. We must try not to drift off into daydreams during a familiar reading. God gives us special graces if we listen when he speaks to us.

In fact, we share the privilege of the disciples, to whom Jesus said: "Blessed are the eyes which see what you see! For I tell you that many prophets and kings desired to see what you see, and did not see it, and to hear what you hear, and did not hear it" (Lk 10:23–24).

Our Lord was talking about his own words and actions. He included in this privilege not only those who lived with him but all the people down through the ages who would do their best to get to know him by studying the accounts of his life, guided by the teaching and Tradition of the Church.

Next comes the *Homily*. The readings and Psalm we have heard have been chosen to illustrate a theme. This theme may be explained by the priest in his homily. Jesus' words and actions, which are sometimes hard to understand, are explained in light of the Church's teaching. The priest may talk about how we can apply what Jesus said and did to our own lives, and how understanding the Gospel can help us decide how to think and act.

At Sunday Mass, and on Holy Days or solemn (special) feasts, the sermon, or homily, is followed by the *Creed*, recited by everyone together. The Creed is a statement of what all

Catholics believe. We have listened to Sacred Scripture, and the priest has explained it and applied it to practical cases; now it is time to express our faith in what God has revealed and taught us. In reciting the Creed, we testify that we believe what God has revealed to men. We worship God, the author of all truth, with our minds.

The Creed is followed by the *General Intercessions* or *Prayers of the Faithful*. These prayers are for the needs of the Church, for our public authorities, for the salvation of the world, for those oppressed by any need, and for our local community and families.

This concludes the Liturgy of the Word.

"Man shall not live by bread alone, but by every word that proceeds from the mouth of God."

Matthew 4:4

"Speak, for your servant hears."

1 Samuel 3:10

Liturgy of the Word
First Reading
Responsorial Psalm
Second Reading
Gospel
Homily
Profession of Faith (Creed)
Prayers of the Faithful

Q. 85 *What does the Liturgy of the Word include?*
The Liturgy of the Word includes readings from the Old Testament, Psalms, Epistles, and the Gospel, a homily, the profession of faith, and the Prayers of the Faithful (CCC 1349).

Q. 86 *What is the homily?*
The homily is an exhortation to accept the Word of God proclaimed in the readings, and to put the Word of God into practice (CCC 1349).

STAINED GLASS WINDOWS: THE POOR MAN'S BIBLE

In the Middle Ages, the majority of people were illiterate. Because they could not read and (without the printing press) Bibles were very expensive, the only time they heard the Word of God from the Bible was at Mass. However, in many great European churches, especially Gothic cathedrals such as Notre Dame and Chartres, the stained glass windows became a sort of 'poor man's Bible.' They depict stories from the Old Testament, Gospels, Acts of the Apostles, and lives of the saints. Even if they were unable to read or afford a Bible, anyone could enter these churches and immerse themselves in the events of the Bible through these great works of art.

Preview

In the next lesson, the students will learn about the Creed and the Prayers of the Faithful.

CHAPTER TWENTY-THREE: SPEAK LORD, YOUR SERVANT IS LISTENING
LESSON FOUR: PRAYERS

Aims

The students will learn that, at Sunday Mass and on special feasts, we recite the Creed. The Creed is a summary of our Faith and a statement of what we believe as Catholics.

They will learn that following the Creed are the intercessions, or Prayers of the Faithful. These prayers are for the Church, public authorities, and the salvation of the world.

Materials

• *Activity Book*, p. 92

Optional:
• "Glorious things of thee are spoken," *Adoremus Hymnal*, #563

Begin

The Liturgy of the Word reveals God's work in salvation history. In the first reading, we see God preparing his people from the beginning of time for the coming of the Savior. In the second reading, we see God working through the early Church. In the Gospel, we see the fulfillment of the Old Testament and the reason for the New Testament in the Person of Jesus Christ—in his teachings and miracles. The Word of God is his revelation; Jesus is the Word made flesh—the perfection of God's revelation—God himself, in the Second Divine Person.

Develop

1. Finish reading the chapter from the student text.

2. At Sunday Mass and on Holy Days, the homily is followed by the Creed. The Creed is the summary of salvation history. It is the key to reading the Scriptures. It is our profession of faith and identifies us as believers and Christians. It says we are who we are because of what we believe. We say: "I believe." This makes it a personal expression of the faith we have. If this is said in truth, then it affects how we live—we must follow the moral life or else we show we do not really believe. If we speak truly, then we will follow the teachings of the Church and live a sacramental life, for these are founded upon our belief in Jesus. If we speak truly, we will be a prayerful people, for we are not just a people, but a People of God in relationship with him.

3. The Creed is said in unison. As Catholics, we all believe the same things. We cannot choose some teachings, but not others. We must believe all of the teachings because Jesus taught them to us—and Jesus is God. We profess our Faith together, for we are the Christian community. We are his people and together we are united in faith.

4. The Prayers of the Faithful express the prayers of the universal Church, and of a particular church community. We pray for the various needs of the Church, leaders of the Church, government leaders, the sick, and the deceased. (Note: the Prayers of the Faithful are prayers of petition.)

5. Have the students write a set of Prayers for the Faithful. They may personalize them, including specific people in their prayers, e.g., Pope, bishop, government leader, sick friends or family, deceased friends, family, souls in purgatory. Include these prayer intentions in your prayers at the end of class.

Reinforce

1. Have the students work on *Activity Book* p. 92 (see *Teacher's Manual*, p. 287).

2. The students may write more Prayers of the Faithful.

3. Have the students work on the Memorization Questions from this chapter. They should review for their quiz.

Conclude

1. Lead the students in singing "Glorious things of thee are spoken," *Adoremus Hymnal*, #563.

2. End the class by praying for the intentions of the students. Ask each student to read one of the petitions on his list of prayers for the faithful.

him, to know and love him better. The more we think about Jesus' life and words, the more we learn about him. We can never go over the Gospels too many times; for every word and action is the word and action of God himself as he lived and walked among men.

We must pay attention during the readings. We must try not to drift off into daydreams during a familiar reading. God gives us special graces if we listen when he speaks to us.

In fact, we share the privilege of the disciples, to whom Jesus said: "Blessed are the eyes which see what you see! For I tell you that many prophets and kings desired to see what you see, and did not see it, and to hear what you hear, and did not hear it" (Lk 10:23–24).

Our Lord was talking about his own words and actions. He included in this privilege not only those who lived with him but all the people down through the ages who would do their best to get to know him by studying the accounts of his life, guided by the teaching and Tradition of the Church.

Next comes the *Homily*. The readings and Psalm we have heard have been chosen to illustrate a theme. This theme may be explained by the priest in his homily. Jesus' words and actions, which are sometimes hard to understand, are explained in light of the Church's teaching. The priest may talk about how we can apply what Jesus said and did to our own lives, and how understanding the Gospel can help us decide how to think and act.

At Sunday Mass, and on Holy Days or solemn (special) feasts, the sermon, or homily, is followed by the *Creed*, recited by everyone together. The Creed is a statement of what all

Catholics believe. We have listened to Sacred Scripture, and the priest has explained it and applied it to practical cases; now it is time to express our faith in what God has revealed and taught us. In reciting the Creed, we testify that we believe what God has revealed to men. We worship God, the author of all truth, with our minds.

The Creed is followed by the *General Intercessions* or *Prayers of the Faithful*. These prayers are for the needs of the Church, for our public authorities, for the salvation of the world, for those oppressed by any need, and for our local community and families.

This concludes the Liturgy of the Word.

"Man shall not live by bread alone, but by every word that proceeds from the mouth of God."

Matthew 4:4

101

Liturgy of the Word
First Reading
Responsorial Psalm
Second Reading
Gospel
Homily
Profession of Faith (Creed)
Prayers of the Faithful

Q. 85   *What does the Liturgy of the Word include?*
The Liturgy of the Word includes readings from the Old Testament, Psalms, Epistles, and the Gospel, a homily, the profession of faith, and the Prayers of the Faithful (CCC 1349).

Q. 86   *What is the homily?*
The homily is an exhortation to accept the Word of God proclaimed in the readings, and to put the Word of God into practice (CCC 1349).

102

THE CREED: A SUMMARY OF SALVATION HISTORY

I believe in God, the Father almighty, Creator of heaven and earth: Gen 1–3, Old Testament.

and in Jesus Christ, his only Son, our Lord, who was conceived by the Holy Spirit, born of the Virgin Mary, suffered under Pontius Pilate, was crucified, died, and was buried; he descended into hell; on the third day he rose again from the dead; he ascended into heaven, and is seated at the right hand of God the Father almighty; from there he will come to judge the living and the dead: Matthew 1:1– Acts 2.

I believe in the Holy Spirit (Acts 2), the holy catholic Church (the Epistles), the communion of saints (Revelation), the forgiveness of sins (Gospels), the resurrection of the Body, and life everlasting. (Revelation). *Amen.*

"The Creed is the spiritual seal, our heart's meditation and an ever-present guardian; it is, unquestionably, the treasure of our soul."

—Saint Ambrose

The Creed that we pray together at Sunday Mass is called the Nicene Creed. The Creed that we typically pray at the beginning of the Rosary is called the Apostles' Creed.

Preview

In the next lesson, the students' understanding of the material covered in this chapter will be reviewed and assessed.

Aims

The students' understanding of the material covered in this chapter will be reviewed and assessed.

Materials

- Quiz 23, Appendix, p. A-33

Optional:
- "Glorious things of thee are spoken," *Adoremus Hymnal,* #563

Review and Enrichment

1. The students must know that the Liturgy of the Word includes:
   - First Reading
   - Responsorial Psalm
   - Second Reading
   - Gospel
   - Homily
   - Profession of Faith (Creed)
   - Prayers of the Faithful

2. The students should understand that the readings of the Mass are selected to draw out a theme and that the readings are related to one another.

3. The students should know that the readings for the Mass come from the Bible.

4. The students should know the four Gospels.

5. The students should know the Creed.

6. The students should be able to write prayers for the faithful.

7. The students should understand that the Word of God is revealed to us through the Liturgy of the Word.

Name:

Speak Lord, Your Servant is Listening   **Quiz 23**

Part I: Number the parts of the Liturgy of the Word to indicate their proper order and give a brief description of each.

<u>5</u> Homily: <u>The priest explains the readings we have just heard.</u>

<u>2</u> Responsorial Psalm: <u>Psalm that is read or sung with a refrain we repeat.</u>

<u>7</u> Prayers of the Faithful: <u>Prayers for the needs of the Church and the world.</u>

<u>1</u> First Reading: <u>Usually taken from the Old Testament.</u>

<u>4</u> Gospel: <u>The record of what Jesus said and did on earth.</u>

<u>6</u> Profession of Faith: <u>The Creed; a statement of what all Catholics believe.</u>

<u>3</u> Second Reading: <u>Taken from the Epistles.</u>

Part II: Answer the following in complete sentences.

1. During the Introductory Rites we speak to God. Who speaks to us during the Liturgy of the Word?
   <u>During the Liturgy of the Word God speaks to us.</u>

2. What do we learn from the Old Testament?
   <u>From the Old Testament we learn the history of creation and of God's chosen people, the Hebrews. Answers may also include that we hear prophecies of the coming Savior.</u>

3. What do the little crosses that we make on our forehead, lips, and heart before the Gospel indicate?
   <u>The crosses that we make on our forehead, lips, and heart before the Gospel indicate that the Word of our Lord is to be in our thoughts, on our lips, and in our hearts.</u>

Faith and Life Series • Grade 6 • Appendix A   *A-33*

Assess

1. Distribute the quizzes, and read through them with the students to be sure they understand the questions.

2. Administer the quiz. As the students hand in their work, you may orally quiz them on the Memorization Questions from this chapter.

3. After all the quizzes have been handed in, you may wish to review the correct answers with the class.

Conclude

1. Lead the students in singing "Glorious things of thee are spoken," *Adoremus Hymnal,* #563.

2. End the class by leading the students in praying the Gloria (see *Teacher's Manual,* p. 279).

Name:_____

The Liturgy of the Word

Answer the following questions in complete sentences.

1. What happens during the Liturgy of the Word?
   During the Liturgy of the Word, God speaks to us.

2. How many readings are there at Sunday Mass?
   There are three readings at Sunday Mass.

3. Where is the first reading from?
   The first reading is from the Old Testament or the Acts of the Apostles.

4. What follows the first reading?
   The Responsorial Psalm follows the first reading.

5. Where is the second reading from?
   The second reading comes from the Epistles.

6. What is the third reading called?
   The third reading is called the Gospel.

7. What is this reading about?
   This reading is about what Jesus said and did on earth.

8. What follows the third reading?
   After the third reading is the homily.

Name:_____

The Gospel

Answer the following questions in complete sentences.

1. Why do we stand for the Gospel?
   We stand for the Gospel to show our reverence for the words of Jesus.

2. What do we sing before the Gospel?
   We sing the Alleluia.

3. What does the priest say?
   The priest says: "The Lord be with you."

4. What is our response?
   We respond: "And with your spirit."

5. Then what does he say?
   Then he says: "A reading from the holy Gospel according to Matthew (or Mark, Luke, or John)."

6. What actions follow these words?
   The priest makes the Sign of the Cross on the Lectionary, and then on his forehead, lips, and heart.

7. What does this mean?
   This means that the Word of God is to be in our thoughts, on our lips, and in our heart.

8. What is a homily?
   A homily is an exhortation to accept the Word of God proclaimed in the readings, and to put it into practice.

Name:_____

Speak Lord, Your Servant is Listening

Number these parts of the Liturgy of the Word in their proper order and give a brief description of each one.

_2_ Responsorial Psalm: a Psalm is sung with a refrain we repeat.

_5_ Gospel Reading: taken from the Gospel. Relates the words and actions of Jesus.

_8_ Prayers of the Faithful: prayers for the needs of the Church, our public authorities, etc.

_3_ Second Reading: taken from the Epistles.

_1_ First Reading: taken from the Old Testament or Acts of the Apostles.

_7_ Profession of Faith: the Creed. A statement of what all Catholics believe.

_6_ Homily: exhortation to accept and put into practice the Word of God proclaimed in the readings.

_4_ Gospel Acclamation: Alleluia sung before the Gospel.

Name:_____

The Creed and the Intercessions

Answer the following questions in complete sentences.

1. What is a creed?
   A creed is a statement of belief. A Catholic creed, then, is a statement of what all Catholics believe.

2. Why do we all say the Creed together?
   Answers will vary.

3. What is our response to the Prayers of the Faithful?
   Our response is "Lord, hear our prayer."

4. Write out three sample intercessions.
   Answers will vary.

5. Write out the Apostles' Creed.
   I believe in God, the Father almighty, Creator of heaven and earth, and in Jesus Christ, his only Son, our Lord, who was conceived by the Holy Spirit, born of the Virgin Mary, suffered under Pontius Pilate, was crucified, died, and was buried; he descended into hell; on the third day he rose again from the dead; he ascended into heaven, and is seated at the right hand of God the Father almighty; from there he will come to judge the living and the dead.
   I believe in the Holy Spirit, the holy catholic Church, the communion of saints, the forgiveness of sins, the resurrection of the body, and life everlasting. Amen.

TEACHER'S NOTES

TEACHER'S NOTES

CHAPTER TWENTY-FOUR
LIFT UP THE CUP OF SALVATION

Catechism of the Catholic Church References

"Amen": 1061–65
Celebration through the Ages: 1345–47
Liturgy: 1349, 1355, 2770, 1350, 1388, 1383–87

Movement of the Celebration: 1348–55, 1408
Presence of Christ in the Eucharist: 1373–81, 1410, 1418
Signs of Bread and Wine in the Eucharist: 1333–36, 1412

Scripture References

Holy, Holy, Holy: Rev 4:8

Blessed Is He Who Comes in the Name of the Lord: Mt 21:9

Summary of Lesson Content

Lesson 1

The Liturgy of the Eucharist begins with the Preparation of the Gifts.

Bread and wine that will become the Body and Blood of Christ are brought forward from the people.

The bread and wine symbolize the unity of man with God.

Lesson 2

The Prayer over the Gifts acknowledges God's goodness and asks for God's blessing.

The washing of hands by the priest signifies the purity with which we should approach the Eucharist.

In the Mass the laity are asked to pray that this sacrifice will be acceptable to God the Father for the praise and glory of his name, for our good, and the good of all his Church.

Lesson 3

The preface begins the Canon.

The Sanctus or Holy, Holy, Holy unites our prayers with the entire Communion of Saints.

People stand to give praise and kneel to express adoration and reverence.

Lesson 4

The priest extends his hands over the gifts and invokes the Holy Spirit to come upon them and make them holy so they can become the Body and Blood of Christ. This is called the Epiclesis.

The Consecration occurs when the priest says: "This is my Body" and "This is the chalice of my Blood." At the Consecration, the bread and wine become Jesus truly present. This change in what is present is called transubstantiation.

The Doxology is followed by the great Amen.

Chapter Twenty-Four: Lift Up the Cup of Salvation
Lesson One: The Gifts

Aims

The students will learn that the Liturgy of the Eucharist begins with the Preparation of the Gifts.

They will learn that bread and wine that will become the Body and Blood of Christ are brought forward from the people. The bread and wine symbolize the unity of man with God.

Materials

- *Activity Book*, p. 93

Optional:
- "Of the glorious Body telling," *Adoremus Hymnal*, #392

Begin

Go through the structure of the Liturgy of the Eucharist. Play a review game so the students know the structure:
Offertory:
      Preparation of the Altar
      Preparation of the Gifts
      Offering of the Gifts
      Washing of the Hands
      Prayers of the Gifts

Eucharistic Prayer:
      Preface
      Sanctus
      Prayer of Thanksgiving
      Invocation of the Holy Spirit
      Consecration
      Offering to the Father
      Doxology

Develop

1. Read paragraphs 1–5 from the student text.

2. Review that the matter of the Eucharist is bread and wine. These are the gifts brought forward during the Offertory.

3. Discuss that the bread used for the hosts is made from wheat and water. It must be unleavened (no yeast). Wheat must be harvested and ground into flour to make bread. The bread is made from many grains of wheat, just as many people make up the Mystical Body of Christ. It is a sign of the unity of the People of God's Church.

4. Discuss that the wine used for the Mass is made from grapes which were crushed in order to become wine. This should remind us that we need to die to ourselves so that Christ can live in us and work through us.

5. Review the proper way to receive the Eucharist under both forms.

6. At Sunday Mass, a collection is taken during the Offertory and brought forward with the gifts. This is one way to support the church in its financial needs. The collection from the Mass maintains the church building (e.g., plumbing, electrics, cleaning), lay staff salaries (e.g., Youth Minister, Organist), the mission Church, various charities, the diocesan offices, etc. It is a sacrificial gift of the People of God. We work hard for our money and it is a sacrifice of our labor. We should give from our excess, but also from what is necessary to us.

7. Often during the Offertory, we sing a hymn. Ask the students to name some appropriate hymns for the the Offertory.

8. Optional: have the students visit a convent/monastery that makes Communion hosts.

Reinforce

1. Have the students work on *Activity Book* p. 93 (see *Teacher's Manual*, p. 299).

2. The students may work on the Memorization Questions and Words to Know from this chapter (see *Teacher's Manual*, p. 293).

Conclude

1. Teach the students to sing "Of the glorious Body telling," *Adoremus Hymnal*, #392.

2. End the class by leading the students in praying the Apostles' Creed (see *Teacher's Manual*, p. 396).

CHAPTER 24

Lift Up the Cup of Salvation

"When he was at table with them, he took the bread and blessed and broke it, and gave it to them. And their eyes were opened and they recognized him; and he vanished out of their sight."

Luke 24:30–31

The LITURGY OF THE EUCHARIST begins with the *Preparation of the Gifts*. Bread and wine are brought up to the priest from the people. The priest accepts them, places them on the altar, and with special prayers offers them to God.

All of the words and actions are rich with meaning. Whenever God wants to do something for us, he always does it in a way that helps our understanding; he uses a sign on one level that shows us what is happening on a higher level.

The bread and wine brought forward from the people will soon become the Body and Blood of Jesus. The bread is made up of many grains of wheat and the wine of many grapes, just as the people, though many, are made into the one Body of Christ through the mysteries of the Eucharist. We, though many, share the one Bread and are made one.

The grapes were crushed in order to become wine, and the wheat was ground into flour to make bread. When we think of this, we can remember that we must die to ourselves, to our sins and faults, and live a new life in Christ.

At this time in the Mass we should be offering ourselves to God: our whole selves,

including our joys and sorrows. A hymn may be sung that can help us understand the actions and the signs.

103

The prayers during the Preparation of the Gifts acknowledge God's goodness as Lord of all creation and the goodness of creation itself. They ask God's blessing on these gifts which are to become for us the Bread of Life and our spiritual drink. After the priest offers the bread, and again after he offers the wine, the people respond, "Blessed be God for ever."

The *Washing of the Hands* of the priest signifies the great purity with which we should approach the Eucharist. It is a prayer to God to wash away our sins as we come close to him.

The priest then invites the people to pray that our sacrifice may be accepted by God, the almighty Father.

The people respond with a prayer that our sacrifice may be accepted at the hands of the priest for three purposes: 1. the praise and glory of God's name; 2. for our benefit; and 3. the good of all the Church. This prayer can remind us that in all that we do, God's glory must be considered first; our good and the good of all the Church, though very important, come after. With his hands extended, the priest then says a prayer that the gifts will be acceptable and pleasing to God. The people stand for this prayer and give consent to it by saying, "Amen."

The Eucharistic Prayer

Now comes the high point of the Mass, called the *Eucharistic Prayer* or *Canon*. It

is in this part of the Mass that bread and wine become the Body and Blood of our Lord and the sacrifice is offered to God.

The prayer begins with the *Preface*, a consideration of the coming sacrifice in light of the liturgical season of the year or of a feast day. It ends as we join our voices to those of the angels in heaven in the hymn called the *Sanctus*:

"Holy, Holy, Holy Lord God of hosts. Heaven and earth are full of your glory. Hosanna in the highest. Blessed is he who comes in the name of the Lord. Hosanna in the highest."

The word **"hosanna"** (a Hebrew word meaning "save us") is a special exclamation of joy in the salvation God has promised to us. It expresses our joyful expectation of God coming to us as our salvation.

The people, who were standing to give praise, now kneel and remain kneeling for the most solemn part of the Mass.

The priest extends his hands over the gifts and invokes the Holy Spirit, asking him to come upon them and make them holy so that they may become the Body and Blood of our Lord Jesus Christ. Then he continues with the *Consecration*, in which he says: "This is my Body . . . this is the chalice of my Blood." At this moment, the bread and wine become the Body and Blood of Jesus.

The priest holds up the consecrated Host and then the chalice with the Precious Blood; as he holds them up for the people to adore, he and the people offer the Holy Sacrifice, Christ's Body and Blood, to our heavenly Father.

This is the part of the Mass where we are called on to proclaim our belief in this great mystery of our faith—that Jesus really is present on the altar now.

The Eucharistic Prayer also contains prayers

104

THE EUCHARIST IN THE CODE OF CANON LAW

The *Code of Canon Law* outlines what type of bread and wine are to be used in the Eucharist.

Can 924 – 1. The Most Sacred Eucharistic Sacrifice must be offered with bread and with wine, in which a little water must be mixed.

2. The bread must be only wheat and recently made so that there is no danger of spoiling.

3. The wine must be natural from the fruit of the vine and not spoiled.

Can 926 – In accord with the ancient tradition of the Latin Church, the priest is to use unleavened bread in the celebration of the Eucharist whenever he offers it.

I am God's wheat and shall be ground by the teeth of wild animals. I am writing to all the churches to let it be known that I will gladly die for God. . . . I am God's wheat and shall be ground by their teeth so that I may become Christ's pure bread.

—Saint Ignatius of Antioch

Preview

In the next lesson, the students will learn about the Prayers over the Gifts.

CHAPTER TWENTY-FOUR: LIFT UP THE CUP OF SALVATION
LESSON TWO: PRAYERS OVER THE GIFTS

Aims

The students will learn that the Prayer over the Gifts acknowledges God's goodness and asks for God's blessing.

They will learn that the washing of hands by the priest signifies the purity with which we should approach the Eucharist. In the Mass the laity are asked to pray that this sacrifice will be acceptable to God the Father for the praise and glory of his name, for our good, and the good of all his Church.

Materials

- *Activity Book*, p. 94

- Missals (with Offertory Prayers)

Optional:
- "Of the glorious Body telling," *Adoremus Hymnal*, #392

Begin

Review the things necessary for a sacrifice:
- Priest: who mediates between man and God. He offers prayers on behalf of the people and offers sacrifice to God. At Mass, the priest also acts in the Person of Christ and offers Jesus in the Eucharist to us in Holy Communion, uniting God and man.

- Victim: bread and wine, which will become the Body, Blood, Soul, and Divinity of Jesus.
- Altar: The altar of the Lord, both table and sacrificial altar (a symbol of the Cross, and of Christ himself).

Develop

1. Read paragraphs 6–9 from the student text.

2. Using a missal, read the Offertory Prayers said by the priest. Often we do not pay close attention to what is said during these important prayers. They are very rich in meaning and help us to understand the Sacrifice of the Mass.

3. After the priest offers the bread and wine to God, we say "Blessed be God forever." We are uniting our voices with the priest in offering God praise and uniting our will with that of the priest in the Sacrifice of the Mass. Just as the priest is offering God the bread and wine (which symbolizes us), we should offer ourselves to God in the Sacrifice of the Mass. We can offer all we are, all we have, and all we do for his greater glory. The priest asks God to accept these gifts, which we offer with humble and contrite hearts. Discuss humility and contrition.

4. The priest washes his hands, and says: "Wash me, O Lord, from my iniquity and cleanse me from my sin." This reminds us of our Baptism (as when we bless ourselves with holy water). We should ask God to purify us, too, at this time, as we are united with the priest in this offering to the Father.

5. Next, the people stand. The priest invites the people to pray that our sacrifice will be acceptable to the Father. We respond: "May the Lord accept the sacrifice at your hands for the praise and glory of his name, for our good and the good of all his holy Church." We acknowledge that the priest is our mediator and we ask God to accept the sacrifice as a worthy sacrifice at the hands of his servant the priest. We also ask to share in the benefits of the Sacrifice of the Mass. We end by saying: "Amen," which means: "I believe this to be true," or "so be it." This is the end of the Offertory, which is followed by the Eucharistic Prayer.

Reinforce

1. Have the students work on *Activity Book* p. 94 (see *Teacher's Manual*, p. 299).

2. The students may work on the Memorization Questions and Words to Know from this chapter.

Conclude

1. Lead the students in singing "Of the glorious Body telling," *Adoremus Hymnal*, #392.

2. End the class by leading the students in praying the Apostles' Creed (see *Teacher's Manual*, p. 396).

The prayers during the Preparation of the Gifts acknowledge God's goodness as Lord of all creation and the goodness of creation itself. They ask God's blessing on these gifts which are to become for us the Bread of Life and our spiritual drink. After the priest offers the bread, and again after he offers the wine, the people respond, "Blessed be God for ever."

The *Washing of the Hands* of the priest signifies the great purity with which we should approach the Eucharist. It is a prayer to God to wash away our sins as we come close to him.

The priest then invites the people to pray that our sacrifice may be accepted by God, the almighty Father.

The people respond with a prayer that our sacrifice may be accepted at the hands of the priest for three purposes: 1. the praise and glory of God's name; 2. for our benefit; and 3. the good of all the Church. This prayer can remind us that in all that we do, God's glory must be considered first; our good and the good of all the Church, though very important, come after. With his hands extended, the priest then says a prayer that the gifts will be acceptable and pleasing to God. The people stand for this prayer and give consent to it by saying, "Amen."

The Eucharistic Prayer

Now comes the high point of the Mass, called the *Eucharistic Prayer* or *Canon*. It

104

is in this part of the Mass that bread and wine become the Body and Blood of our Lord and the sacrifice is offered to God.

The prayer begins with the *Preface*, a consideration of the coming sacrifice in light of the liturgical season of the year or of a feast day. It ends as we join our voices to those of the angels in heaven in the hymn called the *Sanctus*:

"Holy, Holy, Holy Lord God of hosts. Heaven and earth are full of your glory. Hosanna in the highest. Blessed is he who comes in the name of the Lord. Hosanna in the highest."

The word "**hosanna**" (a Hebrew word meaning "save us") is a special exclamation of joy in the salvation God has promised to us. It expresses our joyful expectation of God coming to us as our salvation.

The people, who were standing to give praise, now kneel and remain kneeling for the most solemn part of the Mass.

The priest extends his hands over the gifts and invokes the Holy Spirit, asking him to come upon them and make them holy so that they may become the Body and Blood of our Lord Jesus Christ. Then he continues with the *Consecration*, in which he says: "This is my Body . . . this is the chalice of my Blood." At this moment, the bread and wine become the Body and Blood of Jesus.

The priest holds up the consecrated Host and then the chalice with the Precious Blood; as he holds them up for the people to adore, he and the people offer the Holy Sacrifice, Christ's Body and Blood, to our heavenly Father.

This is the part of the Mass where we are called on to proclaim our belief in this great mystery of our faith—that Jesus really is present on the altar now.

The Eucharistic Prayer also contains prayers

Liturgy of the Eucharist
OFFERTORY
Preparation of the Altar
Preparation of the Gifts
Offering of the Gifts
Washing of the Hands
Prayers over the Gifts
EUCHARISTIC PRAYER (CANON)
Preface
Sanctus
Prayer of Thanksgiving
Invocation of the Holy Spirit
Consecration
Offering to the Father
Doxology

for the Church, for the living, and for the dead. Then the priest takes the chalice and the paten with the Host and, lifting them up, says:

"Through him, and with him, and in him, O God, almighty Father, in the unity of the Holy Spirit, all glory and honor is yours, for ever and ever."

This prayer is called a **Doxology**. The people respond with "Amen," which means that they fully assent to the prayer of the priest, and the sacrifice is complete.

Words to Know:

hosanna   Doxology

"First of all, then, I urge that supplications, prayers, intercessions, and thanksgivings be made for all men."

1 Timothy 2:1

105

Q. 87   ***When do the bread and wine become the Body and Blood of Jesus?***

The bread and wine become the Body and Blood of Jesus at the moment of the Consecration (CCC 1353, 1376).

Q. 88   ***After the Consecration is there anything left of the bread and wine?***

After the Consecration neither the bread nor the wine is present any longer, but there remain only the appearances of bread and wine (CCC 1376).

Q. 89   ***What is the change from bread and wine into the Body, Blood, Soul, and Divinity of Jesus called?***

The change from bread and wine into the Body, Blood, Soul, and Divinity of Jesus is called transubstantiation (CCC 1376).

106

TEACHER'S NOTES

Preview

In the next lesson, the students will begin learning the Eucharistic Prayers.

Chapter Twenty-Four: Lift Up the Cup of Salvation
Lesson Three: Eucharistic Prayer

Aims

The students will learn that the preface begins the Canon.

They will learn that the Sanctus, or Holy, Holy, Holy, unites our prayers with the entire Communion of Saints. People stand to give praise and kneel to express adoration and reverence.

Materials

- *Activity Book*, p. 95

- Missals with Eucharistic Prayer

Optional:
"Of the glorious Body telling," *Adoremus Hymnal*, #392

Begin

Explain that the Eucharistic Prayer is the high point of the Mass. This is the part of the Mass when transubstantiation occurs (the bread and wine become the Body, Blood, Soul, and Divinity of Jesus). Emphasize the need to pay close attention. (This is not the time of the Mass to go to the bathroom!) It is very important to allow others to pray at this time.

Review proper gestures for this part of the Mass.

Develop

1. Read paragraphs 10–13 from the student text.

2. Review the preface and the responses:
The Lord be with you. And with your spirit.
Lift up your hearts. We lift them up to the Lord.
Let us give thanks to the Lord our God. It is right and just.

3. The students should be aware that there are several Eucharistic Prayers currently accepted by the Church. The Eucharistic Prayer is sometimes called the Canon. The oldest of the Eucharistic Prayers is the Roman Canon.

4. The priest then expresses our intention to worship God in justice and in union with the angels and saints. Read this prayer from some of the Canons and have the students compare them. If possible, have them side-by-side, so the students can discuss their content.

5. The students should know the Sanctus both in English and in Latin. They may learn this prayer to music, if it is sung at your parish. We kneel after the Sanctus.

6. The parts of the Mass are not just made-up. They are taken from Scripture. For example, the "Holy, Holy, Holy" is taken from Rev 4:8. The "Blessed is he who comes in the name of the Lord" is from Matthew 21:9. It is important that the students understand that these prayers are taken from Scripture and reflect the Tradition of the Church. The students may research other prayers to find them in the Scriptures. A Bible-search program or a search on the web is helpful for this. If possible, assign different prayers to the students and have each of them report back to the others.

Reinforce

1. Have the students work on *Activity Book* p. 95 (see *Teacher's Manual*, p. 299).

2. Have the students look up the prayers of the Mass in the Bible, using a computer search program as in Develop 6.

3. Have the students work on the Memorization Questions and Words to Know from this chapter (see *Teacher's Manual*, p. 297).

Conclude

1. Lead the students in singing "Of the glorious Body telling," *Adoremus Hymnal*, #392.

2. End the class by leading the students in praying the Apostles' Creed (see *Teacher's Manual*, p. 396).

The prayers during the Preparation of the Gifts acknowledge God's goodness as Lord of all creation and the goodness of creation itself. They ask God's blessing on these gifts which are to become for us the Bread of Life and our spiritual drink. After the priest offers the bread, and again after he offers the wine, the people respond, "Blessed be God for ever."

The *Washing of the Hands* of the priest signifies the great purity with which we should approach the Eucharist. It is a prayer to God to wash away our sins as we come close to him.

The priest then invites the people to pray that our sacrifice may be accepted by God, the almighty Father.

The people respond with a prayer that our sacrifice may be accepted at the hands of the priest for three purposes: 1. the praise and glory of God's name; 2. for our benefit; and 3. the good of all the Church. This prayer can remind us that in all that we do, God's glory must be considered first; our good and the good of all the Church, though very important, come after. With his hands extended, the priest then says a prayer that the gifts will be acceptable and pleasing to God. The people stand for this prayer and give consent to it by saying, "Amen."

The Eucharistic Prayer

Now comes the high point of the Mass, called the *Eucharistic Prayer* or *Canon*. It is in this part of the Mass that bread and wine become the Body and Blood of our Lord and the sacrifice is offered to God.

The prayer begins with the *Preface*, a consideration of the coming sacrifice in light of the liturgical season of the year or of a feast day. It ends as we join our voices to those of the angels in heaven in the hymn called the *Sanctus*:

"Holy, Holy, Holy Lord God of hosts. Heaven and earth are full of your glory. Hosanna in the highest. Blessed is he who comes in the name of the Lord. Hosanna in the highest."

The word "**hosanna**" (a Hebrew word meaning "save us") is a special exclamation of joy in the salvation God has promised to us. It expresses our joyful expectation of God coming to us as our salvation.

The people, who were standing to give praise, now kneel and remain kneeling for the most solemn part of the Mass.

The priest extends his hands over the gifts and invokes the Holy Spirit, asking him to come upon them and make them holy so that they may become the Body and Blood of our Lord Jesus Christ. Then he continues with the *Consecration*, in which he says: "This is my Body . . . this is the chalice of my Blood." At this moment, the bread and wine become the Body and Blood of Jesus.

The priest holds up the consecrated Host and then the chalice with the Precious Blood; as he holds them up for the people to adore, he and the people offer the Holy Sacrifice, Christ's Body and Blood, to our heavenly Father.

This is the part of the Mass where we are called on to proclaim our belief in this great mystery of our faith—that Jesus really is present on the altar now.

The Eucharistic Prayer also contains prayers

104

for the Church, for the living, and for the dead. Then the priest takes the chalice and the paten with the Host and, lifting them up, says:

"Through him, and with him, and in him, O God, almighty Father, in the unity of the Holy Spirit, all glory and honor is yours, for ever and ever."

This prayer is called a **Doxology**. The people respond with "Amen," which means that they fully assent to the prayer of the priest, and the sacrifice is complete.

Words to Know:
hosanna   Doxology

Liturgy of the Eucharist

OFFERTORY

**Preparation of the Altar
Preparation of the Gifts
Offering of the Gifts
Washing of the Hands
Prayers over the Gifts**

EUCHARISTIC PRAYER
(CANON)

**Preface
Sanctus
Prayer of Thanksgiving
Invocation of the Holy Spirit
Consecration
Offering to the Father
Doxology**

"First of all, then, I urge that supplications, prayers, intercessions, and thanksgivings be made for all men."

1 Timothy 2:1

105

SAINT PASCHAL BAYLON: SAINT OF THE EUCHARIST

Saint Paschal Baylon was a Franciscan friar who lived in the late sixteenth and early seventeenth centuries. He worked as a shepherd in his youth and very early on had a reputation for sanctity. It is said that he walked barefoot and lived very simply, with much fasting and prayer, and that he taught himself to read and write so that he could pray the Little Office of Our Lady, a prayer book commonly used by the laity at that time. He was also noted for his devotion to the Eucharist. When he was unable to attend daily Mass, he would stop whatever he was doing when Mass began and kneel in prayer, facing the direction of the church where the Sacrifice was being offered. Later he joined the Franciscans and continued to be noted for his holiness and devotion to the Blessed Sacrament. He would assist at Masses in the chapel all day and pray there all night. Often when the other friars came into the chapel for morning Mass, they found him asleep on his knees. As soon as he awoke, he eagerly assisted at the first morning Mass again. At one point he travelled through Protestant territories in France and was almost killed for his devotion to the Eucharist and the Catholic Faith. Despite his austere life, he was also noted for his great joy. His superior once said that, even after living with Saint Pascal for many years, he never found even the least fault in him.

Meditate well on this: Seek God above all things. It is right for you to seek God before and above everything else, because the majesty of God wishes you to receive what you ask for. This will also make you more ready to serve God and will enable you to love him more perfectly.

—Saint Paschal Baylon

Preview

In the next lesson, the students will learn about the Consecration of the Eucharist.

Chapter Twenty-Four: Lift Up the Cup of Salvation
Lesson Four: Consecration

Aims

The students will learn that the priest extends his hands over the gifts. He invokes the Holy Spirit to come upon them and make them holy so they can become the Body and Blood of Christ. This is called the Epiclesis.

They will learn that the Consecration occurs when the priest says: "This is my Body" and "This is the chalice of my Blood." At the Consecration, the bread and wine become Jesus truly present. This change in what is present is called transubstantiation. The Doxology is followed by the great Amen.

Materials

- *Activity Book*, p. 96

Optional:
- "Of the glorious Body telling," *Adoremus Hymnal*, #392

Begin

The Consecration is the most sacred part of Mass. It is the prayer that changes the bread and wine into the Body and Blood of Jesus. It is the form of the Sacrament. (Review that the matter is bread and wine and the form is the words of Jesus, "This is my Body…This is the chalice of my Blood".) This change is called transubstantiation. Today, we will learn the most sacred parts of the Canon.

Develop

1. Finish reading the chapter (paragraphs 14–18).

2. During the Epiclesis, the priest extends his hands over the gifts. He calls the Holy Spirit to come down upon them to make them holy, so that they may become the Body and Blood of Jesus Christ. With his hand, he traces a cross in the air over the gifts.

3. Next is the Consecration. Up to this point the priest speaks in the third person, but during the Consecration, he speaks in the first person because it is Jesus speaking through the priest (who is another Christ—or acting in the Person of Christ).

4. The priest recounts the events of the Last Supper and is acting out these same events as he says the very words of Jesus at the Last Supper: "This is my Body," "This is the chalice of my Blood." With these words, Jesus is made present. At the Consecration of each of the species, the priest genuflects in adoration. We should make an act of adoration as well, such as the one that Saint Thomas said: "My Lord and my God."

5. We then proclaim the mystery of faith. There are three options. The students should learn all three.

6. We pray for our deceased members of the Church.

7. Next is the Doxology: "Through him, and with him, and in him, O God, almighty Father, in the unity of the Holy Spirit, all glory and honor is yours, forever and ever." This should only be said by the priests. We unite our prayers with them by saying "Amen." With this, the Canon is complete. After the Doxology, we stand.

Reinforce

1. Have the students work on *Activity Book* p. 96 (see *Teacher's Manual*, p. 299).

2. The students may work on the Memorization Questions and Words to Know from this chapter and prepare for the chapter quiz.

Conclude

1. Lead the students in singing "Of the glorious Body telling," *Adoremus Hymnal*, #392.

2. End class by leading the students in praying the Apostles' Creed (see *Teacher's Manual*, p. 396).

The prayers during the Preparation of the Gifts acknowledge God's goodness as Lord of all creation and the goodness of creation itself. They ask God's blessing on these gifts which are to become for us the Bread of Life and our spiritual drink. After the priest offers the bread, and again after he offers the wine, the people respond, "Blessed be God for ever."

The *Washing of the Hands* of the priest signifies the great purity with which we should approach the Eucharist. It is a prayer to God to wash away our sins as we come close to him.

The priest then invites the people to pray that our sacrifice may be accepted by God, the almighty Father.

The people respond with a prayer that our sacrifice may be accepted at the hands of the priest for three purposes: 1. the praise and glory of God's name; 2. for our benefit; and 3. the good of all the Church. This prayer can remind us that in all that we do, God's glory must be considered first; our good and the good of all the Church, though very important, come after. With his hands extended, the priest then says a prayer that the gifts will be acceptable and pleasing to God. The people stand for this prayer and give consent to it by saying, "Amen."

The Eucharistic Prayer

Now comes the high point of the Mass, called the *Eucharistic Prayer* or *Canon*. It

is in this part of the Mass that bread and wine become the Body and Blood of our Lord and the sacrifice is offered to God.

The prayer begins with the *Preface*, a consideration of the coming sacrifice in light of the liturgical season of the year or of a feast day. It ends as we join our voices to those of the angels in heaven in the hymn called the *Sanctus*:

> *"Holy, Holy, Holy Lord God of hosts. Heaven and earth are full of your glory. Hosanna in the highest. Blessed is he who comes in the name of the Lord. Hosanna in the highest."*

The word **"hosanna"** (a Hebrew word meaning "save us") is a special exclamation of joy in the salvation God has promised to us. It expresses our joyful expectation of God coming to us as our salvation.

The people, who were standing to give praise, now kneel and remain kneeling for the most solemn part of the Mass.

The priest extends his hands over the gifts and invokes the Holy Spirit, asking him to come upon them and make them holy so that they may become the Body and Blood of our Lord Jesus Christ. Then he continues with the *Consecration*, in which he says: "This is my Body . . . this is the chalice of my Blood." At this moment, the bread and wine become the Body and Blood of Jesus.

The priest holds up the consecrated Host and then the chalice with the Precious Blood; as he holds them up for the people to adore, he and the people offer the Holy Sacrifice, Christ's Body and Blood, to our heavenly Father.

This is the part of the Mass where we are called on to proclaim our belief in this great mystery of our faith—that Jesus really is present on the altar now.

The Eucharistic Prayer also contains prayers

Liturgy of the Eucharist
OFFERTORY
Preparation of the Altar
Preparation of the Gifts
Offering of the Gifts
Washing of the Hands
Prayers over the Gifts
EUCHARISTIC PRAYER (CANON)
Preface
Sanctus
Prayer of Thanksgiving
Invocation of the Holy Spirit
Consecration
Offering to the Father
Doxology

for the Church, for the living, and for the dead. Then the priest takes the chalice and the paten with the Host and, lifting them up, says:

> *"Through him, and with him, and in him, O God, almighty Father, in the unity of the Holy Spirit, all glory and honor is yours, for ever and ever."*

This prayer is called a **Doxology**. The people respond with "Amen," which means that they fully assent to the prayer of the priest, and the sacrifice is complete.

Words to Know:
hosanna   Doxology

"First of all, then, I urge that supplications, prayers, intercessions, and thanksgivings be made for all men."

1 Timothy 2:1

Q. 87 *When do the bread and wine become the Body and Blood of Jesus?*

The bread and wine become the Body and Blood of Jesus at the moment of the Consecration (CCC 1353, 1376).

Q. 88 *After the Consecration is there anything left of the bread and wine?*

After the Consecration neither the bread nor the wine is present any longer, but there remain only the appearances of bread and wine (CCC 1376).

Q. 89 *What is the change from bread and wine into the Body, Blood, Soul, and Divinity of Jesus called?*

The change from bread and wine into the Body, Blood, Soul, and Divinity of Jesus is called transubstantiation (CCC 1376).

TEACHER'S NOTES

Preview

In the next lesson, the students' understanding of the material covered in this chapter will be reviewed and assessed.

CHAPTER TWENTY-FOUR: LIFT UP THE CUP OF SALVATION
REVIEW AND ASSESSMENT

Aims

The students' understanding of the material covered in this chapter will be reviewed and assessed.

Materials

- Quiz 24, Appendix, p. A-34

Optional:
- "Of the glorious Body telling," *Adoremus Hymnal*, #392

Review and Enrichment

1. The students should know all the parts of the Liturgy of the Eucharist:

OFFERTORY
- Preparation of the Altar
- Preparation of the Gifts
- Offering of the Gifts
- Washing of the Hands
- Prayers over the Gifts

EUCHARISTIC PRAYER:
- Preface
- Sanctus
- Prayer of Thanksgiving
- Invocation of the Holy Spirit
- Consecration
- Offering to the Father
- Doxology

2. The students should know the appropriate gestures and the correct responses to the parts of the Mass.

Name:

Lift Up the Cup of Salvation   **Quiz 24**

Part I: Number the parts of the Liturgy of the Eucharist to indicate their proper order and give a brief description of each.

4 Preface: begins the Eucharistic Prayer and considers the coming sacrifice in light of the liturgical season or feast day.

9 Doxology: the priest lifts the chalice and paten and glorifies God

7 Consecration: the priest says "This is my Body . . . This is my Blood" and the bread and wine become the Body and Blood of Jesus

2 Washing of the Hands: the priest washes his hands, signifying the great purity with which we should approach the Eucharist

5 Sanctus: a special exclamation of joy in the salvation God has promised to us

6 Invocation of the Holy Spirit: the priest asks the Holy Spirit to come upon the gifts and make them holy so they may become the Body and Blood of Jesus

1 Preparation of the Gifts: the priest accepts the bread and wine and places them on the altar and offers them to God

8 Offering to the Father: the priest and people offer Christ's Body and Blood to the Father

3 Prayer over the Gifts: the priest asks God's blessing on the gifts that will become the Eucharist

Part II: Answer the following.

1. What does the word *hosanna* mean?
The word hosanna means save us.

2. Give another name for the Eucharistic Prayer.
Another name for the Eucharistic Prayer is the Canon.

A-34   *Faith and Life Series • Grade 6 • Appendix A*

Assess

1. Distribute the quizzes, and read through them with the students to be sure they understand the questions.

2. Administer the quiz. As the students hand in their work, you may orally quiz them on the Memorization Questions from this chapter.

3. After all the quizzes have been handed in, you may wish to review the correct answers with the class.

Conclude

1. Lead the students in singing "Of the glorious Body telling," *Adoremus Hymnal*, #392.

2. End class by leading the students in praying the Apostles' Creed (see *Teacher's Manual*, p. 396).

Chapter Twenty-Four: Lift Up the Cup of Salvation
Activity Book Answer Keys

Name:_____

The Preparation of the Gifts

Answer the following questions in complete sentences.

1. What is brought forward to the priest during the Preparation of the Gifts?
   Bread and wine are brought forward to the priest.

2. What does the priest do with the gifts and what will happen to them?
   The priest accepts them, places them on the altar, and with special prayers offers them to God. They will become the Body, Blood, Soul, and Divinity of Christ.

3. Of what are these gifts made?
   The bread is made up of many grains of wheat and the wine of many grapes.

4. What other gifts can we offer to God?
   We can also offer ourselves, including our joys and sorrows, to God.

5. Why might a song be sung?
   Answers will vary.

Name:_____

Preparing for the Sacrifice

Answer the following questions in complete sentences.

1. When the priest offers the bread and wine to God, what is our response?
   Our response is "Blessed be God forever."

2. Why does the priest wash his hands?
   The priest washes his hands to symbolize the great purity with which we should approach the Eucharist.

3. We are then invited to pray that the sacrifice may be accepted by God. What do we pray?
   We pray that our sacrifice will be accepted at the priest's hands for the praise and glory of God's name, for our benefit, and for the good of all the Church.

4. Of what does this prayer remind us?
   The prayer reminds us that God's glory must come first in all we do.

5. What gesture does the priest use when he is praying over the gifts?
   The priest extends his hands over the gifts as he prays over them.

6. How do the people give their consent?
   The people give their consent by saying "Amen."

7. What is the next prayer called?
   The next prayer is called the Eucharistic Prayer or Canon.

Name:_____

The Parts of the Mass

Explain what happens during the parts of the Mass listed below.

OFFERTORY
Preparation of the Altar:
The altar is prepared for the holy sacrifice that is about to take place.
Preparation of the Gifts:
The priest accepts the bread and wine and places them on the altar.
Offering of the Gifts:
The gifts are offered to God.
Washing of the Hands:
The priest washes his hands, signifying the great purity with which we should approach the Eucharist.
Prayers over the Gifts:
Ask God's blessing on the gifts that will become the Eucharist.

EUCHARISTIC PRAYER
Sanctus:
We all pray this together. It is a special exclamation of joy in the salvation God has promised to us.
Invocation of the Holy Spirit (Epiclesis):
The priest prays that the Holy Spirit will come upon the gifts and make them holy.
Consecration:
The priest says the words of institution and the bread and wine become Jesus, Body, Blood, Soul, and Divinity.
Doxology:
The prayer with which the priest offers Jesus to the Father.

Name:_____

The Eucharistic Prayer

Answer the following questions in complete sentences.

1. What is the high point of the Mass?
   The high point of the Mass is the Eucharistic Prayer or Canon.

2. What happens during this prayer?
   During this prayer, the bread and wine become Jesus and the sacrifice is offered to God.

3. How does this prayer begin?
   This prayer begins with the Preface.

4. Write out the hymn of praise which joins us in singing with all the angels in heaven.
   Holy, Holy, Holy Lord God of hosts. Heaven and earth are full of your glory. Hosanna in the highest. Blessed is he who comes in the name of the Lord. Hosanna in the highest.

5. What does "hosanna" mean?
   Hosanna means save us.

6. How does the priest invoke the Holy Spirit?
   The priest invokes the Holy Spirit by extending his hands over the gifts and asking the Holy Spirit to come upon them.

7. What words are said in the Consecration?
   "This is my Body . . . this is the chalice of my Blood."

8. What is the Consecration?
   The Consecration is the part of the Mass where the bread and wine become Jesus.

TEACHER'S NOTES

CHAPTER TWENTY-FIVE
COME TO THE TABLE OF THE LORD

Catechism of the Catholic Church References

Fruits of Communion: 1391–1401, 1416
Holy Communion: 1355, 1382–90, 1415, 1417
Jesus Teaches How to Pray: 2607–15, 2621
Liturgy:1349–50, 1355, 1384–8, 2770
Liturgical Celebration of the Eucharist:
      Celebration through the Ages: 1345–47
      Movement of the Celebration: 1348–55, 1408
Lord's Prayer:
      "Our Father who art in heaven": 2777–96,
      2797–2802
      "Hallowed be thy name": 2807–15, 2858
      "Thy kingdom come": 2816–21, 2859

"Thy will be done on earth as it is in heaven":
2822–27, 2860
"Give us this day our daily bread": 2828–37, 2861
"Forgive us our trespasses as we forgive those who
trespass against us": 2838–45, 2862
"Lead us not into temptation": 2846–49, 2863
"But deliver us from evil": 2850–54, 2864
Final Doxology: 2855–56, 2865
Lord's Prayer as Summary of the Whole Gospel:
2761–72, 2773–76
Presence of Christ in the Eucharist: 1373–81, 1410, 1418
Signs of Bread and Wine in the Eucharist: 1333–36, 1412

Scripture References

Our Father: Mt 6:9–13
Passages on Peace: Jn 14:27; Phil 4:7; Mt 5:23–24

Healing of Centurion's Servant: Mt 8:5–13
Healing of Ten Lepers: Lk 17:12–19

Summary of Lesson Content

Lesson 1

After the great Amen, we join in praying the Our Father. This is a prayer that Jesus himself taught us to pray. The Our Father unites us in God's family.

Lesson 3

"Lord I am not worthy," expresses our humility and awe before God present in the Eucharist.

After the Communion antiphon, Holy Communion is distributed to those worthily disposed.

Before receiving Communion, we should make a sign of reverence, such as bowing. The response to "The Body of Christ" is "Amen." This is our act of faith and assent of the will.

Lesson 2

The exchange of peace echoes the resurrected Christ.

The Agnus Dei (Lamb of God) calls us to Communion in the Paschal Meal sealing the New Covenant in the Body and Blood of Christ.

Lesson 4

After we receive Communion, the Eucharistic presence of our Lord remains in us for about 10–15 minutes. This is a time to unite ourselves, delve into this divine intimacy, and offer prayers of thanksgiving.

The prayer after Communion is followed by the final blessing. Mass is ended, and a closing or recessional hymn is sung.

Chapter Twenty-Five: Come to the Table of the Lord
Lesson One: Our Father

Aims

The students will learn that, after the Great Amen, we join in praying the Our Father. This is a prayer that Jesus himself taught us to pray. The Our Father unites us in God's family.

Materials

- *Activity Book*, p. 97

Optional:
- Calligraphy pens and paper

- "O Lord Jesus, I adore thee," *Adoremus Hymnal*, #513

Begin

From the Bible, read the story of Jesus giving the Apostles the Our Father, Matthew 6:9–13. The students may dramatize this story.

Develop

1. Read paragraphs 1–4 from the student text.

2. The Our Father is the model prayer that Jesus gave us. It summarizes the Gospels. It contains all the "spiritual ingredients" we need to move us into a close and loving family with God. Below, we will review the petitions of the Our Father:
OUR FATHER, WHO ART IN HEAVEN, HALLOWED BE THY NAME: We call God "our Father," rather than "my Father," because we are his children through the Church. All people in the Church are God's children. We acknowledge that God is in heaven. However, God is all present: he is everywhere. We think of God as in heaven, for heaven is our greatest desire where we can be perfectly happy and in union with God. When we say: Hallowed be thy name, we ask that all people will know and honor God and realize the sacredness of his name. This calls us to recognize the truths of the Faith.
THY KINGDOM COME: We want the reign of Christ to be present on earth, so we can live in his love.

THY WILL WE DONE ON EARTH AS IT IS IN HEAVEN: We surrender our will to God. If all people did this here on earth, it would be like heaven.
GIVE US THIS DAY OUR DAILY BREAD: We ask for God to provide for our needs and, in a special way, we recognize Jesus in the Eucharist offered daily at Mass.
AND FORGIVE US OUR TRESPASSES AS WE FORGIVE THOSE WHO TRESPASS AGAINST US: We ask to be forgiven as much as we forgive.
AND LEAD US NOT INTO TEMPTATION: Let not the world or our flesh lead us to sin and distract us from God's ways.
BUT DELIVER US FROM EVIL: Give us God's divine protection against all spiritual evils, including Satan and the demons.

3. Learn to sing the Our Father.

Reinforce

1. Have the students work on *Activity Book* p. 97 (see *Teacher's Manual*, p. 311). The students should meditate upon the Our Father and write down their meditations.

2. Have the students work on the Memorization Questions from this chapter (see *Teacher's Manual*, p. 307).

3. Optional: Do a craft to reinforce memorization of the Our Father; e.g., copy the prayer in calligraphy.

Conclude

1. Teach the students to sing "O Lord Jesus, I adore thee," *Adoremus Hymnal*, #513.

2. End class by leading the students in the Agnus Dei (on the facing page).

CHAPTER 25

Come to the Table of the Lord

"And they held steadfastly to the apostles' teaching and fellowship, to the breaking of bread and the prayers."

Acts 2:42

The Communion Rite follows the Eucharistic Prayer in the Liturgy of the Eucharist. The sacred victim, accepted by the Father—since it is his own divine Son—is now given back to us as the greatest gift we can receive.

At the conclusion of the Eucharistic Prayer, after the people say "Amen," the priest puts down the chalice and the paten with the Host and says: "At the Savior's command and formed by divine teaching, we dare to say..."

Then we join in the *Our Father* in order to praise God and place our petitions before him. This is the prayer that our Lord himself taught us as the model for all our prayers. It is certainly fitting, as we pause in the action of the

Mass, to reach out to God the Father with these words in which Jesus taught his Apostles to pray simply, with confidence and love.

The Our Father, called the perfect prayer, contains all the spiritual ingredients we need to move us into a close and loving family, the People of God. Jesus taught us to say "our" Father, not "my" Father, because God wishes to live with us in a community. As God has said so many times in the Old Testament: "I will be your God and you will be my people."

My Peace I Give You

Saint Paul, in his letter to the Philippians, speaks of the peace of God "which passes all understanding" (Phil 4:7). This priceless treasure of peace is Christ's gift to us. At the Last Supper, Christ says: "Peace I leave with you; my peace I give to you; not as the world gives do I give to you. Let not your hearts be troubled, neither let them be afraid" (Jn 14:27).

At this point in the Mass, we may offer each other a sign of Christ's peace, the peace of forgiveness and the reassurance of having

107

his mercy and love. To preserve this gift we must seek to live in peace every day with family and friends and everyone we meet.

As the *Rite of Peace* ends, the priest takes the Host and breaks it over the paten. He places a small piece in the chalice, saying quietly: "May this mingling of the Body and Blood of our Lord Jesus Christ bring eternal life to us who receive it."

Meanwhile, everyone prays: "Lamb of God, you take away the sins of the world, have mercy on us . . . grant us peace."

Jesus, of course, is the "Lamb of God;" he takes away the sins of the world. The Paschal lamb that is eaten by Jewish families to celebrate the Passover, which freed the Israelites from the Egyptians, is a symbol of the true Paschal Lamb who frees us from the slavery of our sins.

I Am Not Worthy

Close to Communion now, we repeat the words of a Roman centurion who once asked Jesus to save one of his servants from death. The centurion did not consider himself worthy to receive Jesus. He asked that Jesus simply give the word and his servant would be cured. Jesus marveled at this man's faith and granted his request. Now we, too, say as the centurion did:

"Lord, I am not worthy that you should enter under my roof, but only say the word and my soul shall be healed" (see Mt 8:8).

Then the priest takes Communion, and the *Communion Antiphon* is recited or sung.

Finally we go up to receive Holy Communion. The priest holds the Host before the communicant, and says: "The Body of Christ," to which the communicant answers: "Amen." When we say "Amen" we are saying: "Yes, I

108

believe that this is really Jesus Christ."

If we are unable to receive Communion for some reason, we should use the time to pray and ask Jesus to be present with us.

Giving Thanks

Receiving Holy Communion allows us to be alone with God in a private way. It is one of the best chances we have to thank Jesus for everything he gives us—especially the gift of his Body and Blood.

There is an incident in the Gospel in which Jesus cures ten lepers. They were cured as they were on their way to show themselves to the priests as Jesus directed. Only one of them returned to Jesus to thank him.

Let's remember to be grateful to Jesus for coming to us in Holy Communion. How do we welcome him? Do we receive him on our tongue or in our hand and then close our minds and hearts to him? Do we at least keep him company for five or ten minutes?

When Communion has been distributed, the priest cleans the paten over the chalice

SAINT AGNES

Saint Agnes, an early martyr for purity, lived and died in Rome. Many of the young noblemen of Rome sought to marry her, but she refused every one, saying that she had consecrated herself to a heavenly husband. This occurred in the early fourth century during the persecution of Diocletian, when simply being a Christian was punishable by death. After Agnes' rejections, some of the young men were so upset that they denounced her as a Christian. They had discovered that the heavenly husband to whom she had consecrated herself was Jesus. Roman officials tried everything from bribery to torture to make Agnes recant, but she refused. Finally, the officials told her that she must either reject her faith in Christ or be killed. Saint Agnes remained true to her faith, and it is said that she accepted her martyrdom as joyfully as a bride on her wedding day—after all, she was going to meet her beloved. Saint Augustine and Saint Ambrose say that she was thirteen at the time of her death.

The Agnus Dei in Latin is:
Agnus Dei, qui tollis peccata mundi, miserere nobis.
Agnus Dei, qui tollis peccata mundi, miserere nobis.
Agnus Dei, qui tollis peccata mundi, dona nobis pacem.

Preview

In the next lesson, the students will learn about the Rite of Peace.

CHAPTER TWENTY-FIVE: COME TO THE TABLE OF THE LORD
LESSON TWO: PEACE BE WITH YOU

Aims

The students will learn that the exchange of peace echoes the resurrected Christ.

They will learn that the Agnus Dei (Lamb of God) calls us to Communion in the Paschal Meal sealing the New Covenant in the Body and Blood of Christ.

Materials

• *Activity Book*, p. 98

Optional:
• "O Lord Jesus, I adore thee," *Adoremus Hymnal*, #513

Begin

"Peace I leave with you; my peace I give to you; not as the world gives do I give to you. Let not your hearts be troubled, neither let them be afraid" (Jn 14:27).

Discuss how the peace of the world and Jesus' peace are not the same thing.

Can you have world peace when we are at war?
Can you have Jesus' peace when we are at war?
What is the difference?
Read: Jn 14:27; Phil 4:7; Mt 5:23–24.

Develop

1. Read paragraphs 5–9 from the student text.

2. After the Our Father, we exchange a sign of peace. Usually, we extend our hand to shake hands with the people immediately surrounding us, saying: "Peace be with you" or "The Peace of Christ." The peace we extend is the reassurance of having Jesus' mercy and love. Therefore, we must strive to live Christ's peace in our families, our work places, our school, our church, etc.

3. The Fraction Rite is the breaking of the Eucharistic Host. It is important to understand that as the Host is broken, Jesus is not broken. He is truly and wholly present in each of the parts of the Sacred Host.

4. The priest then mingles the Sacred Host in the Precious Blood in the chalice, saying, "May this mingling of the Body

and Blood of our Lord Jesus Christ bring eternal life to us who receive it."

5. Meanwhile, the congregation is praying the Agnus Dei: the Lamb of God. The students should know the Agnus Dei that is said/sung at Mass.

6. Review how Jesus is the Lamb of God (Jn 1:29) and review the Passover lamb, the sacrifice which freed the Israelites from slavery just as Jesus frees us from our sins.

7. Teach the students what the priest says after the Our Father, and consider these words: Deliver us, Lord, we pray, from every evil, graciously grant peace in our days, that, by the help of your mercy, we may be always free from sin and safe from all distress, as we await the blessed hope and the coming of our Savior, Jesus Christ.

Reinforce

1. Have the students work on *Activity Book* p. 98 (see *Teacher's Manual*, p. 311).

2. The students may work on the Memorization Questions from this chapter (see *Teacher's Manual*, p. 307).

Conclude

1. Lead the students in singing "O Lord Jesus, I adore thee," *Adoremus Hymnal*, #513.

2. End class by leading the students in the Agnus Dei (see *Teacher's Manual*, p. 303).

CHAPTER 25

Come to the Table of the Lord

"And they held steadfastly to the apostles' teaching and fellowship, to the breaking of bread and the prayers."

Acts 2:42

The Communion Rite follows the Eucharistic Prayer in the Liturgy of the Eucharist. The sacred victim, accepted by the Father—since it is his own divine Son—is now given back to us as the greatest gift we can receive.

At the conclusion of the Eucharistic Prayer, after the people say "Amen," the priest puts down the chalice and the paten with the Host and says: "At the Savior's command and formed by divine teaching, we dare to say…"

Then we join in the *Our Father* in order to praise God and place our petitions before him. This is the prayer that our Lord himself taught us as the model for all our prayers. It is certainly fitting, as we pause in the action of the

Mass, to reach out to God the Father with these words in which Jesus taught his Apostles to pray simply, with confidence and love.

The Our Father, called the perfect prayer, contains all the spiritual ingredients we need to move us into a close and loving family, the People of God. Jesus taught us to say "our" Father, not "my" Father, because God wishes to live with us in a community. As God has said so many times in the Old Testament: "I will be your God and you will be my people."

My Peace I Give You

Saint Paul, in his letter to the Philippians, speaks of the peace of God "which passes all understanding" (Phil 4:7). This priceless treasure of peace is Christ's gift to us. At the Last Supper, Christ says: "Peace I leave with you; my peace I give to you; not as the world gives do I give to you. Let not your hearts be troubled, neither let them be afraid" (Jn 14:27).

At this point in the Mass, we may offer each other a sign of Christ's peace, the peace of forgiveness and the reassurance of having

107

his mercy and love. To preserve this gift we must seek to live in peace every day with family and friends and everyone we meet.

As the *Rite of Peace* ends, the priest takes the Host and breaks it over the paten. He places a small piece in the chalice, saying quietly: "May this mingling of the Body and Blood of our Lord Jesus Christ bring eternal life to us who receive it."

Meanwhile, everyone prays: "Lamb of God, you take away the sins of the world, have mercy on us . . . grant us peace."

Jesus, of course, is the "Lamb of God;" he takes away the sins of the world. The Paschal lamb that is eaten by Jewish families to celebrate the Passover, which freed the Israelites from the Egyptians, is a symbol of the true Paschal Lamb who frees us from the slavery of our sins.

I Am Not Worthy

Close to Communion now, we repeat the words of a Roman centurion who once asked Jesus to save one of his servants from death. The centurion did not consider himself worthy to receive Jesus. He asked that Jesus simply give the word and his servant would be cured. Jesus marveled at this man's faith and granted his request. Now we, too, say as the centurion did:

"Lord, I am not worthy that you should enter under my roof, but only say the word and my soul shall be healed" (see Mt 8:8).

Then the priest takes Communion, and the *Communion Antiphon* is recited or sung.

Finally we go up to receive Holy Communion. The priest holds the Host before the communicant, and says: "The Body of Christ," to which the communicant answers: "Amen." When we say "Amen" we are saying: "Yes, I

108

believe that this is really Jesus Christ."

If we are unable to receive Communion for some reason, we should use the time to pray and ask Jesus to be present with us.

Giving Thanks

Receiving Holy Communion allows us to be alone with God in a private way. It is one of the best chances we have to thank Jesus for everything he gives us—especially the gift of his Body and Blood.

There is an incident in the Gospel in which Jesus cures ten lepers. They were cured as they were on their way to show themselves to the priests as Jesus directed. Only one of them returned to Jesus to thank him.

Let's remember to be grateful to Jesus for coming to us in Holy Communion. How do we welcome him? Do we receive him on our tongue or in our hand and then close our minds and hearts to him? Do we at least keep him company for five or ten minutes?

When Communion has been distributed, the priest cleans the paten over the chalice

---

COMMUNION RITE

The Lord's Prayer (Our Father)
Rite of Peace
Breaking of the Bread
Lamb of God (Agnus Dei)
Communion of the Priest
Communion Antiphon
Communion of the People
Prayer after Communion

CONCLUDING RITE

Blessing
Closing Hymn (Recessional)

and then cleans the chalice itself. The people have a chance to pray quietly. The priest may sit down for a time to continue the silence and thanksgiving. Then, standing at the chair or at the altar, the priest says the *Prayer after Communion*, which asks that our share in the Eucharist be fruitful.

The *Blessing* in the name of the Blessed Trinity follows, and then the priest declares: "Go forth, the Mass is ended."

The people answer: "Thanks be to God."
There may be a *Closing Hymn (Recessional)* as the priest leaves the altar.

After Mass, we should try to spend some time—however brief—alone with Jesus. We may pray for ourselves; for the Church, the Pope, priests, and religious; for our families, friends, and others. A prayer book with a selection of prayers for thanksgiving after Communion may be helpful.

Q. 90 *Who is the Lamb of God?*
Jesus is the Lamb of God, whose sacrifice takes away the sin of the world (CCC 608).

109

PRAYERS OF THE MASS

After the Agnus Dei, the priest breaks the Host over the paten and places a small piece of the Host in the chalice. This is called the mingling of the Body and Blood. Afterward, he silently prays one of two prayers:

1. Lord Jesus Christ, Son of the living God, who, by the will of the Father and the work of the Holy Spirit, through your Death gave life to the world, free me by this, your most holy Body and Blood, from all my sins and from every evil; keep me always faithful to your commandments, and never let me be parted from you.

2. May the receiving of your Body and Blood, Lord Jesus Christ, not bring me to judgment and condemnation, but through your loving mercy be for me protection in mind and body, and a healing remedy.

Preview

In the next lesson, the students will learn about reception of Holy Communion.

Chapter Twenty-Five: Come to the Table of the Lord
Lesson Three: Communion

Aims

The students will learn that by saying, "Lord I am not worthy," we express our humility and awe before God present in the Eucharist.

They will learn that, after the Communion antiphon, Holy Communion is distributed to those worthily disposed. Before receiving Communion, we should make a sign of reverence, such as bowing. The response to "The Body of Christ" is "*Amen.*" This is our act of faith and assent of the will.

Materials

- *Activity Book*, p. 99

Optional:
- "O Lord Jesus, I adore thee," *Adoremus Hymnal*, #513

Begin

Read from the Bible the story of the Centurion's servant being healed: Mt 8:5–13. You may have the students dramatize this passage.

Discuss with the students:
- The Centurion's faith
- Jesus' ability to work miracles from a distance
- Our own unworthiness before God

Develop

1. Read paragraphs 10–13.

2. After the Agnus Dei, the priest elevates the Eucharist and says: "Behold the Lamb of God, behold him who takes away the sins of the world. Blessed are those called to the supper of the Lamb." We reply: "Lord, I am not worthy that you should enter under my roof, but only say the word and my soul shall be healed."

3. The priest then receives Communion, saying: "May the Body of Christ keep me safe for eternal life. May the Blood of Christ keep me safe for eternal life." When the priest receives Holy Communion, the Communion antiphon is said or sung.

4. The priest then distributes Communion. If there is a large number of people receiving, concelebrating priests and deacons help to distribute Communion. In some parishes, there are also extraordinary ministers of Holy Communion. These are lay people who are commissioned and specially trained by the diocese to distribute Communion when there is an

extraordinarily large number of people in the congregation, and the number is too large for the ordinary minister(s) to distribute Communion in a timely manner. Often priests and deacons will also visit the homebound or those in the hospital or nursing home to celebrate Mass or simply to bring them Communion so they can receive our Lord..

5. If one is worthy/properly disposed, he may receive Holy Communion. The priest will hold up the Host and say: "The Body of Christ." One may receive on the hand or the tongue after replying: "Amen." If Communion is offered under both species, the chalice will be offered and the priest will say: "The Blood of Christ." Again, the reply is "Amen." We will review the steps for worthy and reverent reception of Holy Communion in another chapter. It is important to understand that if one receives only the Sacred Host, that he nonetheless receives the Body, Blood, Soul, and Divinity of Jesus—the whole of Jesus. If one receives only a piece of the Host, this is also true. Likewise, if one receives from the chalice alone, he receives the Body, Blood, Soul, and Divinity of Jesus.

Reinforce

1. Have the students work on *Activity Book* p. 99 (see *Teacher's Manual*, p. 311).

2. The students may work on the Memorization Questions from this chapter.

Conclude

1. Lead the students in singing "O Lord Jesus, I adore thee," *Adoremus Hymnal*, #513.

2. End class by leading the students in praying the Agnus Dei (see *Teacher's Manual*, p. 303).

his mercy and love. To preserve this gift we must seek to live in peace every day with family and friends and everyone we meet.

As the *Rite of Peace* ends, the priest takes the Host and breaks it over the paten. He places a small piece in the chalice, saying quietly: "May this mingling of the Body and Blood of our Lord Jesus Christ bring eternal life to us who receive it."

Meanwhile, everyone prays: "Lamb of God, you take away the sins of the world, have mercy on us . . . grant us peace."

Jesus, of course, is the "Lamb of God;" he takes away the sins of the world. The Paschal lamb that is eaten by Jewish families to celebrate the Passover, which freed the Israelites from the Egyptians, is a symbol of the true Paschal Lamb who frees us from the slavery of our sins.

I Am Not Worthy

Close to Communion now, we repeat the words of a Roman centurion who once asked Jesus to save one of his servants from death. The centurion did not consider himself worthy to receive Jesus. He asked that Jesus simply give the word and his servant would be cured. Jesus marveled at this man's faith and granted his request. Now we, too, say as the centurion did:

"Lord, I am not worthy that you should enter under my roof, but only say the word and my soul shall be healed" (see Mt 8:8).

Then the priest takes Communion, and the *Communion Antiphon* is recited or sung.

Finally we go up to receive Holy Communion. The priest holds the Host before the communicant, and says: "The Body of Christ," to which the communicant answers: "Amen." When we say "Amen" we are saying: "Yes, I believe that this is really Jesus Christ."

If we are unable to receive Communion for some reason, we should use the time to pray and ask Jesus to be present with us.

Giving Thanks

Receiving Holy Communion allows us to be alone with God in a private way. It is one of the best chances we have to thank Jesus for everything he gives us—especially the gift of his Body and Blood.

There is an incident in the Gospel in which Jesus cures ten lepers. They were cured as they were on their way to show themselves to the priests as Jesus directed. Only one of them returned to Jesus to thank him.

Let's remember to be grateful to Jesus for coming to us in Holy Communion. How do we welcome him? Do we receive him on our tongue or in our hand and then close our minds and hearts to him? Do we at least keep him company for five or ten minutes?

When Communion has been distributed, the priest cleans the paten over the chalice

---

COMMUNION RITE
The Lord's Prayer (Our Father)
Rite of Peace
Breaking of the Bread
Lamb of God (Agnus Dei)
Communion of the Priest
Communion Antiphon
Communion of the People
Prayer after Communion
CONCLUDING RITE
Blessing
Closing Hymn (Recessional)

and then cleans the chalice itself. The people have a chance to pray quietly. The priest may sit down for a time to continue the silence and thanksgiving. Then, standing at the chair or at the altar, the priest says the *Prayer after Communion*, which asks that our share in the Eucharist be fruitful.

The *Blessing* in the name of the Blessed Trinity follows, and then the priest declares: "Go forth, the Mass is ended."

The people answer: "Thanks be to God."

There may be a *Closing Hymn (Recessional)* as the priest leaves the altar.

After Mass, we should try to spend some time—however brief—alone with Jesus. We may pray for ourselves; for the Church, the Pope, priests, and religious; for our families, friends, and others. A prayer book with a selection of prayers for thanksgiving after Communion may be helpful.

> **Q. 90** *Who is the Lamb of God?*
> Jesus is the Lamb of God, whose sacrifice takes away the sin of the world (CCC 608).

> **Q. 91** *When the Host is broken into several parts, is the Body of Jesus Christ broken?*
> When the Host is broken into several parts, the Body of Jesus Christ is not broken, but only the appearances of the bread; the Body of our Lord remains whole and entire in each of the parts (CCC 1377).
>
> **Q. 92** *Is only the Body of Jesus Christ present under the appearances of bread and only his Blood under the appearances of the wine?*
> No, under the appearances of the bread Jesus Christ is present whole and entire, in Body, Blood, Soul, and Divinity; and the same under the appearances of the wine (CCC 1374, 1390).

WHEN *NOT* TO RECEIVE HOLY COMMUNION

You should not receive Holy Communion:

1. if you are not Catholic.

2. if you do not believe in the Eucharistic presence of our Lord.

3. if you are in mortal sin.

4. if you have not kept the fast.

5. if you have not been prepared to receive Holy Communion, or made your First Holy Communion.

6. if you are not in union with the Catholic Church for some reason.

Preview

In the next lesson, the students will learn about offering prayers of thanksgiving.

Chapter Twenty-Five: Come to the Table of the Lord
Lesson Four: Thanksgiving

Aims

The students will learn that, after we receive Communion, the Eucharistic presence of our Lord remains in us for about 10–15 minutes. This is a time to unite ourselves, delve into this divine intimacy, and offer prayers of thanksgiving.

They will learn that there is a prayer after Communion, followed by the final blessing. Mass is ended and a closing or recessional hymn is sung.

Materials

• *Activity Book*, p. 100

Optional:
• "O Lord Jesus, I adore thee," *Adoremus Hymnal*, #513

Begin

From the Bible, read the story of the healing of the ten lepers (Lk 17:12–19). The students may dramatize this passage.

Discuss how the students can show their thanks to God for his wondrous gift of himself in the Holy Eucharist.

Develop

1. Finish reading the chapter with the students, paragraphs 14–21.

2. How should we receive Communion? In what spirit? How should we be with Jesus once we receive him? Have the students recommend some prayers to say.

3. Remind the students that when we receive Holy Communion, Jesus remains physically present within us as long as the species remains, approximately 10–15 minutes.

4. The priest cleans the paten over the chalice and purifies the vessels. He silently says: "What has passed our lips as food, O Lord, may we possess in purity of heart, that what has been given to us in time may be our healing for eternity."

5. When Communion is over and the altar is cleared, we stand to pray the prayer after Communion, which will change with each day of the liturgical year.

6. Often on Sunday there will be announcements.

7. The priest then gives a final blessing in the name of the Blessed Trinity, and the priest declares: "Go forth, the Mass is ended." The people respond: "Thanks be to God."

8. There may be a closing hymn. During this hymn, the priests leave the altar. This is called the recessional.

9. After Mass, we should try to spend some time, however brief, alone in thanksgiving with Jesus before we greet our neighbors and spend time with friends and family.

10. You may discuss traditions that people may have for Sunday activities after Mass: e.g., Sunday Brunch.

Reinforce

1. Have the students work on *Activity Book* p. 100 (see *Teacher's Manual*, p. 311).

2. The students should work on the Memorization Questions from this chapter and review for the quiz.

Conclude

1. Lead the students in singing "O Lord Jesus, I adore thee," *Adoremus Hymnal*, #513.

2. End class by leading the students in praying the Agnus Dei (see *Teacher's Manual*, p. 303).

his mercy and love. To preserve this gift we must seek to live in peace every day with family and friends and everyone we meet.

As the *Rite of Peace* ends, the priest takes the Host and breaks it over the paten. He places a small piece in the chalice, saying quietly: "May this mingling of the Body and Blood of our Lord Jesus Christ bring eternal life to us who receive it."

Meanwhile, everyone prays: "Lamb of God, you take away the sins of the world, have mercy on us . . . grant us peace."

Jesus, of course, is the "Lamb of God;" he takes away the sins of the world. The Paschal lamb that is eaten by Jewish families to celebrate the Passover, which freed the Israelites from the Egyptians, is a symbol of the true Paschal Lamb who frees us from the slavery of our sins.

I Am Not Worthy

Close to Communion now, we repeat the words of a Roman centurion who once asked Jesus to save one of his servants from death. The centurion did not consider himself worthy to receive Jesus. He asked that Jesus simply give the word and his servant would be cured. Jesus marveled at this man's faith and granted his request. Now we, too, say as the centurion did:

"Lord, I am not worthy that you should enter under my roof, but only say the word and my soul shall be healed" (see Mt 8:8).

Then the priest takes Communion, and the *Communion Antiphon* is recited or sung.

Finally we go up to receive Holy Communion. The priest holds the Host before the communicant, and says: "The Body of Christ," to which the communicant answers: "Amen." When we say "Amen" we are saying: "Yes, I believe that this is really Jesus Christ."

If we are unable to receive Communion for some reason, we should use the time to pray and ask Jesus to be present with us.

Giving Thanks

Receiving Holy Communion allows us to be alone with God in a private way. It is one of the best chances we have to thank Jesus for everything he gives us—especially the gift of his Body and Blood.

There is an incident in the Gospel in which Jesus cures ten lepers. They were cured as they were on their way to show themselves to the priests as Jesus directed. Only one of them returned to Jesus to thank him.

Let's remember to be grateful to Jesus for coming to us in Holy Communion. How do we welcome him? Do we receive him on our tongue or in our hand and then close our minds and hearts to him? Do we at least keep him company for five or ten minutes?

When Communion has been distributed, the priest cleans the paten over the chalice

---

The Lord's Prayer (Our Father)
Rite of Peace
Breaking of the Bread
Lamb of God (Agnus Dei)
Communion of the Priest
Communion Antiphon
Communion of the People
Prayer after Communion

CONCLUDING RITE

Blessing
Closing Hymn (Recessional)

and then cleans the chalice itself. The people have a chance to pray quietly. The priest may sit down for a time to continue the silence and thanksgiving. Then, standing at the chair or at the altar, the priest says the *Prayer after Communion*, which asks that our share in the Eucharist be fruitful.

The *Blessing* in the name of the Blessed Trinity follows, and then the priest declares: "Go forth, the Mass is ended."

The people answer: "Thanks be to God."

There may be a *Closing Hymn (Recessional)* as the priest leaves the altar.

After Mass, we should try to spend some time—however brief—alone with Jesus. We may pray for ourselves; for the Church, the Pope, priests, and religious; for our families, friends, and others. A prayer book with a selection of prayers for thanksgiving after Communion may be helpful.

> **Q. 90** *Who is the Lamb of God?*
>
> Jesus is the Lamb of God, whose sacrifice takes away the sin of the world (CCC 608).

> **Q. 91** *When the Host is broken into several parts, is the Body of Jesus Christ broken?*
>
> When the Host is broken into several parts, the Body of Jesus Christ is not broken, but only the appearances of the bread; the Body of our Lord remains whole and entire in each of the parts (CCC 1377).

> **Q. 92** *Is only the Body of Jesus Christ present under the appearances of bread and only his Blood under the appearances of the wine?*
>
> No, under the appearances of the bread Jesus Christ is present whole and entire, in Body, Blood, Soul, and Divinity; and the same under the appearances of the wine (CCC 1374, 1390).

THE EUCHARIST: THE GREATEST TREASURE OF THE CHURCH

Review the quotes on p. 245 and p. 247. The saints all realize that the Eucharist is the greatest treasure of the Church. That is because God himself is present in the Eucharist. Jesus promised "I am with you always," "I am the bread of life; he who comes to me shall not hunger, and he who believes in me shall never thirst," "he who eats my flesh and drinks my blood has eternal life, and I shall raise him up on the last day," "he who eats me will live because of me," "he who eats this bread will live forever" (Mt 28:20; Jn 6:35, 54, 57, 58). These promises are fulfilled in the Eucharist, our greatest treasure.

Preview

In the next lesson, the students' understanding of the material covered in this chapter will be reviewed and assessed. There will be a quiz and unit test.

CHAPTER TWENTY-FIVE: COME TO THE TABLE OF THE LORD
REVIEW AND ASSESSMENT

Aims

The students' understanding of the material covered in this chapter will be reviewed and assessed.

Materials

- Quiz 25, Appendix, p. A-35

Optional:
- "O Lord Jesus, I adore thee," *Adoremus Hymnal*, #513

Name: _____

Come to the Table of the Lord   Quiz 25

Part I: Number the parts of the Communion Rite to indicate their proper order in the Mass and give a brief description of each.

2 Rite of Peace: <u>We may offer each other a sign of Christ's peace.</u>

8 Prayer after Communion: <u>Prayed by the priest; asks that our share in the Eucharist be fruitful.</u>

1 Lord's Prayer: <u>The Our Father; the prayer that Jesus taught us.</u>

4 Agnus Dei (Lamb of God): <u>Occurs during the Breaking of the Bread, we pray, "Lamb of God, you take away...."</u>

10 Closing Hymn: <u>Is sung at the end of Mass as the priest leaves the altar.</u>

7 Communion of the People: <u>We receive Communion.</u>

3 Breaking of the Bread: <u>The priest breaks the Host over the paten and places a piece of the Host in the chalice.</u>

9 Blessing: <u>The priest prays a blessing in the name of the Blessed Trinity.</u>

6 Communion Antiphon: <u>Is recited or sung.</u>

5 Communion of the Priest: <u>The priest receives Communion.</u>

Part II: Answer in complete sentences.

1. In the Gospels, who said, "Lord, I am not worthy to have you come under my roof..."?
<u>The words "Lord, I am not worthy to have you come under my roof..." were said by a Roman centurion who asked Jesus to save one of his servants.</u>

2. After receiving Jesus in Holy Communion, do we need to thank him for coming to us in Holy Communion?
<u>Yes, we need to thank Jesus for coming to us in Holy Communion.</u>

Faith and Life Series • Grade 6 • Appendix A   *A-35*

Review and Enrichment

1. The students need to know the order of the Communion Rite:
- The Lord's Prayer
- Rite of Peace
- Fraction Rite (Breaking of the Bread)
- Lamb of God (Agnus Dei)
- Communion of the Priest
- Communion Antiphon
- Communion of the People
- Prayer after Communion
- Blessing
- Closing Hymn

2. The students should understand the petitions of the Our Father.

Assess

1. Distribute the quizzes and read through them with the students to be sure they understand the questions.

2. Administer the quiz. As they hand in their work, you may orally quiz the students on the Memorization Questions from this chapter.

3. After all the quizzes have been handed in, you may wish to review the correct answers with the class.

Conclude

1. Lead the students in singing "O Lord Jesus, I adore thee," *Adoremus Hymnal*, #513.

2. End class by leading the students in the Agnus Dei (see *Teacher's Manual*, p. 303).

Name:_____

The Lord's Prayer

Write out the seven petitions of the Our Father and explain them. The first petition is written for you.

Our Father who art in heaven,

1. Hallowed be thy name. Explanations will vary.

2. Thy kingdom come.

3. Thy will be done...

4. Give us this day our daily bread.

5. Forgive us our trespasses...

6. Lead us not into temptation.

7. Deliver us from evil.

Faith and Life Series • Grade 6 • Chapter 25 • Lesson 1   97

Name:_____

The Rite of Peace

Answer the following questions in complete sentences.

1. What does Saint Paul teach us about God's peace?
   Saint Paul says that God's peace "passes all understanding."

2. What did Jesus say about his peace at the Last Supper and what does this mean?
   Jesus said, "Peace I leave you, my peace I give to you; not as the world gives do I give peace to you."
   Explanations will vary.

3. What do we say when we offer each other the sign of peace?
   We say "Peace be with you."

4. What gesture can we use to give the sign of peace?
   Answers will vary; shaking hands is most common.

5. How must we preserve the gift of peace?
   To preserve this gift, we must live in peace every day with family, friends, and everyone we meet.

6. If we all call God "Father," what is our relationship to each other?
   If we all call God "Father," we are brothers and sisters.

7. Is it necessary to live a life of peace and love in the Christian family?
   Yes.

8. Whom can we imitate in giving peace?
   We can imitate Jesus in giving peace.

98   *Faith and Life Series • Grade 6 • Chapter 25 • Lesson 2*

Name:_____

Communion Rite

Answer the following questions in complete sentences.

1. What does the priest say to us before we receive Holy Communion?
   The priest says, "The Body of Christ."

2. What is your response and what does this mean?
   Our response is "Amen." It means "Yes, I believe that this is Jesus."

3. What two ways may you receive Holy Communion in the Host?
   We may receive Communion on our tongue or in our hands.

4. What does the priest say when he offers you the Precious Blood?
   The priest says, "The Blood of Christ."

5. What is your response?
   Our response is "Amen."

6. With what attitude must we receive Holy Communion?
   Answers will vary.

Faith and Life Series • Grade 6 • Chapter 25 • Lesson 3   99

Name:_____

The Holy Mass

Find the following parts of the Mass in the puzzle below.

Sanctus	Second Reading	Eucharistic Prayer
Washing of the Hands	Gospel	Rite of Peace
Responsorial Psalm	Offertory	Preface
Homily	Communion Antiphon	First Reading
Preparation of the Altar	Profession of Faith	The Lord's Prayer
Lamb of God	Liturgy of the Word	Prayer of Thanksgiving
Opening Prayer	Introductory Rites	Offering to the Father
Entrance Antiphon	Prayer after Communion	Breaking of the Bread
Communion of the People	Invocation of the Holy Spirit	Blessing
Prayers over the Gifts	Gloria	Greeting of the People
Penitential Rite	Doxology	Offering of the Gifts
Communion of the Priest	Consecration	Liturgy of the Eucharist
Preparation of the Gifts	Prayers of the Faithful	Communion Rite

```
C I P R A Y E R S O F T H E F A I T H F U L P E C O L E B T E C
W N C O M M R E S P O N S O R I A L P S A L M P O F I O R H E E
A T R P R A Y E R A F T E R C O M M U N I O N T R M F T F E E C
S R R P R A Y E R S O V E R T H E G I F T S C O A M E U R A L L
H O O C O M M U N I O N O F T H E P E O P L E P Y U R G K O O E
I D G P R A Y E R O F T H A N K S G I V I N G E I N Y I N O S C
N U L C O M M U N I O N A N T I P H O N M M L P H O G R G D E T
G O C O P R E P A R A T I O N O F T H E A L T A R O G O S P A O
O F T R F I R S T R E A D I N G O S P E L I B M E N O F G P E P
F R O I M T P E N I T E N T I A L R I T E T L B F R F I T T N E
T A M A M E U C H A R I S T I C P R A Y E R E O A I T H O T I N
H Y O C O N S E C R A T I O N R I C P C O S F C T H E T H Y E I
E R R O F F E R T O R Y M D O X O L O G Y M S G E E W H E P N P
H I S T P R O F E S S I O N O F F A I T H I O T A G O R H A G R
A T G R E E T I N G O F T H E P E O P L E D R N I P R R H P R A
T E O S A N C T U S E C O N D R E A D I N G Z E T F D A N E N Y
D S S A C O P R E P A R A T I O N O F T H E G I F T S T A C I A
S E T P E M M C O M M U N I O N O F T H E P R I E S T H D H N Y
L I T U R G Y O F T H E E U C H A R I S T H O M I L Y E R A G E
I N V O C A T I O N O F T H E H O L Y S P I R I T A E R O L Y
```

100   *Faith and Life Series • Grade 6 • Chapter 25 • Lesson 4*

TEACHER'S NOTES

UNIT SIX TEST
CHAPTERS 22–25

CHAPTER TWENTY-TWO: COME INTO THE LORD'S PRESENCE SINGING FOR JOY

CHAPTER TWENTY-THREE: SPEAK LORD, YOUR SERVANT IS LISTENING

CHAPTER TWENTY-FOUR: LIFT UP THE CUP OF SALVATION

CHAPTER TWENTY-FIVE: COME TO THE TABLE OF THE LORD

Aims

The students' understanding of the material covered in this unit will be reviewed and assessed.

Materials

• Unit 6 Test, Appendix, pp. A-36 and A-37

Assess

1. Distribute the unit tests and read through them with the students to be sure they understand the questions.

2. Administer the test.

3. After all the tests have been handed in, you may wish to review the correct answers with the class.

Name: _____

Unit 6 Test   **Chapters 22–25**

Part I: Yes or No.

1. <u>Yes</u> Is the Mass the re-presentation of Jesus' Sacrifice of the Cross?

2. <u>Yes</u> Does Christ preside over every Mass?

3. <u>Yes</u> In the Sacred Liturgy do we take part in the worship of God that goes on in heaven with the angels and saints?

4. <u>No</u> Does coming to Mass make us better than the rest of mankind?

5. <u>Yes</u> Are we in need of forgiveness when we come to Mass?

6. <u>Yes</u> Does the Church have its own special calendar?

7. <u>No</u> Should we drift off into daydreams during a familiar reading at Mass?

8. <u>Yes</u> Do the ground wheat and crushed grapes used to make the bread and wine used at Mass remind us that we must die to ourselves and live a new life in Christ?

Part II: Answer in complete sentences.

1. What do we do to be outwardly and inwardly prepared to come to Mass?
   <u>To be outwardly prepared to come to Mass we wear suitable clothes. To be inwardly prepared to come to Mass we understand and think about our purpose in coming to Mass, which is to offer the Holy Sacrifice of the Mass with the priest and to be nourished by the Word of God and the precious Body and Blood of Jesus. (Other answers may be acceptable.)</u>

2. What are the two main parts of the Mass?
   <u>The two main parts of the Mass are the Liturgy of the Word and the Liturgy of the Eucharist.</u>

3. Why do we stand when the Gospel is read at Mass?
   <u>We stand when the Gospel is read at Mass to show our reverence for the words of Jesus.</u>

4. What do the little crosses that we make on our forehead, lips, and heart before the Gospel indicate?
   <u>The crosses that we make on our forehead, lips, and heart before the Gospel indicate that the word of our Lord is to be in our thoughts, on our lips, and in our hearts.</u>

5. After receiving Jesus in Holy Communion, do we need to thank him for coming to us in Holy Communion?
   <u>Yes, we need to thank Jesus for coming to us in Holy Communion.</u>

Name: _____

Unit 6 Test (continued)

Part III: Number the parts of the Mass to indicate their proper order and give a brief description of each.

<u>12</u> Lamb of God (Agnus Dei): <u>occurs during the Breaking of the Bread, we pray, "Lamb of God, you take away . . ."</u>

<u>2</u> Gloria: <u>we offer God praise, honor, and adoration, addressing the Father, Son, and Holy Spirit</u>

<u>4</u> Profession of Faith: <u>the Creed, a statement of what all Catholics believe</u>

<u>10</u> Consecration: <u>the priest says "This is my Body . . . This is my Blood" and the bread and wine become the Body and Blood of Jesus</u>

<u>7</u> Washing of the Hands: <u>the priest washes his hands, signifying the great purity with which we should approach the Eucharist</u>

<u>14</u> Blessing: <u>the priest prays a blessing in the name of the Blessed Trinity</u>

<u>8</u> Sanctus: <u>a special exclamation of joy in the salvation God has promised to us</u>

<u>1</u> Penitential Rite: <u>the priest invites the people to think of their sins and be sorry for them and we acknowledge our sins together</u>

<u>9</u> Invocation of the Holy Spirit: <u>the priest asks the Holy Spirit to come upon the gifts and make them holy so they may become the Body and Blood of Jesus</u>

<u>11</u> Lord's Prayer (Our Father): <u>the prayer that Jesus taught us</u>

<u>5</u> Prayers of the Faithful: <u>prayers for the needs of the Church and the world</u>

<u>13</u> Communion of the Priest: <u>the priest receives Communion</u>

<u>6</u> Preparation of the Gifts: <u>the priest accepts the bread and wine and places them on the altar and offers them to God</u>

<u>3</u> Gospel: <u>the record of what Jesus said and did on earth</u>

TEACHER'S NOTES

CHAPTER TWENTY-SIX
PREPARING OUR HEARTS FOR JESUS

Catechism of the Catholic Church References

Grace of Baptism: 265, 1262–74, 1279–80
Holy Communion: 1355, 1382–90, 1415, 1417
Jesus as Our Teacher and Model of Holiness: 468–69, 516, 518–21, 561
Last Supper: 610–11, 621

Preparation:1385–87
Sacrament of Penance and Reconciliation: 1422–84, 1485–98
Sin: 1456, 1458, 2120

Scripture References

Parable of the Wedding Banquet: Mt 22:1–13

Washing of Feet: Jn 13:1–15

Summary of Lesson Content

Lesson 1

We express our faith in Christ's presence in the Eucharist by saying "Amen" when we receive Holy Communion.

We should unite ourselves with Jesus in Holy Communion and offer ourselves, in union with Christ, to the Father.

Lesson 2

We must properly prepare to receive Holy Communion.

We must follow Jesus' example. Just as Jesus washed his disciples' feet at the Last Supper, so too we must receive him with purity and innocence of soul.

Lesson 3

We should always be ready to meet Jesus—either in Holy Communion or at the unknown hour of our death.

We should follow Jesus' teaching. We should be prayerful people who live charitable lives.

We must share in God's life of grace. If we are in mortal sin (and therefore have killed the life of grace in our soul) we must receive the Sacrament of Penance.

Lesson 4

We should strive to learn more about Jesus.

We should forever grow in love for Jesus.

We should strive to receive Holy Communion often, with sincere and humble hearts, trusting in Christ's great love for us.

Chapter Twenty-Six: Preparing Our Hearts for Jesus
Lesson One: Truly Present

Aims

The students will learn that we express our faith in Christ's presence in the Eucharist by saying "Amen" when we receive Holy Communion.

They will learn that we should unite ourselves with Jesus in Holy Communion and offer ourselves, in union with Christ, to the Father.

Materials

- *Activity Book*, p. 101

Optional:
- A video about Saint Thérèse of the Child Jesus, see www.faithand lifeseries.com and click the downloads tab for audio-visual resource suggestions

- "Panis angelicus," *Adoremus Hymnal*, #523

Begin

You may review how Saint Thérèse of Lisieux prepared to receive her First Holy Communion. Show a video about Saint Thérèse of the Child Jesus. Begin the lesson by reading from the box, "Saint Thérèse of Lisieux and Her First Holy Communion," on p. 317, at right.

Develop

1. Read paragraphs 1–3.

2. Have the students make presentations on their First Holy Communion, or interview a classmate on his First Holy Communion. Questions might include:
- What did you do to prepare in the years before you received this Sacrament?
- What did you do to prepare that day?
- What did you wear?
- When did you receive Penance?
- What did you pray before and after?
- Did you make visits to Jesus in the tabernacle?
- Did you attend catechism classes?
- Did your family have any special traditions?
- Did you fast?
- What were you most excited about?
- Where did you receive Communion?
- From which priest? etc.

3. Our "Amen" when we receive Holy Communion is an act of faith. It is our profession of belief that Jesus is present in the Eucharist and affirms all that the Catholic Church teaches.

4. Jesus calls us to receive him in the Holy Sacrament. He wants us to be united with him in this great Sacrament. It is very good to receive Communion often. The effects of this Sacrament in our lives include union with God and his Church, forgiveness of venial sins, strength to overcome future sins, and an increase in grace.

5. Mass is offered daily at church. Have the students learn the times for daily Mass in the parish. Discuss the great value of coming to daily Mass. At Mass we learn the Scriptures, we are united with Christ, and we make each day holy, consecrating our lives to Jesus.

Reinforce

1. Have the students work on *Activity Book* p. 101 (see *Teacher's Manual*, p. 325).

2. Have the students work on the Memorization Questions from this chapter.

Conclude

1. Teach the students to sing "Panis angelicus," *Adoremus Hymnal*, #523.

2. End class by leading the students in praying the Anima Christi found on *Student Text* p. 113 (see the facing page).

CHAPTER 26

Preparing Our Hearts For Jesus

"They said to each other, 'Did not our hearts burn within us while he talked to us on the road, while he opened to us the Scriptures?'"

Luke 24:32

When we go up to receive Holy Communion, the priest holds the Host before us and says: "The Body of Christ," to which we respond: "Amen." We are expressing our belief in the Real Presence of Jesus before us under the appearance of bread. We are also remembering that we have been called to unite ourselves with him in this most Holy Sacrament.

All of us are aware of our need for Jesus in our daily lives. Usually we feel this need most when we are suffering or struggling with a difficult problem. Jesus wants us to have confidence in him and not to worry:

Therefore I tell you, do not be anxious about your life, what you shall eat, nor about your body, what you shall put on. For life is more than food, and the body more than clothing.... Instead, seek his kingdom, and these things shall be yours as well (Lk 12:22–23, 31).

Receiving Jesus in Holy Communion should be a special occasion for us every time. Like all special occasions, we have to prepare for it. Before you take a big test you put in extra time studying. Or when a special friend comes to visit, you make sure everything is tidy or perhaps even make some sort of gift to give that friend. We must also prepare to receive Jesus in Communion.

Preparing to Receive the Holy Eucharist

Jesus once told a parable about a king who gave a wedding banquet for his son. He invited everyone, rich and poor alike, until his hall was filled. When the king came in to meet his guests, he found one man who had not dressed properly for the wedding feast. When questioned, the man had nothing to say. The king's orders were: "Bind him hand and foot, and cast him into the outer darkness, where there will be weeping and gnashing of teeth" (Mt 22:13).

We will displease Jesus also if we go to Holy Communion without first being properly prepared.

We should always look to the example of Jesus to show us what is necessary. Remember how, at the Last Supper, Jesus washed the feet of his Apostles? This was a sign that we are to

111

receive him with purity and innocence of soul. We are all aware of our unworthiness to receive such a gift, but like the Roman centurion we have confidence that Jesus will make us pleasing in his sight.

So how do we prepare our hearts to receive Jesus? It isn't something we do quickly just before we go to Mass. We should always be ready to meet Jesus. This means that we try to live according to Jesus' teaching. As followers of Jesus, our lives should be filled with prayer and good works. We should be unselfish and always ready to share with anyone in need. And most importantly, we must preserve that special life of grace in us which we first received in Baptism. If we lose that supernatural life through serious (mortal) sin, we should immediately ask God for forgiveness and renew his life in us by going to confession.

The more we know about Jesus, the more we will love him and try to please him and want to be with him. We should receive him in Holy Communion often, with a sincere and humble heart, trusting in his great love and desire to be united with us.

112

Q. 93 *Is it good and useful to receive Holy Communion frequently?*
It is very good and useful to receive Holy Communion frequently, even every day, provided it is done worthily (CCC 1389).

Q. 94 *How often must a Catholic take part in Mass?*
A Catholic must take part in Mass every Sunday and Holy Day of Obligation (CCC 1389).

Q. 95 *How often must a Catholic receive Holy Eucharist?*
A Catholic must received Holy Eucharist at least once a year during the Easter season (CCC 1389).

Anima Christi
Soul of Christ, sanctify me.
Body of Christ, save me.
Blood of Christ, inebriate me.
Water from the side of Christ, wash me.
Passion of Christ, strengthen me.
O good Jesus, hear me.
Within thy wounds hide me.
Suffer me not to be separated from thee.
From the malicious enemy defend me.
In the hour of my death call me
And bid me come unto thee,
That with thy saints I may praise thee
For ever and ever. *Amen.*

113

SAINT THÉRÈSE OF LISIEUX AND HER FIRST HOLY COMMUNION

Saint Thérèse calls the day of her first Holy Communion "the most wonderful day of my life." In her autobiography, the *Story of a Soul*, she describes it in great detail. As she received, she prayed "I love you, and I give myself to you forever." Then she was overcome with tears. She relates that as she received Jesus she "disappeared like a drop of water lost in the mighty ocean" and was filled with all the joy of heaven, a joy so deep she could not contain it. She was filled with a tranquil happiness for the rest of the day as she realized that "only the first day of Communion in Eternity will never end."

Preview

In the next lesson, the students will learn about preparing to receive the Eucharist.

CHAPTER TWENTY-SIX: PREPARING OUR HEARTS FOR JESUS
LESSON TWO: PREPARATION

Aims

The students will learn that we must properly prepare to receive Holy Communion.

They will learn that we must follow Jesus' example. Just as Jesus washed his disciples' feet at the Last Supper, so too we must receive him with purity and innocence of soul.

Materials

- *Activity Book*, p. 102

- Bibles

Optional:
- "Panis angelicus," *Adoremus Hymnal*, #523

Begin

Read the parable of the wedding banquet (Mt 22:1–13). Have the students draw renderings of this parable.

Develop

1. Read paragraphs 4–6 from the student textbook.

2. Read John 13:1–15. Dramatize this passage with the students by washing their feet. Afterward, discuss this teaching with the students:
- Why did Jesus wash the feet of the disciples?
- What does washing remind us of? (It reminds us of cleanliness, purity, and Baptism.)
- Why would Jesus wash their feet before the Last Supper?
- Why did the Apostles not wash Jesus' feet?
- Why did Jesus say: "You are not all clean"?

3. Discuss sacrilege. Sacrilege is the profanation of something holy or sacred. It is a grievous mortal sin. We would commit sacrilege if we vandalized a church, or if we received Holy Communion in mortal sin. Sacrilege is a serious wrong. We must never presume that we have the right to receive Communion when we are in mortal sin. We must not be too

proud to receive the Sacrament of Penance first. We must know when not to go to Communion at Mass (even if we think people are staring at us, or thinking bad things about us). It is more important to be pleasing to God and never to offend him with a sacrilege.

4. We are told we must prepare for Holy Communion. Discuss how we can prepare:
- Before we get to the church
- Outwardly
- Inwardly

5. Sometimes we are too well aware of our unworthiness of such a great gift of the Eucharist. We might be afraid to go to Communion, even if we are properly disposed (for example if we have only venial sins). Jesus will make us pleasing in his sight by forgiving our venial sins and perfecting our souls with his grace.

Reinforce

1. Have the students work on *Activity Book* p. 102 (see *Teacher's Manual*, p. 325).

2. You may give the students time to work on the Memorization Questions from this chapter.

3. The students may study the events of Holy Week to see the extensive liturgical preparations leading up to the Easter Eucharist.

Conclude

1. Lead the students in singing "Panis angelicus," *Adoremus Hymnal*, #523.

2. End class by leading the students in praying the Anima Christi found on *Student Text* p. 113 (see the facing page).

CHAPTER 26

Preparing Our Hearts For Jesus

"They said to each other, 'Did not our hearts burn within us while he talked to us on the road, while he opened to us the Scriptures?'"

Luke 24:32

When we go up to receive Holy Communion, the priest holds the Host before us and says: "The Body of Christ," to which we respond: "Amen." We are expressing our belief in the Real Presence of Jesus before us under the appearance of bread. We are also remembering that we have been called to unite ourselves with him in this most Holy Sacrament.

All of us are aware of our need for Jesus in our daily lives. Usually we feel this need most when we are suffering or struggling with a difficult problem. Jesus wants us to have confidence in him and not to worry:

Therefore I tell you, do not be anxious about your life, what you shall eat, nor about your body, what you shall put on. For life is more than food, and the body more than clothing. . . . Instead, seek his kingdom, and these things shall be yours as well (Lk 12:22–23, 31).

Receiving Jesus in Holy Communion should be a special occasion for us every time. Like all special occasions, we have to prepare for it. Before you take a big test you put in extra time studying. Or when a special friend comes to visit, you make sure everything is tidy or perhaps even make some sort of gift to give that friend. We must also prepare to receive Jesus in Communion.

Preparing to Receive the Holy Eucharist

Jesus once told a parable about a king who gave a wedding banquet for his son. He invited everyone, rich and poor alike, until his hall was filled. When the king came in to meet his guests, he found one man who had not dressed properly for the wedding feast. When questioned, the man had nothing to say. The king's orders were: "Bind him hand and foot, and cast him into the outer darkness, where there will be weeping and gnashing of teeth" (Mt 22:13).

We will displease Jesus also if we go to Holy Communion without first being properly prepared.

We should always look to the example of Jesus to show us what is necessary. Remember how, at the Last Supper, Jesus washed the feet of his Apostles? This was a sign that we are to

111

receive him with purity and innocence of soul. We are all aware of our unworthiness to receive such a gift, but like the Roman centurion we have confidence that Jesus will make us pleasing in his sight.

So how do we prepare our hearts to receive Jesus? It isn't something we do quickly just before we go to Mass. We should always be ready to meet Jesus. This means that we try to live according to Jesus' teaching. As followers of Jesus, our lives should be filled with prayer and good works. We should be unselfish and always ready to share with anyone in need. And most importantly, we must preserve that special life of grace in us which we first received in Baptism. If we lose that supernatural life through serious (mortal) sin, we should immediately ask God for forgiveness and renew his life in us by going to confession.

The more we know about Jesus, the more we will love him and try to please him and want to be with him. We should receive him in Holy Communion often, with a sincere and humble heart, trusting in his great love and desire to be united with us.

112

Q. 93 *Is it good and useful to receive Holy Communion frequently?*
It is very good and useful to receive Holy Communion frequently, even every day, provided it is done worthily (CCC 1389).

Q. 94 *How often must a Catholic take part in Mass?*
A Catholic must take part in Mass every Sunday and Holy Day of Obligation (CCC 1389).

Q. 95 *How often must a Catholic receive Holy Eucharist?*
A Catholic must received Holy Eucharist at least once a year during the Easter season (CCC 1389).

Anima Christi
Soul of Christ, sanctify me.
Body of Christ, save me.
Blood of Christ, inebriate me.
Water from the side of Christ, wash me.
Passion of Christ, strengthen me.
O good Jesus, hear me.
Within thy wounds hide me.
Suffer me not to be separated from thee.
From the malicious enemy defend me.
In the hour of my death call me
And bid me come unto thee,
That with thy saints I may praise thee
For ever and ever. *Amen.*

113

MAUNDY THURSDAY

Also known as Holy Thursday, this is the day on which we commemorate the Last Supper. During this Mass, the priest washes the feet of twelve men, as Jesus washed the feet of the Apostles at the Last Supper as an example of service and humility. Even the Pope washes people's feet on Holy Thursday. After the Mass, the Eucharist is exposed for adoration so that we may "stay and keep watch" with Jesus as he asked his Apostles (see Mk 14:38). At midnight, Jesus is taken away and the tabernacle is left empty until Easter, just as Jesus left the realm of the living for the three days he was in the tomb.

Preview

In the next lessons, the students will learn always to be ready to receive Holy Communion.

CHAPTER TWENTY-SIX: PREPARING OUR HEARTS FOR JESUS
LESSON THREE: BE READY

Aims

The students will learn that we should always be ready to meet Jesus—either in Holy Communion or at the unknown hour of our death. We should follow Jesus' teaching. We should be prayerful people who live charitable lives.

They will learn that we must share in God's life of grace. If we are in mortal sin (and therefore have killed that life of grace in our soul) we must receive the Sacrament of Penance.

Materials

• *Activity Book*, p. 103

Optional:
• "Panis angelicus," *Adoremus Hymnal*, #523

Begin

Discuss how we meet Jesus:
• Through Holy Communion (sacramentally)
• At the hour of our death

Either means can bring blessing or condemnation. We need to be ready. Today, we will learn how to prepare.

Develop

1. Read paragraph 7 from the student text.

2. Have the students imagine they are alone and suddenly Jesus is with them. How would they feel? (Would they be happy? Sad? Afraid? etc.) What would they say? ("Finally!", "I'm sorry," etc.) What might Jesus say? ("Thank you, my faithful servant," or "You have not followed my plan for you," etc.) This depends only upon each individual—and ultimately, when we stand before Jesus, we are alone and we cannot hide from the truth. We cannot make excuses or change reality. God knows everything.

3. How can we prepare to meet Jesus?
• Follow his commandments
• Receive the Sacrament of Penance regularly
• Want to meet him regularly (just as we want to spend time every day with our best friend)
• Look forward to receiving him

Have the students give practical ideas of how to prepare to meet Jesus.

4. We do not only meet Jesus, we invite him into ourselves. We receive him. How do we receive an important guest into our homes? What do we do?
• Dress up
• Clean the house
• Plan what we might talk about
• Wait until the guest arrives to eat dinner (avoid snacking)
• Have good conversation (not just talking about the weather, but about things important to us and our guest)
• Share what is going on in our lives, talk, and listen
• Thank the guest for coming, etc.
How then should we prepare our hearts to receive Jesus? What should we do especially for him? Perhaps it is something that we are not already doing.

Reinforce

1. Have the students work on *Activity Book* p. 103 (see *Teacher's Manual*, p. 325).

2. Have the students work on the Memorization Questions from this chapter.

3. If possible, arrange for the students to receive the Sacrament of Penance if they wish.

Conclude

1. Lead the students in singing "Panis angelicus," *Adoremus Hymnal*, #523.

2. End class by leading the students in praying the Anima Christi found on *Student Text* p. 113 (see the facing page).

CHAPTER 26

Preparing Our Hearts For Jesus

"They said to each other, 'Did not our hearts burn within us while he talked to us on the road, while he opened to us the Scriptures?'"

Luke 24:32

When we go up to receive Holy Communion, the priest holds the Host before us and says: "The Body of Christ," to which we respond: "Amen." We are expressing our belief in the Real Presence of Jesus before us under the appearance of bread. We are also remembering that we have been called to unite ourselves with him in this most Holy Sacrament.

All of us are aware of our need for Jesus in our daily lives. Usually we feel this need most when we are suffering or struggling with a difficult problem. Jesus wants us to have confidence in him and not to worry:

Therefore I tell you, do not be anxious about your life, what you shall eat, nor about your body, what you shall put on. For life is more than food, and the body more than clothing.... Instead, seek his kingdom, and these things shall be yours as well (Lk 12:22–23, 31).

Receiving Jesus in Holy Communion should be a special occasion for us every time. Like all special occasions, we have to prepare for it. Before you take a big test you put in extra time studying. Or when a special friend comes to visit, you make sure everything is tidy or perhaps even make some sort of gift to give that friend. We must also prepare to receive Jesus in Communion.

Preparing to Receive the Holy Eucharist

Jesus once told a parable about a king who gave a wedding banquet for his son. He invited everyone, rich and poor alike, until his hall was filled. When the king came in to meet his guests, he found one man who had not dressed properly for the wedding feast. When questioned, the man had nothing to say. The king's orders were: "Bind him hand and foot, and cast him into the outer darkness, where there will be weeping and gnashing of teeth" (Mt 22:13).

We will displease Jesus also if we go to Holy Communion without first being properly prepared.

We should always look to the example of Jesus to show us what is necessary. Remember how, at the Last Supper, Jesus washed the feet of his Apostles? This was a sign that we are to

111

receive him with purity and innocence of soul. We are all aware of our unworthiness to receive such a gift, but like the Roman centurion we have confidence that Jesus will make us pleasing in his sight.

So how do we prepare our hearts to receive Jesus? It isn't something we do quickly just before we go to Mass. We should always be ready to meet Jesus. This means that we try to live according to Jesus' teaching. As followers of Jesus, our lives should be filled with prayer and good works. We should be unselfish and always ready to share with anyone in need. And most importantly, we must preserve that special life of grace in us which we first received in Baptism. If we lose that supernatural life through serious (mortal) sin, we should immediately ask God for forgiveness and renew his life in us by going to confession.

The more we know about Jesus, the more we will love him and try to please him and want to be with him. We should receive him in Holy Communion often, with a sincere and humble heart, trusting in his great love and desire to be united with us.

112

Q. 93 *Is it good and useful to receive Holy Communion frequently?*
It is very good and useful to receive Holy Communion frequently, even every day, provided it is done worthily (CCC 1389).

Q. 94 *How often must a Catholic take part in Mass?*
A Catholic must take part in Mass every Sunday and Holy Day of Obligation (CCC 1389).

Q. 95 *How often must a Catholic receive Holy Eucharist?*
A Catholic must received Holy Eucharist at least once a year during the Easter season (CCC 1389).

Anima Christi
Soul of Christ, sanctify me.
Body of Christ, save me.
Blood of Christ, inebriate me.
Water from the side of Christ, wash me.
Passion of Christ, strengthen me.
O good Jesus, hear me.
Within thy wounds hide me.
Suffer me not to be separated from thee.
From the malicious enemy defend me.
In the hour of my death call me
And bid me come unto thee,
That with thy saints I may praise thee
For ever and ever. *Amen.*

113

MORTAL SIN

The *Catechism of the Catholic Church* 1033 states: "We cannot be united with God unless we freely choose to love him. But we cannot love God if we sin gravely against our neighbor or against ourselves. . . . To die in mortal sin without repenting and accepting God's merciful love means remaining separated from him forever by our own free choice. This state of definitive self-exclusion from communion with God and the blessed is called 'hell.'"

Remind the students that it can be very hard to confess mortal sins but we must never choose to remain separated from God. Jesus is always ready to forgive us in the Sacrament of Penance.

Preview

In the next lesson, the students will learn ways that we may constantly grow in our love for Jesus.

Chapter Twenty-Six: Preparing Our Hearts for Jesus
Lesson Four: Loving Jesus

Aims

The students will learn that we should strive to learn more about Jesus.

They will learn that our love for Jesus should grow forever. We should strive to receive Holy Communion often, with sincere and humble hearts, trusting in Christ's great love for us.

Materials

- *Activity Book*, p. 104

Optional:
- "Panis angelicus," *Adoremus Hymnal*, #523

Begin

Review the Great Commandment:
You shall love the Lord your God with all your heart, with all your soul, with all your strength and all your mind; and your neighbor as yourself.

How can we do this? How can we love with our:
- hearts?—emotional love (familiarity; e.g., recognize God's gifts and actions through others)
- souls?—spiritual love (prayer)
- strength?—love with the will (decision)
- mind?—intellectual love (know God)

Develop

1. Finish reading the chapter with the students.

2. How do we get to know people?
- From what they say
- From what they do
- From what others say about them
- From spending time with them, etc.

3. How have we met Jesus in our lives?
- From our parents/families
- From religion class
- In the Eucharist, etc.

4. How can we learn about Jesus?
- Read the Scriptures (see how the Old Testament points to Jesus, read about him and his life and teachings in the Gospels, read what the Apostles say about him in the New Testament)

- Read the lives of the saints
- Ask friends, family, parishioners, priests, religious, etc.

5. How can we spend time with Jesus?
- Frequent Communion
- Prayer
- Remember that he is always with us and remain in his presence, etc.

6. What is meant by "frequent Communion"?
- At least weekly (We are obliged to go to Mass on Sundays and Holy Days of Obligation; it would be great if we could worthily receive Communion every time!)
- Daily
- We are obliged to receive Communion worthily at least once a year during the Easter season

Reinforce

1. Have the students work on *Activity Book* p. 104 (see *Teacher's Manual*, p. 325).

2. Give the students time to work on the Memorization Questions from this chapter and to prepare for the quiz.

3. Have the students learn about saints who have a great love for Jesus in the Eucharist.

Conclude

1. Lead the students in singing "Panis angelicus," *Adoremus Hymnal*, #523.

2. End class by leading the students in praying the Anima Christi found on *Student Text* p. 113 (see the facing page).

receive him with purity and innocence of soul. We are all aware of our unworthiness to receive such a gift, but like the Roman centurion we have confidence that Jesus will make us pleasing in his sight.

So how do we prepare our hearts to receive Jesus? It isn't something we do quickly just before we go to Mass. We should always be ready to meet Jesus. This means that we try to live according to Jesus' teaching. As followers of Jesus, our lives should be filled with prayer and good works. We should be unselfish and always ready to share with anyone in need. And most importantly, we must preserve that special life of grace in us which we first received in Baptism. If we lose that supernatural life through serious (mortal) sin, we should immediately ask God for forgiveness and renew his life in us by going to confession.

The more we know about Jesus, the more we will love him and try to please him and want to be with him. We should receive him in Holy Communion often, with a sincere and humble heart, trusting in his great love and desire to be united with us.

112

Anima Christi
Soul of Christ, sanctify me.
Body of Christ, save me.
Blood of Christ, inebriate me.
Water from the side of Christ, wash me.
Passion of Christ, strengthen me.
O good Jesus, hear me.
Within thy wounds hide me.
Suffer me not to be separated from thee.
From the malicious enemy defend me.
In the hour of my death call me
And bid me come unto thee,
That with thy saints I may praise thee
For ever and ever. *Amen.*

113

TITLES FOR THE EUCHARIST

- *Eucharist*: The Greek word meaning thanksgiving is *Eucharist*.
- *Lord's Supper*: This title is a reference to Jesus' Last Supper and an anticipation of the wedding feast of the Lamb in the heavenly Jerusalem.
- *Breaking of Bread*: This serves as a reminder that Jesus broke bread at the Last Supper and the disciples recognized him in the breaking of the bread at Emmaus (Lk 24:13–35).
- *Memorial*: The Eucharist is a memorial of Jesus' Passion and Resurrection.
- *Holy Sacrifice*: It makes present the one sacrifice of Christ.
- *Holy and Divine Liturgy*: The Eucharist is the center of the Church's Liturgy.
- *Most Blessed Sacrament, Bread of Angels, Bread from Heaven, Medicine of Immortality, Viaticum*
- *Holy Communion*: By this Sacrament we are made sharers in the Body of Christ.
- *Holy Mass* (Missa): The Latin *Missio* means sending forth or mission. At the end of Mass the priest expresses our mission when he says, "Go forth, the Mass is ended."
- *Source and Summit of Christian Life*: All of the other Sacraments and the entire life of the Church are bound up in the Eucharist because it is Christ himself.

A soul enkindled with love is a gentle, meek, humble, and patient soul.
—Saint John of the Cross

Preview

In the next lesson, the students' understanding of the material covered in this chapter will be reviewed and assessed.

CHAPTER TWENTY-SIX: PREPARING OUR HEARTS FOR JESUS
REVIEW AND ASSESSMENT

Aims

The students' understanding of the material covered in this chapter will be reviewed and assessed.

Materials

- Quiz 26, Appendix, p. A-38

Optional:
- "Panis angelicus," *Adoremus Hymnal,* #523

Name: _____

Preparing Our Hearts for Jesus   **Quiz 26**

Part I: Yes or No.

1. <u>Yes</u> Do we need Jesus in our daily lives?

2. <u>No</u> Are we always aware of our need for Jesus?

3. <u>Yes</u> Does Jesus want us to have confidence in him?

4. <u>No</u> Do we have any reason to worry if we have confidence in Jesus?

5. <u>Yes</u> Do we displease Jesus if we receive Holy Communion without being properly prepared?

6. <u>Yes</u> Should we receive Holy Communion often?

Part II: Write a paragraph about the ways we can follow Jesus in our daily lives that help us to be prepared to receive him in Holy Communion. Consider the following:

prayer, good works, confession, learning about Jesus
What does the parable about the king who gave a wedding banquet for his son teach us about being prepared?

_____

_____

_____

_____

_____

_____

_____

_____

_____

_____

_____

_____

_____

_____

A-38   *Faith and Life Series • Grade 6 • Appendix A*

Review and Enrichment

1. The students should know that they must prepare to receive Jesus in the Eucharist.

2. The students should be familiar with examples of how to prepare for Holy Communion, such as:
   - The parable of the wedding feast
   - The washing of the Apostles' feet at the Last Supper

3. The students should know about meeting Jesus:
   - In Holy Communion
   - At the hour of our death

   Either way can bring blessing or condemnation, depending on our disposition.

4. The students should know how to grow in love for Jesus.

Assess

1. Distribute the quizzes and read through them with the students to be sure they understand the questions.

2. Administer the quiz. As they hand in their work, you may orally quiz the students on the Memorization Questions from this chapter.

3. After all the quizzes have been handed in, you may wish to review the correct answers with the class.

Conclude

1. Lead the students in singing "Panis angelicus," *Adoremus Hymnal,* #523.

2. End class by leading the students in praying the Anima Christi (see *Teacher's Manual,* p. 323 or p. 397).

Name:_____

Communion with Jesus

Answer the following questions in complete sentences.

1. What belief are we expressing when we say "Amen"?
   We are expressing our belief in the Real Presence of Jesus before us under the appearance of bread.

2. When do we usually most feel a need for Jesus in our daily lives?
   We usually most feel a need for Jesus when we are suffering or struggling with a difficult problem.

3. Does the Eucharist help us to grow in trust and love for Jesus?
   Yes.

4. How should we prepare ourselves before receiving Jesus in Holy Communion?
   Answers will vary: pray, think about whom we are about to receive, etc.

Faith and Life Series • Grade 6 • Chapter 26 • Lesson 1   101

Name:_____

Preparing for Communion

Answer the following questions in complete sentences.

1. Would Jesus be displeased if we went to Holy Communion but were not properly prepared? What parable tells us this?
   Yes. The parable about the poorly dressed man at the wedding banquet tells us this.

2. What did Jesus do to show us the need for a clean soul?
   Jesus showed us the need for a clean soul by washing the disciples' feet at the Last Supper.

3. How can we prepare our hearts to meet Jesus? Should we always be ready?
   Answers will vary. Some examples (from the Student Text, p. 112) are to live according to Jesus' teachings, pray, do good works, be unselfish, share with anyone in need, and preserve the gift of sanctifying grace within us.

102   *Faith and Life Series • Grade 6 • Chapter 26 • Lesson 2*

Name:_____

Receiving your Guest

Compare receiving a guest into your home to receiving Jesus in Holy Communion.

RECEIVING A GUEST INTO YOUR HOME	RECEIVING JESUS INTO YOURSELF
• Would you make an effort to dress up?	Answers will vary.
• Would you clean your house before he arrived?	
• Would you think about your time together?	
• Would you wait until he arrived to eat dinner?	
• Would you take time alone with him?	
• Would you share your heart and thoughts with him?	
• Would you tell him what is going on in your life and ask for his help in certain areas?	
• Would you thank him for coming?	

Faith and Life Series • Grade 6 • Chapter 26 • Lesson 3   103

Name:_____

Anima Christi

Write a prayer to Jesus in the Eucharist.
Answers will vary.

Write out the Anima Christi.

Soul of Christ, sanctify me.
Body of Christ, save me.
Blood of Christ, inebriate me.
Water from the side of Christ, wash me.
Passion of Christ, strengthen me.
O good Jesus, hear me.
Within thy wounds hide me.
Suffer me not to be separated from thee.
From the malicious enemy defend me.
In the hour of my death call me
And bid me come unto thee,
That with thy saints I may praise thee
For ever and ever. Amen.

104   *Faith and Life Series • Grade 6 • Chapter 26 • Lesson 4*

TEACHER'S NOTES

TEACHER'S NOTES

CHAPTER TWENTY-SEVEN
COME LORD JESUS

Catechism of the Catholic Church References

Holy Communion: 1355, 1382–90, 1415, 1417
Participation:1385–87
Precepts of the Church: 2041–43

Reception of Jesus: 1373–77, 1413
Sacrilege: 2120
Viaticum: 1524–25

Scripture References

Peter as Pope: Mt 16:13–20; Jn 21:1–29

Authority: Lk 10:16; Is 22:20–25

Summary of Lesson Content

Lesson 1

Jesus gave the Church the authority to administer the Sacraments.

The Sacraments work ex opere operato. The benefit we receive from them depends upon our interior disposition.

To receive Communion worthily, one must be in the state of grace, have the right intention, and observe the Eucharistic fast.

Lesson 3

To receive Communion reverently, we should make a sign or gesture of reverence, such as bowing, before we receive our Lord.

We should offer thanksgiving to Christ after receiving him.

In the United States the "Easter duty" requires us to receive Communion worthily at least once a year between the First Sunday of Lent and Trinity Sunday.

Lesson 2

To be in the state of grace one must be free from mortal sin. To receive the Eucharist in the state of mortal sin is called a sacrilege and brings condemnation upon the recipient. We must intend to receive Jesus with faith, understanding, reverence, and a desire for his spiritual treasures.

The Eucharistic fast is for one hour preceding Holy Communion. Only water and medicine are permitted.

Lesson 4

Viaticum is the last Eucharist we receive before death. *Viaticum* means "provisions for the journey." It is the final preparation for the journey from life on earth to life in heaven.

Chapter Twenty-Seven: Come Lord Jesus
Lesson One: Church Authority

Aims

The students will learn that Jesus gave the Church the authority to administer the Sacraments. The Sacraments work ex opere operato. The benefit we receive from them depends upon our interior disposition.

They will learn that, to receive Communion worthily, one must be in the state of grace, have the right intention, and observe the Eucharistic fast.

Materials

- *Activity Book*, p. 105

- Bible

Optional:
- "Soul of my Savior," *Adoremus Hymnal*, #522

Begin

Review the installation of Peter as the first Pope. Read from the Bible passages in which Jesus places Peter in charge of the Church (Mt 16:13–20 and Jn 21:1–20). The students may dramatize these two passages, draw them, or write about Peter being made the first Pope.

Develop

1. Read paragraphs 1–3 from the student text.

2. Discuss the power of the keys: they bind and loose. What does that mean? In ancient times, when a master gave his keys to his steward, the steward acted with the master's authority. He cared for the master's house. He made decisions that would be acceptable to the master. He decided who came and went from the house and protected it until the master returned. You may read about an example of this in Isaiah 22:20–25.

3. Jesus gave the keys of the Kingdom to Peter. Are these physical keys? No. However, it was a sign of the authority of Jesus over the Kingdom of God. Peter has the authority to make decisions in the Church until the return of Christ. He has the power to let people in, or to keep people out (this is only done by grace—so Peter has the authority to decide if/when/how the Sacraments are dispensed). Peter also has the duty to protect the Kingdom from error in teaching and abuse in practice. We see that the office of Peter then is to govern the people and make/uphold rules, teach the Faith without error, and sanctify through the Sacraments.

4. When Peter died, his authority was passed on to the next Pope, and so on, down to the present day. The authority of Peter always resides in the Pope of the Catholic Church. Read what Jesus said about this authority: Lk 10:16.

5. The Church, in union with the Pope, has the authority to make rules or laws that must be upheld. Examples include the Code of Canon Law, the precepts of the Church, directives of a diocesan bishop, etc. Included in these are rules about the celebration/reception of the Sacraments, including how to receive Holy Communion worthily.

Reinforce

1. Have the students work on *Activity Book* p. 105 (see *Teacher's Manual*, p. 337).

2. The students should research the authority of the papacy and ways it has been exercised in history.

3. You may wish to give the students time to work on the Memorization Questions and Words to Know from this chapter (see *Teacher's Manual*, p. 335).

Conclude

1. Teach the students to sing "Soul of my Savior," *Adoremus Hymnal*, #522.

2. End class by leading the students in praying the Suscipe (from the *Spiritual Exercises* of Saint Ignatius of Loyola; see *Teacher's Manual*, p. 331).

CHAPTER 27

Come Lord Jesus

"And for their sake I consecrate myself, that they also may be consecrated in truth."

John 17:19

Jesus once asked his disciples, "Who do you say that I am?" Peter answered, "You are the Messiah, the Son of the living God." Jesus rejoiced at this answer because, he said, it was a revelation from God.

Jesus then declared that he would make Peter the Rock, or foundation, upon which he would build his Church. And he said, "I will give you the keys of the kingdom of heaven, and whatever you bind on earth shall be bound in heaven, and whatever you loose on earth shall be loosed in heaven" (Mt 16:19).

The authority to "bind and to loose" includes the authority to administer the Sacraments. In other words, the Church has the power to make rules about these matters. The Church sets the times and circumstances for the Eucharistic sacrifice and for distribution of Holy Communion. She teaches us that there are three necessary conditions for the *worthy* reception of Holy Communion. We must:

1. be in the state of grace;
2. have a right intention;
3. observe the Eucharistic fast.

Let us look at these conditions.

State of Grace

The Church asks us, out of reverence for Christ, to be in the **state of grace**. This means that we may not go to Communion if we have committed a mortal sin and have not yet confessed it. To receive Communion in mortal sin would be another mortal sin, called *sacrilege*, the misuse of something holy. To receive Jesus without being in the state of grace would make us like that man in Jesus' parable who came to the wedding feast without being properly dressed.

Right Intention

To have the right intention, we must be aware of the meaning of the Eucharist: that it is Jesus himself whom we receive under the appearances of bread and wine. This means that we should desire to receive him and do so with humility and modesty, recognizing the fact that God is our Creator and we are his creatures.

How we behave at Mass, especially at Communion time, should reflect all these important attitudes. Looking around and talking to friends expresses disrespect and ignorance and gives a bad example.

We must intend to receive Jesus with faith, understanding, reverence, and a strong desire for the spiritual treasures which are to be had in the Blessed Sacrament.

Eucharistic Fast

The **Eucharistic fast** is a means of preparing to receive Jesus with ample time and consideration. It is a sign of our willingness to free ourselves from our own desires so that we can live as true followers of Christ.

We observe the fast by eating no food and drinking no liquids except water and medicine for one hour before receiving Communion. Those who are advanced in age or suffer from any infirmity, as well as those who take care of them, can receive the Holy Eucharist even if they have taken something during the previous hour.

Thanksgiving

Because the gift we receive in the Eucharist is so great, we should make a sincere thanksgiving afterwards. We may do so in set prayers or in our own words. We may also express thoughts and hopes and fears, our troubles and our joys, our needs and our petitions.

Obligation

After all we have said about how wonderful this Sacrament is, it may be a surprise that the Church has had to make a rule that requires all the faithful to receive the Eucharist at least once a year during the Easter season. The obligation is binding on all who have made their first Communion.

Viaticum

Communion given to one who is dying is called **Viaticum**, a Latin word meaning "provisions for a journey." It is well named. All through life Holy Communion has helped us get ready for a holy death. Viaticum is the final preparation for the journey from life on earth, through death, to life in heaven.

So one departs for that Kingdom about which Saint Paul said: "No eye has seen, nor ear heard, nor the heart of man conceived, what God has prepared for those who love him" (1 Cor 2:9).

We shall thank God then for every worthy and ardent Communion we have received.

Words to Know:
state of grace   Eucharistic fast
Viaticum

Sweetest Jesus, may your most Sacred Body and Blood be the delight and sweetness of my soul, safety and firmness in every temptation, joy and peace in every tribulation, light and strength in every word and work, and final protection in death. *Amen.*

—Saint Thomas Aquinas

114

115

PAPAL ELECTIONS

The Holy Father is elected by the College of Cardinals. This College cannot exceed 120 Cardinals and all must be under the age of eighty. The ceremonies begin with a Solemn Mass in Saint Peter's Basilica, after which the Cardinals go to the Sistine Chapel, where all the voting takes place. At the Chapel, they pray the *Veni Creator* and begin the elections, which must be kept entirely secret. All of the participants must stay within the Vatican and they cannot have any contact with anyone outside the College. A special section of rooms, called *Domus Sanctae Marthae*, was built recently to house the Cardinals during the elections. Both the *Domus Sanctae Marthae* and the Sistine Chapel are closed to all outside persons during the elections. The Cardinals vote by secret ballot and the Holy Father must be elected by a two-thirds majority. If they do not reach the majority, they vote again, twice in the morning and twice at night, until they do. If they do not reach a majority after several days, they spend one day in prayer and reflection, and then resume voting. Once the Holy Father has been elected, they ask his consent and what name he will take. All of the Cardinals then make an act of homage and obedience to the new Pope, after which the Holy Father greets the people in Saint Peter's Square and gives his apostolic blessing.

—Adapted from Pope John Paul II, Apostolic Constitution *Universi Dominici Gregis*

CONCLAVE

When the college of cardinals meets to elect a Pope they meet in conclave, or enclosed behind locked doors. The word *conclave* comes from the Latin *cum clave*, which means "with a key."

Preview

In the next lesson, the students will learn about preparations before Communion.

Chapter Twenty-Seven: Come Lord Jesus
Lesson Two: Before Communion

Aims

The students will learn that to be in the state of grace one must be free from mortal sin. To receive the Eucharist in the state of mortal sin is called a sacrilege, and brings condemnation upon the recipient. We must intend to receive Jesus with faith, understanding, reverence, and a desire for his spiritual treasures.

The Eucharistic fast is for one hour preceding Holy Communion. Only water and medicine are permitted during this fast.

Materials

- *Activity Book*, p. 106

Optional:
- "Soul of my Savior," *Adoremus Hymnal*, #522

Begin

The Church teaches that to receive Holy Communion worthily we must meet three requirements. We must be free from mortal sin (in the state of grace); have the right intention (know whom we are about to receive); and observe the Eucharistic fast. We will review these three requirements today.

Develop

1. Read paragraphs 4–9.

2. Go through each of the requirements for worthy reception of Holy Communion:

- STATE OF GRACE: This means being free from mortal sin. As a review, mortal sin requires a grave wrong (it is qualified by the object, intention and circumstance—if any of these three is evil, then the action itself is evil), knowledge that is it wrong, and the intention and will to do this wrong. All three are necessary for a sin to be mortal.

- You may guide the class through an age-appropriate examination of conscience, and arrange for them to go to confession. The steps to a good confession include: knowledge of sins; sorrow for sin; amendment and commitment not to sin again; confession to a priest in the Sacrament of Penance; receiving and doing penance.

- HAVE THE RIGHT INTENTION: We must know whom we receive in Holy Communion: Jesus himself! We should have humility, modesty, and purity of heart. We must see ourselves in light of Christ and receive him with love and devotion. This also includes the need for preparation before we come to church (the way we dress, the way we live all week, etc.), our interior preparation (consider the mysteries of the Mass, be in the state of grace, etc.), and our outward preparation (the way we behave, our reverence, etc.).

- EUCHARISTIC FAST: We observe a fast by eating no food and drinking no liquid for an hour before Holy Communion. The exceptions to this fast are water and medicine. The sick, aged, and their care givers are dispensed from the fast. The Eucharistic fast should help us to hunger for our Lord—the true Bread of Life.

Reinforce

1. Have the students work on *Activity Book* p. 106 (see *Teacher's Manual*, p. 337).

2. Arrange for the students to receive the Sacrament of Penance.

3. The students may work on the Memorization Questions and Words to Know from this chapter (see *Teacher's Manual*, p. 335).

Conclude

1. Lead the students in singing "Soul of my Savior," *Adoremus Hymnal*, #522.

2. End class by leading the students in praying the Suscipe (on the facing page).

CHAPTER 27

Come Lord Jesus

"And for their sake I consecrate myself, that they also may be consecrated in truth."

John 17:19

Jesus once asked his disciples, "Who do you say that I am?" Peter answered, "You are the Messiah, the Son of the living God." Jesus rejoiced at this answer because, he said, it was a revelation from God.

Jesus then declared that he would make Peter the Rock, or foundation, upon which he would build his Church. And he said, "I will give you the keys of the kingdom of heaven, and whatever you bind on earth shall be bound in heaven, and whatever you loose on earth shall be loosed in heaven" (Mt 16:19).

The authority to "bind and to loose" includes the authority to administer the Sacraments. In other words, the Church has the power to make rules about these matters. The Church sets the times and circumstances for the Eucharistic sacrifice and for distribution of Holy Communion. She teaches us that there are three necessary conditions for the *worthy* reception of Holy Communion. We must:

1. be in the state of grace;
2. have a right intention;
3. observe the Eucharistic fast.

Let us look at these conditions.

State of Grace

The Church asks us, out of reverence for Christ, to be in the **state of grace**. This means that we may not go to Communion if we have committed a mortal sin and have not yet confessed it. To receive Communion in mortal sin would be another mortal sin, called *sacrilege*, the misuse of something holy. To receive Jesus without being in the state of grace would make us like that man in Jesus' parable who came to the wedding feast without being properly dressed.

Right Intention

To have the right intention, we must be aware of the meaning of the Eucharist: that it is Jesus himself whom we receive under the appearances of bread and wine. This means that we should desire to receive him and do so with humility and modesty, recognizing the fact that God is our Creator and we are his creatures.

How we behave at Mass, especially at Communion time, should reflect all these important attitudes. Looking around and talking to friends expresses disrespect and ignorance and gives a bad example.

We must intend to receive Jesus with faith, understanding, reverence, and a strong desire for the spiritual treasures which are to be had in the Blessed Sacrament.

114

Eucharistic Fast

The **Eucharistic fast** is a means of preparing to receive Jesus with ample time and consideration. It is a sign of our willingness to free ourselves from our own desires so that we can live as true followers of Christ.

We observe the fast by eating no food and drinking no liquids except water and medicine for one hour before receiving Communion. Those who are advanced in age or suffer from any infirmity, as well as those who take care of them, can receive the Holy Eucharist even if they have taken something during the previous hour.

Thanksgiving

Because the gift we receive in the Eucharist is so great, we should make a sincere thanksgiving afterwards. We may do so in set prayers or in our own words. We may also express thoughts and hopes and fears, our troubles and our joys, our needs and our petitions.

Obligation

After all we have said about how wonderful this Sacrament is, it may be a surprise that the Church has had to make a rule that requires all the faithful to receive the Eucharist at least once a year during the Easter season. The obligation is binding on all who have made their first Communion.

Viaticum

Communion given to one who is dying is called **Viaticum**, a Latin word meaning "provisions for a journey." It is well named. All through life Holy Communion has helped us get ready for a holy death. Viaticum is the final preparation for the journey from life on earth, through death, to life in heaven.

So one departs for that Kingdom about which Saint Paul said: "No eye has seen, nor ear heard, nor the heart of man conceived, what God has prepared for those who love him" (1 Cor 2:9).

We shall thank God then for every worthy and ardent Communion we have received.

Words to Know:
state of grace   Eucharistic fast
Viaticum

Sweetest Jesus, may your most Sacred Body and Blood be the delight and sweetness of my soul, safety and firmness in every temptation, joy and peace in every tribulation, light and strength in every word and work, and final protection in death. *Amen.*

—Saint Thomas Aquinas

115

116

THE SUSCIPE

Take, O Lord, and receive all my liberty, my memory, my understanding, and my entire will, all that I have and possess. Thou hast given all to me, to thee O Lord, I return it. All is thine; dispose of it according to thy will. Give me thy love and thy grace, for this is enough for me.

Preview

In the next lesson, the students will learn about proper reception of Holy Communion.

Chapter Twenty-Seven: Come Lord Jesus
Lesson Three: Reception of Communion

Aims

The students will learn that to receive Communion reverently, we should make a sign or gesture of reverence, such as bowing, before we receive our Lord. We should offer thanksgiving to Christ after receiving him.

They will learn that in the United States the "Easter duty" requires us to receive Communion worthily at least once a year between the First Sunday of Lent and Trinity Sunday.

Materials

- *Activity Book*, p. 107

Optional:
- "Soul of my Savior," *Adoremus Hymnal*, #522

Begin

Review the three requirements of worthy Communion as learned in the last lesson. To receive Communion worthily, we must be in the state of grace, have right intention, and observe the Eucharistic fast. Have the students explain each of these three requirements.

Develop

1. Read paragraphs 10 and 11.

2. Review reverent reception of Holy Communion:
   - Come up the aisle with hands folded.
   - Bow/genuflect before receiving the Eucharist (usually when you are next to receive Holy Communion).
   - Hold up your hands to make a throne/manger for our Lord or have your hands folded to indicate that you will receive on the tongue.
   - Respond to the priest saying: "Amen" (while gazing upon the Eucharist).
   - Make the Sign of the Cross.
   - Fold your hands and return to your pew.

3. Offering thanksgiving after Communion: we should return to our pew, close our eyes, and pray to our Lord, with whom we are now united in Communion. We should offer prayers of thanksgiving for this, the greatest gift you have now received. We should offer ourselves to God, in union with Jesus in the Sacrifice of the Mass. It is also a good time to offer God our petitions and intercessions. If we cannot think of anything to pray, we should just rest in Jesus' presence. We must not, however, waste this precious time by looking around, talking, or simply not paying any attention to our Lord whom we have just received as our guest!

4. Go over various prayers that can be prayed silently after Communion. The students can research some, or you may use the examples given (see the box "Prayers for After Communion," at right, or the inset box in the student text). The students should write their own post-Communion prayers.

5. Review the Easter duty. We are obliged to receive the Eucharist worthily once a year during the Easter season.

Reinforce

1. Have the students work on *Activity Book* p. 107 (see *Teacher's Manual*, p. 337).

2. The students should write post-Communion prayers.

3. The students may work on the Memorization Questions and Words to Know from this chapter (see *Teacher's Manual*, p. 335).

Conclude

1. Lead the students in singing "Soul of my Savior," *Adoremus Hymnal*, #522.

2. End class by leading the students in praying the Suscipe (see *Teacher's Manual*, p. 331).

Eucharistic Fast

The **Eucharistic fast** is a means of preparing to receive Jesus with ample time and consideration. It is a sign of our willingness to free ourselves from our own desires so that we can live as true followers of Christ.

We observe the fast by eating no food and drinking no liquids except water and medicine for one hour before receiving Communion. Those who are advanced in age or suffer from any infirmity, as well as those who take care of them, can receive the Holy Eucharist even if they have taken something during the previous hour.

Thanksgiving

Because the gift we receive in the Eucharist is so great, we should make a sincere thanksgiving afterwards. We may do so in set prayers or in our own words. We may also express thoughts and hopes and fears, our troubles and our joys, our needs and our petitions.

Obligation

After all we have said about how wonderful this Sacrament is, it may be a surprise that the Church has had to make a rule that requires all the faithful to receive the Eucharist at least once a year during the Easter season. The obligation is binding on all who have made their first Communion.

Viaticum

Communion given to one who is dying is called **Viaticum**, a Latin word meaning "provisions for a journey." It is well named. All through life Holy Communion has helped us get ready for a holy death. Viaticum is the final preparation for the journey from life on earth, through death, to life in heaven.

So one departs for that Kingdom about which Saint Paul said: "No eye has seen, nor ear heard, nor the heart of man conceived, what God has prepared for those who love him" (1 Cor 2:9).

We shall thank God then for every worthy and ardent Communion we have received.

Words to Know:

state of grace   Eucharistic fast
Viaticum

Sweetest Jesus, may your most Sacred Body and Blood be the delight and sweetness of my soul, safety and firmness in every temptation, joy and peace in every tribulation, light and strength in every word and work, and final protection in death. *Amen.*

—Saint Thomas Aquinas

115

116

PRAYERS FOR AFTER COMMUNION

- SAINT ISIDORE, seventh century: "What is better than the Blood and Body of Christ?"
Sample Prayer: *Lord Jesus, you are the best food anyone can offer. When I receive you in Communion, you change me from the inside out. Help me to become more loving like you.* Amen.

- SAINT JOHN OF DAMASCUS, eighth century: "The bread and the wine are not merely symbols of the Body and Blood of Christ but the deified Body of the Lord."
Sample Prayer: *Lord Jesus, I believe it is truly you I receive in the Eucharist. You said that anyone who eats your body and drinks your blood will have eternal life. Help me to follow you so that I will be with you both now and forever.* Amen.

- BLESSED TERESA OF CALCUTTA, twentieth century: "The world is so hungry for God, and when Jesus came into the world he wanted to satisfy that hunger. He made himself the Bread of Life, so small, so fragile, so helpless, and as if that was not enough, he made himself the hungry one, the naked one, the homeless one, so that we can satisfy his hunger for our love."
Sample Prayer: *Lord Jesus, teach me to see you in other people. Let each little kindness I do for someone else be a gift for you. You have given so much to me. Help me give to you in return.* Amen.

He who eats my flesh and drinks my blood abides in me, and I in him.

—John 6:56

Preview

In the next lesson, the students will learn about Viaticum.

Chapter Twenty-Seven: Come Lord Jesus
Lesson Four: Viaticum

Aims

The students will learn that Viaticum is the last Eucharist we receive before death. *Viaticum* means "provisions for the journey." It is the final preparation for the journey from life on earth to life in heaven.

Materials

- *Activity Book*, p. 108

Optional:
- "Soul of my Savior," *Adoremus Hymnal*, #522

Begin

Review the meeting of Jesus in Holy Communion and at the time of our death.

It has been said that one Mass in which we participate in this life will be much more effective for us than a Mass said for us after our death. We know that receiving the Eucharist prepares us for death and anticipates heaven. It perfects the soul and unites us with Jesus.

Develop

1. Finish reading the chapter.

2. Years ago, the Anointing of the Sick was known as "Last Rites." This Sacrament was reserved for people on their death-beds. The Anointing of the Sick is no longer reserved for the dying, but now is administered to the aged, the gravely sick (e.g., not a cold, but for illnesses like cancer or before surgery), and those in danger of death.

3. The preparation for our heavenly homeland usually involves three Sacraments: Penance, Anointing of the Sick, and Eucharist.

Penance: if one is conscious, he may receive the Sacrament of Penance and be absolved from his sins. If one is unconscious and in danger of death, the priest may give apostolic pardon, absolving the sins of that person.

Anointing of the Sick: the matter is the anointing with the oil of the infirm and laying on of hands. The form is the words of the priest: "Through this holy anointing, may the Lord in his love and mercy help you with the grace of the Holy Spirit. May the Lord who frees you from sin save you and raise you up." We answer, "Amen." The Anointing of the Sick strengthens us to accept God's will either in restoration to health or in death.

Eucharist: The last Eucharist we receive is called *Viaticum* or "provisions for the journey." It is food for the soul, to unite us with Christ as we pass through death to eternal life.

4. Every church has a tabernacle in which the Blessed Sacrament is reserved. The reserved consecrated Hosts serve to provide Communion to take to the sick and those absent for Communion outside of Mass; to foster Eucharistic devotion; and for adoration of the Blessed Sacrament.

Reinforce

1. Have the students work on *Activity Book* p. 108 (see *Teacher's Manual*, p. 337).

2. Take the students to visit Jesus in the Eucharist reserved in the Tabernacle.

3. You may wish to give the students time to work on the Memorization Questions and Words to Know from this chapter.

Conclude

1. Lead the students in singing "Soul of my Savior," *Adoremus Hymnal*, #522.

2. End class by leading the students in praying the Suscipe (see *Teacher's Manual*, p. 331).

Eucharistic Fast

The **Eucharistic fast** is a means of preparing to receive Jesus with ample time and consideration. It is a sign of our willingness to free ourselves from our own desires so that we can live as true followers of Christ.

We observe the fast by eating no food and drinking no liquids except water and medicine for one hour before receiving Communion. Those who are advanced in age or suffer from any infirmity, as well as those who take care of them, can receive the Holy Eucharist even if they have taken something during the previous hour.

Thanksgiving

Because the gift we receive in the Eucharist is so great, we should make a sincere thanksgiving afterwards. We may do so in set prayers or in our own words. We may also express thoughts and hopes and fears, our troubles and our joys, our needs and our petitions.

Obligation

After all we have said about how wonderful this Sacrament is, it may be a surprise that the Church has had to make a rule that requires all the faithful to receive the Eucharist at least once a year during the Easter season. The obligation is binding on all who have made their first Communion.

Viaticum

Communion given to one who is dying is called **Viaticum**, a Latin word meaning "provisions for a journey." It is well named. All through life Holy Communion has helped us get ready for a holy death. Viaticum is the final preparation for the journey from life on earth, through death, to life in heaven.

So one departs for that Kingdom about which Saint Paul said: "No eye has seen, nor ear heard, nor the heart of man conceived, what God has prepared for those who love him" (1 Cor 2:9).

We shall thank God then for every worthy and ardent Communion we have received.

Words to Know:

state of grace   Eucharistic fast
Viaticum

Sweetest Jesus, may your most Sacred Body and Blood be the delight and sweetness of my soul, safety and firmness in every temptation, joy and peace in every tribulation, light and strength in every word and work, and final protection in death. *Amen.*

—Saint Thomas Aquinas

115

116

Q. 96	*What is necessary for the worthy reception of Holy Communion?*

For the worthy reception of Holy Communion three things are necessary: first, to be in the state of grace; second, to recognize and to consider whom we are about to receive; third, to observe the Eucharistic fast (CCC 1385–87).

Q. 97 *What does it mean to be in the state of grace?*
Being in the state of grace means to be free of all serious sin (CCC 1861).

Q. 98 *How should we receive Holy Communion?*
We should receive Holy Communion reverently and prayerfully. We must be reverent in our behavior and even in our clothing, remembering that we are receiving Jesus Christ as our guest (CCC 1386–87).

Q. 99 *What does the Eucharistic fast require?*
The Eucharistic fast requires one who is to receive the Holy Eucharist to abstain from any food or drink (except for water or medicine) for one hour before Holy Communion (CCC 1387, CIC, Canon 919).

Q. 100 *In danger of death, may one receive Holy Communion even without fasting?*
Yes, in danger of death one may receive Holy Communion without fasting (CCC 1387, CIC, Canon 919, 921).

Q. 101 *What is Viaticum?*
Viaticum is "food for the journey": one's last reception of Holy Communion as he is about to leave this life. It is the Sacrament of passing from death to life (CCC 1524).

117

SAINT JOSEPH, PATRON OF A HAPPY DEATH

Saint Joseph, husband of Mary and foster father of Jesus, is the patron of the universal Church and of a happy death. The Gospel of Matthew tells us that Joseph was "a just man" (Mt 1:19). It also tells us of Joseph's love for Mary and the way he travelled all the way to Egypt at the word of an angel to protect Jesus. There is a tradition in the East that Jesus and Mary were present at Joseph's death. With that company, his death must have been a happy one. Although we cannot have Mary and Jesus physically with us, we can receive Jesus in Viaticum and, through the other Sacraments, our prayers, and the intercession of Saint Joseph and Saint Mary, we can have a happy death.

Preview

In the next lesson, the students' understanding of the material covered in this chapter will be reviewed and assessed.

Chapter Twenty-Seven: Come Lord Jesus
Review and Assessment

Aims

The students' understanding of the material covered in this chapter will be reviewed and assessed.

Materials

- Quiz 27, Appendix, p. A-39

Optional:
- "Soul of my Savior," *Adoremus Hymnal*, #522

Name: _____

Come Lord Jesus   Quiz 27

Part I: Explain what each of these terms mean in regard to receiving Holy Communion.

state of grace: <u>To receive Communion we must be free of mortal sin.</u>

right intention: <u>We must have the right intention in order to receive Holy Communion worthily. (Or, We must intend or desire to receive the Body and Blood of Jesus.)</u>

Eucharistic fast: <u>We must fast for one hour from all foods and liquids except water and medicine before receiving Communion.</u>

thanksgiving: <u>After receiving Communion, we should thank God for giving us so great a gift.</u>

obligation/Easter duty: <u>The Church requires all the faithful who have received their First Communion to receive the Eucharist at least once a year during the Easter season.</u>

Viaticum: <u>Communion given to one who is dying. It means "provisions for the journey."</u>

Part II: Write a prayer of thanksgiving to Jesus for allowing us to receive him in Holy Communion.

_____

_____

_____

_____

_____

_____

_____

_____

_____

_____

_____

_____

Faith and Life Series • Grade 6 • Appendix A   *A-39*

Review and Enrichment

1. Review the things necessary for a worthy reception of Holy Communion:
   - Be in the state of grace.
   - Have the right intention.
   - Observe the Eucharistic fast.

2. Review reverent reception of Holy Communion and the devotion of post-Communion prayers.

3. The students should be familiar with the Easter duty.

4. The students should know what Viaticum is and why the Blessed Sacrament is reserved in the tabernacle.

Assess

1. Distribute the quizzes and read through them with the students to be sure they understand the questions.

2. Administer the quiz. As they hand in their work, you may orally quiz the students on the Memorization Questions from this chapter.

3. After all the quizzes have been handed in, you may wish to review the correct answers with the class.

Conclude

1. Lead the students in singing "Soul of my Savior," *Adoremus Hymnal*, #522.

2. End class by leading the students in praying the Suscipe (see *Teacher's Manual*, p. 331).

CHAPTER TWENTY-SEVEN: COME LORD JESUS
ACTIVITY BOOK ANSWER KEYS

Name:_____

Church Teaching on the Eucharist

Answer the following questions in complete sentences.

1. To whom did Jesus give the keys? What do these keys symbolize?
   <u>Jesus gave the keys to Peter. They symbolize authority.</u>

2. Who has authority over the administration of the Sacraments?
   <u>The Church has authority over the administration of the Sacraments.</u>

3. Who gave her this authority?
   <u>Jesus gave her this authority.</u>

4. What kinds of rules does she make?
   <u>She makes rules about the times and circumstances for the Eucharistic sacrifice and for the distribution of Holy Communion.</u>

5. How often must we receive Holy Communion?
   <u>We must receive Holy Communion at least once a year during the Easter season.</u>

6. Who is bound by this rule?
   <u>Everyone who has made their First Communion is bound by this rule.</u>

Name:_____

For a Worthy Reception . . .

Answer the following questions in complete sentences.

I. Be in a state of grace.
1. Can we receive Holy Communion in a state of mortal sin?
   <u>No.</u>

II. Have the right intention.
2. What is the right intention to have when receiving the Holy Eucharist?
   <u>We must receive the Eucharist with humility and modesty.</u>

3. Must we believe in the Real Presence (Jesus' Body, Blood, Soul and Divinity, truly present in the Eucharist) in order to receive Holy Communion?
   <u>Yes.</u>

III. Observe the Eucharistic fast.
4. What is the Eucharistic fast?
   <u>The Eucharistic fast is a means of preparing to receive Jesus with ample time and consideration.</u>

5. How long must we fast?
   <u>We must fast for one hour.</u>

6. From what must we fast?
   <u>We must fast from all food and drink.</u>

7. What can we consume during the Eucharistic fast?
   <u>We can consume water and medicine.</u>

Name:_____

Come Lord Jesus

Find the words about receiving Holy Communion in the puzzle below.

worthily	receive	reception	life of grace
faith	sacrilege	preparation	right intention
Sacrament	desire	reverence	Eucharistic fast
penance	respect	humility	state of grace
Communion	Viaticum	Bread of Life	

```
R R E C E I V E L R E V E R L D
R E V E R E N C E R E V C A R G
E S U P R E O S M G O E H I R E
D P E C P H I A E H R A G I A C
E E S C H A T C H U T H E C A H
C C S R I A N U M T T C C C H
O T H I O R R O C I I I A E
M A Y G R A A I N L L I R G S
M V L B R E E T S I S F G R F A
U I R E A P N T Y T Y T E O C
N A H T T P R E O Y I E O I R A
I T T P R I I C E N T I N L C
O P O Z A A C R U A F A I T A M
N N W O R T F U M I G N L T S E
  O O N L G K R E M V R E V S T
  B R E A D O F L I F E P E N A N
```

Name:_____

Viaticum

Answer the following questions in complete sentences.

1. What is Viaticum?
   <u>Viaticum is Holy Communion given to someone in danger of death.</u>

2. What does Viaticum mean?
   <u>Viaticum means "provisions for the journey."</u>

3. For what does "Viaticum" prepare us?
   <u>Viaticum prepares us for a holy death and our final journey.</u>

4. What is our final journey?
   <u>Our final journey is a journey from love on earth, through death, to live in heaven.</u>

5. What shall we thank God for upon our death?
   <u>Upon our death, we shall thank God for every worthy and ardent Communion we have received.</u>

TEACHER'S NOTES

CHAPTER TWENTY-EIGHT
HIS ABIDING PRESENCE

Catechism of the Catholic Church References

Abiding Presence: 1378, 1418, 1088, 1313–17, 737, 1380–81

Adoration of Jesus in the Eucharist: 1378–81, 1418

Holy Communion: 1355, 1382–90, 1415, 1417

Jesus as True God and True Man: 464–70, 480–83

Places Favorable to Prayer: 2691, 2696

Scripture References

Abiding Presence of Jesus: Jn 14:13–21

Summary of Lesson Content

Lesson 1

Transubstantiation is the change from bread and wine to the Body and Blood of Christ.

The Eucharist contains Christ truly and wholly present, true God and true man.

Lesson 2

Jesus in the Eucharist is reserved in a tabernacle. At church, we genuflect to Jesus in the tabernacle.

We should make visits to Jesus in the Blessed Sacrament.

Lesson 3

Eucharistic devotion is encouraged by the Church.

Exposition of the Blessed Sacrament allows for adoration of our Eucharistic Lord.

Benediction is the blessing of the faithful with Jesus in the monstrance.

Lesson 4

Many of the saints promulgated devotion to Jesus in the Eucharist.

Spiritual communion is a prayer to unite ourselves with Jesus in the Eucharist, at a time when we cannot physically receive him as we do at Mass in Holy Communion.

CHAPTER TWENTY-EIGHT: HIS ABIDING PRESENCE
LESSON ONE: TRULY PRESENT

Aims

The students will learn that transubstantiation is the change from bread and wine to the Body and Blood of Christ.

They will learn that the Eucharist contains Christ wholly present, true God and true man.

Materials

• *Activity Book*, p. 109

Optional:
• "Tantum ergo," *Adoremus Hymnal*, #393

Begin

Review what the students have already learned about transubstantiation (see the Chalk Talk on facing page). They should clearly understand that the bread and wine no longer remain and only Jesus is present: Body, Blood, Soul, and Divinity, under the appearances of bread and wine. They should also know that transubstantiation occurs during the Consecration in the Eucharistic Prayers of the Mass.

Develop

1. Read paragraphs 1 and 2.

2. Teach the students different names for the Holy Eucharist. Have the students each select one and create a poster honoring Christ under this title:
 • The Blessed Sacrament
 • Holy Communion
 • The Bread of Angels
 • Bread from Heaven
 • Medicine of Immortality
 • Viaticum
 • The Body of Christ
 • The Sacred Host/Precious Blood

3. When we speak of the Real Presence, this phrase traditionally refers to the Body and Blood of Christ present in the Eucharist. Open to grace, we experience Christ in all creation, within ourselves, within all people (Jn 14:18–20; 17:23, 26; Col 1:27), and (in a special way) in the poor and the suffering (Mt 25:30). We experience Christ in the Church (Mt 18:20) and in the liturgical celebrations of the Church. At Mass we experience Christ in:
 • The priest
 • The Scriptures
 • The assembly
 • The Eucharist

4. Jesus is really and truly present in the Eucharist and in each of its parts. He is present Body, Blood, Soul, and Divinity. His presence remains as long as the species remains. At Mass, the Precious Blood must all be consumed; however, the Sacred Hosts are reserved in the tabernacle for the faithful.

Reinforce

1. Have the students work on *Activity Book* p. 109 (see *Teacher's Manual*, p. 349).

2. The students may design a suitable tabernacle for our Lord.

3. Have the students work on the Memorization Questions and Words to Know from this chapter.

Conclude

1. Teach the students to sing "Tantum ergo," *Adoremus Hymnal*, #393.

2. End class by leading the students in praying the Act of Spiritual Communion from the student text p. 119.

CHAPTER 28

His Abiding Presence

"As the Father has loved me, so have I loved you; abide in my love."

John 15:9

We have seen that through transubstantiation Jesus changes bread and wine into his Body and Blood.

The Eucharist is Jesus, Body, Blood, Soul, and Divinity. Jesus is both God and man, and he comes to us in Holy Communion. We receive his divinity as well as his humanity. We can truly say that God becomes our food.

Jesus promised his disciples that he would not leave them orphaned. Indeed, he has instituted a way to stay with us at all times. Jesus is present in the Blessed Sacrament, which is kept in the tabernacles of our churches around the world. A lamp, called the sanctuary lamp, is kept burning there as long as the Blessed Sacrament is in the **tabernacle**.

Here, then, Jesus remains, night and day. He is truly Emmanuel—God with us. He dwells with us full of grace and truth.

We profess our faith in Jesus' presence in the Blessed Sacrament by our behavior in church. Our behavior should include reverent actions: genuflecting, blessing ourselves with holy water, bowing our heads.

We are encouraged to visit the Blessed Sacrament when we have time and a church or chapel is open. The prayer we say there—our conversation with Jesus—is an extra act of love that we offer him freely, and it will bring us special graces.

Eucharistic Worship

The Church has always encouraged devotion to the Blessed Sacrament. There are a number of forms of special Eucharistic worship outside of the Mass, which is, of course, the fountainhead of all the others.

One such form is a Eucharistic procession in which the Blessed Sacrament is carried through the streets with solemnity and reverence, accompanied by singing. Parishes often hold processions on the feast of *Corpus Christi*.

The most common forms of Eucharistic worship outside the Mass, however, are **Exposition** and **Benediction**. The consecrated Host

May the Blessed Sacrament be praised and adored forever.

118

is put in a **monstrance** and placed on the altar for the faithful to see and adore.

During the Exposition there are prayers and hymns, and usually Jesus is honored with incense. We express our profound adoration before the Real Presence of Christ.

At the end, the priest or deacon lifts the monstrance and blesses the faithful with it in the Sign of the Cross. This is called "Benediction."

Special Devotion

Throughout the ages there have been many saints who have had great devotion to Jesus in the Eucharist. Saint Thomas Aquinas wrote many beautiful hymns for Eucharistic worship.

There is a saint of modern times, Saint Peter Julian Eymard, who founded a religious congregation dedicated to the perpetual adoration of the Real Presence of Christ in the Blessed Sacrament. Priests of this order are called the

Blessed Sacrament Fathers. The Blessed Sacrament is always exposed in their religious houses for perpetual adoration.

Words to Know:

tabernacle	Exposition
Benediction	monstrance

Act of Spiritual Communion

My Jesus, I believe that you are in the Blessed Sacrament. I love you above all things, and I long for you in my soul. Since I cannot now receive you sacramentally, come at least spiritually into my heart. I embrace you and unite myself entirely to you; never permit me to be separated from you.

Q. 102 *Is Jesus Christ present in all the consecrated Hosts in the world?*
Yes, Jesus Christ is present in all the consecrated Hosts in the world (CCC 1377).

Q. 103 *Why is the Most Holy Eucharist kept in the churches?*
The Most Holy Eucharist is kept in the churches so that the faithful may adore it, so that they may receive it in Communion, and so that they may recognize in the Holy Eucharist the perpetual assistance and presence of Jesus Christ in the Church (CCC 1378–79).

Q. 104 *Where in the church is the Holy Eucharist kept?*
The Holy Eucharist is kept in a tabernacle, as a worthy place for the presence of the Lord and a place to be recognized by the faithful in Eucharistic devotion (CCC 1379).

119

TEACHER'S NOTES

CHALK TALK: TRANSUBSTANTIATION

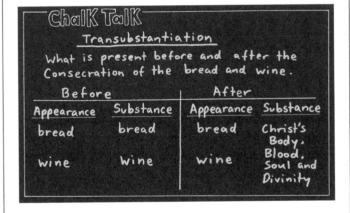

Preview

In the next lesson, the students will learn about Jesus' abiding presence.

Chapter Twenty-Eight: His Abiding Presence
Lesson Two: Abiding Presence

Aims

The students will learn that Jesus in the Eucharist is reserved in a tabernacle. At church, we genuflect to Jesus' presence in the tabernacle.

They will learn that we should make visits to Jesus in the Blessed Sacrament.

Materials

- *Activity Book*, p. 110

- Bibles

Optional:
- "Tantum ergo," *Adoremus Hymnal*, #393

Begin

Read John 14:13–21. Have the students meditate upon this passage and discuss how it refers to the Blessed Sacrament. Have the students explain the passage to you. You may assist them when they are stuck or do not have the necessary vocabulary.

Develop

1. Read paragraphs 3–6 from the student text.

2. Discuss where the tabernacle is in the church. It should be conspicuous. It has a sanctuary lamp which is lit to remind us that Jesus is present. Some parishes also use a tabernacle veil to signify Christ's presence and to honor him.

3. Discuss the qualities of a tabernacle. It should be made of fine materials (usually gold or silver). It should be solid and opaque (not see through). It should be immovable. It should be locked (to protect the Eucharist from theft). It should be in a place of honor.

4. Review that Jesus' presence remains as long as the species remain. So, the Sacred Hosts are reserved after Mass in the tabernacle for two important reasons:
   - To take Communion to the sick
   - For devotional worship

5. When we are in the presence of Christ in the tabernacle, or if we pass in front of it, we signify our faith and love by genuflecting. To genuflect is to kneel down on our right knee. We genuflect when we enter and leave church or Eucharistic chapel.

6. We should visit the Blessed Sacrament often—even daily. We are encouraged to visit regularly to pray whenever the church/chapel is open. Just as 2000 years ago, people could have heard Jesus' message from friends or neighbors but they chose to go to him to be in his presence—so too, we can go to him, be in his presence, and bring him our love and prayers. Devotion to the Blessed Sacrament gives us many graces for it brings us before our Lord. It is an extra act of love that we freely offer him and which will lead us to love more deeply and to participate more fully in the Holy Mass.

Reinforce

1. Have the students work on *Activity Book* p. 110 (see *Teacher's Manual*, p. 349).

2. Take your students to visit Jesus in the Blessed Sacrament. Ensure that they are genuflecting properly.

3. The students may work on the Memorization Questions and Words to Know from this chapter.

Conclude

1. Lead the students in singing "Tantum ergo," *Adoremus Hymnal*, #393.

2. End class by leading the students in praying the Act of Spiritual Communion from the student text p. 119.

3. Arrange with a priest to hold an Adoration service for the students at the next class. Ask him to explain the vessels and vestments used.

CHAPTER 28

His Abiding Presence

"As the Father has loved me, so have I loved you; abide in my love."

John 15:9

We have seen that through transubstantiation Jesus changes bread and wine into his Body and Blood.

The Eucharist is Jesus, Body, Blood, Soul, and Divinity. Jesus is both God and man, and he comes to us in Holy Communion. We receive his divinity as well as his humanity. We can truly say that God becomes our food.

Jesus promised his disciples that he would not leave them orphaned. Indeed, he has instituted a way to stay with us at all times. Jesus is present in the Blessed Sacrament, which is kept in the tabernacles of our churches around the world. A lamp, called the sanctuary lamp, is kept burning there as long as the Blessed Sacrament is in the **tabernacle**.

Here, then, Jesus remains, night and day. He is truly Emmanuel—God with us. He dwells with us full of grace and truth.

We profess our faith in Jesus' presence in the Blessed Sacrament by our behavior in church. Our behavior should include reverent actions: genuflecting, blessing ourselves with holy water, bowing our heads.

We are encouraged to visit the Blessed Sacrament when we have time and a church or chapel is open. The prayer we say there—our conversation with Jesus—is an extra act of love that we offer him freely, and it will bring us special graces.

Eucharistic Worship

The Church has always encouraged devotion to the Blessed Sacrament. There are a number of forms of special Eucharistic worship. One such form is, of course, the fountainhead of all the others.

One such form is a Eucharistic procession in which the Blessed Sacrament is carried through the streets with solemnity and reverence, accompanied by singing. Parishes often hold processions on the feast of *Corpus Christi*.

The most common forms of Eucharistic worship outside the Mass, however, are **Exposition** and **Benediction**. The consecrated Host

May the Blessed Sacrament be praised and adored forever.

118

is put in a **monstrance** and placed on the altar for the faithful to see and adore.

During the Exposition there are prayers and hymns, and usually Jesus is honored with incense. We express our profound adoration before the Real Presence of Christ.

At the end, the priest or deacon lifts the monstrance and blesses the faithful with it in the Sign of the Cross. This is called "Benediction."

Special Devotion

Throughout the ages there have been many saints who have had great devotion to Jesus in the Eucharist. Saint Thomas Aquinas wrote many beautiful hymns for Eucharistic worship.

There is a saint of modern times, Saint Peter Julian Eymard, who founded a religious congregation dedicated to the perpetual adoration of the Real Presence of Christ in the Blessed Sacrament. Priests of this order are called the Blessed Sacrament Fathers. The Blessed Sacrament is always exposed in their religious houses for perpetual adoration.

Words to Know:

tabernacle   Exposition
Benediction   monstrance

Act of Spiritual Communion

My Jesus, I believe that you are in the Blessed Sacrament. I love you above all things, and I long for you in my soul. Since I cannot now receive you sacramentally, come at least spiritually into my heart. I embrace you and unite myself entirely to you; never permit me to be separated from you.

Q. 102   *Is Jesus Christ present in all the consecrated Hosts in the world?*
Yes, Jesus Christ is present in all the consecrated Hosts in the world (CCC 1377).

Q. 103   *Why is the Most Holy Eucharist kept in the churches?*
The Most Holy Eucharist is kept in the churches so that the faithful may adore it, so that they may receive it in Communion, and so that they may recognize in the Holy Eucharist the perpetual assistance and presence of Jesus Christ in the Church (CCC 1378–79).

Q. 104   *Where in the church is the Holy Eucharist kept?*
The Holy Eucharist is kept in a tabernacle, as a worthy place for the presence of the Lord and a place to be recognized by the faithful in Eucharistic devotion (CCC 1379).

119

TEACHER'S NOTES

QUALITIES OF A TABERNACLE

There are certain characteristics a tabernacle must have. A few are mentioned here. Because a tabernacle contains Jesus, who must be protected, it must be of solid, immovable, non-transparent material and it must be kept locked. Because Jesus is reserved in the tabernacle for private devotion, the tabernacle must be kept in a place that is easily visible, beautiful, and appropriate for prayer. We must do all that we can to create an appropriate place to house our Lord. Tabernacles should be placed in the sanctuary, although not on the altar on which the sacrifice takes place. It may also be in a chapel that is connected to the church and visible.

Preview

In the next lesson, the students will learn about Eucharistic worship.

CHAPTER TWENTY-EIGHT: HIS ABIDING PRESENCE
LESSON THREE: EUCHARISTIC WORSHIP

Aims

The students will learn that Eucharistic devotion is encouraged by the Church.

They will learn that Exposition of the Blessed Sacrament allows for adoration of our Eucharistic Lord. Benediction is the blessing of the faithful with Jesus in the monstrance.

Materials

- *Activity Book*, p. 111

Optional:
- "Tantum ergo," *Adoremus Hymnal*, #393

- Monstrance, humeral veil, thurible, and incense

- Prayers for Adoration and Benediction. You may have music such as Gregorian chant to foster meditation.

Begin

Before class, arrange for Adoration of the Blessed Sacrament with a parish priest. Ideally, before the Eucharist is exposed for adoration, he will explain the vestments and vessels used for Adoration and Benediction.

Develop

1. Read paragraphs 7–11 from the student text.

2. Explain to the students that Adoration has been arranged for them and that Father will explain the rite and vestments/vessels used in this devotion when you get to the chapel. One difference that they will encounter is the double genuflection. When the Eucharist is exposed, instead of genuflecting with one knee, we kneel with both knees on the floor and make the Sign of the Cross.

3. Take the students to Adoration and Benediction, even if it is just 15 minutes to make them familiar with this devotion. Explain that adoration is prayer before the exposed Blessed Sacrament and is a silent loving gaze upon our Lord. It is a time for meditative prayer. Benediction comes from the Latin word for blessing. The priest lifts the monstrance with Jesus in it, and blesses the people tracing a big cross in the air with the monstrance.

4. Discuss the students' experience of Adoration and Benediction. Tell them when your parish has Adoration.

5. Explain the tradition of Eucharistic processions (usually on Corpus Christi). Some parishes process the Eucharist throughout the parish boundaries on the feast of the Body and Blood of Christ. A great procession occurs with incense, and bells, and a parade of people follow the the Blessed Sacrament through the streets. As the Eucharist passes people on the street, they stop and kneel in adoration! It is a great sign of faith and honor to our Eucharistic King.

6. You may teach the students the chaplet of the Blessed Sacrament as on p. 345.

Reinforce

1. Have the students work on *Activity Book* p. 111 (see *Teacher's Manual*, p. 349).

2. You may wish to give the students time to work on the Memorization Questions and Words to Know from this chapter.

Conclude

1. Lead the students in singing "Tantum ergo," *Adoremus Hymnal*, #393.

2. End class by leading the students in praying the Act of Spiritual Communion from the student text p. 119.

CHAPTER 28

His Abiding Presence

"As the Father has loved me, so have I loved you; abide in my love."

John 15:9

We have seen that through transubstantiation Jesus changes bread and wine into his Body and Blood.

The Eucharist is Jesus, Body, Blood, Soul, and Divinity. Jesus is both God and man, and he comes to us in Holy Communion. We receive his divinity as well as his humanity. We can truly say that God becomes our food.

Jesus promised his disciples that he would not leave them orphaned. Indeed, he has instituted a way to stay with us at all times. Jesus is present in the Blessed Sacrament, which is kept in the tabernacles of our churches around the world. A lamp, called the sanctuary lamp, is kept burning there as long as the Blessed Sacrament is in the **tabernacle**.

Here, then, Jesus remains, night and day. He is truly Emmanuel—God with us. He dwells with us full of grace and truth.

We profess our faith in Jesus' presence in the Blessed Sacrament by our behavior in church. Our behavior should include reverent actions: genuflecting, blessing ourselves with holy water, bowing our heads.

We are encouraged to visit the Blessed Sacrament when we have time and a church or chapel is open. The prayer we say there—our conversation with Jesus—is an extra act of love that we offer him freely, and it will bring us special graces.

May the Blessed Sacrament be praised and adored forever.

118

Eucharistic Worship

The Church has always encouraged devotion to the Blessed Sacrament. There are a number of forms of special Eucharistic worship outside of the Mass, which is, of course, the fountainhead of all the others.

One such form is a Eucharistic procession in which the Blessed Sacrament is carried through the streets with solemnity and reverence, accompanied by singing. Parishes often hold processions on the feast of *Corpus Christi*.

The most common forms of Eucharistic worship outside the Mass, however, are **Exposition** and **Benediction**. The consecrated Host

is put in a **monstrance** and placed on the altar for the faithful to see and adore.

During the Exposition there are prayers and hymns, and usually Jesus is honored with incense. We express our profound adoration before the Real Presence of Christ.

At the end, the priest or deacon lifts the monstrance and blesses the faithful with it in the Sign of the Cross. This is called "Benediction."

Special Devotion

Throughout the ages there have been many saints who have had great devotion to Jesus in the Eucharist. Saint Thomas Aquinas wrote many beautiful hymns for Eucharistic worship.

There is a saint of modern times, Saint Peter Julian Eymard, who founded a religious congregation dedicated to the perpetual adoration of the Real Presence of Christ in the Blessed Sacrament. Priests of this order are called the Blessed Sacrament Fathers. The Blessed Sacrament is always exposed in their religious houses for perpetual adoration.

Words to Know:

tabernacle   Exposition
Benediction   monstrance

Act of Spiritual Communion

My Jesus, I believe that you are in the Blessed Sacrament. I love you above all things, and I long for you in my soul. Since I cannot now receive you sacramentally, come at least spiritually into my heart. I embrace you and unite myself entirely to you; never permit me to be separated from you.

Q. 102 *Is Jesus Christ present in all the consecrated Hosts in the world?*

Yes, Jesus Christ is present in all the consecrated Hosts in the world (CCC 1377).

Q. 103 *Why is the Most Holy Eucharist kept in the churches?*

The Most Holy Eucharist is kept in the churches so that the faithful may adore it, so that they may receive it in Communion, and so that they may recognize in the Holy Eucharist the perpetual assistance and presence of Jesus Christ in the Church (CCC 1378–79).

Q. 104 *Where in the church is the Holy Eucharist kept?*

The Holy Eucharist is kept in a tabernacle, as a worthy place for the presence of the Lord and a place to be recognized by the faithful in Eucharistic devotion (CCC 1379).

119

TEACHER'S NOTES

CHAPLET OF THE BLESSED SACRAMENT

The Chaplet of the Blessed Sacrament is prayed using a chaplet of thirty-three beads (representing all the years of Jesus' life on earth), and a Blessed Sacrament medal with the words "Jesus in the Blessed Sacrament, have mercy on us" on it. Begin by making a spiritual communion on the medal:

As I cannot now receive thee, my Jesus,
in Holy Communion, come,
spiritually into my heart,
and make it thine own forever.

On each of the beads, pray:

Jesus in the Blessed Sacrament, have mercy on us.

—Approved May 30, 1911 by Pope Pius X

Preview

In the next lesson, the students will learn about the saints and their devotion to the Eucharist.

CHAPTER TWENTY-EIGHT: HIS ABIDING PRESENCE
LESSON FOUR: THE SAINTS AND THE EUCHARIST

Aims

The students will learn that many of the saints promulgated devotion to Jesus in the Eucharist.

They will learn that spiritual communion is a prayer to unite us with Jesus in the Eucharist, at a time when we cannot physically receive him as we do at Mass in Holy Communion.

Materials

- *Activity Book*, p. 112

Optional:
- "Tantum ergo," *Adoremus Hymnal*, #393

Begin

Many saints had a great devotion to the Blessed Sacrament; in fact, it could be said that it was precisely because of their devotion to the Blessed Sacrament that many became saints. If we remember that the Eucharist is Jesus, we can under- stand how spending time with him, loving him, and centering our lives on him would make us holy. Today, we will learn about some of the saints with special devotion to the Blessed Sacrament.

Develop

1. Finish reading the chapter, paragraphs 12–13, from the student text.

2. Have the students research various saints who had a strong devotion to the Blessed Sacrament. The students should be able to report upon these saints. Some suggested saints may be found in the box on p. 347, at right.

3. Spiritual communion is a devotional prayer, through which one unites himself with Jesus in the Eucharist when he is not able to receive him sacramentally. One invites Jesus into his heart and renders it like Jesus' heart.

4. Forty hours' devotion is a popular Eucharistic devotion which commemorates the forty hours Jesus was entombed. It originated in Milan in 1534 and was propagated by the Jesuits under Saint Ignatius. By the end of the 18th century, it had spread to many countries. Saint John Neumann is said to have established this devotion in the United States. Ideally the forty hours are uninterrupted and continue for three days (day and night). The first and third days include liturgies of the Blessed Sacrament, the second day a liturgy for peace; the solemn closing for the forty hours includes the Litany of the Saints, a procession, and Benediction.

5. Perpetual Adoration is a devotion held in some parishes in which adoration occurs twenty-four hours a day, seven days a week. Usually people sign up for an hour to pray before our Lord.

6. Many beautiful hymns have been written to honor the Eucharist. We have studied many of them in the past few chapters. Your class could perform a concert singing these hymns for another class, or simply sing them before the Blessed Sacrament as an act of love.

Reinforce

1. Have the students work on *Activity Book* p. 112 (see *Teacher's Manual*, p. 349).

2. Have the students twork on the Memorization Questions and Words to Know from this chapter, and prepare for the chapter quiz and unit test.

3. The students may sing a Eucharistic hymn before the Blessed Sacrament or perform a concert for the First Communion class.

Conclude

1. Lead the students in singing "Tantum ergo," *Adoremus Hymnal*, #393.

2. End class by leading the students in praying the Act of Spiritual Communion from the student text p. 119.

CHAPTER 28

His Abiding Presence

"As the Father has loved me, so have I loved you; abide in my love."

John 15:9

We have seen that through transubstantiation Jesus changes bread and wine into his Body and Blood.

The Eucharist is Jesus, Body, Blood, Soul, and Divinity. Jesus is both God and man, and he comes to us in Holy Communion. We receive his divinity as well as his humanity. We can truly say that God becomes our food.

Jesus promised his disciples that he would not leave them orphaned. Indeed, he has instituted a way to stay with us at all times. Jesus is present in the Blessed Sacrament, which is kept in the tabernacles of our churches around the world. A lamp, called the sanctuary lamp, is kept burning there as long as the Blessed Sacrament is in the **tabernacle**.

Here, then, Jesus remains, night and day. He is truly Emmanuel—God with us. He dwells with us full of grace and truth.

We profess our faith in Jesus' presence in the Blessed Sacrament by our behavior in church. Our behavior should include reverent actions: genuflecting, blessing ourselves with holy water, bowing our heads.

We are encouraged to visit the Blessed Sacrament when we have time and a church or chapel is open. The prayer we say there— our conversation with Jesus—is an extra act of love that we offer him freely, and it will bring us special graces.

May the Blessed Sacrament be praised and adored forever.

118

Eucharistic Worship

The Church has always encouraged devotion to the Blessed Sacrament. There are a number of forms of special Eucharistic worship outside of the Mass, which is, of course, the fountainhead of all the others.

One such form is a Eucharistic procession in which the Blessed Sacrament is carried through the streets with solemnity and reverence, accompanied by singing. Parishes often hold processions on the feast of *Corpus Christi*.

The most common forms of Eucharistic worship outside the Mass, however, are **Exposition** and **Benediction**. The consecrated Host

is put in a **monstrance** and placed on the altar for the faithful to see and adore.

During the Exposition there are prayers and hymns, and usually Jesus is honored with incense. We express our profound adoration before the Real Presence of Christ.

At the end, the priest or deacon lifts the monstrance and blesses the faithful with it in the Sign of the Cross. This is called "Benediction."

Special Devotion

Throughout the ages there have been many saints who have had great devotion to Jesus in the Eucharist. Saint Thomas Aquinas wrote many beautiful hymns for Eucharistic worship.

There is a saint of modern times, Saint Peter Julian Eymard, who founded a religious congregation dedicated to the perpetual adoration of the Real Presence of Christ in the Blessed Sacrament. Priests of this order are called the Blessed Sacrament Fathers. The Blessed Sacrament is always exposed in their religious houses for perpetual adoration.

Words to Know:

tabernacle	Exposition
Benediction	monstrance

Act of Spiritual Communion

My Jesus, I believe that you are in the Blessed Sacrament. I love you above all things, and I long for you in my soul. Since I cannot now receive you sacramentally, come at least spiritually into my heart. I embrace you and unite myself entirely to you; never permit me to be separated from you.

Q. 102 *Is Jesus Christ present in all the consecrated Hosts in the world?*

Yes, Jesus Christ is present in all the consecrated Hosts in the world (CCC 1377).

Q. 103 *Why is the Most Holy Eucharist kept in the churches?*

The Most Holy Eucharist is kept in the churches so that the faithful may adore it, so that they may receive it in Communion, and so that they may recognize in the Holy Eucharist the perpetual assistance and presence of Jesus Christ in the Church (CCC 1378–79).

Q. 104 *Where in the church is the Holy Eucharist kept?*

The Holy Eucharist is kept in a tabernacle, as a worthy place for the presence of the Lord and a place to be recognized by the faithful in Eucharistic devotion (CCC 1379).

119

TEACHER'S NOTES

EUCHARISTIC SAINTS

Many saints are known for their devotion to the Blessed Sacrament. The following are just a few of the hundreds of saints that could be listed here.

- Saint Clare of Assisi
- Saint Thomas Aquinas
- Saint Peter Julian Eymard
- Blessed Jacinta and Blessed Francisco (from Fatima)
- Saint Isidore

Preview

In the next lesson, the students' understanding of the material covered in this chapter will be reviewed and assessed. There will be a quiz and unit test.

Chapter Twenty-Eight: His Abiding Presence

Review and Assessment

Aims

The students' understanding of the material covered in this chapter will be reviewed and assessed.

Materials

- Quiz 28, Appendix, p. A-40

Optional:
- "Tantum ergo," *Adoremus Hymnal*, #393

Review and Enrichment

1. The students must know the real and abiding presence of Christ in the Eucharist.

2. The students should know that the Eucharist is reserved in a tabernacle. They should be familiar with the requirements of a tabernacle.

3. The students should be familiar with various forms of Eucharistic worship and devotion, including:
- Adoration
- Benediction
- Spiritual Communion
- Visits to the Blessed Sacrament
- Chaplet of the Blessed Sacrament
- Eucharistic Processions
- Perpetual Adoration

4. The students should know various names for the Blessed Sacrament.

5. The students should know of some saints with a great love for the Eucharist.

Name: _____

His Abiding Presence   Quiz 28

Part I: Yes or No.

1. <u>Yes</u> Is it Jesus who changes bread and wine into his Body and Blood through transubstantiation?
2. <u>Yes</u> Is the Eucharist Jesus in his entirety, Body, Blood, Soul, and Divinity?
3. <u>Yes</u> Do we receive the divinity of Jesus as well as his humanity?
4. <u>No</u> Did Jesus leave his disciples orphaned?
5. <u>Yes</u> Is Jesus present in the tabernacles in our churches?
6. <u>Yes</u> Is Jesus in the tabernacle night and day?
7. <u>Yes</u> Should we visit Jesus in the Blessed Sacrament?
8. <u>Yes</u> Does speaking to Jesus in the Blessed Sacrament bring us special graces?

Part II: Answer in complete sentences.

1. What is a sanctuary lamp?
   A sanctuary lamp is a lamp which is kept burning as long as the Blessed Sacrament is in the tabernacle.

2. What kind of reverent actions should our behavior before the Blessed Sacrament include?
   Answers may vary. Reverent actions before the Blessed Sacrament should include genuflecting, blessing ourselves with holy water, and bowing our heads.

3. What is a Eucharistic procession?
   A Eucharistic procession is when the Blessed Sacrament is carried through the streets with solemnity and reverence, accompanied by singing.

4. What is Exposition?
   Exposition is when the consecrated Host is put in a monstrance and placed on the altar for the faithful to see and adore. During Exposition there are prayers and hymns.

5. What is Benediction?
   Benediction is at the end of Exposition when the priest or deacon lifts the monstrance and blesses the faithful with it by making the Sign of the Cross.

A-40   *Faith and Life Series • Grade 6 • Appendix A*

Assess

1. Distribute the quizzes and read through them with the students to be sure they understand the questions.

2. Administer the quiz. As they hand in their work, you may orally quiz the students on the Memorization Questions from this chapter.

3. After all the quizzes have been handed in, you may wish to review the correct answers with the class.

Conclude

1. Lead the students in singing "Tantum ergo," *Adoremus Hymnal*, #393.

2. End class by leading the students in praying the Act of Spiritual Communion from the student text p. 119.

Chapter Twenty-Eight: His Abiding Presence
Activity Book Answer Keys

Name:_____

His Abiding Presence

Answer the following questions in complete sentences.

1. What happens during transubstantiation?
   During transubstantiation, Jesus changes bread and wine into his Body and Blood.

2. Who comes to us in Holy Communion?
   Jesus comes to us in Holy Communion.

3. What does the Eucharist nourish?
   The Eucharist nourishes our souls.

4. Will Jesus ever leave us orphaned? Why?
   No. Jesus will not leave us orphaned because he is always with us, present in the Blessed Sacrament.

5. How can we profess our faith in Jesus' presence?
   We can profess our faith in Jesus' presence by genuflecting, blessing ourselves with holy water, and bowing our heads.

6. Can we visit Jesus in the Blessed Sacrament?
   Yes.

7. Why is it important to pray in front of the Blessed Sacrament?
   It is important to pray with the Blessed Sacrament because the prayer we say there is an extra act of love that we offer Jesus freely, and it will bring us special graces.

8. When can you go and visit the Blessed Sacrament?
   We can visit the Blessed Sacrament whenever the church or chapel is open.

Name:_____

Reposition of the Blessed Sacrament

Answer the following questions in complete sentences.

1. What is a tabernacle?
   A tabernacle is a container in our churches in which the Blessed Sacrament is reserved.

2. What is kept in the tabernacle?
   The Blessed Sacrament is kept in the tabernacle.

3. Does every Catholic church have a tabernacle?
   Yes.

4. Why is the Most Holy Eucharist kept in the churches?
   Answers will vary.

5. Is Jesus Christ present in all the consecrated Hosts in the world?
   Yes.

6. How can you tell if the Blessed Sacrament is in the tabernacle?
   A sanctuary lamp will be kept burning near the tabernacle whenever the Blessed Sacrament is reserved within.

Name:_____

Eucharistic Worship

Answer the following questions in complete sentences.

1. Can we worship the Eucharist?
   Yes.

2. Name two forms of Eucharistic worship.
   Exposition and Benediction are two forms of Eucharistic worship.

3. Has the Church always encouraged a devotion to the Blessed Sacrament?
   Yes.

4. When is the Eucharist carried in procession?
   The Eucharist is carried in procession on the feast of Corpus Christi.

5. What does this symbolize?
   Answers will vary.

6. What is Exposition?
   Exposition is the ceremony in which the Sacred Host is placed in a monstrance on or above the altar for adoration.

7. What is Benediction?
   Benediction is a Eucharistic devotion to Jesus in the Blessed Sacrament in which a priest or deacon blesses the faithful with the monstrance.

8. When might incense be used?
   Incense might be used during Exposition.

9. Name some hymns whose words show a devotion to the Blessed Sacrament.
   Answers will vary.

Name:_____

Spiritual Communion

Answer the following questions in complete sentences.

1. What is spiritual communion?
   Spiritual communion is a prayer we pray to unite ourselves to Jesus in the Eucharist at a time when we cannot physically receive him as we do at Mass.

2. How can we make a spiritual communion?
   We make a spiritual communion by praying a prayer of spiritual communion.

Write out a prayer of spiritual communion and memorize it.
   Sample prayer taken from Student Text, p. 119:

   My Jesus, I believe that you are in the Blessed Sacrament. I love you above all things, and I long for you in my soul. Since I cannot now receive you sacramentally, come at least spiritually into my heart. I embrace you and unite myself entirely to you; never permit me to be separated from you.

TEACHER'S NOTES

UNIT SEVEN TEST
CHAPTERS 26–28

> ### CHAPTER TWENTY-SIX: PREPARING OUR HEARTS FOR JESUS
> ### CHAPTER TWENTY-SEVEN: COME LORD JESUS
> ### CHAPTER TWENTY-EIGHT: HIS ABIDING PRESENCE

Aims

The students' understanding of the material covered in this unit will be reviewed and assessed.

Materials

• Unit 7 Test, Appendix, pp. A-41 and A-42

Assess

1. Distribute the unit tests and read through them with the students to be sure they understand the questions.

2. Administer the test.

3. After all the tests have been handed in, you may wish to review the correct answers with the class.

Name: _____

Unit 7 Test **Chapters 26—28**

Part I: Answer in complete sentences.

1. When the priest holds the Host before us and says: "The Body of Christ" and we respond, "Amen", what are we expressing?
   <u>When the priest holds the Host before us and says: "The Body of Christ" and we respond, "Amen", we are expressing our belief in the Real Presence of Jesus in the Eucharist.</u>

2. What does the parable about the king who gave a wedding banquet for his son teach us about being prepared to receive Holy Communion?
   <u>The parable about the king who gave a wedding banquet for his son teaches us that we will displease Jesus if we go to Holy Communion without first being properly prepared.</u>

3. What is the most important way to prepare our hearts to receive Jesus?
   <u>The most important way to prepare our hearts to receive Jesus is to preserve the life of grace in us (stay in a state of grace).</u>

4. How does Jesus fulfill his promise to stay with us at all times?
   <u>Jesus fulfills his promise to stay with us at all times by being present in the Blessed Sacrament which is kept in the tabernacles of our churches around the world.</u>

5. What is a Eucharistic procession?
   <u>A Eucharistic procession is when the Blessed Sacrament is carried through the streets with solemnity and reverence, accompanied by singing.</u>

6. What is Exposition?
   <u>Exposition is when the consecrated Host is put in a monstrance and placed on the altar for the faithful to see and adore. During Exposition there are prayers and hymns.</u>

7. What is Benediction?
   <u>Benediction is at the end of Exposition when the priest or deacon lifts the monstrance and blesses the faithful with it by making the Sign of the Cross.</u>

Part II: Explain what each of these terms mean in regard to receiving Holy Communion.

1. state of grace: <u>To be in a state of grace means to be free from mortal sin.</u>

Name: _____

Unit 7 Test (continued)

2. right intention: <u>We must have the right intention in order to receive Holy Communion worthily. (Or, We must intend or desire to receive the Body and Blood of Jesus.)</u>

3. Eucharistic fast: <u>We must fast from food and drink, except water or medicine, for one hour before receiving Holy Communion.</u>

4. thanksgiving: <u>After receiving Holy Communion, we should thank Jesus for coming to us and giving us so great a gift in his Body and Blood.</u>

5. Easter duty: <u>The Church requires all the faithful who have received their First Communion to receive the Eucharist at least once a year during the Easter season.</u>

6. Viaticum: <u>This is another name for Communion given to one who is dying. The word means "provisions for the journey".</u>

Part III: Yes or No.

1. <u>Yes</u> Does Jesus want us to have confidence in him?

2. <u>No</u> Do we have any reason to worry if we have confidence in Jesus?

3. <u>Yes</u> Do we displease Jesus if we receive Holy Communion without being properly prepared?

4. <u>Yes</u> Should we receive Holy Communion often?

5. <u>Yes</u> Is Peter the rock upon which Jesus built his Church?

6. <u>Yes</u> Is it disrespectful to talk to friends during Mass?

7. <u>Yes</u> Does God become our food in the Eucharist?

8. <u>Yes</u> Is it Jesus who changes bread and wine into his Body and Blood through transubstantiation?

9. <u>Yes</u> Is the Eucharist Jesus in his entirety, Body, Blood, Soul, and Divinity?

10. <u>Yes</u> Do we receive the divinity of Jesus as well as his humanity?

11. <u>No</u> Did Jesus leave his disciples orphaned?

12. <u>Yes</u> Is Jesus present in the tabernacles in our churches?

13. <u>Yes</u> Is Jesus in the tabernacle night and day?

14. <u>Yes</u> Should we visit Jesus in the Blessed Sacrament?

15. <u>Yes</u> Does speaking to Jesus in the Blessed Sacrament bring us special graces?

TEACHER'S NOTES

TEACHER'S NOTES

CHAPTER TWENTY-NINE
PASSAGE INTO ETERNITY

Catechism of the Catholic Church References

Christian Holiness: 2012–16, 2028–29
Death: 1028, 1021, 2299, 1020, 1006
Forms of Penance in Christian Life: 1434–39
Heaven: 1023–29, 1053
Hell: 1033–37, 1056–57
Individual Judgment: 1021–22, 1051
Last Judgment: 1038–41, 1051–52, 1059

Man as Body and Soul: 362–68, 382
Prayer for the Dead: 1032, 1055
Purgatory: 1030–32, 1054
Sacrifice: 2099–2100
Satisfaction for Sin: 1459–60, 1494
To Die in Christ Jesus: 1005–14, 1018–19, 1020, 1052

Scripture References

Creation and Fall: Gen 2:4—3:24
Readiness to Meet Jesus:
    End Times: Mk 13:30–37
    Maidens and Lamps: Mt 25:1–13

Marriage Feast: Mt 22:1–14
Second Coming: Mt 24:36–44
Thief: Lk 12:35–40

Summary of Lesson Content

Lesson 1

Death is a consequence of Original Sin. Death is the separation of the body and the soul. The body will die without the life of the soul. The soul will live forever—it is a spiritual being.

Jesus died so that we can live with him forever in heaven, should we choose to believe in him and follow his commands.

Lesson 2

Our prayers, reception of the Sacraments, moral life, and works of charity prepare us for a good death.

With the life of grace, we can hope in life united with Jesus forever in heaven.

Lesson 3

Particular Judgment occurs at the moment of our death. Jesus is the judge.

We will know the good and bad we have done in our life; the perfect justice of God and of our eternal reward in heaven or hell; and the presence of the Divine Judge, Jesus.

Lesson 4

We do not know the time of our death, so we should always be ready.

We must develop a spiritual life of prayer and the Sacraments. We must live according to God's will and keep his commandments. We must know and love God through the study of our Faith.

We should love and serve God generously in this life.

CHAPTER TWENTY-NINE: PASSAGE INTO ETERNITY
LESSON ONE: DEATH

Aims

The students will learn that death is a consequence of Original Sin. Death is the separation of the body and the soul. The body will die without the life of the soul. The soul will live forever—it is a spiritual being.

They will learn that Jesus died so that we can live with him forever in heaven, should we choose to believe in him and follow his commands.

Materials

- *Activity Book*, p. 113

- Bible

Optional:
- "May flights of angels lead you on your way," *Adoremus Hymnal*, #573

Begin

From the Bible, read the account of the Fall and the curses that accompanied the Fall in Genesis 2:4—3:24. The students may draw on the board, depicting the Creation as you read it to them. Help them to understand the superiority of man over all the other creatures and the gravity of Original Sin.

Develop

1. Read paragraphs 1–3.

2. Review that man is a body-soul unity created by God. Review the qualities of both the body and the soul:
- Body/Material: It enables us to move around, to feel, to see, to taste, to smell, to hear, etc. Matter is limiting (e.g., if you continue to put things in a box, eventually the box will be full).
- Soul/Spiritual: It enables us to think/know/learn, to love, to communicate, etc. The human soul is immortal and without physical limits (e.g., you can always love more).

3. Review the effects of Original Sin:
- Suffering and death
- Disharmony of the flesh (concupiscence, and disharmony between male and female, and man and animals)
- Loss of grace and separation from God
- Labor needed to learn things, etc.

4. Death is the separation of the body and the soul. This separation leaves the body without any life (it is limited) and it returns to dust. The soul, however, is immortal since it is spiritual. It lives forever in our eternal reward.

5. After the Fall, man lost grace and was not able to go to heaven. The souls of the dead went to the realm of the dead. (This is where Jesus went between Good Friday and Easter Sunday—the Creed says, he descended to the dead, or to hell. He went there to bring the souls of the just into heaven as he opened its gates.) Now, because of Jesus' suffering, death, and Resurrection, we know that heaven is opened and the souls of the just may anticipate this glory!

6. We should see value in suffering and a good death, united to Jesus.

Reinforce

1. Have the students work on *Activity Book* p. 113 (see *Teacher's Manual*, p. 363).

2. Take the students to visit a funeral home and learn proper funeral etiquette. They should become familiar with a Catholic Funeral Rite and interment.

3. Have the students work on the Memorization Questions and Words to Know from this chapter (see *Teacher's Manual*, p. 359).

Conclude

1. Teach the students to sing "May flights of angels lead you on your way," *Adoremus Hymnal*, #573.

2. End class by leading the students in praying the Prayer of Saint John Vianney (see *Teacher's Manual*, p. 357).

PART THREE
The Last Things

CHAPTER 29

Passage into Eternity

"Truly, truly, I say to you, he who hears my word and believes him who sent me, has eternal life; he does not come into judgment, but has passed from death to life."

John 5:24

We are all children of Adam and Eve; we are all made up of body and soul, and condemned by Original Sin to the eventual parting of body and soul that we call death. This parting leaves the body without any life, and it falls back to dust. But the soul does not fall back into nothingness; the soul was made to live forever.

God gave us his very own Son to take the penalty of death upon himself to redeem us from sin. Through Jesus we have the hope of living in heaven with God, although we must still undergo bodily death.

The bishops of the Catholic Church at the Second Vatican Council wrote: "Through Christ and in Christ the riddle of sorrow and death grow meaningful. . . . Apart from his gospel, they overwhelm us."

The mystery of death can only be answered by faith. With faith, we see death as it really is. Jesus said to his Apostles,

"Let not your hearts be troubled; believe in God, believe also in me. In my Father's house are many rooms; if it were not so, would I have told you that I go to prepare a place for you? And when I go and prepare a place for you, I will come again and will take you to myself, that where I am you may be also. And you know the way where I am going" (Jn 14:1–4).

Every prayer we have ever said, every Sacrament we have received, every good work we have ever done, every grace we have been given, helps to prepare us for the moment of death.

We ought to face death with hopeful joy, for Jesus said to Martha: "I am the resurrection and the life; he who believes in me, though he die, yet shall he live, and whoever lives and believes in me shall never die (Jn 11:25–26).

123

Something strange is happening—there is a great silence on earth today, a great silence and stillness. The whole earth keeps silence because the King is asleep. The earth trembled and is still because God has fallen asleep in the flesh and he has raised up all who have slept ever since the world began. God has died in the flesh and hell trembles with fear. . .
I am your God, who for your sake have become your son. Out of love for you and for your descendants I now by my own authority command all who are held in bondage to come forth, all who are in darkness to be enlightened, all who are sleeping to arise. I order you, O sleeper to awake. I did not create you to be held a prisoner in hell. Rise from the dead, for I am the life of the dead. Rise up, work of my hand, you who were created in my image. Rise, let us leave this place. . . .
For your sake I, your God, became your son; I, the Lord, took the form of a slave; I whose home is above the heavens, descended to the earth and beneath the earth. For your sake, for the sake of man.

—From an ancient homily
on Holy Saturday

JESUS' DESCENT INTO HELL

The Apostles' Creed teaches "He descended into hell; on the third day he rose again." The *Catechism of the Catholic Church* explains that hell refers to the place of the dead. While heaven was closed, all of the dead, just and unjust, resided in what is called *Sheol* in Hebrew or *Hades* in Greek. In the three days between Jesus' death and Resurrection, the human soul of Jesus, united to his Divine Person, went into the depths of the dead to rescue the just souls. Jesus did not put an end to hell and damnation but brought to salvation those who had died in God's friendship. (See the *Catechism of the Catholic Church*, paragraphs 631–637, and the Bible, Eph 4:9–10; 1 Pet 3:18–19; 4:6.)

Preview

In the next lesson, the students will learn how to prepare for a happy death.

355

Chapter Twenty-Nine: Passage into Eternity
Lesson Two: Happy Death

Aims

The students will learn that our prayers, reception of the Sacraments, moral life, and works of charity prepare us for a good death.

They will learn that, with the life of grace, we can hope for life united with Jesus forever in heaven.

Materials

• *Activity Book*, p. 114

• Funeral Rite, Appendix, pp. B-30–B-32.

Optional:
• "May flights of angels lead you on your way," *Adoremus Hymnal*, #573

Begin

Often, people fear death because we do not know everything about it. We are anxious about how our bodies and souls will separate and we are saddened by the loss of loved ones who have gone before us. However, we should not fear or be sad about death, for we have in Jesus' Resurrection the hope of eternal life! We know that Jesus conquered death and gives us a share in his life.

Develop

1. Read paragraphs 4–6.

2. Jesus said "I am the resurrection and the life; he who believes in me, though he die, yet shall he live" (Jn 11:25). What does this really mean?
   • If we believe in Jesus (that he is God), then we will believe what he has revealed.
   • We will follow his commandments and teachings.
   • We will respect the authority he gave to Peter and his Church.
   • We will receive the Sacraments which he instituted so that we can share in his life of grace.
   • We will love one another and do good works out of this love.
   • We will be filled with faith, hope, and love.
   • We will desire and anticipate all that he promised.
Have the students give specific examples of how our faith affects our lives and prepares us for eternal life.

3. We know that to go to heaven, we must have Jesus' life of grace in our soul. Grace is something that we have, or do not have. If we are in mortal sin, we do not have grace because our sinful actions have killed that grace in our souls. If we have confessed our sins, God restores that grace and we must nurture it.

4. How do we get grace necessary for salvation?
   • Baptism, Penance, and Anointing of the Sick

5. How do we grow in grace and strength?
   • Sacraments
   • Prayer
   • Good works
Have the students give examples.

6. Just as we prepare for a journey, so too we prepare for our journey from life through death to eternal life.

Reinforce

1. Have the students work on *Activity Book* p. 114 (see *Teacher's Manual*, p. 363).

2. Review (if you have not already done so) the Funeral Rite of the Catholic Church.

3. You may discuss how important it is to visit our sick and elderly and to help them prepare to meet Jesus.

4. Have the students work on the Memorization Questions and Words to Know from this chapter (see *Teacher's Manual*, p. 359).

Conclude

1. Lead the students in singing "May flights of angels lead you on your way," *Adoremus Hymnal*, #573.

2. End class by leading the students in praying the Prayer of Saint John Vianney (on the facing page).

CHAPTER 29

Passage into Eternity

"Truly, truly, I say to you, he who hears my word and believes him who sent me, has eternal life; he does not come into judgment, but has passed from death to life."

John 5:24

We are all children of Adam and Eve; we are all made up of body and soul, and condemned by Original Sin to the eventual parting of body and soul that we call death. This parting leaves the body without any life, and it falls back to dust. But the soul does not fall back into nothingness; the soul was made to live forever.

God gave us his very own Son to take the penalty of death upon himself to redeem us from sin. Through Jesus we have the hope of living in heaven with God, although we must still undergo bodily death.

The bishops of the Catholic Church at the Second Vatican Council wrote: "Through Christ and in Christ the riddle of sorrow and death grow meaningful. . . . Apart from his gospel, they overwhelm us."

The mystery of death can only be answered by faith. With faith, we see death as it really is. Jesus said to his Apostles,

"Let not your hearts be troubled; believe in God, believe also in me. In my Father's house are many rooms; if it were not so, would I have told you that I go to prepare a place for you? And when I go and prepare a place for you, I will come again and will take you to

myself, that where I am you may be also. And you know the way where I am going" (Jn 14:1–4).

Every prayer we have ever said, every Sacrament we have received, every good work we have ever done, every grace we have been given, helps to prepare us for the moment of death.

We ought to face death with hopeful joy, for Jesus said to Martha: "I am the resurrection and the life; he who believes in me, though he die, yet shall he live, and whoever lives and believes in me shall never die (Jn 11:25–26).

123

Particular Judgment

Jesus, who knows our every thought, will judge each of us individually as soon as our souls leave our bodies. This is called the **Particular Judgment**. The truth of his verdict will be made clear to us. With complete clarity we will immediately be aware of three things: 1. the exact balance of good and bad in our life and what we truly are; 2. the perfect justice of our future lot, in heaven or hell; and 3. the presence of the Divine Judge, Jesus.

Saint Paul says: "He will render to every man according to his works: to those who by patience in well-doing seek for glory and honor and immortality, he will give eternal life; but for those who are factious and do not obey the truth, but obey wickedness, there will be wrath and fury" (Rom 2:6–8).

Readiness

Jesus compares us to servants awaiting the return of the master of the house. He said, "Watch therefore—for you do not know when the master of the house will come, in the evening, or at midnight, or at cock-crow, or in the morning" (Mk 13:35).

Jesus recommends a healthy awareness of the reality of death. It should not be a morbid thought; we just have to face facts. If we prepare ourselves for death, we will find joy and peace of mind that death cannot destroy.

We prepare for death by taking advantage of the means our loving Father in heaven has given us. We do our best to live according to his will. We develop a spiritual life of prayer and the Sacraments. We study the truths of our religion in school or in a class at our

124

THE GRACE OF A HAPPY DEATH

"These all died in faith, not having received what was promised, but having seen it and greeted it from afar, and having acknowledged that they were strangers and exiles on the earth. For people who speak thus make it clear that they are seeking a homeland. If they had been thinking of that land from which they had gone out, they would have had opportunity to return. But as it is, they desire a better country, that is, a heavenly one. Therefore God is not ashamed to be called their God, for he has prepared for them a city" (Heb 11:13–16). This passage refers to the patriarchs, but it applies to us, too. We are "strangers and exiles on the earth," and we are journeying to "a better country." CCC 1392 teaches, "What material food produces in our bodily life, Holy Communion wonderfully achieves in our spiritual life. . . . Christian life needs the nourishment of Eucharistic Communion, the bread for our pilgrimage until the moment of death, when it will be given to us as viaticum." At the end of our earthly pilgrimage, the Church offers us three final Sacraments. First, Penance, in which our sins are forgiven and our relationship with God is made right. Second, the Anointing of the Sick, which also forgives sins, strengthens us, and prepares us to meet God. Finally, we receive the Holy Eucharist as Viaticum, food for the journey from death to eternal life.

I love you, O my God, and my only desire is to love you until the last breath of my life.
—Saint John Vianney

Preview

In the next lesson, the students will learn about Particular Judgment.

Chapter Twenty-Nine: Passage into Eternity
Lesson Three: Particular Judgment

Aims

The students will learn that the Particular Judgment occurs at the moment of our death. Jesus is the judge. We will know the good and bad we have done in our life, the perfect justice of God and of our eternal reward in heaven or hell, and the presence of the Divine Judge, Jesus.

Materials

- *Activity Book*, p. 115

Optional:
- "May flights of angels lead you on your way," *Adoremus Hymnal*, #573

Begin

Review how we can prepare for a happy death:
- Live a moral life
- Live a sacramental life
- Pray
- Have faith, hope, and love
- Receive the Anointing of the Sick

Have the students give other examples.

Develop

1. Read paragraphs 7 and 8.

2. What is the Particular Judgment? It is the moment of truth at the end of our lives when we will be judged by Jesus (the highest authority). On what will we be judged? We will be judged on our thoughts, words, actions, and omissions. God knows all of these. (You may review the Confiteor).

3. If Jesus is judging us on our thoughts, words, deeds, and omissions, and we have free will, it is we who determine our eternal reward (heaven or hell) by how we live here on earth.

4. The Particular Judgment is immediate upon our death. We will know with certain clarity three things:

- The exact balance of good and bad in our life and what we truly are—Often we deceive ourselves because we do not want to know the truth. We think that our sins are not as bad as others, or we can rationalize them (I had to do this because . . .). When we commit venial sin, it disposes us to commit mortal sins; the change may be so gradual that we might not realize how bad we have become. Our actions determine our being (a person who steals things is a thief, a person who lies is a liar, a person who commits adultery is an adulterer, a person who sins is a sinner).

- The perfect justice of our future lot (heaven or hell)—We merit either heaven or hell by how we live our lives. When we see our lives in the fullness of the truth we will understand God's justice and accept our eternal reward.

- The presence of the Divine Judge, Jesus—Jesus is the judge, and we will know this and the certainty of the truths he revealed while on earth. We should rejoice at being in the presence of God!

Reinforce

1. Have the students work on *Activity Book* p. 115 (see *Teacher's Manual*, p. 363).

2. Review that each tconfession is like a mini-judgment. We judge ourselves, repent of our sins, and our sins are forgiven. God's mercy is beautiful, but we must seek it here on earth for when we are dead, it is too late.

3. Have the students work on the Memorization Questions and Words to Know from this chapter.

Conclude

1. Lead the students in singing "May flights of angels lead you on your way," *Adoremus Hymnal*, #573.

2. End class by leading the students in praying the Prayer of Saint John Vianney (see *Teacher's Manual*, p. 357).

CHAPTER 29

Passage into Eternity

"Truly, truly, I say to you, he who hears my word and believes him who sent me, has eternal life; he does not come into judgment, but has passed from death to life."

John 5:24

We are all children of Adam and Eve; we are all made up of body and soul, and condemned by Original Sin to the eventual parting of body and soul that we call death. This parting leaves the body without any life, and it falls back to dust. But the soul does not fall back into nothingness; the soul was made to live forever.

God gave us his very own Son to take the penalty of death upon himself to redeem us from sin. Through Jesus we have the hope of living in heaven with God, although we must still undergo bodily death.

The bishops of the Catholic Church at the Second Vatican Council wrote: "Through Christ and in Christ the riddle of sorrow and death grow meaningful. . . . Apart from his gospel, they overwhelm us."

The mystery of death can only be answered by faith. With faith, we see death as it really is. Jesus said to his Apostles,

"Let not your hearts be troubled; believe in God, believe also in me. In my Father's house are many rooms; if it were not so, would I have told you that I go to prepare a place for you? And when I go and prepare a place for you, I will come again and will take you to myself, that where I am you may be also. And you know the way where I am going" (Jn 14:1–4).

Every prayer we have ever said, every Sacrament we have received, every good work we have ever done, every grace we have been given, helps to prepare us for the moment of death.

We ought to face death with hopeful joy, for Jesus said to Martha: "I am the resurrection and the life; he who believes in me, though he die, yet shall he live, and whoever lives and believes in me shall never die (Jn 11:25–26).

123

Particular Judgment

Jesus, who knows our every thought, will judge each of us individually as soon as our souls leave our bodies. This is called the **Particular Judgment**. The truth of his verdict will be made clear to us. With complete clarity we will immediately be aware of three things: 1. the exact balance of good and bad in our life and what we truly are; 2. the perfect justice of our future lot, in heaven or hell; and 3. the presence of the Divine Judge, Jesus.

Saint Paul says: "He will render to every man according to his works: to those who by patience in well-doing seek for glory and honor and immortality, he will give eternal life; but for those who are factious and do not obey the truth, but obey wickedness, there will be wrath and fury" (Rom 2:6–8).

Readiness

Jesus compares us to servants awaiting the return of the master of the house. He said, "Watch therefore—for you do not know when the master of the house will come, in the evening, or at midnight, or at cockcrow, or in the morning" (Mk 13:35).

Jesus recommends a healthy awareness of the reality of death. It should not be a morbid thought; we just have to face facts. If we prepare ourselves for death, we will find joy and peace of mind that death cannot destroy.

We prepare for death by taking advantage of the means our loving Father in heaven has given us. We do our best to live according to his will. We develop a spiritual life of prayer and the Sacraments. We study the truths of our religion in school or in a class at our

124

---

parish, and afterwards we go on reading on our own and learn more about these truths.

Of course, we are aware that we often fail to keep God's laws, in little things if not in big; and so we must often turn to God's mercy and love. Knowing all this, the Church tells us how we can make up for our sins. We can offer prayers, especially the Rosary; we can do charitable deeds for others; we can do penance and offer sacrifices (for example, give up a dessert or second helping or give up having our own way about a game we are playing with others).

Above all, we should serve God generously, not measuring everything with the minimum required by law. For Jesus said: "With your own measure it will be measured out to you again."

The closer we come to Jesus through prayer and acts of love, the more confidence we will have in his care for us and his mercy. If we live for him, we will learn more and more to see death as the beginning of a new and wonderful life with God.

Words to Know:
Particular Judgment

Prayer for the Dead
Eternal rest grant to them, O Lord, and let perpetual light shine upon them. May they rest in peace.

Q. 105 *What happens to each of us at the end of life?*
At the end of life each of us will die, our body and soul will be separated, and we will face a Particular Judgment (CCC 1005, 1022).

Q. 106 *On what will Jesus Christ judge us?*
Jesus Christ will judge us on the good and evil that we have done in life, including our thoughts, and things we failed to do in response to God's grace (CCC 1021, 1868).

Q. 107 *What happens to each man after the Particular Judgment?*
After the Particular Judgment, those who love God and are perfectly holy go immediately to heaven to be with him. Those who love God but still need purification go to purgatory until they are ready to be with God in heaven. Those who have rejected God, through dying in mortal sin, go to hell (CCC 1022).

125

SAINT JUAN DIEGO

Saint Juan Diego is known as the man to whom Mary appeared as Our Lady of Guadalupe, but even before the apparition he lived a life of holiness. He lived fourteen miles south of Mexico City and every morning he awoke before dawn and walked all the way to the city to go to daily Mass. It was on one of these journeys that our Lady appeared to him. Also, when his uncle became very sick during the apparitions, Saint Juan tried to skip a meeting with our Lady to care for him. However, Mary stopped him on his way. The saint told her about his uncle, and she told him not to worry, she would take care of him. Saint Juan trusted our Lady and did as she asked. His uncle was healed just as she had said.

Preview

In the next lesson, the students will learn about readiness for death.

Chapter Twenty-Nine: Passage into Eternity
Lesson Four: Readiness

Aims

The students will learn that we do not know the time of our death, so we should always be ready. We must develop a spiritual life of prayer and the Sacraments. We must live according to God's will and keep his commandments. We must know and love God through the study of our Faith.

They will learn that we should love and serve God generously in this life.

Materials

- *Activity Book*, p. 116

Optional:
- "May flights of angels lead you on your way," *Adoremus Hymnal*, #573

Begin

Review how we can prepare for death and what will happen at the moment of death (separation of body and soul). Review the Particular Judgment. Help the students to understand that once we are dead, we can no longer repent of our sins.

Develop

1. Finish reading the chapter with the students, paragraphs 9–14.

2. Jesus tells us stories about anticipating our meeting with Jesus and Particular Judgment:
- End Times: Mk 13:30–37
- Maidens and Lamps: Mt 25:1–13
- Marriage Feast: Mt 22:1–14
- Second Coming: Mt 24:36–44
- Thief: Lk 12:35–40
The students should read these passages and dramatize them or write meditations based upon them.

3. We should be aware that we will die and we do not know when. Often, when we are young, we think that we will live until a very old age. Some people die young, too. It is important that we accept this and are ready—for we do not know the day or the hour.

4. To be ready for death we must:
- Be in and stay in the state of grace:
We should seek confession as soon as we commit a grave sin. Do not wait, out of pride. We should be sorry for our sins and seek reconciliation with God as soon as we can.

- Know our Faith. Pope Benedict XIV said:
"A great number of those who are condemned to eternal punishment suffer that everlasting calamity because of ignorance of those mysteries of Faith which must be known and believed in order to be numbered among the elect." We have a grave responsibility to know our Faith, so we can live in relationship with God.

- We should live in a way pleasing to God (with others):
We should follow God's will, live a sacramental life, keep his commandments, pray, and be holy.

Reinforce

1. Have the students work on *Activity Book* p. 116 (see *Teacher's Manual*, p. 363).

2. The students may work on the Memorization Questions and Words to Know from this chapter and prepare for their quiz.

Conclude

1. Lead the students in singing "May flights of angels lead you on your way," *Adoremus Hymnal*, #573.

2. End class by leading the students in praying the Prayer of Saint John Vianney (see *Teacher's Manual*, p. 357).

CHAPTER 29

Passage into Eternity

"Truly, truly, I say to you, he who hears my word and believes him who sent me, has eternal life; he does not come into judgment, but has passed from death to life."

John 5:24

We are all children of Adam and Eve; we are all made up of body and soul, and condemned by Original Sin to the eventual parting of body and soul that we call death. This parting leaves the body without any life, and it falls back to dust. But the soul does not fall back into nothingness; the soul was made to live forever.

God gave us his very own Son to take the penalty of death upon himself to redeem us from sin. Through Jesus we have the hope of living in heaven with God, although we must still undergo bodily death.

The bishops of the Catholic Church at the Second Vatican Council wrote: "Through Christ and in Christ the riddle of sorrow and death grow meaningful. . . . Apart from his gospel, they overwhelm us."

The mystery of death can only be answered by faith. With faith, we see death as it really is. Jesus said to his Apostles,

"Let not your hearts be troubled; believe in God, believe also in me. In my Father's house are many rooms; if it were not so, would I have told you that I go to prepare a place for you? And when I go and prepare a place for you, I will come again and will take you to

myself, that where I am you may be also. And you know the way where I am going" (Jn 14:1–4).

Every prayer we have ever said, every Sacrament we have received, every good work we have ever done, every grace we have been given, helps to prepare us for the moment of death.

We ought to face death with hopeful joy, for Jesus said to Martha: "I am the resurrection and the life; he who believes in me, though he die, yet shall he live, and whoever lives and believes in me shall never die (Jn 11:25–26).

123

Particular Judgment

Jesus, who knows our every thought, will judge each of us individually as soon as our souls leave our bodies. This is called the **Particular Judgment**. The truth of his verdict will be made clear to us. With complete clarity we will immediately be aware of three things: 1. the exact balance of good and bad in our life and what we truly are; 2. the perfect justice of our future lot, in heaven or hell; and 3. the presence of the Divine Judge, Jesus.

Saint Paul says: "He will render to every man according to his works: to those who by patience in well-doing seek for glory and honor and immortality, he will give eternal life; but for those who are factious and do not obey the truth, but obey wickedness, there will be wrath and fury" (Rom 2:6–8).

Readiness

Jesus compares us to servants awaiting the return of the master of the house. He said, "Watch therefore—for you do not know when the master of the house will come, in the evening, or at midnight, or at cockcrow, or in the morning" (Mk 13:35).

Jesus recommends a healthy awareness of the reality of death. It should not be a morbid thought; we just have to face facts. If we prepare ourselves for death, we will find joy and peace of mind that death cannot destroy.

We prepare for death by taking advantage of the means our loving Father in heaven has given us. We do our best to live according to his will. We develop a spiritual life of prayer and the Sacraments. We study the truths of our religion in school or in a class at our

124

---

parish, and afterwards we go on reading on our own and learn more about these truths.

Of course, we are aware that we often fail to keep God's laws, in little things if not in big; and so we must often turn to God's mercy and love. Knowing all this, the Church tells us how we can make up for our sins. We can offer prayers, especially the Rosary; we can do charitable deeds for others; we can do penance and offer sacrifices (for example, give up a dessert or second helping or give up having our own way about a game we are playing with others).

Above all, we should serve God generously, not measuring everything with the minimum required by law. For Jesus said: "With your own measure it will be measured out to you again."

The closer we come to Jesus through prayer and acts of love, the more confidence we will

have in his care for us and his mercy. If we live for him, we will learn more and more to see death as the beginning of a new and wonderful life with God.

Words to Know:
Particular Judgment

Prayer for the Dead

Eternal rest grant to them, O Lord, and let perpetual light shine upon them. May they rest in peace.

Q. 105 *What happens to each of us at the end of life?*
At the end of life each of us will die, our body and soul will be separated, and we will face a Particular Judgment (CCC 1005, 1022).

Q. 106 *On what will Jesus Christ judge us?*
Jesus Christ will judge us on the good and evil that we have done in life, including our thoughts, and things we failed to do in response to God's grace (CCC 1021, 1868).

Q. 107 *What happens to each man after the Particular Judgment?*
After the Particular Judgment, those who love God and are perfectly holy go immediately to heaven to be with him. Those who love God but still need purification go to purgatory until they are ready to be with God in heaven. Those who have rejected God, through dying in mortal sin, go to hell (CCC 1022).

125

STEPS FOR DISCERNMENT— KNOWING GOD'S WILL

- Pray and receive the Sacraments often. Have a deep relationship with God.

- Know yourself and the gifts God has given to you. He will use them.

- Search the desires of your heart; God will speak through them (see Ps 37:4).

- Be open and ready to follow *wherever* God leads and to serve him generously.

- Although it will not always be easy, you should have peace, joy, and a sense of rightness.

Preview

In the next lesson, the students' understanding of the material covered in this chapter will be reviewed and assessed.

CHAPTER TWENTY-NINE: PASSAGE INTO ETERNITY
REVIEW AND ASSESSMENT

Aims

The students' understanding of the material covered in this chapter will be reviewed and assessed.

Materials

- Quiz 29, Appendix, p. A-43

Optional:
- "May flights of angels lead you on your way," *Adoremus Hymnal*, #573

Review and Enrichment

1. The students should know that man is a body-soul unity. Because of Original Sin, man will die. At death, the body and the soul will be separated. The body will no longer have life. The soul will live forever.

2. The students should know how to prepare for death.

3. The students should understand that at the Particular Judgment the soul will immediately be aware of :
- The balance of good and bad in our lives
- The perfect justice of our future lot
- The presence of Jesus, the Divine Judge

4. The students should understand the need of readiness for death. Considering death is not sad or morbid. It is a way to help us live good lives and encourage us to:
- Stay in the state of grace
- Know our Faith
- Live in a way pleasing to God

Name:

Passage into Eternity   **Quiz 29**

Part I: Answer in complete sentences.

1. What is death?
   Death is the separation of the body and the soul.

2. What happens to the body after death?
   Without the soul to give it life, the body returns to dust.

3. What happens to the soul after it leaves the body?
   The soul goes to God for judgment and enters into eternity.

4. What is the Particular Judgment?
   The Particular Judgment is the immediate and individual judgment by Christ of each of us at our death.

5. At the Particular Judgment we will be immediately aware of what three things?
   At the Particular Judgment we will be aware of:
   1. the exact balance of good and bad in our life and what we truly are,
   2. the perfect justice of our future lot in heaven or hell, and
   3. the presence of the Jesus, the Divine Judge.

Part II: Yes or No.

1. No   Should we fear death?

2. Yes   Should we be aware of death as something that we must all experience?

3. Yes   When we die, will we be judged for what we have thought, said, done, and failed to do?

4. No   Is God unfair in his judgment of us?

5. Yes   Are there things we can do right now, like living a good life and receiving the Sacraments on a regular basis, to prepare us for death and judgment?

6. Yes   At the hour of our death, will we be at peace if we have done our best to please God and have asked for his mercy for the times we failed to obey him?

Faith and Life Series • Grade 6 • Appendix A   *A-43*

Assess

1. Distribute the quizzes and read through them with the students to be sure they understand the questions.

2. Administer the quiz. As they hand in their work, you may orally quiz the students on the Memorization Questions from this chapter.

3. After all the quizzes have been handed in, you may wish to review the correct answers with the class.

Conclude

1. Lead the students in singing "May flights of angels lead you on your way," *Adoremus Hymnal*, #573.

2. End class by leading the students in praying the Prayer of Saint John Vianney (see *Teacher's Manual*, p. 357).

Name:_____

Passage into Eternity

Answer the following questions in complete sentences.

1. What two parts does a human being consist of?
   A human being consists of a body and soul.

2. What happens at death?
   At death, the soul and the body separate.

3. What happens to the body?
   The body dies and falls back to dust.

4. What happens to the soul?
   The soul lives forever.

5. Why do we have hope?
   We have hope because Jesus took the penalty of death upon himself and redeemed us from sin.

Faith and Life Series • Grade 6 • Chapter 29 • Lesson 1   113

Name:_____

Death and Faith

Answer the following questions in complete sentences.

1. How did Jesus show us that he has power over death?
   Jesus showed us that he has power over death by his Resurrection.

2. What did Jesus tell us about his Father's house?
   Jesus told us that his Father's house has many rooms and he is preparing a place for us.

3. Will we be alone in heaven?
   No.

4. How can we prepare for our deaths?
   We can prepare for our deaths by praying, receiving the Sacraments, doing good works, and receiving graces from God.

5. What did Jesus tell Martha, which gives us hope?
   Jesus told Martha "I am the resurrection and the life; he who believes in me, though he die, yet shall he live, and whoever lives and believes in me shall never die."

114   *Faith and Life Series • Grade 6 • Chapter 29 • Lesson 2*

Name:_____

The Particular Judgment

Answer the following questions in complete sentences.

1. On what will Jesus judge us?
   Jesus will judge us on the good and evil that we have done in life, including our thoughts, and things we failed to do in response to God's grace.

2. What happens to the soul at the Particular Judgment?
   At the Particular Judgment, those who love God and are perfectly holy go immediately to heaven to be with Jesus. Those who love God but still need purification go to purgatory until they are ready to be with God in heaven. Those who have rejected God through dying in mortal sin go to hell.

Faith and Life Series • Grade 6 • Chapter 29 • Lesson 3   115

Name:_____

Readiness

Answer the following questions in complete sentences.

 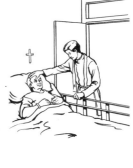

1. Should we be aware that we will die someday?
   Yes.

2. How can we prepare ourselves for a happy death?
   We can prepare for a happy death by living according to God's will, developing a spiritual life of prayer and the Sacraments, and studying the truths of our religion.

3. What has God given us to help us make up for our sins?
   God has given us the Sacrament of Penance and the chance to offer prayers, acts of charity, and penances to help us make up for our sins

4. How can we grow closer to Jesus? Why is this good?
   We can grow closer to Jesus through prayer and acts of love. This is good because it will give us more confidence in his care for us and his mercy.

116   *Faith and Life Series • Grade 6 • Chapter 29 • Lesson 4*

TEACHER'S NOTES

CHAPTER THIRTY
HEAVEN—PURGATORY—HELL

Catechism of the Catholic Church References

Attributes of God Shown in Creation: 293–95, 315, 341
God Creates an Ordered and Good World: 299
Heaven: 1023–29, 1053
Hell: 1033–37, 1056–57
Man's Freedom: 1730–42, 1743–48

Man's Vocation to Beatitude: 1718–24, 1726–29
Purgatory: 1030–32, 1054
Reality of Sin: 386–87, 413
Satisfaction for Sin: 1459–60, 1494
Ways of Knowing God: 31–38, 46–48, 286

Scripture References

Heaven in Scripture:
 Father's House: Jn 14:1–4; 1 Cor 2:9; 1 Jn 3:2
Purgatory in Scripture: Mt 5:23–26; Rom 5:1–5; 1 Cor 3:10–15; 2 Mac 12:39–46; Rev 6:9–11; 1 Pet 3:18–19

Hell in Scripture:
 Those Cast into Hell: Mt 25:41–46
 Enemies: Mt 5:22
 Those who Reject Jesus: Mt 10:28–33
 Tempting to Sin: Mk 9:42–48
 Unfaithful Servant: Lk 19:12–27

Summary of Lesson Content

Lesson 1

Heaven is our goal. We live on this earth in anticipation of union with God in heaven.

Heaven is the greatest joy. It is being with God forever, loving God, and sharing in God's own life.

Living a holy life on earth keeps us more attuned to God and increases our desire for heaven and our confidence that we can get there.

Lesson 2

Those who die in the state of grace, free of all sin or attachment to sin and all debt for sin go to heaven.

Those who die in the state of grace, but with venial sins or unpaid debts for sin will eventually go to heaven after they are purified in purgatory.

Purgatory is a state of purification and penance where souls are cleansed and freed from sin and the punishment due to sin.

Lesson 3

The Communion of Saints includes the Church Triumphant, the Church Suffering, and the Church Militant.

The Church Triumphant are the saints in heaven.
The Church Suffering are the holy souls in purgatory.
The Church Militant are the faithful on earth who strive to get to heaven.

Lesson 4

Those who reject God through mortal sin condemn themselves to hell.

Hell is real. It is a state of eternal suffering and separation from God.

Chapter Thirty: Heaven—Purgatory—Hell
Lesson One: Heaven

Aims

The students will learn that heaven is our goal. We live on this earth in anticipation of union with God in heaven. Heaven is the greatest joy. It is being with God forever, loving God, and sharing in God's own life.

They will learn that living a holy life on earth keeps us more attuned to God, increases our desire for heaven, and gives us confidence to get there.

Materials

- *Activity Book*, p. 117

- Bible

- Litany of the Saints, Appendix, pp. B-33 and B-34

Optional:
- "Hail, Queen of Heaven, the ocean star," *Adoremus Hymnal*, #539

Begin

Read from John 14:1–4. Have the students discuss what heaven must be like:
- Who is there?
- Why is it the greatest place?
- Will we be happy? Why?

The students may depict heaven as they imagine it.

Develop

1. Read paragraphs 1–8 (up to Purgatory).

2. Man is created to be in God's friendship and to live with God for all eternity. That is how it was in the Garden of Eden. Adam and Eve walked with God—and they would never have died. It is only because of Original Sin that this was lost; by the death and Resurrection of Jesus, this friendship and eternal reward were restored.

3. Saint Paul says: "What no eye has seen, nor ear heard, nor the heart of man conceived, what God has prepared for those who love him"(1 Cor 2:9). Saint John says, "We are God's children now; it does not yet appear what we shall be, but we know that when he appears we shall be like him, for we shall see him as he is" (1 Jn 3:2). Bearing in mind these quotes, explain to the students the glory we shall see in heaven and that the happiness we will obtain will be beyond all we can imagine.

4. Review the Communion of Saints. This includes the faithful on earth (the Church Militant), the holy souls in purgatory (the Church Suffering), and the angels and saints in heaven (the Church Triumphant or Victorious). Let us focus on the souls in the Church Triumphant:
- They are triumphant because they live in the presence of God.
- God's pure spirits, the angels, are in heaven (review the choirs of angels).
- The canonized saints are in heaven—those canonized by the Church.
- Mary is the Queen of Heaven.
- The saints are in heaven—all those who died in God's grace and are with him forever, sharing in God's own life.

5. Review that the saints/angels in heaven can pray for us and ask God to give us his graces, as intercessors. You may pray the Litany of the Saints (see Appendix, pp. B-33 and B-34).

Reinforce

1. Have the students work on *Activity Book* p. 117 (see *Teacher's Manual*, p. 375).

2. The students may depict heaven.

3. The students may create their own litany of the saints.

4. Have the students work on the Memorization Questions and Words to Know from this chapter (see *Teacher's Manual*, p. 371).

Conclude

1. Teach the students to sing "Hail, Queen of Heaven, the ocean star," *Adoremus Hymnal*, #539.

2. End class by leading the students in praying a Hail Mary (see *Teacher's Manual*, p. 396).

CHAPTER 30

Heaven–Purgatory–Hell

"Then the King will say to those at his right hand, 'Come, O blessed of my Father, inherit the kingdom prepared for you from the foundation of the world.'"

Matthew 25:34

Heaven

We cannot know much about heaven, only the little we have been told. Yet every time we look at a crucifix we are reminded that Christ was stripped of everything men hold dear and opened his arms on the Cross to gain for us our everlasting future of unimaginable happiness.

This does not mean that we should not try to think about true happiness, but only that we should always recall that the real thing will be far greater than anything we can think of. We can never make a mistake by exaggerating the happiness of heaven. We can make a great mistake by thinking of it too little. An even greater mistake would be to make heaven sound boring.

Living close to God prepares us for heaven in many ways. Not only does it merit reward, but as the years go by we become more attuned to God and the things of heaven, and that increases our desire to reach heaven and our confidence that we will get there. "O taste and see that the LORD is good!" (Ps 34:8).

The purpose of your life and mine is to see God in heaven someday. But that is not something that is easy to imagine; in fact, we cannot imagine God, since he is a pure spirit and we can only imagine things we have seen. So how can you get an idea of it? You can get an idea about it by thinking about the beauty and design and order and truth and goodness and power of the world about you. God created every good thing in the world and set it all in order. So the goodness, truth, and beauty of creation give us some idea of God; he is like all these things, but he is infinitely more good, true, and beautiful than all of them. We also have an idea of heaven through everything Jesus said and did.

So now we can ask ourselves this question: What is heaven? And we can say this: Heaven is being with God forever and loving God and living God's own life—which means that we are so united to God that with him we see what he sees, know what he knows, and love how he loves, according to our fullest human capacity. It means that God will make us like himself!

We will not be bored, not for a moment. Eternal life, therefore, means not only living forever, but living *God's life* forever!

God says: "My people will be filled with my good things."

Purgatory

It's easy to waste time out of thoughtlessness. We should use the minutes, hours, and days to grow in the spiritual life, to come close to God. Our spiritual life begins at Baptism, which removes the punishment for Original Sin but leaves us still with wounds in our nature.

Our life after Baptism, if it is a life of prayer, Sacraments, and good works, will heal our wounds even more; if it is a life of sin and vice, it will deepen them.

There is a book about the spiritual life called *Ascent of Mount Carmel*, by Saint John of the Cross. Growing spiritually is compared to climbing a great mountain. The higher we climb, the more we change. Some people climb all the way to the top and are rewarded with such union with God that they go straight to heaven when they die.

Purgatory can also be compared to the ascent of Mount Carmel. Those who die as God's friends—in the state of grace, free of all sin or attachment to sin, free of all debt to make up for sin—go immediately to heaven when they die. But what about those who die as God's friends, in the state of grace, but with venial sins or unpaid debts for past sins, all forgiven but not yet worked off?

They are not yet ready for heaven. Only what is completely holy can enter heaven. What happens to them?

They go to a place of purification and penance called purgatory where their souls are cleansed and freed of the unpaid debt of sin. Being purified hurts, both here and hereafter; there is no way to be healed and grow that is free from pain. But we can avoid a purgatory in the hereafter by accepting our purgatory here. We can be healed and purified and make up for our sins by doing penance and by humbly accepting the difficulties and sufferings that come to us in life.

In purgatory, there is one thing on everyone's mind: God. The soul there desires God with a greatness that is hard for us to imagine. The souls in purgatory know with absolute certainty that they are saved and are going to heaven. They fear no more danger to their salvation. They are being made ready for union with God, and so they must be cleansed of any obstacles to that perfect union. These obstacles to union are like rust, remains of sin that hinder the soul from

enjoying God. Saint Catherine of Genoa tells us that the rust diminishes as the soul becomes healthier under the rays of divine sunlight. So there is great happiness as well as great suffering in purgatory.

The saints in heaven are called the **Church Triumphant**, the souls in purgatory are called the **Church Suffering**, and the faithful on earth are called the **Church Militant**. All together we form the one Church of Christ. We on earth can help the souls in purgatory by praying for them, sacrificing for them, and offering Masses for them.

Hell

Jesus told us that just as those who do the will of the Father will receive the reward of eternal happiness, those who reject the Father and refuse to do the will of God will be condemned to eternal punishment. "Depart from me, you cursed, into the eternal fire prepared for the devil and his angels" (Mt 25:41). The condemned are those who die without repenting of their mortal sins.

Many people like to think that hell does not exist. They say that God would never send anyone to a place of everlasting torment since he loves us so much. It is true that God does not want people to go there. But he made us with a free will so that we could freely choose to love God. Any persons in hell have freely chosen to love only themselves and have chosen not to love God; they are, of their own choosing, utterly alone.

The loss of God is the greatest pain in hell. We were made for God, but since the souls in hell have totally rejected him there is nothing left for which they can hope. And what makes their suffering in hell even greater is that each one there will realize that he alone is the cause of his own damnation.

God offers everyone the grace to repent and turn to him. We should always remember to pray for those who are near death so that they will seek the mercy that God extends to them.

Words to Know:
Church Triumphant   Church Suffering   Church Militant

"For what does it profit a man, to gain the whole world and forfeit his life? For what can a man give in return for his life? For whoever is ashamed of me and of my words in this adulterous and sinful generation, of him will the Son of man also be ashamed, when he comes in the glory of his Father with the holy angels" (Mark 8:36–38).

BATTLE OF THE ANGELS

"And another sign appeared in heaven; behold, a great red dragon. . . . His tail swept down a third of the stars of heaven, and cast them to the earth . . . . Now war arose in heaven, Michael and his angels fighting against the dragon; and the dragon and his angels fought, but they were defeated and there was no longer any place for them in heaven. And the great dragon was thrown down, that ancient serpent, who is called the Devil and Satan, the deceiver of the whole world—he was thrown down to the earth, and his angels were thrown down with him. And I heard a loud voice in heaven, saying, 'Now the salvation and the power and the kingdom of our God and the authority of his Christ have come'" (Rev 12:3–4, 7–10).

Preview

In the next lesson, the students will learn about purgatory.

Chapter Thirty: Heaven—Purgatory—Hell
Lesson Two: Purgatory

Aims

The students will learn that those who die in the state of grace, free of all sin or attachment to sin and all debt for sin go to heaven.

They will learn that those who die in the state of grace, but with venial sins or unpaid debts for sin will eventually go to heaven after they are purified in purgatory. Purgatory is a state of purification and penance where souls are cleansed and freed from sin and the punishment due to sin.

Materials

• *Activity Book*, p. 118

• Bibles

Optional:
• "Hail, Queen of Heaven, the ocean star," *Adoremus Hymnal*, #539

Begin

Review that only those perfected in God's grace may go to heaven. Many of us share in God's grace, but we are not perfect. Review that, with sin, there is the stain of sin (which is removed with absolution) but also the temporal punishment for sin. This debt for sin must be repaid before we can enter heaven.

Develop

1. Read paragraphs 9–14 from the student text.

2. Purgatory is a state of purification. It cleanses the souls of those who died in the state of grace from venial sins and the temporal punishment due to sin. It is a process which allows the souls that are saved to achieve the holiness necessary to enter heaven.

3. Is purgatory in Scriptures? Read and discuss the following passages.
• Rom 5:1–5 (Why does Saint Paul rejoice in his sufferings?)
• 1 Cor 3:10–15 (What should be the foundation of our life? If Jesus is the foundation of our life, where will we go after death? How will the deeds or words of those going to heaven be tested?)
• Mt 5:23–26 (What does Jesus ask us to do? What will we avoid if we do what he asks? There is an expression that refers to the "debt of sin." What does Jesus mean when he says "You will never get out until you have paid the last penny"?)
• 2 Mac 12:39–46 (What is the noble deed done by Judas? Why should we pray for the dead?)

Also read Revelation 6:9–11 and 1 Peter 3:18–19.

4. Discuss indulgences with the students. An indulgence is a "remission before God of the temporal punishment due to sins whose guilt has already been forgiven, which the faithful Christian who is duly disposed gains under certain prescribed conditions through the action of the Church, which, as the minister of redemption, dispenses and applies with authority the treasury of the satisfactions of Christ and the saints" (Paul VI, Indulgentiarum Doctrina, 1). There are partial indulgences, which remove part of the temporal punishment due to sin, and plenary indulgences, which completely remove all of our time in purgatory.

Reinforce

1. Have the students work on *Activity Book* p. 118 (see *Teacher's Manual*, p. 375).

2. Allow your class the opportunity to obtain a plenary indulgence. Note: you can obtain indulgences for those in purgatory as well.

3. Have the students work on the Memorization Questions and Words to Know from this chapter (see *Teacher's Manual*, p. 371).

Conclude

1. Lead the students in singing "Hail, Queen of Heaven, the ocean star," *Adoremus Hymnal*, #539.

2. End class by leading the students in praying a Hail Mary (see *Teacher's Manual*, p. 396).

CHAPTER 30

Heaven–Purgatory–Hell

"Then the King will say to those at his right hand, 'Come, O blessed of my Father, inherit the kingdom prepared for you from the foundation of the world.'"

Matthew 25:34

Heaven

We cannot know much about heaven, only the little we have been told. Yet every time we look at a crucifix we are reminded that Christ was stripped of everything men hold dear and opened his arms on the Cross to gain for us our everlasting future of unimaginable happiness.

This does not mean that we should not try to think about true happiness, but only that we should always recall that the real thing will be far greater than anything we can think of. We can never make a mistake by exaggerating the happiness of heaven. We can make a great mistake by thinking of it too little. An even greater mistake would be to make heaven sound boring.

Living close to God prepares us for heaven in many ways. Not only does it merit reward, but as the years go by we become more attuned to God and the things of heaven, and that increases our desire to reach heaven and our confidence that we will get there. "O taste and see that the LORD is good!" (Ps 34:8).

The purpose of your life and mine is to see God in heaven someday. But that is not something that is easy to imagine; in fact, we cannot imagine God, since he is a pure spirit and we can only imagine things we have seen. So how can you get an idea of it? You can get an idea about it by thinking about the beauty and design and order and truth and goodness and power of the world about you. God created every good thing in the world and set it all in order. So the goodness, truth, and beauty of creation give us some idea of God; he is like all these things, but he is infinitely more good, true, and beautiful than all of them. We also have an idea of heaven through everything Jesus said and did.

So now we can ask ourselves this question: What is heaven? And we can say this: Heaven is being with God forever and loving God and living God's own life—which means that we are so united to God that with him we see what he sees, know what he knows, and love how he loves, according to our fullest human capacity. It means that God will make us like himself!

We will not be bored, not for a moment. Eternal life, therefore, means not only living forever, but living *God's life* forever!

God says: "My people will be filled with my good things."

Purgatory

It's easy to waste time out of thoughtlessness. We should use the minutes, hours, and days to grow in the spiritual life, to come close to God. Our spiritual life begins at Baptism, which removes the punishment for Original Sin but leaves us still with wounds in our nature.

Our life after Baptism, if it is a life of prayer, Sacraments, and good works, will heal our wounds even more; if it is a life of sin and vice, it will deepen them.

There is a book about the spiritual life called *Ascent of Mount Carmel*, by Saint John of the Cross. Growing spiritually is compared to climbing a great mountain. The higher we climb, the more we change. Some people climb all the way to the top and are rewarded with such union with God that they go straight to heaven when they die.

Purgatory can also be compared to the ascent of Mount Carmel. Those who die as God's friends—in the state of grace, free of all sin or attachment to sin, free of all debt to make up for sin—go immediately to heaven when they die. But what about those who die as God's friends, in the state of grace, but with venial sins or unpaid debts for past sins, all forgiven but not yet worked off? They are not yet ready for heaven. Only what is completely holy can enter heaven. What happens to them?

They go to a place of purification and penance called purgatory where their souls are cleansed and freed of the unpaid debt of sin. Being purified hurts, both here and hereafter; there is no way to be healed and grow that is free from pain. But we can avoid a purgatory in the hereafter by accepting our purgatory here. We can be healed and purified and make up for our sins by doing penance and by humbly accepting the difficulties and sufferings that come to us in life.

In purgatory, there is one thing on everyone's mind: God. The soul there desires God with a greatness that is hard for us to imagine. The souls in purgatory know with absolute certainty that they are saved and are going to heaven. They fear no more danger to their salvation. They are being made ready for union with God, and so they must be cleansed of any obstacles to that perfect union. These obstacles to union are like rust, remains of sin that hinder the soul from

enjoying God. Saint Catherine of Genoa tells us that the rust diminishes as the soul becomes healthier under the rays of divine sunlight. So there is great happiness as well as great suffering in purgatory.

The saints in heaven are called the **Church Triumphant**, the souls in purgatory are called the **Church Suffering**, and the faithful on earth are called the **Church Militant**. All together we form the one Church of Christ. We on earth can help the souls in purgatory by praying for them, sacrificing for them, and offering Masses for them.

Hell

Jesus told us that just as those who do the will of the Father will receive the reward of eternal happiness, those who reject the Father and refuse to do the will of God will be condemned to eternal punishment. "Depart from me, you cursed, into the eternal fire prepared for the devil and his angels" (Mt 25:41). The condemned are those who die without repenting of their mortal sins.

Many people like to think that hell does not exist. They say that God would never send anyone to a place of everlasting torment since he loves us so much. It is true that God does not want people to go there. But he made us with a free will so that we could freely choose to love God. Any persons in hell have freely chosen to love only themselves and have chosen not to love God; they are, of their own choosing, utterly alone.

The loss of God is the greatest pain in hell. We were made for God, but since the souls in hell have totally rejected him there is nothing left for which they can hope. And what makes their suffering in hell even greater is that each one there will realize that he alone is the cause of his own damnation.

God offers everyone the grace to repent and turn to him. We should always remember to pray for those who are near death so that they will seek the mercy that God extends to them.

Words to Know:
Church Triumphant   Church Suffering
Church Militant

> "For what does it profit a man, to gain the whole world and forfeit his life? For what can a man give in return for his life? For whoever is ashamed of me and of my words in this adulterous and sinful generation, of him will the Son of man also be ashamed, when he comes in the glory of his Father with the holy angels" (Mark 8:36–38).

HOW TO GET A PLENARY INDULGENCE

Conditions for receiving a plenary indulgence:
1. Sacramental confession
2. Reception of Communion
3. Pray for our Holy Father
4. Fulfill one of the proscribed devotions for a plenary indulgence. For example:
   - Adoration of the Blessed Sacrament for at least 1/2 hour
   - Scripture readings for at least 1/2 hour
   - Way of the Cross recited
   - Rosary prayed in a church or with a family group or religious community

Preview

In the next lesson, the students will review the Communion of Saints.

126

127

128

CHAPTER THIRTY: HEAVEN—PURGATORY—HELL
LESSON THREE: COMMUNION OF SAINTS

Aims

The students will learn that the Communion of Saints includes the Church Triumphant, the Church Suffering, and the Church Militant. The Church Triumphant are the saints in heaven. The Church Suffering are the holy souls in purgatory. The Church Militant are the faithful on earth who strive to get to heaven.

Materials

- *Activity Book*, p. 119

  Optional:
  - "Hail, Queen of Heaven, the ocean star," *Adoremus Hymnal*, #539

Begin

The Mystical Body of Christ, the Church of Christ, and the Communion of Saints, all refer to the same thing—all those who are united in Christ:

- The faithful on earth
- The holy souls in purgatory
- The just in heaven

Develop

1. Read paragraph 15.

2. The souls in the Church Triumphant: (Review)
   - They are triumphant because they live in the presence of God.
   - God's pure spirits, the angels, are in heaven.
   - The canonized saints are in heaven—those canonized by the Church.
   - The saints are in heaven—all those who died in God's grace and are with him forever, sharing in God's own life.

3. The Church Suffering: (Review)
   - These are the holy souls in purgatory.
   - These souls are saved and died in the state of grace.
   - They are being purified of their venial sins and punishments due to sin.
   - They are growing in holiness so they can enter heaven.

4. The Church Militant: (Review)
   - These are the faithful of Christ here on earth.
   - These souls are striving for salvation: belief (Creed), right living (moral life), and Christian life (with others, through the Church) are essential.

5. Not all people are born Catholic and the Church teaches that there is "no salvation outside the Church." This means that the Church is the dispenser of grace. Many people, however, share in this treasure through the one Baptism, faith in God, or following their consciences. The Church has the fullness of the means of salvation.

6. Teach how the Communion of Saints interacts: those on earth can pray for each other, for those in purgatory, and can ask for the intercession of those on earth, in purgatory, and in heaven. Those in purgatory cannot pray for themselves and need the prayers of those on earth and in heaven.

Reinforce

1. Have the students work on *Activity Book* p. 119 (see *Teacher's Manual*, p. 375).

2. The students may depict the Communion of Saints

3. Have the students work on the Memorization Questions and Words to Know from this chapter.

Conclude

1. Lead the students in singing "Hail, Queen of Heaven, the ocean star," *Adoremus Hymnal*, #539.

2. End class by leading the students in praying a Hail Mary (see *Teacher's Manual*, p. 396).

enjoying God. Saint Catherine of Genoa tells us that the rust diminishes as the soul becomes healthier under the rays of divine sunlight. So there is great happiness as well as great suffering in purgatory.

The saints in heaven are called the **Church Triumphant**, the souls in purgatory are called the **Church Suffering**, and the faithful on earth are called the **Church Militant**. All together we form the one Church of Christ. We on earth can help the souls in purgatory by praying for them, sacrificing for them, and offering Masses for them.

Hell

Jesus told us that just as those who do the will of the Father will receive the reward of eternal happiness, those who reject the Father and refuse to do the will of God will be condemned to eternal punishment. "Depart from me, you cursed, into the eternal fire prepared for the devil and his angels" (Mt 25:41). The condemned are those who die without repenting of their mortal sins.

Many people like to think that hell does not exist. They say that God would never send anyone to a place of everlasting torment since he loves us so much. It is true that God does not want people to go there. But he made us with a free will so that we could freely choose to love God. Any persons in hell have freely chosen to love only themselves and have chosen not to love God; they are, of their own choosing, utterly alone.

The loss of God is the greatest pain in hell. We were made for God, but since the souls in hell have totally rejected him there is nothing left for which they can hope. And what makes their suffering in hell even greater is that each one there will realize that he alone is the cause of his own damnation.

God offers everyone the grace to repent and turn to him. We should always remember to pray for those who are near death so that they will seek the mercy that God extends to them.

Words to Know:
Church Triumphant   Church Suffering
Church Militant

"For what does it profit a man, to gain the whole world and forfeit his life? For what can a man give in return for his life? For whoever is ashamed of me and of my words in this adulterous and sinful generation, of him will the Son of man also be ashamed, when he comes in the glory of his Father with the holy angels" (Mark 8:36–38).

Q. 108 *What is eternal life?*
Eternal life is the reward of living forever with God in the happiness of heaven. The souls of those who die in grace and God's friendship enter heaven after death, either immediately or after purification (CCC 1022).

Q. 109 *What is heaven?*
Heaven is our eternal enjoyment of God, who is our happiness, with the angels and the blessed (CCC 1023–24).

Q. 110 *What is purgatory?*
Purgatory is the temporary state of purifying suffering after death for those who die in God's friendship, but who do not yet have the holiness needed to be with God in heaven (CCC 1030–31).

Q. 111 *What is hell?*
Hell is the eternal suffering of separation from God (CCC 1033–35).

Q. 112 *Is it certain that heaven and hell exist?*
Yes, it is certain that heaven and hell exist. God has revealed this, frequently promising eternal life and happiness with him to the good, and threatening the wicked with damnation and eternal fire (CCC 1024, 1034).

Q. 113 *How long will heaven and hell last?*
Heaven and hell will last forever (CCC 1029, 1035).

SAINT CATHERINE OF GENOA: *TREATISE ON PURGATORY*

After ten years of marriage to a worldly husband, Saint Catherine of Genoa was granted an overwhelming vision of God and the true state of her sinfulness. She experienced the fire of purgatory and saw what the souls in purgatory see. The details of these visions were written down many years later by Saint Catherine's confessor, Fr. Marabotti, in the *Treatise on Purgatory*. In it, the saint describes the souls in purgatory as free of all self-love and longing only for the presence of God. Knowing that they suffer as a result of their sins, the only desire of souls in purgatory is to be with God in Paradise.

"The souls in purgatory are entirely conformed to the will of God; therefore, they correspond with his goodness, are contented with all that he ordains, and are entirely purified from the guilt of their sins."

—Saint Catherine of Genoa
Treatise on Purgatory

"We must not wish anything other than what happens from moment to moment, all the while, however, exercising ourselves in goodness."

"If it were given to a man to see virtue's reward in the next world, he would occupy his intellect, memory and will in nothing but good works, careless of danger or fatigue."

—Saint Catherine of Genoa

Saint Catherine was born in Genoa in 1447 and died in 1510 having left behind significant insights on mysticism. She was canonized in 1737.

Preview

In the next lesson, the students will learn about hell.

CHAPTER THIRTY: HEAVEN—PURGATORY—HELL
LESSON FOUR: HELL

Aims

The students will learn that those who reject God through mortal sin condemn themselves to hell.

They will learn that hell is real. It is a state of eternal suffering and separation from God.

Materials

- *Activity Book*, p. 120

- Bibles

Optional:
- "Hail, Queen of Heaven, the ocean star," *Adoremus Hymnal*, #539

Begin

Before beginning this lesson, explain clearly to the students that the souls who go to hell choose this for themselves by the way that they live on earth (review: we are judged on our thoughts, words, actions, and omissions).

Develop

1. Finish reading the chapter (paragraphs 16–19).

2. Hell is real. It is a state of eternal suffering in which the condemned are banished from the presence of God. We find evidence of hell in the Scriptures:
   - Those cast into hell: Mt 25:41–46
   - Enemies: Mt 5:22
   - Those who reject Jesus: Mt 10:28–33
   - Tempting to sin: Mk 9:42–48
   - Unfaithful servant: Lk 19:12–27

Have the students read and discuss these passages. Can the students see the evil done in each action, which merits condemnation?

3. The loss of God is the greatest pain in hell. We were made for God and to live with him forever, so to reject God irrevocably gives the soul nothing to hope for.

4. Each soul is alone in his own condemnation. Imagine being alone for a week—seeing no one, speaking to no one, having no one to share your joys and sufferings with. So it is in hell—only forever. There are no "friends" in hell. Since one chooses to go to hell by choosing self over God and everyone else, he is condemned to isolation.

5. Discuss God's tremendous mercy. God does not desire that even one soul be condemned to hell. He offers his mercy to all who seek it during their lives. His loving mercy is so great that it can forgive all of men's sins! Certainly that is greater than even our worst sins. We must never despair. We must turn to Christ to seek his mercy in the Sacrament of Penance.

6. We should pray for those near death. We should pray that they receive the Anointing of the Sick and God's mercy.

Reinforce

1. Have the students work on *Activity Book* p. 120 (see *Teacher's Manual*, p. 375).

2. The students may work on the Memorization Questions and Words to Know from this chapter and review for their quiz.

Conclude

1. Lead the students in singing "Hail, Queen of Heaven, the ocean star," *Adoremus Hymnal*, #539.

2. End class by leading the students in praying a Hail Mary (see *Teacher's Manual*, p. 396).

enjoying God. Saint Catherine of Genoa tells us that the rust diminishes as the soul becomes healthier under the rays of divine sunlight. So there is great happiness as well as great suffering in purgatory.

The saints in heaven are called the **Church Triumphant**, the souls in purgatory are called the **Church Suffering**, and the faithful on earth are called the **Church Militant**. All together we form the one Church of Christ. We on earth can help the souls in purgatory by praying for them, sacrificing for them, and offering Masses for them.

Hell

Jesus told us that just as those who do the will of the Father will receive the reward of eternal happiness, those who reject the Father and refuse to do the will of God will be condemned to eternal punishment. "Depart from me, you cursed, into the eternal fire prepared for the devil and his angels" (Mt 25:41). The condemned are those who die without repenting of their mortal sins.

Many people like to think that hell does not exist. They say that God would never send anyone to a place of everlasting torment since he loves us so much. It is true that God does not want people to go there. But he made us with a free will so that we could freely choose to love God. Any persons in hell have freely chosen to love only themselves and have chosen not to love God; they are, of their own choosing, utterly alone.

The loss of God is the greatest pain in hell. We were made for God, but since the souls in hell have totally rejected him there is nothing left for which they can hope. And what makes their suffering in hell even greater is that each one there will realize that he alone is the cause of his own damnation.

God offers everyone the grace to repent and turn to him. We should always remember to pray for those who are near death so that they will seek the mercy that God extends to them.

Words to Know:
Church Triumphant   Church Suffering
Church Militant

"For what does it profit a man, to gain the whole world and forfeit his life? For what can a man give in return for his life? For whoever is ashamed of me and of my words in this adulterous and sinful generation, of him will the Son of man also be ashamed, when he comes in the glory of his Father with the holy angels" (Mark 8:36–38).

128

Q. 108 *What is eternal life?*
Eternal life is the reward of living forever with God in the happiness of heaven. The souls of those who die in grace and God's friendship enter heaven after death, either immediately or after purification (CCC 1022).

Q. 109 *What is heaven?*
Heaven is our eternal enjoyment of God, who is our happiness, with the angels and the blessed (CCC 1023–24).

Q. 110 *What is purgatory?*
Purgatory is the temporary state of purifying suffering after death for those who die in God's friendship, but who do not yet have the holiness needed to be with God in heaven (CCC 1030–31).

Q. 111 *What is hell?*
Hell is the eternal suffering of separation from God (CCC 1033–35).

Q. 112 *Is it certain that heaven and hell exist?*
Yes, it is certain that heaven and hell exist. God has revealed this, frequently promising eternal life and happiness with him to the good, and threatening the wicked with damnation and eternal fire (CCC 1024, 1034).

Q. 113 *How long will heaven and hell last?*
Heaven and hell will last forever (CCC 1029, 1035).

129

SAINT FAUSTINA

Born in Poland in 1905, Helena Kowalska was a poor girl who received little education. Before turning twenty, she joined the Congregation of the Sisters of Our Lady of Mercy in Warsaw and was given the name Sr. Maria Faustina. As she lived, worked, and prayed in the convent, Saint Faustina began to have visions of Jesus, who talked to her about his divine mercy. He told her to have an image painted of himself. In this image, he wanted two rays of light, red and white, to come from his heart, and he asked that the words "Jesus, I trust in you" be painted underneath the image. The two rays of light signify the blood and water which poured from Jesus' heart when the soldier pierced his side (Jn 19:34). Jesus said that the water represents Baptism, by which we are made righteous and the blood represents his Precious Blood, which gives life to our souls. The image presents visually the message of divine mercy that Jesus gave to the world through Saint Faustina. Jesus is reminding us that, in his mercy, he died for all of us that we may live. If anyone turns to him and repents, Jesus will forgive him, no matter how many his sins. Many dioceses celebrate the feast of Divine Mercy (Divine Mercy Sunday) on the first Sunday after Easter. This is a day for us to bring to mind the infinite mercy of God, call upon him, trust in him, and thank him for his mercy.

How many souls have been consoled by the prayer *"Jesus, I trust in you"*. . . . This simple act of abandonment to Jesus dispels the thickest clouds and lets a ray of light penetrate every life.

—Pope John Paul II
from the homily at the Mass for
Saint Faustina's Canonization

Preview

In the next lesson, the students' understanding of the material covered in this chapter will be reviewed and assessed.

CHAPTER THIRTY: HEAVEN—PURGATORY—HELL
REVIEW AND ASSESSMENT

Aims

The students' understanding of the material covered in this chapter will be reviewed and assessed.

Materials

- Quiz 30, Appendix, p. A-44

Optional:
- "Hail, Queen of Heaven, the ocean star," *Adoremus Hymnal*, #539

Review and Enrichment

1. The students should know the Communion of Saints: those in heaven, purgatory, and on earth.

2. The students should understand the concepts of heaven, hell, and purgatory.

3. The students should know that we choose our own eternal reward based upon our thoughts, words, actions, and omissions.

Name: _____

Heaven—Purgatory—Hell　　　　Quiz 30

Part I: Answer in complete sentences.

1. What is the final purpose of our life?
   The final purpose of our life is to see God in heaven.

2. What is heaven?
   Heaven is being with and loving God forever.

3. Will heaven be boring?
   No, heaven will not be boring, not even for a moment.

4. When does our spiritual life begin?
   Our spiritual life begins at Baptism.

5. What is purgatory and how can we help the souls there?
   Purgatory is a temporary state of purifying suffering after death for those who die in God's friendship, but who are not yet holy enough for heaven. We can help the souls in purgatory by praying for them, sacrificing for them, and offering Masses for them.

6. What is the Church Triumphant?
   The saints in heaven are the Church Triumphant.

7. What is the Church Suffering?
   The souls in purgatory are the Church Suffering.

8. What is the Church Militant?
   The faithful on earth are the Church Militant.

9. Who are the condemned?
   The condemned are those who die without repenting of their mortal sins.

10. Does hell exist?
    Yes, hell exists.

11. What is the greatest pain in hell?
    The greatest pain in hell is the loss of God.

A-44　　　　　　　*Faith and Life Series • Grade 6 • Appendix A*

Assess

1. Distribute the quizzes and read through them with the students to be sure they understand the questions.

2. Administer the quiz. As they hand in their work, you may orally quiz the students on the Mcmorization Questions from this chapter.

3. After all the quizzes have been handed in, you may wish to review the correct answers with the class.

Conclude

1. Lead the students in singing "Hail, Queen of Heaven, the ocean star," *Adoremus Hymnal*, #539.

2. End class by leading the students in praying a Hail Mary (see *Teacher's Manual*, p. 396).

Chapter Thirty: Heaven—Purgatory—Hell
Activity Book Answer Keys

Name:_____

Heaven

Answer the following questions in complete sentences.

1. What do we know about heaven?
   We know that Jesus sacrificed himself on the Cross to gain for us a future of unimaginable happiness.

2. Is it certain that heaven exists?
   Yes.

3. What is heaven?
   Heaven is our eternal enjoyment of God, who is our happiness, with the angels and the blessed.

4. How does God prepare us for heaven?
   God prepares us for heaven by making us more attuned to God, which increases our desire to see him in heaven.

5. What is the purpose of your life?
   The purpose of our lives is to see God in heaven.

6. What is eternal life?
   Eternal life is living God's life forever.

Faith and Life Series • Grade 6 • Chapter 30 • Lesson 1   117

Name:_____

Purgatory

Answer the following questions in complete sentences.

1. What is purgatory?
   Purgatory is the temporary state of purification and penance where souls are cleansed from the unpaid debt of sin.

2. Who goes to purgatory?
   Those who die as God's friend but with venial sons or unpaid debts of past sins that have been forgiven go to purgatory.

3. Do the souls in purgatory stay there for ever? (If not, where do they go?)
   No. Souls in purgatory go to heaven.

4. How can we work off at least some of our purgatory here on earth?
   We can work off at least some purgatory by accepting our purgatory here by doing penance and humbly accepting the difficulties and sufferings that come to us in life.

5. What does every soul in purgatory desire?
   Every soul in purgatory desires to be with God.

6. Do souls suffer or are they happy in purgatory? Why?
   Souls suffer and are happy in purgatory because they know that they are being prepared to go to heaven but they are not there yet.

118   *Faith and Life Series • Grade 6 • Chapter 30 • Lesson 2*

Name:_____

Communion of Saints

God wills each of us to be eternally happy with him in heaven. Describe the state of the souls in heaven, those in purgatory, and the faithful on earth.

Heaven:
   Answers will vary.

   Major points are:
   – Eternally happy with God

Purgatory:
   – Being purified so that they can enter heaven

Faithful on Earth:
   – Able to choose to follow God and prepare for heaven or not

Faith and Life Series • Grade 6 • Chapter 30 • Lesson 3   119

Name:_____

Hell

Answer the following questions in complete sentences.

1. What is hell?
   Hell is the eternal suffering of separation from God.

2. Who goes to hell?
   Those who reject the Father and refuse to do the will of God will go to hell.

3. Is it certain that hell exists?
   Yes.

4. How long does one spend in hell?
   One spends eternity in hell.

5. What is the greatest pain in hell?
   The greatest pain in hell is the loss of God.

6. Who causes a person to go to hell?
   A person freely choosing not to love God causes that person to go to hell.

120   *Faith and Life Series • Grade 6 • Chapter 30 • Lesson 4*

TEACHER'S NOTES

CHAPTER THIRTY-ONE
HE SHALL COME AGAIN

Catechism of the Catholic Church References

Beatific Vision: 163, 2548–50, 2557
Christ's Resurrection and Ours: 992–1004, 1015–17
Christian Beatitude: 1720–24, 1728–29
Heaven: 1023–29, 1053
Hell: 1033–37, 1056–57
Last Judgment: 1038–41, 1059
Man as Body and Soul: 362–68, 382

Purgatory: 1030–32, 1054
Resurrection of the Body: 988–91
Second Coming: 440, 671–72, 675, 677–82, 830, 988, 1031–32, 1038–41, 1060, 1107, 1130
To Die in Christ Jesus: 1005–14, 1018–19, 1020, 1052

Scripture References

Ascension: Acts 1:1–11

Scripture References for Second Coming: Lk 21:8–36; Mk 13:5–37; 2 Pet 3:10; Rev 21—22; Mt 7:13–14

Summary of Lesson Content

Lesson 1

Jesus will come again in glory.

At the time of Jesus' Ascension, two angels told the Apostles that Jesus will come in the same way as they saw him go into heaven.

Lesson 2

At the Second Coming Jesus will come again in great splendor.

He will come to judge the living and the dead at the General Judgment.

Purgatory will no longer exist and the resurrection of the body will occur so that all may share in the eternal reward of the soul (either heaven or hell).

Lesson 3

At the General Judgment, the justice of God will be known by all. The just will be rewarded, the unjust will be damned.

Jesus Christ will be fully vindicated, exalted, glorified, and honored.

Lesson 4

We should all strive to live our lives in anticipation of the truths of the Last Days.

Saint Paul compares the spiritual life to a race.

CHAPTER THIRTY-ONE: HE SHALL COME AGAIN
LESSON ONE: SECOND COMING

Aims

The students will learn that Jesus will come again in glory.

They will learn that, at the time of Jesus' Ascension, two angels told the Apostles that Jesus will come in the same way as they saw him go into heaven.

Materials

- *Activity Book*, p. 121

- Bibles

Optional:
- "I heard the voice of Jesus say," *Adoremus Hymnal*, #579

Begin

Review the timeline of Jesus' life. Include major events, such as:
- Virginal Conception
- Nativity
- Finding in the Temple

- Baptism in the Jordan
- Time of Preaching and Miracles
- Last Supper/Crucifixion/Resurrection
- Ascension

Develop

1. Read paragraph 1 from the student text.

2. Read Acts 1:1–11. This is the account of the Ascension and the promise of the Second Coming. Discuss what the Second Coming may be like.

3. Find passages in the Bible that teach about the Second Coming.
Luke 21:8–36 and Mark 13:5–37 (signs of the time)
- Wars and tumult
- Nation will rise against nation, and kingdom against kingdom
- Great earthquakes
- Famine and pestilence
- Terrors and great signs from heaven
- They will persecute you
- This will be a time for you to bear testimony

2 Peter 3:10
- It will be immediate, loud, and the earth will be consumed
Revelation 21—22
- There will be a new heaven and earth
- Wedding of the Lamb
Matthew 7:13–14
- The "narrow gate" leads to eternal joy
It is by these signs that we will know that Jesus is returning.

4. Have the students discuss the joy of Jesus' return. Would we recognize him? We know that Jesus will come in glory. How do we envision the glorious Jesus?

5. Will we be ready for Jesus' Second Coming? What can we do? We recognize the signs that Jesus will come again. We can pray for his return. We can always be ready through the moral life and sacramental life.

Reinforce

1. Have the students work on *Activity Book* p. 121 (see *Teacher's Manual*, p. 387).

2. The students may depict the Second Coming of Christ.

3. You may give the students time to work on the Memorization Questions and Words to Know from this chapter (see *Teacher's Manual*, p. 381).

Conclude

1. Teach the students to sing "I heard the voice of Jesus say," *Adoremus Hymnal*, #579.

2. End class by leading the students in praying Eternal rest, grant unto them O Lord (on the facing page).

CHAPTER 31

He Shall Come Again

"And when I go and prepare a place for you, I will come again and will take you to myself, that where I am you may be also."

John 14:3

Saint Luke records in the Acts of the Apostles that at Jesus' Ascension into heaven, two angels stood by the disciples and said to them, "Men of Galilee, why do you stand looking into heaven? This Jesus, who was taken up from you into heaven, will come in the same way as you saw him go into heaven" (Acts 1:11).

One day, when we least expect it, Jesus will appear in the heavens in great splendor and majesty, and all the armies of heaven with him. At this **Second Coming**, the trumpets will sound, the dead will rise, and the whole human race will be assembled before the judgment seat of Christ; the books will be opened and the judgment will begin. Every man's deeds, even the most secret, will be made known. Everyone will see and appreciate the holiness of the just, whether they hardly ever sinned or were great sinners and overcame their sins. Everyone will see and appreciate the justice of God in banishing the unrepentant from his sight, into hell forever.

The just, who served God with body and soul, in good times and bad, in good health and sickness, in joy and in sorrow, in pleasure and pain, will now receive a wonderful, glorious reward. They have tried hard to do something beautiful for God; now God will do something beautiful for them. It is true that they already see God, and this is called the Beatific Vision because it is a vision, a knowledge, which "beatifies" us, or makes us *completely* happy. Nevertheless, the souls in heaven are not yet all that God made them to be. Man was not made to be a disembodied spirit; man is a creature composed of body and soul. The body and soul will be brought together again at the Second Coming. It is the whole man who will enjoy heaven or suffer in hell. There will no longer be any need for purgatory.

One of the reasons for the judgment at the end of the world, called the **General Judgment**, is to make clear to everyone the wisdom, knowledge, graciousness, mercy, patience, loving kindness, and justice of the Lord of history in his dealings with all men. All shall be satisfied that it was well done. Then the just, who so often suffered at the hands of the unjust, will be honored, and the unjust who refused to ask God's forgiveness will be covered with shame and disgrace.

Above all, Jesus Christ the Savior, who suffered such humiliations, will be fully vindicated, exalted, glorified, and honored. His splendor will be so great that he

will light up the whole City of God. In the City of God, the new Jerusalem, the heavenly city, the whole universe will be renewed and set free from anything unfitting or harmful. Then those who have loved God and lived in his light will be united with him in heaven. And the just will have tremendous powers of mind and body to enjoy it all.

This is the goal toward which we are all striving. Remember how Saint Paul compared the life of a Christian to an athlete's? Let us work toward our goal so that we can say with him:

I have fought the good fight, I have finished the race, I have kept the faith. From now on there is laid up for me the crown of righteousness, which the Lord, the righteous judge, will award to me on that Day, and not only to me but also to all who have loved his appearing (2 Tim 4:7–8).

Words to Know:

Second Coming   General Judgment

We proclaim your Death, O Lord, and profess your Resurrection until you come again.

130

131

SAINT VINCENT FERRER: SAINT OF THE APOCALYPSE

Following the spirit of Saint Dominic, Saint Vincent joined the Dominican order in 1367. He began his apostolic work lecturing at universities in Catalonia and Barcelona and later worked for Pope Clement VII in Avignon. Although he was given such exalted roles, Saint Vincent longed to work among the people and fulfill the Dominican charism of preaching. In 1399, he fell ill. As he lay in bed, he had a vision of our Lord along with Saint Francis and Saint Dominic. They told Saint Vincent that he was to leave the comfort of the papal court and go out to preach. After the vision, Saint Vincent regained his health and went forth from Avignon.

The saint then travelled through Spain, France, Italy, Germany, and Flanders, and possibly even England, Scotland, and Ireland. As he travelled, he preached to thousands of people, including followers of Islam, Judaism, and lapsed Catholics. A favorite topic of Saint Vincent was the Last Judgment. Because we never know when the day will come, we must always be prepared. Through his preaching and many miracles (especially healings), thousands of people were converted. Saint Vincent died at the age of seventy after a life of preaching and service.

Eternal rest, grant unto them, O Lord; and let perpetual light shine upon them. May their souls, and the souls of all the faithful departed, through the mercy of God, rest in peace. Amen.

Preview

In the next lesson, the students will learn about the General Judgment.

Chapter Thirty-One: He Shall Come Again
Lesson Two: General Judgment

Aims

The students will learn that, at the Second Coming, Jesus will come again in great splendor. He will come to judge the living and the dead at the General Judgment.

They will learn that purgatory will no longer exist at the Second Coming. The resurrection of the body will occur, so that all may share in the eternal reward of the soul (either heaven or hell).

Materials

- *Activity Book*, p. 122

Optional:
- "I heard the voice of Jesus say," *Adoremus Hymnal*, #579

Begin

Review the signs that Jesus is about to return. Discuss the reality of the Second Coming. Ask them to name a prayer that tells us of Jesus' return. (The Creed, the prayer after the Our Father at Mass, etc.)

Develop

1. Read paragraphs 2–4 from the student text.

2. At the Second Coming, the trumpets will sound, the dead will rise, and the whole human race will be assembled before Jesus for the General Judgment.

3. At the General Judgment, every man's deeds, even the most secret, will be made known. Everyone will see and appreciate the holiness of the just—whether they had hardly ever sinned or were great sinners that overcame their sins. Everyone will see and appreciate the justice of God in banishing the unrepentant from his sight into hell forever.

4. We might be embarrassed when we think about our sins being revealed before everyone, but at that time, we will not mind for it will give great glory to God in showing his mercy and grace to help us overcome our sins.

5. With the General Judgment comes the resurrection of the body (see the Creed). Every man is a body-soul unity, and the body of each person will be raised up and reunited with his soul.

6. The glorified resurrected body is our own and will be like Jesus':
- Lucid: It is beautiful and perfect.
- Agile: It can move through space at the speed of thought.
- Immortal: It will not die again.
- Impassible: It is incapable of suffering.
- Spiritual: The will rules the body perfectly.

7. Every body will be resurrected and united with the soul—even those of the condemned. For the condemned, spiritual suffering will also become physical suffering for eternity.

8. There will no longer be a need for purgatory.

Reinforce

1. Have the students work on *Activity Book* p. 122 (see *Teacher's Manual*, p. 387).

2. The students may depict the General Judgment.

3. The students may write a poem about the resurrection of their own bodies.

4. You may give the students time to work on the Memorization Questions and Words to Know from this chapter.

Conclude

1. Lead the students in singing "I heard the voice of Jesus say," *Adoremus Hymnal*, #579.

2. End class by leading the students in praying Eternal rest, grant unto them O Lord (see *Teacher's Manual*, p. 379).

CHAPTER 31

He Shall Come Again

"And when I go and prepare a place for you, I will come again and will take you to myself, that where I am you may be also."

John 14:3

Saint Luke records in the Acts of the Apostles that at Jesus' Ascension into heaven, two angels stood by the disciples and said to them, "Men of Galilee, why do you stand looking into heaven? This Jesus, who was taken up from you into heaven, will come in the same way as you saw him go into heaven" (Acts 1:11).

One day, when we least expect it, Jesus will appear in the heavens in great splendor and majesty, and all the armies of heaven with him. At this **Second Coming**, the trumpets will sound, the dead will rise, and the whole human race will be assembled before the judgment seat of Christ; the books will be opened and the judgment will begin. Every man's deeds, even the most secret, will be made known. Everyone will see and appreciate the holiness of the just, whether they hardly ever sinned or were great sinners and overcame their sins. Everyone will see and appreciate the justice of God in banishing the unrepentant from his sight, into hell forever.

The just, who served God with body and soul, in good times and bad, in good health and sickness, in joy and in sorrow, in pleasure and pain, will now receive a wonderful, glorious reward. They have tried hard to do something beautiful for God; now God will do something beautiful for them. It is true that they already see God, and this is called the Beatific Vision because it is a vision, a knowledge, which "beatifies" us, or makes us *completely* happy. Nevertheless, the souls in heaven are not yet all that God made them to be. Man was not made to be a disembodied spirit; man is a creature composed of body and soul. The body and soul will be brought together again at the Second Coming. It is the whole man who will enjoy heaven or suffer in hell. There will no longer be any need for purgatory.

One of the reasons for the judgment at the end of the world, called the **General Judgment**, is to make clear to everyone the wisdom, knowledge, graciousness, mercy, patience, loving kindness, and justice of the Lord of history in his dealings with all men. All shall be satisfied that it was well done. Then the just, who so often suffered at the hands of the unjust, will be honored, and the unjust who refused to ask God's forgiveness will be covered with shame and disgrace.

Above all, Jesus Christ the Savior, who suffered such humiliations, will be fully vindicated, exalted, glorified, and honored. His splendor will be so great that he

will light up the whole City of God. In the City of God, the new Jerusalem, the heavenly city, the whole universe will be renewed and set free from anything unfitting or harmful. Then those who have loved God and lived in his light will be united with him in heaven. And the just will have tremendous powers of mind and body to enjoy it all.

This is the goal toward which we are all striving. Remember how Saint Paul compared the life of a Christian to an athlete's? Let us work toward our goal so that we can say with him:

I have fought the good fight, I have finished the race, I have kept the faith. From now on there is laid up for me the crown of righteousness, which the Lord, the righteous judge, will award to me on that Day, and not only to me but also to all who have loved his appearing (2 Tim 4:7–8).

Words to Know:
Second Coming   General Judgment

We proclaim your Death, O Lord, and profess your Resurrection until you come again.

> **Q. 114** *Will Jesus Christ visibly return to earth?*
> Yes, Jesus Christ will visibly return to this earth at the end of the world to judge the living and the dead, at the General Judgment (CCC 680–82).
>
> **Q. 115** *What awaits us at the end of the world?*
> The resurrection of the body and the General Judgment await us at the end of the world (CCC 1016, 1038).
>
> **Q. 116** *What does "resurrection of the body" mean?*
> The "resurrection of the body" means that our bodies will be transformed by the power of God and reunited with our souls, so that we will share in the eternal reward or punishment we have merited (CCC 997–99, 1005).

ASSUMPTION OF MARY

CCC 966: The Assumption of the Blessed Virgin is a singular participation in her Son's Resurrection and an anticipation of the resurrection of other Christians.

At the General Judgment, we will be given glorified bodies. It can be hard for us to understand what that means, but we have an example to look to in Mary. She was human like us, but she was immaculate. Therefore, we can see in her some of what we will one day have. When the course of her earthly life was finished, she went to heaven, body and soul. In the same way, we will one day live in heaven and our souls will be reunited with our bodies. Mary is our example, our intercessor, and a sign of our hope.

Preview

In the next lesson, the students will learn about the vindication of Christ.

Chapter Thirty-One: He Shall Come Again
Lesson Three: Vindication

Aims

The students will learn that, at the General Judgment, the justice of God will be known by all. The just will be rewarded; the unjust will be damned.

They will learn that Jesus Christ will be fully vindicated, exalted, glorified, and honored.

Materials

- *Activity Book*, p. 123

Optional:
- "I heard the voice of Jesus say," *Adoremus Hymnal*, #579

Begin

Review the events of the General Judgment and answer to the best of your ability any questions that the students may have.

Assure the students that this will be a great and wonderful day. It is not to be feared. It is a day when we will be in the glory of Christ.

Develop

1. Read paragraph 5 from the student text.

2. Saint John tells us of the glorious vindication of Christ on the Last Day: "Then I looked, and I heard around the throne and the living creatures and the elders the voice of many angels, numbering myriads of myriads and thousands of thousands, saying with a loud voice, "Worthy is the Lamb who was slain, to receive power and wealth and wisdom and might and honor and glory and blessing!" And I heard every creature in heaven and on earth and under the earth and in the sea, and all therein, saying, "To him who sits upon the throne and to the Lamb be blessing and honor and glory and might for ever and ever!" (Rev 5:11–13).

3. On the Last Day, Christ will be recognized as Lord and Savior. Why is this necessary? Don't all people recognize this already?

- No, the Jewish people did not recognize Jesus as the Messiah, and the Islamic people (Muslims) see Jesus as only a prophet. Many other religions do not accept Jesus as Lord and Savior. But, if we recall, salvation is offered to all people who live in union with God (so it is possible for people of other faiths to go to heaven—more difficult, but possible). Therefore there is a great need for all to know and worship Christ the Lord.

4. In the Church and in heaven, we recognize Christ as King. We also recognize Mary as our Queen—Queen of Heaven and Earth. Mary is the Mother of Jesus and our spiritual Mother. Help the students foster devotion to the Blessed Mother. Set up a classroom altar and have a May crowning.

5. Pray a litany of saints. Pray for the deceased members of the students' families.

Reinforce

1. Have the students work on *Activity Book* p. 123 (see *Teacher's Manual*, p. 387).

2. The students may work on the Memorization Questions and Words to Know from this chapter.

Conclude

1. Lead the students in singing "I heard the voice of Jesus say," *Adoremus Hymnal*, #579.

2. End class by leading the students in praying Eternal rest, grant unto them O Lord (see *Teacher's Manual*, p. 379).

CHAPTER 31

He Shall Come Again

"And when I go and prepare a place for you, I will come again and will take you to myself, that where I am you may be also."

John 14:3

Saint Luke records in the Acts of the Apostles that at Jesus' Ascension into heaven, two angels stood by the disciples and said to them, "Men of Galilee, why do you stand looking into heaven? This Jesus, who was taken up from you into heaven, will come in the same way as you saw him go into heaven" (Acts 1:11).

One day, when we least expect it, Jesus will appear in the heavens in great splendor and majesty, and all the armies of heaven with him. At this **Second Coming**, the trumpets will sound, the dead will rise, and the whole human race will be assembled before the judgment seat of Christ; the books will be opened and the judgment will begin. Every man's deeds, even the most secret, will be made known. Everyone will see and appreciate the holiness of the just, whether they hardly ever sinned or were great sinners and overcame their sins. Everyone will see and appreciate the justice of God in banishing the unrepentant from his sight, into hell forever.

The just, who served God with body and soul, in good times and bad, in good health and sickness, in joy and in sorrow, in pleasure and pain, will now receive a wonderful, glorious reward. They have tried hard to do something

beautiful for God; now God will do something beautiful for them. It is true that they already see God, and this is called the Beatific Vision because it is a vision, a knowledge, which "beatifies" us, or makes us *completely* happy. Nevertheless, the souls in heaven are not yet all that God made them to be. Man was not made to be a disembodied spirit; man is a creature composed of body and soul. The body and soul will be brought together again at the Second Coming. It is the whole man who will enjoy heaven or suffer in hell. There will no longer be any need for purgatory.

One of the reasons for the judgment at the end of the world, called the **General Judgment**, is to make clear to everyone the wisdom, knowledge, graciousness, mercy, patience, loving kindness, and justice of the Lord of history in his dealings with all men. All shall be satisfied that it was well done. Then the just, who so often suffered at the hands of the unjust, will be honored, and the unjust who refused to ask God's forgiveness will be covered with shame and disgrace.

Above all, Jesus Christ the Savior, who suffered such humiliations, will be fully vindicated, exalted, glorified, and honored. His splendor will be so great that he

130

will light up the whole City of God. In the City of God, the new Jerusalem, the heavenly city, the whole universe will be renewed and set free from anything unfitting or harmful. Then those who have loved God and lived in his light will be united with him in heaven. And the just will have tremendous powers of mind and body to enjoy it all.

This is the goal toward which we are all striving. Remember how Saint Paul compared the life of a Christian to an athlete's? Let us work toward our goal so that we can say with him:

I have fought the good fight, I have finished the race, I have kept the faith. From now on there is laid up for me the crown of righteousness, which the Lord, the righteous judge, will award to me on that Day, and not only to me but also to all who have loved his appearing (2 Tim 4:7–8).

Words to Know:
Second Coming   General Judgment

We proclaim your Death, O Lord, and profess your Resurrection until you come again.

131

Q. 114 *Will Jesus Christ visibly return to earth?*
Yes, Jesus Christ will visibly return to this earth at the end of the world to judge the living and the dead, at the General Judgment (CCC 680–82).

Q. 115 *What awaits us at the end of the world?*
The resurrection of the body and the General Judgment await us at the end of the world (CCC 1016, 1038).

Q. 116 *What does "resurrection of the body" mean?*
The "resurrection of the body" means that our bodies will be transformed by the power of God and reunited with our souls, so that we will share in the eternal reward or punishment we have merited (CCC 997–99, 1005).

132

ALL SAINTS' DAY AND ALL SOULS' DAY

On November 1, we celebrate All Saints' Day. This is a Holy Day of Obligation. The purpose of this day is to commemorate all saints, known and unknown. Although the Church has canonized thousands of people, she knows that there are others she has not officially recognized. On All Saints' Day, we commemorate both.

All Souls' Day is celebrated on November 2. On this day, we remember our faithful departed and pray for the souls in purgatory. At Mass on All Souls' Day, the priest may wear black vestments to commemorate all the souls who have died in Christ but still need to be purified in purgatory.

Preview

In the next lesson, the students will learn about the spiritual life.

CHAPTER THIRTY-ONE: HE SHALL COME AGAIN
LESSON FOUR: CHRISTIAN LIFE

Aims

The students will learn that we should all strive to live our lives in anticipation of the truths of the Second Coming.

They will learn that Saint Paul compares the spiritual life to a race.

Materials

- *Activity Book*, p. 124

Optional:
- "I heard the voice of Jesus say," *Adoremus Hymnal*, #579

Begin

Arrange for outdoor games, such as races and challenges, which can be used as examples of the spiritual life.

If the weather is not cooperating, play indoor hand-eye coordination games.

Develop

1. Finish reading the chapter with the students (paragraph 6).

2. The spiritual life is the journey of faith that we make on earth, and which prepares us for heaven. We enter the spiritual life at Baptism. In the last chapter we learned that Saint John of the Cross wrote about the spiritual life in the *Ascent of Mount Carmel*. There are many good books on the spiritual life.

3. Review that the spiritual life generally develops through three stages:

- *Purgative way*: The primary stage in mental prayer, according to the teaching of Saints Teresa of Avila and John of the Cross. The soul's chief concern in this stage of perfection is an awareness of its sins, sorrow for the past, and a desire to expiate the offenses against God.

- *Illuminative way*: The intermediary stage between purification and union on the path to Christian perfection. Also

called the "Way of the Proficients," the main feature of the Illuminative Way is an enlightenment of the mind in the ways of God and a clear understanding of his will in one's state of life.

- *Unitive way*: The third and final stage of Christian perfection, beyond the purgative and illuminative. Its principle feature is a more or less constant awareness of God's presence, and a habitual disposition of conformity to the will of God. Although commonly regarded as the last stage in the spiritual life, it is recognized that the three traditional levels of progress in holiness are not chronological. They may be present, in greater or lesser degrees, at any point in a person's growth in sanctity.

From the *Pocket Catholic Dictionary* by John A. Hardon, S.J.

4. Saint Paul compares the Christian Life to a race. An athlete needs practice, diet, and talent in order to be a winner!

Reinforce

1. Have the students work on *Activity Book* p. 124 (see *Teacher's Manual*, p. 387).

2. Parallel the life of an athlete with the spiritual life (What does he eat? What do we feed our souls? How does he exercise? How do we exercise spiritually? How does he prepare for a race? How can we?) Organize the students in a relay race.

3. The students may work on the Memorization Questions and Words to Know from this chapter and prepare for the quiz.

Conclude

1. Lead the students in singing "I heard the voice of Jesus say," *Adoremus Hymnal*, #579.

2. End class by leading the students in praying Eternal rest, grant unto them O Lord (see *Teacher's Manual*, p. 379).

CHAPTER 31

He Shall Come Again

"And when I go and prepare a place for you, I will come again and will take you to myself, that where I am you may be also."

John 14:3

Saint Luke records in the Acts of the Apostles that at Jesus' Ascension into heaven, two angels stood by the disciples and said to them, "Men of Galilee, why do you stand looking into heaven? This Jesus, who was taken up from you into heaven, will come in the same way as you saw him go into heaven" (Acts 1:11).

One day, when we least expect it, Jesus will appear in the heavens in great splendor and majesty, and all the armies of heaven with him. At this **Second Coming**, the trumpets will sound, the dead will rise, and the whole human race will be assembled before the judgment seat of Christ; the books will be opened and the judgment will begin. Every man's deeds, even the most secret, will be made known. Everyone will see and appreciate the holiness of the just, whether they hardly ever sinned or were great sinners and overcame their sins. Everyone will see and appreciate the justice of God in banishing the unrepentant from his sight, into hell forever.

The just, who served God with body and soul, in good times and bad, in good health and sickness, in joy and in sorrow, in pleasure and pain, will now receive a wonderful, glorious reward. They have tried hard to do something beautiful for God; now God will do something beautiful for them. It is true that they already see God, and this is called the Beatific Vision because it is a vision, a knowledge, which "beatifies" us, or makes us *completely* happy. Nevertheless, the souls in heaven are not yet all that God made them to be. Man was not made to be a disembodied spirit; man is a creature composed of body and soul. The body and soul will be brought together again at the Second Coming. It is the whole man who will enjoy heaven or suffer in hell. There will no longer be any need for purgatory.

One of the reasons for the judgment at the end of the world, called the **General Judgment**, is to make clear to everyone the wisdom, knowledge, graciousness, mercy, patience, loving kindness, and justice of the Lord of history in his dealings with all men. All shall be satisfied that it was well done. Then the just, who so often suffered at the hands of the unjust, will be honored, and the unjust who refused to ask God's forgiveness will be covered with shame and disgrace.

Above all, Jesus Christ the Savior, who suffered such humiliations, will be fully vindicated, exalted, glorified, and honored. His splendor will be so great that he

130

will light up the whole City of God. In the City of God, the new Jerusalem, the heavenly city, the whole universe will be renewed and set free from anything unfitting or harmful. Then those who have loved God and lived in his light will be united with him in heaven. And the just will have tremendous powers of mind and body to enjoy it all.

This is the goal toward which we are all striving. Remember how Saint Paul compared the life of a Christian to an athlete's? Let us work toward our goal so that we can say with him:

I have fought the good fight, I have finished the race, I have kept the faith. From now on there is laid up for me the crown of righteousness, which the Lord, the righteous judge, will award to me on that Day, and not only to me but also to all who have loved his appearing (2 Tim 4:7–8).

Words to Know:
Second Coming   General Judgment

*We proclaim your Death, O Lord,
and profess your Resurrection
until you come again.*

131

Q. 114 *Will Jesus Christ visibly return to earth?*
Yes, Jesus Christ will visibly return to this earth at the end of the world to judge the living and the dead, at the General Judgment (CCC 680–82).

Q. 115 *What awaits us at the end of the world?*
The resurrection of the body and the General Judgment await us at the end of the world (CCC 1016, 1038).

Q. 116 *What does "resurrection of the body" mean?*
The "resurrection of the body" means that our bodies will be transformed by the power of God and reunited with our souls, so that we will share in the eternal reward or punishment we have merited (CCC 997–99, 1005).

132

SPIRITUAL CLASSICS

Many of the saints have left us great spiritual writings to help guide us in the spiritual life. The following is just a small list of many that could be chosen.

- Saint Augustine of Hippo   *Confessions*

- Saint Ignatius of Loyola   *Spiritual Exercises*

- Saint Teresa of Avila   *Interior Castle*
  Way of Perfection

- Saint John of the Cross   *Dark Night of the Soul*
  Ascent of Mount Carmel

- Saint Louis de Montfort   *True Devotion to Mary*

- Saint Francis de Sales   *Introduction to the Devout Life*

- Saint Thérèse of Lisieux   *Story of a Soul*

Preview

In the next lesson, the students' understanding of the material covered in this chapter will be reviewed and assessed.

CHAPTER THIRTY-ONE: HE SHALL COME AGAIN
REVIEW AND ASSESSMENT

Aims

The students' understanding of the material covered in this chapter will be reviewed and assessed.

Materials

- Quiz 31, Appendix, p. A-45

Optional:
- "I heard the voice of Jesus say," *Adoremus Hymnal*, #579

Name: _____

He Shall Come Again   **Quiz 31**

Part I: Yes or No.

1. <u>Yes</u> Will Jesus come in splendor at the Second Coming?
2. <u>Yes</u> Will the whole human race be present at the Second Coming?
3. <u>Yes</u> Will the dead rise at the Second Coming?
4. <u>Yes</u> Will all of our deeds, even our most secret deeds, be made known at the General Judgment?
5. <u>Yes</u> Will the beatific vision make us completely happy?
6. <u>No</u> Will only our souls exist after the Second Coming?
7. <u>Yes</u> Will the General Judgment make clear to everyone the wisdom, knowledge, graciousness, mercy, patience, loving kindness, and justice of the Lord in his dealings with all men?
8. <u>No</u> Will anyone be upset with the way Jesus will judge us?

Part II: Saint Paul compared living the spiritual life to running a race. Write a paragraph explaining what the saint and the athlete have in common. Think about the following things: the need for self-discipline, the need for perseverance, the need to keep one's eyes on the prize.

_____
_____
_____
_____
_____
_____
_____
_____
_____
_____
_____
_____
_____
_____
_____
_____
_____
_____

Faith and Life Series • Grade 6 • Appendix A   *A-45*

Review and Enrichment

1. The students should know that Christ will come again in glory.

2. The students should be familiar with the events of the General Judgment.

3. The students should know about the resurrection of the body and the qualities of the resurrected body.

4. The students should know that Christ will be vindicated. They should know that Christ is the King (and Mary is the Queen) of Heaven.

5. The students should have a basic understanding of the spiritual life and its development.

Assess

1. Distribute the quizzes and read through them with the students to be sure they understand the questions.

2. Administer the quiz. As they hand in their work, you may orally quiz the students on the Memorization Questions from this chapter.

3. After all the quizzes have been handed in, you may wish to review the correct answers with the class.

Conclude

1. Lead the students in singing "I heard the voice of Jesus say," *Adoremus Hymnal*, #579.

2. End class by leading the students in praying Eternal rest, grant unto them O Lord (see *Teacher's Manual*, p. 379).

CHAPTER THIRTY-ONE: HE SHALL COME AGAIN
ACTIVITY BOOK ANSWER KEYS

Name:_____

He Shall Come Again

Write a brief essay on what will happen when Jesus comes again.

Answers will vary but should be based on p. 130 of the Student Text.

General Judgment I

Write a paragraph explaining the General Judgment.

Answers will vary but should be based on p. 130 and 131 of the Student Text.

General Judgment II

Answer the following questions in complete sentences.

1. Will all people come to know and recognize Jesus Christ as the Savior?
   Yes.

2. Will Jesus be vindicated and exalted?
   Yes.

3. Who will share in the glory of God?
   The just will share in the glory of God.

4. What will the just experience?
   The just will experience the beatific vision.

5. How will we be like the angels?
   We will be like the angels because we will have great powers of mind and body to enjoy all that God has done.

General Judgment III

Read Chapter 31 from your student text. What did Saint Paul have to say about our goal? Explain Saint Paul's analogy or write your own.

Saint Paul says: "I have fought the good fight, I have finished the race, I have kept the faith. Henceforth there is laid up for me the crown of righteousness, which the Lord, the righteous judge, will award to me on that Day, and not only to me but also to all who have loved his appearing."

Answers will vary regarding the explanation.

TEACHER'S NOTES

CHRISTMAS SEASON SUPPLEMENT
ANGELS WE HAVE HEARD ON HIGH

Christmas and its celebration hold a place of particular importance in the minds and hearts of young people. It is essential, therefore, that they always be conscious of what is at the heart of this celebration. Either at the end of the school year, or at the appropriate time in the liturgical calendar, you may wish to review this supplemental material with your students.

Take the time to have the students read through pp. 135–137 in the student textbook. Ask them to reflect on how these seasons are important during our Christian pilgrimage. Have the students work on *Activity Book* p. 125 (see the facing page).

TEACHER'S NOTES

Angels We Have Heard on High

> "Glory to God in the highest, and on earth peace among men with whom he is pleased!"
>
> Luke 2:14

Legend has it that Saint Francis of Assisi put together the first manger scene for Christmas with figures to inspire devotion—and that was about eight hundred years ago. The story of the birth of the Son of God has an endless appeal. For, considering who Jesus is, he chose for himself the humblest possible birth. He had every right to be born in a palace; he was born in a stable. He had every right to many servants; at most he had an ox and a donkey.

The Son of God did not come into the world with power and glory. He did not come to establish an earthly kingdom. He came to redeem the human race from sin. His birth was the first step toward that end.

The Gospel tells us that the birth of Jesus came in "the fullness of time," that is, at the time God had chosen and prepared. He chose a virgin, Mary of Nazareth, to be the Mother of his Son, and let her remain a virgin before and after his birth. Isaiah the prophet had written: "Therefore the Lord himself will give you a sign. Behold, a virgin shall conceive and bear a son, and shall call his name Immanuel" (Is 7:14).

God chose Mary from among all Jewish women to be the Mother of his Son. He also protected her from Original Sin, which has been passed on to every other descendant of Adam, except Jesus himself. Mary possessed God's grace from the first moment of her existence. It would not have been fitting for God

the Son to receive his humanity from a sinful woman. Mary's conception without Original Sin is called the Immaculate Conception. "Immaculate" means "pure" or "spotless."

Mary's soul, then, was pure and spotless. She was "full of grace" because God had saved her from Original Sin and all actual sin. She never sinned—not once, not even in the smallest way. She loved God so much. Mary was first in importance, after Jesus, among all the people who played a major role in God's plan of redemption. But she was not an earthly princess. She lived with her parents in a small town of Nazareth. She was betrothed to a man named Joseph, a carpenter.

135

Mary was still a young girl, betrothed to Saint Joseph, when God sent an angel to her on a very special mission. She must have been startled. The archangel Gabriel told her not to be afraid. He told her that she had found favor with God and had been chosen to be the Mother of the Savior. He told her that she would conceive the Child by the power of the Holy Spirit; thus, she would always remain a virgin. Furthermore, the Child would be called "Son of God."

Mary's answer was: "Behold, I am the handmaid of the Lord; let it be to me according to your word" (Lk 1:38).

Then the angel left her, and God worked the miracle in which his only Son was conceived in her womb without an earthly father. When it became clear that Mary was going to bear a child, the same angel, Gabriel, told Joseph, Mary's betrothed, that Mary was with child by the Holy Spirit. This Child, he told Joseph, was to be named Jesus, because he would save his people from their sins. The angel told Joseph not to be concerned.

Joseph was relieved to hear the angel's message. He had been anxious about his life with Mary. He had not understood about Mary

conceiving a child without a human father, and he had wondered about God's plan for him as Mary's husband. Now Joseph and Mary together prepared for the Child's birth.

Not long before the Child was due, the Roman emperor decreed that there should be a census of the whole empire. Joseph had to take Mary with him to Bethlehem, the town of his ancestors, to register there for the census.

This involved a trip of about ninety miles, which must have been uncomfortable for Mary in her condition. Then, after the dusty, crowded roads, they found the houses and hotels in Bethlehem already filled. After asking everywhere, Joseph led his beloved wife to a stable, a cave in a hillside where she would be out of the cold night air and have privacy; and there, in that stable, the Son of God was born. There he gave his first cry and was laid down to sleep on some straw in a manger. He was wrapped in strips of cloth called swaddling clothes.

In the fields on some nearby hills, unusual things were happening. Angels came to some shepherds and told them to go to the stable to see the newborn Savior of the world. When the angels disappeared, the shepherds did what they had been told and found the Child. They were the first to see him. These shepherds weren't very powerful or important people, but they had what is always needed to find Jesus: humility. When they saw him, Luke tells us, they "understood" what they had been told about the Child.

Who Is Jesus?

When Jesus cried, or felt chilled, or became hungry, it was God crying, or feeling chilled, or becoming hungry. He is the Son of God made man—that is, true God and true man. Before becoming man, he had eternal, infinite life with God the Father and God the Holy Spirit in the Blessed Trinity. This life was never interrupted; even after becoming man he remains God.

136

Jesus is one Person, God the Son, with two natures, divine and human. As God, he can do everything God can do (know everything, create out of nothing, raise the dead, be everywhere, live eternally, love without limit), and as man he can do everything man can do—which is surely much less than what God can do.

The act by which the Son of God became man is called the Incarnation—which means, literally, taking on flesh. This happened when he was conceived in the womb of the Blessed Virgin Mary, and it was revealed for all the world to see when he was born.

That's how much God loved us—enough to become one of us.

Q. 117 How did God prepare Mary to be the Mother of his Son?

God prepared Mary to be the Mother of his Son by preserving her from Original Sin, which means that she was filled with grace from the moment of her conception. This is called the Immaculate Conception (CCC 491).

Q. 118 What is the mystery of God made man called?

The mystery of God made man is called the Incarnation (CCC 470).

Q. 119 Did the Son of God cease to be God when he became man?

No, the Son of God did not cease to be God when he became man. God is eternal (CCC 470).

Q. 120 Is Jesus true God and true man?

Yes, Jesus is true God and true man. He has two natures: human and divine (CCC 464).

Q. 121 Is Jesus two persons?

No, Jesus is one Divine Person, the Second Person of the Blessed Trinity (CCC 466).

137

Angels We Have Heard on High

Read the prayer below. Then explain how it shows Mary's role in salvation history.

THE ANGELUS

V. The angel of the Lord declared unto Mary,
R. And she conceived of the Holy Spirit.
   Hail Mary. . . .
V. Behold the handmaid of the Lord,
R. Be it done unto me according to thy word.
   Hail Mary. . . .
V. And the Word was made flesh,
R. And dwelt among us.
   Hail Mary. . . .
V. Pray for us, O holy Mother of God,
R. That we may be made worthy of the promises of Christ.

Let us pray. Pour forth, we beseech thee, O Lord, thy grace into our hearts, that we to whom the Incarnation of Christ thy Son was made known by the message of an angel, may by his Passion and Cross be brought to the glory of his Resurrection. Through the same Christ our Lord. *Amen.*

Answers will vary.

Faith and Life Series • Grade 6 • Supplement 1

125

CHRISTMAS SEASON SUPPLEMENT
FRUIT UPON THE BOUGH: THE MISSION

The Advent and Christmas seasons are our introduction to the life of Christ. Take time to have the students read pp. 138–140 in the student textbook. Ask them to think about and discuss the redemptive mission of Jesus and how this was gradually revealed. Have the students work on *Activity Book* p. 126 (see the facing page).

TEACHER'S NOTES

Fruit Upon the Bough: The Mission

"... for my eyes have seen your salvation which you have prepared in the presence of all peoples, a light for revelation to the Gentiles, and for glory to your people Israel."

Luke 2:30–32

In his great mercy God gave to us his own Son to restore us to his friendship. Christ came into the world as an infant, bore witness to the will of the Father, taught us the complete truth about God, and was himself the perfect model of all we should be.

We call this Christ's mission. Even in Jesus' infancy, God began to reveal this mission to the world. We have seen how the shepherds were invited to come and see the

newborn Savior. Not long afterward, other things happened that showed that God was letting people know about Jesus' mission.

When Jesus was eight days old, Saint Luke tells us he was circumcised in accordance with Jewish law; when he was forty days old, he was presented to the Lord in the temple in Jerusalem. His parents offered in sacrifice two young pigeons, as the law directed.

Then a most unusual thing happened. A very devout old man named Simeon was led by the Holy Spirit to the Child in the temple and took him into his arms. Through the Holy Spirit he recognized the Messiah. With great joy Simeon blessed God, saying that now he could die in peace because he had seen the Savior both of the Jews and Gentiles. Mary and Joseph marveled at what was being said.

Then the shadow of the Cross fell across the group—the Cross which was still far in the future. Simeon turned to Mary and said: "Behold, this child is set for the fall and rising of many in Israel, and for a sign that is spoken against (and a sword will pierce through your own soul also), that thoughts out of many hearts may be revealed" (Lk 2:34–35).

Simeon saw a full picture: power, glory, and suffering. The Child was a sign that

---

would be opposed—and Mary, His mother and the Mother of the Church, would have a unique share in his sufferings. God was filling in the picture of his plan of redemption.

Shortly afterward, three kings or wise men from the East came to see the Child and give him gifts. God had told them to follow a bright star to find the newborn King of the Jews. Their visit was added testimony to the greatness of the newborn Savior; it was also testimony to the all-out fury which would oppose him.

King Herod, a vicious man insanely jealous of his power, heard from the wise men that a new King had been born, and all his darkest passions were aroused. Intending to kill the Child, he instructed the wise men to report back to him after they had found the Child. But the wise men were warned against Herod in a dream, and they went home by another route after their visit.

When Herod learned of this, his rage and suspicion knew no bounds. He sent his soldiers to Bethlehem and the surrounding area with orders to kill all the boys there who were two years old and younger, being certain that the newborn King would perish in the holocaust.

However, the Holy Family escaped the clutches of this bloodthirsty tyrant. Joseph had been warned in a dream of the coming danger. An angel commanded him to take mother and child and seek safety in Egypt and to stay there until he was told it was safe to come home.

Joseph obeyed immediately—that very night—and so they escaped. The children who died were Christ's first martyrs. We call them the Holy Innocents.

Not everybody is called to give his life for Christ—though many have. But it is sometimes as difficult to live for Christ as it is to die for him. It may even be harder. Take the case of a person with a serious illness who nevertheless has to bear heavy responsibilities. Think of Pope John Paul II, who had to

resume the burdensome task of the papacy after being so badly wounded. That must be harder than dying.

Another Stage

When Jesus was twelve years old, Luke tells us, he went to Jerusalem with his parents for the feast of the Passover. Unknown to them, he stayed behind when they set out on their return. At the end of the day they discovered he wasn't with them and returned immediately to Jerusalem to look for him. The third day they found him in the temple, deeply involved in conversation with the teachers of the law, listening to them and asking them questions. Everyone who heard him was amazed at his wisdom.

Mary asked him why he had done this. He answered, "Didn't you know that I must be about my Father's business?" His parents did not understand. Afterwards he returned with them to Nazareth and lived in obedience, and Mary thought over all these things while he "increased in wisdom and in stature, and in favor with God and man" (Lk 2:52).

The unfolding of Christ's mission was often mysterious, even to his parents. In the temple he had said, in effect, that he had reached adulthood, like turning eighteen or twenty-one in our society. According to Jewish law he was a man; and now that Jesus was an adult, the Father wanted his Son's witness in the temple. He wanted his Son's wisdom to be known. But only this hint was given when

Jesus was young; we hear no more until he is thirty years old and begins his public life. "Let your light shine before men," he was to say; and when he was twelve years old, he had begun to do so.

Until he entered upon his public life, Jesus lived quietly in poverty and humility, obedient in all things to the authority of his parents. His whole life is a mystery of redemption.

> **Q. 122** *In what ways is Jesus' whole life a mystery of redemption?*
> Jesus' whole life is a mystery of redemption by God's act of becoming man in the Incarnation which brought us a share in his life, by Jesus' obedience which atoned for our disobedience, by Jesus' miracles and healings through which he bore our infirmities, and by his death and Resurrection which justifies man (CCC 517).

Name:_____

Fruit Upon the Bough: The Mission

Fill in the crossword puzzle with the words that tell about God's plan for our salvation.

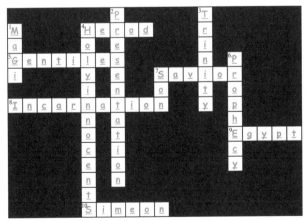

Across
4. The king who ruled the Jews at the time of Christ's birth.
5. A word for persons who are not Jews.
7. Another word for "Redeemer."
8. A word meaning "made flesh."
9. Where Joseph took the Holy Family for safety.
10. The holy Jew who recognized the baby Jesus as the Messiah.

Down
1. The three wise men are also called the three _____.
2. The occasion on which Jesus was first taken to the temple.
3. God is a unity and a _____.
4. The children that were killed in Bethlehem.
6. Simeon's prediction about Jesus was a _____.
7. The Second Person of the Blessed Trinity is God the _____.

Liturgical Colors and Vestments

ALB: a full-length white tunic worn by the priest when offering Mass.

AMICE: an oblong piece of white cloth worn by the priest under the alb covering his shoulders.

CHALICE: the cup-shaped vessel used at Mass to contain the Precious Blood of Christ.

CHASUBLE: the outer garment worn by the priest celebrating Mass.

CIBORIUM: a vessel with a lid used to hold the consecrated Hosts which we receive in Holy Communion.

CINCTURE: a cord tied around the waist of the alb.

COPE: a large semi-circular cloak worn by the priest at Benediction and in processions.

CORPORAL: a square white linen cloth on which the paten and chalice are placed during Mass.

CRUETS: small bottles or vessels that contain the water and wine used during Mass.

DALMATIC: the outer garment worn by a deacon at Mass or other liturgical celebrations.

FINGER TOWEL: a cloth used by the priest to dry his hands during the Mass.

HUMERAL VEIL: a long, oblong piece of cloth worn like a shawl over the priest's shoulders during Benediction when the priest holds the monstrance.

LAVABO DISH or FINGER BOWL: a shallow dish for the water used when the priest washes his hands at Mass.

PALL: a stiff, square card covered with white linen used to cover the chalice at Mass.

PATEN: a plate of precious material on which the Body of Christ is placed during Mass.

PURIFICATOR: a small white linen towel used by the priest to purify the chalice and paten after Communion.

alb

amice

chalice

chasuble

ciborium

cincture

cope

corporal

141

STOLE: a long, narrow strip of cloth worn around the priest's neck during Mass; it is the same color as the chasuble.

VESTMENTS: special garments worn by the clergy at all liturgical celebrations. At Mass these include the amice, alb, cincture, stole, and chasuble. For Benediction the cope and humeral veil are used.

LITURGICAL COLORS

The different colors used throughout the liturgical year for vestments and decorations in the Church symbolize various truths and sentiments of the Faith.

WHITE: symbolizes purity, joy, innocence, holiness, and glory; it is used during the Christmas and Easter seasons, for feasts and commemorations of Christ (other than the Passion) and for feasts and memorials of Mary, the angels, and saints who were not martyrs, and it may be used for Masses of the dead.

RED: symbolizes fire and blood; used for celebrations of the Passion, Palm Sunday, Good Friday, for Pentecost, for feasts of the Apostles and evangelists, and for feasts of martyrs.

GREEN: symbolizes life and hope; used for days which are not feasts during Ordinary Time (the time after Epiphany up to Ash Wednesday and after Pentecost up to Advent).

VIOLET: symbolizes penitence and sorrow; used during the penitential seasons of Advent and Lent. It may also be used for Masses of the dead.

ROSE: is an indication of a more joyful celebration, and is used on Gaudete Sunday during Advent and Laetare Sunday during Lent.

BLACK: symbolizes mourning; it may be used in Masses for the dead and on All Souls' Day.

142

cruets

dalmatic

finger towel

humeral veil

pall

paten

purificator

stole

TEACHER'S NOTES

Words to Know

ABSTINENCE: a form of penance such as refraining from eating meat.

ADORATION: giving praise and honor.

ADVENT: the liturgical season starting four Sundays before Christmas, during which we prepare for the birth of Jesus.

APOSTASY: the rejection by a baptized person of the Christian Faith.

AVARICE: excessive desire for wealth; greed.

BEATITUDE: the promise of true happiness made by Jesus to those who follow him faithfully.

BENEDICTION: When the priest blesses the people with Jesus in the Blessed Sacrament.

BLASPHEMY: the sin of speaking about or to God in a scornful or irreverent way.

CHASTITY: the virtue of ordering sexual pleasures according to the Sixth and Ninth Commandments.

CHURCH MILITANT: the members of the Church on earth.

CHURCH SUFFERING: the souls in purgatory.

CHURCH TRIUMPHANT: the saints in heaven.

CONSCIENCE: our ability to know and judge what is right or wrong.

COVENANT: a solemn agreement.

CULPABLE IGNORANCE: not knowing something that one ought to know.

CURSING: the sin of expressing hope that evil or harm will happen to someone or something.

DECALOGUE: the Ten Commandments given to Moses by God.

DETRACTION: the sin of telling something without sufficient reason about another person that is true but harmful to that person's reputation.

DIOCESE: the part of the Church over which a bishop has authority.

DIVINE OFFICE: the prayer of the Church using Psalms, hymns, and readings. It is called the Liturgy of the Hours because parts of it may be prayed at different times of the day.

DOXOLOGY: A prayer of adoration and praise, said especially in honor of the Blessed Trinity. The prayer said by the priest after the Consecration: "Through him, with him, in him. . ." is an example of a doxology.

ENVY: the sin of being resentful or saddened by another's success.

EUCHARIST: the real Body and Blood of Jesus under the appearances of bread and wine.

EUCHARISTIC FAST: abstinence from food and drink one hour before receiving Holy Communion. Water and medicine do not break the Eucharistic fast. The aged, the sick, and those who care for them may receive the Eucharist even if they have taken something during the previous hour.

EXPOSITION: the ceremony in which the Sacred Host is placed in a monstrance on or above the altar for adoration.

FALSE WITNESS: the giving of untrue testimony about another; lying about someone.

FASTING: doing penance by eating less food than usual.

143

FLATTERY: false praise.

FRAUD: the sin of deceiving another in order to deprive him of something he rightfully owns.

GENERAL JUDGMENT: the universal judgment of the entire human race at the end of the world.

GOSSIP: the sin of idle or malicious talk about others.

HERESY: the willful denial of a truth of Faith.

HEROIC VIRTUE: the performance of extraordinarily virtuous actions.

HOLY DAYS OF OBLIGATION: certain days, besides Sundays, when Catholics are required to take part in Holy Mass.

HONOR: to respect and reverence someone or something.

HOSANNA: a Hebrew word meaning "save us." It is a special exclamation of joy at the salvation God has promised us.

IDOLATRY: the sin of worshipping something other than God.

IMMACULATE CONCEPTION: Mary's conception free of the stain of Original Sin. Through the grace of God, Mary was free from Original Sin from the moment of her conception.

IMPIETY: the sin of lacking reverence or proper respect for God.

IMPURITY: sexual pleasure in thought or action that is against the Sixth or Ninth Commandments.

INTERCESSOR: someone who pleads or prays for another.

LAST SUPPER: the last meal Jesus had with his Apostles, at which he gave us the Eucharist, the Mass, and the priesthood.

LENT: the liturgical season of penance in preparation for Easter.

LITURGY: the public ceremonies of the Church used for worship.

LITURGY OF THE HOURS: see Divine Office.

MAKE SATISFACTION FOR: making up for some wrong-doing.

MEMORIAL: the recalling or remembrance of a past event.

MONSTRANCE: a special vessel used to hold and display the Sacred Host for adoration.

MURDER: the sin of killing someone wrongfully.

MYSTERY: a divinely revealed truth which we can never fully understand.

OATH: a declaration calling on God as a witness to the truth of what is being said.

OBLATION: the offering of something in an act of worship.

PARTICULAR JUDGMENT: the individual judgment by Christ of each human being at the moment after death.

PASSOVER: the Jewish feast commemorating the deliverance of the Israelites from Egypt.

PATRON SAINT: a special saint chosen to intercede for a particular person or group.

PENANCE: something done to make up for sin.

PRAYER: the raising of the mind and heart to God; talking with God.

PRECEPT: a particular rule or command.

RASH JUDGMENT: the sin of judging another's behavior as wrong without enough evidence.

REVERENCE: honor and respect.

SABBATH: the day of rest and worship; it is celebrated on Saturday by the Jews and on Sunday by Christians.

144

SACRAMENT: a sign given by Jesus that gives us grace.

SACRIFICE: the offering up of something to God.

SAINTS: holy people, particularly those whom the Church has declared to be in heaven.

SANCTITY: holiness.

SCANDAL: the sin of giving bad example which leads another into sin.

SECOND COMING: the return of Jesus at the end of the world as he promised at his Ascension.

SELF-DENIAL: the act of giving up something we desire for a higher motive.

SLANDER: the sin of saying something false about another which harms his good name.

STATE OF GRACE: being free of mortal sin and possessing God's grace.

STEALING: the sin of taking the property of another; this is a sin against the Seventh Commandment.

SUICIDE: the act of killing oneself; this is a sin against the Fifth Commandment. (However, if someone commits suicide without full knowledge and consent, his responsibility before God is lessened, even though the act is still wrong.)

SUPERSTITION: belief that creatures have supernatural powers.

TABERNACLE: a container in our churches in which the Blessed Sacrament is reserved.

TEN COMMANDMENTS: the laws given to us by God.

TRANSUBSTANTIATION: the complete change of substance of the bread and wine into the Body and Blood of Christ.

USURY: the sin of taking excessive interest for a loan of money.

VIATICUM: Holy Communion given to someone in danger of death.

VICAR OF CHRIST: the Pope, who takes the place of Jesus on earth.

VICTIM: the thing offered to God in a sacrifice.

VOLUNTARY DOUBT: the sin of willfully doubting some religious truth when there is enough reason to believe it.

VOW: a solemn promise made to God of something good and pleasing to him.

WORSHIP: giving honor, praise, and sacrifice to God.

145

TEACHER'S NOTES

Prayers

THE SIGN OF THE CROSS

In the name of the Father, and of the Son, and of the Holy Spirit. *Amen.*

OUR FATHER

Our Father who art in heaven, hallowed be thy name. Thy kingdom come. Thy will be done on earth, as it is in heaven. Give us this day our daily bread, and forgive us our trespasses, as we forgive those who trespass against us, and lead us not into temptation, but deliver us from evil. *Amen.*

HAIL MARY

Hail Mary, full of grace, the Lord is with thee. Blessed art thou among women, and blessed is the fruit of thy womb, Jesus.

Holy Mary, Mother of God, pray for us sinners now and at the hour of our death. *Amen.*

GLORY BE

Glory be to the Father, and to the Son, and to the Holy Spirit. As it was in the beginning, is now, and ever shall be, world without end. *Amen.*

MORNING OFFERING

O Jesus, through the Immaculate Heart of Mary, I offer thee my prayers, works, joys, and sufferings of this day in union with the Holy Sacrifice of the Mass throughout the world.

I offer them for all the intentions of thy Sacred Heart: the salvation of souls, reparation for sin, the reunion of all Christians.

I offer them for the intentions of our Bishops and of all Apostles of Prayer, and in particular for those recommended by our Holy Father this month. *Amen.*

THE APOSTLES' CREED

I believe in God,
  the Father almighty,
  Creator of heaven and earth,
  and in Jesus Christ,
  his only Son, our Lord,
  who was conceived by the Holy Spirit,
  born of the Virgin Mary,
  suffered under Pontius Pilate,
  was crucified, died, and was buried;
  he descended into hell;
  on the third day he rose again
  from the dead;
  he ascended into heaven,
  and is seated at the right
  hand of God the Father almighty;
  from there he will come to judge
  the living and the dead.
I believe in the Holy Spirit,
  the holy catholic Church,
  the communion of saints,
  the forgiveness of sins,
  the resurrection of the body,
  and life everlasting. *Amen.*

ACT OF FAITH

O my God, I firmly believe that thou art one God in three Divine Persons: Father, Son, and Holy Spirit. I believe that thy Divine Son became man and died for our sins, and that he will come to judge the living and the dead. I believe these and all the truths that the Holy Catholic Church teaches, because thou hast revealed them, who can neither deceive nor be deceived. *Amen.*

ACT OF HOPE

O my God, relying on thy infinite goodness and promises, I hope to obtain pardon of my sins, the help of thy grace, and life everlasting, through the merits of Jesus Christ, my Lord and Redeemer. *Amen.*

ACT OF LOVE

O my God, I love thee above all things, with my whole heart and soul, because thou art all good and worthy of all my love. I love my neighbor as myself for the love of thee. I forgive all who have injured me and ask pardon of all whom I have injured. *Amen.*

ACT OF CONTRITION

O my God, I am heartily sorry for having offended thee. I detest all my sins because of thy just punishments, but most of all because they offend thee, my God, who art all good and deserving of all my love. I firmly resolve, with the help of thy grace, to confess my sins, to do penance, and to amend my life. *Amen.*

THE ANGELUS

V. The angel of the Lord declared unto Mary.
R. And she conceived of the Holy Spirit.

Hail Mary. . . .

V. Behold the handmaid of the Lord.
R. Be it done to me according to thy word.

Hail Mary. . . .

V. And the Word was made flesh.
R. And dwelt among us.

Hail Mary. . . .

V. Pray for us, O holy Mother of God.
R. That we may be made worthy of the promises of Christ.

Let us pray. Pour forth, we beseech thee, O Lord, thy grace into our hearts, that we, to whom the Incarnation of Christ thy Son was made known by the message of an angel, may by his Passion and Cross be brought to the glory of his Resurrection. Through the same Christ our Lord. *Amen.*

MYSTERIES OF THE ROSARY

The Joyful Mysteries

1. The Annunciation.
2. The Visitation.
3. The Nativity.
4. The Presentation.
5. The Finding in the Temple.

The Sorrowful Mysteries

1. The Agony in the Garden.
2. The Scourging at the Pillar.
3. The Crowning with Thorns.
4. The Carrying of the Cross.
5. The Crucifixion.

The Glorious Mysteries

1. The Resurrection.
2. The Ascension.
3. The Descent of the Holy Spirit.
4. The Assumption.
5. The Coronation.

Optional: The Luminous Mysteries

1. The Baptism of Christ in the Jordan.
2. The Wedding Feast of Cana.
3. The Proclamation of the Kingdom of God.
4. The Transfiguration of Our Lord.
5. The Institution of the Holy Eucharist.

LITANY OF LORETO

Lord, have mercy on us.
  Christ, have mercy on us.
Lord, have mercy on us.
Christ, hear us.
  Christ, graciously hear us.
God the Father of heaven,
  have mercy on us.
God the Son, Redeemer of the world,
  have mercy on us.
God the Holy Spirit,
  have mercy on us.
Holy Trinity, One God,
  have mercy on us.

Holy Mary, *pray for us.**
Holy Mother of God,
Holy Virgin of virgins,
Mother of Christ,
Mother of divine grace,
Mother most pure,
Mother most chaste,
Mother inviolate,
Mother undefiled,
Mother most amiable,
Mother most admirable,
Mother of good counsel,
Mother of the Church,
Mother of our Creator,
Mother of our Savior,
Virgin most prudent,
Virgin most venerable,
Virgin most renowned,
Virgin most powerful,
Virgin most merciful,
Virgin most faithful,
Mirror of justice,
Seat of wisdom,
Cause of our joy,
Spiritual vessel,
Vessel of honor,
Singular vessel of devotion,

**Pray for us* is repeated after each invocation.*

Mystical rose,
Tower of David,
Tower of ivory,
House of gold,
Ark of the covenant,
Gate of heaven,
Morning star,
Health of the sick,
Refuge of sinners,
Comforter of the afflicted,
Help of Christians,
Queen of Angels,
Queen of Patriarchs,
Queen of Prophets,
Queen of Apostles,
Queen of Martyrs,
Queen of Confessors,
Queen of Virgins,
Queen of all Saints,
Queen conceived without Original Sin,
Queen assumed into heaven,
Queen of the most holy Rosary,
Queen of peace,

Lamb of God, who take away the sins of the world, *spare us, O Lord.*
Lamb of God, who take away the sins of the world, *graciously hear us, O Lord.*
Lamb of God, who take away the sins of the world, *have mercy on us.*

Pray for us, O holy Mother of God.
  That we may be made worthy of the promises of Christ.

Let us pray: Grant, we beseech Thee, O Lord God, unto us Thy servants, that we may rejoice in continual health of mind and body; and, by the glorious intercession of blessed Mary ever virgin, may be delivered from present sadness, and enter into the joy of Thine eternal gladness. Through Christ our Lord. *Amen.*

THE STATIONS OF THE CROSS

1. Jesus is condemned to death.
2. Jesus carries his Cross.
3. Jesus falls the first time.
4. Jesus meets his Mother.
5. Jesus is helped by Simon of Cyrene.
6. Veronica wipes the face of Jesus.
7. Jesus falls a second time.
8. Jesus speaks to the women.
9. Jesus falls a third time.
10. Jesus is stripped of his clothes.
11. Jesus is nailed to the Cross.
12. Jesus dies on the Cross.
13. Jesus is taken down from the Cross.
14. Jesus is placed in the tomb.

PRAYER FOR THE POPE

Father of Providence, look with love on *N.* our Pope, your appointed successor to Saint Peter on whom you built your Church. May he be the visible center and foundation of our unity in faith and love. Grant this through our Lord Jesus Christ, your Son, who lives and reigns with you and the Holy Spirit, one God, for ever and ever. *Amen.*

PRAYER FOR A BISHOP

Lord our God, you have chosen your servant *N.* to be a shepherd of your flock in the tradition of the Apostles. Give him a spirit of courage and right judgment, a spirit of knowledge and love. By governing with fidelity those entrusted to his care may he build your Church as a sign of salvation for the world. We ask this through our Lord Jesus Christ, your Son, who lives and reigns with you and the Holy Spirit, one God, for ever and ever. *Amen.*

PRAYER FOR VOCATIONS
by POPE JOHN PAUL II

O Jesus, our Good Shepherd, bless all our parishes with numerous priests, deacons, men and women in religious life, consecrated laity and missionaries, according to the needs of the entire world, which you love and wish to save.

We especially entrust our community to you; grant us the spirit of the first Christians, so that we may be a cenacle of prayer, in loving acceptance of the Holy Spirit and his gifts.

Assist our pastors and all who live a consecrated life. Guide the steps of those who have responded generously to your call and are preparing to receive holy orders or to profess the evangelical counsels.

Look with love on so many well-disposed young people and call them to follow you. Help them to understand that in you alone can they attain to complete fulfillment.

To this end we call on the powerful intercession of Mary, Mother and Model of all vocations. We beseech you to sustain our faith with the certainty that the Father will grant what you have commanded us to ask. *Amen.*

PRAYER FOR UNITY OF THE CHURCH

Almighty and merciful God, you willed that the different nations should become one people through your Son. Grant in your kindness that those who glory in being known as Christians may put aside their differences and become one in truth and charity, and that all men, enlightened by the true faith, may be united in fraternal communion in the one Church. Through Christ our Lord. *Amen.*

ANIMA CHRISTI

Soul of Christ, sanctify me.
Body of Christ, save me.
Blood of Christ, inebriate me.
Water from the side of Christ, wash me.
Passion of Christ, strengthen me.
O good Jesus, hear me;
Within thy wounds hide me;
Suffer me not to be separated from thee;
From the malignant enemy defend me;
In the hour of my death call me,
And bid me come to Thee,
That with Thy Saints I may praise Thee
for ever and ever. *Amen.*

MEMORARE

Remember, O most gracious Virgin Mary, that never was it known that anyone who fled to thy protection, implored thy help, or sought thy intercession, was left unaided. Inspired with this confidence, I fly unto thee, O Virgin of Virgins, my Mother: to thee do I come, before thee I stand, sinful and sorrowful. O Mother of the Word Incarnate, despise not my petitions, but in thy mercy hear and answer me. *Amen.*

PRAYER TO SAINT MICHAEL

Saint Michael, the Archangel, defend us in battle. Be our protection against the wickedness and snares of the devil. May God rebuke him, we humbly pray, and do thou, O prince of the heavenly hosts, by the power of God, thrust into hell Satan and the other evil spirits who prowl about the world seeking the ruin of souls. *Amen.*

EXAMINATION OF CONSCIENCE

How have I acted toward God? Do I think of God and speak to Him by praying to Him each day?
Do I speak of God with reverence?
Do I go to Mass on Sunday?
Do I do all I can to make Sunday a day of rest and joy for my family?
Do I participate in Mass, or do I tease or distract others by laughing, talking, or playing?
Do I pay attention to my parents, priests, and teachers when they talk to me about God?
How have I acted toward others?
Do I obey my parents and teachers quickly and cheerfully, or must I be reminded many times?
Do I tell my parents or those in authority over me that I am sorry and ask them to forgive me when I have not minded them?
Do I obey the rules of my home and school?
Do I help my brothers, sisters, and classmates when they need my help?
Am I kind to everyone?
Did I hit, kick, or in any way hurt others on purpose?
Am I willing to play with everyone?
Did I make fun or say mean things to anyone?
Do I do all my classwork and my chores at home well?
Do I take care of my health by eating the right food, etc.?
Do I think or do bad things or say bad words?
Do I tell the truth?
Do I say things about other people that are not true?
Did I cheat in class or in a game?
Did I steal or keep things that are not mine?
Am I willing to share my things with others?
Do I return things that I have borrowed?

THE PRAYER OF FATIMA

O my Jesus, forgive us our sins, save us from the fires of hell, and lead all souls into heaven, especially those in most need of thy mercy. *Amen.*

SPIRITUAL COMMUNION

My Jesus, as I cannot receive thee now in the Most Holy Blessed Sacrament, I ask thee to come into my heart, and make it like thy heart. *Amen.*

PRAYER TO MY GUARDIAN ANGEL

Angel of God, my guardian dear, To whom God's love commits me here, Ever this day be at my side, To light and guard, to rule and guide. *Amen.*

Art Credits

cover *Triptych with the Ascension of Christ, Last Judgment and Pentecost* (detail), Fra Angelico, Scala/Art Resource, NY
9 *Christ's Entry into Jerusalem,* Fra Angelico, Scala/Art Resource, NY
14 *The Presentation of the Tablets of the Law to the Hebrews,* Raphael, Scala/Art Resource, NY
18 *Sacrifice of Abel and Melchisedek* (detail), Ravenna (mosaic), Cameraphoto Arte, Venice/Art Resource, NY
22 *The Angelus,* Millet, Erich Lessing/Art Resource, NY
26 *The Coronation of the Virgin,* Fra Angelico, Erich Lessing/Art Resource, NY
27 *Saint Maximilian Kolbe,* Knights of the Immaculata
27 *Saint Charles Lwanga,* The White Fathers of Africa
27 *Saint John Bosco,* The Salesian Fathers
31 *Moses Fastening His Sandal on Mount Sinai,* Ravenna, Scala/Art Resource, NY
34 *Triptych of the Resurrection with Saint Sebastian* (detail), Memling, Erich Lessing/Art Resource, NY
44 *The Adoration of the Magi* (detail), Gentile da Fabriano, Erich Lessing/Art Resource, NY
49 *Sir Thomas Moore,* Holbein, copyright The Frick Collection, New York
50 *Delivering the Keys of the Kingdom to Saint Peter,* Perugino, Scala/Art Resource, NY
55 *Massacre of the Innocents,* Fra Angelico, Scala/Art Resource, NY
58 *Christ Cleansing the Temple* (detail), El Greco, Samual H. Kress Collection, image courtesy of the Board of Trustees, National Gallery of Art
62 *Marriage of the Virgin,* Fra Angelico, Scala/Art Resource, NY
65 *Homage of a Simple Man; St. Francis Giving His Mantle to a Poor Knight; Dream of the Palace* (detail), Giotto di Bondone, Scala/Art Resource, NY
67 *Saint Francis Preaching to the Birds,* Giotto di Bondone, Scala/Art Resource, NY
70 *Christ Interrogated by Pilate,* Duccio, Scala/Art Resource, NY
75 *Christ Healing the Blind Men of Jericho* (detail), Ravenna, Scala/Art Resource, NY
81 *Last Supper,* Rosselli, Scala/Art Resource, NY
84 *Christ Crucified between Two Thieves,* Rembrandt, Metropolitan Museum of Art, Gift of Felix M. Warburg and his family, 1941
86 *Supper at Emmaus,* Raphael, Scala/Art Resource, NY
91 *Farewell of the Apostles,* Duccio, Scala/Art Resource, NY
94 *Christ Risen from the Tomb,* Bergognone, Samuel H. Kress Collection, image courtesy of the Board of Trustees, National Gallery of Art
112 *Christ Washing the Feet of the Apostles,* Fra Angelico, Nicolo Orsi Battaglini/Art Resource, NY
116 *Communion of the Apostles,* Fra Angelico, Nicolo Orsi Battaglini/Art Resource, NY

124 *Resurrection of Lazarus,* Giotto di Bondone, Scala/Art Resource, NY
127 *The Last Judgment,* Fra Angelico, Erich Lessing/Art Resource, NY
131 *Disputa* (detail), Raphael, Scala/Art Resource, NY
135 *Annunciation,* Fra Angelico, Nicolo Orsi Battaglini/Art Resource, NY
136 *Adoration of the Magi,* Fra Angelico, Scala/Art Resoruce, NY
138 *Circumcision of Christ,* Fra Angelico, Nicolo Orsi Battaglini/Art Resource, NY
139 *Flight into Egypt,* Fra Angelico, Nicolo Orsi Battaglini/Art Resource, NY

PHOTOGRAPHS

36 "The Old Cathedral in Lincoln," photo courtesy of Kristen Harr
38 "Postcards from Italy (series)," istockphoto.com/Crazy D
47 "US Flag with International Flags XXL," istockphoto.com/Dan Cardiff
97 "Pope Benedict XVI Holds Final Mass for World Youth Day 08," Handout/Getty Images News/Getty Images
98 "Honduras Celebrates 500th Catholic Mass," Getty Images/Getty Images News/Getty Images
101 "A Roman Catholic Priest Fr. Rico Sabanal," Jay Directo/AFP/Getty Images
103 "Modern Wineries Have Ancient Roots In The Holy Land," David Silverman/Getty Images News/Getty Images
104 "Cardinal Francis Arinze Conducts a Mass in Washington," Alex Wong/Getty Images News/Getty Images
105 Photo courtesy of Gerald Augustinus
107 "Churches Celebrate the Beginning of Lent," Peter Macdiarmid/Getty Images News/Getty Images
108 "Pope Benedict XVI Celebrates Mass At Nationals Stadium," Win McNamee/Getty Images News/Getty Images
109 "Asian Girl Praying," istockphoto.com/Ximagination
118 "Florida Church Exhibits Monstrance Blessed by Pope John Paul II," Joe Raedle/Getty Images News/Getty Images
123 Photo courtesy of Kristen Harr

Faith and Life series: *Following Christ*
Appendices

God Gives Us the Law   **Quiz 1**

Part I: Fill in the blanks.

1. Every man has the law in his heart to do _____ and avoid _____ .

2. Our _____ is the ability to judge if an action is right or wrong.

3. God established a _____ with the Israelites and gave them his laws.

4. God's laws known as the Ten Commandments are also called the _____ .

5. Man has _____ _____ so that he can love and obey God.

6. Jesus taught us that _____ is the foundation of all law.

7. Jesus said that all of the commandments can be summed up in this: Love _____ above all things with our whole mind, heart and soul and love our _____ .

8. We _____ when we choose to break God's law.

Part II: Write the Ten Commandments in order.

1. _____

2. _____

3. _____

4. _____

5. _____

6. _____

7. _____

8. _____

9. _____

10. _____

The First Commandment in Our Own Day Quiz 2

Part I: Fill in the word that matches the definition.

apostasy	detachment	idolatry
impiety	superstition	heresy

1. _____ the belief that creatures have supernatural powers
2. _____ the lack of reverence or proper respect for God
3. _____ the willful denial of a truth of Faith
4. _____ the rejection of the Christian Faith by a baptized person
5. _____ the sin of worshipping something other than God
6. _____ the ability to let go of things when God asks it of us

Part II: Answer in complete sentences.

1. What can we learn from the story of the rich young man?

2. What are five things in today's world that can easily end up competing with our love for God and become idolatrous?

Part III: Yes or No.

1. _____ In the age before Christ did the sacrifice of the Hebrews please God?

2. _____ In the age before Christ could the sacrifice of the Hebrew people make up for sin?

3. _____ Can man alone make up for sin?

4. _____ Did God have to become man in order to make up for sin?

Prayer—Hidden Treasure   **Quiz 3**

Part I: Answer in complete sentences.

1. What is prayer?

2. What are the three forms of prayer?

3. What are three prayers that we pray as Catholics?

Part II: Write the Mysteries of the Rosary in the correct order.

Joyful Mysteries   Sorrowful Mysteries
1. _____   1. _____
2. _____   2. _____
3. _____   3. _____
4. _____   4. _____
5. _____   5. _____

Glorious Mysteries   Luminous Mysteries
1. _____   1. _____
2. _____   2. _____
3. _____   3. _____
4. _____   4. _____
5. _____   5. _____

Part III: Write a paragraph on one of the following topics.

1. How can we stay focused when we pray?
2. What is the Divine Office or Liturgy of the Hours and who must pray it?
3. What is the spiritual life?

_____

_____

_____

_____

_____

Name: _____

Saints—They Made the Most of It — Quiz 4

Part I: Define the following:

conversion   Church Triumphant   intercede   patron saint

1. _____

2. _____

3. _____

4. _____

Part II: Answer in complete sentences.

1. What role does Mary have in heaven?

2. What is the only way to be happy?

3. What is the only cure for the unhappy man?

Part III: Yes or No.

1. _____ Is each of us called to be a saint?

2. _____ Are the saints close friends of God?

3. _____ Can our hearts rest in anything besides God?

4. _____ Should we pray to our patron saint and to our guardian angel?

5. _____ Are the saints powerful intercessors?

6. _____ Is there any happiness more wonderful than heaven?

Part I: Fill in the blanks with the correct words from the Word Bank.

Word Bank:

good	evil	Decalogue
law	free will	judge
image	conscience	Ten Commandments

God created man in his _____ . It is written upon man's heart to do _____ and avoid
_____ . Man's _____ helps him to _____ right from wrong. To help
us form our conscience, God revealed himself and gave us his _____ . He also gave us
_____ _____ so that we can love and obey him and live in his friendship. God's law
is summarized in the _____ , also known as the _____ .

Part II: Answer the following questions.

1. What kind of sin is the result of deliberately breaking a commandment in a serious way?

2. Besides doing something seriously wrong, what two other things are necessary for a sin to
   be a mortal sin?

3. Does the First Commandment require all men to acknowledge God as the one true God,
   Creator and Lord of all things and to worship and adore him as our God?

Part III: Matching.

1. __ being irreverent or irreligious	a. superstition
2. __ worshipping a false god	b. impiety
3. __ believing in an error or denying a truth	c. heresy
4. __ placing faith or trust in something other than God	d. detachment
5. __ being able to let go of things	e. idolatry

Part IV: Answer in complete sentences.

1. What are we required to do by the First Commandment?

2. What does the First Commandment forbid?

3. What is prayer and how should we pray?

4. What are the two forms of prayer?

5. What is a saint?

6. What is the Church Triumphant?

Part V: Write the Ten Commandments in order.

1. _____
2. _____
3. _____
4. _____
5. _____
6. _____
7. _____
8. _____
9. _____
10. _____

The Holy Name   **Quiz 5**

Part I: Fill in the blanks.

1. The Second Commandment forbids any lack of respect, or _____ , toward God in the use of his most Holy Name.

2. When Moses asked God for his name, God said, "I _____ WHO I _____ ."

3. _____ is the verbal abuse or scorn toward God himself or to the Blessed Virgin, the other saints, or holy things.

4. An _____ calls on God to witness to the truth of what we are saying.

5. A _____ is a solemn declaration committing oneself to do something.

Part II: Yes or No.

1. ____ Is it permissible for someone to take an oath when he is involved in a legal proceeding that requires it?

2. ____ Should we ever take an oath lightly or falsely?

Part III: Answer in complete sentences.

1. What vows do religious brothers and sisters make?

2. What kind of vow does a married couple make?

3. Are the objects used for Mass, such as the altar, chalice, and paten considered to be holy? Why or why not?

4. How should we treat the people, places, and things consecrated to God?

Name: _____

The Lord's Day   **Quiz 6**

Part I: Answer in complete sentences.

1. Which commandment requires us to give one day a week to God?

2. Why do the Jewish people observe the Sabbath on Saturday?

3. Why do Christians celebrate the Lord's Day on Sunday?

4. What is the main way that we worship God on the Lord's Day.

5. Since Sunday is supposed to be a day of joy and refreshment, what sorts of things can we do on Sundays?

Part II: Fill in the blanks.

1. The _____ is a Holy Day, which is consecrated or dedicated to God.

2. We are commanded not to do any _____ work on Sundays and Holy Days.

3. To miss Mass on Sunday is a _____ sin unless there is a serious reason.

Part III: Match the date with the corresponding Holy Day of Obligation.

___ All Saints   a. January 1
___ Christmas   b. forty days after Easter
___ Assumption   c. August 15
___ Immaculate Conception   d. November 1
___ Ascension   e. December 8
___ Mary, Mother of God   f. December 25

The Cross and True Riches

Quiz 7

Part I: Answer in complete sentences.

1. Why should we practice self-denial?

2. Give three examples of acts of self-denial.

3. What is the most perfect kind of self-denial?

4. On days the Church requires abstinence, what are we not to do?

5. On days the Church requires us to fast, what are we to do?

6. What is the penitential season in the Church year that prepares us to celebrate the birth of Christ?

7. What is the penitential season in the Church year that prepares us to celebrate the Passion, death, and Resurrection of the Lord?

Part II: Yes or No.

1. ____ Is it always easy to do good?
2. ____ With the power of God is it possible to do good and even love our enemy?
3. ____ Can practicing self-denial strengthen our ability to do good with the help of God?
4. ____ Can our cross be a penance we choose for ourselves or suffering that God allows in our life?
5. ____ Can penance make up for past sin and help prevent future sin?
6. ____ Is it good to practice self-denial on Fridays?

Name:

Part I: Answer the following in complete sentences.

1. What duties do parents have?

2. What does it mean to honor?

3. How do the roles of care giving change as parents and children get older?

4. What must unite a family and make it holy?

5. Who should we look to as our model for family life?

Part II: Yes or No.

1. _____ If a child is disrespectful of his parents, is he honoring his parents?

2. _____ Does the Fourth Commandment require us to respect and obey government authorities and teachers?

3. _____ Should we pray and sacrifice for our parents?

4. _____ Do grown-ups have to respect their parents?

5. _____ Can a society survive if family life is not strong and healthy?

6. _____ Can the Christian family survive without love for God and neighbor?

7. _____ Is prayer necessary for family unity and peace?

Part I: Yes or No.

1. _____ Must we be reverent toward God's most Holy Name?

2. _____ Is God's name "I AM WHO I AM"?

3. _____ Is blasphemy the verbal abuse or scorn toward God or by extension to the Blessed Virgin Mary or the saints?

4. _____ Are cursing and blasphemy the same thing?

5. _____ Must we be respectful while we are in a church?

6. _____ Is it permissible to take an oath without serious reason?

7. _____ Does an oath call on God to witness to the truth of what we are saying?

8. _____ Is a vow in religion a promise made for a religious reason?

9. _____ Do religious brothers and sisters vow poverty, chastity, and obedience?

10. _____ Do married people make a vow of fidelity to each other?

Part II: Answer in complete sentences.

1. What is the Second Commandment and what does it mean?

2. What is an oath?

3. Why do Christians celebrate the Lord's Day on Sunday?

4. List five ways to keep the Lord's Day holy.

5. Which commandment requires us to give one day a week to God? Write out this commandment.

6. What are we commanded not to do on Sundays and Holy Days?

7. What are three ways of practicing self-denial?

8. What are the two penitential seasons of the Church?

9. On which days does the Church require us to fast?

10. What does it mean when the Church requires us to fast?

11. What age group is bound to fasting?

Part III: Match the date with the corresponding Holy Day of Obligation.

____ All Saints   a. January 1
____ Christmas   b. forty days after Easter
____ Assumption   c. August 15
____ Immaculate Conception   d. November 1
____ Ascension   e. December 8
____ Mary, Mother of God   f. December 25

Citizenship—Rights and Duties   **Quiz 9**

Part I: Fill in the blanks.

1. A _____ is a society of people united under a common government or authority.
2. The _____ _____ includes all the things in a society that allow people to have what they need in order to be truly happy.
3. _____ is the virtue of love of one's country.
4. Saint Paul says, "There is no authority except from _____ ."
5. The government is supposed to use its _____ as God intends.

Part II: Yes or No.

1. ____ Does the government exercise a rightful authority over us?
2. ____ Does the government's authority come from God?
3. ____ Is it acceptable for the government to demand something of us that is against God's law?
4. ____ Should the government respect God's law?
5. ____ Is there more than one kind of legitimate government?
6. ____ Is it important for the government to respect and promote the rights and well-being of all the people?
7. ____ Is patriotism in keeping with Christianity?
8. ____ Does patriotism include the promotion of the true welfare of the whole country and its citizens?
9. ____ If the government declares an action to be legal, does that mean that the action is moral?
10. ____ Is it permissible to support immoral laws?

Part III: Compare the duties of the government with those of citizens.

DUTIES OF THE GOVERNMENT	DUTIES OF CITIZENS

Church Authority—Our Fathers in Faith   Quiz 10

Part I: Answer the following in complete sentences.

1. Who founded the Catholic Church?

2. What was the means that Jesus chose to remain with us always and to lead us to heaven?

3. Who was the first Pope?

4. In what ways does the Pope answer moral questions and address himself to current problems?

Part II: Fill in the blanks.

1. A _____ is the chief authority in his own diocese.

2. The bishop has authority as long as he remains in union with the _____ .

3. The bishop shares some of his authority with the _____ and _____ of his diocese.

4. The Church is often referred to as our _____ _____ Church because she exists to give us life and to provide for our well-being and development until we reach our final goal.

5. We should have a great reverence and _____ for the Church because Jesus gave us the Church as a sign of his love for us.

Part III: Write out the five precepts of the Church.

1. _____

2. _____

3. _____

4. _____

5. _____

Respect Life   **Quiz 11**

Part I: Yes or No.

1. ____ Are the body and soul essential to the human being?
2. ____ Is murder a mortal sin?
3. ____ Does murder violate the God-given right to life of the one who is murdered?
4. ____ Is abortion the killing of an unborn baby?
5. ____ Is abortion murder?
6. ____ Is euthanasia the killing of the elderly or the sick?
7. ____ Is euthanasia murder?
8. ____ Must sick or elderly people be given normal or ordinary treatment to be kept alive?
9. ____ Is careless driving a sin against the Fifth Commandment?
10. ____ Is it acceptable to risk our lives by doing foolish stunts when we are encouraged by a dare or a desire to show off?
11. ____ Is it a sin to eat and drink too much?
12. ____ Is the improper use of medicines and other drugs wrong?

Part II: Answer in complete sentences.

1. What is the Fifth Commandment?

2. What are three examples of situations when killing is not the same as murder?

3. What sorts of things should you do to take care of yourself?

Part III: Fill in the blanks.

1. To take an innocent human life is called _____ .

2. The _____ Commandment makes it clear that it is wrong to take innocent life.

3. _____ , the act of killing oneself, is always wrong.

Charity toward All   **Quiz 12**

Part I: Yes or No.

1. _____ Must we have goodwill toward everyone?
2. _____ Must we have good feelings about everyone?
3. _____ Can we love our enemies by wishing them well and treating them justly?
4. _____ Must we like our enemies?
5. _____ It is wrong to wish that another person be hurt and suffer, or perhaps be killed?
6. _____ Should we show respect and consideration for our enemies?
7. _____ When we suffer the sting of harsh words or ill treatment from others can we offer the pain to God for the one who hurts us?
8. _____ Is all anger wrong?
9. _____ Can just anger help us to stand up for the rights of the oppressed or come to the defense of someone?

Part II: Answer the following in complete sentences.

1. What other actions does the Fifth Commandment prohibit besides murder?

2. What are some of the dangers of anger?

3. What is the sin of scandal?

Part III: Fill in the blanks.

1. The _____ Commandment prohibits actions that cause deliberate injury to another human being.

2. To _____ someone is to wish evil to someone.

3. Jesus says: " _____ your enemies, do good to those who hate you, bless those who curse you, pray for those who abuse you" (Lk 6:27–28).

4. Saint Paul wrote: " _____ those who persecute you; bless and do not curse them . . . Repay no one evil for evil, but take thought for what is noble in the sight of all" (Rom 12:14–17).

Part I: Fill in the blanks.

1. _____ is giving a fully conscious and deliberate bad example or encouragement meant to lead another person into sin.

2. To take an innocent human life is _____ .

3. Murder is a _____ sin.

4. _____ , the act of killing oneself, is always wrong.

Part II: Yes or No.

1. _____ Just because the government decides something is legal, does that mean that it is moral?

2. _____ Are abortion and euthanasia murder?

3. _____ Must sick or elderly people be given normal or ordinary treatment to be kept alive?

4. _____ Is it morally acceptable to risk our lives by doing foolish stunts when we are encouraged by a dare or a desire to show off?

5. _____ Is it a sin to eat and drink too much?

6. _____ Must we wish well to everyone?

7. _____ Must we feel good about everyone?

8. _____ Does Jesus ask us to forgive those who hurt us?

9. _____ Should we care about the well-being of people in other countries?

Part III: Answer the following in complete sentences.

1. What should the government do for its citizens?

2. What does a good citizen do?

3. Whose authority is greater, the government's or God's?

4. How should we treat our enemies?

5. Why is scandal wrong?

6. What is hatred?

Part IV: Matching.

1. __ a successor of the Apostles
2. __ the first Pope
3. __ rules the Church on earth on behalf of Christ
4. __ the Body of Christ
5. __ rules of the Church
6. __ geographic area governed by a bishop

a. Vicar of Christ
b. Church
c. Saint Peter
d. diocese
e. precepts of the Church
f. bishop

The Sacred Flame   **Quiz 13**

Part I: Fill in the blanks.

1. To maintain our self-respect and respect for others we have to do what we know is right and avoid what we know is _____ .

2. The _____ and _____ Commandments require us to respect ourselves and others, and especially married life and the family.

3. All our actions start in our _____ , so we should see the importance of properly directing our thoughts and desires.

4. God has designed human sexuality to be enjoyed only in _____ and only in the proper way.

5. The proper use or control of our sexual powers is called _____ .

6. A chaste person will avoid anything that might be a _____ against purity.

7. _____ is sexual thought or action that is against the Sixth or Ninth Commandments.

8. Chastity requires that we practice self-_____ and self-_____ .

Part II: Answer the following.

1. Write out the two commandments that pertain to chastity.

2. How do these two commandments guide us?

3. Why has God designed human sexuality to be enjoyed only in marriage?

4. What sorts of things does a chaste person avoid?

Part III: Yes or No.

1. ____ Has God reserved the joys of human sexuality for marriage?

2. ____ Is it a serious sin to use sexual powers outside of marriage?

3. ____ Does God want to give those who marry an actual share in the creation of a new human being?

Name:

Ownership

Part I: Define each term.

1. stealing (theft):

2. restitution:

3. fraud:

4. usury:

5. envy:

6. avarice:

7. justice:

Part II: Write a paragraph about Saint Francis of Assisi and his spirit of poverty.

_____

_____

_____

_____

_____

_____

_____

_____

Backed by Truth **Quiz 15**

Part I: Matching.

1. ___ idle talk about the faults of others	a. slander/calumny
2. ___ lying under oath	b. detraction
3. ___ saying something false about another	c. rash judgment
4. ___ pretending to be better than you are	d. gossip
5. ___ judging another's character without enough evidence	e. false witness
6. ___ giving untrue testimony about another	f. hypocrisy
7. ___ deliberately deceiving someone	g. perjury
8. ___ using the truth to harm another	h. lying

Part II: Write a paragraph about what you should do when you are tempted to gossip or listen to gossip. Be sure to explain what gossip is and why it is wrong.

_____

_____

_____

_____

_____

_____

_____

_____

_____

_____

_____

_____

_____

The Beatitudes — Quiz 16

Part I: Match the two parts of each beatitude and give an example of how to practice each one (either in your own life or from the life of a saint).

1. ___ Blessed are the poor in spirit,	a. for they shall be satisfied.
2. ___ Blessed are those who mourn,	b. for they shall obtain mercy.
3. ___ Blessed are the meek,	c. for they shall be called sons of God.
4. ___ Blessed are those who hunger and thirst for righteousness,	d. for they shall be comforted.
5. ___ Blessed are the merciful,	e. for theirs is the Kingdom of Heaven.
6. ___ Blessed are the pure in heart,	f. for they shall inherit the earth.
7. ___ Blessed are the peacemakers,	g. for theirs is the Kingdom of Heaven.
8. ___ Blessed are those who are persecuted for righteousness' sake,	h. for they shall see God.

1. _____

2. _____

3. _____

4. _____

5. _____

6. _____

7. _____

8. _____

Name: _____

Unit 4 Test   # Chapters 13–16

Part I: Yes or No.

1. ____ Do the Sixth and Ninth Commandments command us to be pure?

2. ____ Does the Seventh Commandment require us to respect the property of others?

3. ____ Are we allowed to own stolen property, even if we didn't steal it ourselves?

4. ____ Are we allowed to claim as our own something that belongs to someone else?

5. ____ Is copying someone else's homework considered stealing?

6. ____ When we borrow something, must we return it in the same condition in which we received it?

7. ____ Can a person who has his heart set on material possessions pay attention to the Kingdom of God?

8. ____ Are we ever allowed to tell a lie?

9. ____ Should we listen to people who gossip?

Part II: Fill in the blanks.

1. All have the right to have their possessions safe from _____ , damage, and destruction.

2. If I have taken something that does not belong to me, I must return what I have _____ or replace it if I can, and confess my sin if the matter is serious.

3. If I purposely damage or destroy property, justice demands that I make restitution, that is, _____ for the damage.

4. _____ requires me to share what I have with those who need decent food, clothing, and shelter.

5. _____ involves giving everyone his due, what he has a right to receive.

6. Every human being has a right to _____ , _____ , and _____ .

7. A _____ is a blessing or special happiness promised by Jesus to those who follow him.

Part III: Answer the following.

1. What is the Seventh Commandment?

2. What is the Tenth Commandment?

Part IV: Matching.

1. ___ idle talk about the faults of others

2. ___ lying under oath

3. ___ saying something false about another

4. ___ pretending to be better than you are

5. ___ judging another's character without enough evidence

6. ___ giving untrue testimony about another

7. ___ deliberately deceiving someone

8. ___ using the truth to harm another

a. slander/calumny

b. detraction

c. rash judgment

d. gossip

e. false witness

f. hypocrisy

g. perjury

h. lying

---

1. ___ Blessed are the poor in spirit,

2. ___ Blessed are those who mourn,

3. ___ Blessed are the meek,

4. ___ Blessed are those who hunger and thirst for righteousness,

5. ___ Blessed are the merciful,

6. ___ Blessed are the pure in heart,

7. ___ Blessed are the peacemakers,

8. ___ Blessed are those who are persecuted for righteousness' sake,

a. for they shall be satisfied.

b. for they shall obtain mercy.

c. for they shall be called sons of God.

d. for they shall be comforted.

e. for theirs is the Kingdom of Heaven.

f. for they shall inherit the earth.

g. for theirs is the Kingdom of Heaven.

h. for they shall see God.

At the Last Supper

Part I: Yes or No.

1. _____ Did all of Jesus' followers accept his saying when he told them that he would give them his Body to eat and his Blood to drink?
2. _____ At the Last Supper, did the Apostles receive Jesus in Holy Communion?
3. _____ Is the Eucharist only a symbol?
4. _____ Is the Eucharist truly Jesus?
5. _____ Did Jesus make the Apostles priests at the Last Supper?
6. _____ Does the priest offer the same sacrifice that Jesus offered at the Last Supper and on the Cross?

Part II: Fill in the chart.

BEFORE THE WORDS "THIS IS MY BODY ... THIS IS MY BLOOD"		AFTER THE WORDS "THIS IS MY BODY ... THIS IS MY BLOOD"	
APPEARANCE	SUBSTANCE	APPEARANCE	SUBSTANCE
Bread			
Wine			
This change is called: _____			

Part III: Fill in the blanks.

1. The _____ commemorated God's rescue of his chosen people from slavery in Egypt.
2. The sacrifice that frees man from sin is the _____ and death of our Lord Jesus Christ.
3. The word _____ is used to indicate the total offering of a victim or gift in a sacrifice.
4. In the oblation of Jesus Christ, he was both priest and _____ .
5. In Holy Communion we receive the _____ , _____ , _____ , and _____ of Jesus.
6. We call Jesus' presence in the _____ the Real Presence.

Part IV: Answer the following in complete sentences.

1. The slavery of the Hebrew people is an image of what other kind of slavery?

2. What are the four purposes of offering a sacrifice?

Name: _____

The Living Sacrifice

Part I: Yes or No.

1. ____ Is the victim offered at Mass the same victim offered on Calvary?
2. ____ Does Jesus die again at every Mass?
3. ____ Does Jesus make his Body and Blood present on earth under the appearances of bread and wine?
4. ____ Does Christ bring his sacrifice before us in a real way at Mass?

Part II: Answer in complete sentences.

1. What are two reasons Jesus gave us the Sacrament of the Eucharist?

2. What is the most perfect prayer?

3. What are the four ends of the Mass?

Part III: Write a paragraph explaining *one* of the four ends of the Mass.

_____

_____

_____

_____

_____

_____

_____

_____ _____

_____ _____ ___

_____

_____

_____

_____

_____

The Feast of God   **Quiz 19**

Part I: Yes or No.

1. _____ Is Mass a sacred banquet?

2. _____ Is Mass the re-presentation of Christ's sacrifice on Calvary?

3. _____ Is the Mass like any ordinary celebration?

4. _____ Is the Mass a sacred celebration?

5. _____ Can there be friendship without respect?

Part II: Answer in complete sentences.

1. What do we celebrate at Mass?

2. With what kind of attitude should we approach the Mass?

3. How can we express our reverence for the Mass?

4. In the Old Testament sacrifices, what did the people have to do in order to complete the religious ritual?

5. Why is the Mass the one and only perfect sacrifice?

6. Why is the Mass considered a feast and a sacred banquet?

7. What two things does "our daily bread" refer to in the Our Father?

Part I: Yes or No.

1. ____ Was Jesus' teaching on the Eucharist readily accepted by all?

2. ____ Did Jesus lose many disciples after his teaching on the Eucharist?

3. ____ Did Peter accept Jesus' teaching on the Eucharist?

4. ____ Is Jesus' Flesh real food?

5. ____ Is Jesus' Blood real drink?

6. ____ Did Jesus speak of his Body and Blood only symbolically?

7. ____ Does the Eucharist nourish our souls?

8. ____ When we receive the Eucharist, do we receive the life of Christ?

Part II: Answer in complete sentences.

1. What sorts of things did Jesus do to help people believe in him?

2. What did Peter say in response to Jesus' teaching on the Eucharist when Jesus asked the twelve if they would also go away?

3. What happens when we receive the Eucharist worthily?

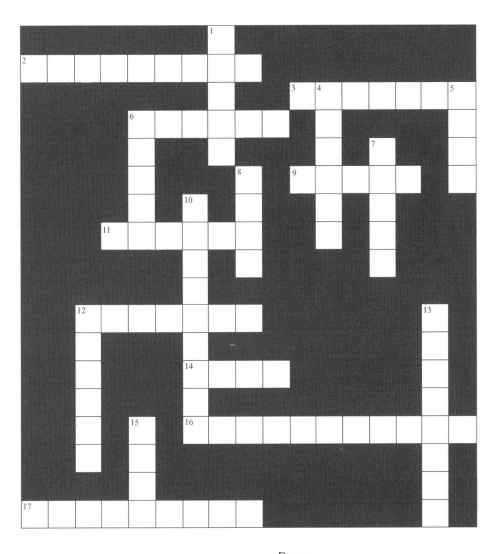

Across

2. Joseph of _____ took the body of Jesus and buried it in a tomb.
3. Jesus was buried in haste because they had to prepare for the _____ .
6. On the first day of the week, some women set out for the tomb with _____ .
9. An angel informed the women that Jesus had _____ from the dead.
11. The Apostles were in hiding for fear of the _____ leaders.
12. After the Resurrection, Jesus breathed on the Apostles and gave them the power to _____sins.
14. Jesus asked Peter three times "Do you _____ me?"
16. Through his Resurrection Jesus brought us the new life of _____ grace.
17. Jesus told his Apostles that they were to be his _____ to all nations.

Down

1. Jesus appeared among the Apostles and said " _____ be with you".
4. On the first day of the week some women went to _____ the body of Jesus.
5. Jesus' Resurrection is a sign of _____ that we too will one day rise from the dead.
6. When the women arrived to the tomb the great _____ had been rolled back.
7. The Apostle _____ set out to see for himself and found the empty tomb.
8. The Apostle _____ went along with Peter.
10. The angel told the women to go tell the news to Jesus' _____ .
12. Jesus said to Peter: " _____ me".
13. Forty days after his Resurrection, Jesus _____ to heaven.
15. Jesus made Peter the first _____ .

Part I: Fill in the chart below comparing the Passover to Christ's Last Supper and Crucifixion.

PASSOVER SACRIFICE	CHRIST'S SACRIFICE
- slavery of the Hebrew people - God frees the Hebrews - Passover lamb - the lamb is slaughtered - eat the lamb	- _____ - _____ - _____ - _____ - _____

Part II: Answer in complete sentences.

1. What is transubstantiation?

2. What is an oblation?

3. What do we call the presence of Jesus in the Eucharist?

4. What is the greatest power of the priesthood?

5. What are two reasons Jesus gave us the Sacrament of the Eucharist?

6. What are the four ends of the Mass?

7. With what kind of attitude should we approach the Mass?

8. How can we express our reverence for the Mass?

9. What happens when we receive the Eucharist worthily?

Part III: Yes or No.

1. ____ When the bread and wine are changed into the Body and Blood of Christ, can we see the change?

2. ____ Is the whole Jesus present in the Eucharist?

3. ____ Is Mass a sacred banquet?

4. ____ Is Mass the re-presentation of Christ's sacrifice on Calvary?

5. ____ Does Jesus die again every time we go to Mass?

6. ____ Was Jesus' teaching on the Eucharist readily accepted by all?

7. ____ Did Peter accept Jesus' teaching on the Eucharist?

8. ____ Did Jesus make Peter the first Pope?

9. ____ Jesus truly died on the Cross, but is he still dead?

10. ____ Was the risen Jesus a ghost?

11. ____ After the Resurrection did Jesus give the Apostles the power to forgive sins?

12. ____ After forty days, did Jesus ascend into heaven?

13. ____ Did the Resurrection of Jesus bring new life?

14. ____ Does Jesus' Resurrection give us hope that we too will rise from the dead?

15. ____ Does the Resurrection of Jesus help us to believe that he is God?

Come into the Lord's Presence Singing for Joy Quiz 22

Part I: Answer in complete sentences.

1. What do we do to be outwardly prepared to come to Mass?

2. What do we do to be inwardly prepared to come to Mass?

3. In the Sacred Liturgy do we take part in the worship of God that goes on in heaven?

4. What are the two main parts of the Mass?

5. Are we in need of forgiveness when we come to Mass?

6. From where do the words in the first part of the Gloria come?

7. When we pray the Gloria what type of prayer are we offering to God?

8. What is the liturgical year?

Part II: What are the five parts of the Introductory Rites?

1. _____
2. _____
3. _____
4. _____
5. _____

Speak Lord, Your Servant is Listening   **Quiz 23**

Part I: Number the parts of the Liturgy of the Word to indicate their proper order and give a brief description of each.

___ Homily: _____

___ Responsorial Psalm: _____

___ Prayers of the Faithful: _____

___ First Reading: _____

___ Gospel: _____

___ Profession of Faith: _____

___ Second Reading: _____

Part II: Answer the following in complete sentences.

1. During the Introductory Rites we speak to God. Who speaks to us during the Liturgy of the Word?

2. What do we learn from the Old Testament?

3. What do the little crosses that we make on our forehead, lips, and heart before the Gospel indicate?

Part I: Number the parts of the Liturgy of the Eucharist to indicate their proper order and give a brief description of each.

___ Preface:_____

_____

___ Doxology:_____

_____

___ Consecration:_____

_____

___ Washing of the Hands:_____

_____

___ Sanctus:_____

_____

___ Invocation of the Holy Spirit:_____

_____

___ Preparation of the Gifts:_____

_____

___ Offering to the Father:_____

_____

___ Prayer over the Gifts:_____

_____

Part II: Answer the following.

1. What does the word *hosanna* mean?

2. Give another name for the Eucharistic Prayer.

Part I: Number the parts of the Communion Rite to indicate their proper order in the Mass and give a brief description of each.

___ Rite of Peace: _____

___ Prayer after Communion: _____

___ Lord's Prayer: _____

___ Agnus Dei (Lamb of God): _____

___ Closing Hymn: _____

___ Communion of the People: _____

___ Breaking of the Bread: _____

___ Blessing: _____

___ Communion Antiphon: _____

___ Communion of the Priest: _____

Part II: Answer in complete sentences.

1. In the Gospels, who said, "Lord, I am not worthy to have you come under my roof . . ."?

2. After receiving Jesus in Holy Communion, do we need to thank him for coming to us in Holy Communion?

Name: _____

Part I: Yes or No.

1. _____ Is the Mass the re-presentation of Jesus' Sacrifice of the Cross?

2. _____ Does Christ preside over every Mass?

3. _____ In the Sacred Liturgy do we take part in the worship of God that goes on in heaven with the angels and saints?

4. _____ Does coming to Mass make us better than the rest of mankind?

5. _____ Are we in need of forgiveness when we come to Mass?

6. _____ Does the Church have its own special calendar?

7. _____ Should we drift off into daydreams during a familiar reading at Mass?

8. _____ Do the ground wheat and crushed grapes used to make the bread and wine used at Mass remind us that we must die to ourselves and live a new life in Christ?

Part II: Answer in complete sentences.

1. What do we do to be outwardly and inwardly prepared to come to Mass?

2. What are the two main parts of the Mass?

3. Why do we stand when the Gospel is read at Mass?

4. What do the little crosses that we make on our forehead, lips, and heart before the Gospel indicate?

5. After receiving Jesus in Holy Communion, do we need to thank him for coming to us in Holy Communion?

Name: _____

Unit 6 Test (continued)

Part III: Number the parts of the Mass to indicate their proper order and give a brief description of each.

___ Lamb of God (Agnus Dei): _____

_____

___ Gloria: _____

_____

___ Profession of Faith: _____

_____

___ Consecration: _____

_____

___ Washing of the Hands: _____

_____

___ Blessing: _____

_____

___ Sanctus: _____

_____

___ Penitential Rite: _____

_____

___ Invocation of the Holy Spirit: _____

_____

___ Lord's Prayer (Our Father): _____

_____

___ Prayers of the Faithful: _____

_____

___ Communion of the Priest: _____

_____

___ Preparation of the Gifts: _____

_____

___ Gospel: _____

_____

Part I: Yes or No.

1. _____ Do we need Jesus in our daily lives?

2. _____ Are we always aware of our need for Jesus?

3. _____ Does Jesus want us to have confidence in him?

4. _____ Do we have any reason to worry if we have confidence in Jesus?

5. _____ Do we displease Jesus if we receive Holy Communion without being properly prepared?

6. _____ Should we receive Holy Communion often?

Part II: Write a paragraph about the ways we can follow Jesus in our daily lives that help us to be prepared to receive him in Holy Communion. Consider the following:

prayer, good works, confession, learning about Jesus
What does the parable about the king who gave a wedding banquet for
his son teach us about being prepared?

_____

_____

_____

_____

_____

_____

_____

_____

_____

_____

_____

_____

_____

_____

Name:

Come Lord Jesus

Quiz 27

Part I: Explain what each of these terms mean in regard to receiving Holy Communion.

state of grace: _____

right intention: _____

Eucharistic fast: _____

thanksgiving: _____

obligation/Easter duty: _____

Viaticum: _____

Part II: Write a prayer of thanksgiving to Jesus for allowing us to receive him in Holy Communion.

_____

_____

_____

_____

_____

_____

_____

_____

_____

_____

_____

_____

_____

_____

His Abiding Presence

Part I: Yes or No.

1. ____ Is it Jesus who changes bread and wine into his Body and Blood through transubstantiation?
2. ____ Is the Eucharist Jesus in his entirety, Body, Blood, Soul, and Divinity?
3. ____ Do we receive the divinity of Jesus as well as his humanity?
4. ____ Did Jesus leave his disciples orphaned?
5. ____ Is Jesus present in the tabernacles in our churches?
6. ____ Is Jesus in the tabernacle night and day?
7. ____ Should we visit Jesus in the Blessed Sacrament?
8. ____ Does speaking to Jesus in the Blessed Sacrament bring us special graces?

Part II: Answer in complete sentences.

1. What is a sanctuary lamp?

2. What kind of reverent actions should our behavior before the Blessed Sacrament include?

3. What is a Eucharistic procession?

4. What is Exposition?

5. What is Benediction?

Name: _____

Unit 7 Test

Chapters 26–28

Part I: Answer in complete sentences.

1. When the priest holds the Host before us and says: "The Body of Christ" and we respond, "Amen", what are we expressing?

2. What does the parable about the king who gave a wedding banquet for his son teach us about being prepared to receive Holy Communion?

3. What is the most important way to prepare our hearts to receive Jesus?

4. How does Jesus fulfill his promise to stay with us at all times?

5. What is a Eucharistic procession?

6. What is Exposition?

7. What is Benediction?

Part II: Explain what each of these terms mean in regard to receiving Holy Communion.

1. state of grace: _____

_____

2. right intention: _____

_____

3. Eucharistic fast: _____

_____

4. thanksgiving: _____

_____

5. Easter duty: _____

_____

6. Viaticum: _____

_____

Part III: Yes or No.

1. _____ Does Jesus want us to have confidence in him?

2. _____ Do we have any reason to worry if we have confidence in Jesus?

3. _____ Do we displease Jesus if we receive Holy Communion without being properly prepared?

4. _____ Should we receive Holy Communion often?

5. _____ Is Peter the rock upon which Jesus built his Church?

6. _____ Is it disrespectful to talk to friends during Mass?

7. _____ Does God become our food in the Eucharist?

8. _____ Is it Jesus who changes bread and wine into his Body and Blood through transubstantiation?

9. _____ Is the Eucharist Jesus in his entirety, Body, Blood, Soul, and Divinity?

10. _____ Do we receive the divinity of Jesus as well as his humanity?

11. _____ Did Jesus leave his disciples orphaned?

12. _____ Is Jesus present in the tabernacles in our churches?

13. _____ Is Jesus in the tabernacle night and day?

14. _____ Should we visit Jesus in the Blessed Sacrament?

15. _____ Does speaking to Jesus in the Blessed Sacrament bring us special graces?

Passage into Eternity   **Quiz 29**

Part I: Answer in complete sentences.

1. What is death?

2. What happens to the body after death?

3. What happens to the soul after it leaves the body?

4. What is the Particular Judgment?

5. At the Particular Judgment we will be immediately aware of what three things?

Part II: Yes or No.

1. _____ Should we fear death?

2. _____ Should we be aware of death as something that we must all experience?

3. _____ When we die, will we be judged for what we have thought, said, done, and failed to do?

4. _____ Is God unfair in his judgment of us?

5. _____ Are there things we can do right now, like living a good life and receiving the Sacraments on a regular basis, to prepare us for death and judgment?

6. _____ At the hour of our death, will we be at peace if we have done our best to please God and have asked for his mercy for the times we failed to obey him?

Heaven—Purgatory—Hell   **Quiz 30**

Part I: Answer in complete sentences.

1. What is the final purpose of our life?

2. What is heaven?

3. Will heaven be boring?

4. When does our spiritual life begin?

5. What is purgatory and how can we help the souls there?

6. What is the Church Triumphant?

7. What is the Church Suffering?

8. What is the Church Militant?

9. Who are the condemned?

10. Does hell exist?

11. What is the greatest pain in hell?

He Shall Come Again   **Quiz 31**

Part I: Yes or No.

1. _____ Will Jesus come in splendor at the Second Coming?
2. _____ Will the whole human race be present at the Second Coming?
3. _____ Will the dead rise at the Second Coming?
4. _____ Will all of our deeds, even our most secret deeds, be made known at the General Judgment?
5. _____ Will the beatific vision make us completely happy?
6. _____ Will only our souls exist after the Second Coming?
7. _____ Will the General Judgment make clear to everyone the wisdom, knowledge, graciousness, mercy, patience, loving kindness, and justice of the Lord in his dealings with all men?
8. _____ Will anyone be upset with the way Jesus will judge us?

Part II: Saint Paul compared living the spiritual life to running a race. Write a paragraph explaining what the saint and the athlete have in common. Think about the following things: the need for self-discipline, the need for perseverance, the need to keep one's eyes on the prize.

_____

_____

_____

_____

_____

_____

_____

_____

_____

_____

_____

_____

_____

_____

_____

Our Gestures at Mass

Materials: index cards or small pieces of paper with gestures written on them (see list page B-2); basket or box to hold the cards; bowl of holy water; floor space in which to demonstrate the gestures

Preparation: write the gestures on the index cards or pieces of paper

Direct Aims:

> • to understand gestures as the outward expression of an inner attitude
> • to reflect on the meaning of the individual gestures used at Mass

Indirect Aim: to make our individual gestures of worship more deliberate

What to Do and Say

Say:

> Throughout the centuries, our Church has developed ceremonies in which public worship is offered to God. We call this public form of worship "liturgy."

Write "liturgy" on the board. Say:

> The word *liturgy* comes from two Greek words that mean "people" and "work."

Next to liturgy on the board write "= people + work." Say:

> Liturgy is our main work as People of God. It is the main way we fulfill the primary commandment to love and worship God above all things with our whole selves. Liturgy is important because it is the way we give God , our Creator and Lord, the worship he deserves.

Write on the board "Mass = liturgy." Say:

> The Mass is the most important Liturgy of the Church. How we conduct ourselves during Mass reflects our inner attitude toward God. If I am slouching, not listening, and making gestures of worship sloppily, I am saying with my body that I do not care about God. If am erect, attentive, and making the gestures of worship carefully, I am honoring God with my body. Today, we're going to look at the gestures we make when we are at Mass.

Pass the basket with the cards, and have each student draw one card. Call on the students one by one to come forward and reverently demonstrate the gestures that is on their card. After each demonstration, ask the class:

> Was that done reverently and well? (*If the response is negative, ask the student to repeat the gesture.*)
>
> What do we call this gesture?
>
> During which part of the Mass do we see this gesture?
>
> What is expressed by this gesture?

Our Gestures at Mass *(continued)*

Blessing oneself with holy water
When: entering and leaving a church
What: renewing one's baptismal
    promises (to be a disciple of Jesus)
    and asking for the grace to live
    them out; purifying oneself before
    entering God's presence

Making the Sign of the Cross
When: at the beginning and end of Mass,
when entering and leaving the church
What: uniting ourselves with Jesus and his
death on the Cross, which unites us to God.

Genuflecting
When: passing in front of the tabernacle
What: adoration of the Blessed Sacrament

Kneeling with folded hands
When: during private prayer before the
tabernacle in preparation for Mass; during
the Eucharistic Prayer at Mass; during
prayer after receiving Communion
What: humility before God; adoration of
God

Bowing
When: passing in front of the altar (where
there is no tabernacle behind the altar, one
bows instead of genuflecting when passing
in front of it); during the Creed, when we
say, "By the Holy Spirit was incarnate
of the Virgin Mary and became man."
What: reverence for God and holy thing;
humility before God

Beating the breast with clenched fist
When: during the Confiteor, when we say
"through my fault."
What: sorrow for sin

Standing with hands folded
When: the entrance precession; the Gloria;
the Gospel; prayers of intercession; the
Hosanna; the Our Father; the Lamb of God;
the recessional
What: a sign of respect

Sitting quietly with hands folded
When: during the Old Testament reading,
the Responsorial Psalm, the Epistle, the
homily, the Offertory
What: giving respect to God and others
by listening and paying attention

**Making a small cross with the thumb on the
forehead, lips, and heart**
When: before the Gospel
What: requesting the Word of God to dwell
in one's thoughts, words, and desires

**Carrying something in precession or pro-
cessing**
When: entrance precession; Offertory
procession
What: reverence for God and holy things;
offering something to God

Receiving Communion on the tongue
When: during Holy Communion
What: desire to receive Jesus, dependency
upon God, reverence for the Holy Eucharist

Receiving Communion in the hand
When: during Holy Communion
What: desire to receive Jesus, dependency
upon God, reverence for the Holy Eucharist

**Shaking another's hand or offering some
other gesture of peace**
When: the sign of peace
What: offering the peace of Christ to
another, showing respect for another person
as a temple of the Holy Spirit

Rite of Marriage (from *The Rites of the Catholic Church*, vol. 1)

The Liturgy of the Word proceeds as usual. After the homily, the Rite of Marriage begins.

QUESTIONS
After the Liturgy of the Word, the Rite of Marriage begins. The priest asks the couple:
N. and N., have you come here freely and without reservation to give yourselves to each other in marriage?
R/ *Yes.*

Will you love and honor each other as man and wife for the rest of your lives?
R/ *Yes.*

Will you accept children lovingly from God, and bring them up according to the law of Christ and his Church?
R/ *Yes.*

CONSENT
The priest says to the coupe:
Since it is your intention to enter into marriage, join your right hands, and declare your consent before God and his Church.

The couple joins hands and the bridegroom says:
I, N., take you, N., to be my wife. I promise to be true to you in good times and in bad, in sickness and in health. I will love you and honor you all the days of my life.

The bride says:
I, N., take you, N., to be my husband. I promise to be true to you in good times and in bad, in sickness and in health. I will love you and honor you all the days of my life.

The priest says:
You have declared your consent before the Church. May the Lord in his goodness strengthen your consent and fill you both with blessings. What God has joined, men must not divide.
R/ *Amen.*

BLESSING OF RINGS
Priest:
Lord, bless these rings which we bless + in your name.
Grant that those who wear them
may always have a deep faith in each other.
May they do your will
and always live together
in peace, good will, and love.
We ask this through Christ our Lord.
R/ *Amen.*

Rite of Marriage *(continued)*

EXCHANGE OF RINGS
The bridegroom places the bride's ring on her finger and says:
N., take this ring as a sign of my love and fidelity. In the name of the Father, and of the Son, and of the Holy Spirit.

The bride places the bridegroom's ring on his finger and says:
N., take this ring as a sign of my love and fidelity. In the name of the Father, and of the Son, and of the Holy Spirit.

The Liturgy of the Eucharist is celebrated.

NUPTIAL BLESSING
After the Our Father, the priest prays:
My dear friends, let us turn to the Lord and pray
that he will bless with his grace this woman
now married in Christ to this man
and that through the Sacrament of the Body and Blood of Christ,
he will unite in love the couple he has joined in this holy bond.

Father, by your power you have made everything out of nothing.
In the beginning you created the universe
and made mankind in your own likeness.
You gave man the constant help of woman
so that man and woman should no longer be two, but one flesh,
and you teach us that what you have united
may never be divided.

The rest of the Mass is celebrated

SOLEMN BLESSING
Before the final blessing of the people, the priest gives the couple a special blessing:
May God, the almighty Father, give you his joy and bless you in your children.
R/ *Amen.*

May the only Son of God have mercy on you and help you in good times and in bad.
R/ *Amen.*

May the Holy Spirit of God always fill your hearts with his love.
R/ *Amen.*

And may almighty God bless you all, the Father, and the Son, + and the Holy Spirit.
R/ *Amen.*

Vessels used in the Liturgy

chalice and paten

lavabo

ciborium

monstrance

cruets

Other items used at Mass

lectionary

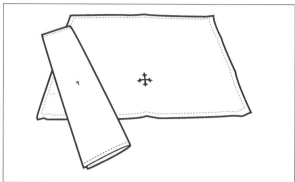

altar linens

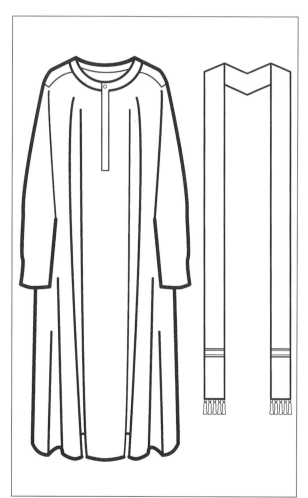

alb and stole

chasuble

The Liturgical Year

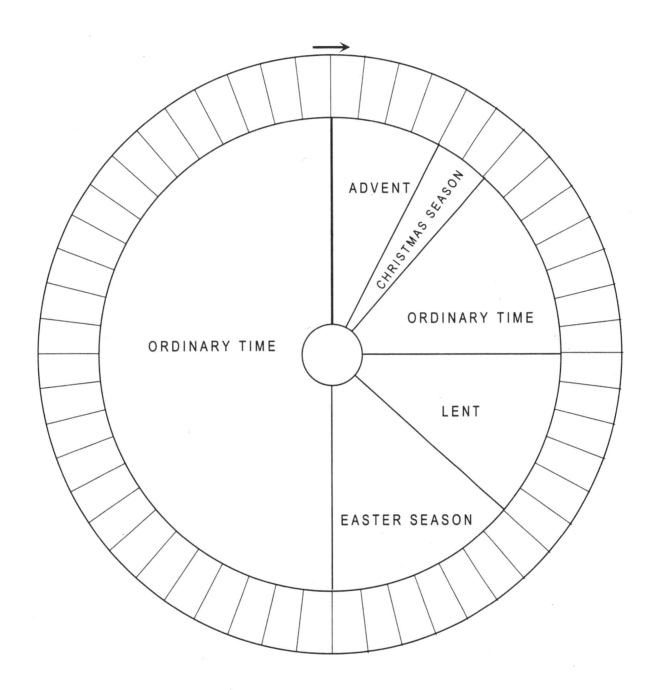

ADVENT

CHRISTMAS SEASON

ORDINARY TIME

ORDINARY TIME

LENT

EASTER SEASON

The Liturgical Year *(continued)*

Materials: photocopies of student worksheet (page B-7), coloring pencils, markers, or crayons (green, violet, rose and red).

Direct Aims

- to understand the central seasons and feasts of the liturgical year

- to understand the liturgical colors

- to see the liturgical year as the story of salvation in miniature

Preparation: Using a copy of page B-7, prepare a sample liturgical calendar that the students can use as a model.

What to Do and Say

Read or review the section on penitential seasons (student text, pp. 40 and 41). Say:

> In her wisdom, the Church has provided a beautiful system of feasts and seasons through which we can learn and live our Catholic Faith. A liturgical calendar helps us to follow the seasons and feasts of the Church's year.

Write "Liturgical Calendar" on the board. Say:

> The word *liturgical* comes from two Greek words that mean "the people's work." For Catholics, our chief work is to worship and glorify God. The liturgical calendar records the different feasts and season of worship that the Church celebrates in the course of a year.

Show the students the calendar you have prepared. Say:

> This is a drawing of the Church's liturgical year, in the form of a circle divided into the fifty-two weeks of the year. The weeks are grouped into seasons, and for each season there is a corresponding liturgical color. The color of the priest's vestments and other church decorations varies according to the season or feast.

Give copies of p. B-7 to the students. Say:

> As we go through the liturgical calendar section by section, you can color in each week with its liturgical color.

Point to the top of your model calendar and say:

> The arrow at the top of the circle marks the beginning of the liturgical year and tells you to follow the weeks in a clockwise direction. The first section consists of the four weeks of Advent.

The Liturgical Year *(continued)*

The first Sunday of Advent is the beginning of the Church year.

> The liturgical color for Advent is violet, a penitential color for a penitential season. Advent is a time when the Church remembers the many centuries of waiting and preparation that the chosen people experienced before the coming of the Savior. The liturgical color for the third Sunday of Advent, however, is rose. This Sunday is also called Gaudete Sunday—in Latin, *gaudete* means "rejoice." Why do we rejoice on this Sunday? We rejoice because this Sunday reminds us that despite the long time of waiting, the chosen people never lost hope that God's Word would be fulfilled. It reminds us also that we are soon to celebrate the birthday of the Savior at Christmas.

Invite the students to color the first four weeks of Advent, using violet and rose. Then point to the next section. Say:

> The next liturgical season is Christmas. The Church celebrates this great feast not only on December 25, but also until the feast of the Epiphany. The liturgical color for this season is white, which is the color of all the major Church celebrations. This section we leave uncolored.

Point to the next (green) section on your calendar. Say:

> After the Christmas season comes a "time between seasons," which we call Ordinary Time. It is neither a preparation for nor a celebration of any special feast or season. The number of weeks in this season can vary depending on the date of Easter, which can be early or later in the spring.

Invite the students to color the section for Ordinary Time green. When they have finished, point to the next (violet) section on your calendar. Say:

> This violet section represents the six weeks of Lent, a season of prayer, fasting, and almsgiving, during which we prepare for the feast of Easter, when we celebrate the Resurrection of Jesus. The season of Lent also has a rose-colored Sunday. The fourth Sunday of Lent is called Laetare Sunday—*laetare* being a Latin word, meaning "rejoice." It is the Church's way of reminding us that no matter how long or difficult the waiting seems, the final victory over sin and death will eventually come. The last Sunday of Lent is Palm Sunday, also called Passion Sunday. Its liturgical color is red, to remind us of Jesus' suffering and death.

Have the students color the Lent section of their calendar. Then point to the next (white) section on your calendar and say:

> Notice how long the Easter season is compared to the Christmas season. The Easter season lasts for seven weeks, ending at the feast of Pentecost. As you see, the color for the Easter season is white. The liturgical color for Pentecost Sunday, however, is red, as a reminder, of the tongues of fire that came upon the Apostles that day.

The Liturgical Year *(continued)*

Have the students color the last week of the Easter season red. Then say:

> The next season in the Church's year is another season of Ordinary Time, whose liturgical color is…[green]. This period of Ordinary Time extends from the first Sunday after Pentecost until the last Sunday of the year. The expression "Ordinary Time" comes from the fact that the Sundays of this period are numbered with ordinal numerals—for example, the Third Sunday of Ordinary Time or the Fifth Sunday after Pentecost.

> The last Sunday of the Church year is the feast of Christ the King. The liturgical color for this feast is white. You can see why this is an appropriate feast for the conclusion of the liturgical year. It reminds us that Christ is truly the King of this world and should be the rule for our daily lives, and that someday all things will find their fulfillment in him at the end of time.

After the students have had a chance to complete the coloring of their calendars, summarize:

> The liturgical calendar is like a miniature picture or timeline of the history of salvation. There is a long period of waiting for the Savior, then a period of celebration when the Savior comes, and then a period when the Savior preaches and teaches and lays the foundation for his Church. Next is the period of trial and suffering, when Jesus gave up his life to redeem us from sin, followed by a period of rejoicing that Jesus has conquered sin and death by rising from the dead, ascending into heaven, and sending the Holy Spirit to his Church. And finally there is the long period of reflection as the Church faithfully awaits the Second Coming of Christ the King.

Trace the liturgical calendar clockwise with a finger and say:

> All these events except the very last—the Second Coming of Christ at the end of time— have been accomplished. The seasons of the Church year remind us that today, we are members of the Church, waiting faithfully—eating the Bread, drinking the Cup, and proclaiming Christ's death until he comes in glory.

Rite of Baptism (adapted from *The Rites of the Catholic Church*, vol. 1)

Gather the students and begin class with the Sign of the Cross.

Welcome the children to the "Baptism" of the doll. Have two children act as parents and two as godparents.

Ask the parents: What name have you given your child? Parents: *N.*

What do you ask of God's Church for N.? Parents: *Baptism.*

Explain to the children that in asking for N. to be baptized, the parents are also responsible for raising N. in the Catholic Faith. It is their duty to help their children keep the commandments of loving God and neighbor.

Ask the parents: Do you clearly understand what you are undertaking? Parents: *We do.*

Ask the godparents: Godparents, are you ready to help these parents in their duty as Christian mothers and fathers? Godparents: *We are.*

Liturgy of the Word: Read the baptism of Jesus: Lk 3:2b–22.

Intercession: R/ *Lord, hear our prayer.*

We pray for N. who will be baptized here today. R/

We pray for N.'s parents. Help them to raise N. according to the Faith. R/

We pray for N.'s godparents, may they support N.'s parents in the rearing of N. R/

We pray for all God's family, united in one Baptism for the forgiveness of sins. R/

We pray that you renew the grace of our Baptism that we may be more faithful to you. R/

Anointing before Baptism (Oil of Catechumens—on the chest):

We anoint you with the oil of salvation in the name of Christ our Savior; may he strengthen you with his power who lives and reigns for ever and ever. All: *Amen.*

Explain that the priest would then bless the water for Baptism. (Bless + this water in which N. will be baptized.) Ask the students what water symbolizes. We drink it for life, we can die in it by drowning, it is fun, it is cool and refreshing, it washes, etc. Make these parallels to the spiritual life: we die and rise to new life with Christ through Baptism, we are washed free from sin, and we are filled with the life of grace, which nourishes our souls.

Renewal of Baptismal Promises (all present may do this): R/ *I do.*

Do you renounce Satan? And all his works? And all his empty show? R/

Do you renounce sin, so as to live in the freedom of the children of God? R/

Do you renounce the lure of evil, so that sin may have no mastery over you? R/

Do you renounce Satan, the author and prince of sin? R/

Do you believe in God, the Father almighty, Creator of heaven and earth? R/

Do you believe in Jesus Christ, his only Son, our Lord, who was born of the Virgin Mary, suffered death and was buried, rose again from the dead and is now seated at the right hand of the Father? R/

Do you believe in the Holy Spirit, the holy Catholic Church, the communion of saints, the forgiveness of sins, the resurrection of the body, and life everlasting? R/

Rite of Baptism *(continued)*

This is our Faith. This is the Faith of the Church. We are proud to profess it, in Christ Jesus our Lord.
All: *Amen.*

Ask the parents and godparents: Is it your will that N. should be baptized in the Faith of the Church, which we have all professed with you? Parents and Godparents: *It is.*

(Pouring water over N.'s head three times): N., I baptize you in the name of the Father, and of the Son, and of the Holy Spirit.
All: *Amen.*

Explain that now N. will be anointed on the crown of the head with chrism to share in the threefold ministry of Christ as priest, prophet, and king.

Next, N. will be clothed in a white garment as a reminder of how pure N. is. Just as we must work hard to keep white clothes clean, so too we must work to keep our soul free from sin. We put on clothes as we are now clothed in Christ. After the child has been clothed, you say:
N. you have become a new creation, and have clothed yourself in Christ. See in this white garment the outward sign of your Christian dignity. With your family and friends to help you by word and example, bring that dignity unstained into the everlasting life of heaven.
All: *Amen.*

Next N. will receive a lighted candle, which represents receiving the light of Christ. Light the candle and give it to the godparents.
Say: Receive the light of Christ. Parent and godparents, this light is entrusted to you to keep burning brightly. This child of yours has been enlightened by Christ. He is to walk always as a child of the light. May he keep the flame of faith alive in his heart. When the Lord comes may he go out to meet him with all the saints in the heavenly kingdom.
All: *Amen.*

Ephphetha (optional) (bless ears and mouth of N.): The Lord Jesus made the deaf hear and the dumb speak. May he soon touch your ears to receive his word, and your mouth to proclaim his Faith, to the praise and glory of God the Father.
All: *Amen.*

Explain that now the newly baptized has been reborn as a child of God, and so together with him, we pray the Lord's Prayer: *Our Father…*

Final blessing:
May almighty God, the Father, and the Son, and the Holy Spirit + bless you.
All: *Amen.*
Go in Peace.
All: *Thanks be to God.*

You may sing a song (example: For all the Saints).

The Papacy

1. St. Peter (Simon Bar-Jona): d. 64 or 67
2. St. Linus: 67–76
3. St. Anacletus (Cletus): 76–88
4. St. Clement: 88–97
5. St. Evaristus: 97–105
6. St. Alexander I: 105–115
7. St. Sixtus I: 115–125
8. St. Telesphorus: 125–136
9. St. Hyginus: 136–140
10. St. Pius I: 140–155
11. St. Anicetus: 155–166
12. St. Soter: 166–175
13. St. Eleutherius: 175–189
14. St. Victor I: 189–199
15. St. Zephyrinus: 199–217
16. St. Callistus I: 217–222
17. St. Urban I: 222–230
18. St. Pontian: 230–235
19. St. Anterus: 235–236
20. St. Fabian: 236–250
21. St. Cornelius: 251–253
22. St. Lucius I: 253–254
23. St. Stephen I: 254–257
24. St. Sixtus II: 257–258
25. St. Dionysius: 259–268
26. St. Felix I: 269–274
27. St. Eutychian: 275–283
28. St. Caius: 283–296
29. St. Marcellinus: 296–304
30. St. Marcellus I: 308–309
31. St. Eusebius: 309–310
32. St. Melchiades: 311–314
33. St. Sylvester I: 314–335
    Most of the Popes before St. Sylvester I were martyrs.
34. St. Marcus: 336–336
35. St. Julius I: 337–352
36. Liberius: 352–366
37. St. Damasus I: 366–384
38. St. Siricius: 384–399
39. St. Anastasius I: 399–401
40. St. Innocent I: 401–417
41. St. Zosimus: 417–418
42. St. Boniface I: 418–422
43. St. Celestine I: 422–432
44. St. Sixtus III: 432–440
45. St. Leo I (the Great): 440–461
46. St. Hilary: 461–468
47. St. Simplicius: 468–483
48. St. Felix III (II): 483–492
49. St. Gelasius I: 492–496
50. Anastasius II: 496–498
51. St. Symmachus: 498–514
52. St. Hormisdas: 514–523
53. St. John I, Martyr: 523–526
54. St. Felix IV (III): 526–530
55. Boniface II: 530–532
56. John II: 533–535
57. St. Agapitus I: 535–536
58. St. Silverius, Martyr: 536–537
59. Vigilius: 537–555
60. Pelagius I: 556–561
61. John III: 561–574
62. Benedict I: 575–579
63. Pelagius II: 579–590
64. St. Gregory I (the Great): 590–604
65. Sabinian: 604–606
66. Boniface III: 607–607
67. St. Boniface IV: 608–615
68. St. Deusdedit: 615–618
69. Boniface V: 619–625
70. Honorius I: 625–638
71. Severinus: 640–640
72. John IV: 640–642
73. Theodore I: 642–649
74. St. Martin I, Martyr: 649–655
75. St. Eugene I: 654–657
76. St. Vitalian: 657–672
77. Adeodatus II: 672–676
78. Donus: 676–678
79. St. Agatho: 678–681
80. St. Leo II: 682–683
81. St. Benedict II: 684–685
82. John V: 685–686
83. Conon: 686–687
84. St. Sergius I: 687–701
85. John VI: 701–705
86. John VII: 705–707
87. Sisinnius: 708–708
88. Constantine: 708–715
89. St. Gregory II: 715–731
90. St. Gregory III: 731–741
91. St. Zachary: 741–752
92. Stephen II (III): 752–757
93. St. Paul I: 757–767
94. Stephen III (IV): 768–772
95. Adrian I: 772–795
96. St. Leo III: 795–816
97. Stephen IV (V): 816–817
98. St. Paschal I: 817–824
99. Eugene II: 824–827
100. Valentine: 827–827
101. Gregory IV: 827–844
102. Sergius II: 844–847
103. St. Leo IV: 847–855
104. Benedict III: 855–858
105. St. Nicholas I (the Great): 858–867
106. Adrian II: 867–872
107. John VIII: 872–882
108. Marinus I: 882–884
109. St. Adrian III: 884–885
110. Stephen V (VI): 885–891
111. Formosus: 891–896
112. Boniface VI: 896–896
113. Stephen VI (VII): 896–897
114. Romanus: 897–897
115. Theodore II: 897–897
116. John IX: 898–900
117. Benedict IV: 900–903
118. Leo V: 903–903
119. Sergius III: 904–911
120. Anastasius III: 911–913
121. Landus: 913–914
122. John X: 914–928
123. Leo VI: 928–928
124. Stephen VII (VIII): 928–931
125. John XI: 931–935
126. Leo VII: 936–939
127. Stephen VIII (IX): 939–942
128. Marinus II: 942–946
129. Agapitus II: 946–955
130. John XII: 955–964
131. Leo VIII: 963–965

The Papacy

(continued)

132. Benedict V: 964–966
133. John XIII: 965–972
134. Benedict VI: 973–974
135. Benedict VII: 974–983
136. John XIV: 983–984
137. John XV: 985–996
138. Gregory V: 996–999
139. Sylvester II: 999–1003
140. John XVII: 1003–1003
141. John XVIII: 1004–1009
142. Sergius IV: 1009–1012
143. Benedict VIII: 1012–1024
144. John XIX: 1024–1032
145. Benedict IX: 1032–1044
146. Sylvester III: 1045–1045
147. Benedict IX: 1045–1045
148. Gregory VI: 1045–1046
149. Clement II: 1046–1047
150. Benedict IX: 1047–1048
151. Damasus II: 1048–1048
152. St. Leo IX: 1049–1054
153. Victor II: 1055–1057
154. Stephen IX (X): 1057–1058
155. Nicholas II: 1059–1061
156. Alexander II: 1061–1073
157. St. Gregory VII: 1073–1085
158. Bl. Victor III: 1086–1087
159. Bl. Urban II: 1088–1099
160. Paschal II: 1099–1118
161. Gelasius II: 1118–1119
162. Callistus II: 1119–1124
163. Honorius II: 1124–1130
164. Innocent II: 1130–1143
165. Celestine II: 1143–1144
166. Lucius II: 1145–1145
167. Bl. Eugene III: 1145–1153
168. Anastasius IV: 1153–1154
169. Adrian IV: 1154–1159
170. Alexander III: 1159–1181
171. Lucius III: 1181–1185
172. Urban III: 1185–1187
173. Gregory VIII: 1187–1187
174. Clement III: 1187–1191
175. Celestine III: 1191–1198

176. Innocent III: 1198–1216
177. Honorius III: 1216–1227
178. Gregory IX: 1227–1241
179. Celestine IV: 1241–1241
180. Innocent IV: 1243–1254
181. Alexander IV: 1254–1261
182. Urban IV: 1261–1264
183. Clement IV: 1265–1268
184. Bl. Gregory X: 1271–1276
185. Bl. Innocent V: 1276–1276
186. Adrian V: 1276–1276
187. John XXI: 1276–1277
188. Nicholas III: 1277–1280
189. Martin IV: 1281–1285
190. Honorius IV: 1285–1287
191. Nicholas IV: 1288–1292
192. St. Celestine V: 1294–1294
193. St. Boniface VIII: 1294–1303
194. Bl. Benedict XI: 1303–1304
195. Clement V: 1305–1314
196. John XXII: 1316–1334
197. Benedict XII: 1334–1342
198. Clement VI: 1342–1352
199. Innocent VI: 1352–1362
200. Bl. Urban V: 1362–1370
201. Gregory XI: 1370–1378
202. Urban VI: 1378–1389
203. Boniface IX: 1389–1404
204. Innocent VII: 1404–1406
205. Gregory XII: 1406–1415
206. Martin V: 1417–1431
207. Eugene IV: 1431–1447
208. Nicholas V: 1447–1455
209. Callisius III: 1455–1458
210. Pius II: 1458–1464
211. Paul II: 1464–1471
212. Sixtus IV: 1471–1484
213. Innocent VIII: 1484–1492
214. Alexander VI: 1492–1503
215. Pius III: 1503–1503
216. Julius II: 1503–1513
217. Leo X: 1513–1521
218. Adrian VI: 1522–1523
219. Clement VII: 1523–1534
220. Paul III: 1534–1549
221. Julius III: 1550–1555
222. Marcellus II: 1555–1555

223. Paul IV: 1555–1559
224. Pius IV: 1559–1565
225. St. Pius V: 1566–1572
226. Gregory XIII: 1572–1585
227. Sixtus V: 1585–1590
228. Urban VII: 1590–1590
229. Gregory XIV: 1590–1591
230. Innocent IX: 1591–1591
231. Clement VIII: 1592–1605
232. Leo XI: 1605–1605
233. Paul V: 1605–1621
234. Gregory XV: 1621–1623
235. Urban VIII: 1623–1644
236. Innocent X: 1644–1655
237. Alexander VII: 1655–1667
238. Clement IX: 1667–1669
239. Clement X: 1670–1676
240. Bl. Innocent XI: 1676–1689
241. Alexander VIII: 1689–1691
242. Innocent XII: 1691–1700
243. Clement XI: 1700–1721
244. Innocent XIII: 1721–1724
245. Benedict XIII: 1724–1730
246. Clement XII: 1730–1740
247. Benedict XIV: 1740–1758
248. Clement XIII: 1758–1769
249. Clement XIV: 1769–1774
250. Pius VI: 1775–1799
251. Pius VII: 1800–1823
252. Leo XII: 1823–1829
253. Pius VIII: 1829–1830
254. Gregory XVI: 1831–1846
255. Bl. Pius IX: 1846–1878
256. Leo XIII: 1878–1903
257. St. Pius X: 1903–1914
258. Benedict XV: 1914–1922
259. Pius XI: 1922–1939
260. Pius XII: 1939–1958
261. Bl. John XXIII: 1958–1963
262. Paul VI: 1963–1978
263. John Paul I: 1978–1978
264. John Paul II: 1978–2005
265. Benedict XVI: 2005–

—see *Catholic Almanac*

Prayer of St. Patrick's Breastplate

I arise today
Through a mighty strength, the invocation of
    the Trinity,
Through a belief in the Threeness,
Through confession of the Oneness
Of the Creator of Creation.

I arise today
Through the strength of Christ's birth and his
    baptism,
Through the strength of his Crucifixion and his
    burial,
Through the strength of his Resurrection and his
    Ascension,
Through the strength of his descent for the
    judgment of doom.

I arise today
Through the strength of the love of cherubim,
In obedience of angels,
In service of archangels,
In the hope of resurrection to meet with reward,
In the prayers of patriarchs,
In preachings of the Apostles,
In faiths of confessors,
In innocence of virgins,
In deeds of righteous men.

I arise today
Through the strength of heaven;
Light of the sun,
Splendor of fire,
Speed of lightning,
Swiftness of the wind,
Depth of the sea,
Stability of the earth,
Firmness of the rock.

I arise today
Through God's strength to pilot me;
God's might to uphold me,
God's wisdom to guide me,
God's eye to look before me,
God's ear to hear me,
God's Word to speak for me,
God's hand to guard me,
God's way to lie before me,

God's shield to protect me,
God's hosts to save me
From snares of the devil,
From temptations of vices,
From every one who desires me ill,
Afar and anear,
Alone or in a multitude.

I summon today all these powers between me
    and evil,
Against every cruel merciless power that
    opposes my body and soul,
Against incantations of false prophets,
Against black laws of pagandom,
Against false laws of heretics,
Against craft or idolatry,
Against spells of women and smiths and
    wizards,
Against every knowledge that corrupts man's
    body and soul.
Christ shield me today
Against poison, against burning,
Against drowning, against wounding,
So that reward may come to me in abundance.

Christ with me, Christ before me, Christ behind
    me,
Christ in me, Christ beneath me, Christ above
    me,
Christ on my right, Christ on my left,
Christ when I lie down, Christ when I sit down,
Christ in the heart of every man who thinks of
    me,
Christ in the mouth of every man who speaks of
    me,
Christ in the eye that sees me,
Christ in the ear that hears me.

I arise today
Through a mighty strength, the invocation of
    the Trinity,
Through a belief in the Threeness,
Through a confession of the Oneness,
Of the Creator of Creation.

—Saint Patrick (c. 377)

The Seder: Introduction

The Seder is the ritual meal that takes place in Jewish homes on the first night of Passover. The service, which commemorates the night God delivered the Hebrews from slavery in Egypt, involves the recitation of special prayers and the consumption of symbolic foods.

The Last Supper of Jesus with his disciples was a Passover Seder. During the meal, Jesus taught that he is the Lamb of God, the perfect sacrifice to the Father, which frees us from the slavery of sin and death. During each Mass, parts of the Last Supper are reenacted; some of the gestures and prayers of the Mass, therefore, come from the Seder service.

Materials:

- large serving platter for Seder tray
- matzah—three whole matzahs for under the Seder tray; additional matzahs for the table
- horseradish—mild creamed horseradish is easiest to use
- celery—two sticks for each participant
- ground apple—about a tablespoon per person
- ground walnuts—about a tablespoon per person
- cinnamon—mix with apples and walnuts to taste
- "wine"—grape juice, about two ounces per person, plus enough to moisten apple-nut mixture
- shank bone—turkey thigh bone, chicken leg or neck bone, or whatever you can get from the butcher; boil to clean and roast till brown
- hard-boiled eggs—1/4 egg per person; plus one whole egg, roasted until brown, for Seder tray
- large cloth napkin—folded in four and stitched closely along the folded sides to form three pockets for holding the matzah that is placed under the Seder tray
- "wine" glasses—one per person
- bowls for salt water—paper nut cups will do; one per person
- bowls for fresh water—short paper cups will do; one per person
- napkins, paper plates, spoons
- two candles, matches
- necktie, yarmulke (skull cap), necklace, shawl
- Bibles or photocopies of Psalms to be recited
- Photocopies of the Seder outline (B-18–B-20)

The Seder: Preparation

Before class, arrange the tables or desks in a U-shape or a rectangle, with the leader's chair at the head, facing the students. Decorate the tables with cloths, plates, and candles of dark blue and white (the colors of the Israeli flag) or white and violet (the color for Lent). A floral arrangement or a ceramic or toy lamb with a ribbon around its neck makes a nice centerpiece. At the head of the table, place a Seder tray, which is a platter with samples of the following symbolic foods:

- **Maror**: Ground horseradish represents the bitter suffering the Hebrew slaves endured at the hands of the Egyptian taskmasters.

- **Karpas**: Cut celery (or another green vegetable) represents spring. It is dipped in salt water, which symbolizes the tears shed by the Hebrews during their slavery.

- **Haroses**: Ground apples and walnuts symbolize the mortar the Hebrews were forced to make for the Pharaoh's buildings.

- **Zeroah**: A lamb shankbone represents the lamb that was sacrificed and eaten on the first Passover. Those who painted their doorways with its blood were "passed over" by the tenth plague, which killed the firstborn of the Egyptians. Zeroah means "arm," for it was the mighty arm of God that compelled Pharaoh to free the Hebrew slaves.

- **Baytzah**: A hard-boiled egg symbolizes the animal sacrifices the Israelites brought to the temple in Jerusalem during holidays such as Passover. The eggs are dipped into salt water, signifying the mourning of the Jews over the destruction of the temple.

Underneath the Seder tray are placed three matzahs (unleavened bread) in a matzah holder or wrapped in layers in a cloth napkin. More matzah is on the table. The matzah represents the bread the Hebrews made in haste before their departure from Egypt.

Set each place with a glass of grape juice, a napkin, a dish of salt water, a spoon, a dish of fresh water, and a plate. On each plate, place two pieces of celery, a spoonful each of horseradish, and apple-nut mixture, and a slice of hard-boiled egg.

The Seder is a family meal. Choose a boy to be the father and give him a necktie and yarmulke (skull cap) to wear. Choose a girl to be the mother, wearing a necklace and shawl. Choose a third student to act the part of the youngest child.

A Seder Outline *abridged and adapted*

Candle-Lighting Ceremony

Usually, the mother of the family leads the candle-lighting ceremony, using two tapers or a special Passover candelabra. She lights the candles and says:

> Blessed are you, O Lord our God, King of the universe, who sanctified us with his commandments and commanded us to kindle the festival lights.

> Blessed are you, O Lord our God, King of the universe, who gave us life and sustained us and brought us to this joyful season.

Opening

The father usually leads the rest of the Seder. He sits at the head of the table and begins the service:

> We have gathered to observe the Passover, the night God delivered Israel from bondage and brought them out of Egypt. Let us proclaim the power, the goodness, and the faithfulness of God.

The First Cup

The father leads the blessing. All raise their cups and say:

> Blessed are you, O Lord our God, King of the universe, who has created the fruit of the vine.

All take a sip.

The First Washing

All participants wash their hands with the water provided. In ancient times, a household servant washed the dusty feet of the dinner guests. At the Last Supper, Jesus himself performed this service and washed the disciples' feet. In modern Jewish households, each person has his own water and towel, or a bowl and towel are carried from person to person by the mistress of the house.

Appetizer: Karpas

The father asks everyone to take some celery, dip it in the salt water, and say:

> Blessed are you, O Lord our God, King of the universe, who has created the fruit of the earth.

All eat the celery. This reminds us of Judas' betrayal.

Yahatz: Breaking the Middle Matzah

The father takes the middle piece of matzah and breaks it into two parts. One part is wrapped up and saved for the end of the meal. The teacher might select some students to "steal" this piece and hide it, a tradition in many Jewish families today. The remaining part is lifted by the father, who says:

> This is the bread of affliction, which God's people ate in the land of Egypt. Let all who are hungry come and eat.

He then places the matzah on top of the others.

A Seder Outline *(continued)*

The Four Questions and the Hagadah

The youngest child asks four questions about why this night is different from all the others:

> Why do we eat only unleavened bread?
> Why do we eat bitter herbs?
> Why do we dip the herbs twice?
> Why do we dine with special ceremony?

The father answers the questions by telling the Hagadah, the story of the Hebrew people from Abraham to Moses. The father, the teacher, or another student reads the narrative:

> In the beginning, our people worshipped idols, but God revealed himself to them and made a covenant with our father Abraham, in which he promised to make him a great nation. Abraham and Sarah had a son, Isaac, in their old age. Isaac's younger son, Jacob, inherited his father's promise. Jacob became the father of Joseph, who was sold into slavery by his jealous brothers. Joseph became great in Pharaoh's service by saving Egypt from famine. His own family came to him for food and settled in Egypt. Many years later, another Pharaoh enslaved the Hebrews. But the people of Israel cried out to God, who heard their cry and sent Moses to lead them to freedom. Moses asked Pharaoh to let his people go. When he refused, God sent ten plagues that compelled Pharaoh to free the Hebrew slaves.

The Showing of the Foods

To make the connection between the story and the foods, the teacher points to each item on the Seder tray and explains its significance (see page B-17).

The First Part of the Hallel

To show thanks for the mighty works of God, the Hallel, or Psalms, are recited. The Hallel includes Psalms 112, 113, and 114. The teacher chooses one to be recited by the class.

The Second Cup

The father leads in taking a second sip of the grape juice. All say:

> Blessed are you, O Lord our God, King of the universe, who has created the fruit of the vine.

The Second Washing

All wash their hands again.

Sources

Kolatch, Alfred J., *The Concise Family Seder* (New York: Jonathan David Publisher, Inc., 1989).

Rosen, Ceil and Moishe, *Christ in the Passover: Why Is This Night Different?* (Chicago: Moody Press, 1980).

A Seder Outline *(continued)*

Eating the Matzah, Maror, and Haroses

The father breaks the original top matzah and the broken half of the middle matzah into enough pieces for all and distributes them. This may be the point at which Jesus said, "This is my Body." Each person holds a piece of matzah while the father says:

> Blessed are you, O Lord our God, King of the universe, who brings forth bread from the earth.

All eat the matzah. Each person takes another piece of matzah from the table, dips it into the maror and the haroses, and eats it. (A spoon may be used for dipping and spreading.) Each person takes a piece of hard-boiled egg, dips it into salt water, and eats it. At this point in the Seder, the table is cleared of the symbolic foods, and the rest of the meal is served.

Grace after Meals

After the meal is finished, Psalm 126 is recited. The father then looks for the hidden matzah or asks the children who hid it to bring it back. He divides it among all the participants, and all eat.

The Third Cup

The father asks the others to raise their cups and say:

> Blessed are you, O Lord our God, King of the universe, who has created the fruit of the vine.

This could be the point at which Jesus said, "This is my Blood."

All sip from their glasses, which are refilled if necessary.

The Second Part of the Hallel

More Psalms are then recited, including Psalms 115 and 135. The teacher chooses one for the class to recite.

The Fourth Cup

The father concludes by asking all to raise their cups one last time and say:

> Blessed are you, O Lord our God, King of the universe, who has created the fruit of the vine.

All drink. The father says:

> Our Seder has ended. Let us go in joy.

The Parts of the Mass

I. INTRODUCTORY RITES

A. Entrance Antiphon or Hymn
B. Greeting of the People
C. Penitential Rite
D. "Glory to God"
E. Opening Prayer (Collect)

II. LITURGY OF THE WORD

A. First Reading, Responsorial Psalm, Second Reading
B. Gospel
C. Homily (Sermon)
D. Profession of Faith (Creed)
E. Prayers of the Faithful

III. LITURGY OF THE EUCHARIST

A. **Offertory**
   1. Preparation of the Altar
   2. Presentation of the Gifts
   3. Preparation of the Bread
   4. Preparation of the Wine
   5. Washing of the Hands
   6. Prayer over the Gifts

B. **Eucharistic Prayer**
   1. Preface and "Holy, Holy"
   2. Invocation of the Holy Spirit
   3. Consecration of the Bread
   4. Elevation of the Host
   5. Consecration of the Wine
   6. Elevation of the Chalice
   7. Prayers for the Church, the living, and the dead
   8. Doxology and Great Amen

C. **Communion Rite**
   1. The Lord's Prayer
   2. Rite of Peace
   3. Breaking of the Bread; "Lamb of God"; "Lord, I Am Not Worthy"
   4. Communion of the Priest
   5. Communion of the People
   6. Prayer after Communion

IV. CONCLUDING RITES

A. Final Blessing and Dismissal

B. Recessional

The Parts of the Mass (continued)

Greeting of the People

"Glory to God"

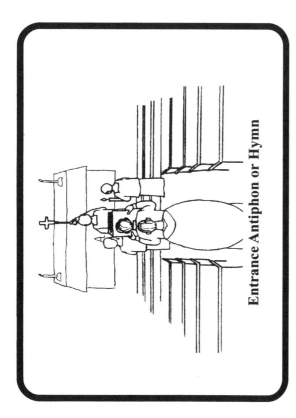

Entrance Antiphon or Hymn

Penitential Rite

The Parts of the Mass *(continued)*

First Reading, Responsorial Psalm, Second Reading

Homily (Sermon)

Opening Prayer (Collect)

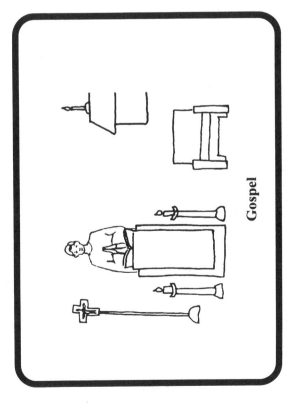

Gospel

The Parts of the Mass *(continued)*

Prayers of the Faithful

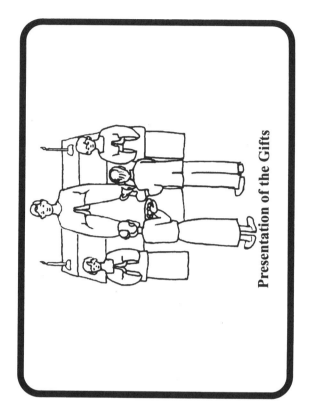

Presentation of the Gifts

Profession of Faith (Creed)

Preparation of the Altar

The Parts of the Mass *(continued)*

Preparation of the Wine

Prayers over the Gifts

Preparation of the Bread

Washing of the Hands

The Parts of the Mass *(continued)*

Invocation of the Holy Spirit

Elevation of the Host

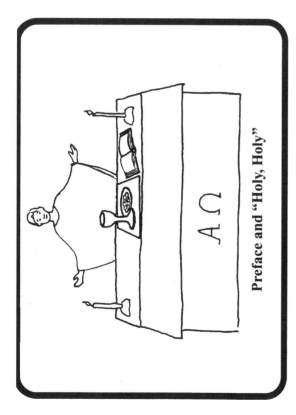

Preface and "Holy, Holy"

Consecration of the Bread

The Parts of the Mass *(continued)*

Elevation of the Chalice

Doxology and Great Amen

Consecration of the Wine

Prayers for the Church, the living, and the dead

The Parts of the Mass *(continued)*

Rite of Peace

Communion of the Priest

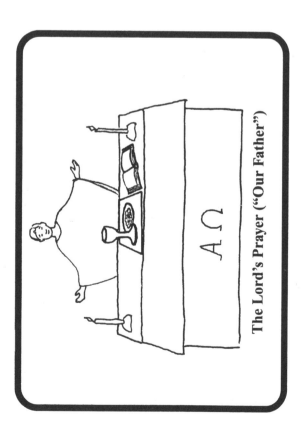

The Lord's Prayer ("Our Father")

Breaking of the Bread; "Lamb of God"; "Lord, I Am Not Worthy"

The Parts of the Mass *(continued)*

Prayer after Communion

Recessional

Communion of the People

Final Blessing and Dismissal

Rite of Funerals (from *The Rites of the Catholic Church*, vol. 1)
Vigil for the Deceased

INTRODUCTORY RITES

GREETING
May the God of hope give you the fullness of peace, and may the Lord of life be always with you.
R/ *And with your spirit.*

OPENING HYMN
Choose an appropriate song.

INVITATION TO PRAYER
My brothers and sisters, we believe that all ties of friendship and affection which knit us as one throughout our lives do not unravel with death.

Confident that God always remembers the good we have done and forgives our sins, let us pray, asking God to gather N. to himself.

Pause for silent prayer.

OPENING PRAYER
O God,
glory of believers and life of the just,
by the death and resurrection of your Son, we are redeemed:
have mercy on your servant N.,
and make him/her worthy to share the joys of paradise,
for he/she believed in the resurrection of the dead.
We ask this through Christ our Lord.
R/ *Amen.*

LITURGY OF THE WORD

FIRST READING
Have one of the students read 2 Corinthians 5:1, 6–10.

RESPONSORIAL PSALM
Have one of the students read Psalm 27.
Between each stanza, all respond: *The Lord is my light and my salvation.*

GOSPEL
Read Luke 12:35–40.

HOMILY
At this point, the presiding priest or deacon would give a homily.

Rite of Funerals *(continued)*

PRAYER OF INTERCESSION

LITANY
Let us turn to Christ Jesus with confidence and faith in the power of his cross and resurrection:

Risen Lord, pattern of our life for ever: Lord, have mercy.
R/ *Lord, have mercy.*

Promise and image of what we shall be: Lord, have mercy.
R/ *Lord, have mercy.*

Son of of God who came to destroy sin and death: Lord, have mercy.
R/ *Lord, have mercy.*

Word of God who delivered us from the fear of death: Lord, have mercy.
R/ *Lord, have mercy.*

Crucified Lord, forsaken in death, raised in glory: Lord, have mercy.
R/ *Lord, have mercy.*

Lord Jesus, gentle shepherd who brings rest to our souls, give peace to N. for ever: Lord, have mercy.
R/ *Lord, have mercy.*

Lord Jesus, you bless those who mourn and are in pain. Bless N.'s family and friends who gather around him/her today: Lord, have mercy.
R/ *Lord, have mercy.*

THE LORD'S PRAYER
With God there is mercy and fullness of redemption; let us pray as Jesus taught us:
All: *Our Father...*

CONCLUDING PRAYER
Lord God,
you are attentive to the voice of our pleading.
Let us find in your Son
comfort in our sadness,
certainty in our doubt,
and courage to live through this hour.
Make our faith strong
through Christ our Lord.
R/ *Amen.*

A member or a friend of the family may speak in remembrance of the deceased.

Rite of Funerals *(continued)*

CONCLUDING RITE

BLESSING

Blessed are those who have died in the Lord; let them rest from their labors for their good deeds go with them.

Eternal rest grant unto him/her, O Lord.
R/ *And let perpetual light shine upon him/her.*

May he/she rest in peace.
R/ *Amen.*

May his/her soul and the souls of all the faithful departed, through the mercy of God, rest in peace.
R/ *Amen.*

If a priest or deacon is present, he will conclude with these prayers:
May the peace of God,
which is beyond all understanding,
keep your hearts and minds
in the knowledge and love of God
and of his Son, our Lord Jesus Christ.
R/ *Amen.*

May almighty God bless you, the Father, and the Son, and the Holy Spirit.
R/ *Amen.*

If a priest or deacon is not available, a lay minister concludes:
May the love of God and the peace of the Lord Jesus Christ
bless and console us
and gently wipe every tear from our eyes:
in the name of the Father,
and of the Son, and of the Holy Spirit.
R/ *Amen.*

CLOSING HYMN
Choose and appropriate song.

Litany of the Saints

Lord, have mercy on us.
Christ, have mercy on us.
Lord, have mercy on us. Christ, hear us.
Christ, graciously hear us.
God the Father of Heaven,
have mercy on us.
God the Son, Redeemer of the World,
have mercy on us.
God the Holy Spirit,
have mercy on us.
Holy Trinity, one God,
haver mercy on us.

Holy Mary,
*pray for us.**
Holy Mother of God,
Holy Virgin of virgins,
Saint Michael,
Saint Gabriel,
Saint Raphael,
All ye Holy Angels and Archangels,
All ye Holy Orders of Blessed spirits,
Saint John the Baptist,
Saint Joseph,
All ye Holy Patriarchs and Prophets,
Saint Peter,
Saint Paul,
Saint Andrew,
Saint James,
Saint John,
Saint Thomas,
Saint James,
Saint Philip,
Saint Bartholomew,
Saint Matthew,
Saint Simon,
Saint Thaddeus,
Saint Barnabas,
Saint Luke,
Saint Mark,
All ye Holy Apostles and Evangelists,
All ye Holy Disciples of our Lord,

All ye Holy Innocents,
Saint Stephen,
Saint Lawrence,
Saint Vincent,
Saints Fabian and Sebastian,
Saints John and Paul,
Saints Cosmos and Damian,
Saints Gervase and Protase,
All ye Holy Martyrs,
Saint Sylvester,
Saint Gregory,
Saint Ambrose,
Saint Augustine,
Saint Jerome,
Saint Martin,
Saint Nicholas,
All ye Holy Bishops and Confessors,
All ye Holy Doctors,
Saint Anthony,
Saint Benedict,
Saint Bernard,
Saint Dominic,
Saint Francis,
All ye Holy Priests and Levites,
All ye Holy Monks and Hermits,
Saint Mary Magdalen,
Saint Agatha,
Saint Lucy,
Saint Agnes,
Saint Cecilia,
Saint Catherine,
Saint Anastasia,
All ye Holy Virgins and Widows,

All ye Men and Women, Saints of God
intercede for us.

Be merciful,
Spare us, O Lord!
Be merciful,
Graciously hear us, O Lord!

Pray for us. is repeated after each invocation.

Litany of the Saints *(continued)*

From all evil,
  O Lord, deliver us. *
From all sin,
From thy wrath,
From a sudden and unprovided death,
From the deceits of the devil,
From anger, hatred, and all ill will,
From the spirit of fornication,
From lightning and tempest,
From the scourge of earthquake,
From pestilence, famine, and war,
From everlasting death,
Through the mystery of the holy Incarnation,
Through thy coming,
Through thy nativity,
Through thy baptism and holy fasting,
Through thy Cross and Passion,
Through thy death and burial,
Through thy holy Resurrection,
Through thine admirable Ascension,
Through the coming of the Holy Ghost, the
  Paraclete,

In the day of judgment,
  *We beseech thee, hear us.***
That thou wouldst spare us,
That thou wouldst pardon us,
That thou wouldst vouchsafe to bring us to true
  penance,
That thou wouldst vouchsafe to govern and
  preserve thy holy Church,
That thou wouldst vouchsafe to preserve our
  apostolic prelate and all ecclesiastical orders
  in holy religion,
That thou wouldst vouchsafe to humble the
  enemies of thy holy Church,
That thou wouldst vouchsafe to give peace and
  true concord to Christian kings and princes,
That thou wouldst vouchsafe to grant peace
  and unity to all Christian people,

That thou wouldst vouchsafe to bring back
  to the unity of the Church all those who
  have strayed away, and lead to the light of
  the gospel all unbelievers,
That thou wouldst vouchsafe to confirm and
  preserve us in thy holy service,
That thou wouldst lift up our minds to
  heavenly desires,
That thou wouldst render eternal blessings to
  all our benefactors,
That thou wouldst deliver our souls and those
  of our brethren, relatives, and benefactors
  from eternal damnation,
That thou wouldst vouchsafe to give and
  preserve the fruits of the earth,
That thou wouldst vouchsafe to give eternal
  rest to all the faithful departed,
That thou wouldst vouchsafe graciously to hear
  us, Son of God,

Lamb of God, who take away the sins of the
  world, *spare us, O Lord.*
Lamb of God, who take away the sins of the
  world, *graciously hear us, O Lord.*
Lamb of God, who take away the sins of the
  world, *have mercy on us.*

Christ, hear us.
  Christ, graciously hear us.
Lord, have mercy on us.
  Christ, have mercy on us,
Lord, have mercy on us.
  Our Father...

And lead us not into temptation,
  But deliver us from evil.

O Lord, deliver us. is repeated after each invocation.
***We beseech thee, hear us.* is repeated after each
invocation.